MW01076807

HENRIK IBSEN

HENRIK IBSEN
THE MAN AND THE MASK

IVO DE FIGUEIREDO
TRANSLATED BY ROBERT FERGUSON

YALE UNIVERSITY PRESS
NEW HAVEN AND LONDON

This translation has been published with the financial support of NORLA, Norwegian Literature Abroad.

First published in English by Yale University Press in 2019.

All translations of Ibsen's poetry by John Northam.

Originally published in Norwegian as *Henrik Ibsen. Mennesket* (2006), *Henrik Ibsen. Masken* (2007), and as the abridged edition *Henrik Ibsen. Mennesket og masken* (2010).

For information about this and other Yale University Press publications, please contact:
U.S. Office: sales.press@yale.edu   yalebooks.com
Europe Office: sales@yaleup.co.uk   yalebooks.co.uk

Set in Minion Pro by IDSUK (DataConnection) Ltd
Printed in Great Britain by TJ International, Padstow, Cornwall

Library of Congress Control Number: 2018956100

ISBN 978-0-300-20881-8

A catalogue record for this book is available from the British Library.

10 9 8 7 6 5 4 3 2 1

CONTENTS

ILLUSTRATIONS

FOREWORD

This book is an edited and abridged edition of my two-volume Norwegian biography of Ibsen, *Henrik Ibsen: The Man* (2006) and *Henrik Ibsen: The Mask* (2007). The abridgement has involved partly a general cutting-down of the text, partly a severe reduction in the length of the notes.

As regards the notes, I have removed almost all references to primary sources – letters, diaries, etc. – while retaining references that contain interesting additional information and, not least, those that indicate the points at which I am indebted to other scholars. It should be noted that, for literary reasons, I do not explicitly engage with the work of other scholars in the actual text. It is therefore important to direct the reader's attention to the notes, and in general to underscore my debt to the work of other scholars of Ibsen's life and work. I would like in particular to mention Tore Rem, who has been my main source for Ibsen's reception in the English-speaking world; and the different perspectives of Ibsen scholars Toril Moi, Atle Kittang, Helge Rønning, Vigdis Ystad, Asbjørn Aarseth and Eivind Tjønneland. I have also made considerable use of the historical perspectives and history of ideas contained in the work of Narve Fulsås and Kjetil Jacobsen. For others who have been helpful, see the Acknowledgements at the back of the book.

In the Afterword I give some account of the historical and literary theory as well as the methodological approach that lies behind this book. I have also included the complete bibliography and list of archives, even though some of the notes may have been removed in the abridgement.

Ivo de Figueiredo
Oslo, 27 September 2018

PROLOGUE

A square in the middle of Skien. To the right the stocks, to the left the town hall with its lockup, also known as 'the loony bin', in the cellar. At the front, on one of the long sides of the rectangular square, lies Stockmannsgården, Henrik Ibsen's childhood home. On the opposite long side are the town's two schools. In the centre of the square stands the church with its steeple. Small boys play and scrap with each other, groups of people stand around chatting, young couples pass by, arm in arm.

The scene is Skien in the 1830s. Not as it was, but as it seems in the memory of an old man looking back. In the winter of 1881 Henrik Ibsen sits down to write his life. He doesn't get very far before giving up, as is usually the case when he tries to write prose. A few pages about his childhood home town are all he manages before the pen is laid aside. But a whole life, and more, is described within these few pages.

He writes about the town he grew up in, the people and places, the episodes he recalls. He writes about his home and his parents, about the stocks in the square which, to his child's eyes, looked like a small creature reaching out to him with its metal arms. About the 'loony bin', where the insane were kept locked up, about the roaring of the waterfall and the piercing whine of the sawmills just outside town – sounds that were like the shrieking of women, or the whine of the blade of a guillotine. It was the dark and the gloomy that fascinated him; he felt at home neither among the gossipy townspeople of Skien nor the rough and tumble of the boys playing in the marketplace.

He wasn't like the others.

This is how Ibsen describes his childhood world. At least, that is what the text seems to convey at first glance. On closer inspection, it becomes clear that besides being a description of childhood, it is also something much more. It is a mythical presentation of the writer's universe, his cosmology. The square in Skien is the world, a cosmos, framed by the house of knowledge (the schools), the house of common sense (the town hall), and those elements that symbolise both incorporation in the cosmos (Stockmannsgården, where Henrik was born) and exclusion from the cosmos (the stocks). And in the middle of it all the church, with its tall steeple, the *axis mundi*. The church is the house of spirit that reigns over it all. Taken together, this is the world of human beings, and beyond it the thundering of the waterfall and the screeching of the saw blades, a constant reminder of chaotic nature that surrounds the cosmos. Chaos, the wildness of nature, which has also hidden itself in the 'loony bin', like a seed of destruction within the cosmos.

This is the world. What about those who inhabit it?

A cosmos must be filled with people and gods. Ibsen is not one of the former, not one of Skien's light-hearted citizens. He is of the family of gods. The gods of poetry. In other words, he belongs in the church steeple.

It is from here that his very first memory comes:

His nursemaid had taken him up the steep stairway to the opening at the top, where the watchman would call out the hours when the clock struck. He sat with his legs dangling over the edge, the arms of a woman safely around his waist. He looked out across the square, at the tops of the hats wandering about down there, the flecked tiles on the rooftops, his mother leaning from the window of the house where he lived, the curtains blowing in the wind. He saw over the rooftop and down into the yard where the horse stood by the stable door, tail twitching. On the wall, a tin bucket flashing in the sunlight.

Henrik sees.

This is how he describes his first impression of the world. He continues, relating how this experience in the church steeple became entwined in his memory with a story he heard a little later. According to this story, a long time ago a dog lived up in the steeple, a black poodle with glowing red eyes. From the church below the poodle could be heard yelping and barking, but it had never been seen save for on one solitary occasion, when a night-watchman made his way up to the opening in the early hours of the morning to cry out that it was one o'clock. Suddenly he fell from the window and plummeted to his death on the cobblestones below. Then the dog appeared in the opening, red eyes glowing in the darkness.

After hearing this story, Ibsen relates, he was never again able to cross the square in Skien without looking up at that opening in the steeple. Ever afterwards he felt himself connected to the church steeple, that unfortunate night-watchman, and not least that black poodle; it seemed to him the connection was closer than the one he felt with the white angel in the church below.

Black poodle, white angel. The angel hung protectively above the devout inhabitants of Skien gathered in the church, over those innocent people who knew nothing of the dark forces of the cosmos. Not like the boy in the window. It was as though a pact existed between him and the poodle, a pact reminiscent of the one Goethe's Faust entered into with the devil, Mephistopheles – Mephistopheles too had first appeared to Faust in the form of a black poodle. A pact in which the boy would be given visionary powers, the power of the word, in return for which he must renounce the innocence and protection to be found beneath the angel's wings. And what he sees in his childhood home is a scenario that is both fearful and romantic, one that involves death and destruction, executions, insanity. A scenario that revealed itself to the small son of the merchant Knud Ibsen but was hidden from the rest of mankind.

He was a writer, and a writer did not belong in church, in the society of others. His home was in the steeple, condemned for all eternity to see the world from outside, from above, to describe it, and the tragedy of human life.

And to feel always the eyes of the devil on his neck.

This is the deeper theme of Ibsen's earliest childhood memories of Skien. There is no childhood, just stories. The ageing Ibsen knew it, that's why he writes a description of childhood that, at the same time, functions as a mythical prelude to his own calling as a writer.

What was it he said, Ibsen, about 'to write, that is mainly a matter of seeing'? He could just as well have said that seeing is mainly about writing.

For someone who intends to write Ibsen's life, this insight is of profound importance. The biographer's obligation is to describe the reality, for example, in deciding which aspects of Ibsen's account of his childhood give reliable information on his life as it was. But it is just as important to see the mythical subtext, in which the ageing Ibsen presents himself as the 'poet-sphinx' to be, the child who sacrificed his childhood for the gift of poetry. It is not about choosing between reality *or* myth but about reality *and* myth – or more precisely, about the reality of the myth. Myths to be understood here, be it noted, not as lies, but as meaningful conceptions of how something is, or how something arose. And in this sense, myths are as true as the reality to which they relate.

The idea of the 'poet-sphinx', which was created by Ibsen himself, has been enhanced by the loyal mediations of literary historians for over a hundred years. We all know the basic components of the Ibsen myth – the story of the suffering artist, the person rejected by bourgeois society after the bankruptcy of the father, the genius who languished as a young apothecary's assistant in Grimstad, and later as a writer and theatre manager in Bergen and Christiania. All the while looking for a recognition that the elite in the cultural backwater that was Norway declined to give him. A pearl in the mire, until he fled abroad and showed what he was capable of with his masterpiece *Brand*, published while he lived in exile in Rome in 1866. An angry writer who writes because his nature forces him to write – not because he *wants* to, but because he *must*. A quiet and introverted man, a man who stays silent while others sound off, but who always holds the world in his sharp gaze, that writer's eye that sees straight to the human heart. Behind that square-cut head and the broad forehead, behind that closed-off face, the most profound thoughts about life and human beings are in ferment.

Such is the myth, and it is false. And true.

Henrik Ibsen's life has been told countless times in writing, in sculpture and paintings; innumerable hands have pressed clay across a mask that bears such an uncanny resemblance to the writer himself. The man and the mask, the reality and the myth. Yet there is no reason to look for the man behind the mask; rather, the mask resembles the hardened exterior of the real self. If we pull away the mask, something of the man comes away with it. Because what is remarkable about Ibsen's life is the way he managed to sublimate his own nature within the myth; he created a self on the basis of his weaknesses as well as his strengths. And it was in this metamorphosis that he captured his own times with such astonishing power.

This physically insignificant man, asocial, inhibited and silent. Who struggled as a joiner of groups and as a theatre manager, who was a political amateur and a semi-educated chancer. A man who treated his fellow human beings badly, who was merciless and absolute in his judgement of others. A man who throughout his life avoided significant commitments except those to his wife and the legal child of their marriage – to whom he was all the more profoundly attached. A shy poseur, a vain Puritan, at one and the same time reserved and aggressive. A man who praised the harmonious and yet was constantly at war with himself. In sum, a jumble of contradictions and an impossible man.

These weaknesses could have been his downfall. Instead, they became his triumph, precisely because, in his own doubts, he found his artistic strength. Because he most certainly was a doubter, but certain in his doubting. Ibsen's feeling of discomfort in the world did not destroy him; instead, as *the pure writer*, raised high above the trivialities of life, he made his name throughout Europe. To an extreme degree he cultivated his role as a writer, careful not to do so at the cost of betraying his business sense. For the educated public he became the exalted writer, the articulator of the riddles people longed to ponder: of the individual's place in the world; of the social and moral forces pressing on the individual from inside and out; of the conditions of human freedom. As a literary project it corresponded closely with his own personal project in life. But it also reflected the widespread cultivation of the personality as being at the centre of life during a period of enormous social and cultural change that characterised the development of modern, bourgeois Europe. So he spoke to his age both by virtue of being the man he was, but also through the works he wrote and the literary image he created.

The powerful and penetrating appeal of the works is interesting enough, but for a biographer, naturally, what is most fascinating is the human metamorphosis; Ibsen's transformation from granite to marble. That he, so uncomfortable and helpless in social settings, should become a star, idolised and admired across an entire continent – the poor son of a merchant in remote Norway turned into a celebrated European writer. And what is most fascinating of all is that the reason for the success of this metamorphosis probably has to be sought in the tension between his social incompetence and his genius; in the artistic flair with which he managed to make use of his weaknesses. One result being that the writing reflected back onto the life. For in the massive cult of personality which arose around Ibsen during the last years of the nineteenth century, his silence was interpreted as wisdom, his aversions as principles, his quarrelsome nature as a necessary outlet for inner spiritual wrestling. Indeed, every aspect of his personality was interpreted in terms of a rhetoric of necessity that transformed every failing into a virtue.

No one knows if Ibsen was ever taken up to the top of the church steeple in Skien. Maybe that whole childhood description is a fiction. For over a century, far more literary historians have trawled the fiction in search of the life than have pondered the fiction in the life. Had they done the latter, they might have noticed how it was Ibsen *himself* who created himself as that boy in the steeple window, the one outside and above life, who wrote because he *had to*, and because a black dog with red eyes never took its eyes off him. Writers of Ibsen's life have often either swirled around in the world of myth, or else they have been 'myth-killers' dedicated to making the life seem less than it is. For the present biographer, however, it has been a matter of some importance to pay as much attention to the myth and the reality of the myth as to reality itself. In other words, this is a book about Ibsen's life, but it is also a book about the myth of Ibsen that has taken shape over more than a century now, and which is impossible to ignore. The myths are real enough, and for that reason they should be neither fostered nor killed off. One must lift them up and look behind them. And then carefully put them back.

In all likelihood the present biographer will also contribute to the construction of myths. It is impossible to write history without at the same time writing stories, impossible to describe reality without constructing it through literary approaches and narrative structures, impossible to seduce the reader while at the same time revealing one's tricks.

It cannot be otherwise. It will be the task of others to reveal these myths.

I shall not do it.

I

SKIEN

THE HOUSE OF IBSEN

He was not the first. Eighteen months earlier, Marichen had given birth to a son named Johan, but he died shortly after Henrik's arrival. They met in the doorway, so to speak, between life and death. It seems that Henrik almost turned and followed his brother out.

But the boy chose life, and all the signs were that he made the right choice.

Henrik Johan Ibsen was born on 20 March 1828, in Skien, a provincial town on the remote fringe of northern Europe. Yet he was also born into a world that was as European as any other, an expanding and successful bourgeoisie that was in the process of making the century its own across the whole continent. The century of the bourgeoisie, the age of freedom, of the individual, in which all inherited privilege and barriers stood ready to fall, in which anyone could sell his soul and gain the whole world – or lose both.

By birth, then, Henrik Ibsen was both provincial and European. His mother was Marichen Cornelia Martine Ibsen, née Altenburg. Though the name is German, the family had been in Norway for generations. It could boast many respectable names and titles, but it was her father Johan Andreas Altenburg, a sea captain, corn-dealer and merchant, who made the fortune that meant that Henrik Ibsen's mother was born into a comfortable home in the year 1799. His father, Knud Ibsen, was also born into the home of a prominent sea captain. He never knew his own father, who was lost at sea just a month after his son's baptism in 1797. Knud's mother, Johanne Cathrine Plesner, remarried the following year, to Ole Paus, a local man of good reputation, a ship-owner and later a landowner. It was on his stepfather's farm at Gjerpen that Knud grew up, with eight half-brothers and sisters.

Sea captains, ship-owners, landowners or whatever they liked to call themselves – they were all essentially merchants. Skien was the town of the bourgeoisie. The civil servants were few in number, but powerful, and even among them it was traditional to take part in the commercial life of the town. With some 2,000 inhabitants by the mid-1830s, Skien has been described as an 'average small timber town'. Nothing could be more misleading. In the first place, Skien was not small but the capital of a vibrant region of Norway, a town that had been growing through its shipping, its timber trade and its sawmills since the sixteenth century. Over the course of the nineteenth century it would emerge as an industrial powerhouse in the creation of modern Norway. During the same period the population had risen rapidly; by the 1840s it was still growing by comparison with the population growth in the rest of the country. Seventy-three thousand people lived in the region in 1845, and it was this population that formed the basis for one of Norway's largest elite environments, a circle of families living in large town houses, country homes and houses connected to the sawmills and the ironworks.

This was the world into which Henrik Ibsen was born, and with this world pale in his memory he would many years later describe his home town as a thriving environment with an upper class that lived partly in the town and partly on the large estates surrounding it, joined by ties of family and friendship which they cultivated at balls and dinner parties all year round. Over the centuries Skien had become a melting pot for a merchant aristocracy, urbane and European in its cultural outlook, and the old rural culture of the local villages. Art, literature and music enjoyed great prestige; Skien could boast art collections and extensive private libraries. Music was an important part of social life, literature was enjoyed in the town's reading circle, and Danish theatre groups regularly performed at the Limie Hall.

Yes, Skien was just another provincial town in Europe, but only to the degree that it is meaningful to relate the notion of provinciality to places and environments. Neither economic, political, intellectual nor cultural capital are divided proportionately along an axis from the centre to the periphery in Norway which, in a European context, is notable for the number of its strong local societies. Simply because one lived in Christiania rather than Skien, Arendal, Stavanger or Bergen did not mean one was in a significant sense more European.

But Skien was a continental town beyond the orientation and habits of its elite. The town and the district also partook of the same *experience* as the rest of the continent, and this was more pronounced here than in Norway as a whole. This experience was one of modernisation and urbanisation, and in due course an industrialisation that entailed a marked expansion of the lower class and the upper middle class, in which the latter attempted to adopt the same cultural values and lifestyle as the elite. In the town in which Henrik Ibsen grew up there were sawmills, tobacco factories, ship-owners and seamen. There were merchants and traders, factory-owners, workers, artisans – everything that pertained to a nineteenth-century European urban civilisation, if on a reduced scale.

It is as part of this young, bourgeois urban society that we find Knud Ibsen, one of many upwardly aspiring merchants who emerged with the fall of the big trading aristocracies in the crisis that followed the end of the Napoleonic Wars.

The era of the big trading houses was passing, to be replaced by a broad and variegated urban bourgeoisie, a world in which every opportunity lay open for the ambitious and the upwardly aspiring.

Knud Ibsen started with something rather more than just his two bare hands, but he still needed to work to keep his family in reasonable style – as the capitalist ethic demanded. His income increased regularly and rapidly from the time he started work, in 1821, as a clerk in the office of his uncle, Knud Plesner. A few years later he was running his own business in Stockmannsgården, an elegant, white-painted mansion on the town square with a view of the church and the stocks, salvation and ruin. Like most of the local shopkeepers he retailed a variety of lines from the first floor of his home: French wines, spices, sugar, wool and cotton products, glass, ivory, mirrors, lace, along with numerous other products, most of them bought from Hamburg, Flensburg or Newcastle. In addition he was extensively involved in the export of timber and spirits.

It seems odd that some expressed doubts about whether Knud Ibsen was a good match for Marichen. There were hints that the marriage was an arranged one, decided on by their parents while both were still children. Knud's step-father, Ole Paus, was the brother of Marichen's mother Hedvig, and the two practically grew up together. But Knud's candidacy was impressive enough in its own right. His reputation was that of an able and respectable businessman, sociable and witty, though with a quick temper and a sharp tongue when roused.

Of Marichen we know less. Her character and even her appearance lie hidden in the shadows of history, or rather: her shadow is all we know of her – a silhouette cut in black cardboard. Like most shadows, it doesn't reveal much; a young girl posing stiffly in a classic high-waisted empire-style dress, her hair pinned up and the hint of a turned-up nose. A young girl from a well-to-do family probably raised to be dutiful and self-sacrificing in the tradition of the time. She is said to have been introverted and modest, with wise and thoughtful eyes; but also a cheerful and vivacious girl, fond of drawing and painting, who excited adverse comment by heading off to the theatre evening after evening whenever the Danish travelling troupes played at the Limie Hall.

So that's what they were like in their youth, shy Marichen and brusque Knud, before the cloak of seriousness descended over them. And whether it was common sense or love that played the decisive role, the two got married in Skien in the year 1825, in the same year that Knud opened for business in Stockmannsgården.

If Knud was a catch for Marichen, there is no denying that she was even more of a catch for him. Marichen's father, who died a year before the marriage, had been one of the town's most prominent men and, besides the distillery at Lundetangen, also owned property in the town and surrounding area. He ran the business from Altenburggården, an elegant manorial home with its own warehouse, stables and barns at the foot of Hundevadtsbakken in the centre of town, a place renowned for its hospitality, with dinner parties and large numbers of guests and visitors. After the death of her husband, Marichen's mother carried on the business, but she had to give up in 1830, with the properties and what was left of the assets being divided between her two daughters, Marichen and her older sister Christine.

Knud Ibsen now took over the Altenburg family's property, including the distillery. At a stroke this elevated him to the highest social class in Skien, and by 1834 he was the sixteenth biggest contributor of tax in the town. In the course of a few years he had become one of the town's most prominent and responsible men. Seen thus, he was the personification of the mentality of his age and his environment, one in which inheritance was of less importance than the talent to utilise one's abilities. And this was the most important inheritance he left to *his* children:

The belief that a self-made man could conquer the whole world.

***

In time little Henrik was joined by other brothers and sisters. Brother Johan Andreas arrived in 1830, his sister Hedvig Katrine the following year, and finally Nicolai Alexander and Ole Paus in, respectively, 1834 and 1835.

When Henrik was three the family moved from the first floor in Stockmannsgården to Marichen's childhood home in Altenburggården. Here Knud maintained the traditions of hospitality and entertaining established in the time of his father-in-law. Malicious rumours later arose, to the effect that his socialising was extravagant and wasteful. But strictly speaking it would have been more surprising had he *not* conducted a social life proper to his position and status. And Knud Ibsen knew what was required of him. He was thirty-six years of age and in his prime. He must have loved the sophisticated life that chance now afforded him, the feasts, the hunting parties, the horse-racing – he owned several mounts himself. In his son's words, he took enormous pleasure in putting on a show of 'limitless hospitality in his own house'. Soon he had also acquired a summer place, Erlands Venstøp, a fine old farmhouse in empire style some three kilometres outside town. His wife carried on painting and visiting the theatre, he joined the town's reading circle, all the pastimes natural to a couple of their class. For Marichen all this must have been a continuation of the comfortable life into which she had been born, while for Knud it would seem a fitting reward for all his hard work – as well as that large slice of sheer good fortune.

Hedvig, the daughter of the house, later described her childhood home as a 'cultured and cosmopolitan household'. Life for the children was rich and lively. There were always people around, visitors arriving from far away, and at Christmas and during the February market the house was full. The market was the highlight; the boys saved up for months to buy honey cakes, and watch the tightrope walkers and the conjurors. As he grew older, one can also imagine that Henrik began accompanying his mother to the Limie Hall. Otherwise the year was a round of one dinner party after another, with balls and concerts. To the soughing of twirling gowns and lively piano playing, in the smoke from roasting beef and a hundred cigars, the ties between the town's more affluent families were bound in social, economic and cultural community.

The world was a secure place. Or appeared so when viewed from knee height.

So how did the catastrophe come about?

THE FALL

As late as 1833, Knud Ibsen gives surety for a friend for a large loan of 75 spesidaler, the action of a man secure in his own liquidity. Two years later there is nothing left, the business and the properties have all been lost.

Things were already beginning to unravel by the summer of 1834. And once the process has started it all happens very quickly indeed. In June the large boiler in the distillery is sealed by the authorities, probably because Knud has been unable to pay the duty. For the rest of the summer and the autumn he is forced to sign bonds for his creditors, and he neglects to pay his tax bills and fire insurance. In December the distillery at Lundetangen comes under the auctioneer's hammer. With that it becomes obvious to all what is happening.

The speed and extent of Knud Ibsen's decline as a businessman suggest unwise investments, combined with unfavourable economic fluctuations. He may, like a number of other merchants, have been part-owner of a ship that went down and lost him a lot of money. The more likely cause was the distillery, which lacked the capacity necessary to run it at a profit. Large-scale investment was required, and once the duty on spirits was raised then the whole enterprise was effectively doomed.

Was he the author of his own misfortune?

Very little is known of Ibsen's business activities during these years, but there is nothing to suggest that there was anything dubious about his reputation as a businessman. His fate was far from unique – almost all the distilleries in the region failed during these years. Rise and fall is the pulse of capitalism. Knud Ibsen lived at a time when the capitalist economy was young, and especially the petit-bourgeois strain of capitalism he practised. By the end of the

1830s the crisis was being felt by all, with one merchant after another suffering the same fate, until finally, in 1840, Nils Aall himself, one of the last of the great trade magnates, was declared bankrupt.

That Knud Ibsen's ruin was a fact as early as 1835, several years before the general depression that washed over the Skien fjord, *can*, of course, suggest that he was an incautious investor or quite simply a poor businessman. But it would be wrong to distinguish too sharply between the waves of depression that occurred at that time. The whole period from 1822, when the crisis occasioned by the end of the Napoleonic Wars was over, to the new bull market that arose in the middle of the 1840s was, in all essentials, a period of prosperity. But its foundations were fragile, and its crises frequent. Moreover the way in which financial affairs were organised at the time made it difficult to run a business without at the same time taking considerable financial risks; the politics of deflation, a shortage of raw materials and the difficulty of obtaining credit meant it was not easy to invest when times were good, and difficult to survive when times were bad. Government legislation and the system of privileges also acted as an effective barrier to steady economic growth.

There were, in other words, structural weaknesses within the economic system that could bring about the ruin of an unlucky businessman, even when times were good. Not until the mid-1840s, when a new and more liberal business policy was adopted, did the capitalist economy finally get on track in Norway.

But by then it was already too late for Knud Ibsen.

THE PUPPET-MASTER

Over the course of the year 1835 Knud Ibsen lost almost everything he possessed in a series of public auctions. His losses were mercilessly reported in the pages of the *Skien and District Weekly Journal* for all to see.

The only small consolation was that he had not been declared bankrupt. This, at least, left him with a shred of honour.

The Altenburggården was among his losses, and in the summer of 1835 the family was obliged to move out to Venstøp. Here Knud Ibsen had hosted many a hunting party for the town's leading citizens, there had been dinner parties, fun and games with the bowling alley. Now the summer home became a fortress, Knud Ibsen's last defence. From here he must try to get back on his feet again – for his family's sake as well as his own. The farmhouse itself was an elegant building, if slightly run-down, and there was plenty of room for Knud, Marichen and the five children. It was here that Henrik would spend eight crucial years of his childhood, from seven until fifteen.

Most of his childhood is lost in obscurity, forgotten or hidden away between memory and myth. We can only suggest the vaguest outlines of Henrik as a small boy, someone who always preferred to be off on his own, where he could read, draw, and let his thoughts run free. At the top of the stairs at Venstøp is a darkened loft, and beneath it a tiny room where a boy could get away from the boisterous fun and games of his brothers and sisters.

Was it here he came to realise it?

That he could give life to the dead?

Henrik sits in the half-dark alone, cutting out cardboard figures of men and women, in beautiful clothes. He glues them onto wooden blocks so that they can stand. He poses them in small groups, some engaged in lively conversation, others in serious discussion, all of them alive, so living that his sister is surprised when he eventually decides to initiate her into the world of his secret cupboard, one which he inhabits alone, with his drawings and his books. The books nourish him, the dolls and drawings enable him to express himself. Maren, who kept the garden at the farm at Mela, used to take Henrik's cardboard creations to the market to sell, along with her berries.

Occasionally the puppet-master himself would emerge from the cupboard to give a performance. And the people would turn up in droves, adults as well as children, to see Henrik entertain them with conjuring tricks and his puppet theatre. One wing of the farmhouse at Venstøp housed a laundry, the servants' quarters and a storage room. The storage room served as his theatre. Henrik arranged the staging in such a way that he and an assistant could manipulate the puppets from their hiding place behind a curtain. It is said that people came from far and wide to attend these shows, and anyone willing to part with a half-shilling could see the knight Fernando rescue the beautiful Isabella of Spain, with her dark curls and rose-red silken dress, from the clutches of the swarthy Moor. An epic European drama, straight from the history books.

One spring day, in the middle of a performance, two local boys decided to disrupt the proceedings, cutting the puppets' strings and precipitating the sudden appearance of the puppeteer himself who, despite being outnumbered, launched a fierce attack on the vandals. The noise attracted the attention of the puppeteer's father, who arrived on the scene and tried to mediate:

'Can't you leave Henrik and his dolls be?'

Hardly a remark that was going to increase the young lad's status among his comrades, yet Henrik must have been grateful to his father, for what greater catastrophe could befall a puppeteer than to have the strings of his marionettes cut?

What greater humiliation for a god than exposure of the complex mechanism by means of which he rules the world?

It has been said of Henrik that he feared scandal more than anything, and that may indeed be true. But it could equally have been the fear of losing control of his creation. For this was about a created world, and about the act of creation. Hedvig recalled one incident when Henrik was building a castle made of snow. The castle was magnificent, but even before it was completed the master-builder himself tore it down. She recalled another occasion on which he was drawing the face on his Hedvig doll, all the while laughing mischievously to himself – not because the face he was painting was ugly, as his sister feared, but at the thought of what an ugly face he *could* have given her, had he been so inclined.

Henrik enjoyed the game, the game of life. He was a spectator rather than a participant – unless he was himself the director. Certainly, he enjoyed swimming in the summer, tobogganing in the winter, and like most other youngsters took part in the Christmas game of trick or treat called *julebukk*. But those who knew him recalled that he preferred to withdraw to his books and his drawings, to his own world. Quiet, serious, introverted, afraid of being laughed at, capable of an explosive rage if he felt he was being teased – something he must have suspected a great deal of the time. Deep souls don't have much appeal in the world of children. His brothers and sisters used to throw snowballs at the wall of the room where Henrik sat reading, until he was driven to come outside and chase them away. He was quite able to get his own back – 'he was really mean and he used to beat us up', one local girl his own age recalled towards the end of her life, admitting too that they used to tease him. 'No one wanted to play with him. He was always on his own.' The boys especially thought he was pompous, and let him know it with their fists. Girls found it easier to be nice to him, but most agreed there was definitely something odd about Henrik. Even when something made him laugh there was something strange about him, the way he sat alone and laughed soundlessly, even though his whole body was shaking.

If there is even a grain of truth in these tales from Henrik's childhood, his need to stage the world was matched by an equally strong need to stage himself. This expressed itself, for example, in a fascination for clothes. The local girls noticed how much he enjoyed visiting the house of the sexton, a man named Lund – not only because the children from the two households were friendly, but also because of the sexton's old father, and in particular his evening dress. Whenever the elegant old gentleman was about to don his velvet trousers, the brown and gold-trimmed silk waistcoat, the starched collar and the buckled shoes, Henrik would politely ask for permission to be allowed to watch. His fascination for beautiful, not to say dandyish apparel, became lifelong, confirming the impression of a shy and rather withdrawn person who, at the same time, wished to attract the attention of others – a duality that must have given him a strong sense of how he wished to manage his own appearance.

Henrik Ibsen was not born to be an artist, he was born to steal apples and run around in Skien's marketplace and in the woods around Venstøp. At the same time there must have been something more, something that pointed ahead, something that, in the perfect wisdom of hindsight, his brothers and sisters and friends were gradually becoming aware of. Memories of a boy with something special about him, who seemed ill at ease in the world, and who shielded himself from it by creating a world of his own.

Through the shadows, where memories and myths meet, this is perhaps the first thing we know about Henrik Ibsen.

He wanted to create, and he wanted to create himself.

VENSTØP

At Venstøp the family were obliged to adopt a frugal lifestyle. There was some income from the farm, but hardly enough. Knud Ibsen was able to keep going with a few odd jobs at the Fossum iron foundry and elsewhere, and he regularly submitted applications for the post of local customs officer in the region. The prospect of a regular job was probably more appealing than starting again from the bottom in business, but his applications were always returned with a polite refusal. For a time he worked for an attorney named Blom, but in the main it was a struggle to keep his creditors away, as the long series of summons and court cases he was involved in throughout the 1830s and 1840s attests.

There can be no doubt that Knud Ibsen suffered under this constant adversity, and the burden of debts, the court cases and the repeated rejection of his job applications must have affected life at Venstøp. Relatives noticed how his cheerful character was gradually replaced by a bitterness. On the plus side, when his businesses failed, friends and relatives rallied round. From a socio-historical perspective there is little to support the assertion that feelings of shame, dishonour and social rejection became associated with Knud Ibsen's name. So many people were ruined, it could happen to the best of men – and it did.[1]

The family no longer had either the money or the occasion to move in Skien's highest social circles. But the respect accorded Knud Ibsen in the days of his affluence did not suddenly turn to contempt once his ruin was a fact. Old business associates willingly provided glowing testimonials whenever he applied for a job. These describe him as capable, honest and upright, firm in character, a decent man whose probity was 'especially praiseworthy'. At Venstøp the family continued to enjoy the company of the local elite, the landowners, the sheriff, the priest. That Knud remained a respected citizen is confirmed by the fact that he was elected a deputy member of the council, and accountant for the local school and poor-relief funds. At Venstøp he hosted meetings of the parish council, and, like the keen huntsman he was, also Skien Shooting Club. There was thus an aura of genteel poverty to life at Venstøp, something which the children, too, would have sensed.

At Christmas, several so-called 'children's dances' were traditionally held. In the Venstøp area there were four that enjoyed particular status: at the homes of Sheriff Pedersen, sexton Lund, Cudrio the storekeeper – and at the Ibsens. Henrik was a keen dancer on these occasions, often dancing with the same girl throughout the evening. And the girls loved the well-mannered gallant, considering it quite an honour when he invited them to dance. Following, you might say, in the footsteps of his father, that old social lion.

The puppeteer was growing out of his cupboard. And once he had left it behind completely he found that he was not the only one cultivating the world of words and pictures.

* * *

From an early age both of Henrik's parents helped him with his reading, and in August 1833, at the age of only five and a half, he began attending Skien's *borgerskole*, a primary school for the children of bourgeois homes, continuing until 1835, when his father could no longer afford the fees. We know less about the years at Venstøp. It was probably beneath Knud Ibsen's dignity to send his son to the local 'paupers' school', and indeed none of the Ibsen children appear in the school records. Henrik probably continued his education at the school attached to the Fossum foundry for the workers' children, or possibly the school run by Christen Lund, the sexton, at Årus, south of Venstøp. Lund was the best-qualified teacher in the region, and was private tutor to the children of the chamberlain, Severin Løvenskiold, at Fossum. Lund and Knud Ibsen were part of the same circle of friends, and the children played together.

Henrik might have gone to either or both of these schools, we just don't know. But the teacher at the foundry school, a man named Hans Isaksen, had a reputation as a very good teacher, so whichever school it was, Henrik was in good hands.

In the spring of 1841, at thirteen years old, he started attending a new private school opened in town by two young theology students, Johan Hansen and W. F. Stockfleth. Even in social terms it was a very acceptable alternative to Skien's long-established Latin School. Here the children of the town's most prominent families received an education in all the usual disciplines except Latin. Henrik, however, was given private lessons by Johan Hansen. Hansen's other special subjects were Norwegian, history and religion, and he is said to have been an outstandingly good teacher. Henrik was, apparently, particularly interested in the religious studies, although a pupil from the same class recalls that he also read a great deal of history.

Henrik Ibsen's education was as good as might be expected, given his family circumstances. Perhaps it was even a little better, for although small, Skien's schools were not bad by contemporary standards. How good a pupil he was is another matter. A good index of *that* might be whether he was sponsored to continue on into higher education by a rich uncle or some other affluent local benefactor. That was common practice where young boys from poor backgrounds showed exceptional promise. The son of Christopher Blom Paus, Knud's stepbrother, later maintained that his father supported Henrik while he studied in Christiania. If this is indeed true, it may well be that he was an outstanding pupil at school. Be that as it may, the atmosphere of a school must have been good for the puppeteer from Venstøp. Whereas before he had cultivated the world of books in the shadowy shelter of the cupboard, he now made friends who shared his interests, boys like Carl Aamodt and the Lieungh brothers, Poul and Hedevall, who would get into a fight with pupils from the Latin School at the drop of a hat, and yet borrowed books from each other and tried their hand at writing poetry.

If he didn't already know it, he found out now how good with a pen he could be.

One of the first victims of the Ibsen wit was a classmate with fiery red hair who was nicknamed 'the astronomer' from his habit of sitting up in a tree or on a wooden fence and peering up at the sky through a telescope. This young man enjoyed showing off his scientific knowledge to his friends and on one occasion had composed a lampoon about Henrik.

He had failed to realise what the whole country would one day come to realise, that one could not ridicule Henrik Ibsen and expect to get away with it. One morning, before the teacher entered the classroom, Henrik displayed a sheet of paper to the class with a very good likeness of the red-headed stargazer, and below it his scientific conclusion:

'Don't believe it's inhabited.'

Throughout his childhood, and as long as the weapons were snowballs and sticks, he had been driven from the field of battle. Now wars could be fought with the pen, and all that ammunition he had been stockpiling in the gloom of his cupboard could be put to good use. And if he dipped the point in poison, victory was a foregone conclusion. There is no one more dangerous than the intellectually mature young princeling. Henrik would continue to rule successive circles of friends, winning victory after victory with his sharp tongue and his sharp pen, before life finally turned the clowning back on him.

Where friends recall a 'bright, irritable character' with a sharp tongue and a quick temper, the teacher remembers a quiet boy with an unusual pair of eyes and an undoubted talent for painting and drawing. Irascible, shy, ironic, rather vain, unusual; what is satire other than a distanced playing with life, dancing jerks in the strings of marionettes? When did the thought arise that art might be something more than a hobby? As of yet, no decision had been taken, but there was a drive. And there was a dream. For a while, between 1840 and 1842, he attended classes in drawing run by the Sunday school, though he was by no means an ever-present attendee – not surprising, bearing in mind that the school was five kilo-metres from Venstøp and classes began at seven o'clock in the morning every Sunday. Later on he was given private tuition in landscape painting by the Telemark artist Mikkel Mandt, and in the years to come he continued to take up his brush at irregular intervals, usually producing landscapes, and using his pen to draw caricatures and cartoons. And yet the dream of writing must, in time, have come to overshadow these other activities, and there is much to suggest that this dream had come to him while he was still in his schooldays.

TRYING YOUR LUCK

Henrik did not complete the curriculum at Hansen and Stockfleth's, probably returning to the *borgerskole* at some point in the year 1842. Here he had started his schooling as a small boy from the home of a businessman on the slide; now he was completing it as the son of a poor man with ambitions to rise up in the world.

On 1 October 1843 he was confirmed in Gjerpen church. According to one story, his father was deeply disappointed that his eldest son was only number three in the queue on the church floor, and persuaded himself that the explana-tion must be that the parents of the two other boys must have slipped the priest a leg of lamb, something he couldn't afford to do himself. The story may well be true, though it says nothing about whether or not the boy himself found it embarrassing to be only third in the queue. Possibly he consoled himself with the priest's comments on him in the report book on the Confirmation classes:

'Reads the Bible very well, and displays a thoughtful nature.'

Nor does it seem likely his father would have been unable to pay for a leg of lamb. Knud Ibsen still had a card or two up his sleeve. Earlier in the autumn he had sold Venstøp, and shortly afterwards the family moved back into town, into an apartment in Snipetorp, an area with a mixed population of working people, craftsmen and small shopkeepers. The apartment was one of two in the building, with a sea captain named Melsom living in the other one. It is unclear whether or not the family moved into Snipetorp as owners or tenants, but within three years Knud Ibsen was sole owner of the property. In other words, his personal drive was still in good shape, and his personal economy recovering – an impression reinforced by the fact that in the spring of 1846 he was planning to put up a new building on the site, a place where he and his son Nicolai could try to get the business up and running again.

Henrik made the move to Snipetorp along with the rest of the family but didn't stay long in the new home. Knud Ibsen's finances were still not sound enough to provide for the whole family, and, like many another boy of

Confirmation age from less affluent families, Henrik had to leave home and start to make his own way in the world. Through a friend, his father had arranged a job for him as an apothecary's apprentice in Grimstad.

What did *he* want?

A friend from his later life claimed that Ibsen had wanted to study medicine, and that the pharmacy was a step along the way to this goal. This may well be true, for in due course he planned to sit his university entrance exam.

But that was still a long way off. His immediate goal had to be to provide for himself.

Henrik left his family and his home town carrying all his worldly possessions in his two hands. What else was he carrying? Was he, as tradition maintains, also carrying with him the mark of the man who had fallen in the world, of bitterness and social shame? Knud Ibsen's ruin has gone down in literary history as one of the great tragedies, his own fate inextricably bound up with the personal and creative development of his literary son: feelings of shame at the disgrace and poverty that had befallen the family; that angst-ridden relationship to his childhood, and his alleged desire to take his revenge on the bourgeois society that had rejected him in his early years.

This theory of social degradation must be a powerful brew, for it has taken a strong hold on a whole line of biographers, all of them determined to provide Ibsen with a childhood as literary and dramatic as he obviously seemed to deserve. And from that perspective, the social degradation theory is true enough, for the role it has played in the myth of the writer's maturity through pain, or more precisely: of an Ibsen whose social criticism was the expression of an inner desire to strike back at the society that had rejected him as a child – a mythology Ibsen would contribute to himself. From a historical perspective, however, this brew turns out be thinner than water. One objection concerns just how much this 'degradation' affected Henrik himself, who was only seven years old when life so shamefully cheated him of his comfortable birthright. Did he have any particular memories of it? Another and more important objection is that the simple fact of the father's ruin would not in itself be enough to bring lasting shame to the Ibsen family – ruin and bankruptcy were much too common for that.

Whatever the effects of the events that befell Knud Ibsen and his family, there is little to be gained from describing these as the results of 'social degradation'. Another matter entirely is the ability of the different members of society to face up to adversity in life. And it is *here*, in the personal chemistry within the family, that the seed of Henrik's reckoning with his home, and with his home town, must be sought, not in over-simplified descriptions of 'social degradation' and rejection. And this reckoning only came later, and it came slowly. When, freshly confirmed, he left the town of his birth he did so simply in order to earn a living; but when he finally said goodbye to his parents, his brothers and sisters and his childhood home, it was forever.

Henrik Ibsen did not carry the mark of defeat on him when he left Skien. He was a true child of the nineteenth century, where the fluctuations of good times and bad times were the rhythm of the age, and where the threat of ruination was the price of freedom. Knud Ibsen lost, Henrik might be able to win.

Henrik Ibsen was a child of the European bourgeoisie. What he carried with him when he left home was upward aspiration. Hadn't it been his goal to take his university entrance exam and become a doctor – this socially degraded youth?

He could be whatever he wanted to be.

II

GRIMSTAD

A YOUNG MAN GOES ASHORE

One day, just before or just after New Year 1843–4, a steamship lay alongside the quay in the little coastal town of Grimstad. On deck stood a young man, strikingly attired in his full Confirmation regalia; a stranger who settled in the town, and who over the next six years would do all sorts of extraordinary things, before disappearing again as suddenly as he had come.

He was carrying with him everything he owned, and it wasn't much. He didn't have much money; or clothes, since he was using his Confirmation suit to travel in. The trunk packed with books probably accounted for most of his worldly goods. A trunkful of books and possibly a pen. Henrik Ibsen was fifteen years old when he arrived in this small coastal town to start work as an apprentice in the apothecary owned by Jens A. Reimann, who ran his modest business from premises at one end of the town's main thoroughfare.

Here he would spend the last years of his youth, in a town that was in every way itself young. Its population had doubled in the course of a few years, a result of the transition from loading port to trading town that took place in 1816. For someone arriving from the old merchant town of Skien the contrast must have been striking. Here little alleyways and snickets wound their way between houses and little patches of garden, the sewage ran through an open canal and there was neither piped water nor street lighting. At night the town was dead and dark, with only a faint light here and there from some room where a family sat gathered round a single wax candle behind the uncurtained windows.

Reimann's shop was in Storgaten, the main street, but far down, and out of the way. A small, two-storey building, one of the oldest in town, with tiny windowpanes and a small surrounding garden. Henrik's quarters were up on the first floor, in the middle of three bedrooms laid out in a line. Sharing the room with him were the chemist's three oldest sons, while the youngest boy slept in the innermost room with his parents. The maids slept in the first room, where the stairs led down into the store. At any moment the chemist might come striding through his room, which wasn't even his alone, and when a customer came calling at night he would have to tiptoe through the maids' room to go downstairs.

The freedom Henrik must have felt as he breathed the sea air on his outward journey was quickly stifled by the children and the maids in these oppressive rooms. No locks on the doors, no place to hide away, no cupboard under the stairs where he could seclude himself with his thoughts and dreams. And things weren't much quieter during the daytime in the shop below. The store itself was in what used to be the house's living room. Beyond it was the kitchen, where Henrik distilled potions, mixed the herbal preparations and sorted the pills, competing for space with the maids as they prepared the household meals.

'At least I can say I'm well content and have never regretted coming here,' he wrote in a surprisingly cheerful manner to his friend Poul Lieungh a few months after his arrival. He had nothing but praise for his employer, although – along with the other employees – he seems to have had a more strained relationship with the lady of the house.

All those who have recalled Ibsen's time in Grimstad speak of work, and more work. The clothes he wore were shabby, and spattered with the potions and powders of his trade. And when he wasn't dispensing pills he was busy dealing with the post, for the town's post office was also part of the chemist's business. When Sunday came around and he finally had some time off he often made his way up to Vesture Virden, a hilltop directly opposite the store, there to sit and read or paint. Sometimes he would row across to Maløya, or hike to the cemetery at Fjære in company with Svein Feldman, an older workman who helped out at the chemist's. A touching friendship developed between the two which lasted until the old man died.

He was very active with the brush, painting whatever took his fancy, and the chemist's was full of his pictures. He drew caricatures of people he met, of those who lived in the house, the customers, and the great and small of the town. And he proudly showed them around.

Gradually his gifts broke the ice and made the inhabitants of Grimstad aware that the new apothecary's apprentice was an unusually talented young man. From the start he had attracted attention through the quickness of his tongue and his impressive skills as a rhymester, and the local boys and girls are said to have flocked around him to hear his latest creations. As soon as work was finished he behaved like most other boys of his age. There were girls to be courted – 'The ladies, though not as gallant as those of Skien, are very acceptable,' he boasted to Poul – and trials of strength with the boys from Vektergården, where the sport lay in lifting heavy metal weights. Snowballs flew between the houses, sledges down the hillsides. And Henrik joined in. He would get roughed up now and then, and had to put up with a bit of teasing – Jørgen Peder, who lived next door, took great pleasure in burying Henrik's face in the snow. But what else could he expect when he arrived in town wearing his Confirmation suit?

But during these early years his circle of friends was small, not least because of the hours he put in at Reimann's shop.

'He spent most of his time in the kitchen with me,' the maid Marie recalled many years later. She remembered him as a quiet, withdrawn boy who could flare up whenever they competed for space on the kitchen table, him to mix his medicines, her to prepare the food.

Quiet and withdrawn, sometimes lonely. But never alone.

IN THE NIGHT

But at night, sitting at the table below the window in the bedroom, in the flickering candlelight, with the sounds of breathing from the sleeping children and maids on all sides, things were different. Then he would read, or write – poems, probably, all of them lost.

Now and then Marie would peer round the door.

'You should go to bed now lad. All that reading isn't good for you.'

But he seldom went to bed until long past midnight. Because this was Henrik Ibsen, so driven by the desire to create that nothing could stand in his way, not the pursuit of his daily bread, which was onerous enough, nor yet the very remoteness of the possibility that his pen might one day release him from his poverty. He never ceased to write, not even during the succession of setbacks and failures that would befall him in the years to come. This strength of will was Ibsen's artistic signature, long before he actually became an artist, sitting up until far into the night on the first floor of the chemist's shop, writing his adolescent verse.

But there were other ways of spending the night.

Else Sophie was her name, and she was hardly what might be termed a good match. Almost ten years his senior, she was the second of the two maids employed by the Reimanns. In general he enjoyed the company of the girls in the house, given all the time he spent with them – Else Sophie, Marie and the nursemaid Katrine. During the day he'd demand a kiss from the girls before he'd sell them caramels, and outdoors he was usually to be seen with girls on the sleigh slide. At night he had to tiptoe through the maids' room on his way to serve customers.

Bare arms above the duvet, the faces of sleeping girls in the flickering light of the candle – what more natural than that he should end up in the embrace of one of them? But why Else Sophie? One obvious answer might be that she was the one who looked after him, who washed and darned his clothes. Marie went home at the weekends, which meant Henrik and Else Sophie spent more time together.

Henrik later attributed the affair to Else Sophie's 'flirtatious behaviour and the fact that we both worked at Reimann's chemist shop'. And that's probably about all it took. But it turned out to be an unhappy affair, because Else Sophie got pregnant. In the summer of 1846 she travelled away, the usual procedure when someone was about to give birth out of wedlock and in shame. Hans Jacob Hendrichssen Birkedalen was born on 9 October 1846, and in the church register the birth was described as 'illegitimate'. A month later Henrik had still not conceded his part in the child's birth. He probably didn't want anything to do with either one of them, mother or child. But Else Sophie brought a case against him in the local court, and towards the end of December Sheriff Preus of Grimstad was instructed to obtain an admission of paternity.

So there's nothing else for it. Henrik 'concedes paternity', but points out that he isn't in any position to make a significant financial contribution:

> I am now in my 20th year; own absolutely nothing, apart from a few shabby items of clothing, shoes and some bed linen, and will shortly be leaving Grimstad Apothecary, where I have worked since the summer of 1843 as an apprentice, with no other source of income than my board and lodging and the above-mentioned necessities of life.

Reimann, as well as others whom the sheriff consulted, confirmed Henrik's poverty, and the sheriff concluded, showing no marked gift for prophecy, that Henrik had, all things considered, 'rather limited prospects'. He was ordered to make an annual contribution of 8 spesidaler until the child reached the age of five, with progressively lower amounts until the boy was fifteen. The unhappy father was informed of these responsibilities by Sheriff Preus on 18 December.

Thereafter paternity became a matter of memories and money. Else Sophie had left town with the boy, and there is nothing to indicate that Henrik wanted any more to do with either of them. Else Sophie and Hans Jacob, the maid's child – neither is mentioned by so much as a single word in his letters and papers. Some have suggested that the whole business created an obsessive shame and guilt in Ibsen, a feeling of nemesis that would pursue him throughout his life – shame over this illegitimate child, something that also crops up over and over again in his plays.[1]

But why should he, a man who hardly ever even mentioned his own father's name again, speak openly of his illegitimate son? Almost without exception, Henrik Ibsen abandoned every significant personal relationship in his life. In light of this, his silence on the subject of the housemaid and her son is not at all surprising, and particularly not after he started a family of his own. And what did he have to be ashamed of? In the period between December 1845 and May 1847 alone, no fewer than thirty-one similar child-support demands were issued in the county, so Henrik and Else Sophie were in good – or not so good – company. Undoubtedly an illegitimate child was a burden to a father (although far more so to the mother!), and undoubtedly there was a degree of shame associated with fathering a bastard. But nineteenth-century morality was a complex arrangement, at once stern and practical. If it was officially regarded as shameful to have a child out of wedlock, it nevertheless happened all the time, and there are no grounds for assuming that this official, public shame proceeded from some intimate and privately experienced feeling of shame.

The loss of a son probably did cause him pain, but it was a pain that never showed itself in the ageing writer's sombre face, and so Hans Jacob Hendrichssen, like Hagar's son, drifts out of Henrik Ibsen's life.

* * *

Christmas 1846 at the Reimanns' must have been a subdued occasion. Maybe Henrik, with his newly acquired financial burden, considered running away, or at least leaving that ill-fated town where the gossip must have spread like wildfire. On the other hand he was still as poor as ever, and the burden of child-support was perhaps, paradoxically, a good reason to hang on to his steady job as long as he could. Because it can't have been much of a Christmas for Reimann either. Business had stagnated over the year, and back in August the shop had been sold at public auction. Reimann appealed against the decision and, for the time being, carried on in business. The new year saw changes that finally put an end to his hopes of continuing but gave new hope to Henrik. In January he travels to Arendal to take his pharmaceutical assistant's examination. He is now entitled to call himself an assistant, and not merely a trainee. The following month Reimann abandons his legal challenge and surrenders the chemist's shop to his creditor, who in turn sells it to Lars Nielsen, Reimann's former trainee, and Henrik's predecessor in the job.

This changes things both for the history of the local apothecary, and for Henrik Ibsen. Lars Nielsen was a young man with drive and ambition, as well as a healthy bank balance. The chemist's shop was moved to a more central location in Østregade, and the range of stock expanded to include groceries and fine wines. Overnight the status of the business rose, but it meant more work for the staff. Nielsen had a number of irons in the fire – he was, among other things, the cashier at Grimstad Sparebank – and he left the day-to-day running of the shop in the hands of his associate.

So now there was plenty of work to do, and a degree of financial security. Else Sophie and his son were out of sight. Henrik could breathe more easily, though the move to Østregade didn't bring about any improvements in his living arrangements. Nielsen rented two rooms on the ground floor from Madam Geelmuyden, using one as the shop and the other as a combination laboratory, duty room, living room and bedroom for Henrik and Nielsen himself. But the situation was still a dramatic improvement. Nielsen was, like

Henrik, a hard worker and a believer in organisation, and only a few years his senior. Although they did not become close friends they shared a mutual respect and a sympathy, although not even Nielsen escaped the lash of his young assistant's tongue: 'the Beast' was the boss's nickname, used whenever he wasn't in the room.

At least there were just the two of them now, and no brood of children or seductive housemaids to disturb his nights. He drew a wage too, and soon made friends – good friends.

THE STEADFAST AND TRUE

In the summer of 1847 Henrik became friendly with a young man who had arrived in town a couple of years earlier. Christopher Due worked as a customs officer in Grimstad and had heard rumours about Reimann's curious young assistant. That two young men of the same age could have lived in the same town for two years without knowing each other tells us much about how withdrawn Henrik Ibsen's life was during his early years in Grimstad. But Lars Nielsen and Due were old friends, and so it came about that one day he called in at the chemist's shop in order to see the mysterious employee with his own eyes.

It was here that they met each other for the first time, Christopher and Henrik, across the counter of the chemist's shop. Two young men, neither one a native of the town, both with the same interests in literature and other intellectual pursuits, both of them chronically short of money. The following summer another young man turned up in Grimstad. Ole Carelius Schulerud was a law student, born and raised in the town. He was the son of Grimstad's custom's officer – Christopher's boss – and intended to continue his law studies from home. He very quickly got to know Henrik and Christopher.

These two, Ole and Christopher, became the 'steadfast and true', Henrik's good friends in Grimstad, who would in the years to come exhibit an unshakeable faith in his talents as a painter and writer. They would meet over punch in the shop's duty room in the evenings and on Sundays, three cocky young men with sharp tongues and big ideas about life and art – which they expressed in a 'wild flight' from the prosaic realities of everyday life in that sleepy coastal town. None of them can have felt especially at home there, Henrik and Christopher because they were newcomers, Ole as a student with memories of the capital fresh in his mind.

What more natural than that they should hang out together, drawn to each other by common interests and a contempt for the comfortably-off contemporaries who surrounded them, those 'empty heads with bulging pockets' as Henrik called them?

In this way Henrik found a sense of belonging in a small circle of intimates, a spiritual place of refuge, a sanctuary for oppositional spirits in the heart of that conformist little town. Their circle gradually attracted a number of other local youngsters who, despite their 'empty heads', were allowed to join, forming a sort of outer circle around the inner core of three. In his memoirs Due describes Henrik as the group's undisputed leader, with his witty rhymes, his mischievous schemes and lacerating tongue.

He must have loved to shock, enjoying the expressions on his friends' faces as they sat playing cards and drinking punch from ointment jars as he abjured all that was holy, not least the conventions of marriage. When he got married, he assured them, he and his wife would live on separate floors, meeting only at meal-times and addressing each other only with the formal 'De'. Other conventions were cut down in those punch-fired evening sessions; he ridiculed the honours system, and mocked the monarchy. Almighty God himself was brought to heel by the deism and pantheism the young chemist's assistant had discovered in Voltaire.

'There was something new and attractive about hearing these smart and unusual observations, these liberated and novel ways of looking at life, many of them new to me, bold as they were and full of paradox,' Due recalled later. Radical, shocking, but always entertaining – that was Henrik around the punch-bowl in the evenings, until his friends, noticing that he seemed tired, and aware of the fact that he liked to sit up late writing, respectfully took their leave of him.

Dancing jerks in the strings of the marionettes. Henrik was in the group, but not of it. Popular, yet somehow elevated above the others, shielded by his irony and his repartee. He made no effort to be liked, though he made sure he was noticed. During these transitional years from boyhood to manhood he grew a thick beard, fashionable enough at the time, and yet still striking in one so young. He was no longer the defenceless little boy in the cupboard under the stairs; the beard symbolises strength, as well as offering protection from the surrounding world. It left the young Ibsen caught somewhere between an uncomfortable shyness and a powerful urge to be seen, to be noticed, torn between his distress at being an outsider and his equally powerful need for a personal freedom that was on a constant collision course with small-town conventions and the limitations imposed by his own poverty.

In more conciliatory moments he might direct his sarcasm against himself and the lowly material conditions of his life, but it was just as likely to be directed at others, and in particular local boys who wanted to be a part of the group but had failed to show the requisite intellectual attributes for entry into the inner sanctum of the triumvirate, conditions of entry formulated by the master of ceremonies himself, Henrik Ibsen. This was the fate of two boys in particular, Daniel Martini and Sigurd Ørbech. On one occasion Henrik wrote a lampoon to the tune of a well-known vaudeville song, illustrated with his own drawings, which he got the hapless Martini to sing, blithely unaware of the fact that he himself was the subject of the lampoon. When at last he did realise he burst into the chemist's shop and threatened to give Ibsen a thrashing. He was a well-built young chap and would have been perfectly capable of it, but Henrik was never one to let his pen or his tongue be guided by such considerations.

Ørbech's fate was to be presented with a verse for inscription on his own future gravestone – in itself a dubious gesture – entitled 'Sigrid Von Finkelbeck's Grave':

When the last brandy bottle was empty
They carried him to his grave;
The flowers that grow there, they say,
Still smell of Finkel to this day!

Henrik certainly got himself noticed in town, but his antics didn't turn people against him. On the contrary, he and Ole and Christopher were always invited along when the other young people organised boat trips on Sundays, played billiards or arranged dances, fancy-dress or otherwise. One of the 'empty heads' even lent him money to buy a suit so that he would be able to attend a ball. Henrik's response was typical: 'In the first place he's stupid enough to lend me the money, and in the second place he's stupid enough to think he'll get it back.'

It was no easy matter, being one of Ibsen's benefactors, as others would find out in the years to come. But balls there were, with punch, tea, coffee and home-made bread. On such occasions Henrik could be on top form. At one 'banquet' he gave a fiery speech denouncing all emperors and kings, and hailed the republic as the only viable form of government.

He might be able to topple monarchs, but asking a girl to dance was a very different matter. What had happened? He had, after all, danced before. Was it manhood and the demons of desire that now made him as inhibited in the presence of young girls as he had formerly been seductively gallant at the inno-cent dances of his childhood? Just how assertive could a poor boy allow himself to be when faced with those small-town young ladies, many of them the daugh-ters of ship-owners? A poor boy who, moreover, had acquired a certain reputa-tion after that unhappy business with Else Sophie Birkedalen? The hint of social inferiority must have accentuated the feeling of distance he felt towards the other young people in Grimstad. And if the story that Henrik once told Due is true – that there were times when he dispensed with the use of under-wear as a way of saving money – then maybe that in itself was reason enough.

* * *

It wasn't very difficult for Henrik, Ole and Christopher to make fun of the small town's respectable citizens. Intellectually speaking, they were big fish in a small pond. In his old age Ibsen admitted that he had probably gone a little too far in his teasing of people whom he did, in fact, like and respect.

And Grimstad had more to offer a young and hungry upstart than Ibsen himself has suggested. If the town was in some ways an insignificant little place it was also cosmopolitan in its own way. It was an affluent town, a shipping town in which most of the young men went to sea, and the young from the better homes received their education in Christiania or abroad – even the girls might find themselves getting a last polish at a finishing school in Europe. The simple and modest southern houses were by no means the whole town; in the surrounding countryside there were many villas and large estates, home to well-established old Grimstad families with names like Bie, Pharo, Holst and Ebbel, many of them with sons and daughters of Henrik's own age of whom some at least shared his cultural and literary interests. When Christopher Due dismissed the town as a materialistic centre for the shipping trade he was ignoring the consequences of this for its cultural standards and its openness to the rest of the world. Shipping brought Grimstad into continual contact with countries like England, Holland, France, Denmark, Sweden, Finland, Russia and Germany.

The image of Grimstad as a cultural backwater reflects the truth that the whole country was actually a cultural backwater at this time. But Europe is wherever Europeans live, and in the European province of Norway the upper class formed a connected social and cultural net that was stretched thinly across the entire country. The Grimstad bourgeoisie's cultural capital included both private libraries and a reading circle that studied not only Dickens, Dumas, Cooper and Scott but also Ludvig Holberg and other Scandinavian writers. Due tells us that Ibsen was a great admirer of Kierkegaard, Oehlenschläger and Voltaire. The town acquired a theatre long before it got its church. The local drama group, of which Reimann was a member, seems to have been more active in the preceding decade, but even in Ibsen's day works by Holberg, Beaumarchais and Johan Ludvig Heiberg, the leading Danish dramatist of the time, were in the repertoire. And the travelling Danish theatre companies performed in Grimstad and neighbouring Arendal, just as they had done in Skien when Henrik was a boy. These Danish troupes reflected the repertoire at the Kongelige Teater in Copenhagen. They performed translated plays by the influential French playwright Eugène Scribe, as well as comedies and vaude-villes by the Kongelige Teater's own dramatists: Heiberg, Thomas Overskou, Henrik Hertz and Jens Christian Hostrup.

Contrary to what has previously been supposed, then, it seems as though Ibsen, while in Grimstad, had access to a broad range of classic and contempo-rary works, not to mention newspapers and periodicals in which literature was discussed and reviewed. No doubt he could also read newspapers published in the capital, especially in view of the fact that for a time the chemist's shop also functioned as the post office. And in Grimstad's literary circles there were subscribers to quality periodicals like *Bien*, and the Danish *Corsaren*. The former published, among other works, pieces by Maurits Hansen, Henrik Wergeland and Johan Sebastian Welhaven. The *Corsaren* also carried literary reviews and was in general a window on the whole cultural world of Danish political and artistic life.

Naturally, much of the cultural life was concentrated within the circle of the most affluent families, and of course, a poor shop assistant was not granted automatic access to this circle. But this was a small world, and in time Henrik became a participant in the cultural life of Grimstad through friendships, visits to the theatre, conversation and the borrowing of books. Lars Nielsen, his employer at the chemist's shop, was among those who invited Henrik in from the cold. Nielsen's parents lived next door to the shop, and Henrik ate his evening meals with the family. Nielsen senior was one of the town's most important men, a sea captain and a ship-owner, and his wife an intelligent woman with strong religious beliefs. Both of them took an interest in Henrik, and Fru Nielsen's friend, a woman named Georgiana Crawfurd, kindly gave the intellectually thirsting young man access to her private library. Here he was able to study the works of Søren Kierkegaard, Henrik Wergeland, Friedrich von Schiller, Gotthold Ephraim Lessing, Johan Wolfgang von Goethe and William Shakespeare.

And all the signs are that he read voraciously.

Over the years scholars have been at pains to try to trace Ibsen's literary influences among the writers he might have read in his youth – no easy task, since he clearly had access to the literary canon of the western world. The influences are more reliably traced backwards, from Ibsen's own writings. But there is little doubt that he imbibed them during the later years of his time in Grimstad.

From about 1848–9 a sort of avalanche seems to have occurred inside him. Social and hormonal, but also creative and intellectual. At the same time as the witticisms were being bandied about in the chemist's duty room and the girls twirled about on the dance floor (oh yes, with the help of Due and others he finally made it onto the dance floor), an artistic and intellectual vein opened up in him, reflecting the much greater creative revolution that was sweeping across the continent of Europe at that time.

Henrik Ibsen entered his *Sturm und Drang* period in the little coastal town of Grimstad, in little Norway, at the same time as the revolution of 1848 was setting Europe on fire – the great fire in Europe and the little one in Grimstad.

From this time onwards, everything would be different.

THE SPIRIT OF 1848

The revolution of 1848 was not one but many revolutions that formed part of a series of greater and smaller uprisings that had washed over the continent of Europe in the wake of the great French Revolution of 1789. In one way or another almost every European land was affected by revolution. The year opened with several uprisings among Italian states demanding free constitutions; next came the February Revolution in Paris. After two days of fighting in the streets King Louis-Philippe was driven from the city and the people proclaimed a new republic.

With that the spark was lit. In the course of the spring there were uprisings in several Italian cities. The Magyars in Hungary rose up against their Hapsburg overlords. The revolution spread to Vienna, capital of the Hapsburg monarchy. Metternich was toppled from power. Germany followed: there was street-fighting in Berlin and other cities, until the Prussian king, Friedrich Wilhelm IV, acceded to the demands of the reformers. Serbs, Bohemians, Croats and Poles rose up, liberal demands for reform were heard in England and Sweden, in Paris the workers marched, Venice declared itself an independent republic, in Italy the Lombards rose up and in Schleswig-Holstein the German-speaking population demanded liberation from Denmark. In Denmark itself absolute monarchy was abolished in 1849. The outbreak of war between Germany and Denmark was the most dramatic manifestation of the 1848 revolution in Scandinavia, but Marcus Thrane's popular uprising in Norway was fanned by the same winds. The rapid and widespread nature of the revolution was at least in part a consequence of the failure of the potato crops over the whole continent the preceding year. Along with a financial crisis the crop failure created a situation of acute famine that drove thousands of Europeans across the sea to America in search of a better life, and fanned the flames of political revolt among those who chose to stay behind.

In many ways the revolution of 1848 was a delayed uprising among European countries, in particular those countries in which the French battle cries of liberty, equality and fraternity were still rhetorical flourishes rather than reflections of reality. The motor behind the revolution was the Industrial Revolution and an increasingly self-assertive bourgeoisie demanding economic liberalism, freedom of expression and free elections. Behind it all lay a new view of human affairs, the demand of the French Revolutionaries for human dignity and, as an extension of it, the ideas of the bourgeoisie on subjects like personality, the individual and the freedom of the individual – ideas echoed in the arts through the Romantic cultivation of the poet-genius. At the same time the lower classes in the countryside rose up, as did the modest but still growing industrial working class, largely consisting of the lower classes from rural towns who had been drawn to the cities and were now living out their new-found freedom as slaves in a capitalist world of industrial overlords. In 1848 Karl Marx wrote his Communist Manifesto.

But there was more. From a continental perspective the revolution was not least a regional and national uprising – ethnic, if you like – in which Europe's smaller and more peripheral nations and peoples rose up against what remained of the old European regimes.

People are right who claim that the spirit of revolution did not have the same appeal to Norwegians as it did to other nationalities. This was probably an effect of the tradition of liberalism the country had already introduced with the constitution of 1814. But even here there were uprisings and demands for political reform. Indeed, the whole of the 'national breakthrough' in Norway was part of a wide stream of ideas and visions that took sustenance from the 1848 revolution. So, too, was Marcus Thrane's movement, and to some extent Scandinavianism (especially in Sweden and Denmark, where Scandinavianism was reinforced by fears of the threat of Russia in the east, and the German states in the south).

The revolution of 1848 was about the small against the great, the periphery against the centre, the new and the young against the old and the failing, the freedom of the individual against the traditional establishment and the heavy hand of despotism.

This was the last large-scale revolution in Europe and, as so often happens, a reaction occurred even before the final echoes of the struggle had died away. The revolution encouraged different kinds of revolt and different ideologies that involved self-contradictions, or the potential for self-contradiction. Thus there were internal contradictions in Norwegian nationalism, as there were between nationalism and Scandinavianism. These differences would become increasingly visible with the passage of years. The revolution was socially heterogeneous, and the generations that were part of it would come to follow very different political and ideological paths. The year 1848 marked a changing of the guard in the hierarchy of power in Europe; the aristocracy suffered a crushing blow, the bourgeoisie improved its position, and the lower class remained the lower class, but under new masters.

In Norway too, a country without an aristocracy, power became vested in an alliance of the bourgeoisie and the civil servants, as Marcus Thrane's supporters would learn to their cost. The revolutionary spirit of 1848 was replaced by reversals and consolidations over the course of the next ten years, where the priority was to ensure capitalist growth and the sovereignty of the world of the bourgeoisie.

* * *

What does all this have to do with a poetically inclined chemist's assistant in Grimstad?

Everything, because Ibsen would absorb the ideas of his age in a way that would remain with him for the rest of his life. Indeed, he would become himself a Norwegian representative of what is often called 'the generation of 1848'. Via the newspapers he could trace the consequences of the revolution both in Christiania and in the wider world. His dismissal of the monarchy and all that was sacred may well have been directly inspired by reports in *Morgenbladet* of the February revolution in Paris. In later life he was open about the fact that the proclamation of the republic in France was the first political event that attracted his serious attention:

> The times were in foment. The February revolution, the uprisings in Hungary and elsewhere, the Schleswig war – all this gripped me powerfully and became a part of my maturing process.

Ibsen composed stirring battle-hymns for the Magyars' tragic struggle for freedom – 'The Magyar is no more, his last great battle has been fought' – and equally stirring paeans to the Danes' war with the German invaders in the struggle over Schleswig.

The complex of currents and ideas of the times took root in him. In his youth he was captivated by the collectivist thought that lay behind national romanticism and Scandinavianism – indeed, for a time even by Marcus Thrane's social revolution – before he gradually came to identify with the deeply felt and subtle demand for freedom of the bourgeois world. This demand for individual freedom and personal autonomy resonated strongly with him, and in time would become the most outstanding characteristic of his work.

But there is more: Ibsen's awakening to his role as a young and aspiring poet also came at a decisive historical moment. In the decades that succeeded the year of revolutions a new and creative spirit emerged from within countries outside the traditional group of trend-setting European cultural lands. Often they were small countries on the periphery of Europe in search of a national identity, countries like the Netherlands, Belgium and the Scandinavian lands. The same thing happened in the United States, especially in the field of literature, and of course in Russia as well, which in this period gave to the world names like Dostoyevsky, Tolstoy and Turgenev. And not least in Scandinavia, where Henrik Ibsen was among the most important exemplars of this peripheral cultural awakening. The phenomenon coincided with the development of a new kind of cultural public life in nineteenth-century Europe, a broad and variegated public life, in which liberal bourgeois societies produced their own artist class, a market-based, dynamic and modern group that provided an overarching firmament for the capitalist, bureaucratic and materialist bourgeois society.

Only rarely have artists, and in particular writers, enjoyed the sort of status that they attained during the decades that coincided with the span of Henrik Ibsen's life. Poets were the priests and the shopkeepers of capitalist society rolled into one. They were to fulfil the role of the poet-genius, responding to a call that elevated them above the material world, at the same time as they by and large lived by the same market principles as any merchant. In the final analysis it was the poets, perhaps for want of something or someone better, who were both to chastise society and to formulate its new ideas, pointing the way forwards towards progress and the future.

The poet's role in society was that of a 'poet-bourgeois', and poet-bourgeois was exactly what Henrik Ibsen would become.

Viewed in the light of this broad perspective on developments that followed the last great revolution in Europe, it becomes easier to see how Lars Nielsen's assistant in his chemist's shop in provincial Grimstad in provincial Norway was actually at the very centre of things, on the crest of a wave of what was to come.

'SCANDINAVIANS AWAKE!'

But it was poetry that came first.

Ibsen was a poet before he became a dramatist, and he remained a poet long after he had committed himself to the theatre. It was here that his talent was most obviously visible, that remarkable talent for chopping and cutting words into rhyming shapes that so impressed those around him – and possibly even impressed himself. His command of drama as a form took considerably longer to acquire.

As was the case in later life, the young Ibsen wrote verse on very different levels that ranged from nonce poems to poems on matters of political and public debate to verse on such perennial preoccupations of the lyricist as love and the problems of art. And then there were poems, often cycles of poems, often described as masterpieces, that were the products of inspiration, profound and rich compositions on a higher level altogether than occasional verse on matters of the day or the quick-witted allegory. To this class belong great poems such as 'In the Picture Gallery', 'On the Heights' and 'Terje Vigen', and – at a stretch – his youthful 'The Miner' – poems that have secured Ibsen's place in literary history as a lyricist.

At his best he could be 'inspired' in his youthful verse too, but if truth be told, most of it was probably in the nature of exercises or formal studies. Thematically the poems range from national romantic evocations of moods in nature and motifs from folk poetry to political battle-songs, but for the most part they are on the subject of love and death, doubt and hope, as well as many on the subject of the artistic calling.[2]

Many of the poems revolve around memories and ideals rather than life itself. There are differing views on the young Ibsen's flight from the world. Do these poems express a 'paradoxical idealism', a striving after ideals that were impossible to realise in this world?[3] Or did he genuinely believe that ideals could be realised through action, even while recognising that life is implacably hostile to the process? What is certain is that a belief in the power of action is clearly present in the political poems, not least those inspired by the revolutions of 1848 and the wave of enthusiasm for Scandinavianism that followed the outbreak of the war between Denmark and Germany over Schleswig.

To the extent to which Ibsen acquired an ideological standpoint in his youth, Scandinavianism was one of its cornerstones. The other was national romanticism, and together these two ideas define his political, cultural and literary attitudes up until the middle of the 1860s. Of the two it was national romanticism that was probably the more prominent. The nationalist thought was more than an ideological position; it was a way of looking at life. The European nationalist breakthrough came late to Norway, but it came good, stimulated by opposition to centuries of cultural pressure from Denmark, and the need to strengthen the young nation with a clear historical and cultural identity. A version of Norwegian national identity had existed for a long time, but it was not until the 1840s that the appeal of the idea grew wider with the appearance of national romanticism. The essence of this was a belief in the existence of a cultural and ethnic community between all Norwegians, a 'national soul' that represented a 'real' Norway, and one which showed itself most clearly in peasant society.

National romanticism had its most powerful impact in the world of the arts, with a series of large-scale arrangements at the Christiania Theatre in March 1849 as its apotheosis. Here the great artists gathered to celebrate the nation; the climax was an epic tableau fashioned after Adolph Tidemand and Hans Gude's painting *Brudefærden i Hardanger*, with a script by Andreas Munch and music by Halfdan Kjerulf.

This high-flown national romantic tableau was the quintessence of the Norwegian cultural scene that Ibsen now entered as a young adult and an aspiring writer.

But the nationalist breakthrough was not solely a phenomenon of the arts. At the same time as it started to become a feature of artistic expression it also became the subject of a scientific examination of the nation's history, its language and its folklore, inspired by the ideas of the German cultural philosopher, Johann Gottfried von Herder. It meant that artists and scientists focused their efforts on the same subject: the nation, and those national treasures that lay hidden deep inside the people. What the people themselves made of it is less clear. In Norway as elsewhere, the elite were the driving force behind the nationalist breakthrough, discovering their raw materials in the country's history and in a native culture that was believed to have been preserved by the common people living out in the rural parts of the country. But in this very belief lay also a contradiction. However enthusiastically one might cultivate peasants and peasant culture, it was a matter of some importance that these expressions of the national spirit be refined into something more appropriate to a higher socio-cultural level. The result was a national romanticism characterised by a tension between 'high' and 'low' versions of it. A further tension existed between the 'national' and the 'classical'. For that part of the elite that consisted of the sons of civil servants in particular, those who rose to positions of social power during the 1830s, it was unthinkable that a cultivation of the national should take place at the expense of the classical heritage of European culture. The task here was, instead, to build the national on the foundations of the classical.

So national romanticism was full of contradictions, and more would emerge as time went by. Influenced by the way in which national romanticism had been put on a scientific footing, and by new aesthetic ideals, Henrik Ibsen too in the 1850s rose up, not against national romanticism as such, but against what he saw as the shallow and superficial version of it promoted by the older generation. In Grimstad he found himself still walking in the footsteps of his forefathers. A number of poems from these years are dense with national romantic motifs, poems like 'Midnight Mood', 'Evening Walk in the Woods' and 'The Miller Lad'. The last of these is dedicated to 'Myllarguten' ('Millerboy'), or Torgeir Augundsson Øygarden, a virtuoso on the Hardanger fiddle who took audiences in the capital by storm with his playing, and is richly spiced with references to enchanted and supernatural beings from Norwegian folklore. It has many similarities to Welhaven's poem of the same title, placing the young Ibsen securely within the prevailing tradition of national romanticism.

In this context the poem 'To Norway's Skalds' (1850) is interesting, because in it Ibsen tries to outline a programme for national-romantic poets. As programmatic statement the poem has probably been overrated – what young man is really able to map out the direction of his whole future at the age of twenty-two? In the poem he attacks the narrow cultivation of the past at the expense of the present:

Why, Bards, so obsessed with a Past so far distant
With long-interred eld, with memories that moulder –

No, the soul of the nation is more likely to be found in the living traditions of the common people in the country villages and towns . . .

Ha, do you not see there the riches that glimmer
A poem of folk-life with beautiful flowers!

Fine words, and not easy to live up to. Because Ibsen himself spent a lot of time poring over mouldering memories; only gradually was he able to liberate himself from the influence of Adam Oehlenschläger and the Romantics. And even though he did, in several plays from the 1850s, explore the world of the folk tale, it was the historical drama that he took to the heights of mastery – for the most part free of mouldering memories.

And yet what is most striking about 'To Norway's Skalds' is the profound identification with the very essence of national-romantic notions of a Norwegian national spirit that awaits only upon the bard's inspirational: 'Be!'

The poet-midwife to the nation. This was the young Ibsen's programme.

So then how could he, in other poems of the same period, unreservedly hail the Swedish king and the ideal of Scandinavianism?

Foreign observers have struggled to understand the relationship between nationalism and Scandinavianism in Ibsen because they have failed to understand the real nature of the nationalist breakthrough in Norway. This is most clearly evident where the impression is given that during his early years Ibsen was, so to speak, faced with a choice between the nationalist project and Scandinavianism (and, later, pan-Germanism) – or, artistically, between national romanticism and other tendencies.

But the question is not only what Ibsen thought but also what he *might* have thought. In mid-nineteenth-century Norwegian society the nationalist breakthrough formed an intellectual ceiling that covered the whole mental landscape. *Beneath* it a number of different tendencies and currents existed, from conservative loyalty to the Union to Norwegian nationalism, which in time came together to form Venstre (the Left). But in one way or another all were nationalist. So when Ibsen hailed Scandinavianism and wrote paeans to the Swedish king at the same time as he was writing plays in the spirit of national romanticism, it is mistaken to interpret these as contradictory ideological projects, for Scandinavianism was regarded as an extension of the nationalist idea.[4] Indeed, it was held that whereas Danish and Swedish culture had been diluted by outside influences, that which was essentially Nordic had been better preserved in Norway, and that therefore Norwegian nationalism also benefited Scandinavia as a whole.

That the Norwegian elite, raised and educated in a Danish – and thus continental – tradition, should turn its back on the large cultures in neighbouring countries was actually an absurd notion. Scandinavianism functioned therefore as a kind of bridge-builder between the national and the continental, and for precisely this reason was hailed by the nationally minded elite of the civil service.

Henrik Ibsen was no exception:

Far in the North a great oak-tree soared, –
The heathen days saw its dawning; –
Deep down in the soil its root explored,
Full noble its heaven-bent awning; –

With its roots highest in the north – in Norway – the branches of the
Scandinavian tribe stretched from the Arctic Ocean to the German border.
And it was primarily Germany that was a threat to the unity of the Nordic
lands. When war broke out in 1848 over Schleswig, Ibsen wrote 'Scandinavians
Awake!', a fiery injunction to Norwegians and Swedes to come to the aid of
their Danish brothers against the Germans.

The conflict between Denmark and Prussia was the only political event that
Ibsen ever became wholeheartedly involved in. And such involvement was not
particularly unusual in 1848; he was still, at the time, a young man afire with the
spirit of the February revolution. And he was not alone; the Schleswig-Holstein
question fuelled the pan-Scandinavian moment in all three lands. When
Denmark finally succeeded in driving the German forces out in January 1851 it
was with the help of Swedish and Norwegian auxiliaries. Essentially, Denmark's
success owed more to the pressure exerted by the European great powers than
to Scandinavian military prowess, but this did nothing to dispel the feeling that
it was a triumph for the Scandinavianist dream, now not only in the form of
poems and after-dinner speeches but also on the field of battle.

If the first Schleswig war enthused and unified the region, the second that
broke out in 1864 proved a very cold shower. This one too would leave its mark
on Ibsen's poetry, although a mark of a very different kind. In both instances
the Danish–German conflict affected more in Ibsen than just his Scandinavianist
faith. Even the warlike youthful poems in support of Denmark conceal other,
deeper motives, motives on the subject of the tensions between ideals and
reality, tensions that spring from a Romantic cultivation of the transgressive
and heroic man of action – for what is it, if not *action*, that bridges the idea and
the real?

But Ibsen was no Lord Byron, the poet who risked his life in the Greek war
of independence against their Ottoman overlords; he was a chemist's assistant
in Grimstad, and his pen was the only weapon he wielded.

* * *

Like the Magyars' 'young generation', Ibsen's Scandinavian brothers in the
south fired him into action – that's to say, into writing poetry. The young
women of Grimstad were, if anything, an even more powerful source of poetic

inspiration. Among them was Sophie Holst, from one of the town's best families, whom he one day invited to be his partner at a dance. His courtship brought him little more than inspiration. She, for her part, found her place in literary history as one of the young 'Sylphs' whom he hid in 'The sea of dreams with the treasures of memory!' The memory of a love that was never reciprocated.

But it was not Sophie who turned out to be the love of his young life. That was Clara Ebbell, with whom Henrik fell head over heels in love in the summer of 1849, and who became the inspiration for a stream of love poems in the course of that autumn. It was said that Clara Ebbell was not among the prettiest of Grimstad's young women, but she was perhaps the most unusual. She was the daughter of a merchant, from one of the town's more prominent families, a serious and intelligent young lady of nineteen who adored music and literature. Of course, and quite properly, Henrik never won her heart. Great love must always involve the worship of a woman who was either his social equal or his superior and whom he could not win, unlike the readily accessible women of a lower social class.

Else Sophie, the maid, and the refined Miss Clara Ebbell came from two different worlds, the one earthly, the other heavenly.

And it was the heavens, the starry heavens, that the young poet aspired to:

Oh Clear [Klare] Star! Despatch a sign
From the heights eternal! –
For the soul's eye twinkle, shine
Friendly, though supernal! –

It's true, as people say, that Ibsen usually wrote poems when he was in love. And in Grimstad it was the heavenly Clara who waved to him in his poetical dreams. In the new year, however, earthbound Clara upped and got engaged to a much older man, a seaman who had given up the sea, and who also happened to be her uncle – a circumstance that brought her young suitor down to earth with a bump. When the poem appeared many years later in print the obvious reference in the opening line to Clara's name – 'Klare Stjerne' (Clear Star) – had been altered to 'Blege Stjerne' (Pale Star).

Love finds its expression in longings and memories; high-flown protestations alternate with melancholy resignation, now and then with sepulchral voices from the grave, as in the gothic 'Dance of Death', in the manner of Goethe and Heine. When Ibsen writes of the 'Spirit-bride of all my dreams' and his 'heart's ideal' – the love that is unattainable – he is also writing of the power of his own emotions, of those moods and longings that nurture his own inspiration and creative power. Was he really in love with Clara, or was it love he was in love with?

And it is the dream of being a poet that is the subject of 'Resignation', from 1847, Ibsen's first known serious poem, and thus a portal into the whole of his life as a writer:

Is the flash from soul's dense darkness,
Breaking through the murk forlorn,
Flaring forth with lightning starkness
Merely for oblivion born? –
Were it vain, all my desiring,
Were my dream but fantasy,
I, denied the soul's aspiring,
Cold and void my poesy! –
Then be mute, ye Intimations! –
If I cannot comprehend, –
Let me, in the ruck of nations,
Live forgotten, and so end!

The thing that matters is the *literary vocation*, an attitude of 'unending challenge' towards life in which the choice is between 'the soul's aspiring' and being 'merely for oblivion born', a theme that recurs allegorically in his next poem, 'By the Sea'. Here the creative power is described as a 'surging foam' that smashes against the cliffs before dying away – 'To the waves' seething leaven/ You've long been consigned!'

'Resignation' and 'By the Sea' are classic examples of poems that seem to tell us something about the poet behind them at the same time as they tell us nothing at all. Many have been tempted to read these poems as windows into the young poet's troubled soul, as a glimpse into the 'hidden' story of the young writer's early years in Grimstad. It's so very tempting to imagine that poor but ambitious young poet as he trudges the streets, or sits alone on Varden, pen in hand on a Sunday, with rebellion smouldering inside him, crushed now by self-doubt, and now exalted by dazzling moments of light. Ibsen, by his own account, put more of himself into his poetry, and especially into the shorter poems, than he ever did into his plays. At a dinner party many years later, when someone voiced the opinion that he had revealed himself in his poetry in a way that was not the case with his plays, his reply was: 'Yes, I should never have let those little devils be published.'

But the poetry is a treacherous source for the life, as is evident from the simple fact that the poems of Ibsen's youth are throughout characterised by an adhesion to the tenets of genre, and an attachment to certain literary influences. A trained eye will soon discover traces of Wergeland, Welhaven, Andreas Munch and Jørgen Moe, as well as foreign writers like the Danish Adam Oehlenschläger, Schiller, Goethe and Kierkegaard. The line 'Let me, in the ruck of nations,/Live forgotten, and so end! – – –' from 'Resignation' sounds, for example, like a clear echo of Schiller's 'Seid umschlungen, Millionene' and Wergeland's treatment of the same idea in the line 'as those happy others,/that rhymed for the millions'.

But if it is difficult to read the life from the text, perhaps the context reveals something about the poet behind it. Because there is no reason to doubt that in his youth, Ibsen himself identified with the role of Romantic poet, and wrote and lived in a tradition in which young poets *should* write longingly and despairingly of their own vocation. So why shouldn't he feel despair too, even if, at the same time, he remained fully conscious of the rules of genre and form? In other words, the young Ibsen's inner life may well have been stormy, but not necessarily as stormy as the poetic form demanded. And if so, then that is something that an analysis of the poet, rather than the poem, will reveal.

There is, moreover, another theme, one that is not expressed openly in the lines themselves, and that is the purely practical aspect of literature as a vocation. From this perspective 'Resignation' can simply be interpreted as the expression of a young man's doubt about whether he has enough talent to be able to live from his writing. Even the idea of a 'literary calling' can be stripped of its Romantic accoutrements and read simply as another version of the sentence 'I want to be a writer'. Another matter altogether was whether he had the ability to do something practical in pursuit of his calling. But if he was himself uncertain of his own talent, his closest friends were in no doubt. After hearing Henrik recite the love poem 'In Autumn', towards the end of 1849, Due was convinced that the poem deserved to be published. Grimstad had no newspaper of its own at that time, but fortunately Due was the local correspondent of *Christiania-Posten*, and he sent the poem in to the capital.

And so it was that, in the face of his own doubts, Ibsen appeared in print for the first time. There was his poem, glowing in the columns of the *Christiania-Posten* of 28 September 1849. And if we are to believe Ibsen himself as he looked back on the occasion in later life, he retired to his room with the paper and 'puffing away/I smoked and I dreamt in sweet contentment'.

THE ART OF BECOMING A WRITER

No matter how much Henrik lived for writing, it is hard to imagine that he saw his own future as a full-time writer. In Norway at that time there were hardly any of them – even the greatest of them, like Wergeland and Welhaven, had to combine their writing with their day jobs. So in the autumn of 1847 Henrik set about studying for his university entrance examination, aware that the academic world would be his best springboard to the capital, and to a life that would enable him to pursue his literary interests.

Grimstad had no school that could offer him the teaching he needed, so his only recourse was to study for the exam privately. The curriculum covered French, German, Latin, Greek, Religion, History, Arithmetic and the 'Native tongue'. Apart from the Greek and the Arithmetic these were subjects with which he had some familiarity from his schooling in Skien. Nonetheless it was a demanding course of study for a young man who not only worked all day in the chemist's shop but then insisted on spending his evenings writing verse.

Henrik began studying under the theology student Emil Bie, and submitted written exercises to a teacher in Christiania. Among these was one entitled 'Why should a nation try to preserve the language and memories of its forefathers?' The subject of the exercise reflects the impact the rise of the nationalist idea had on Norwegian cultural life at this time, and Ibsen echoes the prevailing sentiments of his day when he writes that 'the traditions of the past' and a 'nation's individuality and character' are things that can only evolve 'from generation to generation down through the centuries'. In other words nationalism is something that develops among the people. Equally typical is his insistence on the need to protect a nation's historical heritage and 'continually develop and refine it without ever losing sight of its origins'. The people's inherited treasures must be preserved, at the same time as they are refined and renewed.[5]

The year 1848 was one dedicated to poetry, but in the following year he ploughed new furrows. He continued to write poetry, but now also tried his hand as a writer of prose and drama. The die was cast: strongly influenced by his reading for his exams, and all the impressions created during the year of revolutions, in 1849 he experienced a literary raptus which resulted in his first play. *Catiline*, the story of a nobleman obsessed with the desire to fight against corruption in ancient Rome, was written during three winter months early in 1849. Ibsen worked on it during the small hours, and the central character's tragic uprising mostly takes place at night. Catiline has lived a decadent and irresponsible life, like everyone else in the degenerating Rome around him; among other things, he has been the cause of the death of another. Burdened by shame, he hopes to atone by leading an uprising to topple the government of Rome. But his call to do so is matched by an equally powerful self-doubt. Catiline is a vacillating soul, divided between ambition and power, greatness and immortality on the one hand, and guilt, love and the need for reconciliation on the other. On each of these two sides there is a woman: the gentle and self-sacrificing Aurelia wants him to abandon his plans and retreat to a quiet, healthy and happy life in the country with her, while the priestess Furia stands for the dark longings that eventually cost Catiline his life.

Ibsen may have come across the story during his Latin studies in Skien under Johan Hansen at Hansen and Stockfleth's school; he certainly came across it as part of his studies in Grimstad.[6]

'I devoured those books,' he later wrote.

It is not difficult to see why. Catiline's fate was almost made for revolutionary literature, and Ibsen was certainly not the first to give the material dramatic form.[7] He may also have read some of those who had given the story a literary treatment before him, but most of what he needed would have been there in his Latin curriculum. In particular it seems as though Cicero's accusations against Catiline were what inspired Ibsen to mount this defence of the rebel: the noble revolutionary, the one against the many. Some critics insist that *Catiline* be considered part of Ibsen's whole project on the subject of social and political liberation, and in view of the 1848 revolution there is some justification for this interpretation of the main character's revolt against authority.[8] What is much more striking, however, is the way in which Ibsen distilled the spirit of revolution in such a way as to make it the ethical and existential battleground within a single individual, the individual's struggle against his fate. In this sense Ibsen had already set his personal seal on his debut as a dramatist in this tale of the individual's struggle to find himself in wrestling with forces both inside and outside himself, a battle between doubt and ideal, about a freedom that is opposed by life itself and by what has happened in the past; what finally causes Catiline to plunge the dagger into his own breast is the promise he gave to Furia that he would kill her sister's murderer – a man who turns out to be himself.

Ibsen may have been inspired to write his play by Henning Junghans Thue's primer, *Læsebog i Modersmaalet* (*A Reader for the Mother Tongue*), which was very probably part of his curriculum.[9] According to Thue, what characterised drama as a genre was:

> The struggle between the single-minded forces of the human will, and the implacable demands of necessity ... Tragedy describes the struggle of an exceptional individual against the designs of those who run the world, a struggle in which he is doomed to fail.

In other words, the dramatic conflict involved a struggle between human will and the forces of fate operating outside the individual, and the struggle must be played out within the context of a consistent idea. If Ibsen did indeed read Thue, then these fundamentals spoke to the distant future of his career as a dramatist. And yet it is too simplistic to reduce the young dramatist and poet to nothing more than the sum of his sources and inspirations. Instead, we should try to distinguish between an obvious influence from the historical, literary sources, and Ibsen's own inner dynamic, one in which the influences of the surrounding world are fused with certain 'mental images' deep inside him, that part of his personality which one must describe as original and unique.[10]

While working on the play Henrik was in the habit of reading aloud from the manuscript to Ole and Christopher, who both received further confirmation of their convictions that he had a future as a writer. Christopher offered to make a fair copy of the play, something he did with such fidelity that he even included the dashes Henrik had set down at those points in the text where he was struggling to find the right words.

Now what?

The public must be made aware of the play, but how? The solution lay conveniently close at hand. As it happened, Ole Schulerud was due to return to Christiania in the autumn of 1849 to resume his studies. He took the play with him and handed it in at the Christiania Theatre. The young chemist-poet's *Sturm und Drang* was to be submitted before the highest example of dramatic judgement in the land.

But the theatre was in no rush, and in the meantime the only thing to do was wait – and write. Ibsen had made his decision; it was his pen that was going to raise him up from the obscure world of the chemist's shop and Grimstad. At the beginning of January 1850 he reports proudly to Ole in the capital on his latest projects. There are poems in the spirit of national romanticism, two plays on historical-national themes entitled 'The Northmen' and 'Olav Tryggvason', as well as a short story called 'The Prisoner of Akershus'. He was also gathering most of the poetry written in Grimstad for a collection that he entitled *Assorted Poems from the Years 1848, 1849, 1850*. It seems that the plan was to publish them, but that was as far as things went.

Nothing much the matter with his self-confidence. Even at this early stage he was announcing that the short story he was working on would be his masterpiece. This projected masterpiece, which was never actually finished, was about Christian Lofthuus, the leader of an uprising by the farmers of Agder against the Danish authorities towards the end of the eighteenth century. Once again the theme of revolt was the attraction, relating the story to Catiline and the revolution of 1848, but this time in a more directly nationalist and social-revolutionary context. Ibsen had discovered the story in an old manuscript he chanced to come across and had at once been fascinated. That Lofthuus also happened to be Else Sophie's grandfather was a curious detail that he did *not* share with Ole.

He did, however, reveal that his 'imagined infatuation' for Clara Ebbell was now history. Why imagined? Had he realised that what he had really been in love with was love itself? Or was the disavowal of love a response to the fact that she had preferred the arms of that older, seagoing uncle of hers?

The letter to Ole reveals much about Ibsen's artistic and intellectual state of mind as he languished in Grimstad on the brink of a literary career. If he believed in the call as a driving force of nature from somewhere deep within himself he also had a very practical attitude to the act of writing. He tried everything – poetry, plays, prose. The Latin curriculum had introduced him to ancient Rome; perhaps now it was time to try something in the 'nationalist field'? That he could have been so mistaken as to think his half-completed short story superior to *Catiline* testifies to his uncertainty. For, as time would tell, he sounded notes in *Catiline* that would come to resonate throughout his whole literary career.

But this too is typical of Ibsen, and an important key to understanding the huge command he eventually had over audiences: he had the ability to ride successive waves of literary fashion, to switch between different literary projects with a contemporary relevance, at the same time as he endowed these various enterprises with qualities that gave a consistency to everything he did. He had displayed these for the first time in *Catiline*, without realising he had done so until many years later:

> Much of what my later writing has been about – the contrast between what one wants to do and what one is able to do, between what is willed and what is possible; that is at once the tragedy and the comedy of mankind, and of the individual – all of this is present here in outline.[11]

The contradiction in the winter of 1849–50, however, was mostly that between Ibsen's longing to be a writer and the Christiana Theatre's unwillingness to let him become one. Henrik waited and waited, but no answer came. Finally his patience ran out and he wrote to Ole, who was in no position to influence things one way or the other. Clearly the letter was somewhat intemperate, for shortly afterwards he sent a second letter of apology. Ole would please realise that his letter had been a product of his anxious impatience. All the waiting had created 'an extremely unpleasant mood' – and matters were not improved by the fact that he was still having to count every penny. With his financial obligation to Else Sophie, and the expenses in connection with his Latin lessons and textbooks, the prospect of a royalty fee for his play must have seemed like a small breakthrough in itself. Here, too, the faithful Ole was on hand to help out, on this occasion in the shape of a pair of trousers that he despatched to his impatient friend back home in Grimstad.

The new year was still young when he finally got his answer. On 5 January 1850 Henrik received a letter from Ole. Christiania Theatre had rejected *Catiline*. '*Catiline*'s death sentence – that really hurts,' Henrik wrote back in dejection. But he agreed with his friend that it was no reason to give up. *Catiline* was only the precursor of a whole series of 'plans that we have in this direction.'

These plans were still aimed at making a writer out of Henrik, a project that Ole still found worth his time and his effort, indeed, to such a degree that the following year Henrik was financially dependent on the goodwill of his friend.

So strong was his faith that Ole is said to have offered to abandon his own studies completely in order to devote himself full-time to the promotion of Henrik's work. With the profits he was certain they would make they would be able to realise the dream of travelling through Europe and the Orient which the two of them had so often spoken of in Grimstad.

If the Christiania Theatre would not open its doors to them, then they would have to take matters into their own hands. Ole suggested they sell the publishing rights to the play rather than pay for publication themselves, and Henrik agreed. After a fruitless round of the city's publishers, however, Ole ended up offering to pay for the printing and publishing himself. The most important thing was that the drama be published somehow or other, to prepare the ground for the arrival of Ibsen himself in the capital. He left Grimstad on 12 April, the same day as *Catiline* was published. He had sent a letter enclosing a rather crestfallen Foreword – it was never actually used – in which he expressed the hope that his readers would understand that it was not without 'a very natural trepidation that he offers his work to the public, from whom he nevertheless hoped for the kind of considerate response that a beginner's first effort has a right to expect'.

In other words, may the capital's elite have mercy on him – so the self-confidence that appears in his correspondence with Ole was perhaps not quite as watertight as it seemed. No matter. *Catiline* had been thrown to the wolves. All that was missing was the writer himself.

* * *

Ibsen left Grimstad and never returned. What had he gained from his sojourn there? Were they really the 'six lost years' of biographical tradition? No. Essentially the Grimstad years were a positive experience, despite the difficulties and reversals. In that little town he, Christopher Due and Ole Schulerud formed their own little world, a kind of intellectual diaspora in which the spirits were free and the sky the only hindrance to every extravagant thought about life, the world and themselves. Despite the lack of privacy, he had found the time and space in which to write while working at Nielsen's chemist shop, and in Grimstad he had access to as much literature as he could plough his way through. Together with his childhood reading from Skien it furnished him with the proper foundations for a literary and intellectual life. His arrival in Grimstad had coincided with the end of his childhood, now he was leaving as a literary tyro on the verge of manhood, with a bastard child, a full beard and all. These were not lost years. On the contrary they were highly formative years. Poverty, and the long working days, had not made it an easy life. But it is the artist's way to go through life, not round about life, and if Ibsen's biographers haven't understood this it was something that was patently obvious to Ibsen himself.

It is hard to suppose that leaving Grimstad was a wrench for him. With the exception of Ole Schulerud and Christopher Due he never saw any of the people he had known there ever again, and shortly after his departure he wrote a farewell letter to Due:

> If friendship is dependent on regular company, then ours will end, but if what defines it is the flight of like-minded spirits through the same regions then our friendship can never die.

The letter is interesting for what it tells us about Ibsen's relationships with those close to him. On other occasions he expressed sentiments directly opposed to these, insisting that friendship for him was a matter of physical presence, not least because he had never felt able to give of himself completely in correspondence. Probably his words to Due come closest to the truth. For most of his life Ibsen kept 'regular company' with just a handful of people, principally his wife and the son of their marriage. And if he felt unable to give of himself in letters, it was nevertheless through letters and short visits that he sustained his friendships. He continued for some time to see Ole, but met Christopher again only on a couple of occasions. The remainder of the people he had known in Grimstad became the stuff of memory for him – Jens A. Reimann, Lars Nielsen, seductive Else Sophie, the lovely Clara Ebbel, and all the 'empty heads' that lived there.

Henrik Ibsen was on his way, but he had one last obligation to his past to fulfil, a last farewell to take before dedicating himself completely to a life as a writer.

He travelled home to Skien.

A STROLL ON KAPITELBJERGET

From the time the newly confirmed Ibsen left his home in the winter of 1843–4 until he returned in the spring of 1850 on his way back to Christiania we know of only one occasion on which he visited his family, in the summer of 1845, probably to attend the confirmation of his brother, Johan Andreas. And he likely only visited in April 1850 because his sister Hedvig had asked him to.

The stay of a few short weeks when he was home that spring would be the last time Henrik would see his mother and father, and of his brothers and sisters he met only Hedvig and Ole again. He had never been close to his brothers and sisters. The youngest of them, Nicolai and Ole, had been no more than eight and ten when he left – useful as assistants when he did his conjuring tricks, but not as comrades. It might have been different with Johan, who was just two years younger than Henrik. But the two boys were very different. Johan had little interest in books and preferred to go off hunting with his father. Yet when Johan left for America in 1849, Henrik was the only member of the family he asked his father to pass on a farewell to. And would his father please ask Henrik to write to him?

And then there was Hedvig, just twelve years old when Henrik left for Grimstad. Now she had turned into a young lady of eighteen, and Henrik himself a man of twenty-two. An attachment between them formed that lasted the rest of their lives. Not in the sense that the two were genuinely close, for Henrik made no more effort to stay in touch with her than with the rest of his family. Yet a sort of mutual fondness existed between brother and sister, sustaining at least some sort of connection between Henrik and his roots. Later in life, in sentimental moments, his thoughts would return to that warm-hearted person who had shouldered the responsibility for the family back home. And it was to Hedvig that he confided his innermost dreams one day in 1850, as the two of them walked together through the church ruins on Kapitelbjerget above Snipetorp, with a view across the town and surrounding fields. They were talking of life and what lay ahead of them when Henrik began to speak of the compulsion he felt to reach the greatest attainable heights of clarity and greatness.

'And once you've done that, what will you do then?' Hedvig asked.

'Then I'll die.'

Hedvig was the chosen one, the one he opened up to. What of his parents? By the time Henrik returned for the last time the good days were over forever for Knud and Marichen. After the financial ruin that had occurred in Henrik's childhood his father had struggled and fought to get back on his feet again. And for a time things seemed to be going well. He and Nicolai seem to have managed to make a go of the shop at Snipetorp – the tax records for 1846 show his estimated income as 500 spesidaler, as much as he had earned during the affluent days eleven years previously. Whether he actually earned that much is open to doubt, but the estimate does not support the traditional picture of Knud Ibsen as a broken man.

But it didn't last this time either. Towards the end of 1840 things took another turn for the worse, and in the end Knud Ibsen's business activities were confined to running a small chicken farm in his garden and not much else. The records for 1859 classify him as sick and exempt from tax.

Knud Ibsen could not raise himself again after this second ruin. He had struggled for a long time, but now his strength was gone. If it was any consola-tion, the failures of his career were not his fault alone, neither the original ruin nor the failed attempt to pull himself up again. It was no easy matter for a man of his age and background to find permanent employment, not even as a junior customs officer. For the last years of his life he lived a peripatetic existence, dependent for survival on the help of his half-brothers and sisters. He had to abandon Snipetorp in 1865, and his marriage had been failing for a long time. In the end the couple separated, with Marichen dying in 1869. Johan, the second son, had emigrated to America, and with the failure of the business Nicolai followed him out. Hedvig and Ole had become members of Gustav Adolph Lammers' revivalist movement, to the distress of their father. It is probably at this point in his life that Knud begins to get the reputation of being feckless, irresponsible and vain, responsible for his own ruin and the disappearance of the inheritance from the Altenburg family, a mildly pathetic and hopelessly disorganised individual, sharp-tongued but not good with money. The picture handed down to posterity by the older inhabitants of Skien is of the final sad chapter in Knud and Marichen's last years rather than the good years. Knud Ibsen's tragedy lay not so much in his ruin as in his inability to get back on his feet for a second time. Strictly speaking it was not so much a failure as a gradual sinking down into impotence and lost illusions, burdened by debt, the numerous failed job applications, the court cases, the splits in the family, his growing weakness for alcohol and possibly, too, an element of self-destructiveness in his own nature.

* * *

Why did Henrik break with the family – and what did the breach cost him? Was it quite simply that he no longer *needed* them, now that he was going to be an artist and conquer the world? There may be some truth in that. But he claimed himself that the break was painful, no matter how necessary it might have been: 'there are so many things that stand between me and home,' he wrote to his sister much later, breaking a silence of many years, 'understand this, and do not suppose that in all these long years I have remained silent . . . out of indifference'.

No, indifference was never one of Henrik Ibsen's more obvious qualities. So then what was it? Two different sorts of explanation are usually offered to account for Ibsen's break with his family and his home town. One is based on the social decline of the family, leading to a change in Knud Ibsen that saw him transformed into a domestic tyrant and his wife into a nervous wreck – with Henrik himself heading off into life carrying a deep-seated sense of shame over these developments. Without completely dismissing elements of this first explanation, a second tradition attaches more weight to Ibsen's dislike of the Lammers' revivalist movement that had established itself with dramatic success in the Skien area the year before his return.

'There was a great deal going on in Skien in the 1850s,' one traveller noted a couple of years later. 'Social life was reduced to a minimum, and every conversation at some point or other touched on the subject of Lammers and his movement. And you would definitely not like to cross some of the ladies involved.'

Lammers appealed in particular to women. There are stories of husbands who fought tooth and nail to prevent their homes being invaded by ladies of all ages who had seen the light. Hedvig may well have been among them, a convert to the movement along with Ole, to the despair of Knud – and possibly also Henrik.[12]

There may be something in both explanations, though alone they are patently insufficient. The principal problem with the theory of a social decline is the way it is based on an assumption that financial ruin was inevitably tanta-mount to rejection and shame. Another is that the chronology doesn't add up. The Ibsen family's social decline happened in the mid-1830s, yet they continued to lead a modest and decent life at Venstøp until misfortune struck again in the 1840s. But at that time Henrik was in Grimstad. He did not have first-hand experience of his parents' tragedy, when their marriage broke up and their poverty became extreme. Nor did he have first-hand experience of the effects of the Lammers' movement in Skien apart from those few weeks in 1850. There can be little doubt but that he was repelled by the movement, and perhaps espe-cially by his sister's many attempts to convert him in letters she sent him later in life. Henrik mentions in letters of his own from a later date his 'strong anti-pathy to any closer acquaintanceship with certain spiritual tendencies down there', referring to the Lammers' movement. And yet it is hard to see this anti-pathy as being so strong that it impelled him to break so completely with his origins. Not only did he have very limited personal experience of the Lammers' movement in his youth, but many years later he became personally acquainted with Lammers and his wife while living in Dresden. Reports suggest that he got on very well with the man who had allegedly deprived him of his family.[13]

The deeper explanation must be sought elsewhere, without reference to poverty and an inability to write under such circumstances, unconnected with any view of life or motives involving social disgrace, and beyond the cold fact that he simply did not need his family anymore.

There must have been pain there – a pain within himself, and a pain that kept him apart from his mother and father. Somewhere, in the tension between the son's nature and his parents' nature, there must have been a festering wound that did not disappear, not even after an absence of years. There are signs that something happened to Knud Ibsen after his ruin was a fact, and he may well have become a burdensome presence in his son's mind. While Hedvig is still awaiting Henrik's return to Grimstad she writes to her cousin that her brother's deepest wish is to pay a visit to the family before travelling on to Christiania – 'but he has avoided mentioning it in case his father was against it'. Quite possibly Knud Ibsen became both bitter and temperamental after his ruin, turning into the bad-tempered domestic tyrant of traditional narrative. But even so, a reaction like that has little to do with social 'declassification', that being a social construct. More likely it is a matter of a personal, psychological reaction, of Knud and possibly Marichen's inability to deal with adversity, and to deal with each other in the face of adversity – and the son's inability and later unwillingness to confront the whole business. After all, it wasn't just Henrik who broke with the family. In the course of a few short years the whole Ibsen family fell apart, the entire structure collapsed.

'Our family home broke up after father's ruin,' Ole related laconically towards the end of his life. Many years had passed since he last saw his brother, and he had read scarcely a line of his brother's works.

A pain, but then, what kind of pain? That is something we will never know, as we will never know how much it was the fault of the parents and how much it owed to Henrik's own nature. Nor do we know whether it was a pain that grew slowly, like a tumour, or one that appeared rapidly as the result of some quite definite incident or set of circumstances. There are many possibilities here. Perhaps it was his underage son's illegitimate child that occasioned Knud Ibsen's hostility, or possibly Henrik's radical ideas – the sort of extreme ideas that aroused admiration in the duty room at the chemist's might have met a very different response back home. It's possible Knud Ibsen pressured Henrik to help provide for the family in Skien – he was, after all, the oldest son, and Johan had emigrated to America the year before. There are so many possible explanations that the biographer has no choice but to withdraw in silence.

Many years later Ibsen writes to Bjørnstjerne Bjørnson:

Do you know that I broke with my own parents and my family for my entire life, because I could not remain in a relationship that was based on an understanding that was only partial?

That was his way of writing, but what does it mean? Who does have a relationship of complete understanding with his family? Throughout history, how many Sunday dinners have parents and children suffered through, even where the degree of understanding in the relationship was less than partial? It was probably more to do with his own need to escape from any notion of a joined fate, from the compulsive demands of family membership – something that would be typical of Ibsen throughout his life. The need to be free of any responsibility save the one he owed to his calling.

III

CHRISTIANIA

THE VIKA BOY

On Sunday 28 April 1850 the steamship *Prinds Carl* berthed in Christiania, a city hardly out of its awkward teens, and yet the capital of the land that formed the western branch of the Swedish-Norwegian monarchy, Norway. Modest in size but growing, the town lay uppermost in the fjord, a handful of low, seventeenth-century houses in angular blocks behind the Akershus fortress. Here the city's inhabitants promenaded along the battlements on Sundays, or they travelled out to their country homes in Solli, or went for long walks in Slottsparken, at a pleasant distance from the noise and chaos of the city. The town was growing rapidly, faster than any other large town in Scandinavia. By 1850 there were some 29,000 inhabitants in the city and surrounding regions, and the population was rising as the city's business life expanded. Textile factories and mills and engineering works lined the banks of the river Aker with their dirty red-tiled facades, providing jobs for a growing working class that settled in the crooked and chaotic suburbs that appeared in the city's surrounding areas.

Christiana was changing. In the 1840s the city – and the country – had entered a dynamic phase of modernisation; a class society began to replace the society of inherited status. Industrialisation, a money economy and urbanisation combined to challenge the traditional agricultural way of life in the country towns and villages. But the modernisation process was still far from complete. The first gas pipes had just been laid, the railways didn't arrive until 1853, and a home for the National Assembly would not be built for another thirteen years.

And yet by the middle of the century the city had the recognisable features of a capital; a stock exchange built after the classical model had existed since 1828, and it acquired a university of its own between 1841 and 1852. The royal castle had taken even longer to finish but was complete by 1848. Slottsveien, later renamed Karl Johans gate, formed the spine of the new city as it grew over the succeeding decades.

Just as Norway was in the process of becoming a nation, Christiania was becoming a capital city. What it lacked it was in the process of acquiring. Among the passengers that stepped ashore in Christiania harbour that spring day was a young man who carried with him capital that would prove of immense value to the growth of both city and country. It was in the form of language, ideas and thoughts, some written down in a pile of manuscript papers, others still playing about in that small, rather square head with the serious face almost hidden behind an imposingly full black beard.

Henrik Ibsen had arrived in town, two weeks after his first book had appeared in the bookshops, to pursue his calling as a writer.

Ole Schulerud had invited him to share the little flat he rented in Vinkelgaten 17, on the corner facing Filosofigangen in Pipervigen. The landlady was Ma Sæther, a woman well known locally for her healing powers. Pipervigen – or Vika – was one of those chaotic suburbs that ringed the renaissance town behind Akershus fortress. It lay between the royal castle, the harbour and the amusement park at Klingenberg, its twisted streets hung with washing, alive with the cries of children between the low wooden houses, with here and there a building in brick. As more and more people flocked to the city the settlement gradually expanded upwards towards Ruseløkkbakken, where the infamous 'thieves' quarters' known as Algier and Tunis grew up. Overpopulated, poor and cramped – that was the Vika into which Ibsen moved. Most of the inhabitants were ordinary working people who had moved to the city from the country. Increasingly, as the century progressed, it also became home to students and prostitutes. In the evenings the sons of the city's more affluent citizens would appear on the streets in search of young women less inhibited than those daughters of civil servants with whom they walked arm in arm along the fortress ramparts of a Sunday afternoon.

Vika is often portrayed as a sort of picturesque framing for the young Ibsen's life as he struggled and suffered his way towards his literary destiny. But Vika was so much more than mere framework. Disconcertingly close to the university and the new centre that was emerging between the old settlement and the royal castle, it was also home to a lively social and political environment that the arrival of the students as the century advanced only enriched. Living at Ma Sæther's, Ibsen found himself at the very heart of Vika. The area had been home to rebels before ever he arrived. In her own way Ma herself was something of a rebel, fined several times as a quack, but pardoned on each occasion. In the 1830s Wergeland had hosted secret meetings here with his friends from the opposition Farmers' Party, and it was at Ma Sæther's that the famous revolutionary meeting of 19 May 1836 was held at which the slogan 'Down with the ministers' could be heard ringing from the windows late in the evening. In 1850 the same slogans were once again being voiced, and they brought the young chemist's assistant into contact with some of the most radical personalities of the time.

One was a man named Theodor Abildgaard, another of Ma Sæther's lodgers. Abildgaard was a law student, two years older than Henrik. He had recently become an enthusiastic supporter of Marcus Thrane's workers' movement, joining that summer. He soon rose to positions of prominence in the movement, among them spokesman for the committee charged with formulating proposals for a new constitution. With an equal swiftness he became a member of Ibsen's circle of friends. Among those who must have been awaiting Ibsen's arrival with great anticipation was Paul Botten-Hansen. Four years older than Ibsen, he came from a modest background. At the time of Ibsen's arrival in Christiania, Botten-Hansen was teaching at one of the city's private schools as well as editing *Samfundsbladet*, the organ of the students' union. It carried a review of Ibsen's *Catiline* as early as 13 April.

Botten-Hansen's real passion was neither for the life of a teacher nor of a student, but for books. In his own words he had given himself over 'to the collecting of books instead of the acquisition of some dull meal-ticket, eating once every fourteen days and in the intervening period living either on joy at the books he already possessed, or in anticipation of those he would one day acquire'. From 1851 he tried to sustain himself as a freelance writer, literary critic and magazine editor. It didn't make him rich, of course, but it made him a pioneer in the field of Norwegian literary criticism, and a central figure in Norwegian literary life.

Paul Botten-Hansen was Ibsen's first and most important literary contact in the capital. But he made other friends too in the spring of 1850, people who, like Botten-Hansen, would play their part in saving him from the student life as well as saving Norway from yet another academic.

STUDENT AND WRITER

Officially, Ibsen had come to Christiania to take his university entrance exam, enrol at the university, and then – yes, well, who knows what then? If he had ever seriously considered medicine as a career when he travelled to Grimstad he showed no later signs of it. Perhaps he envisaged some sort of career as an academic that would allow him to write in his free time. What he wanted above all was to live for and from literature as a full-time occupation. If he managed this it would make him Norway's first full-time writer, but there is no evidence that he ever seriously considered this as a possibility. Not yet. So he let common sense rule and set about studying for his exams.

Shortly after arriving in Christiania he enrolled at Heltberg's Latin School, the plan being to study intensively over the next few months and sit his exam at the end of the summer. And Ibsen used the time as best he could to do anything but study. Not very sensible, perhaps, but then there was much about the school itself that could seem less than sensible to the conventional observer, of whom there were numerous examples among Christiania's academic inhabitants.

The oddest thing of all about the school was the headteacher himself, Henrik Anton Schjøtt Heltberg, who habitually wore fur boots, a leather cap and a dog-skin waistcoat. He was a giant of a man, much troubled by rheumatism and asthma, so that he was sometimes bent double with pain behind his lectern. But between these bouts Heltberg could be a passionate and inspired teacher, very different from the popular image of a typical academic. He was of old a supporter of Wergeland, and a devout Latinist with exams that nearly proved it.

In 1846, after several years as a private tutor, he had opened his own Latin School in Christiania offering a two-year course. The school was as eccentric as the man himself.

'The method was the man, and the man was a genius,' as a later pupil once said of him, and there were many who agreed. Nevertheless, the school's primary function was straightforward: to offer pupils a quick and focused course of study aimed at passing the university entrance examination. So it was not surprising that people began calling it 'Heltberg's student factory', or just 'the factory'. What marked the school out as something more than a simple fast track to university entrance was its pupils, mainly country boys, poor people, the not-so-bright, and the odd lazy upper-class youth – the latter less than popular among the other pupils. The result was a melting pot that reflected those far-reaching social changes that were taking place in the middle of the nineteenth century. Far from churning out dutiful royal officials, sons of equally dutiful fathers, Heltberg's was actually a back door into the system for the academics of a new era, to say nothing of the poets of a new era. When Ibsen entered the school in 1850, Aasmund Olavsson Vinje had already been a student there for quite some time. A very young Bjørnson was also in Christiania at the same time, but a poor result from his examination at school at home in Molde meant that he had to wait until the autumn for a place at Heltberg's.

It was here that Henrik Ibsen and Bjørnstjerne Bjørnson met each other, though they did not become friends until later in life. Then enemies, then friends, then enemies again, then friends. Profoundly different from each other, these two would yet remain inextricably bound to each other throughout their lives.

But all that was to come later.

In the spring of 1851 Jonas Lie too enrolled at Heltberg's. By that time Ibsen had left the school, but he and Lie did get to know each other. Thus did four of the most influential Norwegian writers of the next fifty years meet, more or less in front of Heltberg's lectern. All of them young, apart from Vinje, who was thirty-two at the time. Ibsen was ten years younger, though his huge black beard made him look older, while Lie and Bjørnson were mere boys, respectively seventeen and eighteen years of age. Young and talented as they were, they spent as much time on literature as on their studies, giving the rheumatic and asthmatic Heltberg a hopeless task in his efforts to guide this 'flock of young barbarians through the Alpine passes of Latin grammar on the forced march to Rome'.

Not all of them reached Rome – or at least not at the first attempt. Neither Ibsen nor Bjørnson were particularly good students. But Heltberg taught them something else:

> That flock of 'barbarians' he led away
> Had no real goal to buckle down.
> They didn't become 'Latin scholars', nor the slaves of foreign thought,
> But ever more themselves, along the way.
> And that went for all of them. With Honours.

THE GENERATION OF 1848

The friends Ibsen surrounded himself with during that first year in Christiania formed a widely disparate group that together represented a generational shift in Norwegian society. They included radical intellectuals like Abildgaard, freelance writers like Botten-Hansen and Vinje, and aspiring writers like Bjørnson and Lie. Through Botten-Hansen, Henrik also became acquainted with Michael Birkeland who, unlike the others, actually followed the course of study. Like Ludvig Daae, who joined the circle of friends somewhat later, Birkeland would go on to make a name for himself as one of the most influential historians of his day. They were all part of the generation of the 1840s, a generation that would live through profound changes in Norwegian society, and would, in the process, split along a line that divided the defenders of established society from those who opposed it.

The establishment of that era is known to Norwegian historians as the *Embetsmannsstaten*, the Civil Service State, reflecting the dominant position of civil servants in the years between 1814 and 1884, the period between absolute monarchy and the coming of parliamentary rule. In the absence of a Norwegian aristocracy and a sustainable upper class it was the civil servants who acquired a hegemony of power in Norway after 1814. As a social class it was small, socially homogeneous and educated. Approaching the middle years of the century the bourgeoisie gradually evolved into a broad community of businessmen, shopkeepers, industrialists, bankers and ship-owners. This class aspired to the same educational, social and cultural standard as the officials, who were themselves active participants in the economic life of the country, and in due course the officials and this wealthier section of the bourgeoisie became the two pillars on which Norway's upper class depended.

It was in the field of culture and through the codes of social life – of education and cultivation – that the upper class found a way to express itself as the elite. The phenomenon was not unusual in Europe; bourgeois culture was the glue that held together a variegated bourgeoisie that could not base its legitimacy on a centuries-old tradition in the manner of the old European aristocracy.[1] And the large bourgeoisie, all of whom believed themselves superior to workers and domestic servants, pursued the same cultural and social ideals.

The Royal University in Christiania was the bastion of state officialdom and the crucible of public life. It was here people sent their sons, who could expect to graduate to solid positions within the network of the civil service state. These same sons married, in due course, the daughters of other civil servants, producing in turn sons and daughters who went on to enact the same cycle. The university was the place where the regime's social, political and cultural capital was concentrated. Art was in most respects an academic matter, with the divide between literature and science more or less invisible, in the same way as the borders between the various scientific disciplines were unclear. The classic fields of study for the civil service class were law, theology, medicine and philology. Only gradually did the 'newer' subjects like history, archaeology and mathematics emerge as disciplines of their own. In other words, the world of the civil servant was a world of education, anchored in a socially reproductive educational system that united both scientific and cultural capital, and in the final analysis political power as well.

By the middle of the century, however, the exclusivity surrounding this cultural domain was coming under pressure as a new generation of writers and academics from a broader social background and with different prospects for their future began to make its appearance. Botten-Hansen and Vinje were the sons of smallholders, Lie and Daae the sons of civil servants and thus representatives of tradition. The same could be said of Bjørnson too – son of a priest, but from a long line of farmers. Ibsen and Birkeland were from the middle echelons of the merchant class, both from homes that had experienced financial ruin and therefore poorer than their background would actually suggest. For Ibsen this all meant that no great change was involved in his life, no social leap of the sort taken by both Vinje and Botten-Hansen. As the son of a failed businessman the educational course he was now embarked on was the natural one for him, provided he would be able to fund it. In time this new intelligentsia would break open the ring of exclusivity that surrounded state officialdom. In fact, this dramatic development was already under way, stimulated by modernisation, urbanisation and increasing social mobility. Christiania was in the process of establishing a genuine bourgeois public sector that was, in principle at least, accessible to a wide social spectrum, a public forum in the shape of an expanding press and the beginnings of the institutionalisation and professionalisation of cultural life and science.

Within the academic world this development was characterised by continuity and an inner dynamic, while what was happening in the cultural world involved a break, since a completely new system was being established, one based on market forces, the appearance of new institutions, private capital and, in a gradual way, state funding. The watershed came in the 1830s, when Norway had its first public cultural debate in the so-called 'Dæmrings-striden', ('Dawning Debate') involving Welhaven and Wergeland. This new form of public life was, by 1850, still in its infancy, and the degree of accessibility and openness should not be overestimated, particularly if one were, like Vinje, the son of an impecunious smallholder, or had worked as a poor chemist's assistant, like Ibsen. Through the twenty-two-year-old Ibsen's eyes, as he unpacked his suitcase in his room at Ma Sæther's, the public life of the capital city must have seemed daunting, not to say intimidating.

What chance did he have of making it as a writer and a man of letters, with no money, and lacking in the sort of connections that would traditionally open doors for an ambitious young man?

* * *

So Ibsen didn't find the table already laid for him when he arrived in Christiania. If he was to have any hope of living from his writing then he would have to help lay the table himself, take part himself in the process of establishing a cultural public space in which he could operate. And that is exactly what he did, along with Vinje, Bjørnson, Botten-Hansen and the others. The main goal of this generation of intellectuals was to contribute to the development of a broad and independent cultural public space in Norway – independent in the sense that it would be a modern, professionalised cultural field not reliant on the social capital of the civil servant class, and funded partly by the market and partly from state funds.

None of this was going to happen of itself. Ibsen's generation of intellectuals were therefore nation-builders, not only because they studied and wrote about national themes, but also because they were – and had to be, each in his own way – the creators of their own institutions.

When both Ibsen and Bjørnson decided on the theatre it was not merely because of their talent and literary preferences. In reality the theatre was the only developed literary institution in Norway at the start of the 1850s, based as it was on private companies and an audience that had learned to appreciate theatre as part of its education. The few who attempted to carve out a career writing for the market were generally doomed to fail.[2] There were authors, and, with the increase in the general level of literacy, a constantly expanding readership, but there was no network of publishers to speak of, no booksellers or critics, nor any government policy aimed at sustaining this type of cultural life.

But the theatre was important not merely as a literary institution. Here the men and women of the ruling class met to see and be seen, here the cultural and social values of the regime were cemented in ceremonial form, both on the stage and in the auditorium. The theatre was to culture what the Storting was to politics, and voting took the form of standing ovations or ferocious booing and whistling, the classic example being the 'Campbells riot' of 1838, in which Wergeland's play *The Campbells* occasioned an all-out brawl involving Welhaven's 'Danish' party and Wergeland's patriots. So Ibsen's choice of drama involves something more than a simple artistic choice, particularly so when, in due course, he was appointed director and manager of some of the country's theatres. It involved a life in the spotlight in which he had to endure attack from some of the sharpest pens in the country, the judgement of audiences, either in the form of whistles and boos or, worse still, when they simply failed to turn up at all. He was obliged to construct a theoretical and political programme and be prepared to defend it publicly. He was responsible for the finances of the theatre, solving practical problems, and keeping his actors and technicians happy. In sum he was charged with constructing an institutional framework in which to place his writing.

If Ibsen wanted to make a success of things he would have to live with a pen in one hand and a trowel in the other.

HA!

In the first instance he was kept busy enough persuading the world around him that he existed. In the midst of all the excitements and stimulation the capital could offer, one thing obsessed him above all: his calling as a writer, and in particular the fate of his debut as a playwright.

Catiline had not exactly taken Christiania by storm. Of the first print run of 250 it has been estimated that some forty-five were sold. Which is not the same as saying the play sank without trace. Following Paul Botten-Hansen's review in *Samfundsbladet* two more followed, one in the *Christiania-Posten* of 16 May, and the second in *Morgenbladet* on 5 July, before it was finally reviewed in the country's most important literary magazine, *Norsk Tidskrift for Videnskap og Literatur* (*Norwegian Magazine for Science and Literature*), in the month of October. With that, *Catiline* had been reviewed in what were, in 1850, Norway's most important literary forums. The *Morgenbladet* review was particularly significant, not so much because of what was said in the review as because the magazine's acting editor, a professor of philosophy named Marcus Jacob Monrad, had added an editorial comment of his own to the foot of the review.

Monrad's personal attention meant that Ibsen had attracted the notice of the very top of the civil servant state's cultural hierarchy.

What more could a debutant hope for?

Good reviews, of course.

Both the *Norsk Tidskrift for Videnskap og Literatur* and the *Christiania-Posten* were agreed that Ibsen was a promising writer, 'undoubtedly a talent', echoing Botten-Hansen's comments. But there was criticism. Reviewers were irritated by the way the characters constantly feel a need to cry out 'Ha!' at any given moment, and in general criticised the exaggerated intensity of the piece, its 'hysterical pathos' and the stilted, declamatory style of the dialogue. *Catiline* was in the highest degree a product of the expressive, Romantic tradition of exaggerated emotion, with characters who were almost monstrous in their conception, like caricatured incarnations of ideas: self-sacrificing love, greed, lust, murderous doubt.

But Professor Monrad, like the idealist and out-and-out Hegelian he was, appreciated the main thrust of the play: 'the sharply focused conflict between the ethical, the moral principles of the establishment, and the individual's striving towards independence . . .'.

In the light of these qualities the professor was inclined to forgive the young tyro's uncertain rhythms and rhymes, and even *Catiline*'s 'rhetorical excesses' – though these were at times very excessive indeed.

In the main the professor was favourably inclined, and Ibsen had every right to feel well pleased as he slipped the play's good reviews into his pocket. Despite the poor sales figures and some of the critical reservations he had been recognised as a talent by the most discerning critical voices in the capital.

Catiline had triumphed. Ha!

Perhaps the most interesting feature of the reviews is the critics' surprise at the young playwright's choice of theme, or, rather, the fact that he had not chosen a nationalist subject for his play. In Botten-Hansen's view *Catiline* risked neglect because 'the author has – as many people would put it – "turned his back on the national as a theme"'.

So strong was the groundswell of nationalism at that time that a play on a classical theme was regarded as in itself a surprise.

Ibsen cannot have been too surprised at this. Early in 1850 he had already started to revise one of the national-historical themes he had considered during the creative raptus of his last year in Grimstad. Neither 'The Prisoner of Akershus' nor 'Olav Tryggvason' would do; the former remained in its half-finished state as a novel, and no trace remains of the latter. 'Normannerne' ('The Northmen'), however, looked as though it had the potential to be a worthy and topical successor to *Catiline*. Over the Whitsun holidays he turned it into a one-act play and retitled it *The Burial Mound*.

He submitted the play to the Christiania Theatre. It accepted it for production the following autumn.

Ha!

He had clearly found the key. Immediately afterwards he sat down and started work on a new play. The working title was 'Rypen i Justedalen' ('The Justedal Grouse'), a play about a young girl who flees the Black Death to live alone in the deserted Jostedal valley. He had probably come across the story in Andreas Faye's *Norske Sagn* (*Norwegian Folk Tales*) from 1833. The child of nature, dreaming, poetical and spontaneous, was a typically Romantic motif, and the associations with the elves and spirits provided a link to folk poetry.

For unknown reasons, 'Rypen' was never finished, but Ibsen had found his way as a dramatist. If what the Norwegian public wanted was nationalist drama, then by God he was the writer who was going to give it to them!

POVERTY AND SUCCESS

In the autumn of 1850 Henrik and Ole Schulerud moved from Vika to a small, yellow-painted single-storeyed house known as 'Midten', on the corner of Møllergaten and Hospitalgaten. From Ma Sæther's watchful embrace they now entered the embrace of the equally watchful Jomfru Holth, who in turn rented the building from the widow Huusland – all these madams and mistresses and widows kept the youngsters moving to the capital in a firm embrace that was in equal parts maternal solicitude and financial demand.

The move represented quite a step up: Ole had inherited some money. It meant they could even hire a manservant, Kristofer, a luxury not uncommon for students from the affluent homes of civil servants, but which, in the case of Ole and Henrik, was in striking contrast to the rather shabby quarters they lived in. In that crooked and dirty little street-corner house the two friends had to be content with a kitchen, a funny little living room, and a long, narrow room in which there was just space enough for two beds.

If life at Madam Holth's was already cramped and miserable, things hardly improved when Ole's little brother Johan presently moved in with them. He'd shared digs with them earlier, when they were living in Vika, and had turned out to be a mischievous scamp. Ole, mild and tolerant, simply laughed it off, but Henrik was not amused. On one occasion Johan fell ill just as Ole had to make a trip out of town. Henrik was delegated to look after him, and a more unsuitable child-minder could hardly be imagined. When Ole returned a few days later, he found his brother lying exhausted in bed and pleading for food. It turned out Henrik hadn't been feeding him, and Johan had been too stubborn (or weak) to ask. As Johan, tired, and with his belly full, was dozing off he heard his brother remonstrating with Henrik in the living room – the only occasion we know of on which the two friends fell out.

Autumn arrived, and Ibsen's exam results were only fair. On the report, signed in Johan Sebastien Welhaven's elegant hand, it said: 'Very good' in German, 'Good' in French, religion, history, geography, geometry, Latin translation and 'essays in the mother tongue' – which meant in this case Danish – 'Quite good' in Latin, 'Satisfactory' in Latin oral and 'Very poor' in Arithmetic and Greek.

'Very poor' meant, quite simply, that he had failed.

Ibsen had passed part of his entrance exams and now had the right to call himself a student and to join the Students' Union, though he could not begin his studies until he had passed in Arithmetic and Greek. But by now he had found a better way of spending the summer than reading his textbooks; how could he even think about study when he was in the process of making a name for himself as a dramatist at the leading theatre in the country?

At the Christiania Theatre rehearsals continued throughout August and September, and Ibsen expressed his satisfaction with the casting: as well as directing the play, the Dane Christian Ludvig Jørgensen played the part of Bernhard, and the rising Norwegian star Laura Svendsen played Blanca. A total of 557 tickets were sold for the first performance, a very healthy figure. On 26 September the curtain rose for the premiere of *The Burial Mound* at the Christiania Theatre. For the first time in its history the theatre was offering a play by – Brynjolf Bjarme! The use of a pseudonym gave a slight veneer of protection, and Bjarme did his best to keep it up throughout the whole performance.

He took his seat in the innermost and darkest recess of the theatre, hidden behind his huge beard – Brynjolf Bjarme, Henrik Ibsen, Henrik Fullbeard – the man of the moment. Success was no foregone conclusion. Intensely Romantic, *The Burial Mound* was no work of art, neither by contemporary nor current standards, and it is a good deal weaker than *Catiline*. Perhaps he suspected as much himself, though we cannot be sure. But at least there were plenty of 'crumbling ruins' in the spirit of Oehlenschläger. Even the iambic pentameters were a loan from the Danish master, as was the fascination with Old Norse history. But Ibsen was more sympathetic in his attitude towards both Christianity and the culture of southern Europe, and the conflict between the South and the North, heathendom and Christianity, would be a recurrent motif in his work.[3]

Ibsen had no reason to be ashamed of *The Burial Mound*. For one thing, it ran for three performances. That was below average but not unheard-of for a stage play of the time. More to the point, he had made his debut, and a performance at the city's main venue was a triumph in itself. A fee was certainly not guaranteed, but he got one – the theatre paid him 15 spesidaler. In addition he was given a free pass, in itself a sort of free education. It is also worthy of note that two of the performances were for subscribers only, meaning that those who attended were among the most important and loyal supporters of theatre in the capital. And the play had been reviewed at length in the *Christiania-Posten, Morgenbladet* and *Krydseren*. Again, reviews for a new play were by no means guaranteed.

Ibsen's debut wasn't some kind of overnight sensation but a promising start for an unknown young Norwegian dramatist. At the personal level the occasion was an undoubted success; he had, after all, had a play performed on the stage of the country's main theatre. In the course of a few months he had gone from being Henrik Ibsen, an unknown chemist's assistant, to Brynjolf Bjarme, Norwegian dramatist. He continued to use the pseudonym a while longer, but that was largely a formality.

He was Henrik Ibsen. Now *that* was really something.

How sweet would it be if Clara Ebbell turned up on his doorstep one day and knocked on his door?

One autumn day there she was. The engagement to the much older uncle was off, and Clara had come to the capital to escape an uncomfortable atmosphere back home. What did they mean to each other now, the lad from the chemist's shop and the merchant's daughter? If, as has been claimed, Clara was the model for Blanca in *The Burial Mound*, then she still had the muse's power over him. He promised to send her his poems once she was back in Grimstad and did so, six of them, along with his hopes that 'the mood that produced these poems may serve as my excuse for a number of opinions that have, for the most part, been misinterpreted by you'.

What opinions? Was he referring to the provocation his youthful and cocky dismissals of God, marriage, and various other things dear to the heart of the religious Clara had occasioned? That had created distance between them? Or was it yet another attempt to deny his old love? He wrote several poems during this time, and the most powerful of them opens with these lines:

Rock-face, crack and boom and go
Crashing to my hammer-blow;
I must clear a way down yonder
To the goal I dare but ponder.

Deep within the fell's still night
Treasures rich and rare invite,
Precious stones and diamonds blazing
Midst the gold's resplendent mazing.

In the depths here all is peace,
Peace and night that never cease; –

Soon earth's very heart shall clamour
To the smiting of my hammer.

'The Miner' is perhaps the most formally accomplished of all the poems of
Ibsen's youth, even if it uses well-tried lyrical themes. Some have been tempted
to read the poem as a key to Ibsen's innermost mind, burdened down by the
weight of the calling to write that fate had placed upon him. But the key has
been cut by the poet himself; the poems expressed more probably a poetic ideal
that accords perfectly with the heaven-storming Romantic idealism of his
Grimstad days, only this time in a gothic version, with heaven replaced by the
chambers of the earth's heart.

Henrik Ibsen is not the Miner, nor can he be. Yet the poet himself was in the
habit of turning to face the ground when life among his fellow human beings
became too difficult, when the demands made upon him became too great, and
when there were bills to be paid. He did not know it yet, but life would soon
place a millstone around his neck that would weigh him down in a highly non-
poetic fashion.

In the winter of 1851 Henrik sent another poem to Clara, and with that the
contact between them came to an end. As for Clara, well, in time she went off
and married her sailor uncle after all, and by all accounts lived a happy life with
him. On earth, not in the starry firmament. Henrik had his feet firmly planted
on the ground too. Despite his breakthrough with *The Burial Mound* he was still
very poor. Most of his friends were poor too, which is important in understanding the sort of life Ibsen lived during his first year in Christiania. His
poverty must have weighed heavily on him, but it was normal enough for a
young man from his background, and in the circle in which he moved. If he ever
experienced it as uncomfortable and humiliating then he could take comfort in
the fact that his friends were in the same boat and enjoy their company as
equals. Which is what he did. He spent a lot of time with Vinje and Paul Botten-
Hansen in the autumn of 1850. Dark autumn evenings and empty pockets aren't
a happy combination, but now and then things took a turn for the better. On the
rare occasions that Paul received a parcel of smoked mutton and pancakes from
his family in Gudbrandsdalen there would be a party in the little flat:

And then the sparks would really start to fly, with all sorts of criticism and
ironies about life's anomalies and oddities. And when we took to the streets
and saw all those shopkeepers with their bellies full and their heads empty
because all their sense had sunk down into their stomachs, well, you can bet,
life seemed more than a little strange to us.

Yes indeed, life might well have seemed strange to those poverty-stricken
intellectual outsiders as they struggled to maintain their self-respect by

voicing their contempt for these 'empty heads and full bellies', occasionally supplementing this with a plate of home cooking. Presently the idea occurred to them that it just might do these empty heads good to have their faces rubbed directly in life's savage ironies.

Paul Botten-Hansen, Aasmund Olavsson Vinje and Henrik Ibsen decided to start a magazine of their own.

THE MAN

Although Ibsen had written both poetry and drama during 1850, there was little time for such activities the following spring. For most of 1851 he was more journalist than anything else, a profession he never felt completely at home in.

The previous autumn he had regularly attended meetings of the Students' Union literary society, on one occasion reading his own sonnets there. Gradually he acquired a reputation among the students, and presently he became one of the three contributing editors of *Samfundsbladet*, succeeding Botten-Hansen.

The new post was not a particularly demanding one. Over the nine months in which he edited the magazine he wrote a couple of reviews of plays, and began an account of the history of the Students' Union. In fact, his links to the university were on the point of being severed permanently. Ibsen attended Welhaven's lectures on Holberg that spring, but most of his time was spent in the company of people who were neither students nor professors. Through Theodor Abildgaard he was employed as a journalist on the magazine of the Workers' Union, where Vinje already worked. Along with Abildgaard, Ibsen also taught reading and writing for the Christiania Workers' Union School on Sundays.

He appears to have been deeply involved in the movement led by Marcus Thrane. But appearances can be deceptive. Certainly he was one of the few intellectuals who showed any interest at all in Thrane. But he never joined the Christiania Workers' Union, despite taking part in several meetings of the union's steering committee. Undoubtedly he was attracted by the movement's energy, without ever openly supporting its goal of universal suffrage. His involvement probably owed much to his friendship with Abildgaard, as well as the need to earn a little money. Thrane's movement never actually preached real socialism; it was more a lower-class revolt with a strong element of liberal demands for freedom in its programme, in other words, demands that were commonplace in liberal circles. Nor was there much political content to the Sunday school lessons or the journalism – the magazine of the Workers' Union devoted much space to a varied literary content, often in the form of nonce poems and parodies of well-known songs, as well as poems with a vaguely political element to them. Neither books nor plays were reviewed within its pages. The contributions were unsigned, as was the custom of the time, but at least three contributions are usually attributed to Ibsen: two poems, one accompanied by his own illustration, and a satirical drawing.

Of greater significance than either of these magazines was the one Botten-Hansen, Ibsen and Vinje started themselves early in 1851. Posterity associates the venture mostly with Ibsen and Vinje, but in fact it was at Paul Botten-Hansen's initiative, and in the main it was he who ran it.

Botten-Hansen's was never a name to conjure with. He was not interested in posterity. The times and the environment he lived in were good enough for him. And there he was indispensable.

The curious suggestion that the magazine should not have a name appears to have originated with its printer and publisher, Nils Fredrik Axelsen, who envisaged 'a magazine with no name and consisting of various harangues on the subject of what other people think. The drawing must cover both notions. It should depict a man whose appearance makes people laugh.'

It was Ibsen who drew the man who adorned the front cover, a tall, gangly chap striding across Stortorget square, and who presumably made people laugh. Soon people had dubbed the magazine 'Mannen' ('The Man').[4] Ibsen was its regular artist, making him a pioneer in the field of Norwegian weeklies, just as 'The Man' was one of the country's earliest satirical magazines. As is so often the fate of the pioneer, 'The Man' didn't last long. The number of subscribers never exceeded one hundred, and in September of that year, after just nine months, it folded when the printer Axelsen ran out of patience.

In its content 'The Man' was modelled on Danish originals, most notably Meïr Goldschmidt's *Corsair*, which Ibsen may have come across in Grimstad. The formula was a creative mix of genres consisting of editorial comment, articles, cartoons, parodies, articles on aesthetic matters and reviews. Its most prominent quality was its insolence. From the start the idea had been that Ibsen would write poetry and review plays for the magazine – the free pass to the Christiania Theatre that came with the production of *The Burial Mound* the previous autumn made him a natural choice for the job. Most of the poetry he wrote between 1850 and 1851 was printed here, including the only five poems Ibsen deemed worthy of being printed in the collection of poetry he published many years later: 'Musicians', 'In Akershus', 'The Eider', 'Birds and Bird-Trappers' and 'The Miner'.

The profession of literary critic was still in its infancy in Norway, and in later years Ibsen never had much good to say about its practitioners. In his opinion the average critic in the capital was content if he was able to read – and possibly even understand – Johan Ludvig Heiberg's *Prosaisk Skrifter* (*Prose Writings*), and in particular *On Vaudeville* (1826). One overheard discussions on theatrical matters at Treschow's café and Engebrets, then wrote a couple of reviews for *Samfundetsbladet* as a sort of rehearsal before abandoning oneself completely to the task, adopting that spirit of negativity that seemed to be de rigueur for all critics of the time. It was, thought Ibsen, as though the publication of any book at all was considered an outrageous insult that must be repudiated at any cost. He was himself a patron of the cafes he mentions, where those with a passion for the theatre would gather in the evenings after a performance. He read Heiberg for all he was worth, which was, in the early 1850s, quite a lot. But if Ibsen's characterisation of his fellow critics at that time is accurate, his own contributions were very different from theirs. His reviews might be sharply critical, but they were in the main constructive criticism.

Reviewing was not, for Ibsen, a platform from which to make personal points but instead a part of his education as a dramatist.

One of the most interesting features of the 1851 reviews is a new scepticism about writings in the spirit of national romanticism, a scepticism in which he may have been influenced by his new friends Botten-Hansen and, in particular, Vinje. When Vinje mocks the 'moonlight poets' of the previous generation, like Welhaven and Andreas Munch, who 'whine away with what is – coming from them – a ridiculous "worldly-pain"', there are clear connections to Ibsen's poem 'The Lad in the Bilberry Patch' (1850), in which he writes ironically about the naïve city poet's Romantic response to his encounter with a country boy picking blueberries in the woods. But the mocking magpie watching from a tree

knows that the lad isn't really
Enthralled by the blooms' bright hue,
It sees him pick fruit – but it's merely
Sheer need that compels him to.

Ibsen had come a long way from the naïve national romanticism of his Grimstad poem 'The Miller Boy' to 'The Lad in the Bilberry Patch'. His life in Christiania had given him a more cynical and satirical view of the world, and furnished him with a social awareness that, in its turn, conditioned his national romanticism. This is not to say that he rejected national romanticism out of hand, however. This is particularly evident from the way he savaged P. A. Jensen's *Huldrens Hjem* (*The Home of the Huldre*) in the pages of 'The Man', in which he characterises Jensen's attempt to write in the national-romantic style as 'rather forced', and condemns its use of elements from folklore as 'tawdry nationalistic glitter'.

The writer's aim should rather be

to distinguish between the demands of reality and art . . . smoothing down the rough edges of reality before, reproduced as literature, placing it within the framework of art. And in doing so they will realise that nationalism in art cannot be conveyed by inserting trivial versions of scenes from everyday life.

And then, finally, the very essence of national literature: 'the nationalist writer is the one who understands the importance of giving his work a keynote that sounds to us from mountain and valley, from field to seashore, but most of all from within ourselves'.

These are the words of a devout national romantic with a deeply held belief in the power of the writer to interpret the soul of a nation and ennoble it by transforming it into art. P. A. Jensen was offering something different – a *false* and superficial expression of national love.

* * *

In the summer of 1851 Vinje, Ibsen and Botten-Hansen signed a contract with their printer Axelsen, who was still officially publisher of 'The Man'. The contract included a commitment to give the magazine a proper name through a competition that would be paid for by the printer himself. In the event the prize went to the editors, who came up with the name *Andhrimner* – the Æsir's cook in Valhalla in Old Norse mythology. The name posterity now associates with the magazine was actually only its name during the final days of its life.

When Vinje travelled away from the capital in the summer Ibsen assumed responsibility for the political content. In the true spirit of the *Corsair* he lashed out in all directions, attacking not only the politicians running the ministries but, even more fiercely, the opposition. Alarmed by the progress of Thrane's movement, the radical-democratic opposition had gradually withdrawn after 1848. After the Thirteenth Storting assembled in February 1851 with what was presumed to be a radical majority, its inability to act became even more embarrassing. Ibsen directed his bile at this vacillating and feeble response.

In *Norma, or a Politician's Love*, a spontaneous little parody of an opera that appeared in the magazine in June, the liberal Member of Parliament and editor of *Morgenbladet*, Adolf Bredo Stabell, is mercilessly satirised. Stabell is depicted as Severus, the man who cannot choose between the two ladies 'The Opposition' and 'The Party of Government'.[5] Abildgaard must have enjoyed it hugely. He was, of course, on the moderate wing of the Workers' Union that had attempted in vain to take the union into an alliance with the radical members of the Storting.

But not even the union movement was spared Ibsen's pen.

Nothing, it seems, is sacred to him. Much of this, of course, lies in the very nature of satire, where the politician is as much a necessity of life as the lover and the dying are to the poet. Even so, there is no reason to suspect that Ibsen's contempt for politicians, and in particular the self-styled 'people's politicians', was not genuine. Where Abildgaard believed in political compromise, Ibsen turned his back on the whole business completely:

The Storting is for us what Olympus was for the Greeks. Here people have placed their gods, and from their lofty heights these gaze down in majestic silence upon the world, unmoved by the issues of the day, which lie far beneath them, and far beyond them.

In the years before he left Norway, Ibsen nurtured a blazing contempt for representative democracy, as also for that 'spirit of association' that gathered individuals into cliques, groups, and in time into political parties. So it should come as no surprise that Marcus Thrane's movement held little attraction for him.

The connection would come to an abrupt end in the summer of 1851. It was one that would turn out to be crucial in Ibsen's life. Filled with drama, surprises and despair – as well as unexpected opportunities.

SUMMER WITH OSCAR

It all began on the morning of 8 June, with the arrival in Christiania of several hundred Danish and Swedish students to take part in the Scandinavian student congress. The following evening there was a banquet in the Freemasons Hall. Poems were read between the celebratory speeches and the toasts, and Bernhard Dunker, a theatre-lover and the most talented lawyer of his day, gave a long speech in praise of Denmark.

The lawyer's speech was prefaced by a poem, written and declaimed by a young poet who now stood up among the country's leading writers and cultural personalities under his own real name. Ibsen's verse was also in praise of the neighbours in the south:

And Denmark's old defences
In time of strife held out,
The ancient North now senses
Its strong-walled church is stout.

Henrik Ibsen found himself in good company, carried along by this unique gathering in which poor students, poets, generals and other prominent members of society met in a spirit of idealistic enthusiasm and raised glasses – frequently raised glasses – to hail the fellowship of the Scandinavian people. It might have been at his own request that he was there, and he might have been only one among many songwriters at the feast; but it was his talent that had earned him the right to mount the podium.

The following evening there was an excursion to Oscarshall (Oscar's Hall), the summer palace on Bygdøy, just outside the city. Oscar I, the union king of Sweden and Norway, graced the proceedings with his presence, and he invited the gathering – some eleven hundred guests – to join him for a champagne breakfast the following morning on the hill at Dronningberget. General Wedel gave a speech, and a new salvo of speeches, poems and songs was fired off, including one song by Ibsen:

> A gentle breeze with muted song
> Blows through the spruce now . . .

Had he not himself, like the fir tree in Hans Christian Andersen's famous fairy tale, been brought in from the cold to shine among the finest?

> There is a deep, a sorrowing need
> That burdens the forest mind
> It will whisper of its longing
> Of its finest memories
> And of the voice from the heart
> That, banished, finds its echo . . .

Some three weeks after the fraternity of Nordic academics had departed Christiania, the police moved against Marcus Thrane and the workers' unions. Ever since the march to mark the third anniversary of the February revolution in France, the authorities had increased their surveillance of the members of the movement. Abildgaard had been meeting opposition politicians to discuss the possibility of replacing the government with a new, liberal council of state and as soon as the congress of workers' unions had decided to mount another demonstration the police acted. On 7 June, Thrane, Abildgaard and over a hundred others were arrested, and documents and private correspondence seized. In this way the Norwegian working class's first attempt at political organisation was crushed, and the last embers of the February revolution were extinguished.

At home in Møllergaten, Ibsen sat and waited for the police to knock on his door. Would he be summoned as a witness? Might he even be arrested himself? He had, after all, contributed pieces to the Workers' Union magazine and had been a teacher at their Sunday school up until the time of the arrests. Abildgaard had letters from him in his possession – had the police got hold of those? Later he learned that the printer had managed to get rid of the most compromising documents before the arrival of the police, including some probably written by him. Abildgaard had apparently burned the letters sent to him.

It was – or might have been – a fateful moment. Even if the police had learned the full extent of his contacts with Thrane's movement it is by no means certain he would have been jailed – in his own mind he was quite certain he would not have been. But *if* he had ended up in jail then that would undoubtedly have affected him and influenced posterity's perception of him. The man who would later be known as the most dogged individualist in literary history, a cynic who was sceptical of anything with even a whiff of the collective about it, be it parties or unions, would have gone down in history as one of the working-class movement's first martyrs. And who knows but that that, too, might have been a literary inspiration, if of a different kind.

But no one came knocking on his door. Ibsen had nothing to fear from the long arm of the law, not this time. Still, it was a disturbed and disturbing summer, one day joining the king in a toast, the next in fear of being arrested as a political agitator.

Champagne with Oscar I or bread and water with Thrane? Strictly speaking, he had more in common with the latter. Thrane was eleven years older than him, born into a respectable Christiania family. His father had held a trusted position as teller in the Riksbanken, but was arrested for embezzlement shortly after the birth of his son. A couple of years later his grandfather was declared bankrupt, and with that the family's decline was complete. Thrane grew up a talented boy with a vivid streak of rebellion in him. He fell out with his teachers and employers, left school and travelled abroad. Returning home he finally sat for his school-leaving exam in 1840, and thereafter made his living first as a teacher and, later, as a journalist and magazine editor. It was in this latter phase of his career that he developed the radical ideas that turned him into the country's leading political agitator in the aftermath of the 1848 revolution.

So it was that these two, Thrane and Ibsen, both strong, rebellious and artistic men, chose very different social strategies. Both had experienced ruin in the family. But where Thrane dedicated his life and his thought to the class of which he then found himself a member, Ibsen remained loyal to the bourgeois urge to social advancement. He chose the inner world as his battleground, a position that was entirely compatible with all those many glasses of champagne he would drink in the company of kings in years to come, aware that the bubbles rising through his straw-coloured drink symbolised his own rise in the world. Some have suggested that Ibsen thereby betrayed both Abildgaard as a friend and Thrane's social revolution as an ideal in choosing the greater comfort of literary revolution, ridiculing the contrast between the rebellious social criticism of the plays and their creator's fondness for luxury, decorations and the glamour of royalty.

Ridiculous? Perhaps, but it was never Ibsen's purpose to wage war against bourgeois society, neither in life nor in literature. In time he certainly became a rebel, but he was and remained a *bourgeois rebel*, though his writing had qualities that extended far beyond the four walls of the bourgeois living room. And why should he remain committed to Thrane's social revolution when the police raids of the summer of 1851 effectively killed it off? Why abandon the dream of the good life? Among those enthused by the revolution of 1848 only a very few were willing to give up the comforts of bourgeois existence.

It was Thrane who was the exception among the children of the 1848 revolution, one of a small group of Europeans who gave themselves whole to the idea of revolution and were swallowed up by it. After serving his prison sentence he emigrated to America, while men like Karl Marx, Louis Blanc and Alexander Ledru-Rollin lived on as revolutionary vagabonds in a reactionary Europe. Ibsen had no business in their company. He was a child of the bourgeoisie. The drive to self-improvement had been his baptismal gift, and he husbanded it well.

THE PRISONER OF AKERSHUS

As it happens, all this time Ibsen had been struggling hard not to end up behind bars himself. Not as a result of his political beliefs but because he had failed to meet his financial obligations to his illegitimate son. He earned a little from his journalism, a little as the writer of *The Burial Mound,* but not much. He began living off Ole's savings, but these too were soon used up. The first thing to go was the servant, Kristofer. He disappeared the moment Johan moved in – the boy had to be good for something, after all. And Johan waited on the two older tenants as best he could, running errands and making coffee, and when there was a party, boiling eggs for the sandwiches. If any money came into the house there might be cheese, sausage and smoked herring to go with the eggs. And of course, toddy. Meaning friends were very likely to drop in.

But the parties were few and far between. Next to go were their evening meals, which up until that time had been part of their arrangement with Frøken Holth. Now they would sneak out of the house around mealtime, in hopes that the other residents would think they were eating out, before returning after a suitable absence to the coffee and sandwiches Johan had prepared for them.

On one occasion, when Frøken Holth was on her way in to demand the rent, Johan only just managed to warn the others. Ole had time to pull on his jacket and slip out the back door, but Henrik was still in bed.

'Lock the door and say I'm not home,' he ordered the boy.

But Frøken Holth, who suspected something was afoot, pushed her way into the bedroom. Henrik, lying trapped in the bed, was obliged to confess to the lie and promise to put things right.

Johan recalls him at this time as dark and unapproachable, a poverty-stricken intellectual who kept the first edition of his first play in a box, the fruit of the chemist's assistant's *Sturm und Drang,* the tale of Catiline's tragic struggle, of Europe's struggle for freedom in the great revolutionary year of 1848. These were world events that had crossed centuries and oceans to reach the young man as he sat there in the small hours at the shop and bared his heart and his ambitions.

And now here they were, gathering dust in an attic in Christiania.

Another of the fruits of the Grimstad *Sturm und Drang*, however, was not gathering any dust. Hans Jacob Hendrichssen was very much alive and kicking, as was his mother, Else Sophie. If it had been hard enough to provide for an illegitimate son on a chemist assistant's wage, Ibsen was finding out it wasn't any easier as a student and a writer.

His troubles begin in the late summer of 1850. Just as Henrik is putting in the last hours of study before taking his exam – at least, that's what he *should* be doing – he receives a letter from the deputy sheriff of Christiania informing him that his last quarterly payment to Else Sophie has not yet been received. It was a matter of 2 spesidaler. It can't have come as a surprise but it must have been a nuisance all the same. He manages to make the payment at the beginning of August.

First warning; with more to come.[6]

A couple of months later, the same thing happens again, the deadline for the payment passes and he fails to make it until two months later, on 5 December. Second warning. Now he really has entered the vicious circle of the debtor: no sooner has he managed to make one (delayed) payment than it's time for the next instalment. Another payment is due early in the new year, and this time there's real trouble. Weeks pass, and still Else Sophie doesn't get her money.

Inexorably, Ibsen gets crushed between the millstones of debt. At the end of March a distraint order is served on him in Møllergaten, but it seems he is able to talk his way to a postponement. He doesn't manage to make the payment until the beginning of May, by which time, of course, the next instalment is already overdue, and before he is able to pay that, the one after falls due. In May a second order of distraint is issued. This time the process goes through to completion. Nothing of any value is found among his possessions.

That Ibsen couldn't cough up the wretched 2 spesidaler and didn't even own anything worth pawning is eloquent of his poverty. By way of comparison, a day labourer at this time earned in the region of 120 spesidaler per annum.

On 17 June 1851, a few days after that royal champagne breakfast in Oscar's Hall, the axe falls. Henrik Ibsen must have read the official letter in mounting panic:

The chemist (Student) Hendrik Johan Ibsen of Christiania . . . being unable to pay the legally imposed maintenance for a child born out of wedlock to the maid Else Sophie Jensdatter . . . is hereby ordered to serve a period of forced labour at Akershus Fort, one third of the payment for which is to be withheld . . .

Unhappy young writer! In the short story he had started a couple of years earlier he had hailed the rebel peasant leader Christian Lofthuus, a precursor of Marcus Thrane, who had, in his time, been held in Akershus Fort. Now it was his turn to follow in Lofthuus's footsteps, for having got the granddaughter of the great rebel leader pregnant, a martyr to nothing more impressive than his own lust. If the irony ever struck him the taste must have been bitter – and for all the literary potential he saw in Lofthuus's imprisonment there was little trace of poetry to be found in his own wretched predicament.

Two spesidaler was equivalent to a sentence of thirty-four days' forced labour. But all doors were not yet closed. The rules governing the arrangement provided the guilty party with one last chance to pay his debts. Ibsen was given such a chance but again failed to come up with the money, obliging the authorities to serve another order of distraint, finding, as before, that it was futile. Remarkably, he was given yet another postponement, but when he failed to pay up this time the sentence was forced labour, for a period of sixty-eight days.

As autumn set in, the days grew darker, and things weren't much brighter in Henrik's life. Naturally, this is when it comes. The turning point. The thing out of the blue that changes everything.

A FORTUITOUS ENCOUNTER

'As a child, when I first heard the remarkable tales told of Ole Bull's life, I thought he was a god who had come down to earth.'

The actress Oktavia Sperati was not the only one to recall Ole Bull with this kind of awed respect. He *was* like a god, a star in an age when stars were fewer but shone more brightly than those that would come after them. The violinist and nation-builder was Norway's first international celebrity, adored and enveloped in myths that he nourished himself with tales of his countless journeys through Europe and the United States. He played for kings and high society, but above all he was an inspired entertainer and a virtuoso much loved by the general public. Bull was a force of nature, impulsive, creative – but also fickle. He loved to inaugurate grandiose schemes, and carried on in blithe disregard of the bankruptcies that ceaselessly followed in his wake.

In the summer of 1849 he returned home to Bergen to realise his dream of starting a Norwegian-language theatre. A committee was appointed, and a group of local amateurs gathered in the premises of the Drama Society. After a trial performance in November the Norwegian Theatre opened its doors officially on 2 January 1850 with a programme that included Beethoven and Mozart, Holberg's *Den Vegelsindede*, with Bull himself bringing the proceedings to a climax with his own composition for violin and orchestra, *Sæterbesøg*.

The Bergen audience went wild, and at the beginning of September Bull submitted an application for support for the theatre to the National Assembly. Would the Storting show 'its patriotic heart' by allocating an annual sum of 2,000 spesidaler to the new national theatre?

The Storting would not.

The arguments were of a sort to provoke anyone with an artistic turn of mind. How, it was asked, could one give money to the theatre when people were still eating bread mixed with bark? The Liberal politician Johan Sverdrup was in principle not opposed to considering the application, but Søren Jaabæk, representing the farmers, was of the opinion that if nationalism could not sustain itself without public funding, then so be it. And moreover, the demand for a Norwegian, national theatre was not without its problematic side for the Storting. The fundamental tensions in the country's burgeoning nationalism, between high and low, national and continental, were also apparent in the question of a theatre. One could not simply cut all ties to Danish and European theatre for the benefit of a handful of Norwegian dilettantes. When confronted by Danes, the cultural elite was perfectly happy to promote the uniquely Norwegian elements of their shared culture, but within Norway itself it was aspects of European culture, and in particular Danish culture, that divided the elite from the people. Ole Bull's appeal to the Storting envisaged a long-term project, aimed at the establishment of a publicly supported Norwegian theatrical culture in the land. He received the whole-hearted support of the editors of *Andhrimner* and the students of the Royal University in Christiania. At a meeting of the Students' Union, Ibsen – not usually a man given to such things – delivered a speech in passionate support of the project. It may well have been on this occasion that Bull first noticed him. Soon afterwards Bull got in touch and asked Ibsen whether he would consider moving to Bergen to work in the theatre. Henrik Ibsen most certainly would.

Bull's offer is clear proof that Ibsen's entry into public cultural life had been by and large successful. Despite the rejection from Christiania Theatre and some rather patronising reviews of *Catiline*, despite his poverty and feeling like an outsider in the intellectual circles in the capital, Ibsen had been dealt the golden card, the card that is handed out only once in a lifetime.

He was young and promising.

The rejection and mixed reception of *Catiline* had not disheartened him in the slightest and *The Burial Mound* spoke for itself, as did the reviews in *Andhrimner* and his appearance at the meeting of Nordic students. On the other hand, there wasn't exactly a queue of young and promising dramatic talents in the city, and one might reasonably ask where else Bull might have found new blood for his Bergen venture. Nor is there any suggestion that his choice was the result of lengthy deliberations. He was an impulsive man, with a gift for spotting diamonds in the rough – some years later he discovered another new talent in Edvard Grieg. Add to this that Bull had to do something to keep his dream of a theatre alive after the rejection of his application for financing. If he was unable to raise the money, he could at least provide the talent that would, hopefully, secure a commercial and artistic future for the venture.

It seems that Ole Bull *believed* in Henrik Ibsen, and Henrik had the good luck to be taken under his wing. That he was not quite so lucky when it came to possessing the qualities needed to handle all the practical aspects of running a theatre was something that Bergen – if not the whole world – would presently discover. What mattered was that Henrik had been rescued from student life and a starving-in-dusty-garrets existence, forever at the mercy of a series of rather frightening Christiania landladies. Rescued, too, from a spell behind the prison walls of Akershus Fortress, probably with the help of an advance from Bull.

In mid-October, he and Bull boarded the steamship *Gyller* bound for Fredriksvern outside Larvik. From there the journey continued on the *Constitutionen*, and two days later the ship lay to in Kristiansand. The following day Henrik continued alone to Bergen, to devote his services full time to the muse Thalia.

As his ship headed north-west it probably never once occurred to him that the life he was about to begin at the theatre would have anything in common with the sentence of forced labour he had so narrowly avoided in Christiania.

IV

BERGEN

THE CITY BY THE SEA

On 21 October 1851 Henrik Ibsen arrived in Bergen, that strange city that was as much a way of life as it was a city; larger than Grimstad, slightly smaller than Christiania, its gaze directed at itself and at the sea. The maritime route to the world went via Hamburg, and for centuries Bergen had been influenced by the culture and mindset of continental Europe. Bergen people were cosmopolitans, their singing dialect rich in German words and turns of phrase, their culture an urban culture that could seem snobbish to the rest of the world, not that the accusation ever bothered them particularly.

Henrik took lodgings with Helene Sontum, proprietress of one of the city's most reputable boarding houses in Toldbodalmenningen. The boarding house was a favourite with travellers from the British Isles and offered English break-fasts for those who couldn't do without it, which is to say, Englishmen. It was another sign of the city's cosmopolitan nature. But Fru Sontum was more than capable of looking after a lonely young man from the east of the country too. Henrik lived here for some eighteen months, and appears to have been very satisfied; the signs are that Bergen landladies were greatly preferable to those of Christiania. Just ten days after his arrival he composed a wedding song for one of Fru Sontum's sons. Henrik had become a dab hand at these nonce poems, and there would be many more of them during his years in Bergen.

It was here he would embark on his new life as a man of the theatre. Not being local was something of a disadvantage in itself for someone so naturally quiet and introverted; and yet he was Ole Bull's choice, and that was no small thing. When Henrik first arrived in Christiania he was a nobody. Now he had the chance to be a somebody, a man of the theatre, earning a steady wage.

* * *

Like the capital, Bergen had enjoyed a variegated cultural life since the middle of the nineteenth century, which in high degree thrived within a private-public sphere. Significantly there were hardly any cafes in the city, though there were plenty of salons, associations and clubs. The city's musical life was the province of Harmonien and the Philharmonic Society. Art was provided for by the Arts Association, founded by the painter J. C. Dahl, who had also gifted a collection of paintings to the Bergen Museum, which, in turn, doubled as the city's scientific institute. Literary resources included a number of private lending libraries and a few private book collectors. Bergen had quite a few newspapers, the most important in the early 1850s being *Bergens Stiftstidende* and *Bergenske Blade*, with the addition of *Bergens Post* in 1854.

So cultural life thrived in Bergen, even though it was still very much a part of semi-public social life and only minimally institutionalised, and was rather dilettante.

An interest in the theatre was in itself an expression of the city's European outlook. Enthusiasm for the theatre had spread through the eighteenth century from the European aristocracy to the bourgeoisie, and in Norway, which had no aristocracy to speak of, it became the passion of enthusiastic amateurs from the state official class and the upper bourgeoisie. All the drama societies that appeared in Norwegian towns and cities from the 1780s onwards were exclusively upper-class arenas, and Bergen was no exception. Amateur dramatics became a popular pastime, the perfect social vehicle for an upper class desirous of cultivating its networks in an atmosphere of continental sophistication. With its assertive business patriarchy and its close connections with Germany, where the craze for starting drama groups was well established, Bergen was ripe for a group of its own. This duly occurred in 1794 with the establishment of the Dramatiske Selskab. Komediehuset, the society's venue and the first theatre in Norway, was ready for use by the turn of the century. Komediehuset and the Dramatiske Selskab nurtured an enthusiastic local theatrical tradition that only began to wane in the 1830s, and it was during the next decade that Danish theatre groups first began to establish themselves in the city.

So when Bull announced his national theatre it was at a time of change and crisis, with foreign influences threatening to wipe out a relatively young tradition of amateur dramatics in Bergen – as elsewhere in the country. The establishment of the Norwegian Theatre was something new, not only because it would promote a unique and genuinely Norwegian drama, but also because as a public and institutional theatre it would transcend the socially exclusive nature of the dramatic societies. In Bergen there was a vivid interest in the theatre that was shared by ordinary people too, who were inspired by Bull's infectious enthusiasm. People from all walks of life turned up in response to the Norwegian Theatre's advertisement for actors in the summer of 1849 – longshoremen and housemaids along with sons and daughters from the best homes in the city.

Many of those who made their debuts at the Norwegian Theatre in the 1850s – a number of them still not twenty years old at the time – would go on to make their names as stars on the Norwegian stage: Johannes and Louise Brun, Fredrikke Jensen, Lucie Wolf, Andreas Isachsen and others. This was the company Henrik Ibsen would be working with.

THE SORCERER'S APPRENTICE

It would be a mistake to suppose that great expectations were raised by Ibsen's arrival in Bergen. In fact, hardly anyone knew he was coming. But once the theatre committee, the actors and the Bergen public encountered the newcomer, their first reaction was probably surprise as much as anything else. Ibsen had come as the joker in Bull's pack in the battle to win acceptance for the Norwegian Theatre. But how does one actually *use* a joker?

This was the first challenge facing Daniel Danielsen, Knud Nergaard, the brothers Edvard and Ole Bull and the rest of the committee. What on earth were they to do with Ibsen? At a meeting convened a week or two after Ibsen's arrival the details of his contract were discussed and the following was agreed upon:

> The committee hereby engages Hr. Student Henrik Ibsen, who has declared his agreement, to work in the theatre as a dramatist, for which he shall be remunerated in the sum of 20 spesidaler per month as from October 1 this year.

Not exactly a clear statement, and there have been various interpretations of what it actually implied. What seems certain is that, despite the careful wording of the contract, Ibsen must have felt under an obligation to write new, nationalist drama for the Bergen stage. His other duties were more diffuse. For a professional those duties would have included producing and directing. The trouble was that Ibsen had practically no experience at all of such matters. On his arrival in Christiania a year earlier he had hardly even seen a professionally produced play, and when he came to Bergen he had no practical experience of how to run a theatre, apart from what he had managed to pick up during the production of *The Burial Mound*.

Ibsen's lack of experience was not the theatre's only headache. Another was that they already had a director, an experienced headmaster named Herman Laading. Ibsen was therefore obliged to function as Laading's assistant until he had learned a little more about the business of working in a theatre. So during the early part of his years in Bergen, Ibsen was more or less an apprentice – but an apprentice on a regular wage, be it noted. He was being paid 20 spesidaler a month, roughly the equivalent of a teacher's pay, or as much as the best-paid actor in the troupe. If theatrical life in Bergen thus far had little use of him, his own situation at least was now dramatically improved.

Fortunately he got the opportunity to show what he could do as early as November 1851. One of the city's two drama reviewers, a man named Poul Stub, had written an almost contemptuous dismissal of the theatre and its actors. Journalism and the business of reviewing were arenas Ibsen was familiar with, and in four articles in the *Bergens Stiftstidende* he responded to Stub's attack. Stub was, curiously enough, the same teacher to whom Ibsen had sent his essays when he was studying for his entrance examination in Grimstad. Now Stub got his response, and in the superior and acidic style of one of Ibsen's *Andhrimner* contributions the teacher was condemned as a dilettante with a hopelessly negative attitude towards the critic's task:

> If the critic wishes to instruct the actor then he must make it clear *how* the role should be played, and remain silent on the subject of how it should *not* be played.

The city's other critic, Nils R. Eilertsen, didn't fare much better, and had to put up with having his magazine the *Theatrical Companion* dismissed as a 'literary prostitute'. So even before one of his own new plays had seen the light of day Ibsen had managed to seriously offend the city's drama reviewers. Possibly not a very sensible move, but the theatre's own people were no doubt delighted – and perhaps, in the final analysis, that was the most important thing. He had leapt to the defence of the theatre's actors and technicians, and had done so with an academic authority that none of his colleagues could have summoned, with the exception of Laading. In due course Ibsen's own efforts in the theatre would put him at the mercy of the critics; how depressing, then, that 'the art of criticism here is, to put it bluntly, in a very sad state indeed'.

He only appeared on the stage once in the autumn of 1851. On 17 November, Ole Bull gave a benefit concert for the Students' Union's building fund as a thank-you for the support the students had given him earlier in the autumn. Ibsen once again took part, this time with a poem rich in building metaphors that was both a promotion of the cause of the theatre and a paean in praise of Bull himself:

> We might not be building a work that lasts
> As judged by the naked eye,
> Yet we hope that close study will reveal
> A work that silently moves forward.

On the day after the concert Bull convened a meeting of the committee and presented a list of the theatre's 'fundamental ground rules', of which the first stated that its artistic and political goal was the development of a school of Norwegian drama featuring as many 'nationalist elements' as possible. He could not have expressed any more clearly the obligation resting upon Henrik Ibsen to create an 'independent dramatic art' at the Norwegian Theatre in Bergen. And with that Ole Bull disappeared off to America to resume his round of concerts and proceed with various other of his grandiose plans. Early in the new year Ibsen delivered yet another of his prologues, but soon he would have to demonstrate something a little more substantial. He had come to town as Bull's joker, as the sorcerer's apprentice.

Now the sorcerer had left – what had happened to the magic? Over a year had passed since the performance of *The Burial Mound*, and after *Catiline* Ibsen had published nothing. Rumours that he was preparing a collection of poetry for the autumn of 1851 turned out to be a distinct exaggeration. Instead, he was fully preoccupied, learning the art of theatre from the bottom up.

Not surprisingly the ambiguities surrounding his job description and the delegation of duties and talents became more fraught the moment the actual process of putting on plays began. At that time plays were produced in a very different way from what would later be the case. The concept of 'directing' implied the practical work of providing props, costumes, scenery flats, decor and all of those areas that would later be the province of the stage manager and the scenographer. 'Instruction' was the term used to describe the activity most closely resembling that of the modern director, but the concept was still in its infancy. In both the German and the Nordic theatrical traditions there remained a clear distinction between direction given off and on the stage. Away from the stage, during readings, the parts and the play were interpreted for the actor by the 'parts director', and for a long time the convention remained that the actual way the part was played onstage remained the responsibility of the actors themselves. Only slowly did the understanding emerge that directing was something best done by someone outside the acting ensemble, leading to the rise of the modern idea of the director as someone striving to attain an overall conception of *every* aspect of the staging, an independent, creative interpreter of the work ensuring that each production becomes a unique event. France, the leading theatrical country of the period, was the forerunner of this development, reflecting the variegated theatrical world of metropolitan Paris. But in Germany and the Nordic countries too the influence of the director was steadily growing, inspired by the French example and driven forward by names such as Heinrich Laube, Franz von Dingelstedt and Edward Devrient.

The situation at the Norwegian Theatre and the problems surrounding the division of labour between Ibsen and Laading thus reflected the situation in the theatrical culture of mainland Europe. At the start of Ibsen's tenure it was Laading who had the main responsibility for direction on and off the stage; but early in 1852 the committee made it clear that it wanted Ibsen to get more involved in this aspect of the theatre's work too. On 10 February the committee requested that Laading and Ibsen together should try to sort the problem out. The result was that the responsibilities of the director were divided up, with Laading taking on the more general responsibilities for the offstage directing of the actors and their general education, and Ibsen taking charge of the directing of the actual performances and everything else pertaining to props, stage machinery, decor and costume. The new arrangement was formalised in April and was due to be put into practice in the coming autumn.

Finally Ibsen had advanced from assistant and apprentice to a position in which he could actually influence proceedings on the stage. It might have seemed that for a theatre with such modest means at its disposal to employ two paid directors was a curious extravagance. But it looks as though the committee was confident that Ibsen was a worthwhile investment, a confidence that expressed itself in the fact that he and Laading were given joint responsibility for the repertoire for the coming season.

Of still greater significance was the committee's decision to raise Ibsen's wage to 300 spesidaler annually when the renewal of his contract came up for discussion on 13 April; and to sponsor a study-tour of Europe with the aim of learning more about costumes, decor, and the arts of producing and directing – 'in short, more about everything that may be of artistic or technical value to our theatre'.

If anyone had felt a lack of professionalism and knowledge of the European theatre, it was him, and Ibsen must have been thrilled by the offer. Now he was about to realise that old dream he and Ole Schulerud had talked of so many times during those years at the pharmacy.

The dream of travel.

FROM BERGEN TO THE WORLD

The adventure began on 15 April. Ibsen carried with him a letter of introduction from the Bergen sheriff, Christian R. Hansson, the same man who had been dealing with his maintenance payments to Else Sophie. With a regular wage coming in he was now finally able to bring his financial burden under control. In the spring of 1852 he paid one year's support in advance, and throughout his time in Bergen he was generally conscientious in his payments for the support of this unknown son of his.

Now he was about to pay back his debt to Ole Bull and the Norwegian Theatre. He was going to bring the world to Bergen.

He did not travel alone. The committee had also paid for two of the theatre's most talented young actors, Johannes and Louise Brun, to join him. What joy, what celebrations! Johannes twenty years old, Louise two years older, and Henrik himself, just turned twenty-four, heading out into the wide world of European culture. In Copenhagen the plan was to visit the Kongelige Teater. Following that the couple would return home, while Ibsen continued on to Berlin and Dresden.

The committee's instructions were clear. Ibsen was to acquire

> knowledge and experience enough to enable him to assume the post of
> director at the theatre, including the instruction of actors and actresses, as
> well as the arrangement of everything pertaining to the scenery, machinery
> and decor of the stage, the costumes of the performers, etc.

Ibsen was not being sent abroad to grow as a dramatist, but to gain an education as a practical man of the theatre. The result, however, would turn out to be an education in both. There was at that time no direct route from Bergen to Copenhagen, so the journey went via Hamburg. It seems the three did not stay there long, for by 20 April they had landed in Copenhagen. Ibsen rented a room in Reverentsgaden 205, close by the Kongelige Teater in Kongens Nytorv. Bearing in mind the size of the grant he had been awarded the room was impressive. Because he had not come to Copenhagen only to learn. Was he not also an emissary from the world of Norwegian theatre to the country's old colonial overlords? No point in being too humble, then.

One of the first things he did on arriving was to call on the old master himself, Johan Ludvig Heiberg, acknowledged as the leading figure in the cultural world of Denmark and Norway both for his poetry and his drama. As important were his critical and aesthetic essays, which Ibsen had studied in Christiania. By the time Ibsen met him he had given up writing and was in sole charge at the Kongelige Teater.

Heiberg was friendly with sheriff Hansson back home in Bergen, and in his letter of introduction Hansson asked Heiberg to take good care of these three Norwegians, the two Bruns and Ibsen – 'an intelligent and more than averagely talented young writer'. The first meeting between the old and the young writer probably took place in Heiberg's office backstage, between one and three o'clock, part of a ritual the actors referred to as 'the audience', in which the director paced back and forth across the carpet, hands behind his back as he listened to all manner of submissions. In Heiberg's view there was little profit in Ibsen's attending rehearsals at the theatre, for the obvious reason that no plays were currently being readied this late in the season. He did, however, offer the Norwegian free entry to all performances at the theatre, and promised to have him shown around the theatre and educated in its machinery and equipment by Thomas Overskou, their head director.

Ibsen was overwhelmed by his reception. It seemed obvious that there was more scepticism towards the idea of a Norwegian theatre in Christiania than there was in royal Copenhagen. According to Ibsen, the Danes were surprised that the move towards Norwegian theatrical independence had not occurred sooner. And he made good use of his welcome. He studied directing, stage machinery, bought several plays, located sources for costumes and looked for a dancing master to send back home to the theatre in Bergen.

And he saw plays.

'As regards the repertoire, we have been extremely fortunate,' he could report to the committee in the middle of May.

That was putting it mildly. During the weeks he spent in Copenhagen he was able to experience some of the greatest actors of the age in all their glory. He saw the first lady of the Danish stage, Johanne Luise Heiberg, and the great trage-dian and lover Michael Wiehe, he enjoyed the marbled tones of Nicolai Peter Nielsen and the innovative and realistic psychological acting style of Frederik Høedt. There were more than twenty performances at the Kongelige Teater during the time he was there, including four plays by Shakespeare (*Hamlet, King Lear, Romeo and Juliet* and *As You Like It*), as many comedies by Holberg, and several plays produced by the theatre's own writers, including Johan Ludvig Heiberg. He could also see *Earl Hakon* by Adam Oehlenschläger and Mozart's opera *Don Giovanni*. The rest of the repertoire consisted of the usual vaudeville shows and comedies, with Eugène Scribe of course prominently represented.

A week or two after his arrival he also found a dancing master for Johannes and Louise Brun. Ibsen was on a tight budget and had to confer by post with the committee before each outlay. Naturally, he was aware of the theatre's pinched economic state, and yet he was dismayed by the committee's rejection of his request for a wage for the new dancing master, and equally annoyed when his application for an advance on his next month's wages was turned down. The rejection was accompanied by a clear hint that he had been over-spending. Only when he insisted did the committee agree to a small advance, but fortunately for Ibsen the hospitality he enjoyed in Copenhagen was more than generous. The city boasted two theatres besides the Kongelige Teater and Ibsen visited them both. In company with Johannes Brun he was invited to the Royal Court Theatre in Christiansborg. There was a programme of light enter-tainment that evening, but as some sort of compensation King Frederik VII himself was present, and it was the king who closed the proceedings with a speech that was 'a rare mixture of royal dignity and popular appeal'. For Ibsen it was a second royal encounter in little over a year.

The third of Copenhagen's stages was the Casino, in Amaliegade, a private theatre. Here Ibsen attended the premiere of Jens Christian Hostrup's *Master and Apprentice*, a piece of music-theatre notable for its blend of the supernat-ural and everyday realism, with elves and newspaper editors wandering about across the stage. Ibsen was so taken with it that he called on Hostrup at his home in Fredriksberg. It must have been an equally thrilling occasion for him when he met Hans Christian Andersen. In the beginning of June, not long before he was due to leave, he was invited to dinner at the Heibergs' home in Søkvæsthuset. It may have disappointed him to discover that the Danish maestro was more interested in talking about food than about the theatre. But the invitation was an honour in itself, especially for a Norwegian provincial who, just a year earlier, was having to pawn his clothes in order to pay for the sandwiches that were his evening meals in shabby Christiania boarding houses.

Now he was concluding his stay in the city of kings in royal company and conversing on culinary matters with the kings of the Danish theatre.

THE NEW EUROPEAN THEATRE

Naturally these experiences in the citadel of joint Dano-Norwegian culture made an impression on the ambitious but inexperienced Norwegian. And what impressed him most must have been the power of the performances he witnessed, as well as the heavily nationalistic thrust of the repertoire. Although French vaudeville pieces were included, the Danish theatres offered their audiences entire plays on national themes.

Now *that* was more than you could say for good old Norway.

But despite these delights, it is unlikely that Ibsen was equally impressed by absolutely everything he experienced of the Danish theatre world. The letters he sent back to the committee in Bergen are full of praise – but then what stipend reports aren't? Even an apprentice such as he was could see that the stage machinery employed in Copenhagen was hardly first class. As fine as the Kongelige Teater was, it was deficient in many respects. There was something old-fashioned about the whole place, the sets were old and worn, the costumes not especially convincing, the lighting poor – the Christiania Theatre had been using gas lights since 1848, but in Copenhagen the old Argentinian lamps were still in use, supplemented by tallow and wax.

Much more important was the ambivalent impression he must have had of Danish theatre at a time which was then – as it is now – regarded as a golden age. Under the aegis of Johan Ludvig Heiberg much of the spirit of discovery and experiment that characterised Romanticism had been replaced by a more stringent repertoire characterised by classical formalism revamped in the modern and technically accomplished vaudeville tradition. Even though this tradition was realistic in the sense that it reflected the contemporary everyday world of the bourgeoisie, it was still suffused with a harmonising ideal of beauty. One simply did not challenge the audiences' taste, 'crude realism' was eschewed. The aesthetic ideal was a sublimated presentation of life in the form of art – an 'idealised reality', as Heiberg put it. This aesthetic also dominated the acting styles. The actors' gestures and expressions onstage were stylised according to a strict tradition, in which a hand to the forehead meant 'unease', a handkerchief to the eye 'sorrow'. The actors gathered in a semi-circle around the prompt box at the front of the stage, something which the poor lighting made almost mandatory. The lines were delivered in the epic-declamatory style, with faces turned towards the audience. Stress was laid on elegant delivery and diction.

In the years preceding Ibsen's trip to Copenhagen this heavily stylised tradition had come under attack. A notable name among its challengers was the newly recruited Frederik Ludvig Høedt. Høedt had introduced a more radical form of realism and psychological characterisation into his acting, and in doing so influenced his colleagues Nielsen and Wiehe. As a result a deep split had occurred in the theatre. Indeed, according to Johanne Luise Heiberg's memoir, the whole of the 1851–2 season was characterised by a backstage struggle between the two factions.

Ibsen wasn't encouraged to attend the rehearsals, and he didn't get to see the theatre's props and scenery until after the season was over and then only in company with Thomas Overskou, a Heiberg loyalist. Could it be that Heiberg wished to hide the ongoing conflict from his young visitor? Nevertheless, Ibsen can hardly have failed to realise what was going on, if only from Høedt's scandalous performances onstage. Imagine offering audiences a performance so natural and true to everyday life, one which even went so far as to reduce the style so assiduously cultivated by Fru Heiberg to sheer mannerism!

In 1856 Johan Ludvig Heiberg resigned as head of the theatre, and on his death four years later Ibsen wrote a poem in praise of him. A few years later Heiberg's wife also retired from the stage, and she too was honoured with a poem, Ibsen's 'Letter in Rhyme to Fru Heiberg' (1871). But tributes of this kind need not be taken too literally. He recognised her greatness as a stage presence, but above all he was grateful to her because, as director at the Kongelige Teater from 1867, she opened the Danish stage to him. The friendship between them was never as close as some have suggested, but it was a mutually advantageous business relationship.

Well worth a letter in rhyme.

The relationship with Johan Ludvig Heiberg was more complex. In his younger years, Heiberg had rebelled against the majestic Oehlenschläger and opposed the extreme emotionalism of high Romanticism with a nuanced and systematic theory of literature which would, in turn, lead to the more formalised and professional practice of literary criticism. He had also developed a Hegelian systematisation of the literary genres in which drama was exalted above poetry and the epic. A noticeable aspect of his ranking of the genres is that, coincidentally, those forms Heiberg himself mastered occupied the highest places; his favourite genre, the vaudeville, is surprisingly highly rated in his system. His campaign on behalf of vaudeville has to be seen as a reaction against the preceding *staffasjedrama* (tableaux), and a step along the way towards the achievement of a modern, national drama. The realism and relevance of contemporary vaudeville were striking, even if 'raw reality' was eschewed.[1] Heiberg dominated Danish literature and the Danish stage for a generation, and had considerable influence in Norway too, as Ibsen's first theatrical review of any real note shows (of a student production of the vaudeville *The Grønland Asylum* in 1851). In this Ibsen says as little as possible about the contents of the play, and instead concentrates on the degree to which it follows or defies the conventions of the genre. But Heiberg's influence was greater as a window into the Hegelian way of thinking generally, arousing in Ibsen an understanding of the importance of dialectic and contradiction, ideas that would become fundamental features of the Ibsenian drama.

At the time during which Ibsen was in Copenhagen, however, there was little to be had from Heiberg. During his years as theatre manager from 1849 to 1856, personal and political intrigue had led Heiberg to a conservatism that expressed itself in his attitudes to theatre and literature. The rebel became the incarnation of authority, turning into a stumbling block for the progress of realistic drama. He mellowed slightly over time, to a point at which he was prepared to admit that the burgeoning tendencies towards realism, stronger individual portrayals and personal characterisation appeared to reach beyond the confines of his own genre system. But for now the roles were reversed. In the time that was left to him it was Heiberg who would have to learn about the development of drama from Ibsen and his generation, and Ibsen's liberation from Heiberg's influence must have begun as early as 1852. As drama developed, the chains of the Heibergian aesthetic were broken, and Heiberg found himself obliged to paddle along in the wake of history, a distressing fate for a philosopher of the speculative school.

Hans Christian Andersen was among those critical of the Danish theatre, and it was not by chance that he recommended to Ibsen that he spend some time in Vienna once he resumed his travels. There he would have the chance to study the modern art of direction under the innovative Heinrich Laube at the Hofburg Theatre. The idea of Vienna must have been very tempting. But Ibsen was well aware that his funds were insufficient, and there was no more to be had from the committee back home in Bergen.

It meant that he – and the new Norwegian Theatre – were deprived of direct personal experience of one of the most exciting and innovative theatres in Europe. The Royal Court Theatre in Dresden, on the other hand, was well known in Bergen, and on 6 June Ibsen sailed from Copenhagen for the capital of Saxony. Johannes and Louise Brun returned to Norway, as planned. Ibsen had counted on the help of the painter J. C. Dahl once he reached Dresden. Dahl was, after all, not only a native of Bergen but also a professor at the

Dresden Academy of Art, a well-known painter who moved in the best circles. It might have been he who inserted an announcement in the *Centralorgan für deutsche Bühnen* to the effect that Student Ibsen from Norway was in town to study dramaturgy. Dahl himself, however, was away from home travelling, and Ibsen had to spend his first week in Dresden alone.

As he wandered the streets of the city Ibsen had plenty of time to digest his experiences from Copenhagen, as well as savour his first impressions of the old Baroque city. He visited Dresden's Gemäldegalerie in the Johanneum, right next to the elegant Baroque Frauenkirche – an experience recollected in his cycle of poems 'In the Picture Gallery', which he probably wrote the following year and which was first published in 1859:

> I stood once in the gallery, elated,
> Imbibing inspiration from the treasure
> That Art's illustrious sires had dedicated
> To incorruption in kind, generous measure

Within a few years Ibsen would lay down his own brush for good, but the *experience* of pictorial art would always remain an integral part of his own literary project. When Dahl returned to Dresden he invited Ibsen to visit him in his studio, and arranged for him to be shown around backstage at the Hoffteater. Tickets to actual performances he had to pay for himself, but fortunately the prices were reasonable. Ibsen did in Dresden as he had done in Copenhagen, attending performances, studying costumes and generally getting an impression of the way things were done there. The Dresden style was, if anything, even more traditional than in Copenhagen. The beautiful, the harmonic and the ideal dominated. It was all very remote from realism. But Ibsen may well have been impressed by the care that had gone into the choice of costumes, and the realistic and atmospheric scenery and decor. During his stay in the city he had the opportunity to see three Shakespeare productions, including *A Midsummer Night's Dream*, which was not among those he had seen performed in Copenhagen, as well as plays by Friedrich Schiller, Johann Wolfgang von Goethe and Gotthold Ephraim Lessing. Alas, his limited funds meant that he was unable to go to the theatre as often as he had done in Copenhagen.

But he did have one memorable experience. The Polish-born actor Bogumil Dawison was in town, on loan from the same theatre in Vienna that Hans Christian Andersen had recommended to Ibsen. So he got his taste of Heinrich Laube and Vienna after all. Just as Høedt had done in Copenhagen, Dawison provoked audiences with his easy and natural acting style as Hamlet and Richard III. The Germans were stunned by the contrast between the pathos in the lines and the natural, speaking style in which he delivered them.[2] And Ibsen liked what he saw.

The tensions in the Copenhagen theatre world were repeated in Dresden. A few years earlier the ideas of the innovative director Edvard Devrient had influenced the subsequent debate over which way the theatre should be going, though his influence did not extend to the way plays were performed on the stage itself. Like Laube and Franz von Dingelsted, Devrient was a pioneer of the idea of the director as being in overall control of performances that were characterised by realism. If Ibsen read the newspapers during his stay in Dresden he would have formed a clear impression of the degree of public disapproval of the old-fashioned styles still being used at the Hoffteater – exactly the same as in Copenhagen.

Even during his Copenhagen visit Ibsen must have heard talk of *Das moderne Drama* (1852), the new book by the German literary critic Hermann Hettner, but it was not until he arrived in Dresden that he got hold of a copy. It turned out to be an almost programmatic outline for the revitalisation of the drama. It discussed the different forms of drama, but Ibsen would have been especially interested in those passages dealing with historical tragedy and romantic light comedy, both of them genres that he would presently explore in his future works. Historical tragedy must, according to Hettner, be liberated from the prevailing style – a declamatory and tableau-like presentation of a dead past. Instead, it should be a psychological drama of character that appealed to living audiences, a description of the struggle between souls and ideas, between opposing forces. These were sovereign demands, and they should take precedence over all the other usual ingredients – the ceaseless intrigue, the coincidental encounters, confusions over identity, intercepted letters, overheard conversations – all of these should yield to the demands of narrative credibility, the conflict of ideas and the spiritual development of the characters. In Hettner's vision, historical tragedy must be characterised by realism, in the sense of psychological realism. Certainly it was important to capture the spirit of the times, its 'local colour', but Hettner did not demand an exact degree of historical verisimilitude, only a balance between the historicity of a play and its contemporary relevance.

Romantic comedy too should involve opposing forces. What was unique about this genre in Hettner's eyes was the interaction of the worlds of fantasy and everyday life, interweaving with each other throughout in such a way as to make the fantasy seem real and true, and the everyday unreal and comical – just as Shakespeare had done in *A Midsummer Night's Dream*.[3]

Ibsen read and he learned. And even though he would continue for some years to struggle to free himself from confusions of identity and intercepted letters and similar dramaturgical techniques that seem like easy solutions to a later age, what he picked up from Hettner had a lasting influence on his writing.

And yet there are grounds for wondering how great this influence was, taken in isolation. Hettner's book is written in a rather dry and academic style. Instructive, yes, but just how inspiring? Ibsen was probably affected as much by the live theatre he experienced on Danish and German stages; in the interplay between elves and newspaper editors in Hostrup's *Master and Apprentice* he would certainly have detected Hettner's programme – or at least parts of it – converted into dramatic action, as well as in Høedt's and Dawison's vivid and realistic portrayals of Hamlet. Concepts like 'psychology' and 'realism' are fundamental for any understanding of Ibsen's future development, but both should be seen in their historical context. From a twenty-first-century perspective the concept of realism is usually associated with a literary phenomenon of the 1870s and 1880s, while psychology is connected to the development of modern psychology after Sigmund Freud. In the middle of the nineteenth century these two concepts had quite different shades of meaning. Interest in 'psychology' was a part of the age's fascination with the philosophy of personality, the investigation of the soul, and profound descriptions of character in terms of existential qualities and moral imperatives – of which Ibsen and Kierkegaard would be the most celebrated exponents in Scandinavia. There was little such psychology in Scribe, and a wealth of it in Shakespeare and Goethe. Interest in the complex and divided mind had caught on in Denmark as early as the late Romantic period.[4] It can be traced in different ways in the works of writers such as Henrik Hertz, Kierkegaard, Hans Christian Andersen and even in the master of high Romanticism himself, Adam Oehlenschläger, who demonstrated in his drama *Dina*, from 1842, the ability to renew himself, following criticisms by Johan Ludvig Heiberg.

Similarly the idea of 'realism' in writing had its historical preconditions, for the relationship between fiction and reality has been a matter for discussion as long as literature has been produced. In the 1820s Heiberg had offered a realism involving the stock characters of vaudeville but based on the contemporary bourgeoisie and local conditions (both often easily recognisable), and yet still so idealised and stylised that the younger generation of writers were provoked into rebellion. In the same way, by the middle of the nineteenth century Ibsen's understanding of 'realism' – not to speak of Bjørnson's – was still based on an idealism and a beautification that did not become problematic until the appearance of demands for a new and even more radical realism, naturalness and recognisability in the final decade of the century.

History is about continuity, not discoveries. Ibsen and his generation believed that they were living through a period of upheaval, so that their bold dismissal of Oehlenschläger's tragedies and Scribe's vaudevilles was largely the result of their need to create a distance between themselves and their predecessors, and to make space for their own literary projects. Posterity needs to guard against losing sight of the continuity between that which was and that which is to come, between psychology and realism as practised by Ibsen and the tradition he himself was building on. Scribe is a good example. Few dramatists have had a more lasting influence on the stage than he, and yet few have been so universally dismissed by posterity. No, he was not a great psychologist in any sense of the word, but his tight, well-made and commercially successful dramaturgy was an invaluable contribution to the emergence of modern plays with contemporary settings, and Ibsen was among those who learned much from him.

Each in his own way, Hettner, Høedt and Dawison were urging a break with the prevailing theatrical conventions and pointing the way towards a new and more radical realism that laid greater stress on psychology, a more individual portrayal of characters, and delivered a greater overall responsibility into the hands of the director. So there are no grounds for supposing that the artistic profit of Ibsen's sojourn in Copenhagen lay in his fascination for the acting style of Fru Heiberg, no more than it was the traditional theatre of Dresden that held him spellbound. On the contrary, it was the revolutionary trends in European theatre that appealed to him. He learned that something new was afoot, and he was determined to take it back home with him.

THE DIRECTOR

At the beginning of August, Ibsen returned to daily life at the theatre in Bergen. At an extraordinary meeting on 30 August the committee confirmed the 'instructions for the Norwegian Theatre's two directors' it had formulated in the spring. Henceforth Herman Laading would be responsible for the acting, and Ibsen for the way in which plays were staged.

With that the division of labour was complete – or so they thought. In reality conflict was unavoidable. Not surprisingly the older and more experienced Laading took offence at having to leave the staging to young Ibsen. At a time when actors were to learn to play their parts the way they were *supposed* to be played, the role of director of acting was certainly an important one. Another of his tasks was to teach the motley crew of actors, not all of whom were completely literate, how to behave like French aristocrats onstage. Diction and refinement were essential qualities for an actor, and Laading had the background to convey both these qualities to his actors.

But the demarcation of labour between the two men was not clear. As director of staging it was Ibsen's job, besides being responsible for the sets and costumes, to instruct the company in facial expressions and gestures, and where to stand on the stage, as well as to ensure that the interplay between the actors functioned. He was also bound to 'continue the instructing' from their final reading with Laading. In other words, his was the responsibility for the final character of the performance as it was staged. Obviously such an arrangement could lead to conflict between the instructors – all the more so since the two held different ideas on how the acting should be done. Laading preferred 'the conventional French style, which was not entirely free of artificiality', whereas Ibsen wanted to introduce the realistic style of acting he had come across in Copenhagen and Dresden.

The committee was aware of the potential problem and attempted to forestall any difficulties by decreeing that the two instructors should agree on an interpretation of the plays and parts before the work of instructing began. Should this prove unsuccessful, the committee reserved the right to make such decisions itself. It was Laading, however, who, as stage director, had the more prominent role, giving him overall responsibility for the performances and a closer relationship with the theatre committee.

In all likelihood it was assumed that Ibsen would defer to him in these matters, if only out of respect for an older and more experienced colleague. And he almost certainly did so – though probably with a heavy heart, and not without some form of protest.

Henrik Ibsen was not a man to give way easily.

That autumn he settled to serious work as instructor, at the same time as starting work on his first original play for the theatre. Komediehuset, which housed the Norwegian Theatre, was a really rather impressive wooden building. At a pinch it could accommodate audiences as large as those of the Christiania Theatre and the Kongelige Teater in Copenhagen, somewhere in the region of nine hundred. The average number of performances in a season that lasted from October to April was 122. In other words, there were a great many plays, many of them with very short lifespans. Not surprisingly, repeats and revivals made up as much as half of the repertoire. If a play was performed more than four times during the course of a season it was regarded as a success. Audiences were of two types: subscribers, who were usually from the upper class, and the rest, who filled the place on Sundays with their packed lunches and their dogs. The principal hope of audiences was to be entertained. Two-thirds of the repertoire consisted of light romances, vaudevilles and comedies, with serious classics and contemporary dramas being rarities. Ticket sales were the theatre's only source of income, so keeping audiences happy was a matter of financial life or death.

As dramatist and instructor, this became Ibsen's biggest challenge. He was to realise Bull's dream of a new and national theatre, at the same time as satisfying an audience of servants and artisans, tired after a hard week at work and longing to be entertained. It meant that the growth of the Norwegian national theatre took place against a background of chatter, laughter, booing, the sounds of people eating – and the baying of dogs. It wasn't just the

Norwegian Theatre that was in its infancy. Norwegian audiences too were untrained and undisciplined in the culture of the theatre, the less so the lower they stood on the social ladder.

Ibsen could think what he liked about art and its duty to educate audiences, but in the final analysis it was the audiences who decided both the repertoire and the atmosphere in the auditorium. It must have been a very disheartening realisation.

One day a lady stopped him on the street and said she had heard that he was to teach Johannes and Louise and the others how to act and wished him the very best of luck – God be with him.

Ibsen smiled and said he probably needed God's help – 'I'm just learning myself. But don't tell anyone else – maybe they won't notice.'

He was painfully aware of his own lack of experience as a man of the theatre, and obviously the actors didn't let him get away with anything either. Recalling their director in later years they were merciless in their judgement.

'When it came to theatre stuff he was hopeless,' one remembered. 'He was so shy he wouldn't say boo to a goose, never mind *no* to any of the actors. And as for the actresses, dearie me! That Miss Johannesen, Lucie who works at the bank – he quaked in his boots at the mere sound of her voice.'

Several others tell the same story. But is this really fair? Ibsen remained reluctant to talk about his years as a practical man of the theatre in Bergen and Christiania. 'All that upsetting theatre stuff,' as he referred to it in later years.

'His work as a practical man of the theatre left no visible traces,' wrote one of his earliest biographers, Gerhard Gran. 'In the history of our acting traditions he is unimportant.'

Thus the judgement of posterity. But is that really all there is to say?

The reason for this harsh judgement of Ibsen as a practical man of the theatre was, of course, the shadow that would accompany him for much of his adult life, one that would make him appear, by comparison, even smaller and more timid than he really was. The shadow's name was Bjørnstjerne Bjørnson. He would follow in Ibsen's footsteps in Bergen, and later in Christiania, and do so in inimitable Bjørnsonian fashion: voluble, innovative and above all highly visible. But Bjørnson's undeniable importance for the development of the Norwegian stage should not blind us completely to the value of Ibsen's efforts. As Ibsen's journals with their notes and drawings show, his heritage was an important if not always a very obvious one. Through his directing he contributed to the evolution of the role of the director as an independent figure with overall responsibility for the final form of the production. His precise concern for the details of stage decor, costume and scenery made his productions of *The Vikings at Helgeland* and *The Pretenders* textbook examples of how such things should be done.

Much of this was the fruit of his visits to Copenhagen and Dresden – the importance of historically accurate costumes and decor, of a prevailing unity between the scenography and the directing, the careful recording of all instruction. The new realistic, psychological acting style demanded this sort of all-round thinking from a director in ways that had not been necessary with the old idealistic style, in which the players assumed their ordained places at the front of the stage. Part of Ibsen's achievement as a director was to urge Norwegian theatre along in this new direction. This in itself may partially explain the disappointment expressed by some of those who worked under him in Bergen; a play such as *Lady Inger of Østråt*, for example, challenged the actors with complex and complicated characters that they were little qualified to understand.

So Ibsen was rather more than merely 'hopeless' in his backstage manifestation. But at the same time that is exactly what he was. Lacking in skills as a communicator he probably gave his actors more freedom than they knew what to do with, and so left them feeling uncertain. At best he could lecture, but hardly inspire. The emerging idea of the director's real function demanded someone with a very different kind of personal authority from the one nature had provided him with. It left him striving towards a form of theatre based on an inner direction that he himself was unable to provide. He was more at home in the world of onstage directing, reminiscent of those days in his boyhood when he had cut out paper puppets and arranged them in attractive tableaux.

Now those puppets had turned into flesh-and-blood human beings, and as director of his own plays it was his responsibility to lead them in an authoritative manner.

Bjørnson possessed the kind of authority Ibsen lacked. So it is no accident that these two great pioneers of Norwegian theatre left their mark in the fields of, respectively, outer direction, stage direction, and inner direction, acting direction. It was as a writer that Ibsen would be able to communicate his ideas about directing and interpretation in a free and uninhibited way, and it is here, in his own stage directions and in his letters to the directors of his plays, that he would exert his strongest influence as a practical man of the theatre.[5]

IMPISH FUN ON ST JOHN'S NIGHT

As the year 1852 drew to a close, the time approached for Ibsen to make his debut as a dramatist for the Norwegian Theatre in Bergen. Finally he would appear before the people of Bergen with the sort of new, nationalist drama Ole Bull had promised them.

St John's Night was written during the spring and summer of the year, much of it in Denmark and Germany. It is a comedy about the effects of a Norwegian midsummer night on four young people and an old imp. Johannes Birk and Juliane are engaged to be married, although they don't love each other, Julian Poulsen is a student friend of Birk, and Anne is Juliane's stepsister. On the farm in Telemark where the action is set the old gnome decides to celebrate the evening too. He tricks the youngsters into taking a magic potion that opens the sensitive ones to the supernatural world, whereas the less sensitive ones don't understand what's going on and fall asleep. Here, of course, is where the complications arise. It is Juliane and Poulsen who fall asleep, and Anne and Birk who get to visit the golden mansion of the mountain king and experience the dance of the fairies. In other words, they experience the world of Norwegian folklore as real, while the other two miss out on the whole thing. Poulsen, who talks ceaselessly and bombastically of what is 'natural' and 'national' but fails to understand the most profound meanings of these words, is cruelly exposed by the events of the night.

The theme was not particularly original. It has clear parallels with Shakespeare's *A Midsummer Night's Dream* as well as Hostrup's *Master and Apprentice* (which Ibsen had seen in, respectively, Dresden and Copenhagen), Heiberg's *Syvsoverdage* (*7-Day Sleep*), certain poems by Welhaven and bits of Paul Botten-Hansen's *Huldrebryllpet* (*The Huldre Wedding*). His aim was to make a specifically Norwegian play out of a familiar European theme, a Romantic comedy that would entertain audiences at the same time as it conformed to the insights of both Heiberg and Hettner. No exercise in dead nostalgia but a play vibrant with everyday life. Big ideas were opposed to each other, as Hettner had demanded they should be, and in the course of the struggle between them Ibsen took his chance to poke fun at the shallowness of much national romanticism, expressing in his description of Julian Poulsen the ambivalence his own generation felt towards the project, and a scepticism in the face of superficial and false expressions of it.

What sort of response did he anticipate?

Bergen audiences were used to the sort of epic national romanticism associated with Ole Bull and J. C. Dahl, and it was by no means a foregone conclusion that they would enjoy this subtle mockery of a false version of it – especially not when it came from a dour man from the capital. Mocking irony as practised by the editorial board of *Andhrimner* was a world away from the vaudevilles so beloved of Bergen society people. And would that unexpected mixture of fantasy and reality that had created such controversy on the stages of Copenhagen and Dresden do the same thing in Bergen?

The reviews were guarded, but encouraging. The audiences were not. On the first night there was booing and whistling from the packed parquet. The following night most of the seats were empty. *St John's Night* closed – and remained closed for the rest of Ibsen's life.[6] It wasn't a success. But did that make it a flop? Two performances wasn't unusual for a play at the Norwegian Theatre. A problem affecting both Bergen and Christiania in those days was that potential audiences for more than two performances hardly existed. With room for 900 at both venues, filling them was always going to be a struggle. It meant that a popular play risked 'using up' its audience on the first night, and the strong ticket sales for the premiere of St John's Night suggest that this is what happened here.

Ibsen would later experience this dilemma several more times in both Bergen and, later, in Christiania. All of his plays did well and sometimes extremely well on the opening night, with the result that they had very short lives on the stage – precisely because they were initially so popular. This consistent display of curiosity about Ibsen's new plays shows that he was already highly regarded by audiences. But this was scant comfort when it came to the opening of St John's Night. The reaction of audience and critics alike suggests that the play did not meet the expectations of either the committee or the audience for Ibsen's debut in Bergen. Things like that hurt, and for someone as sensitive to criticism as Ibsen was, it must have hurt even more.

In the long run what must have hurt still more was his own feeling that his play had failed to live up to what he himself had expected of it. At first sight Ibsen appears to have been fairly satisfied with it. St John's Night was not a fiasco. It offered a good, representative picture of exactly what he was capable of at that stage in his career. Following the premiere he sent it off to the Christiania Theatre – which rejected it. But in time he must have seen the artistic failings in the play, for St John's Night is the only one of his plays that he expressly rejected. In later years he claimed that 'that rubbish' wasn't even all his own work but a rewriting of something he had been given by the theatre critic Theodor Christian Bernhoft, whom he knew from Christiania. Bernhoft, who died in 1885, did not deny it. Scholars, however, are unanimous in attributing the work to Ibsen alone.

'FLOWERS OF THE FIELD AND POTTED PLANTS'

In the spring of 1853 Ibsen moved out of Madam Sontum's and into two rooms in an annex to the theatre, and for the next four years this would be his home. His time in Bergen thus far had probably been a lonely one. He had no circle of loyal friends and admirers for whom he could shine as in the Grimstad days, and no crowd of like-minded poverty-stricken intellectuals such as he had been part of in Christiania. He was alone, and yet noticed wherever he went, just as had been the case in Grimstad. It was the suit that had attracted attention on his arrival in Grimstad, and his style of dress had not grown any less striking over the years:

'He wore frilly shirts with fancy lace poet's cuffs around his wrists. And when he was out and about he carried a short stick,' according to one source.

That little boy, Henrik the Beardless, who once sat at the feet of old Lund in Venstøp and gaped in admiration at the old man's corduroy trousers and brown and gold-trimmed silk waistcoat, was now a grown man himself. Now it was his turn to dress in style, displaying the same mixture of uncomfortable shyness and a need to be seen as he had done in Grimstad. In the eyes of many he cut a strange and remarkable figure. But not in Rikke Holst's eyes. After Clara Ebbell we don't know the names of any women in Ibsen's life until he became acquainted with Rikke Holst in the spring of 1853 – although we do know that he had asked a young woman to dance the year before. Fanny Riis was the sister of Claus Pavels Riis, author of the hit play *Til Sæters* (*To the Shieling*). She was just sixteen years old, and never forgot her first encounter with Ibsen: 'I thought he was strange,' she wrote later. 'He didn't seem as nice and kind as the others.' He wore his greasy hair swept back, and she noted the strong smell of tobacco when they danced – although, in fact, Ibsen couldn't dance at all. Highly embarrassed, she followed his clumsy lead as best she could, in full view of everyone, before he finally led her to a seat and began a long conversation which Fanny endured, all the while longing to be dancing again – with someone else.

There may have been several such episodes, but if so we know nothing of them. He may well, during the time he lived in the area, have visited Vika prostitutes, a common enough pastime among students in the big city, unless his experience with Else Sophie had put him off the whole business. If that was the case then it was Rikke Holst who got him back on track again.

She was young, fifteen years old and not yet confirmed, a lively girl with brown, laughing eyes. What was it about him? Rikke Holst was attracted to his strangeness, his oddness, and the fact that he was so often alone, and seemed lonely. The pair took walks up to Sverresborg, or beneath the trees by Toldboden, Ibsen usually melancholic and silent save for when he abruptly let loose a torrent of words in furious condemnation of 'convention and hypocrisy', or delivered enigmatic utterances full of paradox and wild assertions. Just as he had done in Grimstad. The difference being that back then he had played these games for an admiring crowd of people his own age, whereas now his audience was a guileless young girl filled with wonder and pity for this little man with his big feelings.

And Rikke listened. What else could she do? She listened as he complained that no one understood him, no one cared about him, and that he would always, always be lonely.

Good thing, then, that he had Rikke Holst.

Just as Clara Ebbell had done, Rikke inspired the lyricist in Ibsen. At least that was how he experienced it; when his heart beat, it usually beat out a rhyme. He wrote a poem for her entitled 'Flowers of the Field and Potted Plants', but Rikke didn't actually want to be a flower of the field. The story goes that in response she sent him a bouquet of auricula, and in return received another poem 'To my Auricula' – anything for love!

In June he proposed to her in verse:

> A word from your lips
> Will seal my future; –
> Do I know the joys of happiness
> In waking dreams only?

Was this desperation? The prayer of a broken young dramatist who wanted to belong, this lonely young oddball with his frilly shirt and his poet's cuffs – she was so young, after all, and the whole thing had happened so fast? Or did he really see in those laughing brown eyes something he could love? They got engaged and cast their rings into the sea. Who could resist a wedding at sea? Rikke's father, as it turned out. He forbade them from seeing each other again. But of course they continued to do so, with Rikke's brother going along as chaperone and lookout. One day Rikke's father surprised them together and exploded with anger, and Henrik took to his heels and ran.

And that was the end of the Rikke Holst saga. Or rather, its beginning: Rikke would go down in literary history, along with Sophie Holst and Clara Ebbell, as one of the young Ibsen's muses.

In time there would be several more of them.

THE BIG LET-DOWN

In the long run, happiness with Rikke couldn't survive the hard realities of life. After the boos from the audience and the tepid critical response to *St John's Night* in the summer of 1853 it was the committee's turn to crack the whip. Since Laading's threatened resignation of the preceding December it had been keeping a careful eye on him.

And with good reason.

Could they afford to lose an experienced, sociable and inspiring figure such as Laading – a man 'born to teach' – for the tight-lipped newcomer Ibsen? Had their support and investment been rewarded? As a way of testing the extent and limits of his talents the committee had allocated him a greater responsibility than originally envisaged in the areas of administration and directing. Was he worth the risk? His debut as dramatist indicated that the answer was, probably not. Ibsen must have been anxious, and he wasn't the only one. In July a formal complaint about his directing was handed to him, and at the end of the month the committee delivered a second letter.

Here it was. Everything Ibsen must have been afraid of throughout the winter and the spring. The whole thing in black and white:

On a number of occasions it has come to the attention of the committee that certain of the obligations pertaining to your position have been either neglected, and subsequently forgotten, or else not carried out to the satisfaction of the theatre.

A list of errors and omissions was appended: imprecision in communications, incomplete directorial lists, cursory attention to scenery – and it might be to the benefit of all if Ibsen could 'develop and extend his contributions as both director and instructor'.

Extend his contributions. That could only mean dealing with the actors – face to face!

At the beginning of August, in a tight-lipped and injured tone, he responds to the criticisms one by one. He has his back to the wall now. Boos and whistles from the audience, his work criticised by the committee – possibly under pressure from Laading, who had threatened to resign again in June. The committee's response was to offer Laading more influence over the way plays were actually directed. The division of labour after these changes is not clear, but the indications are that things continued pretty much as before. The position of the committee, however, was clear: if necessary they would hobble Ibsen in order to keep Laading.

There was more to come. In the autumn of 1853 Ibsen locked horns with one of his actors, Andreas Isachsen. The two had known each other in Christiania. Isachsen was an academic too and had written a couple of plays himself, including the play Ibsen had with him when he arrived in Bergen. In the annals of the theatre's history Isachsen has gone down as its 'evil schemer' and he was clearly not an easy man to get along with. He now voiced his severe dissatisfaction with the quality of the directing. Again Ibsen had to respond, and not long before Christmas he sent a long and detailed letter of complaint to the committee on the subject of the actor, brimming with sarcasm and bitterness.

Adopting a tone like that was hardly the response of a self-assured director complaining of the behaviour of one of his subordinates; indeed, it looked more like a subordinate feeling a need to defend himself to his bosses.

So 1853 ended as it had begun. Everything and everyone was against him. That brief glimpse of early summer light had faded even before the coming of the autumn dark. He had written poetry for Rikke Holst, but it was plays for the theatre he was expected to provide. And as liberating and cheering as it might have been to write poetry, he now faced the more daunting task of once again exposing himself to the judgement of Bergen's theatre audiences, and the theatre committee. Ibsen did something any businessman would understand, something he would come to do again in later years, the only logical thing to do when a new product is simply unavailable: he went to the stockroom. Ibsen played his best card and rewrote *The Burial Mound*, and the revision opened at the Norwegian Theatre on 2 January 1854.

Then, as later, Ibsen showed a businesslike understanding of how to recycle earlier material and put it to good use, without ever sacrificing what he believed to be the prevailing demands of art. Wasn't that exactly what he had done with *St John's Night*, even though the results might have been less than outstanding? He did the same thing now with *The Burial Mound*, giving it a radical rewrite. In this new version the lyrical influence of Oehlenschläger was much reduced and greater attention paid to historical accuracy – Ibsen had obviously read a great deal of Old Norse literature since writing the original version. The main characters were now more clearly defined as individuals and personalities, and the conflict of ideas between Christianity and paganism set in sharper and more psychologically nuanced relief. The actual frame of the story, however, remained unchanged.

Ibsen must have been excited to see what sort of reaction he would get from the audience on opening night, and disappointed to have to confess that he had again failed to turn out a hit. The newspapers didn't even dignify the play with a review but contented themselves with a preview. The audience's reaction was unequivocal: *St John's Night* had managed a two-performance run, *The Burial Mound* was taken off after the premiere. It wasn't performed again for another two years. Even then it only managed one night.

What was the matter with them, those good people of Bergen, who didn't even have the cultural understanding to appreciate a play that had been good enough for audiences in the capital, and was now being offered in an improved version? It must have been some comfort that *Bergenske Blade* printed the entire play as a supplement, making *The Burial Mound* the second Ibsen play to be printed.

LYING TO BLYTT

During these difficult years in Bergen the seasons themselves seemed to bring a certain symmetry to Ibsen's life. Spring usually brought joy in some form or other, filling the troubled poet, before the coming of autumn and the distant appearance of 2 January and the night of the premiere. In the spring of 1852 he had travelled in Europe, and the following spring he got to know Rikke Holst.

Spring 1854 had its own highlight too. In April and May the Norwegian Theatre went on the road to Trondheim, the first occasion ever on which a professional Norwegian theatre had been on tour. Overcoming the intense local rivalry between the two cities, the tour turned out to be a great success. Trondheim audiences reacted enthusiastically to the sound of their own language coming from the stage, and the tour was a clear sign that the Bergen theatre really was a national and not just a local enterprise. The troupe must have been delighted as they stood onstage after the last performance on 2 June and sang the national anthem along with the audience.[7]

In the course of the summer Ibsen had finished another new play. Again he seems to have been convinced that a nationalist theme was the best way to reach his audience. He must have dreaded the whole business, but was perhaps cheered by several changes in the makeup of the committee over the autumn. He hoped to be able to get on better with some of the younger members who had come on board – Herman Baars, Morten Beyer and a merchant named Peter Michael Blytt. It was Blytt who was to prove most important to Ibsen. He also provided posterity with the most detailed description we have of Ibsen's years in Bergen. Like most other people associated with the theatre he was puzzled by this 'quiet, taciturn and modest young man, not very striking in appearance, his gaze usually veiled and hard to read'. Three years into his tenure and Ibsen was still this odd and rather helpless loner, padding silently around in the wings, respected, but not loved, a man who found it hard to make friends, and rather easier to make enemies.

Ibsen's self-confidence must have been desperately low that autumn. Neither *St John's Night* nor the rewritten version of *The Burial Mound* had come up to expectations. He had believed in both, but audiences and critics had remained unmoved.

Best, then, to let the new play sink or swim on its own. Without the author.

He took no chances. One day in September, Peter Blytt opened the door to find the dramatist on his doorstep looking even more shy and uncomfortable than usual. After a few brief and confusing words Ibsen handed his boss a sheaf of papers, a manuscript. Would Blytt be willing to consider this new play, sent to him by a friend of his in Christiania? Would Blytt be prepared to deliver an opinion on whether or not it was worth a production before passing it on to the committee for formal consideration? Blytt didn't just read the manuscript, he devoured it. Who in the world had written it? It had to be Ibsen – but why would the house-dramatist lie about its origins? Blytt was bewildered. He was also convinced that the play, *Lady Inger of Østråt*, was an outstanding piece of national-historical drama, and would be the perfect opener for the theatre's new season in 1855.

Set in the early part of the sixteenth century, Ibsen's new play was both a historical tragedy and a psychological drama of character. Lady Inger struggles desperately to find a way out of the dilemma in which she finds herself, forced to lead a Norwegian-Swedish revolt against the Danish aristocracy of which she is herself a member by marriage. As she fights for her happiness and the happiness of her children in the midst of a game of power-politics she finds herself drawn ever deeper into a network of intrigue that ends in gruesome tragedy.

Lady Inger of Østråt showed what Ibsen had learned during his European trip. Here is the psychological realism that Hettner was looking for, and that Høedt and Dawison displayed in their performances as Hamlet and Richard III. Lady Inger herself is a character of truly tragic proportions and the play is, with the exception of *The Pretenders*, from 1863, the closest Ibsen ever came to being Shakespeare. Structurally the play was much influenced by techniques derived from Scribe – here are purloined letters aplenty, confusions over identity, and the traditional asides necessary to keep the audience abreast of the complexities of the plot.

Ibsen was usually given sole charge of the directing of his own plays, but *Lady Inger* turned out to be different. It was, after all, allegedly the work of another, and from the outset the directing duties were shared with Laading. Ibsen nevertheless managed to introduce, in a modest fashion, some of the ideas he had acquired during his trip abroad. His road to realism, to character-driven drama with an overarching unity, was a gradual process. In the 1850s neither he nor his audiences were ready to abandon the old idealistic formalism, so that what was practised was a hybrid often described as 'picturesque realism'. Close examination of Ibsen's prompt notebooks, his notes for the actors, his ideas for directing, his sketches for the decor and the costumes reveals an almost perfectionist longing to create an overarching sensory unity to the production. The realism was particularly evident in the 'external' directing. In both *St John's Night* and *Lady Inger of Østråt* he introduced a depth to the staging that was a bold advance on the traditional grouping of the actors at the front of the stage. The actors also occasionally faced each other, and not just the audience. For all these reasons, *Lady Inger of Østråt* was at the cutting edge of the struggle between the old drama of the ideal and the new, realistic approach.

Not until rehearsals did Ibsen feel confident enough to confess that he was the writer of the play. It turned out to be something he was prepared to stand behind. Two years later he remained of the firm opinion that it was his best play.

The conventional view of the production of *Lady Inger* in Bergen is that it was yet another failure for Ibsen. But that is not quite the case. Like *St John's*

Night it ran for two nights and was well attended on opening night, with a curtain call for the writer. The only review was mixed, but not without positive comments.[8] Compared with its later box-office appeal, *Lady Inger* could be counted only a moderate success on this occasion. A heavy and rather dark drama of character, it must have seemed unfamiliar to the audience. It may also have made demands on the actors that they were unable to meet. Ibsen's own response to the production is impossible to gauge. Perhaps he was disappointed because his expectations of this particular play had been so high, perhaps its first-night success pleased him, and the curtain call, as did the fact that the chairman of the committee Peter Blytt and several other members clearly appreciated its artistic qualities.

* * *

The signs are that Ibsen got on better with the new committee than he had done with the old one. In particular he must have had confidence in Peter Blytt. The performances of *Lady Inger of Østråt* got 1855 off to a good start for him, and it is not impossible that the play also contributed to a rise in his social status in Bergen. Blytt was one of the most respected merchants in Bergen, and as well as chairman of the theatre committee he was also the director of the Bergen Athenæum. In 1855 he also became chairman of one of the city's exclusive literary societies with the prosaic name the December 22 Society. He invited Ibsen to join.

As in Grimstad, it had taken a few years for the invisible walls surrounding Ibsen to be broken down. And the December 22 Society gave him an excellent entry into Bergen society.

The society met every fourteen days in the autumn and winter for readings and literary discussions. Lectures were given in rotation, and Ibsen's turn came on 27 November 1855. What more natural topic than 'William Shakespeare and his Influence on Nordic Art'? Unfortunately the lecture has not survived, but the title is enough to suggest that Ibsen had his own ideas about a Nordic Shakespearean tradition of which his own *Lady Inger of Østråt* was the latest manifestation. No doubt his choice of subject was influenced too by the fact that in September he was involved in directing a Danish adaptation of Shakespeare's *As You Like It* – an involvement unique in his career.

But if the choice of topic is not a surprise, the mere fact that Ibsen delivered a lecture at all at a gathering of the cream of Bergen society is. At that time cultural life in cities and towns such as Bergen was mostly confined to circles that were a mixture of private and public gatherings. The Norwegian Theatre, which attempted to be a genuinely public institution, was only one part of Bergen's cultural life. But though the theatre was in principle a theatre for all, it was at the same time an important part of the social network of the upper class.

It was a resource for social advancement, not through its public accessibility but as a recruiting ground for the more exclusive circles and clubs with which it was in regular contact. This was true of nineteenth-century bourgeois culture generally: in principle accessible to all, but with internal divisions into groups to which access was exclusive, the price being in part one's financial status, and in part a mastery of certain cultural and social codes.[9]

Ibsen had little money. It made the cultural capital he was slowly accumulating all the more important. It seems that he was welcomed into the society, for just a few weeks later he was invited to compose and recite a prologue in celebration of its tenth anniversary. Further invitations followed.

THE FEAST AT BERGEN

Both the revision of *The Burial Mound* and *Lady Inger of Østråt* attest to the fact that over the years Ibsen had become a serious student of history. *Lady Inger* in particular showed a deep knowledge of Norwegian history, even though, in the spirit of Hettner, he allowed himself considerable artistic freedom with the material.[10] This interest in the past made it natural to follow *Lady Inger* with another historical play, this from a different period. Norway's centuries under the Danish Crown were not really worth spending much time on, in his opinion. The period of the country's greatness preceding it, so well described in the Old Norse sagas, was a different matter. Ibsen knew Snorri Sturluson's *Heimskringla*, but the Icelandic family sagas were unknown to him until he read them in N. M. Petersen's Danish translations which appeared between 1839 and 1844.

Maybe the sagas would provide him with a satisfactory format for national, Norwegian drama?

The breakthrough failed to materialise. He probably found it hard to recreate the epic style of the sagas in the form of a play. Anyway, his voracious appetite as a reader soon led him away from the sagas and into the world of the folk ballads.[11] He discovered Magnus B. Landstad's ground-breaking *Norwegian Folk Ballads*, from 1853, the first extensive collection of folk ballads made in Norway, and quickly realised that the world of the literary romances of the Middle Ages offered more to him as a dramatist than the epic style of the sagas. Perhaps now he would be able to realise his own literary programme, outlined in 'To Norway's Skalds' back in 1850, in which he had loudly though without great originality proclaimed that the folk ballads must be the sources for any truly national literature.

The Feast at Solhaug was written in the summer of 1855 and is a lyrical drama, set in the Middle Ages, and based on something Ibsen had come across in Landstad and Andreas Fayes' collection of folk ballads and tales, and influenced by literary adaptations of such material by Johan Sebastian Welhaven and others. A wedding celebration develops into a fateful drama of love in a catalogue of intrigues fired by dreams of love lost, love awakened, threats, sword-play, and a poisoned chalice that is passed from hand to hand. Two sisters, Margit and Signe, are at the heart of the intrigues, alternately concerned with winning and avoiding their respective suitors. Margit is the one who loses, leaving her sister to enjoy the love of her life while she goes off to live in a nunnery.

The premiere was, as usual, on 2 January, and this time success was complete. The author had to take several curtain calls, and later that same evening members of the public and the theatre's orchestra gathered outside his window to serenade him.

Standing at the window the man of the hour felt something he had not felt for a very long time.

The pure joy of success.

'I do believe,' he confided later, 'that I was sufficiently carried away to give a sort of speech to the gathering; I recall my extreme happiness.'

In later years, Ibsen remembered that the only really sour note was the response of the critics.[12] He said he could never forget the way *The Feast at Solhaug* had been treated by the Norwegian press and used it as an excuse to express his contempt for the general level of literary appreciation in Norway. In fact, *The Feast at Solhaug* was not treated all that harshly, neither in Bergen, Christiania nor Trondheim. Indeed, the response was largely positive, and the only criticisms raised were of a relatively minor sort.

Only one reviewer actually slaughtered the play, and did so comprehensively:

'Here is not a single character with a poetic soul,' Hartvig Lassen wrote in *Aftenbladet*. 'I have read a great many occasional poems that have been copies; but I have never until now seen a play that is in its entirety a copy of another. Because that is what *The Feast at Solhaug* is. This feast isn't held at Solhaug or anywhere else in Norway, it's held at Svend Dyring's house.'

Lassen was accusing *The Feast at Solhaug* of being unforgivably similar to Henrik Hertz's drama *Svend Dyrings Huus* (*Svend Dyring's House*), a play from 1837. One could not make such accusations against Henrik Ibsen with impunity. To be fair, the reviewer in the *Christiania-Posten* had also pointed out similarities between the two plays, though it was only Lassen who made the claim that the play was outright plagiarism.

That was enough for the play's author.

Henrik Ibsen had a particular dislike of being compared to anyone else, and the older he got the more unwilling did he become to concede a literary debt to anyone. The cause was probably a combination of his own sense of self-worth and his image of himself as a writer. More than most, Ibsen brought with him into the world of the modern, market-oriented writer a Romantic insistence on the elevated status of art, and the divine originality of the writer. The effect could be almost comical, for this particular deity was demonstrably a regular wage-earner. Aspiring to the heights, he waded in the trivial, aspiring to art but struggling against the practicalities necessary to achieve it. Searching for a way to create something new, he was condemned to stand on the shoulders of those who came before him.

All the more important, then, to be strongly self-assertive. Let no one think they could get away with accusing Henrik Ibsen of plagiarism.[13]

Bjørnstjerne Bjørnson knew exactly what it was all about. He praised *The Feast at Solhaug* for its lyricism – 'these verses are among the most beautiful and sonorous ever written in Norwegian'. And Ibsen had not been influenced by Hertz. Rather, both dramatists had been inspired by the same folk ballad. Moreover, it was natural for writers to follow in one another's footsteps without that necessarily making them epigones. Bjørnson's defence was fair enough, but he ignores one important fact. As a regular provider of vaudevilles and light comedies Henrik Ibsen had much in common with Heiberg and Scribe, and the points of similarity between *The Feast at Solhaug* and *Sven Dyring's House* owed less to their common origin in a folk ballad than to the prevailing dramatic conventions that characterised the work not only of Scribe, Heiberg and Hertz, but also Ibsen.

It takes one writer to understand another. The two men, Henrik Ibsen and Bjørnstjerne Bjørnson, were still not friends, merely acquaintances from their student days in Christiania. But Bjørnson's warm words of support were certainly conducive to the growth of a friendship.

In the final analysis, the criticism in the newspapers can't have been enough to sour all the praise the play enjoyed, not least from its audiences. Looking back, Ibsen would recall the premiere of *The Feast at Solhaug* as the only happy day he had known in Bergen.

That was an exaggeration. In fact, one good thing led to another. Again, with the advent of spring, life took a turn for the better.

THE EAGLE

The first time Suzannah saw him was one day when she visited the theatre with her friend, Karoline Reimers.

'Which one is Ibsen?' she asked.

Karoline pointed him out.

'Oh my God, he's an old man!'

Karoline laughed – her friend had mistaken Ibsen for the little old man he was conversing with, and she nodded to indicate that she had meant the man with the large black beard.

Suzannah Daae Thoresen was eight years younger than Ibsen and a child at the time of his arrival in Bergen. She was the daughter of pastor Hans Conrad Thoresen and his late wife, Sara Margrethe Daae, and stepdaughter to the pastor's third wife, Magdalene Thoresen. The Thoresen family home was one of Bergen's literary centres, where the lady of the house held salons, and the bookshelves in the pastor's study bulged with books. Suzannah loved literature. Even as a child she was such a voracious reader that her stepmother worried that she knew 'almost nothing about real life on earth'. She and Karoline used the same lending library, and would sit back to back reading on the sofa.

Henrik and Suzannah did not get to know each other properly until 7 January 1856, five days after the premiere of *The Feast at Solhaug*. Magdalene Thoresen had invited the playwright to one of her literary salons. It was not necessarily his first visit to the Thoresen family home, and he may well have met the book-loving young daughter of the house before.

But this, in her twentieth year, was probably the first time he actually *saw* her.

They met again at a ball at a meeting of the Philharmonic Society. Neither of them danced, instead they sat talking together far into the night. When Henrik returned home, he wrote a poem about the evening he had just experienced, about the ball and the dancers, the gentlemen with their 'excited faces' and the ladies who 'smiled so mysteriously', the laughter and exuberance hiding the fact that 'beneath the veiling joy/the sorrows of emptiness lie hidden'.

But one person there stood out for him:

But yes, there is one amongst them,
But one and one only, it's plain.
The eye shows a private sorrow,
I read there both grief and pain.
I read there the dreams whose churning
And wavering never cease,
A heart that's a-throb with its yearning,
A stranger in life to peace.

A poem, in form and content like any other love poem. But on this occasion he really captured the 'bride of his thought'. And held onto her. The indications are that Suzannah had a personality similar to his – as unlikely as that might seem. Not only was she well read, she was also intellectually gifted and a young woman with opinions of her own. She was shy and withdrawn but also temperamental and dramatic, an unforgiving hater, with a penchant for the monumental and the romantic. She disliked social occasions and, again like him, was extremely protective of her private life. Their bedroom door remains eternally closed, and the passion and depths of their love for each other remain matters for them alone. Only one person in a position to gossip did so, their daughter-in-law Bergliot. She writes of a strong bond, fierce quarrels, mutual respect, and above all, a deep loyalty. They were made for each other, which really only means that they had all the necessary requirements for the making of each other.

Two months later it was Karoline's turn to find herself a poet. It was at a gathering in Trondheim, where she stood observing Bjørnstjerne Bjørnson in his natural habitat – at the centre of a crowd of people. Suddenly, in the midst of his stream of talk, he turns and addresses her:

'When my son is born, do you know what I'm going to call him? His name will be Bjørn!'

Naturally the young lady blushed deeply. All through the dinner she sat in silence and listened to the writer's monologue. Silent partly in wonder, but silent also because it was quite impossible to get a word in edgeways.

Thus did these two, Henrik Ibsen and Bjørnstjerne Bjørnson, meet their future wives, the former hesitant, fumbling, and certainly not dancing, the latter winning her heart with a perfectly judged pickup line and a massive display of Bjørnsonian virility. According to family legend, the two young women made a pact, that if one of them should have a son and the other a daughter, the two would marry each other. And that did indeed happen. Just as Bjørnson's first-born really was christened Bjørn – not that *that* came as any great surprise to anyone.

From that point onwards, Ibsen became a regular visitor to the Thoresen house, as well as a number of other houses belonging to Bergen's rich and cultured. Henrik Ibsen had come in from the cold, although it still didn't mean that things were easy for him in the pastor's home. Although not – to put it mildly – renowned for his winning ways, he soon established a close relation-ship with Suzannah's older sister Marie, the second of the two women whom he held in deep and sincere affection. Her older brother Johan Herman would also become important in Ibsen's life, and when Henrik and Suzannah later left Norway to live abroad it was he who took care of Ibsen's affairs back home.

The relationship with his mother-in-law Magdalene Thoresen proved more complex and he remained mercurial to her throughout her life. Her first impressions were of a silent and withdrawn man, clumsy and fumbling. For many years the atmosphere between them was 'cool', perhaps because both were writers and both ambitious – Magdalene Thoresen made her debut anonymously, with the assistance of Bjørnson, in 1860, with a collection enti-tled *Poems by a Lady*. She had by that time already had four plays produced – though not published – at the Norwegian Theatre, three of them during the time Ibsen was there. This mixture of the personal and the professional might well have made their relationship problematic. She may also have been jealous. She was, after all, only thirty-six when Ibsen and Suzannah became a couple, and was known to have a weakness for younger men. When Bjørnson arrived in Bergen she fell head over heels in love with him. Later in life she attempted to seduce a very young Georg Brandes.

Whatever the truth of the matter, Magdalene Thoresen's enthusiasm for her son-in-law rose in proportion as his reputation as a dramatist grew until, like so many female readers and lovers of culture in Europe, she too finally became enamoured of his sphinx-like celebrity and mysterious charisma. Ibsen's attraction for women was something that came relatively late, and by the time it did come he had long since found the woman in his life.

COUSIN NAPOLEON

One good thing did indeed lead to another in that spring of 1856. First success with *The Feast at Solhaug*, and then success with Suzannah Thoresen. In February the committee decided to send the theatre company on yet another trip to Trondheim, this time for three months, for an extensive programme of performances.

Henrik left Suzannah and joined the company for a stormy journey up the coast, with the female members spending most of the trip laid up in their cabins. The troupe arrived in Trondheim late on a Sunday afternoon at the beginning of March. The plan was to perform a long list of vaudevilles and light comedies. But Ibsen was also hoping to put on *The Feast at Solhaug* – provided those back in Bergen were proactive and sent the scenery up by steamboat. The theatre in Trondheim dated back to 1816 and was lacking in many respects, so that even basic standard equipment had to be transported from Bergen if *The Feast at Solhaug* was to be performed. As things turned out, everything was alright on the night and the people of Trondheim were every bit as enthusiastic as they had been two years earlier. Even the reviews in the newspapers were largely favourable. Ibsen must have been very pleased with himself. All the indications are that he really did manage to get on well with the actors in Trondheim, something which had definitely not always been the case.

At the end of March, Ibsen asked to be allowed to return to Bergen in order to 'start work on a new play as soon as possible'. The committee probably understood what lay behind the request when they sent Laading north and granted Ibsen his three weeks' furlough. Once back in Bergen, Henrik and Suzannah got engaged; they were to be married two years later in a ceremony that, according to Magdalene Thoresen, afforded 'not the slightest opportunity for any great display of emotion'. We don't know whether Ibsen really did begin work on his next play during those days in May. Laading sent word from

Trondheim that *The Feast at Solhaug* had been a great success, and afterwards the cast had gathered to raise a glass at the theatre's expense and wish the young couple good luck.[14] The play had also been accepted by the Christiania Theatre and was performed there on 13 March in front of an enthusiastic audience while Ibsen was still up in Trondheim. And as if all this were not enough, a printer named Christian Tønsberg published it in book form six days later. Ibsen now had a third play in print.

Yes indeed, spring really had come to Ibsen's life, and the summer that was to follow was no less remarkable.

That summer Ibsen went on a walking holiday on the Hardanger plateau in south-central Norway with an acquaintance named Carl Johan Anker. It was his first real encounter with the rural way of life and the mountainous Norwegian landscape, the very stuff of Norwegian national romanticism. The experience seemed to him breathtaking. It lingered in his mind 'like a shining memory, one of those jewelled points in a human life which one is still able to conjure up in spirit long, long afterwards'.

Either during the holiday or shortly afterwards Ibsen painted a number of landscapes of which several have survived. It is hard to know how sincere he really was about being a painter; certainly he never took any serious steps in that direction. It leaves him as one of those many writers who flit through the pages of art history on the basis of a youthful flirtation with painting that was presently set aside in order to pursue their primary talent with the pen. With a handful of exceptions Ibsen's paintings are distinctly conventional, the work of a dilettante – no doubt a source of pleasure to him personally but essentially curiosities. This applies also to the landscapes from Hardanger.[15]

* * *

The summer of 1856 could also offer pleasures of a more urbane and cultivated kind. In July and August, Bergen and its theatre were honoured no less than twice with royal visits. In July it was the Swedish crown prince Carl, in company with the young prince of Oranienburg. The committee seized the chance to show the noblest in the land what Norwegian theatre was able to offer. Artistically speaking, everything was well provided for. Not so the royal comfort. The whole theatre had to be refurbished, with, of course, a special box for the royal visitors as well as their own room in which they might enjoy the theatre's hospitality.

The play originally chosen was a vaudeville entitle *Soldaterløier* (*Soldier's High Jinks*). Things had to be kept light-hearted and amusing in order to ensure royal flattery, but shortly before the opening Blytt heard a rumour that the crown prince detested this particular play and regarded it as making fun of the Swedes. In haste the ensemble then began rehearsing Heiberg's *No*, a vaudeville that was every bit as amusing but, it seemed, less hurtful to the crown prince's sensitivities.

And Henrik Ibsen? Naturally, he wrote a prologue, delivered by the ravishing Louise Brun in her white satin gown with gilded belt – twenty verses in unstinting praise of the royal visitor.

And the audience loved it.

Four weeks later came a second outbreak of royalism in Bergen. There had been rumours over the summer that Prince Napoleon, son of King Jerome Bonaparte and cousin of Napoleon III, would be calling in at Bergen on his way up to Iceland. On the afternoon of 23 August the rumours were confirmed as the canons fired a salute to welcome the arrival of the prince's steamboat as it entered the harbour. Bergen's civic reception committee was reconvened in haste, as was the theatre committee once it was known that the prince wished to enjoy some Norwegian theatre in the course of his stay. It would need to be the following day if the prince were to manage it before sailing on.

'Completely impossible' was Ibsen's response when the challenge was put to him. The company was on holiday, and there simply wasn't enough time. Blytt knew his man, however, and suggested that the royal visitor be entertained by a performance of his own play, *The Feast at Solhaug*. And wonder of wonders, even as Blytt was still talking, the impossible became possible. In all haste the players and musicians were summoned, the theatre decorated, the champagne ordered, and the royal command performance duly went ahead.

According to Blytt the prince was delighted by the performance, though he can hardly have understood much of it. After the first act he expressed a desire to greet the performers. Ibsen presented him with a copy of the play, which the prince promised he would have translated into French and performed at the imperial theatre in St Cloud. With that the royal visitor left the premises. Nothing came of his promise to have Ibsen's play translated. Before he left he did, however, award each of the performers a 'Gratifikation af 20 Napoleons d'orer' – and perhaps even the writer of the play received a tip too.

If that was the case, then it would have been Henrik Ibsen's first royal honour, and *that* in itself was certainly worth a day's hard work.

LAST DANCE WITH OLAF LILJEKRANS

As Bergen's summer rain was followed by the autumn rains in the year 1856, Ibsen could look back on a six-month period that had given him more pleasures and satisfactions than all the previous six years combined. The play he wrote that autumn was in many respects a follow-up to *The Feast at Solhaug*, which was hardly surprising. The committee seems to have sensed another success was on the way, paying the dramatist an additional fee of 100 spesidaler for the new play.

The theme of the play wasn't a new one but a development of something he had used in his uncompleted 'The Justedal Grouse' from 1850. On that occasion his source had been Andreas Fayes' story. Since then he had read Landstad's *Norwegian Folk Ballads*, enabling him to retain the basic story of the girl who survived the Black Death and inserting it into a new story based on folk ballads – twelve of them have been identified – which he spiced up with an exciting plot. The result was *Olaf Liljekrans*, about a boy of that name who has been promised in marriage to Ingeborg as a way of ending a long-standing feud between their two families. Naturally, shortly before the wedding the boy goes off and falls in love with someone else, a child of nature named Alfhild, the 'grouse' of the title, whom Olaf believes is really an elf-girl – and with that the complications begin.

After the success of *The Feast at Solhaug* the previous year the Bergen audiences were desperately curious about Ibsen's new play. Tickets were snapped up in record time, and there were even reports of pushing and shoving in the queue. This time too there were only two performances, both very well attended, and ending once again in a curtain call for the writer. Yet it was plain he had not managed to match his previous success. The critics were merciless, and that was more or less the end of *Olaf Liljekrans*.[16] It was never again performed in Ibsen's lifetime, and printed only once his name had become so famous that anything at all with his name on it had become a guarantee of quality.

Olaf Liljekrans was the last of his own plays that Ibsen would produce in Bergen. With six plays behind him he had long since ceased to be 'young and promising' and was, by Norwegian standards, an established dramatist. He was the only dramatist in Norway in the privileged position of having every play he wrote routinely produced on the stage. And even though none of them were really smash-hits, with the possible exception of *The Feast at Solhaug*, his plays had been well received in Bergen.

The question remained, was that enough for him?

He was still not a dramatist but was rather a director of plays in receipt of a wage, with playwriting reduced to the role of part-time activity. He had been living like that for over five years, his writing time restricted by his numerous other obligations. No amount of success in Bergen was going to free him from the chains of that routine.

* * *

A month after the premiere he gives a lecture at the December 22 Society on the subject of 'The Folk Ballad and its Significance in Poetry', in which he argues that folk poetry is not only the nation's richest source of poetry, but also that the folk-ballad was the best starting point for the creation of a national drama.[17]

In scholarly terms the lecture does not have a high reputation; it is at best regarded as an interesting and dilettante pointer towards future studies in the same field. Its starting point is the idea that folk poetry is an expression of a people's character, which is in turn something formed by a people's natural surroundings. Different peoples had different ways of expressing themselves, and what characterised the 'Germanic tribe' was the urge to create an independent folk-poetry, unlike the urge to make art-poetry in the more southerly lands. Owing to the country's isolation and lack of an upper class with European connections, Norway was uniquely qualified to preserve the original mythic content of its folk ballads, and indeed to develop it through the unique combination of Christian and pagan impulses in the verse.[18]

Ibsen here shows the outlines of a Hegelian theory of civilisation, in which paganism's classic, strong epic form finds its antithesis in the lyrical Christian mysticism of the folk ballad, and in which it was the *poets* who were responsible for preserving and ennobling the dying traditions of the folk ballad in the form – the synthesis – of art. As a source for his own writing, however, the importance of the folk ballad was already fading as he stood on the podium on that winter's day in 1857. In that respect his lecture was not a programmatic declaration, but rather a summation of his own search thus far for a national drama. In the final phase of his national-romantic writing he would devote himself fully to saga literature. And it would be on the basis of this, rather than the folk ballad, that he would raise his national drama to mastery, in strict contradiction of the message of his lecture on the folk ballad.

'GET ME A PUBLISHER!'

The spring of 1857 didn't produce much new writing. Ibsen does start work on what would become his saga drama – *The Vikings at Helgeland* – but after a couple of acts he puts it to one side.

Letters, on the other hand, he does write. Important letters.

Following the success of *The Feast at Solhaug* at the Christiania Theatre and Tønsberg's publication of the play, Ibsen had been encouraged to send both *Lady Inger of Østråt* and *Olaf Liljekrans* to the Christiania Theatre. He was still waiting to hear about the latter, but the response to the former gave little grounds for optimism. Unless substantial changes were made to *Lady Inger* the director of the theatre, Carl Borgaard, could hold out no hope of a production. It was common practice to make changes to a script that had been accepted for production, and Ibsen showed himself willing to compromise many times on later occasions. On this occasion he declined to do so, showing just how highly he rated the play.

Nor, it seems, would Tønsberg be publishing *Lady Inger*. Ibsen, in desperation, wrote to his old friend, Paul Botten-Hansen – 'Get me a publisher! I don't care about the small print, I don't even demand a fee, if you can just get someone to publish it.'

What are friends for? Botten-Hansen had published the lecture on the folk ballad in *Illustreret Nyhedsblad* on 10 and 17 May, and over the course of the summer readers could read *Lady Inger of Østråt* in successive issues of the magazine. This was in fact a perfectly acceptable solution, since a magazine often reached a larger readership than was possible with the underdeveloped book market in Norway at the time.[19] Botten-Hansen also challenged Borgaard's decision in the magazine, accusing the Danish director of trying to suppress Norwegian drama. The growth of a national theatre had long been hampered by the inadequacy of local conditions, including poor acting and writing skills. But things were changing. The battle lines were hardening. And Ibsen's play was well worth fighting for, in the opinion of his friends in Christiania.

The insistent tone of Ibsen's letters to Botten-Hansen shows just how important it had become for him to achieve a national breakthrough. And any such breakthrough implied that he must return once more to the capital if he were to have any hope of achieving it. In May his contract with the Bergen theatre expired. It was renewed for one year. But a move was already in the air. Before the summer was over, Ibsen received an offer he could not refuse. In June he applied for leave from the theatre, and on 18 July he travelled to Christiania, with the stated intention of visiting friends. A day or two after his arrival, one of the city's newspapers was able to inform its readers that discussions were taking place between Ibsen and representatives of the Kristiania Norske Theater, the city's young national stage. Ibsen was obliged to write an explanatory letter to the committee back in Bergen. It became apparent that some time before his departure he had learned that the Kristiania Norske Theater was looking for an artistic director, and he had immediately expressed his interest. The day before he was due to leave Christiania, it emerged that he had already accepted an offer of the post, at an annual salary of 600 spesidaler, with the promise of an early pay rise.

Not the most honourable of departures, perhaps, but Ibsen hoped for the committee's understanding:

> I need hardly outline the advantages for me of living in the capital. They are overwhelming.

He admitted that the salary was another important factor, but was keen to stress that he did not want the committee to think that he had betrayed the theatre for the money:

... I shall never forget what I owe to Bergen Theatre; but I have obligations
to myself also, and the conditions at Bergen Theatre have long been difficult
for me, with every new thing I wished to try obstructed in some way. My
hands have never been free, and on a daily basis I have struggled against a
feeling that, for all my hard work, I was actually getting nowhere.

There is no text as honest as a letter of resignation. Finally he was able to say it.
He could get straight to the point and describe his difficulties over the past six
years, which no amount of successful premieres could ever compensate for: the
limited audience potential; the amateur nature of the critical response; conflicts
with the actors; the restricted budget; the rivalry with Laading; and, not least,
his irritation at having to deal with a committee that had the authority to
involve itself in the artistic side of things. He had, moreover, been engaged to be
married for two years now, and his obligations were not only to himself but to
his future wife.

He had served his apprenticeship in Bergen. He had found love and won a
few battles on the stage, but nothing that would secure him a stable future as a
dramatist. He would build on Ole Bull's dream of a Norwegian, national theatre,
but do so this time in the country's capital.

V

CHRISTIANIA

MASTER OF MØLLERGATEN

A city is never the same when you return to it after a long absence. Henrik Ibsen cannot fail to have noticed that Christiania was much changed, on the outside at least. The scruffy little city was beginning to grow up. The old seventeenth-century area behind Akershus fort had been transformed into a modern business quarter. The centre now extended westwards, towards the royal palace. The population was still growing, as were the surrounding suburbs. Over the next ten years it expanded northwards, past the newly established Nytorvet (now Youngstorget) and over towards the Aker river, which would remain the permanent divide between east and west. The old two-storey houses from the era of Danish rule were increasingly giving way to apartment buildings three and four storeys high. Christiania was reaching for the sky.

Once again Ibsen had to find a home, and once again it was the faithful Ole Schulerud who helped him out. Ole had done well. He had completed his law studies and was working as an attorney. He had married his cousin Ulrike and was father to a son now three years old. The little family lived in Christian Hasselgaards' apartment building near Stortorget, a stone's throw from Kristiania Norske Theater in Møllergaten. Ole invited Henrik to move in with them, but within a few weeks he had found his own lodgings another small stone's throw beyond Stortorget, on the corner of Karl Johan and Akersgaten. In August he returned to Bergen to tidy up his affairs there. Suzannah would remain there until they were able to marry.

Then it was back to Christiania to take up the new post, which he did formally on 3 September 1857.

The origins of the Kristiania Norske Theater had connections to his own previous stay in the city. Following his departure six years earlier, the Christiania Workers' Society had started an amateur theatre group to support imprisoned followers of Marcus Thrane. Inspired by this amateur initiative, as well as by the national theatre in Bergen, the Norwegian Drama School Theatre was established in the capital in 1852.

This school, which was renamed Kristiania Norske Theater two years later, had become the subject of a furious public debate. Not so much because it was a Norwegian theatre as because it had the temerity to use spoken Norwegian in its productions – the eastern version of it. A Bergen accent was just about tolerable, but to sophisticated ears the eastern dialect sounded simply vulgar. And as if this welter of regional Norwegian dialects was not enough, plays were even being performed in Ivar Aasen's 'landsmål'. So from its beginning the theatre struggled not only economically but also against ridicule, condescension and poor attendance, which in turn harmed its financial position even further. Sophisticated souls spent their evenings at the Parnassus of the cultured, the Christiania Theatre, with the Kristiania Norske Theater attracting the poorer sections of the population. Surrounded by beer joints and bars on 'dirty, nasty Møllergate', the theatre started life almost as an anti-establishment institution, from the start of the decade dedicated to the idea of 'Norwegianising' the culture, an idealistic enterprise that won the respect of many intellectuals but enjoyed little prestige among the cultural elite.

It was probably the idealistic challenges that made the post interesting to Ibsen as a director. With its precarious finances and its largely uneducated audiences it seemed condemned to offer only the lightest fare to its patrons. This was intolerable for a stage that had as its declared goal the promotion of a native, Norwegian theatre. Finally the leadership was unable to ignore the criticism any longer. Dispensing with the services of the Danish artistic director Jens Cronberg, Henrik Ibsen was duly installed in his place.

Yet again Ibsen was being asked to save a theatre in the name of art and of Norwegian culture.

His starting point was hopeless. Ibsen took up his post as the autumn season of 1857 got under way. Nothing had been prepared for him. There was no repertoire, he did not know the company, had no idea of the extent of the theatre's resources, nor did he possess any knowledge of the typical audiences for the Kristiania Norske Theater that would enable him to compete with the Christiania Theatre in Bankplassen. On top of all this the theatre was struggling financially, its situation not improved by the fact that the Storting had rejected an application for a grant and an interest-free loan the previous spring. Ibsen was, in effect, being asked to flog a dying horse.

Where to begin? As he had done in Bergen, Ibsen decided to open with a Prologue.

On 17 September, Henrik Anker Bjerregaard's *Fjeldeventyret* (*Mountain Adventure*) and Henrik Wergeland's *Efterspil til Fjeldeventyret* (*Sequel to Mountain Adventure*) opened proceedings. The new director's prologue wasn't outstanding but conveyed just exactly the right degree of nationalist pathos to ensure a friendly reception. 'A fine harbinger of what is to come from Hr. Ibsen,' announced *Morgenbladet*. So began the daily grind, with vaudevilles and farces succeeding one another in short order, with the same frantic tempo of rehearsal and performance he had known in Bergen, with two or three plays sometimes being performed on a single evening.

In November, Ibsen does something odd. He sends an application to the Academic College for a Fellowship in Nordic literature.

Did he get cold feet? Was it a moment's doubt about his ability to keep his future wife on what he earned from the theatre alone? Or did he get a sudden and unexpected glimpse into an academic world that held out the promise of a more secure living? The scholarship had recently been established by the Storting to encourage a new field of research, a rarity for the university that Ibsen may have felt duty bound to pursue. Probably his lecture on the folk ballad had encouraged him to believe in his own scholarly abilities – in his application he made special mention of it. Perhaps it was in response to criticism from the leadership of the theatre – at the general meeting of the following summer a degree of displeasure was expressed at results so far, with a call for a greater number of new, original plays in the repertoire – with the exception of *Fjeldeventyret* and Wergeland's *Fjeldstuen* (*The Cabin in the Mountains*), the repertoire of the preceding season had consisted entirely of well-worn old favourites.

Had he landed in exactly the same situation as he had found himself in in Bergen? Would it happen all over again, all those conflicts with the leadership and the company, the never-ending struggle between the demands of art and the demands of the box office? And yet he had greater reason now to have faith in his own work as a dramatist. On 4 November *The Feast at Solhaug* was performed at the Kungliga Dramatiska Teatern in Stockholm, marking the first occasion on which a play by Ibsen was performed outside Norway.[1] The same autumn he finally managed to finish his saga drama *The Vikings at Helgeland* and submitted it to the Christiania Theatre – which duly accepted it for performance. Early in the new year he changes his mind and withdraws his application to the Academic College.

Stick to what you know best.

* * *

In *The Vikings at Helgeland* Ibsen believed he had found the solution to a problem he had struggled with for a long time: how to get a drama out of the lapidary style of the sagas? His solution was to write in a language that closely resembled saga style. The action takes place on the coast of Helgeland in the tenth century and concerns a family feud with the treacherous and deadly Hjørdis as its *primus motor*. The plot is complex but compelling, the characters well defined, and the denouement focused and epic in all its fatal misunderstandings and bloody deaths.

Ibsen's reasons for not giving the play its premiere in Møllergaten were probably related to his assessment of the acting talents of the company and the theatre's technical limitations. It might also have been the case that Henrik Ibsen the *dramatist* was seduced by the prestige and professionalism of a premiere at the country's leading theatre, even though this was, in the eyes of Henrik Ibsen as *head of the theatre*, his competitor. Carl Borgaard, Christiania Theatre's artistic director, had already accepted *The Feast at Solhaug* in 1856. It had been performed there six times that year, and three times the following year. But after the rejection of *Lady Inger of Østråt*, Ibsen's feelings for Borgaard had cooled somewhat, and as he waited and waited for the rehearsals for *The Vikings at Helgeland* to begin his irritation with the director mounted.

Early in March 1858 he goes to see Borgaard at his office to demand an explanation and is told that, although the play has been accepted, the theatre cannot afford to mount a production of it!

Behind this depressing piece of news lay a serious problem for Norwegian dramatists. For an original drama the author received a full fee, whereas old or foreign plays could be performed free of charge. It meant that it made better economic sense for the Christiania Theatre to put on a play by Scribe than one by Ibsen. Ibsen declined to accept the argument. The day after his meeting with Borgaard he writes the first in a series of newspaper articles in which he gives full vent to his anger and indignation. The refusal to perform *The Vikings at Helgeland* had nothing to do with money: what lay behind it was the theatre's opposition to the promotion of the nationalist movement in Norwegian cultural life.

This wasn't about money. It was about Norwegians versus Danes.

This was something the people at the Christiania Theatre had actually understood. At that time the nationalist demands for the theatre were taken seriously in Bankplassen. The move towards an independent Norway could not simply be dismissed as a passing fad; in the course of the few years since Ole Bull had raised the call for a national theatre a large number of Norwegian actors and actresses had emerged from the Norwegian theatres in Bergen and Christiania, and in Henrik Ibsen and Bjørnstjerne Bjørnson, who succeeded Ibsen in Bergen, the movement was rich in both leaders and creators. The 1850s was the decade in which the troops were marshalled and the battle against Danish cultural hegemony in Norway began in earnest.

In this battle the strategy of the Christiania Theatre was to adopt the opponent's cause: the idea of a national theatre would be advanced gradually, from within the walls of the country's leading theatre. In line with this tactic the theatre had mounted a production of *The Feast at Solhaug*, and in the autumn of 1857 it was the turn of Bjørnson's *Between the Battles* and Andreas Munch's *Lord William Russel* (sic). It was claimed, however, that Ibsen's new play would be much too expensive.

Ibsen was by no means dismissive of the nationalist pretensions of his competitor but, like a great many others, he didn't set much store by all its fine promises, the productions of Munch and Bjørnson notwithstanding. In November 1857 Paul Botten-Hansen had severely criticised the theatre leadership for its rejection of *Lady Inger of Østråt*. The previous year Bjørnson had led an organised display of whistling and booing at the Christiania Theatre because it had employed yet another Danish actor and in doing so had broken its promise to make more use of Norwegian actors.

This was the legendary 'theatre battle' of 1856, and its cause was the Christiania Theatre's betrayal of Norwegian acting talent. Now it was all about its betrayal of Norwegian playwriting talent, and in this battle too both Botten-Hansen and Bjørnson were prominent voices. Botten-Hansen wrote a piece of polemic in support of Ibsen, and in April *The Vikings at Helgeland* was published as a supplement to the *Illustreret Nyhedsblad* in 2,200 copies.

Bjørnson's own play *Halte-Hulda* had been rejected by the Christiania Theatre that spring and now he, too, joined in the debate from the other side of the mountains. In the 28 March edition of *Bergensposten* he proclaims the death of such genre favourites as the Scribean comedy, vaudeville, and plays in imitation of Oehlenschläger, and of the Christiania Theatre as an institution, complaining especially of Carl Borgaard, a man who treated authors worse than dogs:

> Is any further proof needed that the time of his particular cultural priest-hood is over, and that his faith itself is sick unto death?

Neither Bjørnson nor Ibsen was being fair to Borgaard; over the previous few years the Dane had consciously tried to strengthen the repertoire with names such as Shakespeare, Molière and other serious dramatists. But he was unable to see the quality in new Norwegian drama and undoubtedly failed the theatre in its self-imposed task of promoting new, specifically Norwegian drama. And that, in the final analysis, was what mattered.

A DREADFUL BURDEN

After the slightly hesitant but still promising start made the previous autumn, the spring of 1858 brought controversy and reversals. Adding to Ibsen's irritation at Christiania Theatre's rejection of *The Vikings at Helgeland* came his disappointment over Meïr Goldschmidt's lukewarm review of the play in the *Corsaren*, and, in February, Johan Ludvig Heiberg's rejection of it at the Kongelige Teater.

But still spring had its joys to offer. The date for his wedding was fast approaching even as he continued to vent his anger at Borgaard in the columns of *Aftenbladet*. His first task was to find a suitable home for the pastor's daughter from Bergen. In April, Ibsen moved from Egertorget to the so-called 'Doctor's Apartments' in Christian Augusts gate 15, close to the university. He then crossed the mountains to fetch his bride-to-be.

Suzannah and Henrik were married on 18 June 1858 after the banns were read three times for the couple in Korskirken. The air that day was warm and humid, with the scent of flowers and laburnum drifting in from outside, seeming to have an almost anaesthetising effect on the guests. Some at least felt in mild distress, despite the happy occasion. The bride had lost her father just eight days earlier, and her stepmother Magdalene Thoresen a husband. For the remainder of her life Magdalene would recall Henrik and Suzannah's wedding day as a day of sorrow.

'Everything, the sounds, the people, the words, the terrible heaviness and an atmosphere the like of which I have never known before or since, even given all the terrible things that happened to me later in my life,' she wrote to Suzannah many years later, in a hopeless attempt to wish her luck on her wedding anniversary.

And Suzannah?

For her it must have been a day of joy and a day of sorrow. The pastor was dead and her childhood home in the process of breaking up. Three years later her stepmother moved away to Denmark with those of her daughters still left at home, in pursuit of a breakthrough as a writer. With that there was nothing left in Bergen for Suzannah. Her future lay with Henrik. We don't know what she made of life in the capital. The traditional narrative describes the young housewife's life as a continual struggle to keep her husband away from bad company and focused on his writing. From the very beginning we get this picture of a wife forcibly holding the pen in her husband's hand, a woman who was her husband's crutch and not much else. In reality Suzannah was, of course, very much more than this. And if he did need to be kept away from bad company, there is plentiful evidence that he enjoyed a lot of good company at this time too, with people who would later be very important for his career.

The move from Bergen to Christiania had revived the urbane Ibsen. The invitations to evening meals in Bergen gave way to an extroverted social life involving cafes, restaurants, societies and meetings. And Ibsen participated – often, but not always – in the quiet and unobtrusive way that people had come to expect of him; 'he very rarely made any contribution to the discussion, and when he did it was always extremely brief,' according to someone who knew him socially at that time. He spent his late afternoons at the L'Orsas cafe, sipping his coffee and reading foreign newspapers. Easier to be inhibited alone with a newspaper behind a cafe table than over a meal.

Sometimes he invited people home, but he preferred to go out to socialise. Among those he saw frequently was Bjørnstjerne Bjørnson, who had returned from Copenhagen in June 1857. Before travelling on to Bergen in November he and Ibsen had struck up a friendship. Ibsen was twenty-nine years old and had written a number of plays that had enjoyed decent runs at the box office, *The Feast at Solhaug* in particular. Bjørnson, four years his junior, had broken through more quickly with *Between the Battles*, in the same year as *The Feast at Solhaug* was performed in Bergen and Christiania. The autumn of 1857 also saw the publication of *Synnøve Solbakken*, Bjørnson's first tale of peasant life, which enjoyed huge success.

From the start the two were competitors, and their friendship was charged with a vigilant tension. Bjørnson had praised *The Feast at Solhaug*, supported Ibsen against the accusations of plagiarism, and sided with him in his difficulties with the Christiania Theatre.

Where was Ibsen when Borgaard gave *Halte-Hulda* the thumbs down? It wasn't in Ibsen's nature to fight other people's battles, but Bjørnson didn't let this trouble him. Towards the end of July 1857 he writes to the influential Danish critic Clemens Petersen and praises his friend to the skies:

Ibsen has arrived from Bergen (read his *The Feast at Solhaug*). I love him!!

Bjørnson is impressed, but not dazzled. He sees that Ibsen's formal mastery also holds dangers for him, in that he risks losing the poetic connection to *life* because he is so preoccupied with language. In his view Ibsen had written *The Feast at Solhaug* in the style of a folk ballad because, 'for me, he is a sort of folk ballad himself', and his language and his themes were so closely modelled on saga style that the characters remained alien, almost seeming like Old Norse gods to the reader. Bjørnson found the epic form of the sagas, including in *The Vikings at Helgeland*, 'dreadfully, chillingly noble'. In doing so he took sides with those such as Heiberg who had rejected the play in Copenhagen on the grounds that attempts to adapt the sagas for the stage simply did not work. Ibsen himself had advanced similar arguments in his lecture on the folk ballad. Bjørnson's criticisms were offered privately to Petersen; publicly he had, of course, defended the play. Ibsen may never have learned of his friend's private thoughts about the work. If he did it must have a been terrible disappointment.

We cannot entirely dismiss the possibility that Bjørnson's observations were disingenuous, influenced by the uncomfortably close connection between the two writers' literary projects. And undoubtedly there *were* similarities between these two plays, especially between the two strong and passionate female characters Halte-Hulde and Hjørdis. Contemporaries wondered who was copying whom; a correspondent in *Aftenposten* claimed openly that Ibsen must have been inspired by *Halte-Hulda* when he wrote *The Vikings at Helgeland*. Bjørnson gave a reading of his play at a gathering at which Ibsen was present in October 1857, and shortly afterwards received a copy of *Vikings*. Neither play was printed until April of the following year, so in practical terms it would have been quite possible for the two men to have been influenced by each other, but the generally accepted conclusion is that they were not.[2]

Bjørnson and Ibsen must have read each other's work closely and followed one another's careers keenly. It leaves open the possibility that Bjørnson's criticism of *The Vikings at Helgeland* contained a fair degree of professional envy, if only of Ibsen's obviously superior formal mastery as a dramatist.

But of course he reveals none of this to Petersen:

> If it were not for the fact that he [Ibsen] is not man enough to believe me free from envy in this matter then I would have told him the truth of this in some quiet moment, taking his hand as I did so.

Why reject an accusation of envy when no such accusation has ever been made, unless there is some small measure of truth in it? Bjørnson was not normally a man to curb his tongue, but faced with a proud and sensitive nature such as Ibsen's he found it prudent to lower his paw. But just how accurate is Bjørnson's characterisation of Ibsen? In an unusually intimate letter to Carl Johan Anker, with whom he had walked on the mountain plateau of Hardangervidda in the summer of 1856, Ibsen reveals a little of what he has struggled with over the years:

> I have often wondered what you really thought of me back then. If you didn't find me enveloped in the kind of repellent chill that makes a close approach difficult . . .

He could be so helpless, so hopelessly clumsy in his relationships with people, that he had not even been able to open up to a friend there on those desolate heights, where there was nothing to hinder him but the soughing of the wind in the heather.

Only later could he open up:

> And yet I found you easier to get on with than anyone else, for there was a youthful spirituality about you, a joy in life, a generosity of spirit which did me good. Hang on to this: believe me, it is not pleasant to see the world from its dark side, and yet, ridiculous as it may seem, there was a time when that was all I wanted. I have longed for, almost prayed for some great sorrow which would really fill my life, give meaning to my existence.

Even though he tries to explain to his friend that he has put his longing for sorrow behind him – 'It was a silly phase of my life, I've fought my way free of it' – this attraction towards grief was much more than a silly phase for Ibsen. It was something that would remain with him all his days.

A NATION'S WARRIOR

Following the theatre debate, the opening of a new season at the Kristiania Norske Theater in the autumn of 1858 was awaited with keen anticipation. Despite criticism for his choice of plays, in the course of his first year Ibsen had not only managed to generate renewed interest in the theatre but had also achieved respectable attendance figures. Ticket sales had brought in 9,000 spesidaler, and the overall income had risen by about 700 spesidaler from the previous year. In most important respects the theatre's finances held firm, and that in itself was no small achievement.

It seems as though the rivalry with the Christiania Theatre had had a stimulating effect, on audiences, on the press, and on the two theatres themselves. Both houses offered a varied programme with a lot of new plays that autumn, although not always of especially high quality. But the audiences turned up, and the newspapers were full of praise.

It seemed the right time to take a chance. Henrik Ibsen had made up his mind to let Danes be Danes and mount his own production of *The Vikings at Helgeland*. The date set for the premiere was 24 November 1858.

It was a gamble. All or nothing.

It turned out to be all.

The theatre was packed, with author and director taking several curtain calls, and the reviews were outstanding. Critics in both *Morgenbladet* and *Aftenbladet* wrote that, with this play, the theatre had exceeded all expectations, while the *Illustrated Weekly Magazine* came to the succinct conclusion that the theatre had passed a significant trial of strength. The staging, direction, diction and scenery were all praised; among the cast Madam Døvle was singled out for praise for her performance as the 'dæmonic' Hjørdis.

A. O. Vinje, writing in *Dølen*, joined in the chorus of praise:

It is tempting to suggest that this is best play ever written here in Norway.

Ibsen had not known such enthusiasm since that happy evening in Bergen, when *The Feast at Solhaug* had been received with such acclaim, and the dramatist himself was serenaded beneath his window. Again, a dinner was held in his honour, with an encomium delivered by Professor Marcus Jacob Monrad. And it didn't end there. In February *The Vikings at Helgeland* was performed in Trondheim, and the following month Bjørnson staged it very successfully in Bergen. It was performed a total of eight times at the Kristiania Norske Theater that season, with another run in the next season. Above average for the times, but still far from being a smash hit. Even so, figures for ticket sales indicate that the play was very well attended each time it was performed.

Despite the high production costs, and the fact that it didn't run for as long as Ibsen might have wished, one would have to conclude that *The Vikings at Helgeland* was a very respectable debut for Ibsen the dramatist at his own theatre.

Perhaps not surprising, then, that he should go on to mount a production of *Lady Inger of Østråt*, a play that he had a high opinion of himself but to which the Christiania Theatre, thus far at least, had given the thumbs-down. It was not particularly successful, being performed only twice. As they had done in Bergen, audiences seemed to find the play a little too heavy. The reviewer in *Aftenbladet* expressed his disappointment at the quality of the acting and, in the spirit of the times, lamented the absence of any 'spirit of reconciliation' that was considered an indispensable conclusion to any successful drama.

That brief observation from *Aftenbladet*'s reviewers was a response to what was, in effect, a literary revolution. Ibsen had broken with the convention that demanded reconciliation, beauty, idealism of any play, including a tragedy. Ibsen had signally failed to meet those requirements in *Lady Inger of Østråt*, a play that was too heavy, too dark, and lacked any glimmer of light or hope.

In making this break, Ibsen had shown that he was a writer on his way towards something – but what?

A 'VEIN OF SILVER RUNNING THROUGH A MOUNTAIN'

A commonly accepted view among literary historians is that the 1850s saw a change in national romanticism that led to a greater degree of realism. The break was partly the result of a raising of social awareness due to the 1848 revolution, partly because of a new and scientific objectivity in how the national breakthrough was viewed, and partly because of new aesthetic ideas that were emerging in Europe. In Norway, Bjørnson was a leading voice in this development, but Ibsen had been wrestling with these new ideas and insights ever since he had arrived in Christiania for the first time in 1850. He came with the works of Oehlenschläger and Welhaven in his trunk, until a meeting with the cynical Vinje divested him of most of his illusions about the nationalist project. The raising of social awareness that came about as a result of Marcus Thrane's movement also served to convince him of the necessity for a renewal of Norwegian national poetry. The conviction is evident in the articles he wrote for 'The Man', as also in the sarcastic remarks directed at the national-romantic figure of Julian Poulsen in *St John's Night*. Ibsen continued to read all the latest history books and books of folklore, so that developments within the field of the humanities became in themselves an incentive to pursue an ever greater degree of realism in literature.

But the demand for realism had other, broader causes too. The social disruption that characterised Europe at the time – the growth of bourgeois, capitalist society, urbanisation, the beginnings of industrialisation and of the modern class society – all these things created new artistic demands for what was recognisable and what was contemporary, for realism and for individualism. In literature this was particularly evident in the novel, and in the theatre through a gradual move from an idealistic style towards realism.

Neither Ibsen nor Bjørnson was in revolt against national romanticism as such; this was more an uprising that took place within the context of the movement itself. The idea of the nation was certainly not set aside. Monarchs and the God-given authority of the aristocracy had shaped pre-revolutionary Europe; in modern, bourgeois society it was the nation state that had taken over this role. And just as the individual in pre-revolutionary Europe was defined in terms of his place in a divine and universally ordered society, the bourgeois individual answered to the Romantic notion of the 'people's individual'.

In terms of the history of ideas, therefore, there is a line that directly connects Ibsen's national-romantic plays to the plays of contemporary life, even if the early phase is often ignored in favour of the later one. Indeed, several biographies give the impression that Ibsen in the 1850s was merely biding his time, waiting to liberate himself from the dreary burden of national romanticism and step forth as the world-famous author of dramas of contemporary life he did indeed become.

A description such as this is, of course, hopelessly anachronistic. As unlikely as it may seen, Henrik Ibsen was indeed something close to a professional 'nation builder' during the earlier period of his writing life.

Ibsen embodied the connection between the old and the new in his writing. *The Burial Mound* had been his contribution to the high Romantic tradition, and in *St Johns Night* he showed the pitfalls of national romanticism. In *Lady Inger of Østråt* he had, with a little help from Hettner and Shakespeare, added historical realism and psychological depth to the genre of historical drama; following this he had returned to his old dream of creating a genuine national drama based on the folk ballad with *The Feast at Solhaug* and *Olaf Liljekrans*. In *The Vikings at Helgeland* he had delivered his most accomplished play so far, with its fast-moving and tightly structured plot and its customised dialogue – there are no monologues here or explanatory asides – and on a human theme that breaks the bounds of both the historical and the national within the context of the play.

But Ibsen's plays were more than illustrations of national romanticism. Or to be more precise, there are elements in the plays of Ibsen's early years that point ahead of and beyond the national-romantic project in both form and content, elements that would twist and turn like veins of silver throughout his entire literary oeuvre.

There is probably some truth in the claim, often made, that Ibsen struggled long and hard to break free of his literary models. 'He only writes well when he is working in the shadow of some recognised literary role model,' was Clemens Petersen's view in 1863. 'When he tries to write with complete independence his work seems odd and strange.'[3] Those veins of silver that would bind his life's work together were, it would appear, not easily detected by Petersen. With the passage of the years they would become ever more visible. Ibsen himself certainly saw them. As we have seen, in the Foreword to a new edition of *Catiline* (1875) he had described the play's ideological theme as 'the contrast between what one wants to do and what one is able to do, between what is willed and what is possible; that is at once the tragedy and the comedy of mankind, and of the individual.'

Was it not this that, behind the layers of immature craftsmanship and the sometimes halting rhymes, shone through in several of his early plays, perhaps most clearly in *Catiline* and *Lady Inger of Østråt*? The human struggle against obstacles that both lie within and are imposed from without, a struggle that, in the final analysis, is about the fundamental demand for self-realisation as an *individual*, at the deepest level about the conditions of human *freedom*?

Had Clemens Petersen read Ibsen's articles on the subject of the theatre written between 1851 and 1863 he would have been able to see that Ibsen was gradually moving towards his own coherent view of what drama should be, and some of it at least he had managed to convey in his own plays. The clearest expression of this was in his review of Andreas Munch's *Lord William Russel* (sic), written in December 1857, an enthusiastic analysis that can also be read as his own programmatic declaration.[4] For Ibsen the most important feature of *dramatic structure* in a drama is the divide between its exterior and its deeper, interior structure. *Dramatic conflict* is something that arises in the interplay between the drama's deepest ideas and its surface.[5] At every level he makes use of contrasts and oppositions, something the form of the drama encourages. These oppositions are often played out in the form of triangular constellations, not uncommonly one in which a man finds himself caught between two women who each represent an oppositional force – the light, loving and self-sacrificing juxtaposed with the dark, demonic and covetous. They are already present in *Catiline*, in the shape of the fair Aurelia and the dark Furia. And as he struggled to create a saga-drama in 1855 these two female figures remained prominent in his thoughts, becoming first the sisters Margit and Signe in *The Feast at Solhaug* before their later incarnation as Hjørdis and Dagny in *The Vikings at Helgeland*.

Aurelia, Furia, Margit, Signe, Hjørdis and Dagny. As a dramatist, women would never cease to fascinate him. He found in them the most complex and enigmatic characters, and more often in the dark women than in the light.

Even in his dramatic machinations he plays off those contrasts and oppositions that point to the deeper levels of conflict in his dramas. A typical Ibsen play makes frequent use of alternations between up and down, in and out, foreground and background – approaches with a clearly symbolic function that he would make very self-conscious use of throughout his literary career.

For Ibsen the demand that a play be based upon a single, fundamental idea appears almost to have programmatic status. But this was not about ideas in the abstract. No, a play should demonstrate 'human conflicts, and woven deep within these, the ideas, competing, defeated or victorious'. It was about people, about the individual's struggle against commonly accepted ideas. The tension could exist on different levels. In *Lady Inger of Østråt* and later in *The Pretenders*, the conflict of ideas is related to the choice individuals make between freedom and responsibility, duty and self-denial, but also to larger cultural and historical choices bound up with the nation and civilisation. With the passage of years this latter dimension would be lost, leaving Ibsen with a drama devoted in its entirety to the individual's struggle with himself or herself and with the world. In this context it is tempting to regard *The Pretenders* as the watershed, with its dual character of large-scale national-historical drama and equally large-scale psychological and ethical drama exploring the tensions between doubt and faith, duty and ambition, in the individual.

* * *

It is not immediately easy to see just where Ibsen stood between tradition and renewal. He rejects both the old, rigidly formal drama in the style of French classicism *and* the banal everyday realism that offered 'the relationship of photography to reality' and not much else. He certainly wanted realism in drama, an 'illusion of reality', but not at the cost of a correspondence between the external reality and an interior idea, in which concern for the ideas and the 'inner realism' (such as psychological credibility) strictly speaking took precedence over 'external realism'. At its heart this idea of drama is a product of the Hegelian thinking which Ibsen inherited from Heiberg. Art should not simply be a straightforward imitation (mimesis) of nature but should offer an idea. And according to Ibsen, this idea could only be found in the 'thousand individual shadings'.

In other words, Ibsen was not a 'realist' in the sense that this word would acquire a few decades later; rather, he was working within the tradition of 'poetic realism', which is the widely used term among literary historians to describe the period preceding the modern breakthrough. Significantly, *The Pretenders* would be followed by two symbolic plays of ideas, *Brand* and

Peer Gynt, which were certainly contemporary, but could hardly be called realistic in form.

More than anything else, the drama was, for Ibsen, a means to approach the
great questions in life through the struggles of fictional characters with themselves and with forces operating on them from within and without, whether it
be Catiline's spiritual struggle between the forces of darkness and light in his
mind, the split in Lady Inger between her concern for the good of the nation
and for her own and her children's happiness, or Hjørdis' struggle with a
demonic urge to power that leads to her own death and the deaths of those
closest to her.

That is how important and how serious art was for Henrik Ibsen.

At the same time he was remarkably faithful to the craft of the theatre and
the conventions of theatrical genres. He wanted a renewal, but one that was
based on tradition. When he made use of such Scribean devices as those endless
confusions and misunderstandings he probably hoped to invest them with
meaning, relating them somehow to the deeper plot-levels of the play – as in
the case of the fatal misunderstanding that leads Lady Inger to take the life of
her own son. Perhaps most striking, in the light of his later production, is his
description of how a play's 'symbolic fundamental idea' should be handled.
Ibsen conveys this by describing how it should *not* be done, which is to say, in
the way that it was usually done:

> Rather than allowing it [the play's idea] to make its way unseen through the
> play, like a vein of silver running through a mountain, it is dragged up into
> the light of day; every development, every line or action points towards it, as
> though to say: 'Look here, here is the meaning – this is the significance of
> what you are seeing!'

Bjørnson had made a similar point in a discussion of the new realistic novel, in
which character was displayed 'not by the straightforward illumination of
words but by expressing the opposite of what is intended, permitting it to be
glimpsed dimly, as though from afar'.

What is being demonstrated here is a more subtle literary technique, a
refined description of character that would hardly have been possible (or relevant) in the plays that were the routine fare of the Norwegian and Danish
stages. Understanding is to be achieved with the cooperation of the reader or
the viewer; there is a riddle to be unravelled, an insight to be attained.

The most striking effect of this new literary approach was its break with the
widely accepted aesthetic of reconciliation. In Norway this found its most
outstanding exponent in Marcus Jacob Monrad, an aesthetic based on a
Hegelian idea that art, in the same way as religion, should offer a 'reconciliation

with the World and with Mortality'. It was art as a kind of 'aesthetic religion' in which beauty and understanding were two sides of the same coin. Art should resolve problems and open a vista to a higher world. This was precisely what Andreas Munch had managed to do in *Lord William Russel* (sic). Munch's play enjoyed a huge contemporary success and represented a breakthrough in the history of Norwegian drama. To a degree neither Ibsen nor Bjørnson could match, Munch managed to write a historical play on a human theme that also spoke directly to contemporary audiences, a play that was both an artistic triumph and a commercial success, not least because he was able to offer his audience the expected resolution of a peaceful and understanding conclusion.

'UP, GET UP IBSEN!'

The production of *The Vikings at Helgeland* in 1858 would be a last glimpse of light for Ibsen for a long, long time. Once again he would experience the wintry side of life, well before the coming of summer. And he who had once prayed for a great sorrow to fill his life with meaning would presently find himself with almost more meaning than he could endure.

Despite the relative success of *The Vikings at Helgeland*, Ibsen still found running the theatre a burden. Isolated successes could not disguise the fact that he had failed to establish himself in any lasting way as a dramatist in Norway. And neither he nor his associates were satisfied with his achievements as head of the theatre. How those endless disputes over the running of the theatre must have wearied him; when he wasn't being criticised by the press and by the competition over in Bankplassen, he was being lambasted by his own committee.

Although Ibsen now commanded a very respectable wage from the theatre, he soon found himself, once again, sinking deeper and deeper into debt. And this time he would find himself dragged to the very bottom. Thus far he was still managing to keep his head above water, though he and Suzannah both had to tighten their belts, and this at a time when Suzannah's stomach was beginning to swell. In the spring of 1859 they had to give up their nice apartment in Kristian Augusts gate and rent rooms from widow Colban in Nedre Bakkehuset, near Pilestredet, on the site where the city's gallows had once stood.

The symbolism of the new address was at least apt: Henrik Ibsen's life had taken a downturn. His earlier sojourn in Christiania had been tough enough, but at least in those days it was more or less what he could expect, given his circumstances. Now, in his second spell in the capital, it was as an experienced dramatist and man of the theatre, head of one of the two most important stages in the city. His poverty must have seemed all the more distressing.

Writing under such circumstances was not easy. Four and a half years would pass between the publication of *The Vikings at Helgeland* in April 1858 and Ibsen's next play, the longest break in his entire career. Perhaps, as some have suggested, brushes and paints became a substitute for the pen during this period. After returning to the capital he had started taking painting lessons from Magnus Thulstrup. Not much came of it, and once he left Norway in 1864 he more or less gave up painting. A family tradition claims that Suzannah had to fight to get him to put his brushes down, and there is much to suggest that this struggle must have taken place in the years around 1860. Their son Sigurd later gave her much of the credit for giving the world a great writer instead of yet another mediocre painter.

His literary impotence was not absolute. For Henrik Ibsen, 'writer's block' didn't mean that he stopped writing, only that he didn't manage to finish anything. He had the ideas for what would later become *Love's Comedy* and *The Pretenders* as early as 1858, but merely in the form of notes and drafts. In 1859 he began work on an ambitious attempt to turn *Olaf Liljekrans* into a libretto, which he entitled *The Mountain Bird*. A couple of years later he approached the composer M. A. Udbye with an invitation to write the music, but the project came to nothing. He wrote a great deal of occasional verse, usually upon request, though some of his finest poems, such as 'In the Picture Gallery' (1859), 'On the Heights' (1860) and 'Terje Vigen' (1862), stem from this period.

These long poems provided him with literary continuity, but he was incapable of going the greater distance of writing a play. Financially he was still just about coping, but the signs of a break-down were plain enough. The dapper and dandyish writer in the frilly shirt front and kid gloves ceased to care about his appearance. He seemed increasingly indifferent towards the bureaucratic side of his work as theatre boss. The drinking got heavier. A government employee who knew him at the time reported that Ibsen was not a man one would want to be seen with in the street. He was quite simply not respectable. In the summer of 1859 that same employee was approached by the editor of *Morgenbladet*, who asked him whether he knew of someone capable of writing a poem for King Oscar I, who lay on his deathbed. The man knew what to do; he would ask Ibsen. Not Bjørnson, because, God knows, Ibsen needed the money more.

He made his way down to Nedre Bakkehuset and knocked on the door:

No answer. So I walked in. He lay there asleep, even though it was late in the day. In his underwear. He'd been out drinking the night before, the dirty pig. Up, get up Ibsen! I shouted. But Ibsen never moved. Up man, get up! There's money to be made!

It took a bucket of cold water to rouse the poet. And naturally, Ibsen wanted to make some money, even though his visitor almost had to drag the poem verse by verse from the uninspired writer. By the time 'A People's Grief' was finally published the deadline had, quite literally, passed – King Oscar was already dead.

Ibsen needed all the money he could lay his hands on. During the few months he and Suzannah rented rooms from widow Colban they fell into arrears on the rent, and the widow took him to court, adding to the list of prosecutions against Ibsen during this period. An occasional verse cannot have paid all that much, yet he produced several more of them. One was for a festival of song in Arendal in June, in which he took part with Vinje and Botten-Hansen. Others were for parties, funerals and student balls. He even wrote verses in celebration of the opening of a school at which his friend Jakob Løkke was headmaster. And when the new king, Carl IV, was celebrated with a torchlight procession in November, Ibsen contributed a 'very charming and extremely Scandinavian' song.

Hack work, in other words. And yet one occasional verse is notable. That autumn sees the death of Ole Schulerud, and on 12 October Henrik Ibsen offers this tribute, standing over his friend's grave:

How soon the bonds were broken,
How soon you passed down into the earth . . .

Many years later he writes to Ole's wife, Rikka:

He was a real friend to me, loyal and true. Looking back there is no one more closely associated with my early years than he.

But the time of the loyal and true friends was over. It was the hour of the wolf.

ART AND COMMERCE

The 1858–9 season turned out to be another good one for Ibsen's theatre – the 11,440 spesidaler that came into the coffers that year was a record. The problem was that the money came largely from plays that were considered of dubious artistic value, whereas the more prestigious productions – including Ibsen's own plays – earned considerably less. Despite highlights such as *The Vikings at Helgeland* the artistic standard was in inverse proportion to the profit made. The conflict between the demands of art and the demands of mammon posed a real problem for Ibsen during his years as dramatist and head of the theatre. It reflected a deeper ideological conflict within both the Norwegian and the wider European cultural arenas.

Whereas bourgeois society felt a need to give legitimacy to its material and capitalist civilisation in the form of an exalted cultural expression, the modern market created in practice a jungle of cultural trivia in response to the demands of a consumer-oriented public. One praised art, but bought entertainment. This is at the historical heart of that worn-out old phrase 'the self-contempt of the bourgeoisie' – a contempt for the materialism that society was actually built on and saturated with, compensated for by a dedicated cultivation of cultural and spiritual life. In a society grown increasingly secular, art in many ways performed the functions once provided by religion. In a world where money and property meant everything, 'materialism' became a dirty word, shadowing the spiritually aspirational elite whichever way it turned.

* * *

Henrik Ibsen's own personal shadow was a man named Rolf Olsen, the man behind, among other things, the box-office smash hit *The Salon* (1848), an entertaining piece of everyday realism with a plot and cast of characters derived from contemporary Christiania. Olsen's goal was to write for the masses, and he knew how to set the cash registers ringing. Naturally this earned him the well-deserved ire of the critics. With hindsight it is easier to see that Olsen contributed to the development of a Norwegian drama that was of and for its time, and that he managed to make the theatre attractive to people outside the restricted world of the cultural elite.[6] But to the sophisticated he was anathema, as he was also to the historians of literature, who ensured that a contempt for the trivial survived well into the next century.

Ibsen and Olsen were personifications of the distinction between 'high' and 'low' in bourgeois cultural understanding, contemporaries representing two different sides of what was actually the birth of modern Norwegian literature; Ibsen stood for what a bourgeois society wished to be, and Olsen for what it in actual fact was. Yet things were not really quite that simple, for Ibsen was no more able than Olsen to ignore the demands of 'the box office' and the despised mass audience. The difference was that Ibsen was less happy about it. In the course of the 1858–9 season he was responsible for the productions of thirty-one plays, of which no fewer than twenty-six were musicals and other light-weight pieces. Only two plays were Norwegian, compared with eighteen French.

But did he really have a choice? As he observed laconically to the committee, 'one learns to be practical in the theatre, one learns to concede the power of circumstances and temporarily at least to abandon the higher goals when this seems unavoidable'.

The same tensions between high and low culture emerged also in the literary criticism he produced during these years. Just as he had in 1851 ridiculed 'Scribe and Company's dramatic sweeties', he complained six years later of 'all this Frenchness', despite the fact that he was producing the plays himself, and ignoring the fact that in the intervening years he had borrowed extensively from Scribe in his own plays. This last is an obvious illustration of the fact that a rigid distinction between high and low culture is untenable; what occurs instead is an exchange of impulses between the two levels.

Yet for Ibsen it was crucial to observe a distance from the demands of the box office.

'Unfortunately one must also to a certain degree take public taste into account,' as he wrote to the theatre committee. Vaudeville and lightweight comedies certainly had their place in the theatre, he admitted, but money was their only justification. Nor was he consistent in his elitism, owing, as he did, a duty of loyalty to his own theatre. In a series of articles entitled 'The Two Theatres in Christiania', written in 1861, he boldly defended his own theatre's role as a vaudeville theatre – 'the Norske Teatret has thus far never pretended to be anything but a people's theatre,' he now says. The Christiania Theatre, on the other hand, was little more than 'a private establishment for an exclusive group' with a 'decidedly cool attitude towards the general public'.

Naturally, behind this surprising expression of solidarity with the Norwegian 'masses' as opposed to the Danophile elite there lay nationalist sentiments. But Ibsen's expressed love of the common people is hardly convincing, and especially not when he was spending so much of his time on literary and stage reviews that despaired of their taste.

* * *

The conflict between art and the box office was actually unavoidable; art could retain its freedom only as long as the coffers were full. That applied to Ibsen the writer as much as it did to Ibsen as head of the theatre. As a serious writer aiming to express himself at the very highest level there were two ways in which he could liberate himself from the constraints of public taste: *within* the market he could write for an audience capable of showing its appreciation for serious writing. If this market were not large enough – and in Norway at that time it was not – he could attempt to educate the audience. The alternative would be to broaden his public appeal, which meant writing for a Scandinavian market. *Independent* of the market he could concentrate on those private or public patrons who were aware of their duty in the face of art.

There is a distinction here between the stage and the printed word. For the novelist there was no tradition of private patronage, which made the struggle to establish state support for writers all the more important. Only in a later age would Norwegian novelists be able to live from their writing alone. Bjørnson's *Synnøve Solbakken* (1857) was a breakthrough in this respect. In four editions that appeared in under three years it sold an unheard-of 4,000 copies. Crucially, this was a joint enterprise involving Norwegian and Danish publishers.

Naturally, the theatre as institution involved a different and much more costly apparatus than the novel. In Europe the theatres had started life under the patronage of the royal and aristocratic courts, a patronage that had gradually turned into the state subsidising of playhouses, reflecting the transition from a closed and elite cultural phenomenon into one more generally accessible to the public at large. This was not the case in Norway, where the theatre had no previous position from which it would have been natural for the authorities to guarantee its transition into a national and public institution. What happened in Norway was that theatre was cultivated by foreigners and by amateurs from the upper class. Practising artists, including writers, enjoyed a modest degree of financial support from the government, but theatres were obliged to survive on the market's own terms.

In the main the route Ibsen chose was the most sensible he could have taken. The drama's double roots in the institutional world of the theatre and the literary world held out some hope at least of a professional career based on the combination of a market consisting of readers and audiences, state funding, and an institutional theatre supported by private individuals who were not solely driven by commercial motives. Ibsen was a man with a great deal of common sense, and he pursued the course of the dramatist with a single-mindedness that few of his literary contemporaries could match. It seems he had little aptitude for the form of the novel, otherwise he might well have tried his hand at that. When Ibsen stopped writing poetry in the 1860s it was not only an artistic choice. He needed to earn money, and poetry was, quite simply, not something that sold especially well.

So Ibsen chose to concentrate on being a dramatist and a man of the theatre. This left him fundamentally dependent not only on the market but also on the state, with all that implied of cultural-political obligations. Not until he moved abroad would he be able to enjoy the private patronage of monarchs and nobles that was still practised on the continent. It was evident to everyone in the theatrical world in the 1850s that the involvement of the state was necessary if a respectable and independent Norwegian theatre was ever to emerge. This was Ibsen's view too. Despite the hatred for the state – and the Norwegian state in particular – that he developed over the years, despite the anarchism and trenchant individualism that would be so characteristic of the mature Ibsen, his fundamental belief remained throughout that it was the duty of the state to guarantee the freedom of the arts.

THE FREEDOM OF ART, THE OBLIGATIONS OF THE STATE

As the 1850s drew to a close, applications for state support for theatres had become a depressing serial on the theme of Norwegian political obstinacy.

Following Ole Bull's application to the Storting in 1851, the Norwegian Theatre had reapplied twice without success. The two Christiania theatres had also submitted applications that turned out to be fruitless, with the Kristiania Norske Theater receiving its latest rejection just before Ibsen took up his post in the summer of 1857.

Now, in the autumn of 1859, he submitted an application himself, hoping that the Storting would allot 2,000 spesidaler annually towards the running of the theatre. Using a rhetoric that owed much to Marcus Jacob Monrad's article of 1854 on the theatre and nationalism, he tries to find the *open sesame* that will have the necessary effect on the country's leaders:

> Over the last fifteen to twenty years the importance of nationalism for the spiritual direction and development of the people has become ever clearer.[7]

Nationalism is the magic word here, a recognition of the fact that a nation's freedom means more than just its political freedom – that 'a people free in spirit and in truth' is an impossibility until people free themselves from a world of 'alien conceptions' and instead devote themselves to finding their own particular national identity. In this process the artists are 'the spiritual eyes of the people'. Having established beyond doubt the importance of art for the nation, Ibsen goes on to make the point that painters, musicians and to some extent novelists too all enjoyed the benefit of state scholarships. Only the theatre remained outside this arrangement, a peculiar situation, given that it was the theatre that combined these other art forms, and to a greater extent than any of them represented a genuine art of the people with a widespread appeal.

Lead, don't follow; control, not submission – that was Ibsen's description of the balancing act required to combine the duties of the artist with the demands of the public. And the solution lay in the provision of cast-iron guarantees on the part of the state. On this point in particular the application was well grounded: Ibsen appends a long list of theatres and opera houses in France, Austria, Germany, Sweden and Denmark, pointing out in each case just how much of their income was derived from ticket sales, and how much from state support. In many cases over half the income came from public funding – as was the case at the Kongelige Teater in Copenhagen – while at the Hoftheater in Dresden the figure was about 40 per cent. The analysis was undoubtedly impressive, and in itself a proof of the obligations incumbent on any nation that regarded itself as civilised.

Among the politicians, opinion on the matter was divided. Frederik Stang, half-brother of the actress Laura Svendsen, was the government minister known to be most keenly interested in the theatre. The difficulty lay in the fact that matters pertaining to the theatre were the province of the Department of

Church Affairs, at that time run by Hans Riddervold, an obstinate philistine who viewed the theatre with an uncompromising distaste that he justified with reference to its uncertain finances, the fire risks, the general aura of disturbance associated with the theatre, as well as, probably, his own religious background. And yet back in 1854, when applications for support from all three theatres in Bergen and Christiania were submitted to the government, Riddervold lost, with the government allocating a grant to the Christiania Theatre alone. In the end, however, the overall victory was his, with the Storting rejecting any form of state support for the theatres. A precedent was established, and Ibsen can hardly have been surprised by the rejection that met his application in 1859.

As a result the Kristiania Norske Theater declared itself bankrupt in 1862. It was immediately taken over by its rival, the Christiania Theatre. In the following year the Norwegian Theatre in Bergen closed its doors, and in 1865 the Throndhjems Theatre had to throw in the towel too after several seasons running at a loss. In this way, after only a few years in existence, the idea of an institutional national Norwegian theatre died. Or at least appeared to. As things turned out, the resumption of the Christiania Theatre's monopoly in the mid-1860s did not lead to a new era of Danish domination in the Norwegian capital. On the contrary, all the resources of Norwegian theatre were now gathered in Bankplassen, and the foundations were laid for what would be a golden age of Norwegian theatre, with Ibsen's own plays as its crowning glory.

In the early 1860s there were few signs of any such coming golden age. Given the incessant struggle his theatre faced, the indifference amounting to downright hostility of the state must have been an appalling provocation for a man such as Henrik Ibsen. If artistic freedom was dependent on the state meeting its obligations, it was looking very much as though the Norwegian authorities intended to stifle the theatre in Norway by resolutely refusing ever to offer any form of state support. Given the strength of the antipathy Ibsen developed towards Norway, and towards the country's politicians and powers-that-be in particular, a reasonable supposition is that what lay behind this was, to a large degree, public policy in regard to national culture – or rather, the lack of any such policy.

A country that killed off its art was no country for Henrik Ibsen.

'NO ARSE AND NO CHEST'

In the summer of 1859 a metaphorical tornado came whirling across the Langfjell mountains and struck the capital like a force of nature. Bjørnstjerne Bjørnson had come to the end of his work in Bergen; now it was time to get Christiania sorted out.

When Ibsen left Bergen he had been deserting a sinking ship. Ole Bull had fallen out with the committee, and the whole project was in disarray. As Ibsen's successor Bjørnson breezed in with a new and adventurous repertoire. He was an inspiration to the performers, revitalised the directing, and he did everything he could to keep the attention of the people of Bergen. And for a time it looked as though he had succeeded; but in the long run he was unable to sustain the public's interest. Disappointed but not downhearted, he returned to Christiania. He didn't stay long in the capital this time either; by May of the following year he had already moved on again. But during his few months there he left an indelible impression, as was his way.

Once again they were together, Ibsen and Bjørnson, after a separation of many years. The reunion was not exclusively a joyous one, not if we are to judge by a letter Bjørnson wrote to Clemens Petersen at around this time:

> If ever Ibsen is able to admit *how small he is* he would be an eminently like-able writer. I've said this to him in as many words, but the only effect has been to make him *envious*. He has subjected me to all manner of minor vexations, and continues to do so.

Gone was the warmth he had shown in his communications with Petersen two years earlier. But how could Ibsen have subjected him to 'all manner of minor vexations' from beyond the Langfjell mountains?

It isn't clear exactly what Bjørnson is referring to, apart from the fact that Ibsen was apparently annoyed at how long it had taken his friend to mount a production of *The Vikings at Helgeland*. Bjørnson may have been digging up old grievances such as the fact that Ibsen had not arranged for a performance of *Between the Battles* when *he* was in Bergen. But there was more to it than that. Bjørnson had just about had enough of Ibsen's anger, his petty-mindedness and his angst-fuelled bitterness:

> Add to this that he's a shabby little chap, with no arse and no chest. And since he has no talent as a public speaker he feels he has to compensate ferociously for this in his writing.

A little chap, with no arse and no chest! Bjørnson certainly knew how to dig the knife in. The only mitigation must be that he was a man as big in love as he was in hate. Ibsen, on the other hand, was a giant at hating, and a dwarf in loving – this being probably the single most distinguishing characteristic between the two of them.

But there was more behind it than even this.

Despite the fact that the Norwegian Theatre in Bergen and the Kristiania Norske Theater were on the same side in the struggle to throw off Danish cultural domination and create a truly Norwegian theatre, there was considerable institutional rivalry between the two of them, just as there was between Bjørnson and Ibsen as writers. This rivalry became public not long after Bjørnson's letter to Clemens Petersen. In Bergen, Bjørnson had suggested that local performers had the best chance of developing a distinctly Norwegian theatre because actors in the capital remained too easily influenced by Denmark. In Møllergaten the claim was greeted with scepticism. In April, Ibsen responded by putting on a farce by Erik Bøgh, in a version adapted by Ibsen himself, in which the Bergen-born Madam Hundevadt enjoyed great success with her parody of Bergen 'sentimentality'. Bjørnson was most definitely not amused.

If it were any consolation, Ibsen didn't have much to amuse him either by the time the theatre opened its doors for the 1859–60 season. The autumn had got off to the worst possible start. He had once again used *The Vikings at Helgeland* as his opening offering. Perhaps the triumph of the year before would be repeated? Moreover, the theatre had invested heavily in new costumes and scenery for the occasion, and naturally they had to be used. But it was obvious that Christiania audiences had seen enough of the tragedy set on the coast of Helgeland, and the play closed after its opening night. With that it was back to the romantic comedies and the vaudevilles. Henrik Ibsen gave the people what the people wanted, plays with alluring titles such as *Husbands in Trouble* and *The Ladies' Knight*. As early as September, *Morgenbladet* had started complaining about the 'fatuous rubbish' that was being offered in Møllergaten. Later the same paper declared, in what was almost an obituary, that the Norske Teatret seemed to have descended 'to the level of an amusement park for the lower classes, a vaudeville theatre'.

The autumn of 1859 wasn't an easy time for Ibsen; and it wasn't much easier for Bjørnson either. Before leaving Bergen he had accepted the offer of the post of political editor of the Christiania newspaper *Aftenbladet*. It was a large step into the world of politics, and seemed to Ibsen tantamount to a betrayal of his literary vocation.

By his own account Bjørnson entered the political world with neither political knowledge nor vision; what he offered instead was instinct and experience. He was active in the Reform Society, one of the first tentative steps towards the formation of political parties in Norway. The contemporary ideal, however, was a free and independent representative, and the Reform Society was either ridiculed or damned as a Jacobite club. As for the other big issue of the winter – the demand for the replacement of a union governor with a native Norwegian prime minister – Bjørnson handled it so clumsily and undiplomatically that by 15 January 1860 he had already effectively been forced out of his new job. His reputation in the capital took a nose-dive. A good thing, then, that he could turn to his tried and trusted friend, the theatre manager, for consolation at such a time.

Or could he?

'DAMN THAT DUTCHMAN!'

Ibsen and Bjørnson each had a burden to bear that autumn, the former theatrical, the latter political. It meant that neither was in any position to give the other solace. There seemed always to be some disagreement or other between the two of them, and that autumn saw the emergence of a new one.

This time it concerned Ibsen's friends.

The last time he lived in the capital Bjørnson had written in an enthusiastic letter to Clemens Petersen that Ibsen and he were members of the same circle of friends. By the time of his return in 1859 he was singing a different tune; now he complained openly about the little 'clique of egotists' whom Ibsen had joined. He was referring to Paul Botten-Hansen and the group of writers and intellectuals who regularly gathered at Botten-Hansen's home in Pipergården on the corner of Rådhusgaten and Kongens gate. Between 1859 and 1863 this group, which has gone down in literary history as the 'Learned Holland', was Ibsen's world. At its core were Paul Botten-Hansen, Henrik Ibsen, the historian Michael Birkeland and the philologist Jakob Løkke. They had known each other since the early 1850s. Ludvig Daae, another historian, did not join them until 1856. In addition to these core members there was a larger secondary group known as the 'batavophiles' (Dutch-lovers) whose members visited the apartment at Rådhusgaten 15 on a more or less regular basis. The Learned Holland was principally a forum in which to cultivate the art of rhetoric and a love for the great classics. The name derives from an occasion on which Daae, in his enthusiasm for Botten-Hansen's collection of books, cried out 'Damn that Dutchman [Hollænderen], he has his spies everywhere!', a quotation from Ludvig Holberg, the Norwegian-Danish dramatist and essayist much admired by members of the group. 'Holland' was Botten-Hansen's living room and Botten-Hansen himself 'the original Dutchman'. When Jonas Lie later described Ibsen as 'the silent heart of the group' he is perhaps being over-generous to his friend. He was certainly among equals in the group, and he was certainly not always so very silent either. He took part in discussions, often on the most bizarre topics such as whether or not fish could suffer from aquaphobia, or whether two plus two still made four on Sirius.

Now Ibsen was back again, with all his 'paradoxes and wild truths', and his friends dubbed him Gert, after Holberg's character in *Mester Gert Westphaler*, in recognition of his bizarre conversational improvisations. In the company of the other members of the Learned Holland he found that intimate forum in which he could express himself openly and freely – a small group of like-minded people, living in a sort of inner exile and cultivating their own difference from the rest of society. From within this group Ibsen could launch verbal attacks on the world around him without necessarily having to be a participant in it. The situation was exactly the same as it had been in Grimstad, and it is clear that what he lacked in Bergen was just such a group of friends. When the members of the Learned Holland were not gathered beneath Botten-Hansen's bulging bookshelves they were living it up in the city's cafes. Ibsen, Birkeland and Botten-Hansen were together almost daily throughout the winter of 1859–60, the hard core of the group, the very 'chapter house' of its cathedral. Birkeland referred to these gatherings as walking 'on the heights', an expression Ibsen would later turn into a striking poetic metaphor far removed from its original meaning, which was quite simply to go out and do the town.

With an equal fervour the group loved literature and learning and despised the materialism with which they claimed society was saturated. Their contempt also implied a cool indifference to politics, especially liberal politics.[8] While Bjørnson was busy establishing alliances with Johan Sverdrup and the people involved in the Reform Society, members of the Learned Holland were sitting in Botten-Hansen's apartment sniggering at the 'materialistic-plutocratic air' in the capital. The aura of spiritual aristocracy within the group was in most respects incompatible with the idea of political parties and democratic reform. Of course, Bjørnson shared their love of literature, but their distant attitude towards political life, their everyday intellectual arrogance and constant irony were distasteful to him. He probably never grasped the subtle balance in the group between witty brilliance and ironic reserve that typified the daily intercourse of the Learned Holland.

'Within that circle people never paid each other admiring compliments,' Dae relates. 'On the contrary the tone was one of merciless criticism.'

Dreadful to relate, but it became almost one of the group's sports to denigrate Bjørnson. Once when he and Vinje were at Botten-Hansen's he tried repeatedly to offend Vinje by calling him a pig. Vinje remained unruffled and appeared to take the insult almost as a compliment, until Bjørnson went on to accuse him of lacking character, an accusation Vinje roundly denied. He didn't mind being called a pig – but characterless? Never!

No, it wasn't easy for Bjørnson.

In the long run, however, it proved difficult for members of the Learned Holland to remain indifferent to politics. Many of them were civil servants, often working at the university, and over the years this led them into a conservative bias. One after another they allowed themselves to be drawn into politics, but not Ibsen. The progressive ideas of the 1848 revolution, which were his generation's most important formative influences, expressed themselves, in his case, in ways other than the political. The contempt for politics was directed particularly at liberal politicians such as Sverdrup. Ibsen had not forgotten the spring of 1851, and the way the Thraneite movement had literally frightened the 1848 revolution out of the liberal opposition in the Storting. Yet he remained impossible to place along the Norwegian political spectrum. He was never a defender of the civil servant state, but neither was he ever a critic of the regime. It had been an easy matter to join in the cry for freedom, not quite so easy to deal with what came afterwards – the demands from those at the bottom of society for an equal voice, the subsequent politicisation, bureaucratisation and reorganisation of society.

Equality became a threat to the freedom that was, in an age of crowds, the unmistakable signature of the individual and the spiritual aristocracy.

SCANDINAVIANISTS AND NATIONALISTS

Of course, Ibsen's association with the Learned Holland caused difficulties in his friendship with Bjørnson. Yet fundamentally they were fighting many of the same battles, and above all shared the cause of promoting Norwegian national culture. On 22 November 1859, Ibsen and Bjørnson jointly founded the Norwegian Society, inevitably reviving memories of the Norwegian Society that had been active in Copenhagen in the eighteenth century and, like its fore-runner, dedicated to the meaning of *being Norwegian*. Bjørnson seems to have regarded the society as a sort of compensation for the defeats he had suffered earlier that autumn, all the more so since several politicians from the now disbanded Reform Society were among the first members of the new society. The goals of the Norwegian Society were not, however, overtly political, but rather 'to encourage a more nationalist direction in literature and the arts'.[9]

Bjørnson was the chairman, Ibsen his more reserved vice-chairman, the society itself a place where 'young, radical, political, literary and artistic forces' came together for discussion, lectures, music, food and drink. But beneath the sociable exterior, the society was riven by a number of tensions.

The society was formed just as the theatre debate flared up again. In November, Bjørnson had attacked the Danish dominance of Norwegian theatrical life, and with the formation of the Norwegian Society the debate became even more heated. The crisis came when the society asked the Christiania Theatre whether it might hire the theatre for the summer months. The plan was to assemble Norwegian actors from the Christiania theatres with those from Bergen and Trondheim. But the Christiania Theatre was not interested in hosting this flowering of Norwegianness on its stage and turned the request down without further ado. When it became clear that the popular Danish actor Anton Wilhelm Wiehe was prepared to resign from the theatre in protest, the crisis was inevitable.

The crisis gave new life to the struggle for a genuinely national cultural and professional arena, at the same time as there was increasing disagreement over exactly what this arena should consist of. By the end of the 1850s the country was on its way out of political stagnation and the next ten years would be characterised by the struggle to leave the union, the opposition of the farmers, and the demand for democratic reform. The demand for clear-cut political positions split the formerly distinct lines of the nationalist breakthrough movement. Ibsen was no more comfortable in the flattering light of national romanticism than he was in the overcast grey of politics, and by his own account he presently broke with the Norwegian Society because reforming politicians had turned it more and more into a 'politicising society'.

But cultural nationalism too became a more complex and politicised issue. In reality the attempt to unite all nationally minded forces within a single organisation was bound to lead to dissension, something that was apparent even during the inaugural phase of the society. Vinje attended the first two meetings. He found attitudes towards the Danish theatre far too negative as well as detecting a similar negativity towards his own particular vision of nationalism. This was at a time when he was in the process of breaking with old friends as his preoccupation with the codification of an authentically native Norwegian language grew – as early as 1859 he was mocking Ibsen for the way he continued to promote Danish at his theatre! With this Vinje staked out his own particular course for a nationalist breakthrough, endorsing the idea of an alternative Norwegian national counter-culture with the promotion of New Norwegian as the country's written language at its core. The movement would in time become part of the broad Left alliance that emerged to challenge the hegemony of the civil servants.

The language question had become particularly contentious during the time Ibsen was living in Bergen. The debate centred on Knud Knudsen's efforts to render the language more Norwegian in its spelling, and Ivar Aasen's promotion of 'landsmålet', or New Norwegian, with which people were now becoming familiar. The theatre in Møllergaten was at the forefront here, with Knudsen as its language consultant, and the use of New Norwegian on the stage.

Theatre was a language issue, and the language issue was a nationalist issue.

All of this created certain difficulties for Ibsen in Christiania. On the one hand he was firmly on the side of 'Norwegianness' in the theatre debate and was fiercely critical of the predominance of Danish culture at the Christiania Theatre. Indeed, he had never before expressed himself with such open hostility towards all things Danish as he did towards the end of the 1850s. 'Seagull's Cry', a poem from January 1859, was perhaps his most overt expression of this:

You nightingale in Denmark's wood,
Why are you vexed that trills
You uttered in yon regions should

Be lost mid pine-clad hills?
Here in the North you have no place,
Abroad your fostering,
By Norway's fjords no kin can trace,
Nor did the glaciers e'er embrace
Your birthright in their ring.

On the other hand, he was wary of what he saw as a potential Norwegian isola-
tionism in regard to the continental and classical traditions, an attitude he
shared with other members of the Learned Holland. Their admiration for Latin
and a classical education had never been in and of itself a barrier to supporting
the nationalist cause. It was, however, seriously incompatible with a form of
Norwegian nationalism that rallied round New Norwegian as its flagship cause.
Ibsen was typically more moderate than Knudsen on the language question,
and entertained towards New Norwegian a scepticism that later turned into
outright hostility.[10] From the language reformers' point of view this scepticism
was completely unjustified. For them there was no incompatibility between a
culture that was uniquely Norwegian and national, and the universal culture of
the rest of Europe – Vinje, to give just one example, was an extremely cosmopolitan man. But for Ibsen and the others of the Learned Holland the connection
between New Norwegian and nationalism was problematic. They therefore
turned to Scandinavianism as a form of compromise between the cosmopolitan
and the specifically Norwegian.

But not even Scandinavianism was free of politicisation. When the question
of the dissolution of the union became acute, the Scandinavianists were
split into one wing that wanted to strengthen the union between Norway and
Sweden, and a Danish-oriented wing that was insistent that Denmark be part
of any future arrangement.[11] Ibsen was among those who supported a cultural
Scandinavianism, and for the whole of his life he avoided the political implications of Scandinavianism as an idea. One could never accuse him of having
a consistent attitude towards Scandinavianism, but it seems as though he
expected matters to develop in accordance with a fundamental dialectic: 'The
"Norwegianness" standpoint is only a passing phase', was his view. 'It presup-
poses a Scandinavianism as its replacement; and following that comes pan-
Germanism.' So if Norwegians should wake up 'one fine day' to discover 'a
German opera house standing on the ruins of Norwegian and the Danish-
Norwegian Theatres then, really, no great harm has been done'.

This was in many ways Bjørnson's view too. He was among the first to utilise
the practical consequences of this new and extended cultural communality,
attaching himself to influential circles in Denmark during his first sojourn
there in 1856–7. In June 1860 he again left Christiania to begin a three-year

journey that included periods of residence in Denmark, Italy, Germany and France. At about the same time he decided to let the Danish publisher Gyldendal publish his future books, since the literary infrastructure in Norway was so underdeveloped.

The Danes may well not have been 'real' northerners, but Norwegian writers were obliged to travel in the service of their art; they had to get out if they wanted to move up. The way to art still pointed south.

Taken together, his involvement with the Norwegian Society and all the glasses of punch enjoyed with the Learned Holland made the winter and spring of 1859–60 the most hectic period of Ibsen's second sojourn in Christiania. Perhaps it is not really so remarkable after all that he seems to have had so little time for work at the theatre? And not really so remarkable either that criticism of the artistic director flared up again. The season had been a thankless shuffling between merciless critics and a fickle public. Which was worse – to have to put up with so much criticism, or to know full well that the criticism was deserved? Significantly, it was at about this time that rumours about Ibsen's drinking began to circulate.

* * *

There was, however, one bright spot. On 23 December 1859, Suzannah had given birth to a baby boy at the Rikshospitalets birth clinic, a publicly funded institution for the use of poor people and unmarried mothers. The boy was named Sigurd, after the warrior and bear-killer from Helgeland. It was his mother's idea, though the name was seldom used at home. Henrik loved to give pet names to the two people closest to him. He called Suzannah either Kat or Ørnen (the Eagle), while Sigurd was Kikkidorian, Grimme-Grimme, plain straightforward Strilen (a person from the countryside near Bergen), or – most commonly – Grimbart. Years later, long after he had become a world-famous writer, and Sigurd the Norwegian prime minister in Stockholm, Henrik could still ask: 'Shouldn't Grimbart be here by now?'

And Grimbart always came. Who needed whom most, the parents or the child, became increasingly unclear as the years went by. The little warrior was always his parents' pride and joy, from the moment he opened his eyes until the time he closed the coffin lids over them, first Henrik, and then Suzannah.

Sigurd was christened on 7 January 1860 at the newly built Holy Trinity church just across the road from Malthegården. Henrik and Suzannah had moved there the previous year, living in a rather shabby apartment in what was otherwise a very fashionable block. Bjørnstjerne Bjørnson and Paul Botten-Hansen were the two godfathers. But of course the joys of fatherhood could do nothing to improve Ibsen's financial position. Quite the opposite. Simple psychology would suggest that it was the poverty and constant debt of these years that were responsible for the penny-pinching pedantry in money matters that would characterise him for the rest of his life, even after the money began to come in. Rather more advanced psychology proposes that it takes a little more than that to change a person. And Ibsen was a man who managed his own affairs, whether they be personal, artistic or financial.

It is actually something of an enigma that he should have managed to get entangled in so much debt at about this time. After all, the move from Bergen to Christiania had more than doubled his annual income. The theatre's accounts show clearly that Ibsen was paid between 635 and 767 spesidaler each season between 1857 and 1862, with the amount he earned from poetry and other writings as a small supplement. That was as much, if not more, than the departmental head of an office earned, and far more than the average hired hand, who had to make do with an annual income of around 29 spesidaler!

And yet it seems it was not enough, and the explanation is probably that Ibsen had accumulated a considerable number of private debts during his years in Bergen, and these continued to burden him after his return to Christiania.[12] In addition he had for several years neglected to pay his taxes, leading to ever larger demands for the payment of back taxes. At one point during 1858 he owed almost as much as he was expecting to earn that year, and over the following years he regularly owed back taxes that amounted to either just over or just under what he earned. Life in Christiania also brought a new round of creditors. The wedding had been expensive for the couple, and social life in the capital was not cheap. Moreover, while Henrik had lived at the theatre's expense in Bergen, in Christiania he had to pay for his own accommodation – and the home had to be furnished. Little Sigurd was a negligible outgoing, but Ibsen's illegitimate son remained a heavy drain on his resources, and continued to be so until the arrangement came to an end in the summer of 1864.

Even so, there is a remarkable discrepancy between income and outgoings. Is it possible that Ibsen's money-sense was 'not particularly acute', as the theatre committee had intimated back in 1852 in connection with his educational travels? A writer with a poor grasp of money – is such a thing possible?

He swore, though, that his son should not suffer the burdens of poverty: 'I'll save every øre I can,' he often said later, 'so that Sigurd will be spared the rabble.' In itself a very noble aspiration.

TOWARDS THE FINAL CURTAIN

For the time being, though, the family remained at the mercy of their creditors. At some point in the spring of 1860 they are forced to move again, this time to a property owned by a carpenter named Grosch on Hegdehaugen, a rise to the west of the city limits. The newly built two-storey timber villa was thoroughly inadequate. There was no water in the house, and the well was home to toads and leeches so they had a long walk to fetch fresh water. The living room leaked whenever it rained, and the wind blew straight through the walls making the wallpaper in the living room balloon out like sails.

Ibsen's career was on a slippery slope, and from the summer of 1860 the Kristiania Norske Theater was headed the same way. The final curtain beckoned.

Despite a healthy income from ticket sales the theatre's overheads were so large that it operated at a loss, and the committee was constantly having to take up new loans. As if that were not enough, the premises themselves were actually unsuitable. As early as the summer of 1859 Ibsen had hinted at the need for a bigger and better theatre. The chance came the next summer. The lending lease on the building was due to run out, but the committee had been offered the chance to buy the building for 15,000 spesidaler. It was an offer that was hard to refuse, even though in hindsight it is easier to see that this is exactly what the committee should have done.

A campaign to raise money for the purchase and development of the property had been launched in the spring of 1859. The following autumn a renewed application for state support was submitted. The collection raised only 3,500 spesidaler and, as we have seen, the application for public funding was rejected. Still, the decision was taken at an extraordinary general meeting in February 1860 to proceed with the purchase of the building, presumably because the choice appeared to be between closure or expansion. The resolution was followed by yet another application for state funding which was, of course, also rejected, though this did not prevent work being started on the rebuilding the next summer.

Ibsen and the other members of the theatre staff must have dreaded the opening of the 1860–1 season. Not surprisingly, the cost of the refurbishment turned out to be far higher than the original estimate. Under the circumstances, the support of the public was crucial, and the responsibility to make sure of it lay principally with Ibsen.

* * *

The opening performance of the season on 11 October wasn't a flop. The programme included a prologue with music performed by Ole Bull; the theatre was full, and afterwards the newspapers wrote enthusiastically of the refurbished premises, painted white and with much more comfortable seating, gilded decorations, and a new curtain featuring a mountain landscape. But why hadn't Ibsen offered a new play for the occasion, instead of trotting out that old warhorse *Tordenskjold* by H. Ø. Blom? And why had the prologue been written by Professor Monrad and not, as one had the right to expect, by the theatre's own artistic director?

Given the personal problems Ibsen was facing at the time, it is not surprising that his work at the theatre suffered. According to Knud Knudsen, who sat on the committee, he could hardly be bothered to attend meetings, probably afraid that he would be asked to provide an account of what had been achieved since the last session. On at least one occasion, the committee met in the back room of the L'Orsas cafe, since it was known that that was where Ibsen was spending most of his time. If Knudsen is to be believed, one member of the committee, a man named Sigvald Petersen, had been even harder in his criticism than he had been himself. Ole Bull had allegedly once remarked that it would be necessary 'to keep a firm grip on Ibsen'. In his annual report to the general assembly in September, Ibsen adopted a tone of weary resignation, offering a litany of excuses for why things turned out as badly as they did.

There can't have been much enthusiasm left in him when it came to the productions scheduled for the remainder of the 1860–1 season, which included plays by both Johan Wessel and Ludvig Holberg. If this wasn't exactly *new* drama it was, at the very least, *Norwegian*. It must have been embarrassing that the Christiania Theatre that same autumn could point to a performance of recent Norwegian drama – *The Feast at Solhaug* had been revived following a run of nine performances in the 1856–7 season. The most interesting performance at the Kristiania Norske Theater that autumn turned out to be a German play, a production of Karl Gutzkow's *Haarpidsk og Kaarde* that Ibsen mounted in November. It was a serious play, and something of a challenge for the company. Fortunately the critics were favourably inclined, although attendance figures were poor. If the repertoire was predominantly light, Ibsen could sometimes take surprising and brave decisions like this. Given the extent of his troubles at the time, it is remarkable how often he was able to produce an inspired piece of verse or a particularly bold production at the theatre.

He managed it again in the spring season of 1861 with a performance of *Mursvendene*, a French play that had taken European theatres by storm. The translator and adaptor Andreas Isachsen transferred the action to Christiania, with scenes and settings that would have been familiar to local audiences, and with the dialogue adapted to reflect local accents. Audiences loved it, while critics complained about the crudity of the language. The play's reception showed again how firmly entrenched the traditional ethic of the dramatic reconciliation was in people's minds; one did not go to the theatre to experience something ugly, 'grubby reality' was not what people wanted to see. If apprentice bricklayers were to be shown onstage then they should be 'idealised' apprentice bricklayers, not apprentices with lime splashed over their faces, or smiths' apprentices with smudged and blackened fingers. It was what the critics and the educated public demanded.

But as spring advanced the audiences declined, and that was the one thing the theatre could not survive. That people failed to turn up to see serious plays

might be put down to the cost of art, but when not even the lightweight material attracted audiences the responsibility was laid at the door of the theatre's
artistic director. The rebuilding of the previous summer had been a costly
undertaking, and now it became apparent to all that the ship was sinking, and
the captain going down with it. One by one the creditors had turned up to
claim their due from any profits, a development with depressing parallels to
Ibsen's own private life. Early in the new year the actors were asked to take a cut
in wages, something they gamely agreed to.

The pressure on Ibsen mounted, and things weren't made any easier by the
fact that he had once again been dragged into another debate about the theatre.

* * *

On 21 March 1861 the first of Ibsen's four articles on the situation of the theatre
in Christiania appeared in *Morgenbladet*. The reasons for it were obvious: the
Kristiania Norske Theater had invested everything in rebuilding the theatre
and appointing a fresh set of actors, and yet still it had not made any inroads on
the status of the Christiania Theatre. With its finances in freefall, the next step
was to win the decisive battle with the help of the press.

Ibsen begins carefully and politely by stating that his intention is to debate
principles, not attack personalities, a promise he manages to keep. In the course
of a broad general history of theatre in Norway he argues that, in its current
incarnation, the Christiania Theatre has nothing more to offer, at the same
time as he praises the historical contribution of both the theatre and its director
Carl Borgaard to Norwegian theatre.[13]

This is important.

Neither Ibsen nor Bjørnson wanted to dispense entirely with the Danish
cultural heritage; but what both wanted was to see their own plays performed
at the largest and most prestigious and professional theatre. Ibsen's loyalty was
not primarily to the Kristiania Norske Theater but to *Norwegian theatre* and
the *theatrical arts* generally. The difficulty was that the Christiania Theatre had
failed on both counts, while his own theatre lacked the necessary resources to
succeed. There is a desperate undercurrent to Ibsen's reasoning: why was it so
difficult to get the relevant authorities and the general public to understand
that *something had happened* in the world of the dramatic arts in Europe?

This was what it was all about – the challenges of art, not the choice between
one theatre and another. He would probably have given his full backing to the
Christiania Theatre as a nationalist enterprise had there been any enthusiasm
for such a project from the theatre's board of directors and the state. But as long
as there wasn't, Ibsen was obliged to continue the struggle from the forum of
the capital's lesser stage. In one sense he was caught between idealism and
professionalism. The situation of the two theatres in Christiana boiled down to

this: the Christiania Theatre had the resources, but it was the Kristiania Norske Theater that had the ideas. But not all the king's horses and all the king's men could put them back together again.

Ibsen's fourth article concludes with the promise of further elucidation of the situation. But time passed, and nothing more was forthcoming. Presently *Morgenbladet* began enquiring about the follow-up.

'Herr Ibsen! Must we ask for a continuation of your series of articles on the theatre?'

Silence.

What had happened to Ibsen?

It had probably all got a bit too much for him, conducting an energetic public debate at the same time as he was struggling in almost every other department of his life. And it was at about this time that his creditors finally began closing in on him. No fewer than ten cases were brought against him in Christiania's assizes during a five-month period in the spring of 1861. The sudden rush of cases was probably a knock-on effect of the first three or four that came to court – three involving tailors, two manufacturers, two from lawyers, and two more demands for unpaid rent.[14]

Even an old case from his cobbler in Bergen from 1852 had not been forgotten – 3 spesidaler and 60 skilling were still owing.

Together the demands amounted to 268 spesidaler, although individually they were small. Presumably Ibsen felt he couldn't spare a single spesidaler, or else the pressure had grown so great that he had simply become indifferent. He was neglecting his work more and more; at the end of February he was severely reprimanded by the committee for having failed to mount a production, and from the close of April to the middle of May there was hardly a single rehearsal. The theatre would just have to look after itself for a while, and the newspaper debate he had started would have to manage without him too. His opponents, however, continued to be active. Even his own actors now openly attacked him. One day he might have read in the newspapers something he must have been dreading: a call to 'Bring back Bjørnson!'

Admiring tales of Bjørnson's achievements in Bergen had already reached the capital. After the turbulent interlude in Christiania in the winter of 1859 and spring of 1860 he had headed off to begin his three-year sojourn in Rome, cutting his ties to the theatre. It was simply a question of time before someone suggested that he was the man to replace Ibsen. The critical strategy succeeded. The average newspaper reader must have got the impression of a general feeling of ill-will towards Ibsen that spring. Even Paul Botten-Hansen conceded that Ibsen needed to buck his ideas up a bit. Coming from a good friend like Botten-Hansen the criticism speaks volumes about Ibsen's reputation as artistic director of the theatre.

He was, quite simply, not up to the job.

BANKRUPT

The autumn of 1861 brought its fair share of criticism and falling audiences too, but gradually the pressure lifted. It seems Ibsen was once again able to summon up his last resources of inspiration to raise the level of the repertoire. Again he found room for some adventurous choices, and another recent German offering, this time Gustav Freytag's *Grev Waldemar*, was performed in Møllergaten. A detail of note is that Suzannah Ibsen was responsible for the translation. So apparently she had other things to do besides force her husband to sit down and write. With a production of Alfred de Musset's *En Fantasie (Un Caprice)*, Ibsen also introduced his audiences to modern French drama of a very different order from the romantic comedies they were used to. Bjørnson came to his assistance too with the play *Kong Sverre*, written the previous spring. It gave Ibsen the chance to offer another new Norwegian drama from the age of the sagas.

This time he was successful. That the success came from the hand of a competitor was, under the circumstances, something he could live with. A breathing space in the midst of all this theatrical misery. If only he had found it as easy to breathe in his private life.

Their precarious financial situation had obliged Henrik, Suzannah and Sigurd to move home several times. After leaving the draughty house on Hegdehaugen in September 1860 they had moved twice. In April 1862 they were on the move yet again, this time to Oslo Strandgate, in the old town. For the remainder of their time in Norway this would be their home. In material terms they had managed to stay afloat, although it had been obvious for some time now that a shipwreck lay not far ahead. The succession of court cases throughout 1861 was exhausting, and took its toll on the family's possessions too, with one creditor after another depriving them of their furniture and property. Ibsen dutifully listed all his possessions for the Christiania Justice of the Peace, but the value came nowhere near to covering what he owed.

At the end of November he fell ill. Seriously ill.

It is not clear exactly what was wrong with him. Magdalene Thoresen described the ailment as 'nervous fever', while in the opinion of his friend Lorentz Dietrichson he had simply been broken by despair. His health had always been good. Ever since his days in Grimstad he had been known for his strength. Now he needed to be looked after like a child – but does he lie down?

'The man will absolutely not accept any help,' his mother-in-law relates. 'He simply will not admit that he is unwell, and refuses to follow any regime but in this as in all other things follows nothing but the dictates of his own indomitable will.'

Ibsen had a cure of his own: 'One night in a fever he got up out of his bed,' Dietrichson relates. 'He pulled on his clothes and hurried out of the house and made his way in pitch darkness to the docks, where he paced back and forth in the most appallingly stormy weather.' On 19 December he again excused himself on the grounds of health from a committee meeting, but in due course he recovered. In Suzannah's opinion it was that storm that cured him. Many years later, at a time when Ibsen's life had become the stuff of myth, this story would grow to the point at which it became an account of the young writer's painful struggle to keep thoughts of suicide at bay – as we all know, a real writer emerges only from suffering. And Ibsen did indeed suffer. But he never wrote less than he did during this time of almost constant suffering.[15]

The spring of 1862 saw the further rapid descent of the Kristiania Norske Theater. Ibsen, now recovered, put on a second play by Bjørnson, the world premiere of *Halte-Hulda*. But audiences found the contrary female lead less attractive than proud King Sverre, and the play ran for only three performances. The season ended in May. On 6 July 1862 it was decided to declare the theatre bankrupt, and it was time to apportion blame for the whole sorry adventure.

Knud Knudsen was in no doubt about where the responsibility lay. The chief cause of the theatre's bankruptcy was the exorbitant cost of the rebuilding, and the responsibility for that lay with the chairman of the committee, Johannes B. Klingenberg. But, he added, Klingenberg was not solely responsible for the failure of the theatre: 'H. Ibsen had also contributed to the decline of the theatre in its last five years of life.'

In other words, Ibsen had been planning the ruination of the theatre since his first day in the job! According to Knudsen, the entire committee was of the view that Ibsen and Klingenberg together had 'destroyed the Norske Teatret'. It was a monstrous accusation, and if it was made to Ibsen's face then it must have hurt him greatly.

A monstrous accusation – but justified? In the unfortunate matter of the rebuilding of the theatre, the decision to go ahead had actually been taken at the theatre's own annual general meeting. But in his annual reports Ibsen had actively promoted the project, and there may have been others besides Knudsen who blamed him. One can hardly doubt that Ibsen struggled to motivate himself during these dark years in Christiania, and with so much criticism of his artistic leadership it would have been surprising if Knudsen was alone in apportioning him some of the blame for what had happened.

But to ask Ibsen to shoulder a greater share of the blame for the theatre's bankruptcy than its other leaders is going too far. With the exception of the final season the box-office receipts increased during his tenure. Unfortunately the income from ticket sales never covered the running costs of the theatre, amplified in recent times as these were by the rebuilding. It was true enough that Ibsen was responsible for a number of costly productions – *The Vikings at Helgeland* alone had accounted for almost half the production costs that season,

500 spesidaler. On the other hand he was explicitly expected to provide plays that were both nationalist and of the highest quality. In sum he failed to meet either the theatre's nationalist or artistic ambitions, but the responsibility for this can hardly be laid at his door alone. And if some aspects of his choice of repertoire were subject to criticism he could also point to a considerable number of good reviews. As a director he also continued the good work he had begun in Bergen in getting the actors to perform as an ensemble, and in improving the quality and the relevance of the scenery.

But there was life after death. That same autumn the Kristiania Norske Theater was resurrected and the actors who had lost their jobs were permitted to arrange performances at the old Møllergaten theatre themselves. The enterprise rapidly gained the sympathy of the public and was well supported throughout the season. Now it was the turn of the Christiania Theatre to worry, for it too had been struggling in recent months. Things could change so quickly in the world of Norwegian theatre. And when a travelling German opera company also began to rent the stage in Møllergaten it proved the last straw for the Christiania Theatre. Once the debts of the Kristiania Norske Theater were paid off it became possible to contemplate a fusion, and after some difficult discussions the two theatres were indeed united in the summer of 1863.

* * *

For Ibsen, too, there would be life after death, although it probably did not seem very likely to him after he received his notice from the theatre, effective from 1 June 1862. The theatre had struggled throughout the spring, and so had he. On 26 May his major creditor, an attorney named Jacob Nandrup, demanded payment of the outstanding debt in full. Ibsen had borrowed money from him on several occasions to cover his debts to other creditors, trapped as he was in this vicious circle, a donkey on a debtor's treadmill. This single large loan had probably been used to pay off most of his earlier, smaller creditors.

Now the day of reckoning had come; Nandrup was owed a whopping 419 spesidaler and 52 skilling, an amount that was completely beyond Ibsen's reach, and by an irony of fate the demand arrived on exactly the same day as he was laid off at the theatre. He had received his last pay packet in May. There was no more money coming in. And as if that were not enough, a large tax demand from the previous year was also outstanding.

So he sits down and makes a list of what he has to offer Nandrup: paintings, dining-room table, sofa-bed, kitchen chairs, knives and forks, sugar bowls – he even lists the flower pots and flowers. Everything, absolutely everything Henrik and Suzannah own, even down to Sigurd's little bed, is neatly noted down on a sheet of paper, a death sentence pronounced over their material lives. In the middle of May he applied to the theatre for payment of the 'hard-won annual wage' that was still owing him. But, threatened as it was by bankruptcy, there was nothing the theatre could do to help. The best he could hope for was patience from Nandrup, and the lethargy of the city's bureaucracy.

And, as luck would have it, the death sentence was never carried out – if it can be described as lucky to live with one's head on the block while waiting for the executioner's axe to fall.

ON THE HEIGHTS

There he was. Unemployed and deep in debt. A theatre boss with no theatre, a playwright who hadn't written a play for four years. And with Suzannah and little Sigurd waiting at home in Oslo Strandgate for a crust of bread to put on the table.

Ibsen did the only sensible thing he could think of. He took to the hills.

In March 1862 he had applied to the Academic Collegium for a travel grant of 120 spesidaler to collect 'any folk ballads as well as older and more recent folk tales that might still survive' in the region of Hardanger and Sogn. Today it might be difficult to comprehend the extent of the fascination that rural Norway and the mountains exerted on the country's urban elite in the nine-teenth century. The mountains were an unknown world located at the heart of Norway, a terra incognita that excited Ibsen's imagination with new sights and new challenges.

At that time a mountain walking trip was considered every bit as much an educational journey as a stay in Copenhagen, Rome or Dresden. Rambling in the Norwegian mountains was becoming the fashion for affluent city dwellers, both native and foreign. Artists and scientists in particular found themselves fascinated by mountain landscapes and the lives of the peasants. For both groups it was about communication, whether it be nature itself, the language or the culture. It was here that the landscape painters discovered the magnificent scenery which they would then recreate in their studios in Düsseldorf and Dresden, here that Faye, Asbjørnsen and Moe collected their folk tales and fairy tales, Landstad his folk ballads, here that Ivar Aaasen came across the splintered remnants of the Norwegian language, and here where Eilert Sundt began his systematic study of the lives and conditions of the common people. And now it was Henrik Ibsen's turn to make the trip, this time as a scholar, to add what he could to Faye's collection of stories – the only field in which he ever revealed any academic aspirations.[16]

On 24 June, Ibsen made the short trip by train to Eidsvoll, and continued from there by steamboat across Lake Mjøsa. Thus far there had been nothing to write home about. The flat landscape surrounding Mjøsa was just not 'Norwegian' enough, monotonous and lacking in drama with its comfortable fields and forests and its equally comfortable natives. But he had to write home regardless, for back in Christiania, Paul Botten-Hansen was waiting for travel descriptions and accompanying sketches to use in the pages of the *Illustreret Nyhedsblad*. He was hoping to find cultural treasures hidden deep within the soul of the people, but pretty soon had to admit that 'there really aren't all that many legends and folk tales left here in Gudbrandsdal'. And the tales he did hear had either been collected before or else were tall stories of recent vintage (as opposed to tall stories from the good old days, in other words, legends).

Was there really not enough material for even a single new collection?

Perhaps the explanation for the disappointing results of the quest lay, as much as anything, in Ibsen's own nature. It's hard to imagine him with the kind of qualities that would encourage strangers to open up to him. Several of those he met during his journey reported that he seemed strikingly withdrawn and silent. Among them were his hosts at Lom rectory, where Ibsen stayed early in July. 'Surely there would be some gems, some kind of spiritual refreshment,' one of the daughters of the house hoped, well aware that their visitor was a real live author. But Ibsen chose to show them the silent and introverted version of himself, and when he travelled on and left them he was as much a stranger as when he had arrived.

For what sort of gems would he have been able to serve up? So far his trip had brought him nothing.

Many years later this young woman met Ibsen again, and to her delight found that he not only remembered her but spoke with pleasure of the fine few summer days he had spent at Lom rectory. He was adept at this. Many are the stories in which Ibsen arrogantly or absent-mindedly appears to ignore people he meets altogether, only for him to provide, many years later, a detailed account of the meeting. He had a remarkable talent for observing people and situations. Indeed, it was probably something he cultivated as part of his calling – the idea of the *poet's eye*. And he must have loved it when he was able to confound people's expectations, and see the confusion on their faces when he showed another side of himself from the one they were familiar with; silent one moment, garrulous the next – but always the observer.

From Lom, Ibsen made his way through Bøverdalen and then followed the hazardous track across Sognefjell. He had different travelling companions along the way, but once over the mountain he headed north on his own until he reached Hellesylt, a tiny settlement huddled up against the mountainside, a place where the sun seldom shone, and where avalanches were not infrequent. Throughout the winter the inhabitants lived in constant danger, not that it seemed to bother them particularly – they had quite simply grown accustomed to it. The village excited Ibsen's curiosity and he stayed there for a couple of weeks. Soon people were whispering about this odd chap who claimed to be a student, and who asked around and dug around and wrote down the answers people gave him.

It was cold on the day Ibsen left Hellesylt and he drank a quick brandy at the way station before heading out. On 18 July he reached Solnør in Skodje, not far from Ålesund. Here, at last, he found what he had set out looking for – folk tales. And luckily for him they had already been collected, by a man named Peder Fylling who lived in the village and was a collector of traditions and old stories. Fylling was a keen amateur historian of the type Norway is rich in, those who have done so much valuable work as collectors without always getting the credit they deserve. Such was Peder Fylling's fate too. Ibsen persuaded him to hand over much of his material to him, probably with a promise of publication. But only four were printed, all in the pages of the *Illustreret Nyhedsblad*, and with no mention of Fylling's name.

With Fylling's manuscript in his rucksack Ibsen must have felt that he had fulfilled the conditions for the award of the grant. On 27 July he left Solnør and headed over Ørskogfjellet and back down into Gudbrandsdal. By early August he was back in Christiania.

* * *

With the exception of the crossing of Hardanger in 1856, this 1862 journey was the only time Ibsen ever went walking in the Norwegian mountains. He really wasn't the outdoor type, and in later life he largely contented himself with strolls along city streets, preferring the view from cafe chairs to the view from mountain peaks. Since the mountains play such a central role in several of his plays and poems, we can safely assume that these walks made a profound impression on him. The mountain walk in particular is clearly visible in Ibsen's work, most notably in *Brand* and *Peer Gynt*. Over the years his whole route has been studied by scholars, journalists and local historians in search of places, people and events that might have inspired him: a priest named O. T. Krogh from Vestnes is said to have been the model for the priest in *Brand*; the little village of Hellesylt the model for Brand's home town; the Ice Church is supposedly in Fanaråken; and the mad but beautiful Ingeborg his model for Gerd. It seems that even his guide, Erik Eriksen, saw something of himself in *Brand* – he remained convinced that he had been Ibsen's model for the small part of 'A Peasant'.

It is doubtful whether all this searching for models and locations has anything important to tell us about Ibsen's work. He was not the kind of writer who works directly from life. He gathered his impressions from the world around him (where else would he have found them?), but in his work he moulded them into ideas and symbols, into art. In some form or other this searching for the roots of his writing in real people and real situations continues to this day, because Ibsen's life has always been as much an object of fascination as his work. Long after his death, the puppeteer continues to pull on the strings.

AIR AND LOVE

Besides filling his lungs with mountain air the walk had left Ibsen with a wealth of impressions. The trip had not been especially remunerative – its only direct result was a handful of travel pieces and drawings in the *Illustreret Nyhedsblad*. And yet he did manage to turn the proposed collection of sagas and stories to some financial advantage. If there is one talent the debtor hones to a fine art it is an ability not to pay off the debt but to postpone the payment. This was what Ibsen did. Not long after his return he signed a contract with Christian Tønsberg for publication of the collection. He then asked the publisher to send the advance of 160 spesidaler directly to Nandrup, keeping him at bay a while longer. Apart from Peder Fylling's rough draft, there was still no manuscript, but that was a mere detail – just as it was a few months later when he made a second, similar deal with a printer named Johan Dahl to publish the same non-existent collection for the same advance against royalties, 160 spesidaler. It was probably this that persuaded the city treasurer, who had decided the time had come to proceed with a foreclosure sale of Ibsen's property to recover the back taxes owing, to withdraw the threat for the time being.

Ibsen had learned the first rule of the debtor: nothing plus nothing is and remains nothing. Lesson number two is that the longer fate is postponed, the harder the blow when it eventually falls. This was another lesson he would presently learn. The city treasurer had advertised the auction in the newspaper, so Ibsen's wretched state of affairs was public knowledge. Ludvig Daae wrote sympathetically in his journal: 'Perhaps the best thing after all is for him to go to Copenhagen.'

Things had got so bad for Ibsen that rumours had begun to circulate to the effect that he was proposing to leave the country. Probably there were quite a few who thought that would be the best solution for him. He had friends, mainly among his fellow Hollanders, who in various ways wanted to help him get back on his feet again.

What did he think?

Ibsen wanted to leave. Of that there is no doubt. But he did not necessarily want to leave for good. In August 1860 he had applied for a royal grant of 400 spesidaler for a six-month trip to London, Paris, Stockholm, Copenhagen and several cities in Germany for the purpose of studying art and literature. He had travelled on the continent once before, and that trip had been richly rewarding. Maybe the same thing would happen again. But his application was rejected, and there had been no more talk after that of travels abroad.

What was he to do here at home? In August 1862 he had written to the authorities at the Christiania Theatre suggesting he be employed as 'House Dramatist'. Did he think they would go for it? They didn't. He began writing drama criticism for *Morgenbladet* and continued to contribute to *Illustreret Nyhedsblad*. But there were few articles in either journal: a handful of reviews, a poem, a couple of articles in which he criticised the Christiania Theatre for the artistic quality of its repertoire at a time when it stood alone on the battlefield.

Under the circumstances he decides to write a comedy.

It was his only hope. At some point he must have realised that his best chance was to write his way out of his predicament. He had written while poor before, and he was certain he could do so again. In 1858 he had written the first act of a prose drama entitled 'Svanhild'. He then put it aside, and probably did not look at it again until early in 1862. By the summer he had a first draft ready, this time in verse. While still at work on what would become *Love's Comedy* he one day encountered Jonas Lie at a cafe called the Petri Kirke and described his new play to him.

'He talked a lot about a scene in the final act,' Lie recalled many years later, 'how at the very moment the bubbling champagne is being raised to the lips the glasses are removed! – The idea puzzled me; I was not enough of a dramatist to be able to envisage the effect.'

Ibsen wanted Jonas Lie to publish *Love's Comedy* in the *Illustreret Nyhedsblad*, of which Lie had been the owner since 1861. Lie had soon begun changing the magazine's profile. He wanted something with a broader popular appeal, less exclusive and with a more varied content. Controversial political material was out, and he wanted less literature. Lie was an editor with an eye for the next thing, and that was something Ibsen certainly approved of, but as it turned out, his new play would be neither popular nor entirely uncontroversial. In June the two men signed a contract whereby Lie agreed to pay Ibsen 100 spesidaler for the right to publish the play in his magazine, once Ibsen had finished it.

For the autumn of 1862 Ibsen literally lived on fresh air and love – the advance for *Love's Comedy* was practically his only income along with the few spesidaler he earned from his articles, and whatever he had left over from his travel grant of the spring. He was also hoping that the Christiania Theatre would buy his play for the net sum of 300 spesidaler. But still Ibsen didn't feel he could let the new play go. Writing didn't come easily during those years, and Jonas Lie had to wait patiently for the third and final act. One story relates that Ibsen used the half-finished manuscript to borrow more money from Nandrup. However, Nandrup demanded he be allowed to read it first, and thereafter insisted that certain lines be dropped as a condition of extending his loan.

Keeping your creditors at bay was one thing, editing a text at the behest of a creditor was quite another. Ibsen must have seethed inwardly, but did as he was bidden – and none of this can have made it any easier to get the play finished.

Jonas Lie wanted the play ready for the New Year edition, as the magazine's gift to its subscribers. But the weeks passed, and he received nothing from Ibsen. Finally Lie had to threaten to provide a final act himself if Ibsen was not forthcoming. That did the trick. *Love's Comedy* was despatched to *Illustreret Nyhedsblad*'s subscribers on 2 January 1863.

This time it wasn't a case of sink or swim. This time Ibsen *needed* it to succeed.

EITHER/OR

On the face of it, *Love's Comedy* is a farce about engagements and extramarital shenanigans set in Fru Halm's lodging house in one of Christiania's more fashionable residential districts, specifically in the garden, where the lodgers and the landlady sing and talk about all manner of things, but mostly about art and love. Two of the tenants, Lind and Falk, are suitors to the landlady's two daughters, Anna and Svanhild, and at the heart of the play is the relationship between the *bon vivant* poet Falk and serious Svanhild, who is searching for love. But there is an ethical and philosophical seriousness beneath the superficial frivolities. Is marriage compatible with the free life of the artist? Are idealism and an artistic calling compatible with the demands and responsibilities of marriage and society? At the beginning of the play Falk seems to be defending the claim of the ideal. If love is to flourish and to inspire art, he insists, then it must do so outside the confines of marriage. The gathering is shocked by his bold talk, but Svanhild is fascinated. She wants to live out her ideal of love with Falk, but it soon becomes apparent that she demands a more responsible kind of love than that which Falk is able to offer her.

The young couple realise that their love can only survive if they part. Svanhild gets engaged to the businessman Guldstad, who is at least able to offer her security. This leaves Falk free to devote himself fully to a life of writing, but now with greater seriousness than ever before. *Love's Comedy* is rich in so many ways. Much is clearly derived from literature; the Svanhild character derives from *Saga of the Volsungs*, the same source as parts of *The Vikings at Helgeland*. But other lines are traceable to Wergeland, Holberg, Camilla Collett's *Amtmandens Døtre*, and not least to Søren Kierkegaard. Its most striking references, however, were to contemporary Christiania, and alert readers could spot references to places such as Kurland, a Kristiania 'Lover's Lane', and institutions such as Hartvig Nissen's girls' school, *Morgenbladet*, the literary magazine *Dølen* and Jens Taastrup Ollendorff's shop selling 'everything for the kitchen'.[17]

Scattering contemporary references such as these was a smart move on Ibsen's part, guaranteeing interest in his play, so much so that it became a kind of parlour game to study the play for these local and personal titbits. Members of the Learned Holland found it very amusing, especially where the references were recognisably to themselves. Paul Botten-Hansen unearthed some lines of verse that quoted directly from his play *The Huldre Wedding*, while Ludvig Daae was almost offended *not* to find any references to himself.[18] In Ibsen's opinion all this went much too far, especially in the irresistible urge to see in Falk and Svanhild a version of himself and Suzannah. In his view this was a grievous distraction from the actual meaning and purpose of his play.

'That book occasioned a great deal of talk in Norway,' he later complained. 'People brought my own personal circumstances into the discussion and my reputation suffered as a result.'

As with *Peer Gynt* later, he was distressed by the number of readers who failed to see anything beneath the satirical exterior of the play. *Love's Comedy* was, after all, more than a comedy and a satire; it was also a drama on the subject of the relationship between life and art, the real and the ideal, duty and freedom.

These were themes Ibsen had tackled before. In the poem 'Paa Vidderne' ('On the Heights'), written towards the end of 1859, a hunter goes off into the hills leaving his mother and his sweetheart waiting behind at home. But the hunter doesn't return home. In the mountains he meets a mysterious stranger who tempts him up onto the heights from where he is to look down and see the little village far below, 'through the ring of thumb and forefinger/to improve the perspective'. Just as though the everyday world and conventional life were a play, and himself a spectator to the whole thing. It was about freedom from the material world, the freedom to make his way up onto the heights in pursuit of a calling. It is not unreasonable to suggest that, at its deepest level, the poem is about an artistic calling, about the poet's freedom to pursue his ideals. But is this longing for freedom presented in a positive light, or is the poem rather about a flight from the world, about an aesthetic life devoid of responsibilities, in which the world is viewed through this comforting perspective, through the ring of thumb and forefinger?

There is no obvious answer, just as there is no obvious answer to the same questions in *Love's Comedy*. Here, too, the tensions are drawn between the social conventions, represented by marriage and life in Fru Halm's garden, and the freedom to pursue a calling. But even here the heedless pursuit of an artistic calling is not presented in an unambiguously positive light – most people will find Falk's personality much too ironic for that. Essentially the problem of a proper interpretation lies in how the lines and characters are viewed: are they to be taken ironically or literally? As comic or tragic? Falk has conventionally been seen as an out-and-out aesthete in the Kierkegaardian sense, with the hunter in 'Paa Vidderne' as his precursor. But put aside the irony, and take Falk literally, and what you get instead is a precursor of Brand, an indomitable idealist who chooses his calling over the demands of society.[19]

We have Ibsen's own word for the existence of a connection between the poem, the play and his marriage. A letter written in 1870 describes the poem as the 'first fruit' of his experience as a married man. And the 'urge to freedom' that runs through the poem was what reached its full expression in the subsequent play. But did this urge to freedom derive from the suffocation of sharing his life with Suzannah? Was there an incompatibility, not only in the play but in Ibsen's life too, between marriage and a literary calling?

Ibsen himself denies it. Marriage had given his life a new depth, he claimed, and Suzannah was, moreover, the only person who believed in *Love's Comedy* when it was published. In other words, Suzannah was the inspiration for his urge to freedom rather than the negative cause of it. Nor can the play be read as a denial of the fact that a literary calling and marriage cannot co-exist; it is, for example, difficult to see the earthy Guldstad as *solely* a comic figure. He has something to offer Svanhild that Falk cannot, and he is moreover unable to offer her his everlasting love.

A harmonising perspective on marriage and home life appeared again in 'Terje Vigen', from February 1862. The long but tightly structured poem has acquired a unique status among Norwegians as a sort of national epic, with its account of the brave seaman who defies all dangers to provide food for his family during the English blockade of Denmark–Norway during the Napoleonic Wars. Terje Vigen became the archetypal Norwegian man, a hugely important figure in the process of Norwegian nation building. As a symbol of the brave seaman the poem has also been of great importance in creating and sustaining the self-image of Norwegians as a seafaring people. To a large extent Ibsen based the poem on material he had become familiar with in Grimstad. But 'Terje Vigen' also features a nationalist and regional motif that relates it to 'On the Heights' and *Love's Comedy*. The hunter in 'On the Heights' leaves his home, but the seaman in 'Terje Vigen' knows the value of home and family. Both made the choice to become themselves, the one by leaving home, the other by finding his way back home. *Love's Comedy* seems to offer both perspectives at the same time – the gain and the loss that come with liberation from conventional life, and the gain and loss that come from holding on to it.[20]

Seen in this light, there may be something in the theory that the play actually proposes two kinds of ideality – that of life, and that of art.[21] Even so, the two kinds of ideality are not presented openly, and are not morally loaded; perhaps the best way of putting it is to say that in this play Ibsen arrived at what would become his signature as a dramatist, a 'divided and questioning duality, the dramatic tension that arises when doubt meets faith, irony encounters enthusiasm, and scepticism boastful pride'.[22]

Seen in perspective – through history's ring of thumb and forefinger – *Love's Comedy* was an impressive achievement. Not simply because Ibsen managed to write a comedy in the middle of a life-crisis. No, what is really impressive is that he managed to write a play that was so rich and so vivid, in dancing and powerful verse, full of witty allusions to literature and to contemporary life. Playful and witty, deeply serious and savagely ironic – *Love's Comedy* is all of this at the same time. It is the play that announces Ibsen's maturity as a dramatist; with the exception of *St John's Night*, it is his first play with a contemporary setting, and of all his plays so far also the one most directly preoccupied with social questions. Overwhelmingly, his earlier characters find themselves confronted by moral dilemmas; but Falk and Svanhild also have to face the massive pressure of society's demands. As a play of ideas, too, the drama pointed ahead to the play that would be his real breakthrough – *Brand*.

This is especially true of Falk's dream of some crushingly 'enormous grief' that might open his eyes to the eternal values. Of course, Ibsen himself had a longing of this kind too which, at its deepest level, has to be understood as a longing for a transcendental liberation from the trivialities of life into something bigger. That he nevertheless depicts Falks's longing with so much irony indicates a certain ambiguity on the subject of the 'enormous grief'.

And yet within a very few years he would know just such an experience, something so strong that it would precipitate an existential crisis that found its final expression in *Brand*. But that lay in the future. At the close of 1862 Ibsen's struggles were with griefs of a far more trivial sort, although they were certainly serious.

He had no job, and very little money.

*　*　*

Following his failed attempt to be employed as house dramatist at the Christiania Theatre in August 1862, rumours continued to circulate suggesting that Ibsen and the theatre remained in dialogue on the subject. In November the matter was resolved. The chairman of the theatre committee, Bernhard Dunker, approached Ibsen and enquired whether he might consider 'assisting the theatre with suggestions for repertoire and casting' from 1 January 1863.

So they did want him after all, if not as their house dramatist.

There was nothing particularly surprising in this development. The venture in Møllergaten was over, and a fusion of the two theatres seemed possible, although practical hindrances still prevented it. The simplest step towards a fusion that would also bring a truly Norwegian theatre a step closer, as well as put an end to the long-running theatrical feud, would be to invite the Kristiania

Norske Theater's unemployed artistic director – who also happened to be one of the Christiania Theatre's most trenchant critics – in from the cold. A note from January refers to his 'taking over the running of the theatre', but in June the job description is much closer to Dunker's original offer to work as the 'artistic advisor in the fields of repertoire and casting'.

In truth by this time Ibsen had had about enough of repertoires, casting, actors and directing. Moreover, the new post was not quite as important as it might have seemed at first sight; he never did get to be an artistic director but instead was subordinate to a committee whose prime objective was to keep the ship afloat until better times came along. In other words, his position was exactly the same as before. If not worse. For his wage at the Christiania Theatre was less than half of what he had been earning as artistic director at Møllergaten. But at least it enabled him to pay off what he still owed in back taxes, his debt being formally declared cleared on 20 February. That was one creditor out of the way. Now there was just Nandrup left.

In fact, with *Love's Comedy* behind him, Ibsen must have longed to let theatre be theatre and get back to writing again. Indeed, for most of the winter and spring he must have been turning over in his mind the ideas that would eventually become *The Pretenders*, though he didn't manage to get anything down on paper until the summer – and then the whole thing came in one single burst of inspiration.

He was a writer. Writing was what he wanted to devote himself to completely. But how to make that happen?

Grants, of course. Government grants. He was beginning to get the hang of it now, the most important and most ambitious literary challenge facing any Norwegian writer: the difficult art of applying for money. In March he submits a grant to the Akademiske Collegium for money to continue with his work of collecting stories and folk tales from the Trøndelag and Nordland regions. Although he was awarded a hundred spesidaler Ibsen never did take that trip, nor any other like it. A few days after submitting this application he sent off another, this time addressed to His Majesty the King and the Norwegian government, in which he requested an annual literary wage of 400 spesidaler.

His supporting argument was crisp and clear: 'To live entirely on the proceeds of one's literary activity is, in this country, impossible.'

A mere two weeks after receiving his application the government passed a unanimous resolution rejecting it.[23] The minister Hans Riddervold spoke for the government when he declared that, despite Ibsen's undoubted literary talent, it was too late in the current session to address a matter that was 'not of crucial importance'. And despite the fact that Ibsen had a great deal of support in the Storting, well canvassed by the tireless Learned Hollanders, the elected representatives followed the government's recommendation and voted 49 to

40 against making the award.[24] In April the Storting had approved by a large majority a similar proposal to award Bjørnson the first purely literary annual grant ever made in Norway.[25]

Henrik Ibsen was 'not of crucial importance' for the nation. Bjørnson was.

Riddervold did, however, remind the house of Ibsen's rejected application for a travel grant of 1860. Bjørnson had been awarded a similar grant in the meantime, and Ibsen was assured that his application would be reconsidered at the next opportunity. In the spring of 1863 Bjørnson returned from his travels abroad full of enthusiasm after his long stay in Rome. Ibsen was encouraged enough to send off yet another application, this time a request for 600 spesidaler for a journey to Rome and Paris to study art and literature.

This time he was lucky, although only to the tune of 400 spesidaler. The dream of writing and of leaving were one and the same dream. His application for an annual grant had contained a veiled threat to move to Denmark as a last resort, since he could see no future in his own country without state support. Through the winter and the spring his urge to travel would receive further stimulation. The reception of *Love's Comedy* had much to do with Ibsen's break with his home country; it was a catalyst for all the repressed frustration and bitterness towards the Norwegian authorities, those same authorities that he had satirised in the play.

The play was quite simply too much for most people.[26] Marcus Jacob Monrad felt that, essentially, it was 'a disturbing break with idealism', Ditmar Meidell condemned the play as 'the regrettable product of literary idleness', and even Paul Botten-Hansen expressed his disappointment that the play was 'devoid of any ideal or conviction'. Not even Bjørnson was particularly enthusiastic about *Love's Comedy*, though not because he found the play immoral in the way Monrad did. Ibsen wasn't protesting against engagements and marriages, in Bjørnson's view, but against all the 'drivel', and especially the drivel spoken 'at weddings, with the aunts and the gossips'. Ibsen was neither for nor against marriage, neither for Straamand nor against Falk, he simply 'allows the contradictions to destroy each other'. And this is what Bjørnson finds impossible to like about the play, that it contains no hero 'who emerges victorious from the struggle, saved from the drivel'. This is important, not just because it shows how much more familiar Bjørnson was with the contemporary aesthetic of reconciliation than Ibsen was, but because this marks a major difference between the two for the whole of their literary lives.

The idealistic and conciliatory Bjørnson, and the doubting and ambiguous Ibsen – in Bjørnson's own words, one who spent too much time on drivel.

The review that would be most important to Ibsen was not written by a Norwegian. In the Danish newspaper *Fædrelandet*, Clemens Petersen both slaughtered the play and hailed the dramatist's genius.[27] And what Petersen praised above all was Ibsen's talent for writing verse – 'Verse is Henrik Ibsen's natural expression.' Which was not to say that Ibsen had managed to use the full register of the metre, for in most other respects Petersen deemed the play a failure.

Rarely can a savage review have been so fondly received. Ibsen wrote a letter to the Dane offering him his heartfelt thanks, for the critical points as much as the praise.

What might have caused such untypical humility?

Clemens Petersen wasn't just anyone. He was *Fædrelandet*'s influential literary critic, and in Denmark *Fædrelandet* was the voice of the liberal elite and as such an important voice in Danish public life. During his first stay in Copenhagen in 1856–7 Bjørnson had been admitted to a literary inner circle of which Petersen was also a member. From the start, the two got on famously, and Ibsen was hoping that now it was his turn to be welcomed in from the cold:

> In particular I would like to thank you because I now see that you are not as critical of me as I had previously felt you to be; this is something I value to a degree that may not be immediately apparent to you, since you can have no way of knowing how spiritually isolated I am up here.

It wasn't just the review of the play, but the fact that Ibsen had been recognised as a writer by someone of Petersen's stature. And if the critic had not exactly gone overboard for the play itself, he had at least been unstinting in his praise of the author's talent. And that was certainly a beginning. Moreover, Ibsen must have been deeply moved by the meditations on the difficulties he faced as a writer in Norway with which Petersen concluded his review. Petersen understood what it was like for him, how he had been

> hounded by theatre committees and journalists. And his friends, his audiences and the authorities sat back and looked on and did nothing, presumably on the grounds that Norway is so rich in talent that it scarcely matters if a few of them go to waste.

If anyone could save him from the gutter, could it be Clemens Petersen? *Love's Comedy* had made Ibsen neither rich nor respected. The combined effects of catastrophic personal finances, problems in the world of the theatre, alcohol, his feeble literary productivity of recent years, and now the reception of *Love's Comedy*, together forced him to take stock of all he had so far built his life and his dreams on. He had sent the play to Trondheim, only to have it rejected. The Christiania Theatre had at least accepted it, but were cautious about putting on a production, in spite of the fact that Dunker had given it his backing.

The Vikings at Helgeland had suffered a similar fate, the difference being that this time *he* was the theatre's artistic consultant. Nor had Ibsen received the 300 spesidaler he had been hoping for. The theatre paid him just 30 spesidaler for the rights, with a percentage of the box-office takings to follow. But since the play was never performed Ibsen was left with just the 30 spesidaler. Even this had the status of a loan that had to be repaid.

THE PRETENDER

A tiny shaft of light is enough to dispel the darkness.

When the government unanimously approved Ibsen's travel grant in September, the nightmare that had been hanging over him for so long had already begun to recede. Despite the fact that he was still heavily in debt – with the knowledge that Nandrup might decide to let the axe fall any time he wanted – and despite the dispiriting response to *Love's Comedy*, it seems almost as though Ibsen's spirits lifted in the summer of 1863 in the direction of something that bears a close resemblance to, well – joy.

Just how this unheard-of change of mood manifested itself, we do not know. But we do know where it took place.

On 12 June, Ibsen boards the steamer *Lindesnæs* to sail to Bergen, to take part in a festival of song. Three choirs from Christiania would be singing the words to his 'Hail Song!' Song festivals such as this were very popular at the time and attracted large crowds. Bergen was in a party mood, people thronged to the city to attend concerts, parties and talks. Ibsen was happy to see old friends such as Peter Blytt again, but the climax must have been Bjørnson's speech at the banquet on 16 June, in which he spoke of reconciliation, the reconciliation of song, at the same time as venomously condemning those trying to sow dissension between the writers:

> And have I not seen this, that my friend Ibsen has been set up against me, to harm me, and I against him, to harm him?

During Bjørnson's absence Ibsen had put on productions of both *Kong Sverre* and *Halte-Hulda*, as well as reviewing his most recent play *Sigurd Slembe* very favourably. And now there he stood on the podium, as big-hearted as only he could be. If we are to believe Ibsen, the festival of song was a single long, warm embrace, highly unfamiliar for a writer and a theatre manager who in recent years had been for the most part an object of public hostility. And it is not unthinkable that Bjørnson's consoling words found a welcome from his audience. Many Norwegians with an interest in literature must have gradually started to feel a certain sympathy for the much-criticised theatre boss Henrik

Ibsen, and wished him well in his quest to be able to devote himself entirely to his writing. One finds expressions of this sympathy here and there in note-books and letters of the time, and most strikingly in the informal support group, with contributors from all over the country, who would a little later provide Ibsen with the money to live in Italy. Back in Christiania he writes a cheerful and warm letter to his host in Bergen, Randolph Nilsen:

> The festival there, and all the dear, unforgettable people I met, had the same effect on me as a particularly pleasant visit to church, and I feel sure that the mood will not be easily dissipated. Everyone was so kind to me in Bergen; it isn't like that here, where a great many people do their best to hurt and pain me as often as they can.

When was the last time a man from the capital so liberally sang the praises of Bergen? Yet the relationship with Bjørnson was not quite as harmonious as the speech at the banquet might have suggested. In a letter to Magdalene Thoresen he complains of Ibsen's behaviour during the festival: 'I made quite an effort to involve him,' he writes, 'but he didn't even visit me.' Then he goes on to list all the things he dislikes about *Love's Comedy*.

It wasn't easy for either of them to find a balance in their guarded friend-ship. Ibsen never felt entirely comfortable about his relationship with Bjørnson, no matter how many overtures Bjørnson made. And the unease was reciprocal. But Bjørnson was at least able to distinguish the man from the issue; Ibsen had to be publicly rehabilitated – that was what his speech had been about. It left him free to moan to Magdalene Thoresen about both his friend's lack of grati-tude and the numerous weaknesses in his work.

Ibsen returned to Christiania happy and eager to get back to creative work again. During late-night sessions with Blytt he had told him of all the things he planned to write. Now he at once set about what would become *The Pretenders*, and had a fair copy of all five acts ready by early September. Not long after-wards he bumped into Johan Dahl, the bookshop proprietor and small publisher, who promised him an advance of 150 spesidaler for the book. That was 50 spesidaler more than Jonas Lie had paid for *Love's Comedy*. Time would show which of the two men had the better commercial instinct.

Ibsen had once again used material he came across in one of P. A. Munch's books as his source, this time his *History of the Norwegian People*, with *Håkon Håkonssons Saga* as a secondary source.[28] The plot of *The Pretenders* is based on dynastic intrigues in Norway in the thirteenth century, but Ibsen takes consid-erable artistic liberties with the material. Following the death of King Inge a number of pretenders to the throne appear, among them the dead king's brother Earl Skule, and the much younger Håkon Håkonsson, who claims to be the king's illegitimate son. The cynical Bishop Nikolas intrigues from the wings. Nikolas was a pretender himself once, and driven on by his lust for power he tries to set Håkon and Skule against each other. Skule, who initially respects Håkon, and doubts the validity of his own claim to the throne, allows himself to be carried away by the bishop's rhetoric. He falls prey to envy and greed, and steals Håkon's 'kingly thought' of uniting Norway into a single kingdom. Civil war breaks out, from which Håkon emerges the victor. And Skule – of course – dies, but not before first carrying out an act worthy of a pretender to the throne. As he faces defeat a change comes over him, and he chooses his own death in order to spare the lives of others and ensure the unification of the kingdom.

Generations of literary historians are agreed that in *The Pretenders* Ibsen wrote a nationalist drama far superior to any he had offered previously. Monrad gave the play a largely enthusiastic review: Ibsen had written a successful drama that genuinely enriched Norwegian literature. Ditmar Meidell was more reserved. In his view the techniques were crude, and the psychology unconvincing.[29] Meidell's assessment is sharply at odds with the usual response to *The Pretenders*. The large-scale nationalist theme with a historical background made a powerful appeal to the nation-building elite of the nineteenth century. More important is the way Ibsen managed to weave a complex drama of character into the historical plot, a genuinely Shakespearean accomplishment. Gone were the rigid saga style and the historical gimmickry. *The Pretenders* describes a struggle between people driven on by big ideas, but also by jealousy, self-recrimination, bitterness and desire. Håkon is clearly the play's protagonist, and Bishop Nikolas its cynical villain, but what is most moving about the drama is the inner struggle that plagues the doubting Earl Skule.

Tradition relates the play and its characters to Bjørnson, Ibsen, and the encounter between the two at the Bergen festival of song. The connection is tempting to make, and not entirely unwarranted. The brooding Skule is often seen as Ibsen, Håkon as Bjørnson, and the call to the throne related to the call to become a writer.[30] And the theme that runs through the play, of doubt and belief in the call, can certainly be related to Ibsen's own vacillating faith in his calling and his status in Norway – reflections on the subject of writing as a vocation appear also, of course, in *Love's Comedy*. And yet it is impossible to gather in all the scattered fragments of Ibsen the man that are strewn across this play, impossible because everything has been remoulded and transformed to serve artistic ends. But the *dramatic problems* that the play discusses are undeniably the fruits of the writer's mind, and it would be naïve to ignore the extent to which Ibsen, in *The Pretenders*, engages in a discussion of ideas and problems that have an obvious relevance to his own personal situation. This, for example, is Jatgejr the Skald's reply to Skule, who has asked where he learned his craft:

Jatgejr: The art of the skald cannot be learned, master.

Kong Skule: Cannot be learned? Then how does it come about?

Jatgejr: I was given the gift of sorrow and that made me a skald.

Kong Skule: So it is the gift of sorrow the skald needs?

Jatgejr: I needed sorrow; it might be that others need faith, or joy – or doubt.

Kong Skule: Doubt too?

Jatgejr: Yes. But the doubter must be strong and in good health.

Kong Skule: And whom would you describe as an unhealthy doubter?

Jatgejr: That would be the one who doubts his own doubt.

Ibsen had possessed the blessed gift of sorrow for a long time, and in his own evolution as a writer he was well on the way to becoming a doubter. A strong, healthy and committed doubter.

* * *

At the end of October he receives written confirmation from the Christiania Theatre of something he must have already been expecting: the theatre wants to perform *The Pretenders*, and it wants the dramatist himself to assist in the production. At the beginning of the month he had asked the Department of Church Affairs to release 100 of the 400 spesidaler of his travel grant, so that he could send his family on ahead of him. On 17 October, Suzannah and Sigurd travel to Copenhagen, where they move in with Suzannah's stepmother, Magdalene Thoresen. Ten days later Ibsen again writes to the department and asks for the rest of the money to be released, as he plans to follow them directly after the premiere.

With his family safely ensconced in Copenhagen, Ibsen took rooms at the Hotel Copenhague in Øvre Vognmandsgate 2 for the duration of the rehearsals and the opening. The theatre had tried to insist that the publication of the play be postponed until after the premiere. But the contract with Dahl had already been signed and *The Pretenders* appeared towards the end of October. The first print run was an ambitious 1,250 copies, from which it was clear that Dahl shared an optimism about the book's prospects with both Ibsen and the theatre. At the time, however, the book did not sell well. The play, on the contrary, gave Ibsen his greatest success so far in the capital when it had its premiere on 17 January 1864. Despite the fact that it ran for five hours it captivated the audience: 'When the curtain fell,' wrote one reviewer, 'there were the usual cries for the author; and when he appeared it turned into a storm of applause.'

It must have tasted so sweet, so sweet.

Not so good that the Norwegian pretender failed to conquer the neighbour in the south. Since his audience with Johan Ludvig Heiberg thirteen years earlier, Ibsen had not managed to attract any significant support in Denmark.

He was still being rejected by the Kongelige Teater, and when one of the minor Copenhagen theatres put on a performance of *The Feast at Solhaug* in December 1861 the occasion went almost unnoticed. When Ibsen left Bergen his aim had been to conquer the capital, and with it, the country. Now he had to win a name for himself in Copenhagen if he were to establish himself as a literary figure in the larger Scandinavian landscape. It was his only hope, given that he was going to have to manage without state support in the form of an annual grant.

Clemens Petersen's review of *Love's Comedy* was a small sign that perhaps now Denmark was ready for him. On the advice of Petersen he accordingly therefore sent a copy of *Lady Inger of Østråt* to the Kongelige Teater in the autumn of 1863, submitting *The Pretenders* a little later.

But the kingdom of Denmark was not so easily won.

The Norwegian-born writer and theatre censor Carsten Hauch's pronouncement on the two plays included words such as 'repulsive', 'impossible' and 'perverse, crude and ugly'.[31] New Norwegian drama, and in particular plays written in the Norwegian language, were still too crude and realistic for Danish tastes, and both submissions were summarily rejected. Ibsen must have been hugely disappointed, and in no way comforted by Clemens Petersen's review of *The Pretenders* once this appeared.[32] In his review of *Love's Comedy*, Petersen had panned the play but hailed its author; in the case of *The Pretenders* he was dismayed by both. Petersen had praised Ibsen's talent as a writer of verse drama and could not forgive him for having written a saga drama in prose. Ibsen had 'failed to understand the nature of his own originality, his own genius, his own talents, and sacrificed them for a subject he has simply chosen'. When it came to themes, a writer ought to follow his intuition, not make conscious choices. And Ibsen's natural metier was verse drama: Clemens Petersen had spoken.

There wasn't much more to be had either from the response of another Danish critic, Carl Rosenberg, writing in the *Dansk Maanedsskrift* in February 1864. Rosenberg admired the grandeur of the plot and the characters, but his overall view was that, in the final analysis, the play was nowhere near what Bjørnson was capable of at his best. No, it really did look as though Denmark wasn't yet ready for Henrik Ibsen. Norwegians, on the other hand, were. The irony of it all was that by this time *he* was just about finished with *them*.

OUT, LEAVE, GO

The staging of *The Pretenders* at the Christiania Theatre was the last time Ibsen was directly involved with the production side of theatre work. Much later he described his years spent in the Norske Teatret as 'abortion on a daily basis', a grotesque if understandable choice of words that nevertheless does scant justice to his apprentice years working there. Bjørnson left the theatre in 1867, following a rather more successful career, and on a brief return a few years later he sighed that 'it cost me dearly when I left the theatre behind, I've never known anything quite like it.' Their temperaments were completely different. Posterity would associate Ibsen with the difficult years of the language struggle, and Bjørnson with its triumphs, in part thanks to Ibsen's own plays.

Thus the unhappy story of Henrik Ibsen's contribution to the Norske Teatret. Unfair, of course, but life itself is unfair, praising after the battle not the soldier who fought in the war, but the emperor who held the prize aloft in his hands.

To get a more balanced picture of Ibsen's experiences as a dramatist and a theatre professional in Bergen and Christiania we need to look more closely at the conditions and prejudices he was faced with at the time. In one sense he was in a privileged position. Seven of the nine plays he had written up until 1863 were performed onstage. This in itself gave him a chance to experiment that few other contemporary Norwegian dramatists enjoyed. In the main his plays received positive reviews, and whereas other dramatists might suddenly produce a box-office hit, Ibsen's writing was seen as a process of steady development. So for literary historians to depict Ibsen the *dramatist* as ignored or rejected in Norway is somewhat misleading. The most difficult problem Ibsen faced during these years, both as dramatist and producer, remained the structural limitations surrounding culture in Norway as a whole. Ibsen must have wished for a generally higher standard of repertoire, of audience, and of criticism. But in all these departments the traditions in Norway were in their infancy, and the kind of theatre Ibsen wanted to see lay some years ahead. Ibsen himself must have understood this. The question is, how much comfort could he derive from such an understanding? The 1850s and 1860s were a period characterised by fumbling and struggling as Norwegian theatre sought to establish and define itself. Everything gained had to be fought for, and it was this perpetual struggle that exhausted him, leaving the gap between what he wanted to achieve and what he was able to achieve a painfully large one.

That another factor may have been his own shortcomings as director and strategist in an institutional setting was perhaps a truth harder to acknowledge.

* * *

The success of *The Pretenders* didn't do much to dispel the dark clouds that lay over Ibsen's mind. Henrik Ibsen was not happy in Norway, and certainly not in Christiania. He was not a happy grass widower as he trudged the freezing streets of Christiania that winter, and in his thoughts he must already have been with Suzannah and Sigurd in what might turn out to be a better life under southern skies.

One evening Ludvig Daae met him walking in the street. Daae, who just a couple of years earlier had refused to believe the rumours of Ibsen's personal decline, now saw the truth of them with his own eyes.

'He looks pretty far gone; tattered coat, tattered hat, and his face almost copper-coloured,' he wrote in his journal. 'It could be just that I caught him on the wrong day, but it upset me.'

Daae was still fond of Ibsen and listened willingly enough to the writer's overwrought claims of plots and deceptions in Norwegian political life. His contempt for Norwegian public life rose like an intoxication – 'but yes, yes, of course, this is Norway, birthplace of giants'. After taking leave of Ibsen, Daae ran into Søren Jaabæk, a prominent figure in the Farmers' Party, of whom he drily noted: 'No worries about poetry in his company.' Poetry at least was something you could count on Ibsen for.

During Ibsen's final few months in Norway it seems almost as though a groundswell of sympathy for him as a man arose. Regardless of what one made of his plays, his talent was generally recognised. Bernhard Dunker is one example. Although he found much in *The Pretenders* that was 'very attractive and good', as much of it again was 'tasteless and unfinished'. In general the most powerful man in the world of Norwegian theatre never did become an uncritical admirer of Ibsen's plays – he didn't like *Brand* (it was philosophy, not poetry!), nor yet *Peer Gynt* (an abortion!), and on reading *The League of Youth* in 1869 he found himself wondering what on earth the dramatist was playing at.

But Ibsen he liked.

Dunker has been described in rather Dickensian terms as a man with 'a nicely shaped head' and a 'dreadful body'. He was widely known and widely disliked for his biting wit, and though he was highly respected as a lawyer and a cultural authority, there was 'something cold, piercing and reptilian about his eyes that, with his slim body and damp handshake, reminded one inescapably of a boa constrictor on legs'.

This two-legged snake was, by all accounts, someone for whom Ibsen had a taste. More importantly, he was someone without whose help he simply would not have been able to leave the country and create a new life for himself as a writer abroad. In the spring of 1864 Dunker and Bjørnson took the initiative for a collection intended to raise money that would supplement the travel grant, which was clearly insufficient. Indeed, Ibsen had already begun to make inroads into it by October, long before his departure. The collection raised the large sum of 700 spesidaler. The names of most of the contributors are unknown, although it seems certain Johan Sverdrup was among them. But with such a large sum the list of donors must have been long.[33]

In the period before a long journey begins it seems often as though the bonds to what one is about to leave start to loosen of their own accord, though the journey itself has not yet started. Among Ibsen's circle of close friends this process had been under way for a long time. 'Holland – ha, the Learned Holland – which is now gone, swallowed up by the tide of time,' Michael Birkeland was complaining to Ludvig Daae as early as November 1861. He had recently been a guest at Paul Botten-Hansen's wedding along with Ibsen and Jakob Løkke. They sat silent and melancholy throughout what was supposed to be a joyous occasion, for they were in no doubt as to who was responsible for the sad fate of the Holland.

'I am very afraid,' Birkeland continues, 'that Fru Hansen has sworn the death of the Holland and all the Hollanders; but I think she will find herself disappointed in the end. Transplanting a tree into new soil is never an easy business.'

Birkeland is not the first to have bemoaned the deadly effect of marriage, not to speak of the husband's ability to thrive as a potted plant. But in point of fact Paul Botten-Hansen was the last of the group's young bachelors. By the end of the 1850s Løkke, Ibsen and Daae had all married. Birkeland himself was engaged to be married just a year before Botten-Hansen and would shortly be a father of three. But all these engagements and marriages are hardly enough to explain the demise of the Holland. What really happened was that the generation of 1848 finally got the chance to start families and careers of their own within the university and the government bureaucracy. One by one they found their niche in life, though not Bjørnson. He created his own niche, becoming almost an institution in his own right. Vinje was another exception. He continued to live the life of a bachelor and an outsider within the alternative wing of Norwegian nationalist thought that would eventually become part of the broad Left coalition (though Vinje would be gone before that came about).

What of Henrik Ibsen?

To understand Ibsen's position and his prospects within Norwegian society it is useful to compare them with those whose situation most closely resembled his. What niche could he occupy or hope to create in the Norway of the 1860s? He had no future in either the university or the state bureaucracy. On a couple of occasions friends had tried to help him find a post, and he himself submitted an application for employment as a Fellow in Nordic Literature. But instead he gambled everything on his writing, obliging him to create his own future in the world of books and the theatre, sponsored by the state in the form of grants and, hopefully, at some point, the award of an annual state grant. But life as a full-time writer was difficult in Norway. A man who wanted to write was obliged to practise a literary rotation in which his own real work as a writer had to give way at times to journalism, lecturing, some magazine editing, some peripheral connection to an institution such as the university, the theatre, or the state bureaucracy, as well as involvement in the political arena.

Such was the career trajectory of the Norwegian literary citizen. Bjørnson followed it to perfection, Ibsen did not. He did not possess the personal qualities necessary to create his own space in Norway, a lack that may be ascribed to a curious form of social incompetence as well as his own artistic and intellectual individuality. Ibsen wanted to be a writer. Nothing else. Perhaps he had no choice. Neither his personality, his social skills nor his literary make-up marked him out as a builder of institutions. And even though Bjørnson could be controversial, he was undoubtedly the more gifted theatre man of the two. Ibsen hated anything that smacked of politics, he was no rabble-rouser, and he disliked journalism. In the thirteen years that had passed since his debut he had been obliged to turn his hand to all sorts of other things besides writing; but as soon as the opportunity arose, he abandoned them all to pursue his career as a writer. He must have been painfully aware of the choice that faced him during his last years in Christiania; and it must have been as clear to all those friends and colleagues who wanted to help him leave the country, who wanted to see him awarded a travel grant, or an annual literary wage – for his own sake, and for the sake of literature.

* * *

On 30 March 1864, as the hour of his departure approached, Ibsen and his friends gathered at the Hotel du Nord. The occasion was both his own farewell party, and to congratulate Paul Botten-Hansen, who earlier that month had been appointed university librarian. This was the last time the Learned Holland met, and the last time Ibsen would see his friend Botten-Hansen. Five years later he would die of pneumonia. At the party Botten-Hansen's friends presented him with a small present, a bound copy of a letter he had sent to his schoolteacher at the age of six, his first literary effort. Paul never did become a writer. Instead he made them.

But it wasn't just Ibsen's friends who made a fuss of him as he was about to leave. Nandrup knew of his plans too, and it seemed to him that now was the time to demand the final repayment of his debts.

Ibsen must have been desperate to get away before the lawyer made his move. Ice prevented any sailings from the Oslo fjord until Friday 1 April, when Ibsen was at last able to board the steamship *Vidar* that took him up to Drøbak, where the postal steamer *Krondprindsesse Louise* lay waiting. Early next morning he was on his way to Copenhagen to be reunited with his family. Just before he left, Nandrup presented his claims for repayment to Dunker, who was in charge of the money raised the previous winter. But of course there was nothing to be had from Dunker – the money was to enable Ibsen to write, not to pay off his creditors!

With that Nandrup finally put the confiscated property up for auction on 2 June 1864, by which time Henrik, Suzannah and Sigurd had already begun their new life in Rome. The axe had fallen, but the prisoner had escaped. Henrik Ibsen was free. He had a substantial sum of money at his disposal, but most of his earthly possessions were gone.

All he owned now was the future.

VI

ROME

OVER THE DYBBØL RAMPARTS

At a dinner at the home of the Russian envoy in London in 1862 a Prussian lieutenant gave a speech that caused no little amusement among the politicians and diplomats present. The lieutenant had been the Prussian emissary from the union of German states for the past eight years and had come to a realisation that he was now immodest enough to share the following with the gathering:

'I will very shortly be obliged to take over as leader of the Prussian government,' he announced. 'Following that I will at the first opportunity declare war on Austria, dismantle the German union, coerce the smaller states and provide Germany with a national unity under the leadership of Prussia.'

One among the guests did not smile at the lieutenant's cocky boast. The British politician Benjamin Disraeli understood that he was perfectly serious. And sure enough: three months later Lieutenant Otto von Bismarck-Schonhausen took over as Prussian minister-president (prime minister) and foreign secretary. Before the end of 1863 he was preparing to take the first step towards a unification of Germany under his leadership that would turn Germany into a major European power.

And that first step involved the Danish-German duchies of Holstein, Lauenburg and Schleswig, which Denmark had defended against separatist rebels and Prussian forces in the first Schleswig war of 1848–51.

When the Danish king Frederik VII died on 15 November 1863 the threat against his country had been building for some time. In December, Prussian troops entered Holstein. An invasion of Schleswig followed. The humiliating defeats of the previous war were to be avenged. It was a one-sided affair in every respect. The great powers had formerly been a barrier to Prussian expansion, but now England, France and Russia washed their hands of the whole business, and the Austrians allowed themselves to be tempted into an alliance, little suspecting that Bismarck's next step would be against them. In Sweden, in the summer of 1863, the king, Carl XV, had promised to support the Danes, but at the last moment the Swedish-Norwegian union decided not to get involved in their 'brother's' war. Militarily, Prussia was now considerably stronger than it had been during the previous confrontation, and German militarism had raised the art of war to the level of a science. Their discipline was ruthless, their equipment modern, and conscription for all had been introduced. A Danish army of only 35,000 faced a better-equipped Prussian-Austrian army that numbered 56,000.

As 1863 came to a close the threat of war hung heavy over Denmark and Denmark's friends in the Scandinavian lands. A rally in support of Denmark was held in the Students' Union in Christiania on 12 December. The following day a poem appeared in the *Illustreret Nyhedsblad* entitled 'A Brother in Need':

> There musters now on Tyraís lines,
> This time, perhaps, the last, –
> A folk beset, a folk that pines,
> Its banner at half-mast.
> Betrayed in dire predicament,
> Betrayed when battle-clad!
> Was this then what the hand clasp meant
> That boded well for Nordic consent
> At Lund and Axelstad?

Henrik Ibsen had not been present at the rallies of Scandinavian students held in Copenhagen (Axelstad) and Lund, only at the one in Christiania back in 1851. But just as Scandinavianism had inspired the passionate verse of his early manhood, so did it return as a source of inspiration on the eve of his departure – but in inverted form. In his youth he had entered Norwegian literary life on a wave of enthusiasm for the Scandinavian cause. Now, while still waiting for the premiere of *The Pretenders* at the Christiania Theatre in January 1865, and just a few months before he was to leave his homeland and embark on the great journey out into Europe, that enthusiasm was replaced by bitterness.

As the autumn of 1863 advanced it became clear that the Danes would not be able to count on any help from the Norwegians and the Swedes. Both Carl XV and his Foreign Minister, Count Manderström, had spoken out about Sweden's obligation to offer support – and thus encouraged Danish hopes; but powerful forces at work in both countries had opposed the idea and effectively tied the king's hands.

Ibsen did not hide his disappointment:

> It was a lie in terms ornate,
> A Judas-kiss, we found,
> When Norway's sons rejoiced of late
> Beside the Danish Sound!

In its original form the poem was longer and coarser. Among other things, Ibsen compared the Norwegian flag to a cholera flag. It seems likely that the editor, Paul Botten-Hansen, had advised him to tone it down somewhat – there was enough dynamite in it as things stood. Just a few years earlier, Ibsen had attacked the Danes in his poem 'Seagull's Cry' during the days of the Norwegian Society; now it was the turn of the Norwegians to suffer a verbal lashing. It was quite a turnaround. Just as Ibsen was about to win the hearts and minds of the Norwegians with *The Pretenders*, probably the most ambitious of all Norwegian national-historical dramas, he began to rage against the inadequacy of his fellow countrymen, cursing them for their betrayal of Denmark.

And there was worse to come.

As late as the winter of 1864, Carl XV was still entertaining a faint hope that the Norwegian Storting would allocate funds for military action, even though his own government had said no. But before the matter had even been debated in the Storting, war had broken out. On 16 January the Prussians delivered an ultimatum, and at the end of the month German troops crossed the Eider and invaded Schleswig. The Norwegian Storting was now Denmark's only hope of support. At a vote on 29 March there was actually a majority to finance military action, but on condition that it would be part of a large alliance of Britain and France, the great powers in the West. Since this was obviously out of the question, the resolution only confirmed that Denmark was now completely isolated. It was a mortal blow to the idea of a Nordic union. Nothing that might later be said or written about the dream could obscure the fact that Denmark had been left to fend for itself against the Prussian army in a battle it was doomed to lose.

On Saturday 2 April 1864, the day after Ibsen left the country, a young student of theology named Christopher Bruun went up to the speaker's rostrum in the Students' Union and condemned his fellow students for their failure to volunteer to fight. His words fell on deaf ears. The fact that so few volunteers joined in the struggle was yet another blow to Scandinavian solidarity.

But Christopher Bruun at least knew where his duty lay; along with a small band of fellow Norwegians he travelled to Denmark, armed and ready to fight.

* * *

And Ibsen travelled too. Not to the war zone, but to join Suzannah and Sigurd who were waiting for him at the home of his mother-in-law Magdalene Thoresen in Copenhagen. In the course of the few days he spent in the city he met Clemens Petersen, whose opinion had meant so much to him when he wrote *Love's Comedy* and *The Pretenders*. They talked together of literature, but the chemistry between them was lacking. Petersen, who loved Bjørnson's passionate temperament, found himself almost depressed in Ibsen's presence –

'I saw a quiet, level-headed and sensible man,' he later told Bjørnson, 'but I saw too that he wore his visor down.'

On 17 April, Ibsen writes home to Bernhard Dunker to thank the lawyer for the money that has been forwarded to him. He doesn't mention the war, but that same day – just a few days before his onward journey takes him to Germany – the fighting around Dybbøl on Jutland intensifies. The beleaguered Danish army was in an untenable position. Practically the entire Danish defensive line came under fire from German artillery, and it became clear that the end could not be far off. It comes on the following day. From first light the thundering of German canon fire rages over the Danish fortifications. Officers and men are killed or wounded. On the morning of 18 April, Prussian troops storm the Danish lines, annihilating every attempt at resistance. Dybbøl was lost, and with it any hope Denmark had of stemming the Prussian tide that was about to wash over the country.

Before the smoke of battle had cleared, and while Danish troops were still retreating to continue the losing battle from defences further inland, Henrik Ibsen travelled to Lübeck, and from there to Berlin. Suzannah and Sigurd remained behind in the Danish capital; the plan was for them to join him in the autumn. Once in the Prussian capital he tried to concentrate as best he could on the cultural experiences on offer, this being, after all, the overt purpose of his trip. He visited the city's museums, its theatres and art galleries. But art could not block out the brutal realities of the world. Towards the end of April he witnessed the parade of victorious German troops through the streets of Berlin, where he saw 'a baying mob wallowing in trophies from Dybbøl, riding astride the gun carriages and spitting into canons, those canons that had received no help and yet had carried on firing until they exploded'.

He needed to get away – to preserve his sanity.

In Berlin he decided on another route. His original intention had been to travel on through France to his destination in Italy. Now it occurred to him that it would make more sense to 'begin at the beginning and trace the historical progress of culture and art through the centuries'. In other words he would head straight for Rome, the capital city of antiquity. His journey took him through Prague and Vienna, then through the mountains and tunnels of the Alps. The mountains seemed to him almost like Purgatory, a transition from the cold dark north to the warm, bright south. The landscape and the light of southern Europe almost literally took his breath away; here was a place where creativity might thrive. After the descent from the mountains his journey took him through Trieste and then on to Venice, where he made a start at learning the language. After six weeks he arrived in Milan, and on the morning of Sunday 19 June he finally reached his destination, Rome, the Eternal City.

THE SCANDINAVIAN

On the day he arrived in Rome, Ibsen at once called on Johan Bravo, consul for the three Scandinavian countries. Bravo was from a Jewish family, raised in Holstein, and was described as 'not a particularly brilliant person, but somewhat comical, and rather touching'. He was a principal member of the city's Scandinavian community, and often the one who introduced newcomers to the city and the community.

Bravo didn't waste any time; he at once took Ibsen down to the premises of the Scandinavian Society and rang the bell.

'Chi è?' cried a voice from within.

'Open up! I have a good friend here to see you!' replied Bravo in his unique brand of broken Dano-German.

'But my dear Herr Consul,' the voice went on, 'I am completely stark naked!'

'God-Devil, just open up, we're all men here!'

This spirited oath did the trick, the door was opened, and there, stark naked, stood one of Ibsen's old friends from his first period in Christiania. Lorentz Dietrichson was a native of Bergen and a childhood friend of Suzannah's. He had been in Rome since 1862, earning his living doing secretarial work at the consulate and as librarian at the Scandinavian Society, where his living quarters were. He was also an unpaid associate professor of literature at Uppsala University. But his main interest was in art; many years later he would become the first holder of a chair in the History of Art in the Nordic Countries. He was in Rome to study classical art, and became an important teacher in this field to Ibsen. That same day he took Ibsen on a tour of the city, and later on in the evening they crossed the Tiber to enjoy the small bars and cafes of Trastevere. They settled in one, a so-called *osteri* within a garden that overlooked the river, enjoying the view and their carafe of Italian wine beneath the vine leaves on that mild Roman evening.

Dietrichson sat there studying Ibsen and wondering: was it just their good mood, or had the bitter and introverted poet he recalled from Christiania changed since the last time they had met? Yes, he had changed. Dietrichson noted how Ibsen could now laugh at the memory of the controversies over *Love's Comedy*, and how he openly expressed his pleasure at the success of *The Pretenders* at the Christiania Theatre. Yet he was unable to hide his anger at what he had seen during the victory parade in Berlin, and at how Norway and Sweden had failed to come to the assistance of their Danish brothers. A few days later Ibsen and Dietrichson along with several other Scandinavians visited an *osteri* called Raffaels Vigne, outside the city. It was a while since he had been in the company of other Scandinavians, and now he gave free rein to his reactions to what he had seen in Berlin. Ibsen began talking about his journey south. Bitter and impassioned, he railed against the betrayal of the Danes and expressed his fervent support for the Nordic cause. 'That afternoon,' writes Dietrichson, 'I think the few of us gathered there in the Roman night felt we were hearing the sound of the Nordic Marseillaise.'

The Nordic Marseillaise, no less. What really happened to Ibsen on his journey from Christiania to Rome?

What was it about the fall of Dybbøl that pained him so deeply?

No other political event ever moved Ibsen as profoundly. During his first years in Rome that Danish defeat became almost an obsession. The obsession can be related partly to his view of life, partly to his own psychic make-up, and partly to his unfolding development as a writer. At the 'view of life' level, the Danish defeat was a blow to one of the most exalted ideals of the age: Scandinavianism, the idea that the three Nordic nations belong together despite a history of vacillating commitment, passionate disagreements, and deep-seated opposition. Precisely because it was so far removed from the world of realpolitik and was largely the passion of idealistic and naïve students, it had retained an attractive and almost virginal purity. And for someone like Ibsen, who detested the smallness and trivialities of realpolitik, this was a quality that exerted an immense appeal.

But now that virginity had been taken. Dybbøl marked the end of the Scandinavian dream. Inevitably it affected his nationalism. All along this had been tied to Scandinavianism, which in turn was a pointer towards mainstream European culture. He had little sympathy for the isolationist and self-sufficient form of Norwegian nationalism, and especially now that it had become so politicised and bound up with issues such as democratisation, the language question, and hostility towards the union. So the essential meaning of the concept of nationalism gradually changed for Ibsen, though it would be some time before the change would be reflected in his writing.

But the pain of Dybbøl also had deeper repercussions.

Dybbøl elicited a highly personal and psychological resonance in Ibsen's ambivalent attitude towards his home country, a compound of fear and bitterness, reminding him of the humiliating years in Christiania, the poverty, the burden of his debts. That his career as a dramatist and man of the theatre had by no means been all bad, and that his troubles as a theatre manager owed something at least to his own personal failings as a leader, did nothing to soften his conviction that he had been rejected by Norway. In the years that followed he would return time and time again to his country's betrayal, even after he was granted an annual writer's wage. His own country's betrayal of Denmark was the catalyst for this reckoning with Norway, this potent brew of measured cultural criticism and rage at the indignities and humiliations, real and imagined, he had experienced at the hands of his own countrymen.

Everything came to a head with Dybbøl.

There are threads leading from this psychological motive that pertain to Ibsen's self-image as an artist, threads that touch on important themes in his writing. One was the tension between action and ideal that he had already broached in his earliest writing, reinforced now by the Kierkegaardian demand to 'be present in life', in which the choice was between a stark 'Either' and 'Or'. Had Ibsen been present at the Students' Union when Christopher Bruun appealed for volunteers for the Danish cause, these tensions would have been even clearer to him. 'When a person abandons his ideal he dies a spiritual death', Bruun had said. Bruun preferred to risk death on the battlefield in the cause of an ideal rather than risk a spiritual death, and Ibsen must have admired his stance. But more significant was the blow Dybbøl dealt to what had been Ibsen's literary enterprise thus far – the pursuit of national romanticism. Once he had lost his faith in the people, it became, in the long run, impossible for him to sustain ideas about a 'spirit of the people' or a 'national collective'. During the course of his stay in Rome he would carry out a ferocious re-examination of that whole nation-building project of which he had once been such a devout adherent.

Dybbøl also had a material effect on Ibsen's literary development at that particular time. It had long been evident to him that his ambitions as a writer required a breakthrough in Denmark – not just in terms of his sales potential in Denmark and Sweden, but as a prerequisite to wider acceptance in Norway.

SUMMER IN GENZANO

At the end of June, Ibsen travelled to Genzano, a country town in the Alban Hills a few miles outside Rome. This was part of the annual life cycle of Scandinavians in Rome, leaving the city at the hottest time of the year not solely to escape the heat but to avoid the risk of disease. Genzano was one of those small, romantic mountain villages so popular among northern Europeans, surrounded by vineyards, olive groves and chestnut and walnut trees that grew along the slopes of what was actually a volcanic crater that reached down to the clear waters of Lake Nemi. Ibsen formed a threesome with the Finnish sculptor Walter Runeberg and Lorenz Dietrichson. These two, along with several others, were Ibsen's company during his first summer in Italy.

One day was very much like the next. Ibsen shared a room with Runeberg. Every morning, while the Finn went out to shop, Ibsen would brew the coffee. Later in the morning Runeberg would disappear into town to sculpt and Ibsen would sit down to write. They ate their evening meal in a rather lugubrious cafe that would regularly be plunged into deepest darkness each time the resident donkey positioned itself in front of the cafe's single small window opening to scratch its behind against the wall. It really was time now for Ibsen to be getting on with work. The winter before his departure from Norway he had been toying with the idea of writing a new historical drama based on the life of the Norwegian-Faroese rebel Magnus Heinesson, who was executed in 1589. He managed to gather some material before leaving the country, but we don't know whether he actually made a start on the work. But this project was certainly his preoccupation while in Copenhagen, and his intention was presumably to continue work on it in Italy.

It shouldn't really surprise us that Ibsen once again showed a fascination for a historical rebel, or that the success of *The Pretenders* should have tempted him to consider writing yet another national-historical drama. But that summer in Genzano had the effect of putting Ibsen on the track of a very different historical subject, and the buccaneering Heinesson was soon forgotten. One afternoon, as several friends were sitting reading and talking on the shady hillside that sloped down to Lake Nemi, Ibsen and Dietrichson fell into conversation about Julian the Apostate, the Roman emperor – Dietrichson happened to be reading a book about Julian's military campaigns. Ibsen was fascinated and remarked that he hoped no one else would make use of the theme before he did. For much of the next ten years he would be preoccupied with the life of the apostate emperor before he was finally able to give the material dramatic form.

And the way he saw it, he would then have written his dramatic masterpiece.

So the Genzano days passed in work, reading, talking, eating and drinking wine in the company of good friends in idyllic surroundings. Among the other Scandinavians living in the town were Lina Bruun and her children Peter and Thea. It seems that both Ibsen the grass widower and Runeberg, who was engaged to be married, developed a violent crush on young Thea, said to have been the model for Agnes in *Brand*, just as her older brother Christopher, who was at the time fighting for the Danes against the Prussians, is one of several suggested models for Brand himself. Lina Bruun did not like Ibsen. He aroused 'bad feelings' in her; she didn't enjoy the way he railed against his own country. Anxiously awaiting the safe return of her son from the war, she let the loud-mouthed, bibulous poet know exactly what she thought of him as she stoutly came to the defence of Norway and Norwegians. In a hopeless attempt to comfort her, Ibsen promised that if her son should fall in battle he would erect a monument to his memory that would put the Norwegian people to shame. Lina's response was that, if he did so, she would bury it with her own hands – she would not tolerate her son's honour being used to shame Norway.

No, Ibsen got on the wrong side of Lina Bruun. But in time she mellowed, as did so many others, in their respect for the enigmatic poet: 'A double-nature such as that is not easy to fathom,' she wrote later. One moment friendly and open, the next 'a malicious glint flashing in his eyes'. An unconfirmed anecdote relates that when Christopher Bruun was reunited with his family in Rome that autumn, he too noted Ibsen's expressed contempt for the way his countrymen had let the Danes down. In that case, Bruun calmly enquired, why had he not volunteered to join the fighting himself? Ibsen had never been particularly courageous in a physical sense, and there is nothing to suggest that such an idea had ever occurred to him. He is said to have responded by telling Bruun that 'we writers have other obligations'.

Did it hurt? Certainly it must have done so at the time. But what is equally certain is that Ibsen never felt any shame about the writer's 'other obligations'. He was not shamed by the pen, just as Christopher Bruun was not shamed by the sword.

DREAMLAND

In September, Ibsen and the other Scandinavians returned to Rome to resume their winter lives. Here he was reunited with Suzannah and Sigurd, now five years old, at the end of their long journey from Copenhagen. It had been almost six months since the couple had last seen each other. A look, a kiss. Not too many words exchanged. The family rented an apartment on the corner of Via dei Due Macelli and Via Capo le Case, in the centre of the 'foreign quarter' around the Spanish Steps. From here it wasn't far to the Caffè degli Artisti and the premises of the Scandinavian Society. And it was around here, in the society's premises, and in the nearby cafes and bars, that most of his life in Rome would revolve.

The Scandinavian community in Rome was in every respect a community of exiles.[1] The Danes were traditionally the dominant group, and the legacy of the years of the great Danish sculptor Bertel Thorvaldsen was still palpable in Ibsen's time. For decades he had been the focal point of the community, a far more charismatic figure than the worthy Johan Bravo. In the main the Scandinavians kept themselves to themselves, inhabiting a Scandinavian world in miniature.

'If Scandinavianism is just a dream back home, out here it is very much a reality', was the contented assertion of the Swedish art historian Carl Nyblom in 1864.

In fact, it was Rome that was the dream.

Rome was a place and a way of life beyond the world, a place in which art, architecture, nature, life itself could be cultivated untrammelled by the din of the world. In the 1860s Rome was as yet untouched by the modernisation that was going on throughout the rest of Europe. There were no dirty factories here, no workers crowded together in tenement slums coated in soot. The exception was the railway, which ran from Frascati in 1856 and three years later from the port town of Civitavecchia. Apart from that, economic stagnation had left Rome looking pretty much as it had looked in the Baroque age, still clustered on the banks of the Tiber. The city wall of ancient Rome lay far from the centre, and between the town and the wall lay the picturesque Campagna, unspoilt countryside only disturbed by the herdsmen with their cattle, the occasional church, and Roman ruins overgrown with moss and ivy. On the horizon: the blue outlines of the Alban Hills. Rome was a peasant society in which ostentatious Renaissance villas bore witness to the old feudal order, while the lavishly ornamented churches announced the city as the centre of the Catholic world. And beneath it all, quite literally, lay history – all those reminders of the former greatness of the Roman empire.

The political constellations made their own contribution to the maintenance of this unique world. The unification of Italy had been proclaimed by 1861, but the Vatican State and Rome, with the backing of the French emperor Napoleon III, had opted to stay independent. Within the city Pius IX reigned, by the grace of God – or probably more accurately, the grace of the emperor. The pope's governance emphasised the contrasts to the modernisation going on outside the tiny state; in 1864 he published the *Syllabus errorum*, a list of the errors of the modern world in which he mounted an all-out attack on liberal and liberalising ideals of freedom such as socialism and communism.

A frozen moment in Rome, a torrent of ideas and events flooding by outside. It could only be a matter of time before it came to an end. For the moment the French guaranteed the city's freedom, but Italian nationalists were clamouring for change. Inspired by heroes of the unification such as Giuseppe Garibaldi and Giuseppe Mazzini, pressure was increasing to take Rome by force and make the city the capital of a united Italy.

Rome was a dream, an eternal moment in the onward rush of history.

And in the same way Rome was outside the world, the Scandinavians living there could feel that they were living outside their own lives. In most respects they were tourists who had come to savour and to admire. They paid a nocturnal visit to the Vatican's collection of sculpture in order to heighten the romantic atmosphere of it all. But in such surroundings, was it really possible to exercise artistic freedom and find genuine creative growth? Ibsen was convinced it was, at least to begin with: 'As yet I still haven't seen much of Rome,' he writes to Bernhard Dunker shortly after his arrival, 'but have the strongest feeling that one can live and work here in an atmosphere of spiritual freedom that is perhaps unparalleled anywhere else in the world.'

So freedom there was – but how was it used? For some, the Roman experience led to an impoverishment rather than an enrichment of their talent, and what they produced was closer to kitsch than art. And naturally, the residents knew how to make the most of this romantic infatuation; handsome young boys and pretty young girls, the very old and the very young who corresponded to the visitors' ideas of Italian street-life, displayed themselves daily on the Spanish Steps. It was here that painters came to find their Madonna, their Saint Sebastian or their 'Italian brigand' who became a feature of innumerable paintings. It wasn't always easy to see any direct connection between these and what was happening in the art world in the rest of Europe. And how much did these Scandinavians actually see of the real lives of the inhabitants of Rome? Who spared a thought for the victims of the Italian brigand? Who wrote letters home on the subject of the dreadful poverty, the appalling sanitary arrangements, the despotic nature of papal rule?

For many Scandinavians with naturally liberal views, this blindness must have been part of the price they paid for their Roman dream: no matter how much they praised the Italian freedom-fighters, or what they really thought of the pope's reactionary autocracy, it was Garibaldi who was the threat, and Pius IX the protector of the dream they were living.

At the same time, Rome was more than merely a romantic utopia. The city boasted a unique collection of artworks from the ancient world, the Renaissance and the Baroque. Michelangelo, Bernini, Raphael – all of these could be admired and enjoyed in the city's churches and galleries. The same was true of architecture. In the autumn of 1864 Dietrichson gave a series of lectures on ancient Rome, arranged as walking tours of the city's historic sites. Ibsen took part in these. This was at a time when archaeologists were beginning to uncover new treasures from the Roman past on an almost daily basis and the Scandinavians must have been hugely impressed with what they saw. The excavation of the Forum Romanum had been started but still had a long way to go. Livestock continued to graze between the marble pillars in these idyllic settings. Traces of ancient Rome were everywhere to be seen in the city, not restored and cossetted but overgrown with moss, crumbled by wind and weather, conjured forth from dream and oblivion – Caracalla's hot springs, Minerva Medica's temple, and those enormous constructions that could still impress across the centuries – the Colosseum, the Pantheon, the Mausoleum of Augustus.

It was all there, for anyone able to see it.

To appreciate fully the power of the Roman experience it is important to remember that people of Ibsen's generation had grown up in an intimate relationship with Europe's classical heritage. And while classical philology and a classical education in Norway were gradually giving way to a more modern education, the ancient world was still one of the pillars of academic life; that much we can see from the Latin syllabus in the textbooks of Ibsen's schooldays. Moreover, he and Bjørnson had both studied Latin under Henrik Heltberg, and a Latin education enjoyed high status among the members of the Learned

Holland. Overall, we might now find the overwhelming force of Ibsen's encounter with Italy hard to comprehend. His close proximity to the classical heritage sheds light both on the apocalyptic nature of Ibsen's response after crossing the Alps and the enormous joy he took in exploring the art world of Rome in the company of Dietrichson.

But great expectations always risk great disappointment. In September he writes to Bjørnson:

> Thank you so much for all the beauty I have imbibed on my journey, it has been so good for me, I can assure you. Here in Rome I have reached a lot of new understandings, though I still haven't developed a taste for antiquity . . .

Bjørnson was not worried. He was convinced that in due course his friend would be able to see 'the individual behind the artistic law'; Ibsen just had to be patient. The enthusiastic tone of Ibsen's letter to Bjørnson is that of the newly converted, but Bjørnson too had struggled when he came to Rome just before Christmas in 1860. Rome was not a confirmation of already established attitudes but a genuine voyage of discovery that forced both men to reconsider and revise their aesthetic points of view and formulate new ones. Perhaps their different responses to the ancient world can be explained by how it contrasted with their opposing psychological needs: whereas the extroverted and spontaneous Bjørnson was attracted to the balance and harmony he found in antiquity, the inhibited and secretive Ibsen found his artistic and emotional release in the individualising expressivity of the Renaissance and the excesses of the Baroque.[2] It's a tempting thought; but the reality is, as usual, more complicated. In time Bjørnson would come to an appreciation of Michelangelo, and in due course Ibsen too was able to see the beauties in antiquity – though perhaps not in quite the way Bjørnson had imagined:

'Increasingly I am able to see the beauty in the sculptures of antiquity, just as you suggested I would in your letter,' he writes to Bjørnson early in 1865. Among the sources of his new-found appreciation was *The Tragic Muse*, one of the nine sculptures from the emperor Hadrian's villa in Tivoli:

> . . . the indescribably exalted, great and contained joy in the expression on the face, the richly garlanded head over which there is something almost supernaturally dizzying and bacchanalian, the eyes, that seem at once to look both inward and yet to penetrate the far distances upon which they are actually focused – that, to me, is Greek tragedy.

Ibsen studied art in search of lessons that could be applied to his own writing. It was typical of him to use the statues of classical antiquity to interpret Greek tragedy. And his understanding of the muse of tragedy points ahead to central features of his own tragedies – the dramatic tension between the harmonious Apollonian and the disruptive Dionysian, the contrast between a person's civilised exterior and his volcanic interior, conveyed via an artistic perspective that looks both within a person and out from that person.

The trouble he initially experienced in appreciating the art of antiquity arose partly because Ibsen found himself unable to see the hand of an original and unique artist behind the work. Michelangelo was another matter – 'in my opinion no one has transgressed more against the laws of beauty than he,' he wrote to Georg Brandes some years later. 'And yet everything he created is beautiful anyway; this is because it shows character.' After seeing Raphael's *Sistine Madonna* in Dresden in 1852, he had written the poem 'In the Picture Gallery'. At that time he was still preoccupied by the aesthetics of idealism, in which a work of art was judged according to the rules of spirituality or beauty it represented. Now he dismisses Raphael – 'his people belong to the time before the Fall'. Michelangelo had no business in Paradise, and neither did Henrik Ibsen.

Ibsen's encounter with the art of antiquity and the Renaissance marked a watershed in his life. Echoes from the Italian art world sound throughout a number of his plays, such as the attraction to the hedonistic world 'with vine leaves in its hair' of plays such as *Ghosts* and *Hedda Gabler* and, of course, in *Emperor and Galilean*. But the art had a liberating effect on him in a more fundamental sense as well. His experience of the Apollonian and the Dionysian in 'The Muse of Tragedy', that tension between inside and outside that he believed he read in the eyes of the muse, goes some way to explaining the structure of his later dramas.[3] And whereas formerly he had tried to write within the conventions of particular genres and specific aesthetic demands, he now actively worked at the transgressional art of breaking these same laws. Ibsen had gone from Heiberg's formalism to a cultivation of precisely those 'sins' that Michelangelo had committed against the classical ideals of the Renaissance and for which he loved him so much. Michelangelo pointed the way forward, away from the universal and inwards towards the individual, something Kierkegaard had also done. Together these influences would combine to bring Ibsen's writing to the decisive turning point that now lay before him.

Intellectual impulses are not enough to create masterpieces; that is the achievement of the hard-working poet alone. But the pleasures and distractions of life at the Scandinavian Society through that autumn of 1864 meant that Ibsen was not yet able to give these new ideas artistic form.

IL CAPPELLONE

Scandinavian artists, writers and scientists had been attracted to Rome since the late 1700s, but the Scandinavian Society was of relatively recent date.

The enterprise developed when libraries of books in Danish, Swedish and Norwegian originally kept at Johan Bravo's house were moved in 1860 to a new location in Palazzo Correa, with the rear of the building abutting the ruins of Augustus' mausoleum. Here the Scandinavian community could read newspapers and study books, take part in organised gatherings, attend dinners and lectures. The society was a little piece of Scandinavia, and the minutes of its committee meetings and complaints protocol tell a tale of endless suggestions, ideas and debates that attest to the lively involvement of the members.

Ibsen soon enjoyed the company of the Scandinavians spending that winter in Rome – Lorenz Dietrichson and his wife, the painter Mathilde Dietrichson (Norwegian), a Danish barrister named Anton Klubien, the Swedish poet and aristocrat Carl Snoilsky, the sculptors Hans Johnsen Budal and Ole Fladager (Norwegian), Jens Adolf Jerichau (Danish) and Walter Runeberg (Finnish), the painters Lars Hansen, Carl Bloch, Ludvig Abelin Schou and Herman Carl Siegumfeldt (Danes), and the Danish art historian Emil Bloch. Lina Bruun was also there with her daughter Thea and two sons, the theologian Christopher Bruun and the artist Peter Bruun. And there were others.

Ibsen spent his first winter in Rome in this company, and an unforgettable time it would turn out to be, rich in laughter and good conversation. Their most regular haunt was the Tritone, where Ibsen held court at the top of the table wearing the broad-brimmed hat that earned him the nickname 'Il Cappellone' among the locals. He was a little older than most of the others and enjoyed holding forth, whether it was raging on the subject of Dybbøl or urging others to starve to death rather than submit to the material demands of bourgeois life – just as the English poet Thomas Chatterton had done, allegedly swallowing the key to his own door in his desperate hunger rather than abandon his literary calling.

Ibsen reeled off his usual array of paradoxes and exaggerations, just as he had done with the Learned Hollanders. If someone claimed that something was as sure as two and two make four, then he was on his feet in an instant: 'But with the greatest respect, are you so absolutely certain that two and two do make four – even on Jupiter?'

That he quickly found his feet in Rome is evident from the fact that he held several official posts in the Scandinavian Society, an involvement that was hardly typical. In December 1864 he became a member of the 'magazine committee', established at his initiative, with the aim of improving the quality and quantity of the newspapers the society subscribed to. Later he kept the accounts for the library, and in January 1866 he had a seat on the committee for the first time, remaining a member until early 1868. In his activities he revealed an aspect of his personality that has often been commented upon, an extraordinary pedantry in quite trivial matters, combined with an almost fanatical willingness to pursue these matters to their most extreme conclusions. There is undoubtedly a great deal of truth in the observation, but it is important to distinguish between the nature of the various issues. There is often a touch of humour and the parodic behind his involvements, and anyway, when the world is small then small things assume greater importance. This was the case in Rome; for example, the wreath of green leaves around the head of the bust of the Danish composer Niels Ravnkilde occasioned a passionate argument that went on for several years, its history traceable through the pages of the society's Complaints Book. Bjørnson made his position very clear:

'Get rid of that greenery, it stinks!'

Ibsen too was fond of filling the Complaints Book with similar contributions. Among other things he displayed a touching concern for the plaster copy of *The Dancer*, one of Thorvaldsen's sculptures that was on display at the society's premises: 'Suggest that the box of adhesive that has been on the Dancer's pedestal since New Year be removed and discarded.'

Later that year, the dancer was in distress again:

'Suggest that the Dancer's left big toe be restored.'

During his early days in Rome Ibsen was remarkably hostile to Germans, and to Prussians in particular. In February 1865 an extraordinary general meeting of the society was called to discuss Ibsen's suggestion that Germans and German speakers be excluded from the organisation. It was a political gesture in support of Scandinavianism, but Ibsen's hatred of Germans was hardly deep-rooted. He had previously spoken warmly of the Germanic people, and within a few years he would become a resident of Germany himself. During that victory parade through the streets of Berlin it seems he was more upset by the vulgarity of the mob's triumphalism than by the Germans in general. Although he never really understood the Prussian mentality and notion of loyalty to the state, in time he found he could forgive the Germans for Dybbøl.

But he never forgave the Norwegians.

'The political conditions back home,' he writes to Bjørnson in September 1864, 'have distressed me greatly and spoilt many a happy hour for me. It was delusion and dreams after all.' During these years there are many attacks on his own country and his own people. It was enough for him to come across a reference to his home country for him to feel like a madman staring 'at a single, concentrated, hopeless dark spot'.

That was how much Ibsen despised Norway.

Through the winter of 1864–5 his view of the Swedes was scarcely any better. He was undoubtedly a Scandinavianist, but Scandinavians themselves hardly impressed him. One day Snoilsky discovered that someone had disfigured the front page of *Illustreret Tidende* in the society's reading room by drawing a rope around the neck of the Swedish Foreign Minister, Count Manderström. As

Manderström was almost the personification of Sweden's broken promises to Denmark, the thrust of the provocation was obvious. Snoilsky was naturally outraged; not only was he Swedish, he also happened to be Manderström's nephew. The matter was formally discussed. Ibsen admitted his guilt in a most shameless fashion and declared himself willing to buy a second copy of the magazine if he were allowed to keep the original, as a souvenir.

The Norwegians were treated similarly, and not necessarily solely on account of Dybbøl. One day, when Ibsen was discussing the language question with the writer Kristofer Janson, their exchange ended with Ibsen throwing a chair at Janson that he only just managed to duck.

'You bloody Bergener!' roared Ibsen. Suzannah sided with Janson, which did nothing to improve Ibsen's temper – 'Well you would, wouldn't you!' he raged, 'You're from Bergen too!'

It all ended amicably, with the two writers strolling arm in arm over the road to drink a cup of chocolate together. Like the story about the rope drawn around Manderström's neck, and all his outbursts on the subject of how the Danes were betrayed, the episode tells us something about his mood at that time. In a letter to his mother-in-law the following year he wrote: 'Here in Rome I encountered all sorts of disgraceful attitudes among the Scandinavians, but you can bet I gave them a piece of my mind and cleared the air; down here I fear nothing. Back home I was afraid standing in the middle of the crowd and feeling their ugly smiles behind my back.'

For good or ill, Rome had liberated him. He raised his whip and he raised his glass. He was marble and he was granite, unpredictable and zealous, furious and content. He kept hidden from most the fact that he was also sensitive, searching and thoughtful.

One in whom he did confide was Bjørnson.

'YOU WON'T BLOODY WELL DIE'

By this time Bjørnson was living and working as a writer in Christiania, and perhaps it was the great physical distance that facilitated the closeness that now developed between them.

Typically it was a misunderstanding that was the catalyst.

When Ibsen left Norway in the spring of 1864 he had applied to the Christiania Theatre for leave of absence from his post as an advisor. His return seemed highly unlikely, but when Bjørnson was then offered the job of artistic director it seemed clear that this would necessarily involve a rejection of Ibsen. And yet when Bjørnson declined the offer in June, Ibsen was then offered the job in his stead. Ibsen's response has not survived, but a note in the minutes of the committee reveals that he did request that he be allowed to retain the advance of 30 spesidaler for *Love's Comedy* until such time as it could be deducted from the fee for his next play.

The committee rejected his request, which can hardly have heightened Ibsen's desire to return to his former place of work. *Love's Comedy*, his child of sorrow, which had taken such a beating in public, and which the theatre had bought only to change its mind about a production, had left him contractually bound to repay an advance he so desperately needed.

Now they wanted him back – but without abandoning their claim.

By his own account Ibsen rejected the theatre's approach unconditionally. But delays in the post meant that it took some time before the theatre was aware of this, and even longer before Bjørnson knew. Bjørnson, in the meantime, had been worrying that Ibsen would get the job instead of him – because, of course, he did actually want it and was only holding out for an improved offer. A misunderstanding arose, with Bjørnson suspecting that Ibsen – for whom he had done so much – was about to repay him by ruining his chances of securing the position.

When in September 1864 Ibsen resumed the correspondence between them, it was because he had finally learned that Bjørnson saw him as a competitor: on 15 August, Bjørnson had written a letter to Dietrichson, which Dietrichson showed to Ibsen, in which he strongly advised Ibsen against returning to the theatre. One thing was that it would look bad to all those who had contributed money to give him a new start if he returned home so quickly. Another was that his was not currently a popular name in Christiania. Bjørnson offered assurances that *he* certainly did not share this scepticism. Ibsen had a future in the theatre, in Bjørnson's opinion, and he himself was not especially anxious to take up a permanent post at the theatre; he wanted the job only for a time, as an experiment. It would be to their mutual advantage if they approached the theatre together, thus enabling both to exploit their own talents to the full.

And so on. Bjørnson flatters away, and trivialises the level of his ambition. Whether Ibsen was genuinely convinced by this, or whether his feelings of gratitude towards Bjørnson inclined him to give way, the result was that he shouldered all the blame for the misunderstanding. He confesses that he has shown himself unworthy of his friend's faith, and explains his failing as an example of his inability to cultivate warm and close relationships:

> I know that this is a failing of mine, this inability to approach intimately and openly those people whose nature requires such absolute giving . . . I can never bear to reveal myself completely, I feel that if I try to express myself I only ever manage to give a false impression of what I am really like deep inside, the real me, so I prefer not to, and this is why sometimes it seems as though we two have as it were stood observing one another at a distance.

How long had that been brewing? Thank God for pen and paper, and for the great distance that separated Rome and Christiania. Had he not made an almost identical confession back in 1858 to Carl Johan Anker during that mountain walk, when he wrote of feeling as though he were enveloped in a forbidding cold? To Anker too he had made this confession only later, and in the form of a letter.

All his life Ibsen regretted how remiss he was in writing letters. But he wasn't; to the extent to which he was able to express his feelings to friends, it was always in the form of written communications.

Bjørnson found such things much easier:

> How often I miss you, Ibsen! I always do, when I'm apart from you, even back during the days when you were in Bergen and I here – but when we do meet, it doesn't work out. Why is that?

Letters between the two are full of enthusiasm, for each other and for art. But Ibsen's money troubles continued, and slowly but surely these must have soured the pleasures of his new life under the Italian sun. He had left Norway, fleeing his creditors. He had found a new way of life, thought new thoughts and seen new sights – wondrous things. Everything was different, apart from this one thing: he was still living from hand to mouth, from day to day. Poverty was a shadow that followed him, three paces behind. The travel grant and the collection couldn't last forever, and Ibsen saw no option but to borrow from friends.

Once again he enters a spiral of debt. Bjørnson does what he can. He sends 100 spesidaler, and again approaches Secretary of State Riddervold to raise the question of a literary wage for Ibsen – 'I praised you to the skies' – and on his friend's behalf submits an application for another travel grant of 500 spesidaler to enable him to go on living in Rome. This time the application was made to the Royal Norwegian Society of Sciences and Letters in Trondheim, accompanied by a letter in which Bjørnson stressed the unfairness of the fact that Ibsen had not been awarded a writer's wage at the same time as he was. Alas, the application was handed in too late. Bjørnson submitted it again, and the following spring Ibsen was awarded a grant, although only of 100 spesidaler, and not at a time when he was most in need of it. Ibsen, meanwhile, had hoped to take over as librarian at the Scandinavian Society after Dietrichson left Rome early in 1865, but nothing came of it.

Back home, Bjørnson was still wracking his brains for ways to help. What if the Christiania Theatre produced an Ibsen play? Or perhaps there was an opening at the university library – 'I'm applying in your name, whether you want the job or not'. Or what about applying for a grant from the Ancker Fund, in Denmark?

Bjørnson urged him to grit his teeth and hold on:

You won't bloody well die, you're tough, courageous, lazy, people like that never die.

Although one can never be completely sure. So in the summer of 1865 Bjørnson allies himself with Johan Sverdrup, Andreas Munch, Bernhard Dunker and Jens Peter Andresen, and another campaign begins to raise enough money for Ibsen to carry on living in Rome. As was the case the year before, Dunker was every bit as central to the campaign as Bjørnson, though that is not always the impression Bjørnson gives.

The response was remarkable. A long list of friends and well-wishers contributed. Several old friends from Bergen were among the names on the list, and in Trondheim the city's wealthiest businessmen gave 53 spesidaler. The district governor in Drammen collected 110 spesidaler from nineteen of the city's wealthiest men. A list of subscribers from Christiania reveals that 37 people contributed 422 spesidaler between them, although the list is undated and may be from the previous year. The collection shows the growth of a feeling of solidarity among Norwegian writers, in the first instance at Bjørnson's initiative, and later enshrined in the statutes of the Norwegian Society of Authors. Secondly, the collections provided rare examples of the way in which private patronage could balance out inequalities in the field of Norwegian culture in the mid-1860s, one in which the market and the state had not yet managed to arrange the support for the cultural life that Norwegians as a nation wished to have.

The collection showed something else too: Ibsen had many, many friends in Norway. Was that something he appreciated?

Throughout the years to come he would insult and offend his homeland, without it always being clear exactly who or what it was he was referring to. But if Norwegian politicians and public bodies did, perhaps, neglect their obligations to Norwegian culture, if their spirits were mean and their thoughts small and all those other valid accusations that Ibsen routinely levelled at his fellow countrymen, one thing at least cannot be denied: Norwegians had not let Henrik Ibsen down, even if Norway had perhaps done so. And in a short while he would, in any event, be given the thing he had above all demanded of the Norwegian state – a writer's annual salary. The irony of it was, of course, that the drama which would eventually compel the state's goodwill had been inspired by hatred of his own country. Its title was *Brand*.

THE REVELATION

At the end of May 1865, Henrik, Suzannah and Sigurd left Rome for Ariccia, not far from Genzano. They kept very much to themselves that summer, as

Henrik needed peace in which to write. He began writing early in the morning, and later in the day took a long walk in Villa Chigli, in an old, overgrown park. In the evenings he would sit on the steps of the church, in the centre of the little village, and savour the cool air.

The conditions were perfect, and yet the writing proceeded slowly. He had started work the previous year on the tragedy of Julian the Apostate, as well as a long poem about a character whom he first called Koll but later renamed Brand. For a time he thought he might be able to finish both within the year, but it was not to be. Julian would in the end require ten years of him, and the poem proved recalcitrant. Ibsen perhaps found some encouragement in Bjørnson's promise to introduce him to the head of the Danish publishing house Gyldendal, Frederik V. Hegel, who was now publishing Bjørnson.

But first he would have to bend his pen to his will!

And again there were money troubles that obliged the family to live a simple, rural life in Ariccia. Suzannah had to prepare their main meals herself on a baker's oven that functioned at thirty degrees, and in the evenings Sigurd would be despatched to buy bread, cheese and wine for their supper. As poverty goes it wasn't exactly dire, but their standard of living fell short of what Suzannah was used to, and what Henrik would have wanted for them all.

Bjørnson tried to cheer him up, get him to see that things weren't all that bad. Hadn't matters taken a turn for the better after he'd left Christiania?

> . . . you're now one of Scandinavia's leading writers, respected, your work awaited with anticipation, you have that wonderful boy, you have your great ideas, you're down there, where you're respected and liked . . .

Couldn't he see that for himself?

It was Ibsen's way to dwell on the dark side of things, clinging on to every bitter memory his life had to offer him. When the light dawned on him that summer, it came as a total surprise. Like a revelation, a blow from God's hand that suddenly revealed to him the shape of everything that had thus far moved formless and unresolved within him. That, at least, is Ibsen's own version of what happened to him in St Peter's one day when he was on a visit to Rome from Ariccia:

> . . . and all at once I had a strong and clear vision of the form in which to say what I had to say. – Now I have jettisoned everything that I have struggled fruitlessly with this past year.

Standing beneath the great dome of St Peter's he knew he must refashion the recalcitrant epic *Brand* as the verse drama *Brand*, an idea that struck him with the force of a revelation. That was how Ibsen described it to Bjørnson. A more prosaic way of looking at it might be that Ibsen, with this story, hoped to convince Bjørnson that he was making good use of the money with which his supporters back home were sponsoring him.[4] In his previous letter he had been careless enough to mention how he could spend days on end just wandering the streets of Rome with no particular aim or purpose in mind. Bjørnson's reply included a veiled accusation of laziness, something that might have motivated Ibsen to claim that his apparently random wandering could indeed be fruitful, that he could be creative in the midst of what looked like idleness. It was hardly coincidental that the revelation occurred in St Peter's. Bjørnson had recommended it to him in an earlier letter: 'As regards St Peter's, I do urge you to pay a visit, several visits, preferably during a Mass, but also when it's very quiet, and on the great feast days; I'll say no more about it, only this: when you're back here again, this above all else is what you will recall from your entire journey abroad.'

In the light of this, Ibsen's story of a revelation in St Peter's seems almost like the result of Bjørnson's invitation to seek just such an experience there. The tale of the revelation in St Peter's can thus be seen as Ibsen's defence of his own creative idleness, a recognition of Bjørnson's perspicacity, and at the same time the expression of a genuine breakthrough in his work on *Brand*.

For there can be no doubt that Ibsen really did find a solution to the formal problems posed by his play at about this time – and whether this was the result of a revelation or not, and took place inside or outside St Peter's, is neither here nor there. As soon as he got back to Ariccia he threw himself into work on the play and wrote in a long, free-flowing rapture. He worked morning and night, something he had never managed to do before, and by the middle of October – after just three months – he had the whole drama finished.

The epic *Brand* had metamorphosed into 'a dramatic poem in rhyme, profoundly serious at heart but with jabs and digs at the rascals'. The fact that it was a verse drama, intended for reading, must have felt liberating to him, who had thus far in his career written for the stage, with all *that* had entailed in terms of frustrations. Both the poem and the drama were the result of a mood that had possessed him ever since witnessing the Prussian victory parade in Berlin. He said later that the desire to chastise the Norwegian people for their cowardice and their betrayal of the claims of the ideal had been born in him then. All would be resolved in *Brand*. The political background is especially evident in the epic version, as in these lines from the opening poem, 'To those complicit':

Now a silence descends over the land
A clammy air veils the mountains,
As though a sorcerer had mixed some dark poison
Enfeebling the people's power.

There is little here of the national-romantic's lyrical pathos in the presence of nature. He turns away now from 'the soul-dead story of our past' and enters 'the foggy world of the moment'. Enough romanticising of the past. What mattered now were the struggles of the day. But much of what was contemporary disappeared anyway as Ibsen converted the theme from epic verse to dramatic poem, at the same time altering the perspective from an outer to an inner, personal conflict. Indeed, most of the overt references to the contemporary conflict were cut. Ibsen was left with a play of ideas centred on moral and existential questions that, reading between the lines, could still be interpreted as a drama of contemporary life.

Brand is the story of a young priest who finds his calling in a remote Norwegian valley settlement towered over by mountains. He preaches a stern and uncompromising faith and a demand that life be lived in pursuit of ideals. The entire play revolves around the priest's attempts to force himself and those around him to live out the unrelenting demands of a creed of 'All or nothing'. He denies the last rites to his mother on her deathbed because she will not give up everything she owns, and refuses to move to somewhere with a milder climate for the sake of his son's health because he will not betray his calling. The son dies, and the mother Agnes dies of grief because Brand refuses to allow her to hold on to mementos of the boy. He demands everything of everyone, including himself. The struggle for ideals is everything, for 'the spirit of compromise is the devil'. Brand manages to get the villagers to join him in building a new church, but on the day of its consecration he realises that it is not here, but up in the mountain, that people should look for God. When they refuse to follow him he journeys alone up the mountain. Here he discovers the 'Ice Church' that the mad local outcast Gerd has told him about. He and Gerd are both swept away in an avalanche and disappear, but before Brand dies he hears a voice intoning these enigmatic words: 'Han er deus caritatis' – He is the God of Mercy.

This was the fruit of the mental upheaval Ibsen had experienced since he left Norway, all that had grown inside him like a foetus and that he had to bring forth into the world.

At the end of September, Ibsen returned to Rome, where he continued to work in the same disciplined fashion as before. 'I am working hard and not going out much,' he writes to his mother-in-law. On 25 October he sends the first four acts of the new play to Gyldendal in Copenhagen. The publisher, Frederik V. Hegel, sends a friendly letter of acknowledgement in which he reminds Ibsen that he must have the remainder of the play by the middle of November if it is to be on the market by Christmas. Hegel offers 30 riksdaler per sheet and a first print run of 1,250, which must have exceeded Ibsen's expectations. Everything seemed to be going his way. Ibsen completes the play, sending the final pages on 15 November, just as Hegel had asked him to.

The cold shower came not long afterwards. Hegel had accepted Ibsen's manuscript on Bjørnson's recommendation. But Bjørnson had led him to expect a
historical drama, probably based on the life of Magnus Heinesson. No one had
told Hegel that Ibsen's plans had changed, and having so much to do in the period
leading up to Christmas he had sent the manuscript to the printers without having
read it – a mortal sin for a publisher. Once he realised that what Ibsen had delivered was not a historical drama but a papal bull of a verse drama, the publisher got
cold feet. On 23 November he writes to tell Ibsen that the play, 'despite all its beauties, might not be understood by the majority of people'. The thematic content of
the play worries Hegel, and he hopes the writer will understand therefore when he
now finds it necessary to reduce both the fee and the promised print run by half.
If Ibsen wants to take his play elsewhere, Hegel assures him he will understand.

It was a cold shower, but that was all. What mattered most of all was that the
play be published, and in a letter of 2 December, Ibsen accepts the revised offer.

The play was on its way, and Christmas was approaching. Ibsen tries to
recapture the spirit of the early days in Rome. Some of the Scandinavians had
moved on, to be replaced by new faces – most of them Danish, along with a few
'repulsive Swedes'. But Ibsen soon realised that life at the Scandinavian Society
bored him. The good humour of the previous winter had gone, and showed no
signs of returning anytime soon.

So he spent most of his time waiting.

Early in December he celebrates publication of the new play in advance. He
writes to Clemens Petersen, urging him to draw attention to the work when it
appears in time for Christmas:

> You once wrote of me that rhyming verse with a symbolic underlay was my
> true metier.

Petersen had made the point in his review of *The Pretenders*. Ibsen had taken
the criticism to heart, and written the sort of play he thought would appeal to
Petersen. Clemens Petersen's approval matters – 'Your response will be decisive
in how my own countrymen respond to the drama, and to the truths that I have
been unable to remain silent about.' The Norwegian critics would not do; if the
truth about Norwegians was to emerge, then he needed the help of a Dane –
preferably two Danes. But as the Christmas bells rang out that year *Brand* had
still not appeared. What on earth was Frederik Hegel playing at?

THE SCORPION'S STING

It looked like being another frugal Christmas for the Ibsens. At the Scandinavian
Society the traditions were upheld, with rice pudding, roast duck, and dancing

round the bay tree, along with endless speeches and toasts in which everyone drank everyone else's health. Then came the ceremonial parade and the raffling of presents, organised in such a way that there was no chance of anyone winning a gift they had themselves contributed. One present, a pair of kid gloves, went to the promising young composer Edvard Grieg, who had recently arrived in Rome. He and Ibsen would get to know each other the following spring.

On 25 December the leftovers from Christmas Eve were eaten, this time without the presence of women and children. The mood was at once much more relaxed – 'Ibsen very drunk,' Grieg noted in his diary. Maybe all those pompous speeches were getting on Ibsen's nerves. He was still angry about the fall of Dybbøl, and sometime in mid-January 1866, after yet another speech in praise of the Nordic countries, his patience ran out. No sooner had a headmaster named Rovsing concluded his speech than Ibsen got to his feet and delivered a riposte in which he suggested that there should be no more fine words on the subject of Nordic unity, since the young men had so signally failed to heed the call when it really mattered.

Since he was only slightly drunk his speech was met with applause by some, whereas others gave vent to their displeasure. The poor teacher tried to explain himself, others joined in, and when the clock struck eleven everybody went home.

What was it that was bothering him – Ibsen? How much did it owe to drink, how much to his own quarrelsome nature, to his hatred of Norwegians and his genuine involvement in Denmark's cause which was now, a year after Bismarck's ultimatum, a lost one? It might have been all of these things, exacerbated by the tensions of waiting – still – for his play to appear. Money was once again beginning to be a problem. January and February pass, and still no *Brand*.

His frustration mounts. Finally he cracks – and complains not to Hegel but to Bjørnson.

'You say Hegel is a man of honour,' he writes in a letter dated 4 March 1866. 'I have had endless difficulties with him and given way at every point, to make sure my book was published in time for Christmas. And yet it wasn't . . .'

At about the same time Hegel in Copenhagen writes a similar letter of distress to Bjørnson:

It's very odd that I don't hear even a word in reply from Herr Ibsen. Here we are in March already, and in all conscience I cannot delay publication any longer. I'll be publishing it in eight days' time, on the terms and conditions originally agreed.

What had happened was this. Hegel had never received Ibsen's letter of 2 December in which he accepted the revised offer; it had quite simply got lost in the post. Hegel assumed that Ibsen was insulted by his offer and had decided not to press for publication. Neither man, it seems, had thought of writing a second letter querying the matter. Not until 7 March does Ibsen again write to Hegel, the same day as that on which Hegel tells Bjørnson that he intends to send *Brand* to the printers and honour his initial commitment to issue a first edition of 1,250 copies. Finally, on 15 March, *Brand. A drama in verse* was published.

Its appearance caused a sensation.

Never before had a single book exerted such a powerful and immediate effect on readers in Denmark, Norway, and even Sweden. *Brand* was read and discussed everywhere, and not least by the young: 'In vain might I try to describe the extraordinary and fascinated passion with which the young people here read and discussed the great writer,' wrote the Swedish poet Gustaf af Geijerstam, speaking for an entire generation of writers who would turn the closing decades of the nineteenth century into a golden age of Scandinavian literature. Everywhere you go in Copenhagen, the *Illustreret Nyhedsblad* told its readers, people are talking about *Brand*, and soon the same would be true of Christiania. And no matter where one stood in discussions of the play, it was hard not to concede that here was a great work of art by a highly original writer. In Denmark, Clemens Petersen responded to Ibsen's plea and reviewed *Brand* in *Fædrelandet* on 7 April. Petersen was clearly impressed by 'this remarkable verse', and found much to praise in it. But throughout the play offered more 'concepts than images', by which Petersen meant that *Brand* was not so much poetry as criticism. Ibsen failed to *show* what it was he wanted to say by means of 'vivid and colourful depictions of reality' but instead resorted to simple postulates – as in the play's famous last line.

Before the review appeared, Petersen had promised Bjørnson he would be gentle with Ibsen, and in reality he had a number of objections to the play besides those mentioned in *Fædrelandet*. He confided to Bjørnson that the play as a whole seemed to him disjointed – 'wild ideas that whirr about rootlessly'. Clemens Petersen would never see the greatness in Ibsen, and yet he had a deep respect for the man's unusual talent.

Much the same could be said of Bjørnson.

'The whole book bores me so much that I've still not managed to read it all the way through,' he replied to Petersen. He regarded *Brand* as an attack on Christianity, and was angered by the lack of clarity in the play and the lack of any reconciliation: 'A single head cannot possibly encompass all this, sometimes it seems to me he has eyes in the back of his neck; because to see simultaneously two things that have nothing whatever to do with each other is, to me, always a repellent form of talent.'

No, being able to see two things at the same time was never Bjørnson's strong point, and his Janus-faced friend's play naturally alarmed him. Bjørnson wasn't the only one who missed a reconciliatory conclusion, and who felt that Ibsen's drama was extreme to the point of hysterical. A young Georg Brandes was impressed by the power in the play and yet objected to the disturbing effect it had on the reader; the effect of literature should be stirring and calming, according to him, it should not throw the reader off-balance. Another who complained of the play's lack of idealism and spirit of reconciliation was Marcus Jacob Monrad, who devoted four separate articles to a discussion of it in the pages of *Morgenbladet*. In his view the play was not really dramatic poetry but abstract rhetoric and satire. In opposition to the drama's main claim that an uncompromising life involved the greatest self-sacrifice he suggested the opposite, that to compromise one's own beliefs involved a greater sacrifice. Ditmar Meidell in *Aftenbladet* was more positive. Despite the play's tendentious quality he admired its daring and strength so much that he foresaw it would occupy 'a permanent and influential place in our national literature'.[5]

What the critics shared was an uncertainty about exactly what kind of literary work this was. Monrad claimed the play was satire, not drama, Clemens Petersen that it was criticism, not poetry. Meidell maintained that it should be read as a 'lyrical dialogue' and not as drama, while Vinje insisted on reading it as a parody – 'I took it to be a joke; otherwise I would have tossed *Brand* straight into the fire.' Bjørnson quite simply loathed it.

What, actually, was *Brand*?

Above all it was a drama that challenged the reader's understanding of what a drama is, and of what kind of message a literary work might convey. We cannot, of course, know what its numerous readers made of Brand's merciless idealism, but the tendency of critics to regard him as the author's mouthpiece and the hero of the drama was probably more pronounced among his contemporaries than in later times. Yet it remains something of a mystery how a literary hero whom the most prominent critics of the day regarded as problematic, indeed, as unacceptable, was able to arouse such widespread enthusiasm among ordinary readers. Some read the work as a nationalist satire, a literary punishment inflicted on Norway for having failed Denmark and hastened the demise of the Scandinavianist ideal. Ibsen undoubtedly intended the drama to be understood in such a way. But it is clear too that there is a larger, overarching quality to the play that transcends its contemporary relevance. Many read *Brand* as a religious drama about Brand's struggle to be true to his calling in a mendacious world.

It was this religious dimension that particularly excited Bjørnson's contempt; at the time he was much preoccupied with Grundtvig, who taught that Christianity could be both 'human and possible' – quite a different view from Brand's. Unsurprisingly, Bjørnson felt a greater empathy for Grundtvig than for

Kierkegaard, while Ibsen felt closer to Kierkegaard. It is hard to say whether or not Ibsen originally intended *Brand* to be a religious drama. In any event, he had no desire at all to see his work reduced in the public perception to the status of a religious pamphlet. In later years he consistently downplayed the religious reading; his only aim had been to depict a 'man of passion', he claimed, someone who fought uncompromisingly against the spirit of compromise. Seen in this light, *Brand* can be read as a symbolic drama of ideas on the relationship between the claim of the ideal and the demands of the real world, alternatively as a tragedy in which the hero is brought down by his finest qualities, or even as a more existential drama of personality, in which, at its deepest level, the conflict lies in Brand's impossible struggle to find freedom in unity and consistency.[6]

In place of freedom and harmony Brand is pursued by constraint and destruction, until finally he is himself destroyed in a terrible avalanche, with the words:

> Answer me, God, in the abyss of death; –
> Does it not matter one whit
> The will of man quantum satis – ?!

At which a voice is heard through the thunderous roar of the avalanche:

> He is deus caritatis!

How should these words be understood? Ibsen never gave any clue; he did, after all, once write that the idea behind a work of art should never be exposed to open view but rather twist its hidden way through it, as a vein of silver runs through a mountain. Does Brand find salvation, or is he condemned – from a religious or ideological perspective? What sort of fate does he actually deserve? What kind of hero is this man, this idealist who sacrifices everything and everyone for a seemingly unloving God? And what kind of writer was Ibsen, to leave his readers in deep confusion over what they should be thinking and feeling?

What did he want, this enigmatic writer, other than to seduce and confuse?

HENRIK HALFBEARD

Ibsen made his real literary breakthrough with *Brand*. He also announced himself as a new kind of writer, with an image and an attitude that would become his trademark: he became the punitive, angry and truth-seeking poet-prophet. The day after *Brand* was published in Copenhagen he wrote to Hegel:

Norwegians and Swedes owe a dreadful guilt of blood to you Danes, and I
feel it is my appointed mission to use the talents God gave me to awaken my
countrymen from their slumbers and force them to see the exact nature of
the great questions in life.

The poet's task was to see through things, 'the hollowness behind all the lies and
self-deceit in our so-called public life, and all those empty and wretched
phrases'. And when the poet was the one best able to do this it was, in part at
least, because he lived abroad. Everything seemed so much clearer, according
to Ibsen, once he had attained sufficient distance from life back home. He gave
his life in exile a deeper significance, one that was related to the writer's calling,
which was to observe human conduct from the outside, and from on high. Just
as prophets returned from the desert to chastise their people, so did the words
of the poet-prophet ring out in his homeland when the bookselling season
came around, in order to 'awaken the people and encourage them to think big'.
He made it clear to his artistic friends in Rome that his task as a poet was not
to bring comfort and succour to his readers:

I shall rage. I shall whip them!

The association of poet and prophet was not arbitrary. Ibsen immersed himself
in theology while working on *Brand* – 'I'm reading nothing but the Bible, it's
powerful and strong!' At a later date he said quite candidly that he regarded the
Old Testament prophets as the literary ideal.

He must have realised early on the nature of the role he was about to assume
in the public life of Denmark and Norway. In the autumn of 1870 he told the
critic Peter Hansen that while working on *Brand* he kept a scorpion under a
beer glass on his desk. When the creature seemed to be ailing he would offer it
a piece of fruit, which the scorpion would attack and inject with its poison, a
process that seemed to revive it. Weren't writers just the same? Was it not a
necessity for him too to assault society with his sting – his literary pen – in
order to live?

One thing is clear: the presence of a scorpion on his desk was no accident.
Ibsen exploited its symbolic value for all it was worth. The letter to Peter
Hansen was not private but a reply to a request for biographical information in
connection with an article Hansen was writing. The letter as a whole seems
part of Ibsen's attempt to construct himself as a writer, one in which the scorpion is given this important symbolic role. He also wrote a poem entitled 'My
Scorpion and I' which he intended to include in the collection of poems that
appeared in 1871.[7] But the story was up and running long before that. In

the 1867 Christmas edition of the Norwegian satirical magazine *Vikingen* a drawing of a scorpion in a glass was dedicated to Ibsen and accompanied with this caption:

> In Brand and Peer Gynt you mocked your land
> Do you not here see the source of your inspiration?

The Norwegian media in general was not notably aware of what Ibsen was up to at any given time down there in Rome, but this tale of the scorpion seems to have made its way back home and in the process became a useful shorthand for Ibsen's whole literary project. So the scorpion served its master well, and was that not perhaps the master's idea all along in acquiring it? If, that is, he really did. The walls of La Locanda Martorelli where Ibsen finished writing *Brand* were decorated with drawings of all the creatures of the Zodiac, including the scorpion, right next to one of the desks. Was it here that the parallel between the writer and the scorpion occurred to him? Was *this* the famous scorpion?

Essentially it matters little. Henceforth Ibsen was the scorpion-writer, the man who injected his poetic poison into the body of society. Not because he wanted to, but because it was in his nature to do so. And in the wake of this breakthrough as a writer and literary actor there came about a very remarkable change in Ibsen's public persona.

Brand changed a great many things – including his appearance.

Writing the play had been difficult. First the hard work of the previous summer. He later wrote of the time as a state of almost permanent ecstasy, with the rhymes pounding away in his head – if they came to him at night then he had to get up to make a note of them. He had been nervous and on edge, but also indescribably happy – full of a sort of 'crusading joy'. He felt utterly fearless. And then that unendurable wait for the play to appear, followed by its unexpected success.

The reviews were mixed, but that did nothing to change the fact that the play was a sensation in Scandinavia. Four editions appeared in the year of publication alone, rather more than three thousand copies, and there would be others in the years to come. Even by Danish standards these were striking figures.[8] And the money started to roll in. An advance of 200 spesidaler found its way into a stocking at the bottom of his chest of drawers, like a treasure to be hidden away – it seems that it never occurred to him to put it in the bank.

And suddenly poverty was banished from Ibsen's life.

For good.

It was in this frame of mind that he replenished his wardrobe and reached for the razor blade. He put aside his old, shabby clothes and donned a new black velvet jacket, a white linen shirt and a pair of kid gloves. The razor then sculpted the neat half-beard to reveal something the world had not seen for over two decades: a narrow and rather gruff line between the bushy sideburns, a line that now and then turned upwards at both ends to reveal an unexpected and irresistible smile: Ibsen's mouth. The change in his appearance was so dramatic that to friends it seemed as though he had become a new person overnight. Lorentz Dietrichson, who had left Rome the previous year, hardly recognised his old friend from the photograph accompanying a letter he received a couple of years later. What really surprised him, however, was not so much the photograph as the hand-writing. The slanting and almost illegible little letters familiar to him over the years were gone, to be replaced by a style that was firm, bold and upright.

Did Ibsen really write this? And that elegant gentleman in the velvet jacket with his neatly manicured beard – could that really be him?[9]

No doubt about it; this was Ibsen – the new Ibsen. Gone was Henrik Wholebeard, that timorous and troubled theatre manager and starving poet. In his place stood Henrik Halfbeard, respected writer, a man with money in his stocking, a man who knew that henceforth he could be whoever and whatever he wanted to be and write whatever he wanted to write. A man who had taken control of his own life and his manifestation in the world.

* * *

Although *Brand* changed many things it did not change everything. Behind that neatly trimmed beard Ibsen was still Ibsen. And he still enjoyed a glass or three. Edvard Grieg has left us a less than flattering portrait of the newly successful writer. At a concert at the Scandinavian Society in the spring of 1866 at which Italian musicians played pieces for piano and strings by Schumann and Chopin, it occurs to a very merry Ibsen that there should be dancing. He has the tables and chairs pushed up against the walls and urges Ravnkilde to sit down and play. But Ravnkilde, like Grieg, thought it somewhat inappropriate to conclude a concert recital with drinking and dancing, and declined. Moreover, the mood of the occasion was subdued on account of the recent death of the young Norwegian composer Rikard Nordraak. Ibsen was so outraged that he took his hat and his cane and left.

'What he's used to,' said Grieg, 'is that whenever we're alone, we jump to it when he says "Play up, you chaps", and what he means by "play" is play anything at all, doesn't matter what. Strange, that such a great man can be so limited.'

Grieg always considered Bjørnson a friend, but never entertained more than a dutiful respect for Ibsen's genius. And Ibsen's lack of musicality did nothing to increase his respect.[10] Ibsen himself was enthusiastic about Grieg, fifteen years his junior, and Grieg had not yet reached the stage in his career where he could manage without the help of the established writer. As it happened Grieg was at the time hoping very much to be appointed concert-master at the Christiania Theatre. Ibsen advised him to write to Bjørnson and Dunker, respectively the manager and the committee chairman of the theatre. But time passed, and no word came from either Bjørnson or Dunker. In June, Grieg approached Ibsen once more and asked him to write to Bjørnson on his behalf, saying that he dared not do so again himself.

Ibsen assures him that he has written to Bjørnson, but advises the young man not to pin his future on the idea of a permanent post at the theatre – 'it would be ungrateful of you to place so little store by your talents as to measure them against such a trivial aim'. Ibsen believed in Grieg – 'an outstanding chap, among those who will shape the future' – and urged him to devote himself completely to his artistic calling. Given his own hard-won experiences of insti-tutional theatre life, this was probably the only advice he could offer.

Grieg never did become concertmaster at the Christiania Theatre, and was thus spared the spirit of compromise. As, most definitely, was Ibsen. A hostile reader of *Brand* might point out the paradox in the fact that freedom from the yoke of materialism seemed to lie in commercial success. To rise above the world one has to conquer it. But if this hardly squares with the image of Brand the world-denying priest, it describes Ibsen very well indeed.

A STATE-APPOINTED SATIRIST

The money that came in from *Brand* was just one of a number of pleasant surprises for Ibsen in 1866. The Norwegian government arranged the rest. Since failing to meet the deadline for a travel grant in March 1865, Ibsen had not applied for further financial support from Norway, nor did he plan to renew his application for the writer's annual wage. But in the spring of 1866 he received a telegram from Michael Birkeland apprising him of the fact that an application would have to be submitted during the current session of the Storting, otherwise it would not be considered until the next parliamentary assembly – not due for another three years! In Birkeland's opinion, Ibsen ought to try an unorthodox approach and send his application directly to the king.

Hearing nothing from their literary friend, he and the other members of the Learned Holland decided to take matters into their own hands. Thus two appli-cations were submitted, one from Ibsen to the king, and one from Michael

Birkeland, O. A. Bachke, Paul Botten-Hansen and Jakob Løkke to the Norwegian government. And as if this were not enough, Bjørnson was in action again. However much he might personally dislike *Brand*, it did not impinge on his wish to secure for Ibsen the same financial support as he himself now enjoyed. Again he spoke to Riddervold, in addition securing the support of friends of his in the Storting to put forward a proposal for the award of a writer's wage. Twenty-eight names were appended to the motion, among them the leaders of the liberal left.

'We cannot,' wrote the parliamentarians, 'stand by and watch passively such a talented and productive soul suffer from the need to provide for the very basics of his existence.' So three separate initiatives were in operation simultaneously. On 15 April, Ibsen submitted an application to the king. Four days later, the Learned Holland delivered an application to the cabinet in Christiania, enclosing a heart-breaking account of Ibsen's struggle while still in Christiania to keep going on a daily basis, and implying that things had not improved much in Italy:

> According to information received, the conditions of his daily life as described are oppressive in the extreme. The money he is able to earn from his literary activity is, perhaps, enough to keep him from dying, but hardly enough to keep a writer alive.

The signatories included as a statement of fact the judgement that 'his literary activities are of great importance for our literature, and in consequence for the development of our national life'. And since last applying for a writer's wage in 1863, Ibsen had written both *The Pretenders* and *Brand*, both of which further enhanced his reputation.

Thus did Ibsen's friends put forward arguments that Ibsen, in his shame, was unable to put forward himself. In his own application he wrote that he was not struggling 'to secure a trouble-free future for myself, but to enable me to carry through a calling that seems to me to address the most important and pressing requirement in Norway today – to wake the people up and enable them to think big'.

The king should know, moreover, that in his own view of his calling, Ibsen regarded himself as 'a warrior under Your Majesty's spiritual banner'.

While the politicians discussed his fate, Ibsen anxiously awaited the result. The nature of his future relationship with his native land would stand or fall by the outcome: 'If this doesn't work out,' he writes to Birkeland, 'then I'm finished with Norway and I won't be submitting any further application.' In that case he would settle in Copenhagen, at some future date, since for the time being he was greatly enjoying life in Rome:

Everything here is absolutely wonderful and marvellous. I've got will-to-work and energy enough to kill a bear.

He had little hope that his application would be successful. But he was wrong. When the vote was taken in the Storting, only four opposed the motion. Søren Jaabæk, leader of the Farmers' Party, was the only one to speak up against it during the brief discussion. He regarded a writer's wage as a business subsidy, and was against it on principle. But as Ludvig Daae had pointed out long ago, when in Jaabæk's company there was never any risk of poetry.

So Henrik Ibsen was saved for the literary life; if it also meant he was saved for his homeland was a much more complex question.

For years he had experienced the natural law that affirms that one debt always gives rise to another. Now he experienced its other side: that once money starts coming in from one source, other sources open up too. In May, a few days before the Storting reached its final decision, the Royal Norwegian Society of Sciences and Letters in Trondheim awarded him 100 spesidaler on the basis of the application he had submitted the previous year with Bjørnson's assistance. On 28 July he also received a supplement to the travel grant of 350 spesidaler from the government – without his even having had to apply! On top of this came the 200 spesidaler he had earned from the first edition of *Brand*, and by May a new edition was already being planned. It must have given him considerable satisfaction to be able to write to Hegel declining the offer of an advance on this second edition. But would Hegel please remember to send three 'nicely bound' copies to two members of the government, Frederik Stang and Georg Sibbern, as well as the king.

It was richly deserved – and not just for these three. Ibsen had formerly felt that he encountered opposition in his homeland; now, in the course of just two years, he found himself in receipt of the handsome support of businessmen, private individuals, the king, the government and the Storting. There could be no doubt that the spineless Norwegians believed that Ibsen would serve the nation and its people by applying himself exclusively to a life of writing. All that was left to do now was get on with it.

A NEW WORKING DAY

Ibsen spent the summer of 1866 with Suzannah and Sigurd in Frascati, another of those small mountain villages outside Rome. This time they lived in much more comfort, in an old mansion with a view of Rome and beyond to the Mediterranean, with mountains and fields stretching away to the east and south.

In the middle of July, Ibsen writes to Paul Botten-Hansen:

Very soon now I'll get down to some serious writing; I'm still grappling with the beast, but pretty soon now I'll have him down and the rest will just write itself.

The 'beast' might have been *Peer Gynt*, which Ibsen mentions for the first time in a letter to Bjørnson in March of that year; or the play about Magnus Heinesson, which he had still not given up on, or his tragedy on the subject of Emperor Julian. Most likely it was Julian, even though he told Bjørnson that *Peer Gynt* was already 'fully formed' in his mind. And yet 1886 came and went without progress on any of these. Instead he busied himself with reprints and translations of earlier works, an occupation that would be an important part of his literary activity in the years to come. In the spring of 1866 he discussed several new editions with Hegel; the publication of his poems was mooted, and there was talk of a German translation of *The Pretenders*.

But the first new edition was not of his drama from the saga age but *Love's Comedy* – a work closely related to *Brand*, and one that had experienced a number of humiliations on its first appearance.

Perhaps, now that *Brand* had beaten the path, perhaps now they would understand?

The autumn 1866 reissue of *Love's Comedy*, its language adapted for a Danish readership, was part of a clear-sighted programme aimed at earning money from previous works and at the same time conquering new markets in Scandinavia. Ibsen was also hoping that *The Pretenders* would break open the German market for him. To Hegel he outlines a vision of 'reviving the old Dano-Norwegian joint literature' – or, why not, a literature that would serve all of Scandinavia, with Copenhagen at its centre? Without relinquishing his contempt for either Norwegians, Swedes or Germans, he now intended to win them over as readers. Was he not a writer-prophet? Was it not his duty to tell the truth, just as it was the people's duty to listen? In a cold and patronising Foreword to a new edition of *Love's Comedy* in May 1867 he regretted that he had published the book in Norway, a country in which literary matters were regarded as 'hardly relevant'. He expressed the hope that in Denmark it would find readers worthy of its quality.

A triumphant payback for the Norwegians, and a friendly greeting to his Danish readers. All thanks to *Brand*.

And it wouldn't be the last time this difficult priest served him well. Christian Tønsberg, Bjørnson and Hegel all invited him to contribute to Christmas publications and magazines that autumn. Ibsen declined, just as he would later decline all such invitations to write articles and contribute to anthologies, or take on the job of editing a magazine. He knew what he wanted now, he wanted to devote himself completely to writing. The money that poured in after *Brand* was managed with the greatest care; when Hegel suggested there would be a fourth edition of *Brand*, he asked him to hold onto the advance for the time being. He had control of his life now, and did all he could to gain control over the future too.

The past was a somewhat more difficult matter. He could try to rise above it, or take his revenge on it with patronising forewords. But he could do nothing to change it, or prevent its constant and haunting returns. It was only now that Ibsen learned what had happened to his property after he had left the country. He had known nothing of Nandrup's auction in the summer of 1864, simply because his friends had decided to spare him the distress when there was nothing they could do to prevent its taking place. The proceeds of the sale were a pathetic 131 spesidaler, not nearly enough to cover his debt to Nandrup. So the spectre of debt still hung over Ibsen. In the summer of 1866 Bjørnson decided that Ibsen was now strong enough to tolerate the truth.

But it turned out he didn't know Ibsen well enough.

'I haven't shed any tears at the loss of the furniture and so on, but to think of my private papers, drafts and notes etc. in the hands of strangers pains me,' he replies to Bjørnson, having in a previous letter rebuked his friend both for having failed to prevent the auction and for not informing him of it. Bjørnson was much offended, and replied that neither he nor any of his friends had known about the auction until it was over. And moreover:

> There was nothing you could have done about it back then – so of what use to warn you?

Then, in a gesture of forgiveness, he throws the accusing letter into the fire – 'you have suffered so much that it excuses your unfairness'.

Naked and exposed in front of strangers, a dreadful embarrassment for such a private person as Henrik Ibsen. But he wanted to protect Suzannah. If Bjørnson should happen to meet Suzannah's sister Marie he must ask her not to mention the auction in any letter to her sister. It would only hurt her, and anyway Ibsen was now, at last, able to 'make everything right again'. *Brand* had made it possible: the four editions that appeared in 1866 earned him over 2,000 spesidaler.

Did he then make sure the debt was paid off once and for all?

Not Ibsen, no.

A month after receiving Bjørnson's letter he gets one from his brother-in-law Johan Herman Thoresen, who is now operating as Ibsen's man in financial matters in Norway and who urges his brother-in-law to use the supplementary travel grant to pay off the increasingly impatient Nandrup. Ibsen hands over half to his creditor. No more than that. Some 350 spesidaler of the debt remains unpaid and continued to accumulate interest. Even with money in the bank he delays as long as possible before finally settling with Nandrup. It was as though he wished to preserve this painful link to his homeland; the debt followed him, like a dark memory from the past. Not until ten years later did he pay off the last instalment of what he owed and meet his last material obligation to his own country.

But whether that also meant an end to the hauntings of the past was another matter.

AN UNPRINCIPLED SCOUNDREL

Christmas Eve 1866 was celebrated in traditional fashion, with dancing round the bay tree, roast duck, and Ibsen in a dangerous mood. Prior to the celebrations there had been rumours that Kristofer Janson would be reading a story in New Norwegian, a potentially provocative gesture of support for those attempting to introduce this as the only authentically Norwegian language. If this turned out to be the case, Ibsen announced, then he would leave the gathering in protest.

The mood during the meal was tense. Would Janson really go through with his politically potent linguistic gesture? And would Ibsen then carry out his threat? Fortunately the diplomatic Janson decided instead to read one of Bjørnson's short stories – in a Bergen accent, granted, but a solution that was acceptable to all.

Ibsen remained in his seat.

It is worth noting that the breakthrough with *Brand* and the definitive end of his poverty did nothing to dampen Ibsen's eccentric antics. The stories of his tactlessness are legion, many of them probably edited for content in the retelling out of respect for the great writer – so that people said that there was so much going on inside him during these years that he 'mingled with the other Scandinavians like a lion of whom the others were actually afraid'. Like the time at Raffaels Vigne early in May 1867. That evening a number of Scandinavians had gathered to say farewell to one of their number. After the meal the Danish painter Johan Lorange decided to help out old Lars Hansen by splitting the bill between the guests. Ibsen objected and began abusing Lorange, a man weakened by a chest infection, and made no secret of the fact that he considered him an inferior painter as well as a man without principles. Lorange shouldn't even be walking on two legs but should get down on all fours! The company was profoundly embarrassed, partly because no one dared to rebuke Ibsen, and partly because no one could deny there was some truth in Ibsen's description of Lorange.

The scorpion's sting. The truth is a poison that none can tolerate.

Undoubtedly there was something of Brand in Ibsen, in particular that irresistible impulse to speak the truth to people's faces, to speak up where others remained silent. But this Brand preached most frequently when drunk. Most of these anecdotes add that Ibsen had had too much to drink at the time. Life in Rome itself might have encouraged such behaviour – whenever men of the Victorian age were removed from the constraints of their natural environment something seemed to happen to them, as countless stories from the European colonies in Africa and Asia bear witness to. Add to this the ready availability of wine and the quarrelsome Protestant side of any Scandinavian was soon exposed.

Although Ibsen didn't really need a dram to cause a scandal. That spring the Scandinavian community was shaken by a rather curious incident occasioned by two newcomers who tended to keep themselves to themselves. And there was undeniably something odd about the Swedish aristocrat Baron Rosen and his young companion Herr Sverdrup, or, more precisely, about the latter. Weren't his clothes rather peculiar? And wasn't his voice a trifle effeminate? Rumours ran rife, and in due course people came to the conclusion that young Herr Sverdrup must actually be a woman. If so, it was in direct contravention of the society's rules, which only allowed the presence of women on specific occasions.

When it finally emerged that Herr Sverdrup was, in fact, Frøken Emma Toll, it was inevitable there would be a backlash. No one was more outraged than Henrik Ibsen. He was deeply offended on behalf of both the female sex and of the society's own laws, and demanded that the baron be expelled from it. He probably didn't have much support – why make a fuss when the unhappy man had admitted the deceit and was, moreover, a rather likeable chap? Why harm his reputation because of a little indiscretion so far away from home? But Ibsen is relentless, revealing once more the striking degree of passion he was willing to expend on relatively trivial matters. As it happened the more conciliatory members of the society managed to drag the business out until such time as the two involved had left the city, at which point the controversy simply disappeared.

Quite what it was that caused Ibsen to fly off the handle like that is hard to say. But the episode sheds an interesting light on his famous defence many years later of women's right to be full members of the Scandinavian Society, a battle to which he brought a similar intensity.

Drunk or sober, Henrik Ibsen was always Henrik Ibsen. Argumentative, teasing, provocative. He had been like that since his youth, the puppeteer never quite able to join in with the others, the one who preferred to observe and confuse, play with the social conventions, and gauge the way people reacted to his own curious impulses and whims. In Rome these impulses seem more unpredictable, more malicious, though it is difficult to draw conclusions from a handful of random anecdotes. Taken together, these stories reveal that Ibsen's need to 'discipline people' had not diminished with the years.

And among those who experienced the effects of this urge more than most were Suzannah and Sigurd.

THE WAD OF COTTON WOOL

Suzannah had placed a wad of cotton wool on the floor. Here, and no further, he was allowed to venture while his mother was out shopping, for the family did not employ a nursemaid. Sigurd would sit there, transfixed by the cotton wool, until she returned. And without crossing that invisible boundary line she had drawn for him.[11]

From an early age he had shown unusual ability. While still in Christiania he had once greeted a family friend with the following words:

'My name is Sigurd Ibsen and I am but nineteen months old.'

In similar fashion he once said of his father's clothes:

'He's fine, but expensive!'

Sometimes he rebelled. He might suddenly decide to push a flower pot off the window ledge, and once he threw his new sailor's cap off the dock. The cap was retrieved, but on board ship away again it went over the railings. Again it was retrieved. As their journey continued by rail he finally managed to get rid of it once and for all, tossing it through an open window. His father merely laughed. Nothing represses rebellion more efficiently and mercilessly than love.

By the age of four Sigurd was able to read, and at six he was already devouring fairy tales and adventure stories before starting on the Bible, the history of the world and Bernhard Severin Ingemann's novels. The boy's linguistic abilities were remarkable. Home was a hothouse, and his parents the keenest of gardeners. They encouraged the boy, nourished him and protected him from the dangers of the world, both real and imagined – everything that lay on the other side of the wad of cotton wool. And in this propitious environment Sigurd flourished, a graceful orchid on a slender stalk – 'this unusual child with his large, dreaming eyes, his shyness, his curious reticence'. This is not to say that he grew up doing as he pleased; his parents had clear goals for his upbringing – not for his education so much as for his character:

'I cannot abide these Jelly Baby types who can't do anything and don't want to either,' Suzannah wrote to her brother later, 'the first rule of being a man is energy and a resolute will. Given that, what his aim in life is doesn't matter, and if I can achieve this in Sigurd I will be content.'

He certainly wasn't going to turn into a Jelly Baby; Suzannah would make quite sure of that! She and Henrik had left their native land. Their son would never have a native land. Instead he grew up in the state of Ibsen, a world of environments, landscapes and languages subject to constant change as his parents moved from place to place. The state of Ibsen had a population of three. Henrik was the regent, Sigurd the adored prince.

What of Suzannah?

The years in Christiania must have been hard for the priest's daughter from Bergen, what with the struggling with creditors, the chronic shortage of money, her husband's creative difficulties, his fondness for alcohol, and those endless problems with the theatre. Her husband's social fall is a matter of literary history, but her family too had experienced a fall. Before Henrik offered her a life of poverty in Christiania she had grown up in a comfortable and cultured home in Bergen. In Rome the family's material conditions finally improved, and from this point on we have several witnesses describing Suzannah's character and appearance – not all of them flattering, to put it mildly. Clemens Petersen had met Suzannah in Copenhagen and was repelled by her ways and her figure, which had begun to fill out: 'She licks her fingers when she eats, and to hold her in your arms and look into her eyes would be like drowning in half-melted fat.'

Petersen wasn't exactly a sight for sore eyes either. He was stout too, with strangely dead eyes and a skin condition that had destroyed his face and deprived him of his eyelashes and eyebrows. But then he was a man, and his appearance an asset of no particular importance.

But the fact that Suzannah didn't live up to contemporary standards of feminine appeal tells us precious little about her nature and her importance for Henrik. He broke off all important relationships in his life, leaving his bonds with the two exceptions all the stronger. There is a persistent rumour to the effect that the intimate side of their relationship came to an end with the birth of Sigurd. As is often the case with rumours, this one too is without solid foundations.[12] As a young man Henrik had often claimed that he and his future wife would occupy separate floors of the house they lived in and address each other by the formal pronoun 'De', but cockiness like that is one of the privileges of the young. And yet it is not unlikely that their marriage seemed more like an intellectual friendship. Suzannah was a very well-read person, and there is nothing to suggest that she used her femininity to make her way in the world. On the contrary, she was noted for her lack of taste in clothing, even though she tried to dress elegantly. In this respect she was the opposite of her stepmother, Magdalene Thoresen, who was open in her sensuality. The relationship between the two had its cooler periods; it may well be that her stepmother's overt sensuality had the effect of cowing Suzannah. Certainly her stepmother's letters seem at times to adopt an intrusive tone.

And it was Suzannah whom Henrik had fallen for, not Magdalene. It was Suzannah who ploughed her way through the parcel of books that arrived every Christmas from Hegel, and many of the loans from the library at the Scandinavian Society were in her name. She was Ibsen's confidante as he worked on his plays, the one who encouraged him in the face of criticism, the one who understood:

'She is exactly the type of person I need,' he later confided to a friend, 'illogical, but with strong poetic instincts, high-minded, with an almost pathological hatred of all petty concerns.'

Well read, but illogical, high-minded but hating the trivial – the characterisation doesn't seem to quite add up. But others have left similar impressions of Suzannah. One of Ibsen's later admirers, Fanny Riis, noted that she could be both tender-hearted and warm in her opinions of others. She too experienced Suzannah as talented and an original thinker, but with a tendency to stubbornness and an overactive imagination. These characteristics in particular could, it seems, lead to heated exchanges with her husband.

'But that simply isn't *true*, Suzannah!' he might exclaim – and they were off.

All in all, she was not so very different from her husband. But if hers was the character he needed, it is by no means certain that *he* was what *she* needed. Yet by her own account, he was. Later in life, in a letter to her brother Herman, she writes that life in exile with her husband has been an unmitigated blessing:

> Ibsen's gifts have developed with an astonishing power, and my contribution to this has been the goal of my life, so that it doesn't matter where I go in the world, so long as I can continue to work at this.

There is no reason to suppose that this is the whole truth behind Suzannah's claim to happiness. But to the outside world she was content to confirm her own mythology, just as he did his – as the woman behind the man, the one who forced him to sit down at his desk each day and write. Maybe that was enough for her. For the homeless, rootless Henrik, she was certainly what he needed. She was the necessary 'other', the one able to make life work out. But love is one thing, actions something else. There are rumours that Suzannah was oppressed by her husband during their early years abroad, and certain episodes seem to bear them out – like the Sunday they took a trip out with some friends. Henrik managed to stop a couple of horse-drawn cabs on the Piazza Barberini, but Suzannah suddenly announced that she didn't want to go. Henrik protested, and when she persisted he thundered:

'Get into the wagon!'

Had Suzannah had any idea of what was to follow, she might have decided to defy her husband anyway – indeed, perhaps that's why she protested in the first place. The Scandinavians passed a lazy afternoon at La Baracca, drinking large quantities of mezzi in the heat. As evening drew near and they were about to head for home, Ibsen was so drunk he had to be supported by Knudtzon and Stramboe, one on each side. This was by no means the first time he was, quite simply, legless.

Back inside the city limits the high-spirited crowd of Scandinavians passed a villa where a dog stood barking at them from behind a barred gate. Ibsen insisted on taking a closer look at the dog, and took Suzannah and Knudtzon along with him. He began tormenting the dog with his stick until it was beside itself with rage. Tiring of this, his attention turned to two little Italian children playing in the street. Suddenly soft-eyed, he began stroking their cheeks.

One moment a lion, the next a lamb; no wonder his friends were on edge in his presence.

There is no doubt that being married to Henrik came at a price, but in the final analysis only Suzannah knew whether that price was worth paying. On many occasions he treated her outrageously, and Suzannah must have felt humiliated and offended. Others too were left with the impression of Ibsen as a controlling husband and father. 'My impression of Ibsen is that he is a big egoist,' wrote the Norwegian N. A. Stang after meeting the couple in the autumn of 1864.

And yet none has given a more pitiless description of Henrik and Suzannah than the young Dane Martin Schneekloth, who saw much of the couple in 1867:

> *He* is domineering, intransigent and self-centred, intensely masculine but with a strange personal cowardice, a man with a powerful urge towards the ideal which, in his everyday life, he is totally incapable of demonstrating, instead restlessly aspiring, restlessly searching, lacking clarity, but with occasional flights of clarity.

His characterisation of Suzannah is not much better:

> *She* is lacking in femininity, she's tactless, but with a steady, hard nature, a compound of intelligence and stupidity, not devoid of feelings, but lacking in humility and womanly love.

They simply could not live together, in Schneekloth's opinion, which was why they were permanently at war with each other. And yet she did love him, if only through Sigurd – 'that poor, emotionally crippled and rather frightening boy.'[13]

Like Clemens Petersen, Schneekloth was no fan of Suzannah, but he was in no doubt about which of them was responsible for their wretched marital life:

He took her from her father's house and led her into this strange world, and instead of devoting his life to finding a way to make amends he devotes all his strength and energy to the demonic pursuit of literary fame. It is distressing to hear of his plans to send his wife and child home so that he may work undisturbed. He lacks the courage to fight his way to success in a domestic setting. He lacks the courage to take the consequences of his own chosen path, to work day in and day out to hold on to her love, to suffer and struggle to learn how to raise his son.

Quite a fusillade – and a good thing for Schneekloth that while he lived his words remained hidden between the covers of his journal.

The spontaneous and uncensored nature of these private observations is what makes his descriptions so interesting, although, of course, one must take the words of a young idealist on the subject of marriage with some caution. But anyone who wants to know something of Ibsen's nature and his relationship to Suzannah should, after careful study of the more objective sources, return with the outbursts of this passionate young man in his journal for a rather different view of the great man. Another point of contrast with most of those who wrote about the years in Rome is that he was not blinded by Ibsen's fame as a writer, which does not mean that he was not an admirer. On the contrary, it was his respect for *Brand* that led the young man to Ibsen's door, and *Brand* is clearly behind the judgement he pronounces on the writer, the man who made idealistic demands of others while failing to live up to them himself.

It was, of course, deeply unfair. Ibsen had never pretended to be a Brand. He was, after all, merely a human being. As were Suzannah and Sigurd.

'HEY, JACOB SHOEMAKER!'

On 5 January 1867, Ibsen sent a Foreword to *Love's Comedy* to Hegel, along with the information that he was now hard at work on his new play, which he hoped to have finished by the summer. The play was *Peer Gynt*, meaning that Emperor Julian was once again postponed, and that Magnus Heinesson had now disappeared from the picture for good.

So it was *Peer Gynt*, although not as quickly as he had at first hoped. For a while things went well, and on 27 March he finished the second act. But then he ran out of steam. As always when writing he needs peace and quiet; all his thoughts are on work, making him even less sociable than usual – which is saying something. Finally he realised that he wasn't going to be able to get much more done in Rome and decided to try to finish the play during the summer in southern Italy – 'I feel the urge to travel in my blood, and even more the urge to be alone.'

Shortly before leaving he met a Dane who would ensure that his loneliness that summer would not be too extreme. Vilhelm Bergsøe was seven years younger than Ibsen at the time he returned for his second stay in Rome in the spring of 1867. Owing to ill-health and failing eyesight he had had to abandon a career as a naturalist, but turning to writing instead he had enjoyed great success with his novel *From the Piazza del Popolo*, based on his own experiences among the Scandinavian community in Rome.

His pleasure was presently soured by reviews of the book, notably one by Clemens Petersen. Disappointed, downhearted and still in poor health, Bergsøe visited the premises of the Scandinavian Society as soon as he arrived in Rome, where he was consoled by Ibsen, who had Petersen's tepid reception of his own most recent book still fresh in his mind.

'Come to the Buffalo this evening,' he suggested, 'and try a wine there that Bissen has obtained from Albano – a couple of carafes of that and you'll forget all about Petersen.'

A bottle of wine is no bad antidote to bad reviews, and when the two men met again that summer in southern Italy there were many of them.[14] On 21 May the Ibsens travelled to Naples, and on from there to the beautiful island of Ischia. They settled in a little country village named Casamicciola on the north side of the island, where Bergsøe was already established, along with his brother and sister and young Martin Schneekloth. The Ibsens took rooms at the Villa Pisano, with a garden adjacent to the garden of the inn where Bergsøe was staying.

Early one morning the Dane heard a voice out on the loggia:

'Hey, Jacob Shoemaker! Are you up yet? Open up, Jacob!'

Who else could it be, crying out in these Holbergian tones in faraway Ischia, but Ibsen? Thereafter they spent a great deal of time together, going for long walks or sitting at the little bar in the Piazza Casamicciola. Ibsen was full of the joys of work now and gave himself over entirely to the disciplines that were becoming almost holy ritual for him. Each morning he rose early and stepped outside to enjoy the first coffee of the day. At ten he sat down at his desk. It meant Suzannah and Sigurd had to leave the premises, because he demanded absolute silence when he wrote. At two he lay down his pen, and after a siesta and a meal read through the morning's work and made a fair copy of it in his elegant, almost calligraphic hand. And with that it was out into the garden once more.

'Hey, Jacob Shoemaker! Damned if it isn't time for another dram!'

He wasn't always in such excellent spirits. Later in the summer Bergsøe writes to a friend complaining about the loneliness of life on Ischia. Despite his daily walks with Ibsen he is suffering the 'pangs of human abstinence'. It seems that those afternoon walks with Ibsen were taken in the deepest silence. In all likelihood *Peer Gynt* was cavorting about in Ibsen's head as they walked. On those occasions when Ibsen did break the silence, it was usually with a reference to the play.

'Could you have a character in a play running about the stage with a casting ladle in his hand?'

'Yes, why not?' replied Bergsøe.

'Yes, but it would need to be a very large casting ladle – one big enough to remould people in.'

Bergsøe knew nothing of the evolving drama he was privy to on such occasions. But he gradually came to a better understanding of the dramatist. Ibsen talked openly and enthusiastically about his own literary calling, and exuded self-confidence. He wasn't writing for the present, he often said, he was writing for eternity. Bergsøe was of a more cautious nature and suggested that such an ambition was perhaps a little on the large side. At which Ibsen exploded:

'Desist from your wretched metaphysics! Deprive me of eternity and you deprive me of everything!'

Seventeen years previously he had taken a walk with his sister Hedvig on Kapitalbjerget above Skien and told her of his dream of what would be the greatest, the most perfect thing. Back in those days he was on the brink of a literary career; now his great breakthrough had been achieved. But the dream remained unchanged – he would devote every waking hour to writing, for that was the greatest, the most perfect thing, that was eternity.

Apart from such outbursts there was little company to be had from Ibsen on these walks. In the evenings he would liven up a bit, as the two of them strolled over the town's piazza to their regular bar. Here the mood would quickly lighten. In the cool evening air, filled with darting fireflies and the scent of the acacias, their tongues soon loosened – well lubricated by a few carafes of wine. 'Oh, if only I dared have one more, if I only dared just one more,' he might say. Quite possibly his need for alcohol was on the excessive side, but it would never again see him lying in the gutter.

In the course of those summer months on Ischia, Ibsen completed the third act of the play and was able to send the whole thing to Hegel at the beginning of August. In the middle of the month he and Suzannah and Sigurd left Ischia and travelled to Sorrento on the mainland, where they took lodgings at the hostel known as Rosa Magra, in the centre of town. Bergsøe followed in due course, and one evening he called on the Ibsen family. It turned out to be a highly interesting evening once the conversation got onto the subject of politics. It seems Ibsen was still able to work himself up into a rage on the subject of Germans and Swedes, as well as Norwegians. And when Suzannah was unwise enough to say something in praise of Swedes, Bergsøe was given an involuntary insight into the inner affairs of the state of Ibsen.

'Keep quiet – I refuse to listen to this. You make me sick!' Ibsen howled, thumping the table so hard he set the wine bottles dancing. Sigurd looked wide-eyed at his father and assured the gathering in his precocious way that he didn't like Swedes either. He knew what he'd do, that eight-year old, if he ever got hold of one of those repulsive Swedes:

'I'd claw their eyes out, because there's a troll inside me too, see.'

Yes indeed, there was plenty of troll in both father and son. And it was trolls Ibsen was using now in the literary reckoning with his homeland he was soon to finish – with, of course, a little salt to rub in the wounds of the Swedes and Germans too. During his two months in Sorrento, Ibsen finished the fourth and fifth acts of *Peer Gynt*, and on 18 October he sent the fair copy of the final act to Hegel in Copenhagen. Then he took a week's holiday with his family in Sorrento.

While still in southern Italy, Ibsen heard rumours that Garibaldi's troops were about to enter the Vatican State with the aim of finally incorporating the Eternal City into the newly created state of Italy. They hurriedly left Naples, hoping to reach Rome before the roads were closed, but were too late. By the time they reached the borders of the Vatican State, the railway connection was broken. The family had to spend fourteen days in the little mountain village of San Germano before they were able to continue their journey to Rome. Here they would spend a last winter in Italy, in a Rome where everything was the same, and yet not the same at all.

The dream of Rome was about to crumble.

THE BUCK RIDE

Ibsen's new five-act play was published in Copenhagen on 14 November 1867. If, with *Brand*, he had managed to fascinate and seduce his Scandinavian readership, then this new play was a worthy follow-up.

Peer Gynt is about the fantastic life of the daydreamer and compulsive liar Peer Gynt, who lives with his mother Åse in impoverished circumstances in a Norwegian village. His father, Jon Gynt, who has squandered the family fortune on drink and the good life, is dead before the play starts. Attending a wedding at Hægstad, Peer absconds with the bride, Ingrid, and runs off into the mountains. After abandoning Ingrid, he comes across three lovesick country girls, and the Greenclad, the Mountain King and his horde of trolls, as well as a formless being who calls himself the Great Boyg. When Peer tries to renege on his promise to marry the king's daughter he is forced to flee again. He meets Solveig again, a girl he had spoken to earlier at the wedding. She has given up everything to be with him. They settle in a cabin at the edge of the forest. Again Peer runs off. This time he stays away for many years, on a journey that brings him to the coast of Morocco. He travels on into the interior, and in the desert he meets the statue of Memnon and the Sphinx, he becomes a prophet among the Bedouin, and is seduced by the Bedouin girl Anitra. Finally he visits the insane asylum in Cairo, where he finds himself hailed as emperor of the insane. Following this he returns home, but not without encountering further drama. The ship sinks, and in the water the Strange Passenger asks for his body to help him in his search for the seat of dreams.

Back home in Norway, Peer encounters the Button Moulder, who proposes to put his soul into the casting ladle unless he is able to demonstrate that he has, all along, been 'himself' in life. Peer heads off to look for witnesses who can prove it, but finds none. His despair increases. The Thin Man says that he does not even deserve hell, like a genuine sinner. Finally he arrives at the cabin where Solveig has been waiting for him all these years. She tells him that he *has* been himself – in her faith, hope and love.

Where did Ibsen get the idea for this incredible tale?

'If it is of any interest to you,' he writes to Hegel in August 1867, 'this Peer Gynt was a real person, who lived in Gudbrandsdal, probably at the end of the previous or the beginning of this century.'

That was about all he knew, and most of it came from Asbjørnsen's *Norske Huldreeventyr og Folkesagn* (*Norwegian Folktales*), which includes a story about a teller of tall tales named Peer Gynt who lived in the mountains. Here we meet the country girls, the Great Boyg, and various other supernatural beings and elements that Ibsen made use of in his drama, along with other scenes and settings he found elsewhere in Asbjørnsen. He may also have heard stories about Peer Gynt during his walking trip through Gudbrandsdal in 1862, noting that Gynt's name was still familiar to the people he met in the valley.[15]

It is of no great consequence whether or not there ever was an actual Peer Gynt. Ibsen was his own fantasist and used the story as raw material, supplementing it with personal encounters and impressions, and introducing a wealth of references taken from literary history.[16] No other Ibsen play is quite so dense in literary allusion – there are parodies of Shakespeare ('My kingdom – half my kingdom for a horse!'), the closing line of Goethe's *Faust* is similarly traduced, and he uses the Bible with an equal freedom. A framework of references welded together to make this deeply original work. Many of the references are used in a spirit of play, but Ibsen's literary debt was also at a deeper level. The relationship between *Peer Gynt* and *Faust* is obvious, and no one could fail to see the Kierkegaardian tension between Peer's ethical obligations to Solveig and to himself, and the aesthetic flight that characterises most of his life.

Literary historians can add a long list of names and titles as influences – Adam Oehlenschläger's *Aladdin*, Paul Botten-Hansen's *The Huldre Wedding*, Bjørnson, Welhaven, Wergeland, Per Daniel Atterbom, Johan Ludvig Heiberg,

Dante, Hans Christian Andersen, Esaias Tegnér, Holberg, and in particular the Danish writer Frederik Paludan-Müller. Traces of Paludan-Müller's influence on Ibsen go as far back as *Catiline*, and are especially in evidence in *Love's Comedy*, *Brand*, *Peer Gynt* and *Emperor and Galilean*. The influence is apparent in the choice of rhymes and rhythms, as well as in the presence of the claim of the ideal in people's characters that is typical of Paludan-Müller's work, notably in *Adam Homo*, which was among the many books Ibsen borrowed from the library of the Scandinavian Society. Along with the numerous literary allusions, the list of books Ibsen borrowed from the library seems to show that, freed now from the burden of running a theatre on a daily basis, he was finally able to expand his acquaintance with the canonical literature of Europe while living in Rome.

He later revealed to Georg Brandes that he had also made much use of his own childhood in *Peer Gynt*. Åse was a version of his own mother, and life in the household of the affluent Jon Gynt was based on his own memories of life at home before his father's financial ruin. Ibsen specified that he had used these characterisations with 'necessary exaggerations', a caveat that hardly altered the rather negative effect his words had on the reputation of his parents, Marichen the good mother and the fickle Knud Gynt. Rarely can literature have so mercilessly traduced a life, reducing it to a few lines of dialogue between stiff covers. Beyond that, any number of lightweight and unreliable characters in Ibsen's own circle of acquaintances have been accorded the dubious honour of having their names put forward as possible models for Peer Gynt. They included Ole Bull, A. O. Vinje, Vilhelm Bergsøe and young Martin Schneekloth, whose exaggerated notion of his own talent was only made palatable by his attractive personality – just like Peer.

Quite a few had a touch of the Gyntian in their nature – including Henrik Ibsen himself.

Just as *Brand* had done, *Peer Gynt* challenged readers' assumptions of what a drama might be. The fact that Ibsen called it 'a dramatic poem' did nothing to lessen the confusion. With these two unclassifiable works Ibsen had demonstrated himself capable of the same sort of 'madness' as Michelangelo. Formally *Brand* was the more traditionally structured of the two, its alternating four-beat iambics and trochaics contrasting with the frequent recourse to doggerel and the free rhythms of the folk ballad in *Peer Gynt*.[17] The writing itself proceeded in a similarly free and unfettered fashion. Indeed, Ibsen had no idea that Peer would be going to Africa until after he had started writing, and as late as September he was asking Hegel to leave the list of dramatis personae open in case a few more minor ones popped up. As had been the case with *Brand*, he worked in a sort of intoxicated ecstasy, with the verses constantly pounding away in his head; on Ischia he frequently rose in the middle of the night to jot down ideas that in the morning turned out to be unusable.

Little wonder that Bergsøe found his companion remote and unapproach-able during the many walks they took together that year.

Appropriately for such a 'wild' piece of work, *Peer Gynt* was given a very mixed reception by readers and reviewers.[18] Bernhard Dunker called it an abortion, and Hans Christian Andersen suggested that it must have been written by a madman. Georg Brandes, who did not review the play until December 1868, read it as a morality play along the lines of Goethe's *Faust*. He found much to admire in Ibsen's incredible talent for making verse and in his command of language, but was repelled by what he took to be its ethical message, by its 'contempt for humanity and its self-hatred', and Ibsen's 'twisted view of life' – 'and yet what bitter pleasure he finds in thus tarnishing the image of human nature!'

Ibsen remained too much for Brandes, who still demanded that literature be soothing and harmonious.

Overall, the Danish critics were more sceptical than those in Norway. Both *Morgenbladet* and *Aftenbladet* gave the book good reviews, although with reservations – Frederik Batsman in *Aftenbladet* expressed a wish that Ibsen would one day offer readers 'something less polemical and nihilistic, something more straightforwardly lovely and aesthetically satisfying'. Ibsen cannot have been surprised that people found his play provocative. *Peer Gynt* was, among other things, a swingeing social satire in verse; the depiction of Hussein in the madhouse scene was, for example, a dig at Count Manderström, the Swedish minister who had come to symbolise for Ibsen the betrayal over Dybbøl. But the satire was mostly directed at his own country, as in Huhu's ridiculing of the New Norwegian language movement, and in the obvious parallel between Norway and the land ruled over by the Mountain King, between the smug self-satisfactions of Norwegian nationalism and the philosophy of the trolls. In the eyes of the language reformers Ibsen had long since aligned himself with the supporters of Dano-Norwegian. And even though Vinje considered Ibsen a much better writer than Bjørnson – 'Ibsen's sharp and brightly polished knife works better for me than Bjørnson's butter knife' – he had been making fun of Ibsen's Dano-Norwegian since 1859. There are those who think *Peer Gynt* contains several jabs aimed at Vinje.

But it was Kristofer Janson, not Vinje, who hit back at Ibsen in the pages of *Aftenbladet*, wondering whether he wouldn't soon tire of 'sitting there spitting and cursing in his kitchen chair'. This was payback from a man whom Ibsen had thrown a chair at during a heated discussion on the language question several years previously.

Bjørnson was another who read *Peer Gynt* as a national satire, and an entirely appropriate one, following Norway's betrayal of Denmark. Even if this play also was a little too highly strung and diffuse for Bjørnson's taste, it was strong, courageous and, not least, very amusing. And even if the meaning of the final scene, with Peer in Solveig's embrace, remained a little unclear, Bjørnson summoned up enough reserves of friendly goodwill to enable him to interpret the scene as one of reconciliation, possibly even in the religious sense. In other words, Bjørnson read the drama as both satirical and a morality play.

Writing to Ibsen in person he is effusive:

'I love your anger, I love your courage. I love your strength, I love your heedlessness.' Ibsen should be in no doubt about what he held in his hands here – 'this is a love letter, nothing more and nothing less'. Big words, big love: Bjørnson cherished Ibsen for his weaknesses as well as his strengths, for *Brand* as well as for *Peer Gynt*.

Clemens Petersen was not quite so indulgent when he reviewed the play in *Fædrelandet* a week after Bjørnson's review had appeared in the *Norsk Folkeblad*. As usual he permitted himself a few warm words about Ibsen's talent, but more forcefully than before he indicated what were, for him, the fatal limitations on this talent. Petersen regarded *Peer Gynt* as a continuation of *Brand*, and so included both plays in his review. In both, Ibsen had been guilty of writing 'prose in verse' instead of 'thinking poetically', and of working from a gallery of types rather than creating unique and living characters. *Peer Gynt* was not poetry, and its riddles were insoluble because they were empty, and the entire play devoid of idealism.

To Hegel, Ibsen affected to be unmoved by the critical hostility; that Norwegians protested did not worry him in the least. But he felt that both Norwegians and Danes made too much of the play's satirical content – 'Why can they not read it as a poem?' Naturally, as an artist, he did not enjoy seeing his work reduced to the status of a political pamphlet. But there again, if Norwegians thought they recognised themselves in *Peer Gynt* – well, if the cap fits, go ahead and wear it.

In reality *Peer Gynt* was much too important to Ibsen for him to remain unmoved; along with *Brand*, this play represents a turning point in his literary career so far, one that involved the final disappearance of that persistent vein of national romanticism that runs through his early plays, and its replacement by a vein that threaded its way inwards towards the human mind.

THE MIND'S SILVER VEINS

Given the number of punches and kicks handed out to Norwegian culture and Norwegian ways in the course of the play it is little wonder that so many read *Peer Gynt* as a satire on Norway and Norwegians. Such a reading persists to this day, though time has relegated it to a secondary position. But even among the play's contemporary readers there were those who highlighted other aspects.

One alternative to the nationalist-satirical reading was to see it as a folk play, with Peer as a sort of Askeladd (Ash Lad), or an Aladdin in more cosmopolitan guise, someone whose journey through life is presented as a fabulous odyssey before he finally wins the princess and the kingdom in Solveig's humble shack. Such a reading, with its echoes of the romance of fantasy, fairy tale and dream, invites a more positive assessment of Peer's character.

There is, however, a third reading, one in which the drama is understood as a morality play patterned on the morality plays of the Middle Ages, with associations to Goethe's *Faust* or Heiberg's *A Soul after Death*. Within this tradition, Peer's flights of fantasy appear as character flaws, and his journey through life as the path of a lost soul – until in the end he finds salvation.[19]

In this light, Peer appears as Brand's polar opposite, the negative image of the priest's character and personality.

A fourth reading ties the play even more closely to *Brand*. In this, both plays are viewed as transitional stages linking Ibsen's national-romantic period with the concentration on the individual and the personality that became the central theme of his later writing.[20] Ibsen had grown up at a time of national romanticism, in which ideas such as 'the nation' had acquired almost metaphysical dimensions, and in his earlier plays much of the dramatic tension lay in the characters' relationship to overarching phenomena such as the nation, and Christianity. Essentially, human beings were a part of something larger than themselves. It was this sense of belonging that Ibsen lost during the years in Rome. Disappointment over Dybbøl precipitated the breakdown of ideas about the national collective, and accentuated his sense of revolt against the nationalist project back home. This revolt is most strongly apparent in *Brand*, in which the priest's fanatical struggle against the collective is opposed by an equally fanatical struggle against – yes, well, what, actually? Arne Garborg was right to wonder what Brand was actually fighting for, beyond his simple demand for wholeness and consistency in people.[21] Once the national collective has been jettisoned, what exactly is it in *Brand* that assumes the role of the overarching element?

The answer depends on the reading. Some might say God, but in that case it is the god of Kierkegaard, independent of the collective. Others will say that *Brand* merely expresses Ibsen's revolt in favour of individuality, but that he has not yet identified a larger entity to which the individual might relate.

* * *

Brand and *Peer Gynt* represent a decisive turning point in Ibsen's oeuvre, a turning inward towards the personality, the individual and the individual's ethical responsibilities. And it is precisely here that he resonates so profoundly with the spirit of his own times. In the 1860s liberalism and belief in the individual had reached its zenith in Europe, and beyond Europe too. In Russia the battle raged against serfdom; America was involved in the civil war that led to the abolition of slavery. It was in this decade that economic liberalism had its real breakthrough, in the form of free-trade agreements and the abolition of privileges. The hero of the age was the industrial entrepreneur, capitalism's own self-made man. All of this brought the individual into central focus, as did the growing opposition to the Church and the authority of Christianity. Charles Darwin's book on the origin of species, published in 1859, was the battering ram of the new scientific thinking, forcing the individual to take responsibility for a definite view of life, even if this entailed a denial of God Almighty himself.

The relationship between faith and knowledge, the focus on the individual's ethical responsibilities, and a philosophising on the subject of the personality as the very essence of life, all these characterised the spirit of the age, and were present in the form of ideas long before Ibsen. Since the beginning of the century, philosophers and poets such as the Norwegian Niels Treschow and the Danes F. C. Sibbern and Poul Martin Møller had represented a school of thought that focused on the philosophy of personality and psychological 'theories of the soul', which also included an interest in the fantastic and the insane, corresponding in this respect to a movement in the times away from the universal and towards the individual.

In the Dano-Norwegian tradition, this tendency is seen as a series of 'laying on of hands', from teacher to pupil, in which Søren Kierkegaard's 'laying on of hands' on Ibsen is seen as the culmination.[22] So the preconditions for Ibsen's turn towards the personality and the individual's ethical responsibility involved much more than just Kierkegaard. Among his own contemporaries there were other influences. Clemens Petersen's programme of poetics was rooted in an ethical idealism and an individualistic poetic vision, and in the autumn of 1867 the Danish philosopher Rasmus Nielsen occasioned an extensive debate when he suggested that faith and knowledge were wholly distinct entities. The debate brought into sharp focus the intolerable burden devolving on the individual to take personal responsibility for his or her own attitude towards life's most profound ethical questions. The freedom of liberalism and the demands of society, faith and knowledge, idea and reality, the individual and the world – opinions were sharply divided on the relationship between these; the common ground was the individual's constitution in the world.

And yet despite these more general preconditions, there can be no doubt that Kierkegaard occupied a unique position in Ibsen's thinking – indeed, that he exercised a crucial influence on Ibsen's development as a poet and a human being. The influence involves the direct adoption of ideas, as well as the more indirect influence of the Danish philosopher's unique style. Kierkegaard's philosophy is not only elegant, witty and literary; it also features a theatrical construction. His play with pseudonyms as mouthpieces for expressing differing approaches to life has been described as 'the first, modern existential theatre'.[23] In the same way, Ibsen's characters represented different attitudes towards life, frequently in their most extreme manifestations, as in the cases of Brand and Peer Gynt.

A great deal has been written on the question of Kierkegaard's more direct influence on Ibsen's texts. It seems certain that he had been reading Kierkegaard since his days in Grimstad.[24] The influence is evident in the case of the poem 'Balminder' ('Ballroom Memories'), but more difficult to pin down elsewhere in the poetry of Ibsen's youth. In a general sense the lyrical attraction to themes such as *memory* and *the longing for sorrow* points towards Kierkegaard's aesthetics, but there are parallels too with the Romantic ideas of the times in general, and in Welhaven's work in particular. There are clear textual parallels between the poet and the philosopher in dramas such as *Lady Inger of Østråt* and *Olaf Liljekrans*, but it is not until Ibsen's second sojourn in Christiania that Kierkegaard moves to the foreground, most strikingly in *Love's Comedy*, *Brand* and *Peer Gynt*, with decreasing effect in the later dramas.

Above all, the influence is most evident in Kierkegaard's ideas on the different stages that become options to human beings as they make their way through life. These stages are partly successive, partly hierarchical, with the *aesthetic* as the lowest of them. This is the natural state of the human being, the stage of spontaneity, with pleasure as its goal, with no thought of responsibility or attitude. But after a time individuals reach a point at which they are in a position to choose their lives (a choice informed by the *angst* that comes with the freedom to choose), meaning that they may elect to remain at the aesthetic stage (either in continuing spontaneity, like Don Juan, or in a more sophisticated fashion, as in the case of Johannes the Seducer), or to proceed to another level of existence. In the *ethical stage* individuals choose to take responsibility for their own lives by relating them to rules governing what is right and what is wrong, and in doing so creating a meaning and a context for life. For the ethical person *guilt* and *regret* – concepts that have no meaning for the aesthetic person – have a regulatory effect on how he or she conducts their life. With the *religious stage* comes a recognition that regret cannot atone for guilt, which thereafter becomes *sin*. In other words, individuals cannot save themselves; sin can only be atoned for by a *sincere* abandonment to God.

Kierkegaard speaks of the transitions between these three stages as 'leaps', and it is of particular interest to note that the 'leap' away from the aesthetic stage is related to 'becoming one's self'. Kierkegaard's philosophy of personality is inextricably related to the question of ethical responsibility, a link which can easily be applied to Ibsen as well. Kierkegaard never presented his philosophy as a coherent and disciplined teaching – his style is more rhapsodic, essayistic, above all literary. This is how Ibsen must have read him, making it unwise to apply a 'Kierkegaardian teaching', which is a later construction, directly onto his own contemporary readership. Ibsen might just as easily have been fascinated by certain isolated aspects of the Kierkegaardian universe, by the elegance of his paradoxes and the power of his concepts, as by the deeper contents of his philosophy. And yet one can hardly doubt that the connection between Kierkegaard's stages and the 'leaps' between them was obvious to Ibsen's contemporary readers, including to Ibsen himself.

* * *

The indications are that it was the journey to Rome, and his experience of Dybbøl's devastated defences, that awoke the ethical being in Ibsen. 'If I were to describe the most significant result of my journey so far,' he writes to Bjørnson in September 1865, having just completed *Brand*, 'then I would say it is that I have rid myself of the aesthetic . . .'

Bjørnson could count himself lucky, he wrote, because – unlike him – he had never been plagued by a need to look at the world 'through the ring of thumb and forefinger', meaning the aesthetician's distant and uninvolved attitude towards life. A human as well as an artistic understanding was involved here, because it was in Rome that Ibsen definitively ended his relationship with the Danish aestheticism represented by Heiberg, and embarked on the divine poetical madness of which *Brand* was the first manifestation.

But it is as unwise to suppose that Ibsen the man lived his life in relation to philosophical categories as it is to suppose that Ibsen the writer contented himself with transcribing another's world of thought into verse.[25] Ibsen always maintained that he had read little of Kierkegaard, and understood even less.[26] On both counts the claim is unlikely, and should be seen as an unwillingness – not uncommon among writers – to admit any literary debt at all to others. But it must have been frustrating for Ibsen to find himself regarded in some quarters as more or less a disciple of Kierkegaard, both because Kierkegaard's ideas in general were in the air at the time, and because Ibsen made so much of this common intellectual currency entirely his own in terms of the form in which he expressed it. His attitude towards the theme of *sorrow* can serve as one illustration of this. In the poetry of his youth, Ibsen's attitude towards the yearning for sorrow had elements that might suggest the aesthetician's despair at the emptiness of life, and both Falk in *Love's Comedy* and Jatgeir in *The Pretenders* associate the call to be a poet with 'the gift of sorrow'. Ibsen's letter to Carl Johan Anker in 1858 is confirmation that he shared this longing. Here he openly concedes that he has longed for, indeed, almost prayed for some great sorrow that would 'give meaning to life'. That he also found the sensation problematic is evident from his assurance that he had now put it behind him, but that it would 'always remain a memory' within him.

Ibsen's personal attitude towards sorrow can probably best be understood in isolation from Kierkegaard. He manifestly did not put his sorrow behind him, but instead endowed it with an ethical seriousness that moves beyond the sense in which Kierkegaard used the term. This is the sense in which he experienced Dybbøl, and in the way he wished that his fellow countrymen might be struck down by some 'national disaster' that would spur them into action.

Ibsen lived always on the wintry side of life, driven on constantly by the longing for some profound experience that might force him, and the rest of the world, into an awakening.

His denial of the influence of Kierkegaard can probably be traced to two main sources, Frederik Helveg and Georg Brandes, who in books published in, respectively, 1866 and 1867, viewed *Brand* from the perspective of Kierkegaardian philosophy – indeed, Brandes calls Ibsen quite simply 'the poet of Kierkegaard'.[27] This was probably enough to make Ibsen afraid that his great breakthrough play was being reduced to a sort of stew of Danish Kierkegaardianism and Norwegian pietism. Additionally there was the fact that Kierkegaard, despite the literary aspects of his style, was a philosopher, not a writer. Ibsen was in no doubt that philosophy was something profoundly different from literature, and that he belonged in this latter category, not the former. He never read deeply in either philosophical or scientific writings, and remained unembarrassed by the fact. For it was the writer's privilege 'above all to *see*, not to reflect'.

'MY BOOK *IS* POETRY'

The divided critical response to *Peer Gynt* had no apparent consequences for its sales. The first print run of 1,250 sold out immediately, and within fourteen days a second printing of 2,000 was necessary. Ibsen had done it again. Readers in Scandinavia had been consumed with an excited anticipation over the follow-up to *Brand*, and Ibsen had not let them down.

There was really only one sour note, and it was a very sour one indeed. Its name was Clemens Petersen. In the late winter of 1868, Ibsen bumps into his old walking companion from Ischia, Vilhelm Bergsøe, at the premises of the Scandinavian Society.

'Have you read what he wrote?' asked Ibsen.

'Who?' responded Bergsøe.

'*Fædrelandet*'s great oracle has passed down his judgement on me as well, so you're not alone any more. He's understood about as much of Peer Gynt as an Eskimo from Lapland, and off he goes and fills his column with a lot of drivel and nonsense. It makes you feel ill just to read it.'

And with that he snapped the pen he was holding in two, muttering 'Hopeless!' And would Bergsøe mind giving him a thrashing next time he was in Copenhagen? Bergsøe couldn't promise to do that – and nor could Bjørnson, who had received a similar commission in a furious letter from his friend in December: a crime, that was the only word for Petersen's review, and may it 'sear and scorch his soul'. Bjørnson must have seen the literary prophet's wild eyes and sternly wagging finger as he read on: 'If this is war, then so be it!' Ibsen would show them. If he wasn't a poet, then he would get a camera and deal with those philistines as a photographer would. One by one he would deal with them, portraying them just the way he had portrayed the language reformers – 'the child in the womb shall not be spared . . .'

In its rage and bitterness the letter was unique; he would never write another one like it again.

'My book *is* poetry; and if it is not, then it will become so. The idea of what poetry is – in our country, in Norway – will submit to my book.'

A rage such as this could have only one source; Ibsen hated Petersen because his attitude towards him had been originally one of the most profound respect. While still at work on *Peer Gynt* he had sent the critic a letter in which he humbly thanked him for his review of *Brand* – for what he had written, and for what lay between the lines. Just as he had done after *Love's Comedy*. Again Petersen had to be told how much his criticism had meant to him. In fact, Petersen's criticism of *Peer Gynt* was not so strikingly different from what he had written about *Brand* – although in the latter case he had shown more respect for Ibsen's literary talent – or at least, that was how Ibsen interpreted it. Essentially what Petersen did in his review of *Peer Gynt* was combine all his arguments around the one central objection he had to both plays, indeed, to Ibsen's writing as a whole, that none of it was real poetry. This was the accusation that Ibsen found intolerable.

At that time Petersen occupied a unique position in Danish cultural life. He was chief reviewer for the country's most influential cultural organ, and the first critic to have a daily newspaper as his main platform. He was a conscientious writer, but entertaining, undeniably stylish and authoritative.[28] There was no getting around him for a man like Ibsen, and not only as a way in to the Danish book market. The *substance* of his criticism was of equal importance. Since his debut as a critic in 1856 he had maintained a clear distance from the regime of Johan Ludvig Heiberg. 'The age of elegance is gone', Petersen had announced, with reference to the formalism, and the stress laid on rules and external form, that characterised the work of a man who was both his own as well as Ibsen's former teacher. According to Petersen, Heiberg and his protégés had turned aesthetics into a 'social grace' and poetry into something 'outside of ourselves, that one brushes and beats, and occasionally dons, like an item of clothing'. Writing was, for Petersen, more than form and technique, but also more than 'an act of reflection'. What he sought instead was 'the poetic in poetry'. He tried to penetrate to the text's deepest levels of ethical, artistic and idealistic content. He demanded of a work of art that it have purpose, seriousness and conscience. Poetry must be *real*, arising from a source of genuine inspiration within the writer himself, and *truthful* in the sense of showing a complete inner consistency in the characters. Above all what characterised Clemens Petersen's literary vision was his understanding of the *ethical*, an understanding that locates him somewhere between the formal-aesthetic poetics of Heiberg, and the psychological and realistic view of literature that arrived with Brandes and the modern breakthrough. In the history of Danish theatrical criticism he is aptly described as 'the defender and critic of the drama of ideas'.

No wonder Ibsen felt attracted; these were the terms of his own revolt against Heiberg, of everything he had learned from the madness of Michelangelo, and not least of the process that lay behind the writing of his two most recent dramas. In his own estimation he had managed to cross the 'yawning chasm' that lies between 'wanting' to write and 'having' to write, and his success in doing so was in no small measure due to Clemens Petersen.

Or at least he thought he had, until Petersen once again – and this time more trenchantly than ever before – denied that *Peer Gynt* was poetry. In other words, Ibsen's cry of 'My book *is* poetry' was a very specific reference to the conception of poetry promoted by Petersen, but which the teacher himself had failed to recognise when it was placed under his own nose! That was how important Clemens Petersen was to Ibsen. The fact that his importance has been so little noted in the field of Ibsen studies is partly because of his close association with Ibsen's great rival Bjørnson, and partly because of Ibsen's later connections with Georg Brandes. But just as Brandes' importance for Ibsen has been exaggerated in the literary histories, the influence of Clemens Petersen's idealism has been underestimated.

So Ibsen had to make do without Clemens Petersen. His hegemony in the cultural life of Denmark was in any event soon over. In March 1869 he had to leave the country following revelations of sexual abuse of boys at the school where he taught. Scandal was inevitable, and Petersen's enemies had a field day, for his harsh and pitiless criticisms had made him many enemies. For a long time afterwards his name and his work were passed over in silence. He settled in the United States, and did not return to his homeland until 1904, an old man, beaten and senile.

As for poetry, things went the way Ibsen had predicted. It was indeed poetry that had to submit to his book, and not the other way round.

Peer Gynt became poetry.

THE END OF A DREAM

In reality, Ibsen's challenge to Bjørnson to thrash Petersen also involved a rebuke: Bjørnson should not only have protested against the review, he should also have expressly denied that he was complicit in it. Bjørnson's involvement was something people might have suspected, and that he was merely hiding behind his own positive review in *Norsk Folkeblad*. He himself entertained no such suspicions, Ibsen assured him, but his whole approach was so paranoid that Bjørnson had every right to feel he was being accused of something.

Bjørnson, who had already declared his devotion in that effusive letter, was no less affectionate this time around. How could Ibsen feel threatened by something as insignificant as a review, he asks patiently? Bjørnson was actually worried about the state of his friend's mental and physical health, given the demented fury of his tirade against Petersen. Perhaps it would be a good idea for Ibsen to get away from Rome for a while? And maybe he should respond to his critics by writing a light entertainment – 'Give them your wine, not your wrath.' And his approach works. Ibsen regrets his 'idiotic outburst' and thanks his friend for his understanding. A rapprochement seems to have occurred, and Ibsen appears to have moved on from Clemens Petersen's review.

But it was all only on the surface.

In reality he never did forgive Petersen, and his relationship with Bjørnson grew increasingly cool. For Ibsen the whole business was an opportunity to relinquish the burden of gratitude he felt towards his supporter and competitor. But the break was not yet in the open, and did not become so until Ibsen did as Bjørnson had suggested, and wrote a light entertainment, but not something as free of wrath as the one Bjørnson had suggested. By early 1868 it was clear to Ibsen that his time in Rome was up; with Garibaldi's entry into the city the Roman dream was in serious danger of ending.

'It would distress me greatly if politics and empty phrase-making became the order of the day here too,' Ibsen had written to his mother-in-law the previous autumn. 'But sooner or later it will happen.'

And he was right about that, though on this occasion Garibaldi's advance turned out to be premature. While the Red Shirts marched on Rome at the end of September 1867 Garibaldi himself was under arrest in Caprera and unable to join his men until he made a dramatic escape, in time for what turned out to be a hopeless struggle against the papal forces and the French army which, having previously withdrawn, now returned to guarantee the freedom of the Vatican State. The expected uprising of the people of Rome never occurred, and in the course of September and October Garibaldi's men were either massacred or fled, blood flowed in the streets of ancient Rome, and Garibaldi himself was once more placed under arrest.

The battle was lost, but not the war. Two years later the pope lost his protector for good once the French found themselves fully preoccupied in dealing with Otto von Bismarck, who had now directed his well-disciplined forces southwards. Thus Pope Pius IX was left to defend his tiny state alone. In September 1870 Rome fell at last, and was incorporated into the Italian state, eternity being compelled to defer to the exigencies of the present.

Ibsen's response to all this was mixed. Garibaldi was a man he admired deeply, a hero who stood for everything Norwegians did *not* stand for – a willingness to make sacrifices, courageousness and resolution in action. It would have been a good thing, in his view, for Norwegians to have been struck by some 'national tragedy', it would have given them the chance to show that they too, like Garibaldi's brave army, were deserving of honour. Rome had given Henrik Ibsen his breakthrough. Its dreamlike and timeless atmosphere had worked a deep magic on him, in stark contrast to his earlier life in Norway. The reality of life in Norway had been burdensome for him. There is nothing to suggest that the ceaseless struggle to live the writer's life had strengthened him – any more than the draining effort to meet his obligations at the theatre, following the cultural and political debates in the newspapers, having to take account of the views of the theatre committee, public taste, and the state's persistent financial stinginess in funding the country's cultural life.

In a predicament like that, a man such as Bjørnson rolled up his shirtsleeves; Ibsen's response had been to pull down the brim of his hat.

Seen from this perspective, Rome offered Ibsen freedom in two quite distinct ways. One was the freedom from every serious personal responsibility save that to his own immediate family; the other was that it provided him, as a writer, with complete independence of any institution. For the first time in his life he had been able to *write for the sake of writing alone*. That he should have written two dramas for reading, rather than stage plays, was one expression of this new freedom. And in Gyldendal's Frederik Hegel, who had accepted *Brand* without even having read it, he had found a publisher prepared to give him complete artistic freedom. Following the commercial success of *Brand* this artistic freedom was assured.

Rome had liberated him – and yet he had to leave the city. The Scandinavian community there had been an environment largely insulated from the trivialities of the world, a place where he devoted himself to the pursuit of writing and the good life. All his days he would recall life in Rome filtered through a veil of nostalgia that eliminated all trace of his money troubles and the alcohol-fuelled spats. In reality the 'golden days' were confined to the first twelve months or so; as early as 1865 he had started to complain of boredom there. At its best the attitude towards poetry and art in the Roman life around him was one of a contemplative and backward-looking sort; at its worst it descended into a parodic cultivation of ancient ideas and Romantic clichés. The writer of revolutionary dramas such as *Brand* and *Peer Gynt* could not be comfortable for long in Rome's soporific dream of classicism, and once Garibaldi's troops had disturbed the papal peace it was only a question of time before Ibsen began packing his suitcase.

The question was, where to go?

Ibsen was not yet ready to return home. Had he done so, he was convinced he would have turned everyone against him within a month of his arrival, or else 'start wearing all sorts of disguises again and become a lie both to myself and to others'. Putting it bluntly, he was not strong enough to live as a Norwegian in Norway. He had made his position clear to Bergsøe:

I am not going back to Norway, until Norway calls for me.

Financially, he was now able to choose to live wherever he wanted, provided banking and a postal service to Norway and Denmark were available. He was a free writer, and what sort of good reasons did a man really need anyway for *not* settling in Norway? Even so, Ibsen did not at this point envisage a lengthy period of exile; sooner or later he would have to return home, he thought – but not just yet. Winter turned to spring in 1868 and the family had still not made a decision; but by April a goal was becoming clear. The family would spend the summer in northern Italy or the Tyrol; after that, everything was flexible.

Rome had given him his freedom. The challenge now was what to do with it.

VII

DRESDEN

SILENCE

On the evening of 31 August 1870 the head of the Prussian General Staff, Helmuth von Moltke, stood on the crest of a hill overlooking the River Meuse and the small French town of Sedan on its further bank. Standing alongside him was the Prussian prime minister, Otto von Bismarck, with King Wilhelm I and his sons. Below them was the French army, ensconced in and around Sedan and the town's old fortress.

Too late the French emperor Napoleon III had learned that Prussian military might was something to be feared. Just a few years previously, the German kingdom was merely one of many such on the patchwork quilt that was Europe; but gradually its power had increased. In 1864 Prussia conquered Holstein, Lauenburg and Schleswig, and in doing so encountered no objections from the French emperor, who saw the strategic value of a counterbalance to Austria's dominant position on the European continent. Along with Russia it was the Habsburgs who stood in the way of his dream of a united Europe, with France at its centre and Paris as the shining capital of the continent. In 1856 the combined forces of France, Austria and England defeated Russia on the Crimean Peninsula. Two years later France, with the support of the Italian nationalist movement, drove the Austrians out of northern Italy.

But the Prussians had plans of their own – if not for a united Europe then for a united Germany. In 1866 they began a brief and effective campaign against Austria, still with the blessing of the French. Not until the defeat of Austria, and the Prussian annexation or enrolment of the northern German states under its leadership, did Napoleon finally realise that he had a new and dangerous competitor in the struggle for hegemony in Europe.

Almost overnight, Prussia had become an industrial and military giant, without the traditions and cultural heritage of France, but more modern, and equally well organised and ambitious.

With the outbreak of the Franco-German war in the summer of 1870, two of the most advanced countries on the continent faced up to each other. Every aspect of nascent modernity – the industrialisation, the long railway links, the well-organised apparatus of government and the capitalist economy, the research and the technology – was brought into play in a way that would reach a preliminary climax in the bloodbath at Sedan. The Prussian forces numbered 120,000 men and 700 powerful canons from the Krupp factory. Strategically and technologically they were superior to the French army, led by the emperor himself. By the end, 3,000 French soldiers lay dead on the field of battle, 14,000 were wounded, and another 21,000 taken prisoner. Victory at Sedan was a decisive moment for the Prussians, and a slaughterhouse for the French. But even after the surrender of Napoleon III, the war was not over. A new army under republican leadership continued the fight, until France was finally obliged to concede defeat in February 1871. In all the war had cost the lives of 140,000 Frenchmen and 47,500 Germans; to these figures must be added the thousands of lives lost with the fall of the Paris Commune.

* * *

On 13 May 1868, more than two years before that bloody September day in Sedan, Henrik Ibsen left Rome with his wife and son. For four years he had been living in the Papal City, still shielded from the barbarities of the outside world by the French emperor. Rome existed beyond time, in a world of dream and forgetfulness all its own. There were no revolts here, no industry, no marching soldiers, or any of the other harsh realities of life that were in the process of changing Europe. He would spend the next few years in Germany, at the heart of a moving stream of events that would shape and change the continent in the name of modernity. The decade that divided *Peer Gynt* (1867) from *The Pillars of Society* (1877) was a time of radical change for Ibsen, and one in which the war between Germany and France put an end to any faith he might once have had in European civilisation.

Henceforth nothing would be as it once had been. Everything was in the process of change – including literature.

The plan was to spend the summer in northern Italy or the Alps. The family journeyed northwards in a leisurely fashion. They spent eight days in Florence, two in Bologna, eight in Venice and as many in Bozen, before eventually arriving at the place where they would spend the rest of the summer – 'the loveliest area I have seen north of the Alps, cheap, accessible, delightful in every way', Ibsen wrote to a friend in Rome. The place was Berchtesgaden in Bayern, a pretty mountain village divided by two small rivers, a fertile spot with picturesque houses and churches ringed around by snow-clad peaks.

Quiet, pretty and cheap – an irresistible combination for Ibsen.

The summer days went by in pleasant and leisurely fashion, with Ibsen walking in the mountains and spending time with his family. He wrote to consul Johan Bravo in Rome that he was contemplating making a start on a new play, although he didn't expect to really get going until late in the summer. Meanwhile the family had decided to spend the winter in Munich and

Dresden, probably out of consideration for Sigurd. The boy was now eight years old, and it was time for him to begin school properly. In Rome his education had been a mixture of teaching at home, private tuition, and his own independent reading. The problem was that there was not a single Protestant school in Rome.

Towards the end of August a letter Ibsen writes to Hegel reveals that he has not been completely idle that summer. With a new edition of *Love's Comedy* out of the way (1867) he felt the time was right for another new edition, this time aimed at the major theatrical venues in Denmark and Sweden. His choice fell on *The Pretenders*, which had enjoyed such success at the Christiania Theatre back in January 1864. Ibsen had had little contact with the theatre since then. So this would be his next project: the conquest of the Scandinavian theatre world. But it wasn't something that could be achieved overnight. The new edition of *The Pretenders* was delayed, and he had only just made a start on his new play.

At the end of August the family left Berchtesgaden and travelled to Munich, where they were able to enjoy 'all the city's marvellous art treasures, and the people's loathing of the Prussians'. For four weeks the family lived at Maximiliansplatz 13, before continuing their journey to Dresden early in October. Here they would spend the winter before travelling back home to Norway.

The plan was to stay one winter; in fact, over six years would pass before they moved on again.

Dresden was the capital of the old kingdom of Saxony, a city characterised by all the transitional phenomena of the late nineteenth century – from feudal state to bourgeois state, from agrarian to industrial society, and from an independent monarchy to incorporation into the Prussian unification of German states that led to the establishment of the empire in 1871. The architecture and town-planning were Baroque, but gradually being supplanted by more modern styles and fashions. It remained dignified and impressive, a city built on both banks of the Elbe, with its spires, its towers and cupolas arching up towards the heavens – especially in the old town, south of the river bend, with its Frauenkirche, one of the largest Baroque churches in Europe, the city's famed art academy, the Königliches Hoftheater and the Zwinger Palace – while in and around these spiritual and cultural institutions the modern world hummed and buzzed in the shape of tramcars, banks, office buildings and business premises. The factories and the workers' housing were located on the outskirts of the city; Dresden was a centre for the production of ceramics, chemicals and pharmaceuticals, as well as tobacco and chocolate.

If Rome was a dream of classicism, then Dresden represented contemporary, modern European reality. During the first part of the century the city had established itself as an important cultural centre in Germany, even though it neither then nor later challenged Berlin or Munich. A colony of Russian revolutionaries contributed to the strongly liberal and radical intellectual atmosphere in the city. The anarchist Mikhail Bakunin moved there in 1844 and worked with the revolutionary author Arnold Ruge, a later associate of Karl Marx. The liberal sympathies among the city's intellectuals were dealt a severe blow by the quashing of the Dresden revolution of May 1849, and the entry of Prussian troops into the city. Strict restrictions that included censorship had been imposed, though these were presently relaxed, and by the end of the 1860s cultural life was once again thriving alongside both liberal and conservative forces. Monarchic conservatism and liberal intellectualism were opposing polarities that were to some extent brought into harmony by a shared patriotism and a dream of German unity that was common to both monarchists and liberals, enhanced by Prussian successes in the Franco-German war of 1870–1.

In this melting pot of new and old styles and ideas, Baroque beauty and dirty factories, the Ibsens made their home in October 1868, moving into an apartment at An der Frauenkirche 6, in the centre of historic Dresden, near the Frauenkirche and the Johanneum, the Renaissance palace where Ibsen had seen works of art when he visited the city back in 1852. All the signs were that Dresden would be a pleasant place to stay the winter – and like Berchtesgaden, it had the advantage of being another 'very cheap place to live'.

The only trouble was that they didn't know anyone there. No Scandinavian community, no prospect of evenings out with the wine and talk flowing.

Only the three of them.

'Do you know of any Danes who intend to spend the winter in Dresden?' Ibsen rather pathetically wrote to Hegel shortly after arriving. 'I long for Scandinavian company; there may be some here, but so far I haven't met any.'

But Ibsen had learned how to spend time in Dresden before. He visited the Königliches Hoftheater, which in his opinion was one of the best in Germany, even if it was 'no match for Copenhagen's Kongelige Teater as regards taste and repertoire'. At the very least the city provided him with peace in which to work, and by the end of October he was able to inform Hegel that he had a complete draft and a revised first act of his new play ready. It was a romantic comedy on the subject of the 'currents and tendencies in contemporary life'. The play was set in Norway, but Ibsen hastened to assure Hegel that it would be of great interest to Danes too. And the title? *The League of Youth, or Our Lord and Co.*

By Christmas he had revised it as far as the fourth act and was still going strong. In the meantime, on the advice of Hegel, the title had changed. He conceded that 'Our Lord and Co' would only result in outrage and accusations of blasphemy that lay well outside the actual intentions of the play and agreed to cut the subtitle and call it just *The League of Youth*.

The play was not ready by the end of the year as he had hoped it would be. Ibsen had several other irons in the fire that winter. In February he applied for a travel grant from the Department of Church Affairs with the aim of spending a year in Sweden in the study of 'the Swedish peoples' attitude towards culture, art and literature' – yet another attempt to cement his reputation as a Scandinavian and not merely a Norwegian writer. In Germany the initiative came from others working on his behalf. As early as the winter of 1864–5 Edvard Grieg's brother John, in a burst of pure enthusiasm, had translated *The Pretenders* into German with the help of his German-born wife, Marie Erhardt. The translation was done in Dresden, where John Grieg had studied, and there was a reading at the premises of the literary society in the city in the spring of 1866. Grieg, however, was unable to find a publisher willing to publish an unknown Norwegian author. In January 1869, Ibsen received a letter from a German travelling salesman named Peter Friedrich Siebold telling him that he was at work on a translation into German of *Brand*.[1] Ibsen was uncertain how to respond but decided in the end not to object and then inundated Siebold with suggestions – could he arrange for a favourably inclined portrait article about him to appear in a Leipzig newspaper, one in which all his achievements in Scandinavia could be mentioned?

> If my name could be introduced to Germans in this way then it would be a
> lot easier to find a publisher for your translation.

And might a translation of *The Pretenders* be interesting as a follow-up project?

> The theme of the play is remarkably apposite in the light of recent
> developments in Germany, the unification of the different parts under a
> single leadership etc.

Ibsen's historical drama about the unification of Norway during the High Middle Ages had appealed strongly to the nationalist elite in Norway in the 1860s. Why should it not exert a similar appeal on the Germans, who were engaged in a parallel process of unification under Prussian leadership? Might not the ongoing formation of a German nation give the play an extended contemporary relevance? Ibsen was convinced it would. At the very least the Germans should know that a successful Scandinavian dramatist on the payroll of the Norwegian state was present among them, ready to sell them the great chastiser Brand and Haakon the reconciler. The irony here, of course, was that Haakon's conciliatory rhetoric was now meant to support German unification, while Brand was roused to fury by the consequences of that very same nationalist impulse for Denmark during the war of 1864.

It couldn't be helped: Ibsen was engaged in a unification process of his very own, one that trumped all other considerations.

CHANGING OF THE GUARDS

It was more important to write a new work than sell old ones, and through the spring of 1869 it was the new play that preoccupied Ibsen. As early as the end of February he had gleefully informed Hegel that the play was finished, but the fair copy was not in fact despatched until 2 May.

In *The League of Youth* Ibsen presents us with a large cast of characters involved in an intricate plot, with the young Steensgaard at its centre. The ambitious lawyer settles in a small Norwegian town, and uses a speech on 17 May, National Day, to attack the owner of the local ironworks, Bratsberg, and announce the formation of a new party, to be called The League of Youth. The crowd hails his speech, and Steensgaard finds himself welcomed into Bratsberg's house, on the mistaken assumption that his speech was in fact an attack on his competitor, a landowner named Monsen. It is only the first in a whole series of misunderstandings and intrigues involving both love and politics. Steensgaard has previously courted Monsen's daughter Ragna, but now finds it more opportune to turn his attention to Bratsberg's daughter, Thora. When Bratsberg at length realises that it was he who was the object of the attack and throws the lawyer out of his house, Ragna once again becomes the chosen one. In among the lawyer's pompous speechmaking and his ignominious volte-faces it emerges that a swindle has been carried out by chamberlain Bratsberg's son Erik that threatens to ruin both Bratsberg and Monsen. Steensgaard thereupon proposes to a rich widow, Madame Rundholmen, but turns his focus back on Thora the moment her father is cleared of involvement in the swindle. Thora, however, like Ragna, and like Madame Rundholmen, finds someone else. It leaves Steensgaard with no option but to leave town, at which everything returns to normal again – save for the number of new, happy couples to be seen around town.

Steensgaard loses everything, but the future is on his side: unscrupulous and opportunistic as he is, does he not possess all the qualities necessary to make a good politician? That, at any rate, is the view of the cynical Daniel Hejre, who closes the play with a quotation from Napoleon, to the effect that 'the most dubious material of all, he says, is that which goes into the making of a politician. Ha ha!'

* * *

Literary historians have always had trouble placing both *The League of Youth* and the play that followed it, *Emperor and Galilean*, within Ibsen's oeuvre. The ordering is quite simply wrong! With a seductive regularity Ibsen's production shows a consistency both in terms of his own inner development and its place in the general scheme of literary periodisations. In his national-romantic period he writes plays on nationalist-historical themes, and with the great dramas of ideas he abandons the civilising project and addresses himself instead to the individual within the context of the ethical idealism that characterised Scandinavia in the 1860s. Following this he enters contemporary life fully with realistic plays with modern settings in the 1870s and 1880s, before entering the final, symbolic phase that closes the century. The pattern is all the more seductive since Ibsen's career was coterminous with the second half of the nineteenth century, so that he appears to be almost a personification of the divisions of the literary history of the period.

If only he had not been inconsiderate enough to write *The League of Youth* before *Emperor and Galilean*, instead of allowing the latter to conclude his series of plays of ideas, and the former to inaugurate his plays of contemporary life. But the ordering is by no means arbitrary, and literary history has as little propensity to move in straight lines as did Ibsen's career as a writer. The two dramas that lie between *Peer Gynt* and *The Pillars of Society* reflect in reality a decade of literary, ideological and personal searching.

This searching is especially notable towards the end of the 1860s, and finds its first expression in a revised orientation towards literary leader-figures and friends.

Following the savaging of *Peer Gynt*, Ibsen lost all faith in Clemens Petersen as an arbiter of literary excellence. The death of Paul Botten-Hansen in July of that same year was, in truth, only the physical end of a relationship that had long since ceased to be a useful one. And if Bjørnson was not actually dead for Ibsen, then their friendship seemed to all intents and purposes to be on its deathbed. In a letter to Hegel, Ibsen confided that the correspondence between them had ceased – 'and for a number of reasons I am unhappy with his behaviour, which does not seem to me to be worthy of an honourable man'.

There can be no doubt that Ibsen regarded Bjørnson as complicit in Clemens Petersen's slaughter of *Peer Gynt*, and that this soured the relationship between them. Nor is there any reason to doubt that the debt of gratitude he owed to Bjørnson oppressed him, every bit as much as his own lack of gratitude must have irritated Bjørnson. From its very beginning the friendship between them had been overshadowed by a sharp sense of competition for readers, recognition and literary themes. Add to this that Bjørnson had once again become involved in politics, this time as editor of the radical *Norsk Folkeblad*, a move that was, for Ibsen, the same as a betrayal of his literary calling.

Sparring between the two had always been a feature of the relationship, not only at the artistic but also at the strategic level. Throughout the 1850s and

1860s both men had kept a close eye on changes taking place in Danish cultural life; at any cost, the goal was to be on the side of the future. Bjørnson's early association with Clemens Petersen and the coterie around the newspaper *Fædrelandet* in 1856–7 gave him a head start here, an advantage later reinforced by his alliance with Frederik Hegel and Gyldendal. Through Petersen, Bjørnson had also associated himself with intellectuals such as Rasmus Nielsen and Rudolph Schmidt, connections that were instrumental in driving an ever greater wedge between him and Ibsen towards the end of the 1860s.

Rasmus Nielsen was an unusual figure in Danish intellectual life. He was a charismatic philosopher who worried deeply about the consequences for the Christian faith of the new advances being made in the sciences. It was from Nielsen and his circle that the Darwinists and Positivists in Denmark encountered their first and most serious opposition, with Nielsen arguing that 'faith' and 'knowledge' were two quite incongruous principles, so that a person might subscribe to the new scientific learning without at the same time abandoning the faith of his childhood.

* * *

Nielsen's circle stood for everything that Georg Brandes would later take a stand against. Brandes was born into a Jewish family in 1842. Along with his brother Edvard he would rise to a position of prominence in Danish and Scandinavian cultural life that was unprecedented. Georg was enormously talented and passionate about literature. He completed a doctorate in aesthetics in 1864 before embarking on an uncertain future as writer and critic. Unlike most of his contemporaries, he took an early interest in the writings of English and French authors, those who promoted in their works the modern virtues of rationalism, empiricism, positivism and a faith in the future and in evolution. In France, Comte had provided much of the philosophical framework for the positivist view of life, in which the empirical and regulatory scheme of the natural sciences was applied to art and the humanities. Philosophy and the view of human life were brought down to earth, differing thus from traditional speculative philosophy, not to speak of the Christian view of the world. Positivism proved easy to harmonise with the inevitable Hegelian dialectic, resulting in a markedly optimistic view of the future in which people, measurability and evolutionary belief were central aspects.

The importance of these new ideas came to Brandes during his first extensive trip abroad to France, in 1866–7. In Paris he met Hippolyte Taine, who had developed a positivistic method of studying literature. Brandes attended the theatre, where he saw plays with contemporary settings. French literature fascinated him, and in particular that school known in France as 'Romanticism' that included names such as Victor Hugo, Théophile Gautier, Honoré de Balzac,

Stendhal, George Sand, Alfred de Musset and Prosper Mérimée. Thirty or forty years previously these writers had introduced a socially involved and politically radical *littérature engagée* that addressed itself both to the old, stiff and formal classicism as well as to the idealistic enthusiasms of German Romanticism. As early as the 1850s Bjørnson described this kind of writing as 'naturalism', but until the advocacy of Brandes these French writers had enjoyed little currency in Scandinavia. In many ways this literature was a response to the new, positivistic worldview. It had a decisive impact on Brandes and the whole modern breakthrough in Scandinavia.

On his return from Paris, Brandes tried to apply the lessons he had learned to his own literary activities. He wrote reviews in the spirit of Taine, and engaged in a debate of unusual bitterness with Rasmus Nielsen and Rudolph Schmidt that left them lifelong enemies. It was at just this point in his life that he becomes a presence in the correspondence between Ibsen and Bjørnson.

'You mustn't put too much trust in Brandes,' Bjørnson warns Ibsen in a letter from Copenhagen of December 1867. 'There is something wrong with a person who does not have faith in God at his centre.' Bjørnson had taken up a position in the struggle between faith and knowledge: 'No, we are witness to the growth of another mighty spirit here, the philosopher Rudolph Schmidt.'

The warning came too late for Ibsen. He too had noticed the exchanges between Brandes and Nielsen and was in no doubt about whose side he was on. Brandes condemned Nielsen's distinction between faith and knowledge as a cowardly avoidance of the difficulties of choice, and the author of *Brand* would have had little difficulty in agreeing with him. Ibsen had actually been curious about Brandes for some time, though not as long as Brandes had been curious about him. Through the autumn of 1864 Brandes read all the plays of Ibsen's youth and was particularly impressed by *The Pretenders*. One of the very first reviews he ever wrote was that mixed response to *Brand* of May 1866. Ibsen, who was more interested in criticism that was constructive rather than merely good, clearly saw something there that was of interest to him. He knew, moreover, that Brandes was at work on a longer study of all his plays. He therefore asked Hegel to pass on his thanks to the young critic, and in enclosing his manuscript of *Peer Gynt* in October 1867 he had asked Hegel to convey his greetings and say that 'I am especially interested to hear his opinion of this'.

Shortly afterwards he wrote to the Danish zoologist Jonas Collin:

. . . I must say I find in G. Brandes an altogether convincing and strong voice. I don't know whether you are a friend or opponent; but it seems clear to me that this man will play a vital part in the sciences and raise the level of cultural life back home.

Prophecies don't come much more accurate than that. But in the early stages the personal contact between them was limited to a brief correspondence on the subject of the suicide of their mutual friend Ludvig David in 1866. Later, Brandes wrote a number of reviews and articles about Ibsen's plays, some of which were collected in expanded form for *Aesthetic Studies*, which appeared in 1868. Then, in the summer of 1869, the correspondence between them resumes. And *now* the magic starts. Now both men – both seekers in their respective roles as writer and critic – find a resolution in the work of the other, or in what they choose to see in the other. And so there was a changing of the guard in Ibsen's literary orientation towards the end of the 1860s. Bjørnson, on the other hand, remained loyal to yesterday's men – Clemens Petersen, Rudolph Schmidt and Rasmus Nielsen. Only later, and after a great deal of soul-searching, did he put himself at Brandes' disposal, as did many another Scandinavian writer in the years to come.

* * *

During this time of upheaval, with old friends and literary mentors being exchanged for new ones, and with the intimacy of Rome replaced by the anonymity of city life in Dresden, Ibsen received a reminder of the roots he had severed many years ago. In the summer of 1869 a letter arrives from his sister Hedvig informing him that their mother is dead.

He puts the letter to one side, doesn't answer it immediately.

It had been nineteen years since the parting in Skien, nineteen motherless years. Did he ever think of her? Miss her? Not until September does he reply, in a letter that bristles with contradictory emotions and responses: Hedvig is not to suppose that he has kept her at a distance through indifference, but so much has passed between them, and between himself and his home. Moreover, he concedes, he is not good at writing letters but must be there in person, close, in order to give more fully of himself.

'But you, you can write. Do it. Do it often!'

He can't write, and he doesn't want to either. His sister's revivalist version of Christianity pains him, not least when she attempts to persuade him to share her beliefs: 'Don't try to convert me,' he warns her. 'I want to be truthful; whatever is to be will surely come to be.' Finally he assures her that he still has the 'warmth of heart that has to be present at the outset, in which a truthful and strong spiritual life is best able to flourish'.

Ibsen was strong enough in spirit alright, if not in faith. But where was the warmth towards his sister? It was one thing to thank her for having looked after their parents, and especially their mother who had now passed away. Hedvig, who had 'so lovingly fulfilled your duties on behalf of all the rest of us. You truly are the best of us!' Pretty words from a distant son and brother who has relinquished all responsibilities save those to his calling as a writer. Finally he says it, in a simple greeting on the reverse of a portrait of himself that he encloses with the letter: 'I believe we have always been close, and we will always remain so.'

And so it was, a bond of goodwill and tenderness that would last a lifetime and tolerate everything – except intimacy. For if it really was the case that he had to be physically near in order to give fully of himself, then there were several opportunities to do so on his trips back to Norway in the 1870s and 1880s, and when he finally returned home permanently in 1891. He never took them, and when the two did eventually meet again, both of them were old.

And then it was she who came to see him.

'SOMETHING GREEN IN THE BUTTONHOLE'

In June 1869 the Ibsens moved from the city centre and out to Königsbrücker Strasse 33, in the Antonstadt district, on the other side of the Elbe. It was a place of villas and parks, but also of factories and housing for workers. Sound as it was, their financial situation did not allow them to go on living in the centre of town, in fashionable sight of the Frauenkirche. In Königsbrücker Strasse the family lived close to a barracks and the Jordan and Timaeus coffee and chocolate factory. A few years previously the light and beauty of Rome had filled Ibsen with creative energy; what did the life in Antonstadt fill him with, other than the sound of bugle calls and the nauseating smell of chocolate?

Writing to Hegel, Ibsen optimistically refers to the new apartment as his summer residence, but for two years it became the family home. Letters reveal nothing of his long-term plans, other than that there was still no prospect of a return to Norway. In all likelihood they had decided to remain in Dresden for the time being out of consideration for Sigurd's schooling. While still waiting for the publication of *The League of Youth*, Ibsen submitted the play to the three main theatres in Norway, Sweden and Denmark. Now was the time. Now the Scandinavian theatre world was about to be conquered in one fell swoop.

For the time being, the author's life was rather more eventful than that of his play. That summer he received an invitation to attend a Nordic orthographic conference in Stockholm. He accepted, hoping at the same time to get the opportunity to promote his play. The conference turned out to be the start of something he could not possibly have dreamt of beforehand – an adventure more fantastic than anything from the fascinating world of orthographic reform that would take him on an incredible journey across two continents in the company of kings, khedives and emperors, with sumptuous banquets, champagne, gold, and dancing beauties under the black desert sky.

And it all started with that orthographic conference. On 20 July he travelled to Stockholm. He had been awarded the travel grant that he had applied for to study Swedish culture and literature, but for the time being he preferred to save the money for a later occasion. Having spoken contemptuously of it over the years, this was his first actual personal experience of Sweden. His aim was to win Swedish hearts; what happened was that the Swedes won his heart.

The aim of the conference was to coordinate spelling in the Scandinavian lands. It came to no directly applicable conclusion but did put forward a number of suggestions that in time affected spelling reforms in the three countries.[2] Ibsen was among those who took the suggestions seriously and adopted the 'Scandinavian orthography'. It supplemented perfectly his own dream of a new pan-Scandinavian literature, a dream that would also have the benefit of enlarging the potential market for his books. In revising *Love's Comedy* he had edited out words and phrases that were peculiarly Norwegian, and in his most recent play had tried to achieve a similar effect. The results were twofold. Henceforth in his writing he would avoid old-fashioned Danishisms in favour of a written language that corresponded more closely to the actual sounds of spoken Norwegian; on the other hand, this former vice-chairman of the Norwegian Society also showed himself willing to remove a number of Norwegianisms in favour of a language that once again approached spoken Danish, a compromise he stuck to for the rest of his life.

In addition to Ibsen the Norwegian delegation consisted of Professor Ludvig Kristensen Daa, Jacob Løkke, and Ibsen's old opponent from the Kristiania Norske Theater, Knud Knudsen. It must also have been pleasing to see old friends from Rome again such as Carl Snoilsky and Lorentz Dietrichson. It was Dietrichson who had made the arrangements in Stockholm for him and found him a couple of rooms in Herkules Backe. Dietrichson was by this time a professor at the Academy of Art in Stockholm and moved in the best circles in town. Through him Ibsen would gain access to the very highest social circles in Stockholm, and hardly a day went by without an invitation to dinner.

'My stay in Sweden has been one long celebration,' Ibsen writes to Hegel. 'Wherever I go I encounter the most remarkable courtesy and friendliness.'

It would be hard to say who was the more surprised – the Swedish upper class, at the sight of this small bearded chap who turned out to be the writer of the strange and powerful *Brand*, or Ibsen, at the overwhelming degree of interest in his person he encountered. And among such people! Since the publication of *Brand* he had, after all, hardly mixed with anyone other than a dissolute gang of Scandinavian artists in Rome.

Now the writer could reap the rewards of the work he had sown.

The young August Strindberg was living in Stockholm at the time of Ibsen's visit. He did not meet Ibsen face to face, and in fact would never do so. But he did not forget the Norwegian's first encounter with Sweden.

'Who does not recall the appearance of the famous poet when he visited Stockholm a few years ago,' he later wrote. 'Wearing a velvet jacket, a white waistcoat with black buttons, collar in the latest style and carrying an elegant cane, a self-ironic smile playing at the corner of his lips he strolled about, always avoiding any deep conversations.'

Henrik Halfbeard, the writer who kept his deepest secrets hidden behind an elegant and worldly exterior, aroused interest and created confusion. Could this really be the creator of the world-denying priest Brand? The women in particular were curious about him. Among those he met during his stay was Fredrika Limnell, whom he visited both at her home in Stockholm and at the family's idyllic country residence Lyran, close to Lake Mälaren. In this household Fru Limnell was the heart of an extensive literary circle, and as such she followed Ibsen's career closely over the years to come.

The climax of his stay was probably the audience with Carl XV, king of Sweden, himself an amateur poet and a painter. Ibsen and he had first met many years earlier, in 1856, when the then crown prince visited Bergen. Following a performance at the Kungliga Dramatiska Teatern, Ibsen was invited to a reception with the king and a number of others. Through a colourful Armenian-Egyptian named Ohan Demirgian, employed by Carl as his Crown Equerry, Ibsen was invited to join a delegation attending the opening of the Suez Canal. The delegates were to travel by train from Paris to Marseilles and then by ship to the African continent. They would be travelling as guests of the Egyptian khedive, Ismail Pasha, with all expenses paid. As extra insurance Ibsen decided to take the remainder of the travel grant intended for the study of Swedish culture – now that he was on 'such a good footing' with the king he did not imagine it could possibly cause any trouble.

What an honour! Were these really the kinds of vistas that had now opened up to him? The stay in Stockholm must have woken the social climber's instincts in him. And now he was going to Egypt as the guest of the khedive! Perhaps no great surprise that at this point it occurred to him to upgrade his own appearance a touch? He hinted as much to Erik af Edholm, the Lord Chamberlain, saying that 'something green in the buttonhole' would probably go down well in Egypt. Edholm took the hint and raised the matter with the king a few days later. Ibsen was thereupon summoned, and duly created a Knight of the Vasa Order.

Henrik the knight. In his youth he had turned up his nose at the whole idea of such decorations. With the years came a change of attitude so great that it was now he himself who had solicited the award.

So Ibsen's first visit to Sweden ended in a friendship with the king, a green ribbon to wear in his buttonhole, and an invitation from the Egyptian royal family in his pocket. It was certainly not what he had been expecting when he arrived. For years he had been furious with the Swedes for the way they had let the Danes down in 1864, and as late as the spring of 1868 he was still calling the Swedes 'our spiritual enemies'. Naturally, he felt a little uneasy about what the Swedes might think of him – indeed, the thought had troubled him ever since the appearance of *Brand*.

Fortunately, Suzannah had allayed his fears.

'It makes me so happy to hear that you are having such a wonderful time,' she writes to him not long after his arrival. 'You see now that I was right, when I told you you should get to know Sweden properly.'

In the event his fears proved unfounded. The Danish actress Johanne Luise Heiberg was probably not the only one to be puzzled by the Swedes' enthusiasm for a writer who could 'hardly be said to have flattered them'. But the Swedes did indeed love him. And how was he supposed to keep his anger burning as he hurried from one dinner invitation to the next? In the years to come, Ibsen's hatred of both Sweden and Germany would be tempered as recognition of his literary talent grew in both countries. It was only his own country he could never forgive.

THE GUEST OF THE KHEDIVE

After a farewell dinner at the Kungliga Dramatiska Teatern at the Hotel du Nord in Carl XII Square, Ibsen left Stockholm on 29 September to return to Suzannah and Sigurd in Dresden.

At about the same time *The League of Youth* was finally published in Copenhagen, and during the autumn and winter the play was performed at the main Scandinavian theatres. As far as Ibsen was concerned the play would have to get along without him for the time being, for he had other things on his mind. Not long after his return to Dresden he left again, on a train bound for Paris, and thence to Marseilles, where he boarded the SS *Moeris* along with eighty-five other guests of the Egyptian khedive.

On 9 October the boat sailed, and for the next few weeks Ibsen led a first-class life. His fellow delegates were Scandinavians, Frenchmen, Germans, Dutchmen and Spaniards, with the English leaving separately the following day. Ibsen shared a cabin with the only Swede, Captain Oscar von Knorring, whom he had previously met in Stockholm. Ibsen also spent much of his time in the company of the only other Norwegian in the party, the Egyptologist Jens D. C. Lieblein, a man who had, at some point, managed to give *Brand* a bad review. Among the other passengers were a young Danish literary historian named Peter Hansen, who later became director of the Kongelige Teater, the French writer and critic Théophile Gautier, as well as assorted academics and journalists from various countries. The service on board was excellent, with four meals a day. Alas, much of it went over the side as the weather was rough and few of the passengers were hardened sailors.

At last, on Friday 13 October, they arrived in Alexandria harbour, and Henrik Ibsen was able to set foot on the African continent – two years after *Peer Gynt*.

Two days were spent sightseeing around Alexandria – Pompey's Pillar, Cleopatra's Needle – before the travellers proceeded by train to Cairo. They spent five days there, with sightseeing from morning to evening: mosques, museums and the graves of the Mamelukes. The citadel with its view across the seething city of countless minarets, its maze of streets and alleyways, filled with the sounds of human voices, the reek of camels, importunate street sellers, all in chaotic contrast to the restrained demeanour of the Europeans. And behind the city: the lazy curving of the Nile, the pyramids' jagged forms against the sky, the faint outlines of the desert mountains in the distance. On a visit to Heliopolis outside the city Ibsen sent a bouquet of flowers to Suzannah at home in Dresden. 'They still smell,' Sigurd wrote back on behalf of his mother. The ten-year-old was bursting with pride over his father and enjoying the attentions of his schoolteachers. Everyone knew that Henrik Ibsen was travelling as a guest of the khedive of Egypt. 'It delights me to hear that you are having such a good time,' he continued in his precocious way, concluding equally formally: 'Do write soon to your devoted son, Sigurd Ibsen.'

After five days in Cairo the guests prepared for the great trip along the Nile. Early on the morning of 22 October four riverboats cast off from the banks, each with a barge in tow. Ibsen and Lieblein were on board the SS *Ferus* in company with von Knorring, seventeen Germans, one Dutchman and one Swiss, with the French and the Spaniards occupying the other boats.

Thus did this motley crowd of Europeans embark on their magical journey into the heart of Africa, bringing all their conflicts along with them, as the Europeans always have done on this continent. Before long the Germans were suggesting that the Prussian flag should be hoisted on their boat, since all the passengers were assumed to be Germanic. The suggestion was voted down, and for the remainder of the trip the Prussians feared that the French would get wind of the humiliating episode. But the French had enough on their minds as it was; they had proudly proclaimed their own ship the admiral of the little cortege but found themselves regularly outdistanced and last ashore each time they put into harbour.

Flooding on the banks of the Nile was unusually severe that year and many of the ports were closed. It meant that Ibsen had to be content to study the Sphinx at a distance. The same went for the ancient ruins in Memphis and Abydos. But there were plenty more statues, ruins and graves to visit. The khedive had provided the party with copies of a guide written by the famed

Egyptologist Mariette, who was at that time leading the excavations around the Sphinx. Life on board was slow and easy. Each evening they put into port, and there were occasional outings inland. On the third day they were shown around the khedive's sugar factories in Roda, powered by English steam-engines. In Asyet, Ibsen and Lieblein went for a walk on their own and came to a school where they were treated to coffee and a display of the pupils' proficiency in French. Wherever they went they encountered the contrasts between the cultures of Europe, Arabia and the ancient world. In just the same way the travellers must have been struck by the discrepancy between the ideas of the Orient the Europeans had brought with them, and the reality they met on the ground. Were these ideas changed by the experience, or was it instead the reality that was coloured by their preconceptions? Maybe the author of *Peer Gynt* took a different view of Egypt after visiting the country in person, though the account he afterwards wrote of the trip still describes the whole experience as an exotic journey through a thousand and one nights.[3]

They were approaching the 26th parallel, and the heat was intolerable. The locals, of course, adapted their clothing to the heat, but only a few of the Europeans removed the odd item of clothing, leaving the rest helpless prisoners of their own dignity. The Arabs knew exactly what to do with the curious Europeans. Wherever they went they were accosted by street-sellers offering more or less genuine historical relics for sale. Ibsen bought part of a mummy, a female hand with a scarab ring. Thus did he journey, hand in hand with history, until the last day of October and the arrival of the French empress, Eugénie, one of several European monarchs who would be attending the opening ceremony in Suez. She arrived in style aboard a large, reddish-pink ship and wearing 'white, as lovely as Egypt's Cleopatra, as the setting sun sheds its golden light over the ship's bunting and carpets and silks'.

Apparently she wasn't quite so lovely when the whole company headed off on an outing into the desert and the makeup ran down over the imperial face in all the heat.

A few days later the expedition reached its goal, Aswan. Ahead of them were the Blue Nile Falls, and beyond them the old Nubian tribal lands and the limitless African continent. Shortly afterwards the empress arrived with her party, and once again the dark, moonlit nights were enriched with displays of fireworks and Bengal lights – 'everywhere life and movement, a strange atmosphere, part European and part Oriental', according to von Knorring.

Finally, on 6 November, the party began its journey back down the river again for the opening celebrations. At a town called Girga, where they paused for a twenty-four-hour stopover, Ibsen left his travelling companions to do some exploring on his own. He had grown tired of the endless bickering between the Germans and the French; these latter were now travelling onboard the *Ferus* because the other boats were overcrowded. The latest from the Germans was that the seating at table ought to be arranged by rank, a suggestion that was voted down as comprehensively as the suggestion about the flag. Ibsen walks alone into Girga, wanders the narrow, dirty streets, watches the Arabs at work, wonders at the poverty of their living conditions, at the simple nature of the products on sale in the bazaars. He notes the Arabs' subservience to their masters, their indifference towards others in their own position, the dull, dreamlike half-life they seem to lead. All the way he is pursued by begging street urchins who are chased away by the adults, only to reappear:

'Bakschis! Bakschis!' – 'Spare change! Spare change!'

By now he has left the town behind and finds himself in a corn field, at the end of which is only the endless desert. The street urchins have disappeared. Ibsen stands alone at the edge of the desert, savours the peaceful silence which, he imagines, can exist only here. Was this not the landscape that created the hermits, those who went out into the desert, not in flight from something but in search of something? Peace. Solitude. The European Henrik Ibsen stands at the edge of the desert and, with civilisation at his back and emptiness before him, he starts to think. It seems to him that if the Arabs are ever to achieve civilisation it can only be through the exercise of a 'shamelessly despotic government'. Any attempt to copy the European model of representational government will only lead to 'a lot nonsense about "human rights"'. He thinks about how nations and civilisations come into being, about who shall lead and who shall follow in this backward society, and that it can only achieve the same strength as European society if it liberates itself from the Europeans' weakness, their nonsense and their empty phrase-making.

All these thoughts run through his head. But his gaze is fixed not on civilisation; it is trained on the vastness of the desert.[4]

The dwelling place of hermits.

* * *

The trip from Cairo had taken about two weeks, but on their return they had the current with them and made the journey in a little over half that time. At the opening ceremony that got under way on 16 November in Port Said, where the Suez Canal runs into the Mediterranean, Ibsen's party were all present. The following morning the main part of the celebrations began, involving a long procession of ships from numerous countries; the Scandinavians travelled on board the Danish corvette the *Nordstjernen*, placed somewhat further back in the line than most of the passengers would have liked: the sense of competition among the European visitors seemed never-ending.

What a show, what a performance. Present were the empress of France, the Austrian emperor, the khedive of Egypt, of course, and princes from Prussia and the Netherlands. The Sultan of Turkey was there, as were ambassadors from Russia and England. The streets and squares were filled with Europeans, Turks, Bedouins, Persians, Arabs, Copts, and Africans of every hue. The formal sailing of the canal began the following day. In al Ismailiyah the harbour and the town were brightly lit and gaily coloured as fireworks shot skywards. In the evening there was a ball at which all the royal guests were present, along with a certain writer from Skien who now found himself in the most exclusive company imaginable, far outranking anything he had known in Stockholm. But in Sweden he had, after all, been the man of the hour. Here he was merely one guest among many, his name known to only a few, and while Lieblein and other Scandinavians delivered speeches on various formal occasions, Ibsen appears to have kept his mouth firmly shut.

The whole thing was a wonderful and quite exotic adventure. But that was as far as it went.

In another couple of days the sailing of the canal was complete. Ibsen returned to Port Said. There a letter awaited him, a missive from far-off Norway that instantly dispelled his sense of magical wonder. The letter was from Suzannah in Dresden, and described the fate of *The League of Youth* at its premiere at the Christiania Theatre on 18 October:

> . . . at the first performance the first three acts were greeted with rapturous applause, but in the fourth, where Bastian says his line about what a nation is, a gang of people in the third row began whistling, led by some students involved in the language debate, what do you think of that?

At the second performance things got worse:

> The whistling began even before Lundestad ends his first speech. Again and again they were drowned out by applause, but they wouldn't stop and the curtain had to be brought down.

What did he think of that? We find out in 'At Port Said', the poem he wrote immediately on his return to Dresden:

> The steamers sailed
> By the Obelisk.
> In the tones of home
> I heard whispered news:
> The mirror-verse I polished
> for manly sluts,
> was spattered back there
> by spotting whistles.

* * *

So *The League of Youth* had not exactly been ignored back home in Norway; that in itself had to be a good thing. But the exact nature of its reception was still not clear to him at this point. In any event, it was time to get home. He was, after all, no adventurer, and the long journey had begun to weary him. He was probably only telling the truth when he later confessed that the best part of the whole trip was sitting at home and reminiscing about it. Von Knorring and Lieblein stayed on a month longer at the khedive's expense, while Ibsen sailed from Alexandria to Marseilles, reaching Paris at the end of November 1869. Here he broke a resolution he had made to himself and remained there for two weeks, at his own expense.

How could he resist it?

PARIS 1869

It would be hard to overstate the importance of Paris for a dramatist in the nineteenth century. The city was the capital of European theatre; everything that would in due course characterise the modern theatre was first manifest there. The problem is, the two weeks Ibsen spent in the French capital are pretty much *terra incognita* in a life that has been otherwise fairly exhaustively documented. What did he get up to in Paris? Did he have any profoundly formative experience, something that might be related to what he later wrote? All we learn from him is that he visited some of the city's art galleries, but he does not say which, or what he saw. Paris had plenty to offer the art lover; he probably visited the Louvre, the Musée du Luxembourg, or some of the many other galleries. He cannot have seen Le Salon, the most important annual exhibition, because that did not open until May.

We don't know whether he attended the theatre. His French was limited, but from his own career as a theatre professional he was familiar with a great many French dramas. The advantage enjoyed by Paris as a centre of the theatrical world was related to the fact that France was a centralised land with Paris a cultural capital that set the standard for the whole nation. The city boasted numerous private theatres, could command large audiences, and it was not uncommon for new plays to be rehearsed thirty or forty times before public performance. Things were otherwise in the decentralised Germany, with smaller court theatres that performed for a limited audience, changed the repertoire frequently, and usually made do with three or four rehearsals. There was also a tradition in Paris for the dramatist to direct his own plays, thus ensuring a close approximation between the author's intentions and the finished product. The technology of the scenery and lighting were, moreover, the most advanced in the world. Every German theatre manager who wanted to experiment with stage realism, techniques of ensemble acting, and a holistic style of direction made it his business to visit Paris. In the 1830s Heinrich Laube, Franz von Dingelstedt and Eduard Devrient had all visited the city. In the autumn of 1869 it was Henrik Ibsen's turn.

The most innovative Parisian stage he might have visited was that of the Théâtre du Gymnase. Since the 1850s its celebrated director Adolphe Lemoine Montigny had been presenting ensemble playing, stage realism and a psychological character interpretation that was more radical than anything else in Europe at that time.[5] Eugène Scribe, in his day, had introduced a modest degree of realism to the theatre in depicting recognisable, bourgeois characters. Montigny went much further, furnishing the stage in realistic fashion and directing his players in the use of natural gesture and a psychological immersion in their parts. Both the acting style and the production techniques were well adapted to the school of new, realistic French drama which concerned itself with both social problems and complex, individual characters.

Because modernism both recognises and indeed encourages the breaking of rules, it is easy to forget how bound the theatre once was to quite explicit ethical, aesthetic and social norms. It meant that every small step in the development of a realistic and naturalistic theatre engendered shock, scandal and furious debate, whether it be a cough from the stage, some folksy expression from the lips of a prima donna, or the more radical and realistic presentation of the lower classes on stage, such as Émile Zola offered in his naturalistic plays from the 1870s. And just as the step from Scribe to Montigny occasioned shock and head-shaking, so the leap from Montigny to Zola did the same.

By the time of Ibsen's arrival in Paris, Montigny's ideas had spread to other theatres, so that Ibsen might have experienced at first hand a realistic drama of contemporary life with modern production values and a natural acting style.[6] The difficulty in trying to substantiate such a possibility is that Ibsen did not write a new drama of contemporary life until *The Pillars of Society* in 1877, eight long years after his brief stay in Paris. Literary historians have expressed surprise that Ibsen never mentioned his debt to French theatre and literature, a surprise that was shared by Ibsen's contemporaries. 'Why not Paris?' Magdalene Thoresen asked him once. 'After all, it's at the centre of modern theatre.'

Yes indeed, why not Paris? Why didn't Ibsen acknowledge and even explicate the importance French drama must have had for him over the years? One obvious possibility is the language barrier, another his unwillingness to go into the question of his literary influences; in other words, he may well have read the French dramatists, and learned from them, but fought shy of conceding their importance for him. A third explanation could be that literary impulses might have worked on him in the same way as philosophical impulses, influencing him by a process of indirect absorption via translations, newspaper articles, conversations, or through intermediaries such as Georg Brandes and Bjørnstjerne Bjørnson. A fourth explanation might be related to his age and his aesthetic education prior to the visit to Paris in 1869. Ibsen was born in 1828. His intellectual life began just after Wergeland's death, so that in many ways he was of the late Romantics' generation. For him, Rome was the natural goal of his educational journey, just as it was Paris for the generation of Norwegian writers that succeeded him. In Rome he had written plays of ideas, and long before he finally took his decisive step in the direction of plays of realism and contemporary life in 1877, Georg Brandes had brought Paris to him.

And yet he *was* there, in Paris, in the autumn of 1869, and we can only guess at the ideas and influences he carried in his head as he sat on the train bound for Dresden and home in the middle of December.

STEENSGAARD AND COMPANY

Home at last from his great adventure Ibsen was able to read the reviews of *The League of Youth*, now that it had been published in all the Scandinavian lands and even staged in Norway. He was not unprepared for criticism, or for the fact that the strongest reactions would probably come from his own countrymen. But the scandal that ensued was only partly caused by the play; it was more that the play caused political tensions to flare up once more between the state officials and a nascent left-wing coalition made up of farmers, language reformers, anti-unionists and other supporters of democratic reform. As had been the case with *Love's Comedy*, spotting Ibsen's left-wing models in the play became a parlour game; Steensgaard, the opportunist, was readily identified as a parody of Bjørnson – indeed, Bjørnson himself was convinced that this was the case.

As was to be expected *Morgenbladet*, which had become by this time Christiania's leading conservative newspaper, staunchly supported Ibsen and interpreted his play as a straightforward political attack on the Left. Kristian Elster, writing in *Aftenbladet*, expressed the ambivalence felt by the young on the left towards Ibsen. Ibsen had been the one who challenged the respectable bourgeoisie's fear of new thoughts and ideals. And now this? A. O. Vinje disliked Ibsen's pompous salvo and expressed his doubts that the country was served by nourishing such snarling aggression. Vinje was not the only one to find it odd that Ibsen's contempt should be funded by the state in the form of an annual writer's wage. Elster denied that Ibsen had suffered all that much at home in Norway. His exile was a voluntary matter and gave no grounds for proclaiming him a martyr. So the narrative of Ibsen's suffering on the road to a literary career in Norway had not yet established itself; there remained a gap between his own autobiographical narrative and the narrative back home in Norway, a gap that would be filled by literary historians and the writers of memoirs as Ibsen's importance increased and the public's cultural memory faded – just the conditions needed for the creation of a literary myth.

Bjørnson had no intention of making any public comment on Ibsen's play. Despite the occasional spats between them, he had never expected such an attack. 'I'm looking forward to *The League of Youth*,' he had written to Ibsen before publication of the play. Now he was hurt – 'not one single syllable from me,' he assured Rudolf Schmidt. If he had to say something, it would be this:

> Apart from people who delude themselves completely surely no one can any longer doubt that Ibsen is a scoundrel.

A few months previously, Ibsen had assured Hegel that he wanted to avoid an open break with Bjørnson, but within the year it came anyway, and it was Ibsen's doing. That Bjørnson should have felt himself betrayed isn't hard to understand. It is likely that he felt not only hurt but threatened. His colleague's success in Denmark was beginning to make inroads into his own status as the 'breath of fresh air from the north'. In the Christmas week of 1870 he reminds Hegel, in slightly wounded terms, that it was he who had brought Ibsen to Gyldendal.

The following winter he comes right out with it:

> I note that Ibsen is now everyone's favourite down there in Copenhagen. Well, if you're looking to *him* for edification then good luck to you!

Critics in Denmark concerned themselves most with the play's literary qualities. Typical in this respect was the reviewer in *Fædrelandet*, who stuck to Clemens Petersen's old line in complaining that the play offered abstract concepts rather than genuine poetry. No doubt the realism was superlative, and the plotting masterly, but the satire was unrelievedly negative. In other words, what was lacking was any positive and reconciliatory element. Seen in this light, Steensgaard could be viewed as a Peer Gynt in the real world.

Not even Georg Brandes was particularly enthusiastic; but in mitigation he moved quite far in the direction of accepting Ibsen's revolt against the 'laws of beauty' that governed the old idealistic aesthetics. In line with this he withdraws his former objections to *Peer Gynt*, claiming now that it will come to be regarded as one of the great works of the century, if one excluded the problematic fourth act. The origin of Brandes' challenge to aesthetic formalism may have been his enthusiasm for the writings of his favourite French critics. But a letter Ibsen wrote to him in the summer of 1869, in which he defends *Peer Gynt* by invoking Michelangelo, may have influenced him too. Michelangelo had broken the 'rules of beauty' but, according to Ibsen, the art he created was still beautiful because it was full of character. In reviewing *The League of Youth* Brandes reveals that he has still not completely liberated himself from his former ways of thinking. Although he praises the play's technical construction, he expresses regret that the truth conveyed is so 'grim', and beauty so conspicuously lacking among the 'gallery of apes' that made up the cast list, not least in the biggest ape of them all – Steensgaard the lawyer.[7]

But one character was exempted from this criticism. Several reviewers comment on Selma, daughter-in-law of Bratberg, the chamberlain, one of the play's minor characters. Here reviewers found a glimmer of light in someone whose character seemed to admit at least the possibility of idealism. Selma is a woman full of longing, but bitter over the way she has been excluded from the affairs of her husband's family: 'How I have thirsted to taste one drop of your sorrows!' she complains to the chamberlain and her husband. And she continues:

> But if I asked, all you ever did was laugh it off. You dressed me up like a doll; you played with me, the way you play with children. Oh, I had such a longing to be entrusted with a burden. I had the seriousness and the longing for all such things that arouse passion and that elevate.

Selma was the only character whom Brandes found really interesting; he thought a whole drama could be written around such a woman's position in the family. The overlooked woman, who feels a longing to be serious and yet is never taken seriously, and so is reduced to the status of a child or a doll in the world of men. Ibsen would return to the idea of the doll-woman; for the time being she was no more than a tragic flicker in the playful world of his light comedy.

* * *

If the publication of *The League of Youth* aroused the ire of Norwegians, the staged version caused even more of a storm. As Suzannah described in her letter, the performance at the Christiania Theatre caused a riot the like of which had not been seen since the infamous 'Campbell riots' of the 1830s. The evening of the first performance itself went off quietly enough with just a few whistlers, but by the time of the second performance two days later the radical youth of the city had organised itself. The chorus of catcalls broke out during the first act, and did not stop until the curtain came down. The performance continued after some delay, but at the end of the fourth act a full-scale riot broke out, with jackets being ripped and cravats flying through the air.

The demonstrators were few in number, but they were young, and they represented a new presence on the political landscape. One of the demonstrators himself highlighted the paradoxical fact that, in principle, he had nothing against Ibsen. On the contrary, there was considerable admiration for the creator of *Brand* among the young of the Left. This ended with the riot of 1869. In the polarising process that was taking place in Norwegian society at that time the young flocked instead around Bjørnson's banner. He had aligned himself with Søren Jaabæk's farmers' movement, and when Johan Sverdrup emerged as a leader of the opposition in the Storting in 1869, Bjørnson hailed him in his poem 'To Johan Sverdrup'. The following spring Bjørnson was elected president of the Students' Union on a wave of leftist radical enthusiasm.

So being labelled the model for Ibsen's Steensgaard had no deterrent effect on him.

As for Ibsen, it was a matter of importance for him to distance himself from both the left and right in politics, and insist that *his* revolution involved 'torpedoing the ark'; the only thing that mattered was the individual human being, and a personality that was whole and incorruptible. And in many respects *The League of Youth* is more about people than politics. Steensgaard is basically a split personality, distinctly a twin brother to Peer Gynt, but not blessed with Peer's charm. So thematically and psychologically there is a clear continuity between this and the preceding play. Other aspects point towards the future. In *The League of Youth* Ibsen took a decisive step in the direction of the realistic drama in terms of language, the nature of the dialogue, and a logical and naturally motivated sequence of events.[8] With a pride that was ill-concealed he told Brandes that he had managed to liberate himself from the use of monologues and asides, and created a dialogue that flowed along naturally. He had also created characters that worked both as individuals and as representative types, a necessary step if he were to achieve both credibility and forceful communication.

His choice of a light comedy for his new realism was probably because the genre was generally regarded as being best suited to drama with a contemporary setting, as in the vaudevilles of Heiberg and Scribe. A *tragedy* with a contemporary setting would have been a much more radical proposition.

But Ibsen's aim was to hit hard, not to entertain. Had he not written to Bjørnson, after the break with Clemens Petersen, that he intended to 'photograph' his contemporaries 'one by one'? And had he not given Hegel notice to expect a play on the subject of the 'Dissensions and currents in contemporary life'? He had been as good as his word, but in his role of photographer he had kept himself hidden and let his pictures do the talking. He had entered the debate of the day, and withdrawn the moment he was required to reveal his own standpoint.

Was it possible to be an active member of society, and at the same time stand outside it? If so then it can only have been as an exercise in literary privilege.

In any case, he had never intended to 'photograph' Bjørnson. Art and life could never be the same thing, he insisted. Even if the artist took his material from real life, there would always be 'a huge difference between the head of the model and the portrait'. The statement is confirmation that Ibsen remained faithful to his credo of the 1850s, that 'external realism' must be secondary to the main idea. The difficulty, though, was that the main idea in this particular play involved an assault on the ideological choices made by men such as Bjørnson and Sverdrup.

It may well never have been his intention to portray them individually; they were simply models, meaning only, of course, that he ended up portraying the lot of them.

'DU TRITTST AUF DEINE HOSE!'

The League of Youth caused Ibsen some unpleasantness, but by way of compensation it remained a favourite on Scandinavian stages for many years to come. Posterity has found its success puzzling, just as posterity has puzzled over how a light comedy could have been taken so seriously on the political level. But this is to underestimate both the theatrical charm of the play and the theatre's role as an arena for public and political debate in the nineteenth century, where what happened among audiences could be just as important as what took place on the stage.

The play opened at the Kungliga Dramatiska Teatern in Stockholm on 11 December 1869.[9] Expectations were high and audiences flocked to the theatre. Ibsen's canny initiative in visiting the Swedish capital turned out to have been a very good investment. The reviews, however, were lukewarm. As elsewhere, critics found the play too bitter, too unforgiving. There was too much realism, too little idealism – although they conceded that it worked better onstage than as a book. Such criticisms, however, were drowned in the roars of approbation from audiences.

'Wherever I go people tell me that The League of Youth has been done brilliantly in Stockholm,' Ibsen writes in the new year, 'and it's no more than I expected from the outstanding performers I met while there.'

Stockholm had been conquered. Now it was Copenhagen's turn. In February 1870, after a great deal of toing and froing the previous autumn, The League of Youth opened at the Kongelige Teater. It was the first time an Ibsen play had ever been performed at the main theatre in Denmark. Finally he had achieved a goal that must have seemed to him, from the very earliest days, the highest conceivable honour for a Norwegian dramatist – to have written a play for the Kongelige Teater in Copenhagen!

No matter that Bjørnson had already realised the same dream twice over, both times with plays directed by Johanne Luise Heiberg. Fru Heiberg had realised just how good Ibsen was back in the winter of 1866, when she read *Love's Comedy* and asked herself: 'Why aren't more people talking about this book?' In 1864, four years after the death of her husband Johan Ludvig Heiberg, Fru Heiberg had retired from the stage. Three years later, she took over the reins as director at the Kongelige Teater. She, who had once been the 'foaming white froth' atop the wave of Danish Romanticism, was alert to what was happening in the world of Norwegian theatre and now became as enthusiastic an admirer of Ibsen's work as her husband had once been sceptical. When Ibsen sent *The League of Youth* to the theatre in the summer of 1869 she accepted it, despite the protests of the theatre's own dramaturge Carsten Hauch.

In general the play was well received by audiences in Copenhagen and it ran for thirteen performances that season, a success that was explained here, too, by the fact that its qualities emerged most successfully when staged. The critics had to admit that bursts of laughter punctuated the evening, and who could claim that a comedy wasn't funny when audiences were laughing all the way through it?

With Steensgaard and company doing well in Denmark, back in Dresden, Ibsen was trying to get used to a life without honours and decorations. It cannot have been easy. Over the previous six months one great event had been succeeded by another. Now the pen lay on his desktop and awaited its master.

The signs are that Ibsen experienced a crisis in the spring of 1870 that affected his literary creativity. That poetic rapture that had enveloped him under Italy's bright skies was a thing of the past. It was only now, as he settled into everyday life in Dresden, that he noticed it.

He had writer's block.

Not that he didn't try. 'As for me,' he wrote to Johan Hermann Thoresen in March, full of self-confidence, 'I'm very busy on literary projects.' And as far as it went, it was true; the problem was that only a very few of these came to anything. In Stockholm, Jacob Løkke had offered to help him in tracking down his early poems for a volume of his collected verse, and in the new year Hegel made the same suggestion. Ibsen was enthusiastic, but didn't do anything about it until Løkke handed over the results of his work the following spring. In the meantime he was trying to capture some of his Egyptian experiences on paper, as he had promised Hegel he would, and – somewhat surprisingly – he had expressed an interest in writing a play with an Egyptian setting with his Swedish travelling companion, Oscar von Knorring, as co-author. The project came to nothing, and the prose account of his travels dried up after a few pages. For almost the whole of 1870 he sent assurances to Hegel that a new drama with a contemporary setting was under way. He says little about the content other than that it would be a 'serious drama set in the present and in three acts'.[10] These were probably his first notes for *The Pillars of Society* (1877), but at some point in the autumn this early draft ended up in the bottom drawer, overtaken by a new idea, or rather, the return of an old one: he would write a libretto for an opera! In 1859 the intention had been to turn *Olaf Liljekrans* into an opera. This time the plan was to write something about the saga king, Sigurd Jorsalfare. Again, nothing came of it.

Why couldn't he get started on the play he *should* have been working on? It had been in the background the whole time, the tragedy of Julian the Apostate. The story had haunted him ever since he had first heard it in 1864, read aloud to him beneath the olive trees of Genzano by Lorentz Dietrichson. But he couldn't find a way into the material, and other projects constantly intruded. By the spring of 1866 he had stopped pretending to Hegel that the tragedy was on its way. In the late winter of 1869 it crops up again in correspondence, but still he can't get a handle on the material. And then, in June of that year, having sent off *The League of Youth*, he announces to his publisher that he is setting about it in earnest. Yet again he is distracted, and for the whole of 1870 no further work on it is done.

The sense of isolation Henrik had felt during the early days in Dresden gradually passed as he and Suzannah came into contact with a number of Scandinavians who were permanent residents of the city. The Norwegian Karl Bomhoff, who worked at Gehe's pharmaceutical factory, describes dinners and gatherings at which the Ibsens were present, along with other Scandinavians from the factory. Ibsen enjoyed the company of the Skien priest Gustav Adolph Lammers, who had long since left the Reformed Church movement and gone back to the State Church. All the signs suggest that he and Ibsen got on well together, despite Ibsen's old dislike of the movement and of his sister's involvement with it in particular. The composition of his social circle is interesting, because it shows Ibsen in the company of the 'men of the new age', industrialists such as Bomhoff and his colleague Oscar Rundquist.

So where social life in Rome had been an almost exclusively artistic affair, in Dresden he was now meeting and enjoying the company of men who represented the modern, industrial world. Yet the sort of companionship he had enjoyed in Rome was not repeated in Dresden; the signs are that in Dresden he spent his time with people who were acquaintances rather than good friends. It meant that, for good or ill, family life became closer and more important. If life with a Henrik Ibsen in full literary flow was hard enough, we can only guess at the sort of difficulties an Ibsen with writer's block presented in the household.

For Sigurd the biggest change from life in Rome must have been his schooling. His father enrolled him in Dr Hölbe's Institute, a school for the children of foreigners that lay one hour's walk from the apartment on Königsbrücker Strasse. The fees must have been a considerable burden. The family had moved from the centre of town to save money, but in principle they were by no means poor: in 1870, Ibsen's total income was roughly 7,500 Norwegian kroner – more than the highest salary attainable for a Norwegian professor.[11] We have no very clear picture of the family's outgoings at this time, though earlier in life Henrik had shown an impressive talent for being poor even while earning a healthy income; he was still paying off the debt to his Norwegian creditor, Nandrup the lawyer. Possibly the parents made sacrifices in their standard of living at home in the interests of Sigurd's education. But one of the consequences was that the boy was not as well dressed as the other pupils, most of whom came from considerably more affluent homes than he did. So despite a marked improvement in financial status following the success of *Brand*, the Ibsens continued to be reminded of their relative poverty as Ibsen pursued his goal of climbing ever higher up the social ladder.

Sigurd was ashamed of himself and his home. 'Du trittst auf deine Hose!' the boys shouted out to him in the street when they saw him approaching in clothes his mother had darned for him. He didn't like to bring friends home from school, pretending to his parents that he didn't want to anyway. A long and penetrating stare from his father exposed the lie, and Sigurd once again felt ashamed, this time for having been ashamed. To compensate he would make up the most fantastic stories: he claimed that his father was the king of the apes, and that his mother was a negress and so never left the house. He had a brother who was kept locked up in a cupboard, and the woman seen outside his house wasn't his mother at all but a lady who lived with them. It was this lady who took the boy with her to Dresden's art galleries and listened to the boy's expositions on each and every single painting until she thought she might pass out. In the evenings he played cards with the king of the apes. Henrik let the boy win every time – apart from once, when he forgot, and left Sigurd the loser. In a rage the boy threw down his cards, and from that point onwards Henrik decided never to play cards with his son again. Instead they turned to chess, a practice that continued for the rest of their lives.

This was Ibsen family life, in which, in due course, the highlights became those occasions on which father would read aloud from his newly completed work. This was another tradition that was observed for the rest of their lives, formal occasions centred on what was, after all, the most important thing of all – Henrik Ibsen's writing.

If Sigurd struggled to find a place between his family and the rest of the world, it seems as though Suzannah soon felt at home in Dresden. According to a family friend she overcame her lack of interest in domestic matters and embraced the role of housewife, inspired by the ideal of the dutiful 'deutsche Hausfrau'. And if she had formerly felt herself oppressed by her husband, the same family friend relates that in time she learned to fight back. In this, it seems, she was helped by her sister Marie, who moved in with the family in 1868 and remained a member of the household until 1872. She was Hans Conrad Thoresen's eldest daughter and Magdalene's stepdaughter. She had been taking care of her brothers and sisters from an early age. A warm and smiling presence, she was very different from the serious Suzannah. Henrik was very fond of Marie, so fond indeed that some have even suggested he felt a 'hidden erotic attraction' to her, as he took her around the museums and art galleries of Dresden.

The bonds between Henrik, Suzannah and Sigurd must have been unusually strong. No one has conveyed this more clearly than the woman Sigurd later married, Bergliot, in her memoir entitled *The Three of Them*. But, according to Lorentz Dietrichson, there was another bond in the family, the special bond between mother and son. Sigurd was Suzannah's best friend – 'the only one who completely understood and treasured her real greatness, understood it and shared its joys and sufferings – the only one'.

So 'the two' lived as a unit within 'the three', with the son at the centre, balancing the marriage between two strong and stubborn personalities, at the same time the mother's ally against the dominant member of the trio, Henrik Ibsen, the writer.

LETTER IN RHYME TO FRU HEIBERG

All things considered, what Dresden had to offer was not hugely important to him. Ibsen had his sights set on Scandinavia again. In the spring of 1870 he planned a trip to Copenhagen and Christiania to conclude the work of collecting his poems. Yet his latest play had stirred up everything he found contemptible about Norwegian society. He must have thought long and hard about his relationship to his native land.

'Judging by the attacks I have seen,' he writes in January, 'the idea up there seems to be that empty phrase-making, vacuity and shabbiness are national peculiarities.'

And yet he had by no means given up the idea of moving back home. But had *he*, by this time, made such a return impossible? With a strained optimism he writes to Hegel that 'if I seem to have lost a few friends up there, my compensation is that I have made even more'.

He had made more friends; the question was, of what value was the friendship of Norwegian conservatives, if all the while he insisted on remaining outside the debates raging within a Norwegian society that would become ever more polarised and politicised in the years to come?

The relationship to Norway must have preoccupied him even more when the chance to return home for good arose that spring. The offer came from the board of the Christiania Theatre. A lot had happened in the theatre world since he had left the country in 1864. When Bjørnson took over the reins at the Christiania Theatre in 1865 he had introduced an almost autocratic regime as he pursued his aim of establishing a genuinely popular theatre based on a repertoire that would also find room for more exalted forms of drama. His efforts were successful, but at a cost. By June 1867 he felt that enough was enough. His attempt to return the following year was rejected by the committee – to the great disappointment of the company. In the spring of 1870 some of the leading performers were in open revolt against the committee's line, and in the autumn of that year they left the company and formed an independent and competing company in the Kristiania Norske theater's old premises on Møllergaten. Bjørnstjerne Bjørnson was in charge.

This was the background to the committee's attempt to attract the services of someone with the reputation and creativity to be able to challenge Bjørnson and his 'strikers' theatre': would Ibsen consider a post as the theatre's new artistic director, in the first instance for a period of at least one year, and with a guarantee that no bureaucratic responsibilities would attach to the job? Ibsen's initial response must have been very sceptical, not least because of the way his previous play had been received. Were he to return to the theatre, he told one member of the committee, he would end up as something he wanted least of all to be – 'a Party man'. He would only bring trouble, and surely that couldn't possibly be in the theatre's interests?

And yet he did not dismiss the offer out of hand; after all, the job might be one way of engineering a triumphant return to his homeland. That it would also mean trouble was almost certainly true, but at least he could count on Bjørnson's support – he had advised his actors to return to their old place of work should Ibsen accept the theatre's offer. Possibly Ibsen worried about the response of the company, for between him and Bjørnson there was little doubt about which one *they* preferred to work under. He assures the company he'll be able to keep the actors disciplined; they should be in no doubt that he would be nothing like as easy-going as he had been the last time he worked with them. Not a very diplomatic promise, and not an especially convincing one either. And on top of everything else, he doesn't actually need the job; this time he really *can* choose writing over the practicalities of running a theatre.

Perhaps it was this that decided him finally to reject the offer. Or perhaps the reason came in a moment of self-insight, revealed in a parenthetical observation of devastating understatement:

I've worked in the theatre before, and I do not flatter myself that I was particularly popular in the job.

So he suggested to the committee that they once again offer the post to Bjørnson. It meant he could say no to a job he didn't really want anyway and at the same time make a gesture of friendly respect towards Bjørnson that didn't cost him anything.

* * *

The family decides to split up for the summer of 1870. Suzannah and Sigurd would spend the school holidays at a spa resort in Bohemia. Suzannah was already beginning to suffer from rheumatism, and in the years to come Sigurd would accompany her to spa towns all over Europe. Ibsen's plan was to go to Copenhagen, there to further advance the cause of his career and taste life as a celebrity following the success of *The League of Youth* at the Kongelige Teater – perhaps even the magic of Stockholm would be recreated?

What of Norway? Having rejected the offer of a job at the Christiania Theatre the only pressing reason for him to go back home was to track down any missing poetry. Or was that a job that could be safely left to Jacob Løkke? In the end he dropped the idea of visiting Norway. The decision came as a relief to him, but not to Suzannah.

'Oh but you absolutely must go to Norway,' she pleaded with him once they had parted company for the summer. 'Don't put it off for another year, it looks as if you simply don't care, and I'm afraid it might harm your career. You can keep your stay short, but do convince yourself and make the trip, because once you are there, I'm sure you'll find it will do you good.'

Suzannah realises that he risks burning his bridges if he doesn't go. She knows that he ought to go home and face the Great Boyg, stand up for who he is, and for his writing. She doesn't mention the fact that the country he seems willing to write off is also *her* country, nor yet that what is at issue is also Sigurd's chance to actually *have* a home country. Suzannah and Sigurd's chances of ever returning home are in the hands of her husband. He must choose for all of them.

But he doesn't want to.

The plan was to travel to Copenhagen in the middle of July. A few weeks before his departure date he wrote a letter to Frederik Hegel. He has realised that Gyldendal publishing house is celebrating its centenary this year, and he has forgotten to offer his congratulations.

It marked a turning point in my life as a writer, as well as in my material conditions, when I got you as my publisher.

And the reply he gets in return is every bit as warm.

'Of course I realise that you overestimate my modest role in your career and in the promotion of new writing,' writes Hegel. 'I have every bit as much reason as you to celebrate the fact of our coming together, my dear Ibsen, and the friendship and respect you have offered me, of which you have given me several proofs.'

Warm words from two men who have known each other for six years but have never yet met. It happens now for the first time. Frederick V. Hegel had joined the Gyldendal Booksellers Company as a young apprentice. He made rapid progress, and in 1850, still only thirty-three years old, he was put in charge of the company. Now aged fifty-three, he was regarded as the leading publisher in Scandinavia. But few publishers can have been born so lucky: without his straining himself in any noticeable way all the great writers of the age flocked to his door. Hegel had a reputation for being a tactful and in every way a correct gentleman, possessed of a good head for business and a warm heart. In almost every extant photograph he poses with a thoughtful furrow in his brow and a faint, inscrutable smile that suggest a refined and aristocratic personality, though in fact his background was modest.

In other words he bore no resemblance to Ibsen at all, if we ignore the fact that both were ambitious and strategically astute producers of books.[12] The meeting between them probably did not bring writer and publisher any closer, with the relationship between them remaining businesslike and cordial, as it had been from the start.

The relationship between Ibsen and Georg Brandes was a much more passionate affair, but *that* particular encounter would have to wait, since Brandes was abroad at the time Ibsen visited Copenhagen. Otherwise his stay was sociable enough. Among other things there was a reunion with Oscar von Knorring, and a meeting with the young writer Laura Kieler and his mother-in-law Magdalene Thoresen, who was now living as a writer in her own country. Her appreciation for the rather dour theatre director who had shown up one day at the pastor's house in Bergen all those years ago had increased in proportion to his success and the spread of his reputation. Now she couldn't speak too highly of his genius – 'everything about Ibsen is great, almost inhumanly great'. Another who thought there was something special about Ibsen was Hans Christian Andersen. He was keen to meet this 'Norwegian poet who doesn't like Norwegians', apparently forgetting that they actually had met, back in 1852. He saw his chance when Ibsen accepted an invitation to dinner from their mutual friend Carl Bloch, who had known Ibsen in Rome. But the evening of 11 August came and went without any invitation arriving from the Danish painter. For a few days Andersen nursed his injured pride at 'Rolighed', the home of a stockbroker named Melchior with whom he was staying, before swallowing it and inviting both Bloch and the Norwegian poet to join him at Melchior's house. Andersen, the master of the fairy tale, had just read *Peer Gynt* and was not enthusiastic about Ibsen's own great fairy tale: 'there is a sort of pathological wildness about the whole thing,' he wrote in his journal, 'it's like the work of a mad writer.'

And it was this mad writer, who was rumoured to be taciturn and even dour when in company, whom he had just invited to dinner!

Who was he, this tight-lipped Norwegian, creator of the fiery Brand and the mad Gynt? The enigma surrounding Ibsen's person was beginning to grow, nourished by the disturbing combination of strength and ambivalence evidenced in the works. Just as it had done in Sweden the preceding autumn. As things turned out, the dinner at Melchior's house was a great success. Ibsen made a good impression on the company and, according to the host, was both friendly and interesting.

The climax of the stay was undoubtedly a gala performance of *The League of Youth* that Johanne Luise Heiberg had arranged in honour of the visitor. Following the success of the play she had suggested a production of *The Pretenders*, but again she encountered opposition from within the company. The play was much too long and too difficult, and the actors were certain that audiences wouldn't like it at all. But Fru Heiberg managed to get her way, once Ibsen had given his permission for cuts to be made. That the choice fell on *The Pretenders* was not unconnected to the fact that Hegel had acquired the rights to the play and published it in a new edition in the autumn of 1870.[13] Ibsen and Hegel were thus able to exploit to the full the opportunities that had arisen at the Kongelige Teater: they followed up the success of *The League of Youth* by relaunching the best of Ibsen's earlier works. The whole thing was carefully planned. Earlier in the summer Ibsen had persuaded the Danish composer Peter Heise, another acquaintance from Rome, to write incidental music for the play, and in January 1871 *The Pretenders*, directed by Fru Heiberg, had its premiere at the Kongelige Teater.

By Fru Heiberg's own account the play was not merely a success; the response to *The Pretenders* was rapturous, the most sensational of its kind since Oehlenschläger's *Earl Hakon*, back in 1807! The reviewers too agreed that the production was a credit to the theatre, though a few dissenting voices questioned the staging – a criticism of Fru Heiberg, not the dramatist.

* * *

The breakthrough achieved by Bjørnson and Ibsen at the Kongelige Teater was more than a personal triumph for the two writers; it shifted the whole centre of gravity of the cultural relationship between Denmark and Norway, indeed, throughout the whole of Scandinavia. There was a general feeling throughout the 1860s in Denmark that theatrical life in the country had stagnated.

'People waited and waited, but no new dramatist appeared,' Fru Heiberg writes sadly in her memoirs.

But something was happening in Denmark's former colony up in the north. Ibsen and Bjørnson entered the world of Danish theatre like a breath of fresh air, and the roughness the Danes had formerly turned their noses up at was now seen as powerful and modern. Among some Danish dramatists the development was seen as distinctly threatening.

'I really do hope,' Holger Drachmann complained eight years after Ibsen's debut at the Kongelige Teater, 'that we shall see an "Oehlenschläger-like" revival in our literature so that we aren't constantly required to move in the wake of these Norwegians.'

These Norwegians – that meant Ibsen and Bjørnson:

'The sheer talent and productivity of these two men have been putting our own literature under pressure for the last fifteen years. It's about time we responded.'

And indeed a great deal had changed in the cultural balance between the two countries since the days when Ibsen paid court to Clemens Petersen. It is illuminating to view this as a post-colonial phenomenon, in much the same way as writers from the former British colonies in Africa and Asia helped to renew literature in Great Britain towards the end of the twentieth century. Perhaps precisely this mixture of provincial rawness and a European frame of reference is an important factor in accounting for the success of *Brand* and *Peer Gynt* in Scandinavia; certainly it is hard to imagine these two plays coming from a Danish dramatist of the time.

The success of the triumvirate of Hegel, Bjørnson and Ibsen surprised others besides Drachmann: 'Whatever Gyldendal publishes almost immediately goes into a second print run,' an astonished Henrik Hertz writes as early as 1867. And just as Hegel was the catalyst for the Norwegian breakthrough in the world of print, Johanne Luise Heiberg was for the stage. In gratitude she was rewarded with the greatest gift any writer can offer: a tribute in verse that made the widow a permanent part of Ibsen's literary universe. 'A Letter in Rhyme to Fru Heiberg' was written during the Easter of 1871, recalling a meeting between the two of them the previous summer. On 10 August, Fru Heiberg had invited Ibsen to dinner at her home in Rosenvænget. Once before, during his study trip of 1852, he had sat at table with her. Then he was there on sufferance, now he was guest of honour. Now it was the hostess's turn to be excited at the prospect of getting better acquainted with the man behind the great writer, and it was this evening that lay behind the letter in rhyme with which Ibsen repaid his debt of gratitude to her:

> For the vision granted me,
> hear my grateful prophecy.
> You shall live for generations
> wondrous, merged with Denmark's reaches, —
> with a night, the Sound's tall beeches
> under Memory's constellations.

In unusually vivid visual terms Fru Heiberg's theatrical talents are likened to a great fleet of ships and pleasure boats, symbolising all the different roles she has played. The fleet enters the waters of the Øresund, while people – the audience – line the banks. But once the procession has passed the ships again glide by through the summer night; now it is *memories* of the actress's roles that take shape, only half-visible in the dim light. And now it is those standing on the banks who must help in delineating the outlines of the different ships, an audience that participates in the process of creation, its memories bringing the actress's roles into sharp relief, bringing artist and audience together in perfect union.

The letter in rhyme melted Fru Heiberg's heart: 'So you have sat down with your lyre and turned your thoughts to a poor soul like me.' And the poem really *is* a most fulsome tribute, not just to Fru Heiberg but to everything Denmark has meant to Norwegian cultural and spiritual life in the past. And yet despite this, no close friendship developed between the poet and the prima donna, even though Ibsen describes sitting at her table as an overwhelming experience:

> Last year's visit I just squandered,
> I stayed dumb;
> Beauty's debt, the whole round sum
> still heart-hoarded, I just wandered
> off again.

Johanne Luise Heiberg hardly felt herself overwhelmed in quite the same way. She must have noticed how silent Ibsen was during the meal, but did not interpret it in an equally poetic fashion. Like many others who met him, she was struck by how astonishingly boring the poet could be at table; for the entire evening she hardly manged to coax a word out of the man.

'I've spoken with Ibsen a number of times now,' she confided to the actor Holm Hansen afterwards. 'But he's a verbal skinflint and only communicates through his printed works.' She found him inhibited and suspicious, a striking contrast to the power of his work: 'It's really quite annoying to sit and freeze in the presence of so much fire.'

Not until the letter in rhyme had transformed the meeting between them into art did the fire flare up again, quite in keeping with the contents of the poem, where Ibsen had turned Fru Heiberg into a myth, turned her into art, and art into reality. Thus she was able to find warmth in the fire of the poem, regardless of the writer's personal chill. In all subsequent literary references to Fru Heiberg and Ibsen the letter in verse has been seen as confirmation of the warm friendship they shared, demonstrating thus the writer's metamorphosis through the act of writing: Ibsen's dour and taciturn presence at the dinner table transmuted into a wondering and awestruck silence at being in the presence of the great Danish prima donna.

THE REVOLT OF THE HUMAN SPIRIT

Before the end of August 1870 Ibsen receives a letter from Suzannah, now back in Dresden with Sigurd. She found the experience depressing, she relates. While they were all away, France had declared war on Prussia. The war had lasted for the whole of the summer and into the winter until French resistance finally collapsed in February 1871, a month after the proclamation of the German empire at Versailles.

Throughout the late summer and autumn Dresden was filled with wounded soldiers and French prisoners of war. The Ibsen family's sympathies were with the French, something that was bound to lead to difficulties since Saxony had just joined the union of north German states under Prussian leadership. Suzannah was shocked at the public mockery and contempt shown for the French people, at the dishonourable way the victors treated their beaten enemies, and at the suspicion that now met everyone who didn't speak German. She and Marie hardly dared speak to each other in the street and kept their sympathies to themselves.

But Sigurd didn't.

'Heart and soul he is francophile,' writes Suzannah to Henrik in Copenhagen, 'and advertises his sympathies at school every day, so he's a real war hero.'

Martyr might have been a better word. Sigurd is said to have been beaten up at school for refusing to support the Germans. He could hardly expect any help from the teachers, who were as patriotic as the German pupils. Henrik must have been beside himself with worry, but fortunately Suzannah was able to ease his mind the following month. At her request the principal of the school had taken steps to ensure that those bullying Sigurd be dealt with. His own letter to his father makes no mention at all of his suffering. It is as though the most important thing of all was to remain unshakably true to his beliefs. Did he think that was what his father expected? Because Henrik too was a man of firm convictions, though also a pragmatist, and one who chose his battles carefully.

Henrik had a touch of Brand, but also of Peer Gynt in his character. The son, it seems, had inherited only Brand's uncompromising streak.

A letter written by Sigurd's mother a few weeks before this gives a more nuanced picture of Sigurd's complex nature, one which mingles common sense with concern:

> In the evenings, when he is tired, he sheds tears and wishes you were here, but yesterday, while we were sitting in the woods, he asked me first if you received your writer's wage every year, and then, if you were writing anything.

Henrik Ibsen was back in Dresden before the end of September. 'No trace of enthusiasm for the war here,' he reports to Hegel. 'Whatever the newspapers are saying about that is pure fiction. The country is suffering dreadfully.' The effects were felt throughout the autumn and winter of 1871. Coal rationing was one thing, the way it affected people's lives another. Many families had lost loved ones on the field of battle, and the hospitals were filled with wounded German soldiers while French officers who had been taken prisoner wandered the city streets like free men.

Once again he puts the tragedy of the emperor Julian to one side and instead tries to write an opera about Sigurd Jorsalfare. But nothing works for him. He blames the war – 'this damn war has a very disturbing effect on me' – but he had been struggling with his writing long before the outbreak of the conflict. Life after Rome had been rich in experiences, but rootless. After the glittering festivities in Stockholm and Egypt, scandal in Norway, and the exhaustion of war-torn Dresden – 'my home among strangers' – a sort of revolt seems to have grown inside Ibsen, a revolt that in the first instance finds its expression in an ever more intense relationship with Georg Brandes. At the end of June 1869 he writes a letter that inaugurates a correspondence between them that continues for years. A strange friendship develops between the two, as strong as it is ambivalent, characterised by a desire on both sides to fight the same battle. But it is noticeable how the two read their own ambitions into each other's writings and doings – valuable for themselves, but not always so appropriate for each other.

Around Christmas, Ibsen writes to Brandes, who has been away travelling for nine months and now lies in a hospital in Rome with a serious bout of typhoid fever. Ibsen gives vent to that sense of revolt that has been building up in him after his return to a Germany at war, a war that has also had dramatic consequences for the holy city of Rome. No longer under the protection of Napoleon III, it has been occupied by Italian troops. Ibsen grieves for all that has been lost:

Rome was the only peaceful place in Europe; the only place that enjoyed real freedom, freedom from political tyranny. I don't think I want to see it again after what has happened. All that lovely spontaneity has been spoiled and is now lost; for every politician who appears down there, an artist will be broken. And that wonderful need for freedom – those days are over now; I have to admit, the only thing I love about freedom is the struggle to achieve it; possession of it is of no interest to me.

Europe was in flames, the French crushed under Bismarck's iron heel, and in the eternal city of Rome the clocks had started to tick again. The feeling of change, of destruction, of evanescence seems to have overcome Ibsen completely, persuading him that he was living through a time of epic change, one in which everything that had formerly been fixed and solid was now melting away:

The old, illusory France has been shattered; now the new and very real Prussia has been shattered too, and we are suddenly entering a new epoch. Ideas will come tumbling down around us too – and probably not before time. We have been living on the crumbs of the revolutionary table of preceding centuries for quite long enough.

So he bids a definitive farewell to the heritage of the great revolutions of 1789, 1830 and especially 1848, which coincided with his own intellectual awakening. Concepts need to be redefined, he now believes. Freedom, equality, fraternity – these words no longer have the same ring about them. That is what the politicians fail to understand – 'and that is why I hate them'. What the world needs is not more revolutions, or at least, not 'external revolutions'. What is called for now is a 'revolution of the human spirit'. And in this Brandes must take a lead, once he has rid his body of the fever.

A revolution of the human spirit. From now on this becomes Ibsen's credo. It's been a long time coming. These are the consequences of *Brand*, *Peer Gynt* and his rejection of the whole nationalist project. Would Brandes be prepared to join him in *that* revolution?

The answer is yes. And no.

In the narrative of literary history, Henrik Ibsen and Georg Brandes stand like two generals in the struggle for the breakthrough of the modern, shoulder to shoulder in the battle for the individual, for freedom and progress.[14] But the narrative is a distortion, a later construction, created once the modern breakthrough was a fact. In the main the contact between them was neither as strong nor as close as the history suggests. The irregular but fruitful exchange of ideas between them that began in the summer of 1869 comes to an abrupt halt a few years later. Between 1876 and 1882 they did not correspond with each other at all. It means that during the years in which Ibsen broke through with his dramas of contemporary life, years in which he also made a name for himself in Germany, there was no contact between him and the leading figure in the 'modern breakthrough'. Nor did Brandes write about Ibsen much during these years. He did not discuss *A Doll's House* until a year after its publication, and then rather negatively. And in the years between 1877 and 1883, while Brandes was living in Berlin, he published not a single word on Ibsen in German.[15] Not until the appearance of *Ghosts* (1881) did he stand shoulder to shoulder with Ibsen, and the great writer and great critic appear like the comrades-in-arms of literary tradition.

The limited nature of the contact between them was not solely because they were so different as individuals – Ibsen Norwegian and prickly, Brandes Danish and cultured, the former a satirist at heart, the latter with little apparent sense of humour. Their view of the world was different. Brandes the academic disliked the writer's disillusionment, his negativity, and his penchant for the obscure and the riddling; he sought clarity of expression, and possessed an optimism about the future that was alien to the other. In *The Men of the Modern Breakthrough* (1883), Brandes likens progress to a 'locomotive belching fire'. Ibsen could never have made such a comparison. What they did have in common was the feeling of being part of a spiritual aristocracy, though even here their elitism expressed itself in different ways. Where Ibsen was the hermetic and dogged individualist, Brandes wanted to be a leader in the field of social struggle. He too was unwilling to lend his name to the political left, but was not against the idea of political parties as such:

> I am not the type of man who joins any political party; the thing is, I am a one-man political party, and the only choice people are really going to have is to join *me*.

Brandes wanted to take an active and leading role in society, to reform its institutions. He was also involved in various ways in countering the social injustices that were part and parcel of a class-based society. It left Brandes split between his feeling for solidarity and his elitism – a problem Ibsen did not have.

Brandes was a player, whereas Ibsen's declared intention was to upend the whole gaming board; in the final analysis, that was perhaps the most important distinction between them.

In fact, so great was the distance between them that at certain periods one might almost suspect Brandes of actively working against Ibsen, passively, by rarely commenting on his writing, and actively, by talking about him in a compromising way.[16] In time the critic would come closer to the older writer's position, but only after years of opposition, and educated by his reading of Nietzsche. In the article entitled 'Aristocratic Radicalism', which Brandes wrote about the German philosopher in 1889, Ibsen's insights from the years around 1870 seem to hover between the lines. The article is in part an explanation of Nietzsche's philosophy, and partly the expression of the view of life that a weary leader of the breakthrough of the modern had arrived at.

In 1871 the gulf between them remains wide. Typically the two responded in quite different ways to the enrolment of the Vatican in the Italian state. Ibsen's tears at the loss of the last refuge of art arouse only contempt in Brandes. In a letter to his parents he writes:

> . . . I don't really give a damn about all that lovely poetic peace they had here; in plain Danish it was nothing but sleepiness, servitude, laziness, and rot; possibly the ruins looked better in that kind of light. But it's too much to ask people to suffer just so the ruins look good.

Brandes' letter to Ibsen has not survived, but he must have expressed something similar in it. Ibsen, at least, certainly reacts as though this is the case in his next letter:

> And now, in your most recent friendly (?) lines to me, you will have it that I am a hater of freedom.

Ibsen then gives an explicit account of his position:

> I would never equate freedom solely with political freedom. What you call liberty, I call liberties; and my idea of the struggle for freedom is quite simply the constant daily effort required to adopt and live out the idea of freedom.

Here he touches upon the unavoidable paradox that lay at the heart of contemporary rhetoric on the subject of freedom. Both Ibsen and Brandes rallied round the banner of freedom, and regarded the struggle for freedom as a progressive idea. But at the same time, the concept of freedom was one of the pillars of the established liberal society that both were a part of, the subject of ordinary, everyday political rhetoric. Ibsen feels an urgent need to distinguish between the banal usage of the conception of freedom he observes in the political world, and the permanent revolutionary sort of freedom that is *his* concern – what he calls the revolt of the human spirit.

'The minority is always right', he could claim; or he could speak longingly of the 'wonderful longing for freedom' the Russians might have felt under the czars, and speak disparagingly of everything that had to do with public-spiritedness, organisations and party politics. Norway's tragedy was that it had lost its aristocracy, because an aristocracy was necessary to build a nation. Norway was a land of headless torsos, plutocrats and clowns – the country had not even managed to hang on to the old spiritual aristocracy of its officials.

He states his position plainly to Brandes:

> My dear friend, the liberals are freedom's worst enemies. Freedom of belief and freedom of thought thrive best under absolutism.

For him the greatest threat to freedom came from 'state societies', and the way these emptied the concept of its most important content. Indeed, to the alarm of Brandes, he goes on to deny the necessity not merely of the state, but of the individual's duty to be a good citizen. 'Get rid of the state! Now there's a revolution I could support.'

In his view the turbulent times through which they were living heralded the end of the organised state, and of more than that, of religion, the moral code, and art in its existing forms. All things were historically conditioned, and all things were about to come to an end. No sooner had Brandes read the letter from his friend than he grabs his pen and writes to his parents, as was his habit whenever the world became difficult:

> His radicalism is completely unprecedented. I get dizzy just reading about all the things he wants to revolutionise.

Any subtleties that might have lain between Ibsen's lines were, it seems, lost on Brandes. He is simply shocked, which irritates Ibsen and makes him even more dogmatic. So any idea that Ibsen was Brandes' promised land as a critic – his 'America', as some have claimed – has to be moderated in light of the fact that their ethical and moral worldviews only partially overlapped. Indeed, one might say that Ibsen *was* Brandes' America, but only with the proviso that Brandes, like Columbus, had originally planned to reach India. Only gradually did they come to accept each other as inhabitants of the same promised land, as 'brothers in arms' in the cause of the modern breakthrough. Even then there remained clear points of distinction between their literary and ethical projects.

THE SPIRITUAL ARISTOCRACY

That Ibsen was probably exaggerating slightly in his correspondence is hinted at in a later letter in which, in a moment of refreshing self-irony, he complains that the socialist Paris Communards have stolen his 'no-state theory' and rendered it unusable. But how should he be properly understood? Ironically or literally?

What actually lies behind Ibsen's 'no-state theory', apart from an obvious desire to provoke Georg Brandes?

The state must be abolished, because it hinders the liberation of the individual, is what he claims. But a third notion is conspicuous by its absence here, and that is the idea of the nation. Previously, before he had confronted his own romantic nationalism, Ibsen had considered the concepts of state and nation to be in intimate relationship with one another, in the sense that the latter legitimised the former. Using an ethnically based definition of nationhood he could still, in 1865, maintain that 'a state can be destroyed, but not a nation'. As long as 'our national spirit' was strong enough, the nation would survive even if the state disintegrated, something the Jewish people had demonstrated over centuries. Ibsen had never had much good to say about the state, and once the nation had been abolished as a unit of civilisation then not much remained to him but the individual. The realisation strikes him all the more forcibly from his front-row seat at so many of the political and military changes that were taking place in Europe throughout the 1860s and 1870s: Denmark's loss of Schleswig and Holstein to Prussia; the formation of a federation of German-speaking states under Prussian leadership; Bismarck's wars against Austria and France and the establishment of the German empire; the Habsburgs' loss of Venice to Italy; and the completion of the unification of Italy with the enrolment of the Vatican State in 1870. For us, looking back through two world wars, it is hard to imagine the monstrous upheaval this series of events – and in particular the Franco-German war – was for contemporaries. For a brief historical moment at least, enthusiasm for the superiority of bourgeois civilisations was silenced. And along with the blood that seeped down through the battlefields many of the ideals that civilisation was based on vanished too – the heritage of the great revolutions.

For Ibsen the conclusion followed naturally. There could be no point in replacing one kind of state with another – 'and for that reason I believe the next great revolution will be aimed at overthrowing the very idea of the state'. In the years to come he became more and more convinced of the correctness of his prediction. In January 1883, Ingvald Undset, father of Sigrid Undset, recalled his conversations with Ibsen in Rome: 'Ibsen no longer recognises nationality, nor anything else either; he is a complete anarchist who wants to see the slate wiped clean – a torpedo under the whole ark. The human race has to start all over again, from the beginning – and begin with the individual!'

The slate wiped clean; that was the real extent of Ibsen's revolutionary thought, and that was the task facing his generation in the transitional times through which they were living – 'what emerges instead will be the future's business; our main task is to blow the status quo to pieces – to destroy it!'

* * *

As a social vision all this is diffuse, not to say replete with inner contradiction. To demand that the state be abolished does not exactly accord with praising 'absolutism', the most authoritarian form of state control. And in practice there seems little doubt that in the 1860s and 1870s Ibsen allied himself increasingly with the conservative forces in society, *with* the establishment and *against* the opposition. This loyalty finds its clearest expression in his correspondence with royalty, in whose presence Ibsen works so hard to abase himself. But it is also apparent in his response to specific social issues. Even though he sympathises with the French, he is scathing about the country's revolutionary tradition, in which punishment and discipline were, in his opinion, sorely lacking. Indeed, Norway should beware its own revolutionaries: 'People who allow Jaabæk and Bjørnson to walk about like free men deserve to be locked up themselves.' Referring to the conservative Norwegian government, he said that he 'supports it with my pen and with all the powers at my disposal'. Even on an issue like Bjørnson's breakaway theatre he took the establishment side, saying that the actors should be punished until they bowed to the will of the management.

Where is the logic in all this? To suggest that his remarks are emotionally motivated exaggerations is no real answer, for they are, after all, the products of reason and, in spite of everything, there is a certain discernible consistency.

Nor does Ibsen's desire to see the state abolished accord with his demand, repeated over the years, for the state to recognise its obligations to the country's cultural life, for example, in the form of subsidised theatres, an annual wage for writers, and national and inter-state agreements aimed at securing copyright for a writer's work. In other words, these demands had, formerly, a clearer ideological basis. In a speech given at P. A. Munch's grave in Rome in the summer of 1865 he had asserted that the state has two functions. One was to ensure the 'welfare of the state society', meaning its material welfare. The other was to provide for 'the life of the nation', which meant encouraging the efforts made by literature, art and the sciences to ensure that the nation earned the right to survive. In tossing aside the concept of the nation it appears that Ibsen's only positive expectation of the state had been that it should provide for its writers!

Probably the best approach is to consider his ideas on the state, the individual and society against the background of his psychological and emotional make-up, his literary project, and his intellectual disposition. Hardly surprising, then, that the picture is a little unclear. But there again, that is quite simply how this man was put together. The signs are that he lacked the basic ability to understand and to relate to complicated social questions and the practical mechanics of political life, and that literary historians have overlooked this, since a lack of talent in one particular department is rarely prominently commented upon in recounting the lives of great men. However extreme his views might seem, it would be wrong to assume he held them alone. It is perfectly possible to find counterparts to Ibsen's views on society in some of the historical and ideological discussions that were taking place among his contemporaries.

With the coming of a modern, class-based industrial society many remained sceptical about the process of democratisation, the politics of the crowd, the rise of political parties and the extensions of bureaucracy, all of which threatened to cast a dull grey veil across life. There were many who supported the demand for freedom while at the same time fearing the tyranny of equality, and doing what they could to hinder the entry of the lowest social class into polite society. The 1860s was the decade when the debate on democratisation, voting rights and constitutional reform erupted onto the European stage. The conservative side feared the rise of the lower class and its influence on the political system. Voting reforms were introduced in Great Britain, Sweden and Denmark, with new constitutions in the latter two cases. All reforms were characterised by the conservative desire to keep the working class under control, a tendency made manifest by a conditional extension of the franchise, and countered by strengthening the influence of the privileged class, and by constitutional reform that strengthened an upper chamber dominated by the elite and closely bound to executive power in the country.

At home in Norway similar proposals were put forward by some of Ibsen's old friends from the Learned Holland, Michael Birkeland, Ole Andreas Bachke and Jacob Løkke. Like Ibsen, all three had been shaped by the revolutions of 1848 but, alarmed by Marcus Thrane's movement and the growth of opposition from the Left, all had gradually turned in the direction of a fundamental and anti-democratic conservatism. Together they contributed a series of articles to *Morgenbladet* in the 1860s in which they suggested a programme of reforms modelled on those being introduced in neighbouring countries. As the situation developed, even the farmers joined the coalition of the Left. Frustration in conservative quarters in Norway in the 1860s and 1870s was widespread; the despotism of the masses was growing, and yet conservatives seemed unable to agree on any kind of sustained response to the threat.

This is another aspect of the real-world political backdrop to *The League of Youth*, although Ibsen makes no specific mention of it.

Ibsen was not alone in looking for an elitist response that could curb the power of the masses. And yet he was different from his old friends from the Learned Holland in that he unfailingly observed a distance from the political debates of his day.[17] He cared little for such matters as the extension of the franchise and constitutional reform, and farmers remained the target of his contempt:

'If only a revolution would break out back home,' he was once heard to exclaim in Rome. 'It would give me the greatest pleasure to man the barricades and start shooting Norwegian farmers.'

By adopting a position well outside any political grouping and ignoring any obligation to be practical and consistent in his political theorising, Ibsen could allow himself to go much further than Birkeland, Bachke and Løkke, firing off one outrageous broadside after another with no attempt at all to suggest a connection between the thought and its practical political application. In doing so he undermined the Hollanders' whole project.

So Ibsen was no party-political animal, any more than he occupied a clearly defined ideological position. And yet it might be profitable to try to establish a functional description that would reveal the fundamental characteristics of an Ibsenian ideology. One possibility would be to call it *aristocratic individualism*, a concept that expresses his profound ambivalence towards modernisation in a way that suggests both the backward looking (aristocratic) and the progressive (individualism). Ibsen was someone who embraced modern society while at the same time being in revolt against it. Socially a child of the petite bourgeoisie, ideologically a child of the 1848 revolution, he identified himself with the self-made man, adaptable, upwardly mobile and striving for freedom. In sum, he reacted at an early stage to many of the natural consequences of modernisation, a reaction in which he was not alone. In the 1800s, and particularly in the later years of the century, a number of writers, philosophers and social thinkers warned of some of the less attractive aspects of the process of democratisation, notably the 'tyranny of equality', 'mob rule' and 'dictatorship of the majority'. Such opposition was not a unified response. On the one hand there were considered analyses such as Alexis de Tocqueville's discussion of the dangers and blessings of democracy in *On Democracy in America* (1835). De Tocqueville, who was of noble birth himself, regarded the democratisation of Europe as inevitable and desirable, while fearing that an equal society would lead to a situation in which people sacrificed their freedom for security under an omnipotent state. Democracy, he thought, in a worst-case scenario, could engender a despotic regime that was milder, but at the same time more comprehensive than any previous regime: the all-powerful state in a democracy 'is not tyrannical, it exerts pressure, it quells, it weakens, extinguishes, renders dull and finally moulds the people into a herd of fearful and obedient animals with the state as its shepherd'.

In other words, democracy's worst enemy was mediocrity, and its longing for security.

Similar sentiments were expressed by John Stuart Mill and Kierkegaard ('The majority is an untruth'). One of those who did not accept the democratic development but instead fought to preserve an aristocracy of the spirit in the face of the despotism of the masses was Thomas Carlyle. In *On Heroes, Hero-worship and the Heroic in History* (1841) and other works he described the great heroic figures who down through the ages had held high the flame of the spirit. The Italian freedom-fighter Guiseppe Mazzini also praised the minority and the exceptional individual, and developed a teaching characterised by pan-Roman nationalism, radical liberalism and heroic elitism.[18] The extent to which Friedrich Nietzsche belongs in this company depends on how one reads him. Read in the way he was in Scandinavia towards the end of the 1800s, he was seen as a believer in the exceptional individual, a man who held the masses in contempt.

Despite the differences between them, what unites these thinkers is that they were all driven by an emotional and instinctive force that opposed them to the more pragmatically oriented conservative politics of containment that developed within the political system.[19] They were rather like prophets communicating a deep unease at the process of modernisation that nevertheless continued on its remorseless way. Not until the twentieth century did these tendencies assume organised form with the creation of political parties or radical groups that fought to shape the new mass societies along elitist lines. In certain countries, such as Germany and Italy, they were briefly successful in choking democracy; in other countries such groups were successfully marginalised as democracy established itself. This was what happened in Norway. Here the Free-Minded Liberal Left established itself as the 'chieftains' party' at the start of the new century, but had run out of steam by the 1920s, when its aristocratic message was taken over by the activists of the Fatherland League. Their mantle in turn was assumed by the fascist National Front, which took the aristocratic line in Norwegian politics to its perverted end in the Ragnarok of the Second World War.

From being a cry for the great man, the loner who could rise above the crowd, aristocratic individualism in the twentieth century turned into an organised aristocratic elitism that was either within or close to the party system. From there the distance was not great to an authoritarian elitism in which the Romantic hero was traded for a lower-class leader with a sovereign contempt for the masses.[20]

Henrik Ibsen was part of the ideological landscape of aristocratic individualism in the 1800s. Formed in the days before the establishment of parliamentary rule, he was one of those solitary figures who warned against the darker sides of democracy. Compared to the aristocratic elitism of the twentieth century his was more radical in its willingness to destroy the status quo, but less radical in its alternative visions of society – to the extent that he had any such vision at all. Ibsen was in many ways a prisoner of his own century. His anger against developments in society was characterised by resignation, his attitude towards the process of modernisation highly ambivalent. He was at once revolutionary and reactionary, almost a personification of what is known as 'the dilemma of freedom', the contradiction between freedom as vision and the inevitable consequences of freedom in real life.[21]

It was a sense of the death of ideas and the collapse of history that lay behind Ibsen's dream of the noble human being, and Nietzsche's belief in the exceptional man. If we are to take Ibsen's extra-literary comments on politics and society seriously, it is hard to ignore the irrationalism, the contempt for the masses, the cultivation of the elite, and a certain affinity with violence and the exercise of power.[22] Taken to extremes it provides a fine ideological thread that links Ibsen's universe of ideas to the vitalism and cults of personality of the leader-figures of the century that followed his.

Had it not been for the writing.

One of the most remarkable things about Henrik Ibsen is the striking gap between his life and his teaching. For him the drama was a psychological and aesthetic laboratory, and even though the Ibsen play often revolves around ethical problems, drama is hardly a medium for the preaching of moral and political ideas. By its very nature, drama is unsuited to the unopposed promotion of ideas and beliefs. The dramatist is forced to pit different views of life against each other without the use of any superior narrative voice; if the audience is to be persuaded of something, this can only happen through the actions and dialogue of the characters on the stage. Theatre is about the play of opposites, in which the characters should, at their best, appear to be complete and rounded creations, regardless of whether they are heroes or villains. This demands both empathy and distance of the dramatist. But if drama is, by definition, polyphonic, then there is no doubt that Ibsen drew more radical conclusions from this realisation than most others. Seen in this light, one might perhaps say that his anti-idealistic, polyphonic and ambivalent plays come close to the very essence of what drama is as a genre.

In much of his writing Ibsen explored the relationship between the individual and society in a way that involved the constant subversion of any position or stance, including even those that most closely resembled his own. A persistent motive is the heroic longing for greatness, for the ennoblement of the individual. But in contrast to Mazzini he did not relate heroism to the nation, nor yet, like Nietzsche, to any theory of the history of civilisation. And he did not cultivate heroes in the way suggested by Carlyle; in his plays they are more likely to fail, not in tragic greatness but instead pathetically stripped of all their illusions. Ibsen preached neither heroism nor a philosophy of power. Instead he undertook a dramatic investigation of the human urge to freedom, the longing to transcend one's own limits, juxtaposing these against values such as responsibility, love and the obligations of everyday life.[23] This is why the character who comes closest to being Ibsen's alter ego, Dr Stockmann in *An Enemy of the People*, is depicted with a distinct irony, and why it is so difficult to abstract political implications from the plays.

Perhaps one could say that Ibsen the writer had a civilising and humanising effect on Ibsen the human being, in that he introduced his own tendencies and inclinations into his work, not in order to promote them but to challenge them.

If this is the case, then it gives a powerful resonance to his famous observation that to write is to sit in judgement over oneself.

Henrik Ibsen was a writer, not a preacher, though at various times his works have been embraced by everyone from socialists and anarchists to fascists and Christians. As a writer his concern was with the constitution of the individual in the world. In that sense, everything he wrote could be described as a critical drama of social life, but in a generalised form that extended beyond any political, institutional or social category. Understood thus, it is tempting to interpret his conservative sympathies and his alliance with the powerful as expressions of a distaste for the very fact of the political struggle. In the final analysis, it was the opposition that dragged politics into the foreground. Then, once the battle had been won, it took the rhetoric of freedom with it as it assumed power, turning it into a power-preserving ideology. For someone dedicated to a permanent revolution of the human mind, political struggle represented a dead end, because the freedom of the individual was so lightly sacrificed and the concept of freedom itself so soon calcified. For Ibsen these effects were indistinguishable from corruption.

The constant noise generated by the social struggle also made it difficult to write, and this is an important factor. For Ibsen, aristocratic individualism was closely bound up with his attitude towards writers and the role of the intellectual. 'What I would wish for you above all is a thorough-going egoism,' he writes to Georg Brandes. 'There could be no better way in which to benefit your society than by transforming the raw metal inside you into something valuable.'

The calling. An author's obligation was to his calling and nothing else.[24]

I have never felt a particularly strong sense of solidarity. I have always just sort of included it as one of the traditional virtues, – and if one had the courage to actually drop it completely then the personality might almost be rid of a certain burden.

So what might seem a form of anarchism is in point of fact an aristocratic individualism closely related to the role of writers and intellectuals in society, as long as 'the masses lack any understanding of higher matters both at home and abroad'. There is then no sense in which this was an anarchism in the sense of developed and constructive social philosophy.[25] Only in occasional glimpses does Ibsen offer alternative models of society, and he does not do even this until a few years later. Those who would make a constructive social thinker out of him blithely ignore the huge contempt with which he regarded the crowd. Summing up, the relationship between the man and the writer can be described thus: where Ibsen *the man* expresses a resigned anger at the way society is developing, Ibsen the *writer* energetically revolutionises European drama, drawing attention to extremely radical ideas in both the individual and in society. From a historical and biographical perspective this is perhaps the most interesting of all the paradoxes that surround the life and work of Henrik Ibsen.

* * *

Little wonder that Brandes was shocked. His aim was not to abolish the institutions of society but to reform them. No doubt he wished he could stand shoulder to shoulder with Ibsen in this struggle, but there were so many things that just didn't seem right between them. He quickly realised that Ibsen was most definitely not someone who was as enthusiastic about the new ideas, the positivism, the advances in the natural sciences, as he had probably expected. On top of that he seemed indifferent to social questions, at best politically naïve and, at worst, deeply conservative. It left him of only limited use to Brandes when the latter began his series of lectures on the main currents in European literature in 1871, an event that would involve him in his first major conflict in Danish public life, and one in which he had need of all the friends he could get.

The problem was that Ibsen did not want to take part in the political debate. He didn't want to expose himself to attack on open ground, preferring instead to fight from his desk.

Brandes genuinely admired Ibsen as a writer, but was repelled by his bitterness, doubtful about his sincerity, and shocked by his attraction to the extreme. And Ibsen found Brandes frustrating in equal degree. He admitted to a friend that his letters to Brandes were reserved. He was irritated by the misunderstandings that arose because they did not know each other, and by the way he felt Brandes did not understand what he meant. In general he was concerned about Brandes' caution and willingness to compromise; to Ibsen the only thing that matters is 'to will what one must'. He saw no evidence that Brandes understood these words.

But what they did have in common was important enough. Ibsen the hermit and Brandes the reformer were united in a belief in the exceptional individual and the duty of the intellectual to lead, beliefs that Ibsen almost certainly reinforced in Brandes (and in that sense he was an important support for Brandes before Brandes set out on his lecture tour of 1871). In the years around 1870 the idea of the spiritual aristocrat was at its strongest in Ibsen, stimulated by the military and political unrest in Europe, strengthened by his correspondence with Brandes, and his own sense of being adrift in the uncertain little patch of European reality in which he had chosen to settle.

Ibsen's 'Balloon Letter to a Swedish Lady', written in Dresden in December 1870 against the background of the Franco-German war, is his most notable artistic expression of this idea. The Swedish lady in question was Fredrika Limnell, who had had Ibsen as a guest at her country home by Lake Mälaren during his visit to Sweden the preceding year. Taking the trip to Egypt as his starting point, he tries to offer a diagnosis of the age by tracing lines back to the greatness of ancient Egypt. Unlike the Nordic and Greek antiquities, ancient Egypt was a dead past, the columns and temples along the banks of the Nile like bones and skeletons in the sand.

> And why?
> Well, the reason's pretty plain.
> Where identity is lacking,
> where the form does not contain
> hatred, pleasure, joy and tension,
> throbbing pulse and blood's bright stain, —
> then the sum of high pretension
> is mere skeleton-like clacking.

A civilisation that obliterated the individual and the personality, a society in which the members had no other call in life but 'plain and simple existence', was doomed to fall. Now it was in the process of happening all over again. What was the expansive and state-centred Prussia if not a new Egypt, with the people as the stones that make up the pyramids, the building blocks of society rather than personalities in their own right?

Prussia would have to be punished; but it is perfectly possible to read the letter in rhyme as a diagnosis of modern society in general. But what was the alternative? Ibsen begins the poem by reminiscing about the heroes of a bygone age such as the Swedish warrior king Gustavus Adolphus, and Peter Wessel the naval hero, before asserting that the longing for 'beauty' still lives. The longing for beauty and the cultivation of heroes, the belief in strong and exemplary ideal figures able to bring greatness to a society, these are key concepts in the vision of the aristocratic individualist. But Ibsen can offer no candidates, and the poem ends in a defence of the poet's withdrawal from social life to a life in artistic exile, one in which art can be cultivated for its own sake:

Shall we join the fun together?
Well, who knows, dear lady whether
doves will bring the card? We'll see.
Till then I wear gloves – kid-leather –
in my chamber's privacy;
till then I shall seek allayment
as a poet garbed in vellum;
that will stir the good-folk's venom,
'heathen's' sure to be my payment;
mobs are my abomination,
I fear dregs, contamination,
I shall bide time's slow rotation
in my spotless wedding raiment

Quite possibly all this wagging of the tail for the aristocracy might be explained by the writer's desire to appeal to the recipient of the poem herself, Fru Limnell. But there is no reason to question the sincerity of his contempt for the crowd and the mob. In aristocratic and monarchical circles he had actually found a place where art *could* be cultivated for its own sake – with kid gloves and vellum. Seen from this angle, Ibsen's social ambitions appear to be not solely a lusting after status and financial security but also the search for an artistic space that would afford complete freedom.

In the final analysis, this was probably what mattered most to him, and what guided his view of the world around him:

The freedom to write.

'I MUST, I MUST'

As emotional as Ibsen is in his correspondence with Brandes, in his long letter to the Dane Peter Hansen of 28 October 1870 he is subdued. What he says, however, is more or less the same.[26]

Peter Hansen was a journalist and critic whom Ibsen had met in Stockholm the previous autumn. The letter remains one of the most frequently quoted in the literature on Ibsen, and with good reason. It comes following a request from Hansen for a brief overview of Ibsen's writing which he probably intended to use in a journalistic context. Although nominally a private letter its address is public. But Hansen doesn't want a straightforward record of the facts; what he wants, he says, is 'the inner story'. And that is exactly what he gets, a concise literary autobiography of the writing so far. This is in the autumn of 1870, following Ibsen's definitive breakthrough in Scandinavia. Ever since the appearance of *Brand* he has in a variety ways, and always thoroughly self-consciously, confirmed his status as a writer, and carefully nurtured the way in which he presents himself in public. The letter to Hansen is a further example of this.

He begins by identifying the source of his own writing:

> All that I have written originates in an atmosphere and a particular set of circumstances; I have never written anything simply because I have found, as one says, 'a good story'.

With these words he defines the core of his literary nature. It is a question of 'necessity'. He writes not because he *wants* to, but because he *has* to. A stream of necessary creativity seems to flow through his life, from a source deep within him, and from the meeting between this stream and the ever-changing world that surrounds him the individual works emerge.

Based on this analysis he then gives an account of the origins of each play. *Catiline*, that drama of revolt, was written in a 'stuffy and very respectable little town, where I found it impossible to express everything that was growing inside me'. *Lady Inger of Østråt* emerged from his infatuation with Rikke Holst, in the same way that *The Vikings at Helgeland*, 'On the Heights' and *Love's Comedy* could be related to a 'longing for freedom' that is resolved in his love for Suzannah. It is surprising to note the importance he ascribes to his wife's love and in particular her support for *Love's Comedy* when it appeared. The beloved and meaningful 'other' is given this 'resolving' function in his writing at a point when all are turned against him – 'And I was excommunicated; everyone was against me' (in addition, the tribute to Suzannah might owe something to a wish to 'cleanse' his marriage from the embarrassingly biographical reading the play was given when it was published). Rejection in its turn gave rise to a new 'atmosphere' that found its resolution in *The Pretenders*. Following the Prussian attack on Denmark the polarisation between writer and society increases, a new atmosphere forms, a furious anger that finds its expression in *Brand*; the sense of compulsion is here reinforced by Ibsen's use of an organic metaphor to the effect that the drama 'grew inside him like a foetus'.

Typically he describes the trip to Rome that was paid for by a travel grant as a 'flight into exile', formulating his own myth of suffering through the idea that he had to flee from his own country to escape persecution and opposition. But of greater significance is the way in which he relates his fate to his writing through a rhetoric of compulsion in which opposition in life created a series of atmospheres that in turn found their expression in his work. A typical feature of this rhetoric is a mysticism rooted in place and nature. Rome, with its 'ideal peace', gave rise to both *Brand* and *Peer Gynt*, each written in what seemed a wine-induced ecstasy. Similarly there is something reminiscent of 'sausages and beer' in *The League of Youth*. Elsewhere he relates the realism of this play to the 'heavy German air', and to Hansen he explains that 'prosaic reality exerts a strong influence on the forms the imagination creates'.

The notion is undeniably striking. Of course life in the Eternal City should produce great dramas of ideas, and the pulsating life of a modern German city give rise to a realistic drama with a contemporary setting. The connection is probably real, but what is interesting is the way that Ibsen in the prose of his letters and in his speeches deliberately encourages the idea of the hand as the tool of the writer's hidden core, and of the work as the product of the encounter between this core and its surroundings. In the same way he relates the striking thematic continuity of his writing to that same rhetoric of necessity, notably in the injunction printed as a Foreword to his *Collected Works* in 1898:

> Only by reading and understanding my entire oeuvre as a single, integrated and continuous whole will one be in a position to appreciate the intended effect of its individual parts. My cordial request to readers is, therefore, quite simply, not to put aside any individual work until later, not to skip anything, but to make the works their own by reading and experiencing them in the same order as that in which I wrote them.

Close to the very end of his active life as a writer he thus binds the whole thing together by relating the first line of the play that opens the collection – 'I must, I must' (*Catiline*) – to the words that end the final play – 'I am free, I am free' (*When We Dead Awaken*). It seems likely that this conscious attitude towards continuity and connection in his writing is something that began to take shape in his mind early in the 1870s. The letter to Peter Hansen is one example. Another is the Foreword to the revised edition of *Catiline* that was published in 1875, in which he points out that even here, in his very first play, he was sounding notes that would be heard again and again in his subsequent works, 'the contrast between what one wants to do, and what one is able to do, between what is willed and what is possible; that is at once the tragedy and the comedy of mankind, and of the individual.'

In this way Henrik Ibsen carefully raised up the two pillars on which his literary project rested: the writing itself and the mythology around him as its author. Under the circumstances it is hardly surprising that he should downplay any literary debt he might have had to other writers. To Hansen he takes the opportunity to deny once again any extensive knowledge of Kierkegaard's work, and he is similarly elusive on the subject of *The Feast at Solhaug* and *St John's Night*, the two plays most directly modelled on the work of others. He was more than happy to talk about the making of the plays and his own working methods; but the deepest roots of his writing lay hidden behind a veil of mystery, not to say metaphysics.

This idea that writing emerged from the innermost depths is no reason to suspect that Ibsen entertained a simple reductionist view of his own writing. On the contrary, he disavows any simplistic conclusions that relate art to reality, the work to the life. He was well aware of the unique and independent nature of art, and knew as well as anyone that the published work of art lived a life of its own. On one occasion he writes to Brandes that 'the intention is none of the critic's business' and concedes that a writer must respect a critic's independent reading. Ideally the work should speak for itself without any prompting from the author at all. However, in that furious response to Clemens Petersen's slaughter of *Peer Gynt*, the one in which he says that 'My book *is* poetry, and if it isn't, then in the future it will be', there is a passage that somewhat complicates the relationship between life and work. The quotation continues thus:

> The idea in our country, in Norway, of what constitutes poetry shall shape itself according to this book. In the world of ideas, nothing is stable; the Scandinavians in our century are not Greeks . . . Summa summarum: I do not want to be either an antiquarian or a geographer, I will not adapt my talents to please anyone. In sum, I have absolutely no intention of taking good advice from a man like Monrad.

Ibsen's words here have been interpreted as showing that he had evolved an almost modernist view of art, one in which the text has the status of something *autonomous*, something that creates its own norm, independent of any references to things outside the world of art.[27] But there is no reason to pull the literary theories of a later era down over Ibsen's Romantic head. Because it as an extension of the Romantic ideal of the writer's exceptional position in society, rather than as an anticipatory modernism, that we need to understand his insistence on the importance of the role of the poet, and his freedom to define what poetry is regardless of any expectations society might have of the nature and function of literature.[28] What is really striking about the statement is how radically he pursues the idea, not least in his willingness to dismiss even tradition itself as an authority for his own writing.

Even though his respect for the literary text debarred him from recognising any authoritative reading of his own works, there were other, more subtle ways of laying claim to ownership of them, as, for example when he relates the birth of the works to the conjoined conceptions of something 'being experienced and something being "lived through"'. The distinction in its most familiar form occurs in a speech Ibsen gave in the autumn of 1874. It is not made in the letter to Peter Hansen from 1870, but it is at around this time that he first begins to use the pairing.[29] In May of that year he writes to Magdalene Thoresen that, in the writing process, he distinguishes between something that has been 'experienced' and something that has been 'lived through'. And in June he stresses the intrinsic worth of art to Laura Kieler when he claims that *Brand* is 'entirely a work of art and nothing but', going on to explain the drama as the result of something 'lived through' – by implication, not something that has merely been 'experienced'.

Something lived through, not something that was merely experienced. Reality is turned into art by a process of sublimation in the writer's mind. To his mother-in-law he explains that 'the moment of poetic conception' takes place when the writer is able to 'raise reality up to the inner and higher level of truth'. In other words, by a process of 'living through'. In this way Ibsen insists on a subtle connection between the work, the writer and reality, and in doing so he is able to maintain property rights over his work at the same time as he defends its independence as art.

* * *

If we add together Ibsen's aristocratic individualism, his views on the independence of art, and the writer's ability to sublimate reality by 'living through' it, a powerful portrait of the writer's unique nature emerges.

The writer stands in some ways outside society and does what he does according to norms he himself establishes by the authority of his genius. In a social sense, Ibsen sees himself as a member of the spiritual elite, writers who had, in his view, a unique ability to interpret reality and the things that preoccupy a society at any given moment. It is easy to overlook the collectivist side of Ibsen the individualist; because what has been 'lived through' is not something the writer lives through uniquely – his public live through it too:

> But no writer lives through things in isolation. What he lives through his fellow countrymen live through with him. For if it were not so, what was it that built the bridge of understanding between the messenger and the recipients of the message?

The point is crucial, and highlights an important proviso in our understanding of Ibsen's idea of writing and the independence of the writer: that independence is *relative*, and depends on what may seem an obvious condition – that in the final analysis the writer is and must be a part of his society.[30] Ibsen does not give us much to go on, but it seems likely that, for him, *the writer and the intellectual exist in an experimental and relatively independent zone on the outer limits of society*. This is the context in which we must understand his self-presentation as the 'poet-prophet' after his breakthrough with *Brand*, the writer who emerges from the desert to educate his people, like an Old Testament prophet.

If we stay with the metaphor then the desert surrounding Israelite society corresponds to this artistic and intellectual zone in Ibsen's modern nineteenth-century society, the region in which new ideas can arise in optimal freedom. And for Ibsen that freedom was best founded on a platform of spiritual aristocracy that was far removed from society's institutions and the daily struggle.

POETRY AND LIES

The connection between Ibsen's attitudes as a spiritual aristocrat and his social ambitions emerged clearly in the autumn of 1870. During his visit to Copenhagen he met a lawyer named Anton Klubien, whom he had known in Rome. Klubien had just the right connections to help Ibsen out with something that had been weighing heavily on him for a while, a matter connected to his social prestige and his reputation as writer and citizen.

It was a question of honours and decorations.

Despite his breakthrough at the Kongelige Teater, Ibsen remained dissatisfied with the way he was treated in Denmark. For one thing, he was not paid the same fees as his Danish colleagues, even though he wrote in what was practically Danish. Another thing: if he was to be treated as a foreign writer then it would be only reasonable for him to be honoured in the same way as his fellow Norwegians Johan Sebastian Welhaven and Andreas Munch had been honoured, with the award of the Order of the Dannebrog. Had not Ibsen argued and defended the Danish cause with his pen every bit as much as they had?

'And I will say this straight out,' he writes to Klubien, 'I am greedy for any recognition of this sort from Denmark.'

Greedy was the word. In Stockholm he had dropped discreet hints about something green to wear in his buttonhole; the following autumn he mounted a full-scale campaign to get himself awarded the Order of the Dannebrog. That he also pursued the award of an order from the Egyptian khedive is easier to understand. The union king's Crown Equerry, Ohan Demirgian, who had secured Ibsen's invitation to Suez, handed out Swedish orders liberally while in Egypt. All the foreign visitors were awarded the Turkish Medjïdjie Order, Turkish because Egypt was at that time a part of the Ottoman Empire. It turned out that Demirgian had exceeded his authority in this instance. His behaviour caused such a scandal in Sweden that he dared not travel home again. Ibsen, who had left Egypt before the handing out of the orders, had been appraised of the situation by von Knorring, but was unable to collect his decoration owing to the scandalous associations with Demirgian's name. Not until the autumn of 1870 did Demirgian return to Sweden, and in November he received a friendly enquiry from Ibsen about the whereabouts of his Turkish decoration.

In other words, all perfectly understandable. And yet there can be no doubt that Ibsen had an unusual fondness for decorations of this kind.

Why did they matter so much to him?

'People are all the same,' the Danish parliamentarian Andreas Frederik Krieger observed drily from the sidelines. 'Now H. Ibsen wants to be decorated – with the Dannebrog, so that next year he'll be a big man in Norway.'

He had hit the nail on the head. Ibsen was convinced that orders and decorations would enhance his prestige in Norway. It had become all the more important to him since several other Norwegian artists had been granted the Norwegian St Olav Order, while he had been ignored. The reasoning is not particularly convincing. Would Ibsen's critics in Norway suddenly become devout admirers were he to inflate his ego even more than he already had?

Did he understand Norwegians at all?

At a dinner in Christiania that same autumn Ibsen's name came up. Someone observed, apparently to general amusement, that the exiled author was to be seen gadding about Dresden in a blue velvet tailcoat with the Vasa Order pinned to his lapel. Now this actually wasn't too far from the truth, and when Ibsen once again started campaigning to get more decorations, it didn't take long for the rumours to start up again. Early in 1871 he realises he has been a little too open in expressing his interest: he asks Klubien to forget the whole business and instead help him to re-establish his reputation. But it is too late: in February he receives the Dannebrog, and a few months later even the Turkish Medjïdjie Order, Third Class.

In the final analysis, Ibsen seems to have been well able to live with such a reputation:

'Now my fellow Norwegians will think my collection of poems twice as good as they did before!' he writes to Hegel in the middle of February 1871, still convinced of his countrymen's admiration for all that glinting silver on his chest.

Yes, and what about that poetry collection? Jacob Løkke had had his work cut out trying to put the collection together back home in Norway. The poems were spread across newspapers, weeklies and special editions, or else they only existed in manuscript form. Ibsen probably waited and watched, his impatience growing, for Bjørnson's *Poems and Songs* had by now appeared, in the summer of 1870, and once again an atmosphere of competition attended upon their literary activities. At last, in January 1871, Løkke was able to send a large package of copies to Ibsen. Ibsen immediately decided to scrap three-quarters of them and set about revising the remainder and adding new ones, including a few taken from his plays. Some time in February the work was complete apart from one final poem, added at the last minute. By March the proofs were ready, and on 3 May *Poems* was published in a first edition of some 4,000 copies.

He had originally intended to call the volume 'Selected Poems', probably to stress that this was a retrospective collection, since the fifty-five poems were spaced evenly across the span of his literary career so far, with the exception of the poems of his youth. None of the poems from the Grimstad collection, *Various Poems*, was included, but that may have been because he had been unable to trace a copy following the auction of his possessions. In all the collection accounted for about a quarter of his total output of poetry, including the poetry taken from the plays. The final two poems included were 'Letter in Rhyme to Fru Heiberg', to which he had just put the finishing touches, and a short poem simply entitled 'Thanks'. Both were poems of gratitude, but the latter was highly personal.

The poem 'Thanks' ('Tak') was addressed to Suzannah, as is clear from the fact that when read backwards the title read 'Kat', one of Ibsen's pet names for his wife:

> Her distress showed when sorrows
> impeded my way —
> her delight was the morrow's
> creative display.
>
> Her home is far yonder,
> on freedom's high seas,
> where poet-craft wander
> sea-mirrored, at ease.

The whole of the myth surrounding Suzannah is contained in these few lines, the notion of the wife who had sacrificed so much for the writer, the one whom he so desperately needed if his life and his writing were to come together successfully. A poetic tribute that sees the wife's complete abnegation in the service of poetry and the poet as a virtue:

> Her aim was inspiring
> My vision's glow
> But how helped the firing
> There's none she'd have know . . .

Ibsen had originally intended to let the poems be expressions of the various stages of his life when he wrote them, but in fact a number of them were almost completely rewritten. In other words, he retouched his literary remembrances in order to give the collection a greater sense of unity.[31] Thus the first poem in the collection, 'Fiddlers', is a presentation of himself as poet, of the sacrifices he has made in order to become a creative writer, and of that duality in his nature that was both a constructive and a destructive force: 'In mighty halls and great churches/I fiddled self-confined,/and torrent-song and terror/have never left my mind.'

The poem that concludes the collection is also autobiographical, and dualistic. In 'The Burnt Ship' he sums up how he left his homeland in order to follow the trail of 'more cheerful gods' in Italy.

And yet:

> for huts of the Norsemen
> from scrub bathed in light
> there rides forth a horseman
> unfailing, each night.

The final verse expresses a sense of physical belonging, a hope, as well as an exquisite calculation. If Ibsen had not actually ridden north every night since leaving home back in 1864 the poem does nevertheless convey a deep attachment to Norway, and that the idea of a journey home had preoccupied him throughout his years in exile. He was still not ready to make that trip, but in this last poem in the collection he wanted to push the door open slightly and admit the existence of this sense of belonging. When he did eventually return home, no one should be in any doubt about where his heart had been all the time he was away.

As regards the reviews, Ibsen was particularly interested in what Georg Brandes might have to say and got Hegel to send him a copy of the collection. Brandes received the book in Italy and at once wrote to his mother, telling her how his initial enthusiasm had turned to disappointment as he made his way through the poems:

> Most of them are *obscure to the point of impenetrability*, many are embarrassing, and the humour almost always a failure. It's all too self-conscious. Too cerebral. There is an air of deliberation about the whole thing. But there are also some very moving portions too, and almost in spite of myself I found myself moved.

Before writing his review, Brandes expressed his reservations in a personal letter to the author, and not long afterwards visited Ibsen in Dresden on his way back to Denmark. So Ibsen cannot have been unprepared for what he read in the pages of the *Illustreret Tidende* of 22 October 1871. 'This is not a rich book,' Brandes wrote, 'and yet it reaches out to something beyond itself, it brings tidings from a spirit with the rare quality both artistically and humanly of striving upwards. So it is a book that enthuses, for, despite its faults, it is so passionate that it communicates passions, and one likes to speak of that which moves one.'

Another Danish critic, Otto Borchsenius, also thought Ibsen 'a greater spirit than he is a writer', and in *Fædrelandet* Rudolph Schmidt predictably claimed that Ibsen's poetry could not compare to Bjørnson's. All in all Ibsen could be satisfied with the reception of his poetry collection; there was less at stake this time too. It sold well, though it seems doubtful that Norwegians thought it 'twice as good' because the author had been awarded the Dannebrog.

It's more likely they allowed themselves to be flattered by his poetic assurance that each night he rode, like a horseman, back to the snowy homes in the north.

'YOU PROVOKE THE DANES . . .'

In July 1871 the Ibsens said goodbye to suburban life in Königsbrücker Strasse and moved back into the centre of Dresden again. Dippoldiswalder Strasse 7 was in a respectable quarter on the other side of the Elbe, near the historic centre of the city. The area was relatively newly established, typically bourgeois, with right-angled streets and large apartment blocks. The Ibsens' new home was close to the so-called diplomatic quarter and in terms of standards of living marked a definite step upwards, a point he did not avoid making to Hegel when informing him of the change of address.

That same month he receives a visit from Georg Brandes, on his way home from travelling abroad. He had sweated himself free from typhoid fever in Rome, fallen in love with a young Danish girl, and even managed to have an affair with his landlady in Sorrento. In Dresden he booked himself in at a shabby hotel and went on a round of the galleries with his friend Julius Lange before eventually calling on the Ibsens.

Brandes recognised Ibsen at once from the portraits, in his shirtsleeves, his head sticking out of the window, although by the time the door was opened the velvet jacket was on, with all its ribbons and medals in place. Ibsen embraced Brandes, hugging him so tightly to his chest that he struggled for breath.

The first meeting.

Brandes found Ibsen good-looking – 'wonderful forehead, long wavy hair, clear eyes'. Both must have been tense; as much as they wished for each other's friendship, the correspondence thus far between them had been characterised by misunderstandings and confusions. So many strong opinions had been expressed, without their being able to see the reaction in each other's eyes. For some two or three hours they chatted together about various things, Ibsen's work, Brandes. A lot about Brandes. That evening they went out together for something to eat and a beer. And what better way to strengthen a friendship than to speak of mutual enemies? Ibsen spoke of how Bjørnson had warned him against Brandes, and of how Bjørnson's friend Rudolph Schmidt had tried to enlist him as co-editor of the periodical *For Ide og Virkelighed* (*Towards Ideas and Reality*). As though he would be willing to take over a seat still warm from Clemens Petersen! Ibsen's suspicions of Bjørnson and his contempt for Schmidt, Petersen and the whole of the old national-liberal guard in Denmark must have warmed Brandes' heart, while the evening must have given both of them the feeling that they were united in their response to the new ideas and the new literature.

In other words, both men discovered just the alliance they had been hoping for and needing. Ibsen was feeling bullish. As they said their goodbyes he called out to Brandes, a smile on his face:

'You provoke the Danes, and I'll provoke the Norwegians.'

Brandes would do more than provoke the Danes; he would declare war on them. But not just yet. When he returned home to Copenhagen in the middle of July, he was full of misgivings and doubts. 'Is it me who is to give the battle order?' he writes in his journal for 22 September. 'Am I really the only leader of the young?'

Shortly afterwards he receives an encouraging letter from Ibsen:

> It occurs to me that you are undergoing the same sort of crisis as I was in the days when I wrote *Brand*. And I feel certain that you too will find the right medicine to drive the sickness from your body.

Ibsen had some advice:

> Hard work is an outstanding cure.

Rarely can Ibsen have offered better advice at a more appropriate time. Brandes soon regained his equilibrium and embarked upon a period of furious literary activity that resulted in the twelve lectures he would come to deliver at the University of Copenhagen in November and December, later expanded and published in six volumes under the title *Main Currents in Nineteenth-Century Literature* (1872–90). Formally it was a literary-historical overview, but few were in any doubt about the lecturer's real aim: to advance a devastating critique of what seemed to him the cultivation of an irrelevant aestheticism, idealism and reaction which, in his view, afflicted most of the literature being created in Denmark at that time. Instead he offered a programme for a new view of literature, one that felt itself duty-bound to address the problems of the real world:

In our time, the proof that a literature is alive is its willingness to debate problems.

It meant a literature that would apply a magnifying glass to institutions such as marriage, and the Church, and to all the social problems that modern life was heir to. The aim of literature should no longer be to please, but to inspire to revolt, and to move the world on. For beneath this problem-oriented view lay an entrenched belief in the future and in progress, in the spirit of positivism, and in equal degree a heroic faith in the writer as the visionary genius able to drag society along in the proper direction. Brandes had wanted to declare war on Denmark. And war was what he got. People flocked to the lectures, drawn both by genuine interest and the strong whiff of scandal. Rumours swirled. Brandes spoke in praise of suicide, it was said, he spoke warmly of novels about broken marriages, and disparagingly about Denmark. His name was on everyone's lips. Danish cultural life, previously so sedate and quiet, was suddenly a bubbling cauldron. Suddenly everyone was involved, not just those inside Auditorium 7 of the university's main building in Frue Plads.[32]

For posterity, Brandes' lectures of 1871 remain the symbol of the breakthrough of a realistic and modern literature in Scandinavia. Naturally, there were precursors, not least from the world of French literature, which he held up for comparison with the prevailing aesthetic in Denmark. But the series of lectures was undeniably a dramatic event. The lecturer's own life was equally dramatic. The lectures, and their subsequent publication, beginning with the first volume in February 1872, aroused a storm of protest. Brandes did indeed discuss such matters as suicide, marriage and the Church. And in criticising the idealised classicism of the Danish sculptor Berthel Thorvaldsen he was also criticising the 'good taste' of the Danish public – obviously a hazardous undertaking. Beneath it all lay a willingness to reduce moral and social conceptions to the level of social, political, geographical and physiological phenomena.

In doing so he brought into focus the conflict between faith and knowledge, between the Christian and the scientific view of the world. His Darwinism was interpreted as hostility to Christianity (reasonably enough), his cosmopolitanism as hostility to Denmark (slightly less reasonably), and his positivism as immoral (totally unreasonably). Brandes' Jewish heritage did nothing to decrease the scepticism with which many viewed him.

And of course he also had supporters. The young Danish writers Holger Drachmann and J. P. Jacobsen announced their support for him, as did other young intellectuals, some wholeheartedly and permanently, others on what turned out to be a temporary basis. But if the young Brandes and his even younger supporters were on the side of the future, they were decidedly not on the side of the present. Their opponents were legion. It was only to be expected that the circles around *Fædrelandet* and *For Ide og Virkelighed* would be against him; more disappointing was the failure of many of his old friends to defend him. In addition he found himself under attack from a large number of leading academics, theologians and newspaper editors.

Not surprisingly, attempts were made to discourage any further such lecturing, and to Brandes' considerable distress he was not appointed to the post of Professor of Aesthetics. Nor was he successful in an application to be appointed a lecturer in aesthetics. He found that most of the press was closed to him; only the periodical *Nyt Dansk Mannedskrift* offered him space in which to reply to his critics. As 1872 drew to a close he was both isolated and unemployed. With very few exceptions, his allies were either young and without influence or they lived abroad.

Ah yes, no doubt about it, the Danes could certainly be provoked.

* * *

Quite what Ibsen may have contributed to Brandes' radical literary programme is not initially easy to see: the literary influences thus far in the life of this monstrously well-read critic had been so many and so various. His positivism was probably something he got from Hippolyte Taine, his involvement in the question of women's rights from the English philosopher John Stuart Mill; Brandes had met both on his travels abroad. The review of *The League of Youth* might indicate Ibsen's role in helping to liberate Brandes from his idealistic aesthetics, but probably his influence was greatest at the personal level. From all that Brandes had thus far written to and about Ibsen, it is tempting to suggest that the Norwegian writer had strengthened Brandes' belief in the personality and the exceptional individual, the idea of a calling, the willingness to confront one's own times and to force through a revolutionary programme without compromise.

Just how strong this influence was emerges most clearly in Brandes' review of *Poems*, a review written in October – and not in his response to the poems, which was conditional, but in his response to the poet:

> Even when alone, he divides more than he unites. He points back to the powers he discovers within himself when, fearlessly and heedlessly, he follows his own nature and his own star. But a star shines only at night. No use in asking Ibsen for a banner; he writes only for himself and for those like him; and he does not provide them with a banner but with an example.

Ibsen was, for Brandes, the poet of loneliness and the dark. But what readers of the review could not have known was that Brandes, in a previous letter to the Norwegian writer, had urged him to raise his flag and take his place in the front ranks of the social struggle. Ibsen refused, and refused so forcefully that Brandes was speechless with admiration for this poet of loneliness, indeed, admired him so greatly that parts of the review are mere paraphrases of Ibsen's most recent letter to him.

So while acknowledging the distance between his own and Ibsen's view of literature and showing a profound respect for Ibsen's integrity, Brandes is not unmoved by the notion of the lonely and incorruptible writer now, when it is *his* turn to hoist his flag and challenge received opinions in Denmark. After the series of lectures was over, Ibsen continued both to enthuse and comfort Brandes with his account of the blessings of loneliness and opposition to which the chosen one is heir.

'No more dangerous book could ever fall into the hands of a writer,' Ibsen wrote after the first volume was published. 'This is one of those books that opens up a chasm between yesterday and today.'

That the liberal press had excluded Brandes from its pages, and the university declined to employ him, was not something Brandes should worry too much about. Would he really want things to be otherwise?

A war such as you are engaged in cannot be waged by a state official.

Ibsen holds nothing back, and is almost triumphalist in relating how all his predictions about the treacherous response of the liberals, and the puzzlement of the masses, have turned out to be correct. But now Brandes must just be strong, and hold on tight – because 'your campaign is good, it's fresh, it's healthy; you are a great and liberating destroyer, a genius'. Ibsen's words must have been heart-warming and encouraging in the midst of so much hostility and opposition, but nothing could alter the fact that the two men's ideas on the role of the intellectual in society were radically different. Brandes did not *want* to be an outsider in society, he wanted to be part of it.

But what did Ibsen do?

While Brandes was busy provoking his fellow countrymen in November and December of 1871, Ibsen was trying to provoke as few people as possible. In November the German periodical *Im neuen Reich*, edited by the writer Gustav Freytag and the historian Alfred Dove, published an attack on him for the anti-German sentiments expressed in his 'Balloon Letter to a Swedish Lady' and 'The Murder of Abraham Lincoln', both of which were included in *Poems*. The attack was in the form of an anonymous appendix to a lengthy article and served as a crude reminder to German readers that there lived among them a Nordic writer whose attitude towards the country that was host to him was hateful, disrespectful and contemptuous. The issue was picked up by, among others, *Constitutionelle Zeitung*, which advised its readers to be more careful in their dealings with non-Germans.[33] Ibsen was forced to respond. In the 23 November issue of *Im neuen Reich* he assures readers that his poem was not intended as an attack on the German people, only on the Prussian politicians responsible for the attack on Denmark.

> A writer can hate ideas, principles and systems; but he cannot hate individuals.

Had he not lived among the Germans for three years now? Did not his own son attend a German school? Had he not worked hard to spread German literature in his own country? Moreover, Suzannah had translated two plays by Freytag, both of which had been performed in Christiania. And as if all this were not enough, readers were told of how he had, on his own initiative, helped a widow who had lost both her sons in the war, just as he continued to pay the school fees for an orphaned child in Dresden. No one could complain that he, a Norwegian, had backed the Scandinavian side in the Dano-German war. He was a true friend of the German people. He goes even further in a letter to Peter Friedrich Siebold, who was translating *Brand* into German.

'You are mistaken if you believe that I cannot see the greatness in a man like Bismarck,' he claims now. 'But I regard him as a hindrance to a good and friendly relationship between Germany and Scandinavia.'

Despite his reservations, Ibsen's view of the Iron Chancellor was changing, as was his whole attitude towards Germany as a nation. He admits as much himself:

> During my long stay in Germany I have changed in many of my attitudes.

What had become of that raging hatred of the Prussians? It is worth noting that the Germans were not the only ones to be provoked by the 'Balloon Letter to a Swedish Lady'. The Norwegian writer Laura Kieler had recited the poem at a gathering at the home of Fredrika Limnell, the woman to whom it was addressed. Kieler never forgot the silence that fell over the gathering of Swedish ladies and gentlemen as she came to the line 'Remember the fallen heroes of Dybbøl'. It made her all the more disappointed to see that in the printed version of the poem the line had been changed, to read 'Kongedybet's brave heroes!' – a sign of Ibsen's willingness to tone down the political references in his writing, this time to accommodate his new-found Swedish friends.

Was that cowardly? Opportunistic?

It might seem that way. But if we look at some of the things he said about writing and society at around this time in context, there is a consistency in the way he tones down his more hostile statements about Swedes and Germans.

Ibsen certainly wanted to revolutionise society through his writing. But in fighting for the revolt of the human spirit he had to be very careful not to be drawn into the political issues of the day. This may have been the thinking behind the change in him. If he wanted to retain his total revolution then he could not afford to become involved in specific conflicts or associated with particular individuals, parties and nations. In short, he wanted to remain at the outer limits of society, and to preserve his right to create on his own terms. It was, quite simply, a question of freedom, in his writing, and in his own person.

And yet Ibsen's responses to German complaints still had an opportunistic air to them. They came at a time when he was on the threshold of a possible breakthrough in Germany. Late in 1872 he receives a letter from P. F. Siebold informing him that the translation of *Brand* is now complete; he also learns that two other translations of the same play are in the offing. Not long afterwards he receives copies of German editions of *The Pretenders* and *The League of Youth*, both translated by Adolf Strodtmann. Word was that a production of the latter was being considered in Vienna, and of *The Pretenders* in both Breslau and Prague.

Something appeared to be happening for him in Germany, and after Germany it would be the turn of Great Britain. In April 1872 he received a letter from a young Englishman who worked at the British Museum. Edmund Gosse had discovered Ibsen's work by chance in a bookshop in Trondheim the previous summer, and was encouraged to explore the Scandinavian languages and literature further. He sent Ibsen a review of *Poems* that had appeared in *The Spectator*, at the same time enquiring whether Ibsen would send copies of *Love's Comedy*, *Peer Gynt* and *The League of Youth* for him to translate into English. Ibsen promptly ordered Hegel to fulfil the request and requisitioned Jacob Løkke, who was living in London at the time, to talk to Gosse about him.

> It is very important for me to become accessible to an English-speaking readership, and the sooner the better.

Edmund Gosse became Ibsen's first intermediary in Great Britain, although in the first instance to no great effect. The translations took a long time; by the following year he had managed only parts of two of the plays. He did, however, write articles about Ibsen's works, and reviewed several of them.

There was no breakthrough in Great Britain this first time around. But Ibsen must have felt that he was starting to make conquests. And, like any general, he had to choose his battles carefully. The situation did not call for him to repel people with polemic but instead to win them over by the power of his writing and the calculated cool of his marketing. In other words, we must view his toning down of possible political provocation in his writing, such as Dybbøl, as the expression of a need to free himself from the small revolutions in order to serve the greater one – the revolt of the human spirit – *and* as part of his commercial strategy as a writer. It was about principles and pragmatism, and just that mixture of the ideological and the opportunistic was typical of Ibsen.

As a man and as a writer it was rarely a question of all or nothing for him, but rather of a little of this and a little of that.

THE EUROPEAN

He continued to worry about his reputation in Germany. By his own account, life in Dresden had not been particularly easy after the Franco-German war and the exchanges in *Im neuen Reich*. But German suspicions did not disappear overnight. Two years later his translator Adolf Strodtmann published a book entitled *Das geistige Leben in Dänemark* (1873). Strodtmann gives what is in many ways a flattering account of Ibsen, but in his Foreword writes that he must be seen as uncompromisingly anti-German.[34]

Immediately after receiving the book Ibsen wrote to the author on the subject of his analysis of the poem 'Norden's Signals'. In this his theme was once again the Schleswig-Holstein question, but Strodtmann should not for a moment believe that this implied any criticism of Germany. Again the Norwegian feels compelled to urge his pro-German sentiments, even more forcefully this time:

> I am, like most Norwegian Scandinavianists, a pan-Germanist. I consider Scandinavianism to be an intermediate phase on the road towards the ultimate goal, the union of the great Germanic tribe.

His fear that Strodtmann's book will make life in Dresden even more difficult drives him to make extreme protestations of loyalty towards Germany. He even acknowledges 'Germany's world-historical mission' – a far cry from his earlier tirades about the Prussians being a nation of waiters. Admittedly, pan-Germanism can easily be interpreted as an extension of Scandinavianism, which can in turn be viewed as an extension of the idea of the nation. This was how both Ibsen and Bjørnson had seen it. But with the breakdown of Ibsen's nationalism the historical and theoretical basis of the analysis disappears. When he now begins to hail the pan-Germanic idea in the 1870s, it is most likely the expression of his pragmatic desire to remain in dialogue with an ever-expanding cultural arena.

Ibsen's courtship of the Germans cannot be explained solely as a strategic manoeuvre aimed at increasing his sales figures, or as the expression of a desire to edit politically controversial elements out of his writing. A third and highly personal motive is involved: he needs the acceptance of the Germans *because he has quite literally made his home among them.* The six years Ibsen spent in Dresden and his subsequent period in Munich have traditionally been passed over lightly by scholars, who maintain that he lived there simply because it was there Sigurd had access to the best education, and there that the cost of living was lowest. But although these were certainly important factors, they tell us nothing about what life in Germany gave him, and what effect it had on him.

What did Germany mean to Ibsen? Although he had a few acquaintances among the local population and some resident Scandinavians, the family lived in the main a quiet and withdrawn life in Dresden. Ibsen felt that Dresdeners were reserved in their dealings with foreigners, and foreigners themselves tended to stick with their own kind.

'I don't have many friends,' he confesses in a letter in the spring of 1872. 'I'd like to have more.'

At least he could regularly welcome Scandinavian friends and acquaintances who called in on the family on their travels through Europe. Hans Christian Andersen visited in April, and in the summer Suzannah's half-sister Dorothea arrived with her husband Conrad Falsen and half-brother Thomas. Thomas Thoresen stayed on until well into the autumn, while Dorothea and Conrad lived in Berlin from 1875 to 1877, where Conrad was employed at the Swedish-Norwegian legation. Henrik must have been particularly interested in his young brother-in-law, for Thomas was a director at the Møllergaten theatre. He was also the author of a number of farces and vaudevilles that had been performed both there and at the Christiania Theatre with considerable success. Throughout their years in Dresden, Henrik and Suzannah had plenty of contact with her family. This was his family now, not least Marie, who had by this time been living with them for several years.

That came to an end in April 1873. To Henrik's disappointment and consternation, Marie travelled back to Norway to seek employment as a teacher. His response came from the fact that she, like Thomas, suffered from tuberculosis. Wouldn't it be better if she stayed with them, wondered Henrik, and moved back to Christiania when they did?

But Marie was adamant, and Henrik bade her a reluctant farewell on her way northward.

If Ibsen's life in Dresden was otherwise quiet, he was by no means dissatisfied with big-city life in itself. He was a regular customer at Brühlsche Terrasse, close to the Frauenkirche, at the restaurants around Wildsdruffer Platz or the Café Francais, where he could read foreign newspapers, even Norwegian and Swedish papers. He also took a modest part in the literary and cultural life of the city and was sometimes in the company of its leading intellectuals, not least at the Literarischer Verein Dresden. Ibsen knew about the society long before he settled in the city. John Grieg's translation of *The Pretenders* had been given a reading there as long ago as 1866. Seven years later, Strodtmann's articles about Ibsen and his translations of *The Pretenders* and *The League of Youth* formed the basis of a short series of three lectures at the society. Ibsen was a member and attended several gatherings, though he is reported to have remained silent during the debates. We do not know how often he attended, or even whom he may have spoken to there.

Literarischer Verein developed from the popular salon culture of the 1830s and 1840s, at the time when Dresden was turning into a major city and undergoing political reforms that ensured a liberal and variegated public life. Artists, authors and intellectuals from all over Germany made their way here. Through them, Ibsen was in contact with a cultural, literary, political and scientific environment more authoritative than any he had previously known.

He also had some contacts outside the society. It seems that one of these was a professor of botany, Matthias Jakob Schleiden. Another was Count Wolf von Baudissin, among the most important translators of Shakespeare and Molière in Germany. He also kept the company of the former Danish minister for Schleswig, Holstein and Lauenburg, Harald Raasløff, and the writer Charles Edouard Duboc, a central member of the literary society and a war correspondent with an extensive personal network among Germany's leading intellectuals. Among the many Russians in the city Ibsen is thought to have met the poet Karolina Pavlova, though there is no evidence that he ever met Fyodor Dostoevsky, who was resident in Dresden from August 1869 to July 1871.[35]

* * *

To sum up, Ibsen's network of contacts in Dresden consisted of people from several nations and from different social strata. Among Scandinavians his contacts included painters, opera singers, office workers and factory owners. Writers, aristocrats and academics from the humanities and the natural sciences were among his German acquaintances. It was a network that reflected Dresden's own identity as a mixture of the old and the new, the feudal and the bourgeois, as well as people from the cultural and industrial worlds. Those who frequented the literary society, for example, included not just writers and intellectuals but also painters, officers, civil servants, teachers, merchants and men of science.

In other words, the city was a genuine European melting pot in which Italian tradesmen, Russians and other Slavic speakers made up large minorities. At the same time it was unmistakably German, and the same was true of the literary society. To the extent that members shared the same ethical and ideological attitudes these might be characterised as a peculiar mixture of enlightened liberal ideas and a thoroughgoing German patriotism that was reinforced by the Franco-German war of 1870–1. Perhaps this combination provides some background for Ibsen's furious attack on liberalism's ideas of freedom in his letters to Brandes, though the degree to which he was upset by German patriotism is unclear. He supported the French, but had no difficulty in being in the company of German patriots. In a letter to Bomhoff he writes enthusiastically of a factory owner named Gehe who kept in his backyard 'the most wonderful apparatus for illuminating buildings', which was intended for use in the celebrations when Paris fell.

Regardless of the apparent size of this social network in Dresden, it is clear that very few of these people were close friends. This must explain the regular descriptions of his life there as isolated and withdrawn. For how could debates in the Literarischer Verein, or architectural illuminations in Gehe's backyard, compare with the warm evenings of wine and laughter in the friendly cafes of Rome?

Maybe there really was something in the heavy sigh he heaved to his old friend from Rome, Fr. G. Knudtzon:

But how can anyone live the sublimely bacchanalian life here, where the spiritual and physical diet consists of sausages and beer.

Well at least one could get away from the place in the summer – if not all the way to Rome, then halfway. On 15 July 1872, Ibsen left Dresden with Suzannah and Sigurd for a holiday in the mountains. They travelled around in Bohemia and Austria before settling in Berchtesgaden, in the Bavarian Alps. It was the second time the family had spent the summer there. A letter from Georg Brandes awaited him when he arrived. In previous correspondence the two men had agreed that it was about time they met up again. The initiative probably came from Brandes. Clearly, Ibsen's support during the storm following the publication of *Main Currents* had meant much to him.

In his letter Brandes says he expects to visit Dresden in September. He also – and quite boldly – invites Ibsen to contribute to a new periodical he is planning. Boldly, because he knows that Ibsen does not like to run with the herd, and knows that he risks embarrassing his friend. But Ibsen's response is remarkably positive; he will indeed put his pen at the disposal of Brandes' fight, suggesting a letter in rhyme 'on the subject of contemporary attitudes to politics, literature and such-like matters'.

It looks as though Ibsen was for once willing to break his rule about committing only to his own writing. To Hegel, who had offered to publish Brandes' magazine, he admits openly that he is looking for something to do on the side, a confession perhaps not unrelated to the fact that it was now three years since his last play had appeared. Brandes' magazine was to be called *The Nineteenth*

Century, and in time it would come to be an important forum for the Brandes brothers' literary activity. Ibsen's contribution was, however, modest.

Returning from Berchtesgaden at the end of August, the family found a new home in Dresden. The address was Grosse Plauensche Strasse 9, in the same quarter as Dippoldiswalder Strasse. Brandes arrived on the doorstep one day in September, as promised, bringing with him the writer and editor Meïr Goldschmidt. Brandes would be staying for three weeks and, unlike the hasty meeting of the previous year, they had time now for long discussions, and conversations over pineapple punch. Ibsen introduced Brandes to the literary society, where parts of *Main Currents* had already been discussed. During these weeks Brandes became 'extremely fond' of Ibsen, feeling now for the first time that he began to know who he really was, and how his complexities, his anger and the inconsistency in what he said and did all actually added up and in their own way made sense. At their previous meeting he had been struck by his friend's good looks; this time he notices in particular a charisma that is both severe and exalted.

> People must think him a very important man, so serious that he rarely smiles, with the sharp edges of the autodidact, and something both threatening and inviting about his person, typical of someone who commands obedience.

His opinions, however, remained unchanged.

'Politically he is very conservative, or more precisely, he is an absolutist,' Brandes tells a friend. Ibsen's contempt for liberals remained as strong as ever, and he was still capable of claiming that it was better to live under the authority of a single great leader than under the lesser authority of many. As naïve as it sounded to Brandes' ears, he listened patiently to Ibsen's ceaseless mockery of false freedom fighters, and his claim that repression is to be preferred because it creates such a 'wonderful longing for real freedom, and the struggle to attain it'.

Unlike before, however, Brandes is no longer shocked by such views. Instead he is fascinated, and particularly when the conversation turns to the subject of writing. He is lost for words to describe how illuminating it is to listen to Ibsen hold forth about the 'psychological nature' of the literature of the future, and of how the great divide is between those works written by a 'personality' and those written by people of mere 'talent', a divide that illustrates the difference between *having* to write and *wanting* to write. In Ibsen's view it was a distinction Brandes had previously failed to understand. Now, however, he felt that Brandes did.

Brandes notices something else. The Norwegian writer appeared more European than he recalled from their previous meeting – 'all of that provincial Norwegian narrow-mindedness has been blown away, and he now has a more appropriate sort of modern cultural sophistication'. It looked as though life in Dresden had changed Ibsen; the Norwegian who had travelled to Rome, there to melt into a semi-bohemian world of Scandinavian artists and writers, had taken the final step of turning himself into a European.

If only he had not suffered such pangs of longing for a little taste of salted redfish from Trondheim.

A HORSEMAN RIDES

'Dresden is, as you know, a fishless place, and we Bergeners suffer dreadfully from the lack of our national dish,' Ibsen wrote to his friend Karl Bomhoff, who had by now left Dresden and was back home in Norway. Would Bomhoff be kind enough to send a large consignment of redfish to him and Suzannah? He may have become a man of the world, but in his heart and his stomach he remained a Norwegian. He was still, moreover, in receipt of the annual writer's wage from the Norwegian state.

In June 1872 his application for a travel grant was rejected by the Department of Church Affairs. Yet another sign of the Norwegian state's failures to acknowledge his achievements, but Ibsen still does not give up on his homeland. He writes several pieces concerning Norway that year. In the same month as he submitted his application, he was invited to write a poem marking the millennial celebrations on 18 July of King Harald Finehair's victory at the battle of Hafrsfjord and the subsequent unification of Norway. After so many years, Ibsen was deeply sceptical of this sudden invitation to participate in such a prestigious event. And when he did finally decide to add his powerful voice to the national festivities, the message he offered was hardly celebratory.

In the poem 'At the Millennial Celebrations July 18 1872' he expresses his gratitude for all the opposition, the anxieties and pains his native land has caused him, all the grief he needed in order to grow:

> My folk, who poured for me a deep potation,
> that bitter-cordial draught wherewith to save
> me, as a poet, from the very grave,
> whence I drew strength to fight in dawn's elation —
> my folk who gave me exile's staff, who gave
> grief's loaded pack, swift shoes of desolation,
> the heavy gear to furnish my retreating —
> I from abroad send home to you my greeting.

It wasn't exactly a thank-you poem. Ibsen deflates the celebrations of the unification of the country with an account in verse of his own flight into exile. It was no doubt a subtle and deliberate gesture, but it was also honestly meant. Norway had given him the gift of sorrow, as he rightly acknowledges, despite the bitterness and recriminations that run through the lines.

When it came to it, it proved hard to control the narrative of his own martyrdom from abroad. Predictably, the committee in charge of the festivities printed the verse, but chose not to have it read in public, as Ibsen had wished. People must have found it hard to swallow the pompous and self-pitying tone of the poem's opening verse. For the satirical magazine *Vikingen* the poem was a gift. Ibsen was depicted standing in front of a mirror, posing with a jug of beer and a bag of money on which was written 'Writer's Wage 400 (spd)'. In the mirror image these items were transformed into a pilgrims' staff and a bottle labelled 'Strength and Health Tonic'. Even his friends found it difficult to take him seriously. 'In his Harald poem Ibsen clambers up onto a ridiculous pedestal,' Jonas Lie conceded, though he could not ignore the poem's literary qualities.

Ibsen was furious, but there was little he could do. What did they actually expect? Was he not being paid a writer's wage in order to tell the truth? Was it, perhaps, not his duty as 'state satirist' to crack the whip over people?

Oh no, there was quite a distance between the heroic kings of the saga age and today's craven and self-indulgent generation!

Following the rejection of his stipend application and the reception given to his millennium poem one might suppose that Ibsen had had enough of his native country for a while. Not so. In October 1872 he writes a letter to Hartvig Lassen, who had been appointed aesthetic consultant and censor at the Christiania Theatre at the beginning of the year. He begins the letter by regretting that he has not yet been asked for permission to allow a production of *Love's Comedy*. Before he left for Rome, the theatre had accepted the play and paid the author a modest advance of 30 spesidaler, specifying that the money be returned should there be no production, which there was not. The time had come to do something about that old humiliation, even at the risk of being rejected yet again. Ibsen pushes his luck; he encloses a list of suggestions for the cast, and proposes that he be paid a fee of 300 spesidaler, precisely the amount he had asked for ten years earlier. Fortunately Lassen accepts the offer, and between then and Christmas their correspondence is devoted to practical aspects of the coming production, with Ibsen almost drowning Lassen in detailed instructions and advice.

This was his way of trying to direct – from Dresden – the event that was supposed to wipe out the memory of the wretched reception the play had been given on its previous outing. But it proved as difficult to control the resurrection of *Love's Comedy* from a distance as it had the presentation of the millennial poem. He was irritated by delays in mounting the production. Not until November 1873, a year after he first contacted Lassen, could the characters Falk and Svanhild be heard declaiming their dialogue in rhyme at the theatre in Bankplassen, and it was a further six months until he received his fee.

* * *

If Ibsen's relationship to his homeland was and remained complex, the same might also be said of his relationship towards his new homeland, Germany. These complexities are not diminished if we look at the most important poems he wrote in the first half of the 1870s. In these he appears to contradict his own opposition to the formation of nations and states, his *tabula rasa*. The millennium poem is not merely a bitter personal salute, it is also a celebration of the unification of Norway. In a draft of the poem he expresses a dream of Scandinavian union in which he hopes to experience 'the rallying post moved east of the Keel,/half on Norway's, half on Sweden's land'. The lines do not appear in the final version, but in the later poems 'Greeting in Song to Sweden' and 'Far Away' (1875) he openly praised the union of Norway and Sweden.

And yet the question is really whether Ibsen's perspective goes beyond the national and Scandinavian, and even the pan-Germanic horizon. For all of these unification projects can be seen as reflections of an overarching utopian vision of the future of European civilisation. In 'A Letter in Verse', the poem Ibsen had promised and finally written for Brandes' periodical in 1875, Europe is likened to a ship that appears to be holding a steady course. But the crew seem oppressed, the passengers apathetic:

> And why? Because a surreptitious doubt,
> sly rumours restlessly keep sneaking out
> from after-deck and fo'c'sle, a farrago:
> they think they're sailing with a corpse for cargo.

The corpse in the hold, Europe's heritage, the dead old thoughts that blunted the passengers' perceptions and left them unable to see that they were heading into new waters:

> Have you not noticed some upheaval's pending?
> Did you not see a period was ending?

One era was at an end, a new one beginning. But Ibsen says little about what the new one will bring: 'Don't press me, friend, to act the necromancer; I'd rather ask; it's not my job to answer.' He was just another passenger, different only in that whereas the others lie sleeping in their cabins in the heat, he sits up, awake, looking into the dawn that is just breaking:

I turned my eyes from that lethargic flailing,
I peered ahead in the refreshing night;
I sought the east where dawn's faint, early light
began to shroud the starlight in its veiling.

Based on this, we can imagine that Ibsen is operating with both a short and a long-term perspective on the future of Europe. In the former, the breakdown of history overshadowed everything else; the continent was at a watershed and the entire status quo had to be brought down. Only the individual could be reformed. In the latter perspective, new models of society would appear, built by a new and improved generation. There are good reasons for supposing that Ibsen operated with this double perspective, but one would have to be very indulgent indeed to ignore the obvious contradictions and illogicalities in these poems.

One episode that demonstrates this clearly is Ibsen's part in the so-called 'Signal dispute' in 1872. In the autumn of that year Bjørnson had once again managed to provoke people, this time with a suggestion that it was time for a reconciliation with Germany now that the Dano-German war was over. Ibsen hurled himself into the debate, writing the poem 'Norden's Signals', in which he attacks Bjørnson with heavy irony:

There's a change in the offing! Talk on, no objection!
The weather-vane's signalled the change in direction.

Was Ibsen any the less of a weather-vane when he accuses Bjørnson of being 'the priest of pan-Germanism' a matter of a mere few months after he himself had sung the praises of pan-Germanism in his letter to Adolf Strodtmann? It is equally embarrassing when he, in the 'Millennium Poem', expresses his admiration for a man such as Bismarck, the bane of the Danes at Dybbøl, while 'Norden's Signals' honours the memory of the fallen Danish soldiers. Precisely this kind of inconsistency makes it tempting to interpret Ibsen's attack on Bjørnson's position as an expression of the rivalry between the two men.

* * *

The sense of living through a period of transition must have filled Ibsen with doubt and uncertainty in the years between 1870 and 1873. Letters and poems written during those years convey this impression. The theme of transition was dealt with on a much larger scale in *Emperor and Galilean*, which Ibsen had rewritten during February 1873. It had finally come to him, the tale of Julian the Apostate that he had been thinking about and working on sporadically since 1864. In Rome he must have studied Latin texts and recent histories, though no notes of any such reading are extant. There are a few drafts and notes from the early years in Dresden, but the material did not open up to him until the summer of 1871.

'I am hard at work on "Emperor Julian",' he had written enthusiastically to Hegel back then. 'This book will be my masterpiece. It occupies all my thoughts and all my time. It will show the positive worldview that critics have been demanding of me for so long.'

There was nothing wrong with his sense of ambition. Throughout most of 1872 he had worked slowly on what would turn out to be a huge drama in ten acts. For a long time he planned to write the play in three parts, but in the autumn he decided to join the first two parts together, as 'Caesar's desertion'. That same autumn he wrote most of the second part of the monumental drama, which he entitled 'Emperor Julian'. By the time Lorenz Dietrichson visited him at the end of the year the work was almost in its finished form. Perhaps in a gesture of gratitude towards the man who had first suggested to him the idea of writing about Julian, Ibsen broke open that ring of 'the three' and allowed Dietrichson to be present when he gave a reading from the as yet unfinished work. Sigurd, to his great annoyance, was on this occasion sent out of the room with instructions to do his Scripture homework.

'I think there's as much religion in father's play as there is in my Scripture homework,' the precocious boy had complained to his mother as she accompanied him from the room.

Ibsen was not a good reader of his work, but as the reading came to a close at around midnight, Dietrichson felt both moved and shaken. When he went to bed that night the characters from Ibsen's play haunted his dreams. But several months remained before the work was ready for publication. Although Ibsen had already made a fair copy of the text in February 1873, he would spend the whole of the spring and the early summer going over it again before being completely satisfied. He wrote to his old Learned Holland friend Ludvig Daae asking him to check the language and the historical facts; it was the first time Daae had heard from him since he had left Norway. At the same time Ibsen resumed the revision of earlier works. Now it was the turn of *Lady Inger of Østråt* and *The Vikings at Helgeland*; both were to be revised and delivered to Scandinavian theatres.

It was vital to keep things moving. His writing block had passed, but it was now almost four years since a new play had appeared, and his bank balance was beginning to suffer. Yet another move in the autumn of 1872, this time to a second-floor apartment at Wettiner Strasse 22, close to the historic centre of Dresden, did not improve his finances. Step by step the family had been moving closer to the elegant buildings in the centre of the city. A rise in the cost of living following the Franco-Prussian War seems not to have put them off.

Quite why the family felt that this was an advantageous time to move is unclear, for 1872 was a bad year for Ibsen, financially speaking. His own account books suggest he was probably using accumulated capital from the income of previous years. The great financial leap forward that could finance a lifestyle more in keeping with the new address did not occur until the following year. And it was the new play *Emperor and Galilean* that paid the bills.

THE WORLD'S EXHIBITION IN VIENNA

Ibsen had plenty to keep him busy in the months leading up to publication. In the spring of 1873 he received an invitation to be a member of the jury judging the art at the World's Exhibition in Vienna.[36] The exhibition itself opened on 1 May, but his attendance was not required until a month later. He accepts the invitation, and tries to send as much of the work he has promised Hegel before leaving. In May he despatches the final part of *Emperor and Galilean*, and directly after that a revised version of *The Vikings at Helgeland*. He plans a more extensive revision of *Lady Inger of Østråt* that he hopes to complete while in Austria.

On Friday 13 June, at nine o'clock in the evening, he gets off the train in Vienna. He at once checks in to the luxurious hotel where he is to stay, just five minutes away from the exhibition area. He even has his own chambermaid. The following day he writes a letter to Suzannah describing the service she provides, and all the benefits he enjoys as a guest, and how much everything costs:

> She brings me coffee whenever I ask for it, as well as French bread and butter for breakfast, for a total cost of 30 Kreutzer or 6 Groschen. I ate breakfast here today, beautifully presented on a silver platter with a doily and serviettes, a full jug of coffee, plenty of milk, bread, butter and sugar, all of it delicious and top quality.

These World's Exhibitions were real nineteenth-century affairs, optimistic manifestations of expansion and progress, in which individuals from different countries gathered to exchange ideas and experiences, as well as demonstrating their own achievements in the fields of technology, architecture and art. The exhibitions in London in 1851 and 1862 and in Paris in 1855 and 1867 had largely been about technology and in particular the century's great advance, the steam engine. The Vienna exhibition was different in that more attention was paid to art and applied art. Austria was not, anyway, particularly noted for its industry, and the participation of England, the United States and France could only be described as modest. The new German empire, on the other

hand, was noticeably present. Ibsen was put on the jury for painting and sculpture, representing both Norway and Denmark. Suzannah learned of how busy
his days were. Up every morning at six o'clock, and two hours later he was
washed and dressed, had eaten breakfast, read the paper and smoked his
morning pipe. By nine he was in session with the painting jury, the discussions
lasting until twelve, after which they crossed the road to a restaurant to enjoy 'a
good meaty meal with excellent beer'. At two he was in session with the sculpture jury, which ended its deliberations at about five. There was no time for an
afternoon rest.

In other words, life was tough for a writer used to a life of routine, so long
as it was his own and not someone else's.

These World's Exhibitions were traditionally patronised by royal goodwill
and a royal presence. Oscar II, the new king of Sweden-Norway, had been an
active advocate of Norwegian and Swedish participation, a royal enthusiasm
that was repeated in other lands, as a way of expressing the alliance between the
monarchy and the new industrial bourgeoisie. In Vienna, Ibsen was introduced
to the Habsburg emperor Franz Joseph, whom he had seen in Egypt, as well as
a number of dukes, counts and barons. Once again he raised his glass with
society's finest, though he wasn't exactly scruffy himself; Fritz von Dardel,
representing Sweden, thought he looked more like a French notary than an
artist. Typically, he preferred to attend the society events, avoiding the large
crowds attending the rest of the exhibition. Suzannah described for her brother
Johan Hermann the exclusive gatherings her husband attended – 'in a word, far
from where *ordinary people*, Ibsen's great fear, are the dominant presence'. As far
as he could he even avoided fellow members of the jury; while the others dined
together, he slipped away to a beer tent to enjoy his beer alone.

* * *

Of what possible professional benefit might the exhibition have been to him?
In an account written for *Morgenbladet* of 30 August he claims that the art
exhibition 'offers a wealth of material illustrating the cultural history of our
own times'. In the main the paintings on exhibition were a pre-Impressionist
mixture of historical studies, portraits, landscapes and genre paintings. They
included forty-nine paintings, the work of twenty-seven Norwegian artists,
most of them resident in Düsseldorf. Later generations have expressed surprise
at Ibsen's praise and concluded that his view of art was 'old-fashioned' because
he did not prefer Impressionism. This is, of course, hopelessly anachronistic,
because the first Impressionist exhibition did not take place until the following
year. Ibsen's view of art did indeed become more and more old-fashioned as
Impressionism, realism and naturalism gradually began to revolutionise
painting, while his own tastes remained relatively unchanged. But in 1873 he

was in tune with the times, not only in his aesthetic preferences but also in his view of theatre and painting as 'sisters in art', something that is well illustrated in the mixture of realism and historical tableaux that characterises *Emperor and Galilean*.[37]

From beginning to end the whole thing was a matter of medals and prestige. But for Ibsen there was at least one artistic surprise: never before had so much eastern European culture, art and applied art been so much in evidence as at the World's Exhibition in Vienna. Certainly, Russian contemporary literature was known in the West; but Ibsen was pleasantly surprised to discover that painters from Russia and Hungary could compare with the best that western Europe had to offer.

Hungary and Russia – both countries would be fruitful markets for his own work in the years to come.

LOVE AND RIGHTS

At the end of July, Ibsen left Vienna, but he did not return home. In the summer heat an epidemic of cholera had broken out in Dresden. Instead he travelled to Pillnitz, just south of the city, where Suzannah and Sigurd were already installed. The family remained here until the end of August.

The little town lay in a wine-producing region on the eastern banks of the Elbe and had several castles, summer residences for the aristocracy and villas for the wealthy industrialists and bankers. Over the years intellectuals and artists such as Alexander von Humboldt, Caspar David Friedrich, Arthur Schopenhauer and Richard Wagner lived in the area. Now it was Henrik Ibsen's turn to look here for peace and quiet in which to work, primarily to get the revision of *Lady Inger of Østråt* under way. But he is still unable to get started. The whole of August is spent in fulfilling obligations left over from the World's Exhibition, and he is constantly visited by friends and acquaintances passing through.

One of these visits turned out to be of considerable importance. In August the new director of the Christiania Theatre, the Swede Ludvig Josephson, announced that he wished to visit Ibsen in Pillnitz and was warmly welcomed.

Ludvig Josephson was an experienced writer, actor and director who had formerly been employed at the Kungliga Dramatiska Teatern in Stockholm. His name had previously been considered for the Christiania job, but his arrival in the Norwegian capital in February 1873 was not greeted rapturously by all, to put it mildly. At the first performance after the Swede's arrival there was organised whistling, with, as it happens, the express support of Bjørnson. The new director was greeted with cries of 'Down with the committee! Get rid of the foreigner!'

But the foreigner remained. For his first production he made a diplomatic choice, Bjørnson's *Maria Stuart*. Josephson's outstanding characteristic was not, however, his diplomacy (Bjørnson's friendship was not easy for him to win), but his artistic excellence. As an ensemble leader he had outstanding qualities, as well as a sharp eye for the best of the new European and Norwegian drama. Gradually the atmosphere changed, from one of scepticism to recognition, and by the time Josephson left the theatre in the summer of 1877 he had succeeded in considerably raising its artistic standard. Not least, his openness in regard to the changing currents in Scandinavian drama made him a natural ally for Henrik Ibsen.

Seeing that *Love's Comedy* was among the theatre's forthcoming productions, he had written to Ibsen and asked whether he might pay him a visit. One August day, as he stood on the deck of the steamer as it berthed in the harbour at Pillnitz, he caught sight of a small figure wandering back and forth along the quayside. The man was elegantly clad in black, with a black hat atop the dark, rather long hair, kid gloves on his hands, and a decorative ribbon in his buttonhole. Everything Josephson had heard about Ibsen so far turned out to be true. Not just the sartorial vanity, but also the formal and very reserved nature. Georg Brandes had noticed the same thing, that Ibsen had not only become a rather snobbish dresser but had started to adopt refined personal mannerisms. Lorentz Dietrichson, who also visited him at Pillnitz, recalled Ibsen telling him that the village girls in the Bavarian Alps had taken him for a Catholic priest and asked to kiss his hand, something he clearly did not object to.

Nor did he have much objection to adding to his collection of orders and decorations, and in particular one that came as a complete surprise: at the coronation the previous year of Oscar II, the new king of Sweden-Norway, he had been awarded the St Olav Order. It meant that he was finally able to pin a glittering prize from his own country onto his already overcrowded lapels.

The contrast with Suzannah seemed all the more striking to Josephson, for while her husband was always dressed up as though for an occasion she inevitably wore simple everyday clothes. Josephson liked them both; he found Ibsen's reserve a lot more reassuring than Bjørnson's larger-than-life persona. And after a few beers most of his reserve disappeared anyway. The goodwill was mutual, and when Ibsen took his farewell of Josephson he did so in the knowledge that he now had an important ally at the Christiania Theatre. On 1 September, the same day that Henrik, Suzannah and Sigurd returned to Dresden, Josephson opened the season with a new production of *The Pretenders* and then began rehearsals for *Love's Comedy* which was on the bill for November.

* * *

On 16 October *Emperor and Galilean* was finally published in all three Scandinavian countries. Hegel had received instructions to send complimentary copies to Oscar II and a number of other people, associates and family. He is less generous as regards his faithful advisors Ludvig Daae and Jacob Løkke; only if Hegel can think of a reason to do so is he to send copies to them. The sales were good. Before long it was clear that the first print run of some 4,000 was not going to be enough and a second printing of another 2,000 was made in December.

These print runs in themselves created publishing history. Ibsen was able to pocket over 10,000 Norwegian kroner, far more than he had ever earned before from any previous single publication. In 1870 his income for the year was 7,500 kroner. Two years later it was down to 2,400. In 1873 his total income was almost 16,000 kroner, over three times what a top Norwegian bureaucrat could earn. By German standards too Ibsen was making a good living. In the mid-1860s an annual income of 1,200 thaler (3,200 Norwegian kroner) was enough to give the members of a bourgeois household a comfortable life, while a professor could earn up to 8,000 Norwegian kroner. Professors did not live extravagant lives, but they clearly belonged to the upper class; in 1875 only 5 per cent of the population of Prussia were taxed for incomes in excess of 2,667 Norwegian kroner. With the exception of two years, Ibsen's income would remain between 10,000 and 20,000 kroner until 1890 (and closer to the latter than the former). In general his income was high and increasing, not least because from 1873 he had started to invest in stocks and shares. In certain years as much as half of his income went to investment, meaning that his capital increased at an even rate, balancing out the variations in his income from year to year.

Security is probably the watchword for Ibsen's finances; he regularly bought shares in banks and trams, but favoured above all else the railways – 'You simply can't make a sounder investment if you don't want to run any risks.'

This is how insufferably boring Henrik Ibsen's economic life had become. There was more drama to be had from his adventures as a debtor, but following the change in his fortunes from 1873 onwards, he finally paid off his old debt to Nandrup, the lawyer. Ever since he had left Norway, the debt had shadowed his life, a constant reminder of the unhappy years in Christiania. In the main he had left it to his brother-in-law Johan Hermann Thoresen to deal with the payments – 'I don't want my name circulating on documents like that'. Now finally, not long before Christmas 1873, he receives news that the debt has been cleared.

'I am debt-free,' he writes in triumph to his brother-in-law, finally liberated from the miseries of the past.

And so he was, at least as far as money was concerned.

* * *

Love's Comedy opened at the Christiania Theatre on 24 November 1873. It must have been quite an occasion for Ibsen. Granted, several of his plays had been performed here in the years since he had left the country. But this was, after all, his first premiere in four years. The play was, moreover, one that many considered unsuitable for the stage. In Ludvig Josephson's capable hands, however, it turned out to be highly suitable. It was performed fifteen times in that season, and in the years to come was revived at regular intervals.

Ibsen had got what he wanted. His honour was restored in Norwegian public life. Against all the odds *Love's Comedy* was a hit. It made it perhaps easier to handle the fact that at about the same time two of his fellow country-men were trying to take advantage of his success. Two years earlier, Ibsen had tried to stop an illegal publication of *The Vikings at Helgeland* and prevented a planned publication of *Lady Inger of Østråt*. The initiative was the work of a printer named Hans Jacob Jensen, former owner of the *Illustreret Nyhedsblad*. During Paul Botten-Hansen's time as editor, these two plays had been offered as offprints, and now the printer was hoping to capitalise on Ibsen's success. Ibsen protested furiously, claiming that he most certainly had not handed over the general publication rights of the plays to the magazine but only the rights for this single printing. He appointed a Christiania lawyer, Emil Stang, to take the printer to court and assumed that would be the end of it, even though the city court spent a long time deliberating the matter.

Jensen was no common fortune hunter but an energetic and capable profes-sional who would in time play a vital role in the development of the Norwegian press. But he was obstinate, as Ibsen learned when he found out, in the autumn of 1873, that the printer was yet again announcing *The Vikings at Helgeland* for sale, even while the court was still debating the legality of the edition. That did it for Ibsen. He had promised Hegel publishing rights to all his old plays, and they had even worked out a publishing timetable in which every new play by Ibsen would be followed by a revised version of one of the old ones, as they had done in publishing *Love's Comedy* after *Brand*. The idea now was for *The Vikings at Helgeland* to follow *Emperor and Galilean*, regardless of what the cheeky printer was planning.

The authorised edition of the saga drama was published at the beginning of December. The city court did not reach its decision until September 1875, and it went in Ibsen's favour. Jensen appealed, but when the case came up at the High Court the following spring he lost again.[38]

THE THIRD KINGDOM

The action in *Emperor and Galilean* spans a period of twelve years, from AD 351 to 363. Young Julian is half-brother to Gallos, heir to the throne. The reigning emperor, Konstanzios (Constantius) has killed the brothers' family, and now Julian fears for his own life. It is a transitional period, a time of tensions between paganism and Christianity. Julian has been raised a Christian, but is agnostic. He travels to Athens to learn more about the old pagan gods but is frustrated in his quest. He does, however, become fascinated by the esoteric teachings of the mystic Maximos on the subject of 'the third kingdom', a kingdom that will arise with its foundations in the ethical seriousness of Christianity, and the learning and life-enhancing joys of paganism. At a séance Maximos is contacted by three spirits. These represent men who, without knowing it themselves, have changed the course of history. The first is Cain, the second Judas Iscariot. The third spirit does not show itself, leading Maximos to believe that it is either himself or Julian.

After the death of Gallos, many believe that Julian, married to the emperor's sister Helena, should be the next emperor. After he wins a great battle in Gaul the emperor is afraid Julian will advance on Rome to unseat him. The emperor sends a basket of poisoned fruit to Helena, who eats from it. She dies, as does the child she is carrying. Now Julian takes the most important decision of his life. He turns his back on Christianity, adopts the worship of pagan gods and marches on Rome. The first part of the double-drama ends at this point.

In the second part it emerges that the emperor has died even before Julian reaches Rome. Julian mounts the throne and declares universal religious freedom, including the freedom to be a Christian. But gradually conflicts arise between the emperor and the Christians, and in the end Julian embarks on a gruesome persecution of them. He has become a tyrant, and as his popularity declines so does his power, and when a campaign against the Persians is unsuccessful his world crumbles. The mood turns against him, and in the end he is killed by an old friend, a Christian. It becomes clear that the persecution of the Christians has strengthened their cause, and that Julian, like Cain and Judas, has served a 'World-will' without realising it.

* * *

Ibsen was not alone in looking forward to the publication of *Emperor and Galilean*; his readers had been too. Many of them were aware of the fact that he had for some years been working on an ambitious drama about Julian the Apostate, a theme that had earlier been treated by the Dane Carsten Hauch and the Swede Victor Rydberg – 'and there really was every reason to expect that, when a writer like Henrik Ibsen had settled on a theme such as Julian's apostasy and his fall, the work would be of monumental importance'.

The long gestation of the play, and the high level of expectation surrounding it, must be the explanation for that large first printing. Overall the play was well received, the few criticisms made all being of the same order. There was general agreement that the play's second part was weaker than the first, with Ibsen's heavy reliance on the historical sources affecting its literary quality. Even today, this is substantially the critical consensus; never before had he undertaken such meticulous background research for a historical play.[39] But most were impressed by the enormous achievement the play represented. In *Aftenbladet*, Kristian Elster described it as 'a superlative spiritual masterpiece'. A rather more restrained Erik Bøgh, well understanding its popularity, was nevertheless moved to suppose that readers too probably gave a sigh of relief on coming to the end of the book:

'Well thank God Henrik Ibsen finally finished *that.*'

For the twenty-two-year-old Arne Garborg, *Emperor and Galilean* was both a deeply influential work and an opportunity for the aspiring writer to liberate himself from his literary model. Shortly after publication he published a study in which he freely admitted the greatness in the play, both in the epic historical subject and in the psychological portrait of Julian. But every bit as interesting as Garborg's analysis of the work is his analysis of the position Ibsen now occupies in Norwegian public life:

He is read with interest, indeed, almost hungrily; readers devour his books with an alacrity that is otherwise quite unknown in our domestic book world. Indeed, the mere rumour of a new work from him is enough to cause an outbreak of excited expectation that is at times almost feverish, and once the book has appeared and been read, then, in the circles in which such matters are of interest, it becomes the sole topic of conversation for a long time afterwards.

Although Garborg's own enthusiasm is readily apparent, the description is literally overwhelming: with most of his great works still to come, Ibsen already occupies this unique place in Scandinavian public life. He was a writer whose every publication now occasioned an almost feverish sense of enthusiastic anticipation. But despite this great interest Ibsen was, in Garborg's view, not really a conventionally 'popular' writer. Rather he exercised an almost supernatural power over his readers that left them shaken and stunned:

One realises that one is in the presence of a mighty spirit; these dizzying ideas, these wild and unpleasant vistas that open up across the world of the night, this merciless and demonic revolutionary who lifts the veil on the corruptions of life.

No doubt about it, Garborg was spellbound by Ibsen; but his reservations are of equal interest. Because, for all the wealth of his thoughts, ideas and images, Ibsen had no answers to offer: 'He is himself only a searcher after truth.' Like others, Garborg was dismayed by Ibsen's negativity, and he protested vigorously against the claim that doubt should be considered a gift. It most certainly was not, in Garborg's view. Doubt was a position, and an unhappy one, because it left Ibsen's writing bound in 'diffusion and darkness'. The writing was no more than 'the huge play of great powers', and failed to elevate itself to the state of true beauty, reconciliation and harmony. Garborg's reservation on this point is particularly revealing in that it shows that the traditional idealistic view of art and literature was still very much alive among Ibsen's contemporaries. The persistence of this backdrop – now irrevocably lost to posterity – has to be understood in order to appreciate how fundamentally disturbing was Ibsen's effect on his first readers.

Informal reactions throughout literary Scandinavia were similarly divided. Ibsen's old friends from the Learned Holland were enthusiastic, in particular Løkke and Daae, his historical advisors. In Copenhagen, Johanne Luise Heiberg was left with a mixture of fascination and sadness. 'If only I had a magic wand,' she wrote after reading the double drama at one sitting. She saw the dramatic potential in the material, but felt that only magic could bring it to the stage.

Bjørnson was less impressed.

'It was a great disappointment,' he relates in a letter. 'I imagine that this marks the end of the Brand stuff (literature's version of avant-garde music!) – and then we'll probably get what he's really a master of – plot-based plays! We need them!'

Georg Brandes reviewed the play in his own magazine, *The Nineteenth Century*. He readily acknowledged the 'beautiful and the profound' in the work, adding that, in Ibsen's ability to bring the material to life through vivid dialogue he was, at times, the equal of Goethe. But Brandes found the drama uneven and diffuse, and expressed polite astonishment at the way the great freedom fighter Julian allowed himself to be restrained by the law of necessity. For Brandes it seemed a religious determinism that annihilated all concepts of personal freedom and responsibility. He had heard the motto from Ibsen himself, the need to *will* what one *must*. He gave his own answer in the review: for him, the freedom of the will was the greatest of them all, and the law of necessity could and should be broken.

* * *

Posterity has inherited this mixture of admiration and reservation for *Emperor and Galilean*. It is often referred to respectfully as Ibsen's 'great work', but the play was not studied in any depth for a great many years. A major problem has been to decide whether the play should be read as a *historical-philosophical* work or a *literary* work. Traditionally the former approach has been taken, inspired by the overwhelming world-historical perspective involved in the drama, and in particular Maximos' obscure prophecy concerning 'the third kingdom'. In choosing to write about the transitional period between the classical antiquity of pagan Rome and the Christianity of the Europe of the Middle Ages, Ibsen was, so to speak, grabbing hold of Western civilisation as it crawled out of the cradle. A more ambitious project for a historical drama could hardly be imagined, and the temptation to ascribe a 'positive view of life' to this most enigmatic of writers, as he himself once claimed the play displayed, has proved hard to resist.

But what was Ibsen really trying to show in his historical play?

The play is clearly based on the Hegelian idea that history progresses by means of a dialectic in which the civilisation of one epoch is challenged by a new one, and in which the conflicts are resolved in a higher synthesis of the two. Thus the paganism of antiquity is challenged by the Christianity of the Middle Ages in the drama, and the prophesied third kingdom is the utopian synthesis. This is not to suggest that *Emperor and Galilean* represented Ibsen's return to Hegelian philosophy. What he did was to make use of a Hegelian dialectic that had long been an intrinsic part of his understanding of history and his technical repertoire as a dramatist as the foundation for his play.[40] But what kind of historical synthesis of civilisations did he envisage? Some have viewed the third kingdom as a Romantic, if only half-glimpsed, vision of a future society in which all conflicts have been resolved.[41] In his own observations on Scandinavianism and pan-Germanism Ibsen had already showed signs of his interest in such harmonising social utopias. Others have read *Emperor and Galilean* in a Christian light and identified the third kingdom as the time of the Second Coming.[42] The play undeniably ends in the triumph of Christianity over paganism, this being, of course, historically the only possible outcome. Still others have noted in the play a Neoplatonic longing for reconciliation, or a meditation around Arthur Schopenhauer's philosophy of the Will, in which the third kingdom appears as an obscure harmonising of two differing ways of expressing the Will in life: between the celebration and denial of life, paganism and Christianity, freedom and necessity.[43]

The problem throughout has been that the play is so full of contradictions, and characterised by so many intertwined conflicts and projects, that it has proved very difficult to confine it within the terms of any complete and authoritative critical model.[44]

If we are to believe Ibsen himself, *Emperor and Galilean* was not meant as a religious drama, any more than *Brand* was. It seemed likely, however, that he was more ambitious for its historical-philosophical perspectives. Perhaps there are grounds for seeing the play as an over-exuberant work of amateur philosophy in which an attempt is made to hide the poor construction of the thought in an outsized project by the use of obscure and mysterious literary turns of phrase. Even though Ibsen believed he was offering his 'positive view of life' in this play, and even if he worked hard to give the whole drama a perspective on the history of civilisations, this might well be better understood as an isolated outcropping of ambition, perhaps even the last dregs of a phase of theorising about civilisations that he had, in actual fact, put behind him. For why should he, in the wake of his reckonings with the prevailing ideologies of his age, the nation-building and the heritage of revolution, turn around and start preaching about social utopias?

To the degree to which *Emperor and Galilean* contains a world-philosophical vision, it is to be found not in the utopia but rather in the unresolved Hegelian scheme. It is easier to suppose that Ibsen's real interest was in the tension between the first and the second kingdoms, and not in the imminent third kingdom, just as he had announced to Brandes that he was less interested in freedom than in the struggle for freedom.[45] His business was, and remained, the revolt of the human spirit, understood as a *permanent revolution* taking place within the individual.

Neither Brandes nor Garborg was particularly enamoured of the play's world-philosophical dimensions. Perhaps they would have been more sympathetic had they chosen to read it on its own dramatic and literary terms.[46] In that case they might have laid greater stress on Julian the human being in his efforts to stake out the course of his fate at a time of change, when one view of life confronts another, and one worldview another. One way to interpret Julian's struggle is to see him as a tragic hero in search of freedom and authenticity, a man who tries to harmonise his life and his actions with what he believes to be historical necessity.[47] The struggle ends in tragedy for Julian because he seeks freedom by elevating himself to the level of a divinity. Paganism appeals to Julian because it leaves space for human autonomy, while Christianity demands sacrifice and the extinction of the self. This is why he hates the Galilean. But the ancient world too is one in which the proud man who raises himself above the law of necessity is punished, and Julian's fall follows the laws of all classical tragedy.

A more radical interpretation of Julian's struggle is to see him as a sceptic who is crippled with anxiety at the thought of freeing himself from the law of necessity, because he sees no alternative to emptiness and meaninglessness. He shuns choice, clings on to every sign that offers hope of a meaning in life (including the vision of the third kingdom), and falls prey to scepticism and an unbridled and theatrical dramatisation of himself and his surroundings; in other words, he arranges existence as a stage play in order to create an appearance of meaning and wholeness. In this sense the drama can be read as a turning point in Ibsen's writing, one in which he takes sharp issue with the idealistic approach to art and literature and turns instead to an exploration of scepticism in the modern age, to the struggle of the individual to find a place in which to stand and to live in meaningful coexistence with others after the breakdown of ideals in the bloody mists of Europe's battlefields and the disappearance of the revolutionary heritage beneath the ruins of the Paris Commune.[48]

* * *

For Ibsen to have returned to historical drama after *The League of Youth* looks like a break in his literary development. But he had never seriously argued against historical drama as such, only against drama that was national-historical. Secondly the tragedy of Julian was, in many ways, an unavoidable enterprise. He had worked on it for so long, and invested so much in a subject that genuinely fascinated him, that he simply could not abandon it.

Thirdly, the choice of Julian's fate is easy to understand in the light of the drama's contemporary subtext. In accordance with Hettner's theories on historical drama, *Emperor and Galilean* was given a historical setting as a way of casting light on the present. No less than Julian, Ibsen felt himself to be living through a period of transition, the modernisation of Europe, in which nations ate each other up, and life in a state choked its individual members as surely as the new sciences and modern mores challenged Christianity's centuries-old grip on the people, and in which the last embers of the great revolutions were dying: 'Ha, and how the ideas will come tumbling down around us then.'

Seen from this perspective, the play can be understood as the literary fruit of Ibsen's move from Rome to Dresden; quite simply, it might have been difficult for him to make use of the Julian theme as long as he was living in Rome, a region outside the boundaries of time. The move to Dresden and proximity to the Franco-German war brought him into brutally close contact with modern reality.[49] For Ibsen it felt natural to put the perspective of history between himself and such close and intrusive events. He tells Edmund Gosse in a letter that what he is describing are things 'which I, in other forms, have lived through, and the chosen historical theme has a closer connection to movements in our own times than one would be inclined to suppose beforehand'.

Emperor and Galilean was as much a contemporary drama as it was a historical drama, and what is more, it was also fully in keeping with Ibsen's orientation towards realistic drama. Gosse was informed of this when he suggested that the play should have been written in verse. Ibsen disagreed. The play was deliberately written in 'the most realistic form', so that readers would be left with a feeling of events that had really taken place. That was why he had done so much research for the play, and that was why he had written it in prose and populated it with a number of everyday characters.

We are no longer living in Shakespeare's time, and among sculptors there is already talk of painting their statues in natural colours.

A new age demanded new forms:

My new play is not a tragedy in the classical sense; I wanted to depict people, and for that very reason I do not have them speaking in 'the tongues of the gods'.

In this way the confrontation with idealism was laid open for a realistic and grounded description of the everyday; all Julian achieves with his idealistic wanderings is to destroy the preconditions for a meaningful relationship between people, and that story demands to be told using the speech of human beings, not of gods. That particular dimension was hardly obvious to contemporary readers; for them, the contemporary relevance of the drama was more obviously connected to the historical watershed they felt themselves to be living through, and the evident parallels to Julian's time. It was typical of the reviewer in *Illustreret Tidende* to view the drama as a commentary on the Danish debate on the subject of faith versus knowledge. Was not Georg Brandes a Julian fighting for the freewill of the individual and for freedom of thought in the new scientific (read: pagan) world picture, freed from the burdensome yoke of Christianity? According to the periodical, discussions about which side Ibsen would be on had been taking place long before publication.

Would Ibsen defend Christianity, or would he relapse into pagan materialism and thus place himself in Brandes' camp?

Well, whose side was he on – Brandes' or Christ's? There was no easy answer. Bjørnson is said to have accused him of atheism, while Erik Bøgh was left wondering why he didn't take either side but left the answer up to the reader. Georg Brandes himself was by no means sure that Ibsen was promoting his cause. He was much provoked by the triumph of Christianity in the play, and what seemed to him its religious determinism. Might he also have wondered whether Julian was a portrait of himself? The thought is tempting, not least because Ibsen, in the same way as Maximos, had been keen to provide the young idealist Brandes-Julian with a 'calling'. And just like Julian, Brandes too experienced the strength of the Galilean when he challenged faith and tradition with his lectures and publications as part of the Danish public debate.[50]

But if the parallel is valid, why does Ibsen let him be destroyed by an apparently invincible Christ?

What else was to be expected? Ibsen had no intention of making things easy for the reader, and in his review of *Poems* Brandes himself had accepted that 'even alone, he divides more than he unites'. Ibsen may well have strewn his letters with bombastic judgements and assessments, but it did not prevent him, as a writer, from choosing to anatomise the struggle rather than take an unequivocal stance on one side or the other. Brandes found the play hard to swallow; and yet it is not a given that it involved a betrayal of him. It all depends on the sort of reading one gives it. Is there not, in spite of everything, a greatness in Julian's struggle? And could the third kingdom not be understood as a recognition of Brandes' historical importance, even if not entirely on his own terms?

If nothing else, Brandes should have realised this: Ibsen would never commit himself to one kingdom or the other; his concern would always be for the dynamic between the two. And it is in this dynamic that the power of the work lies, not in the vague utopia of some impending kingdom.

'COWPATS, NORWEGIAN NORWEGIANNESS AND SMUG SELF-SATISFACTION!'

Be all this as it may, the production of *Love's Comedy* at the Christiania Theatre and the publication of *Emperor and Galilean* got 1874 off to a good start for Ibsen. It was not by chance that it was at this time that he decided to adapt *Peer Gynt* for the stage, with music by Edvard Grieg. The plan was to create a production that could be performed in Christiania, Copenhagen and Stockholm. He writes to the composer on 23 January 1874: 'Would you compose the necessary music?' He then outlines the adaptation, indicates where the musical elements should be, and offers a couple of suggestions for their composition.

Quite a shopping list – and this from a man whom Grieg himself had described as completely unmusical!

Ibsen's suggestions were, as it turned out, not bad; he did, after all, write with the eye of an experienced man of the theatre for what would work onstage. Grieg was convinced and agreed to the commission. Although cool in his assessment of Ibsen as a person, he had always admired him as a writer. Back in 1868 he had celebrated the birth of his first child by setting 'Margrethe's Cradle Song' from *The Pretenders* to music. He must also have been attracted by Ibsen's proposal that they split the fee of 400 spesidaler from the Christiania Theatre between them. Both dramatist and composer were agreed that the music be composed in the spring and summer, though Grieg did not actually get started until the middle of summer.

'*Peer Gynt*'s going very slowly,' he complained to his composer friend Frants Beyer in August, 'and there's no question of my being finished by the autumn.' The task was proving a lot more difficult than he had at first thought it would be.

'It is a dreadfully recalcitrant subject, apart from certain places, for example, where Solveig sings.'

1. The oldest existing photograph of Henrik Ibsen, probably taken in 1860.

2. Lars Nielsen's pharmacy in Østregade, Grimstad. The back room served as Ibsen's and Nielsen's bedroom and living room. *Catiline* was written here in the small hours through winter and spring 1849.

3. During their first months in Christiania in 1850, Ibsen and Ole Schulerud lodged at Ma Saether's in Vinkelgaten 17, in Vika, Christiania's red-light district. The young men lived in the attic above the gate.

Henrik Johan Ibsen

har fremstillet sig til *Examen artium* i *August* 18 50, og paa Grund af de specielle Charakterer, nemlig:

for Udarbeidelse i Modersmaalet . . . *Godt.*
— Latinsk Oversættelse . . . . *Godt.*
— Latinsk Stiil . . . . *Temmelig godt.*
— Latin (mundtlig) . . . . *Maadeligt.*
— Græsk . . . . *Slet.*
— Hebraisk . . . . —
— Tydsk . . . . *Meget godt.*
— Fransk . . . . *Godt.*
— Religion . . . . *Godt.*
— Historie . . . . *Godt.*
— Geographie . . . . *Godt.*
— Arithmetik . . . . *Slet.*
— Geometrie . . . . *Godt.*

erholdt *Hovedcharakteren*: *non contemnendus.*

Christiania, i det philosophiske Facultet *3die September* 18 50.

J. S. Welhaven

p. t. Decan. facult. philos.

Secret. facult. philos.

Mb. 452 f°

4. Ibsens 'Examen Artium' from 1850. This was the academic certificate qualifying students for admission to university in Norway and Denmark – a qualification wasted on Ibsen as it turned out.

5. Suzannah Ibsen photographed around 1860.

6. Sigurd aged four in 1863, the year before the Ibsen family moved to Rome. Sigurd would grow up in Italy and Germany and would feel estranged from his home country for the rest of his life. In many ways, his true home was always the 'state of Ibsen'.

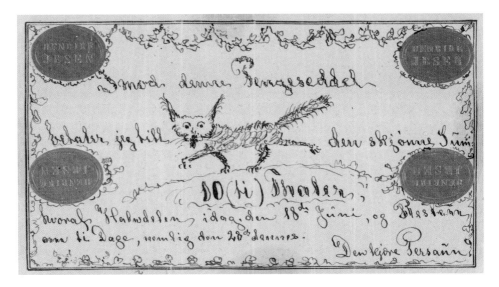

7. One of the 'banknotes' that Henrik gave Suzannah at Christmas and on birthdays in their years of poverty. The cat alludes to Suzannah's pet name, Kat.

8. Ibsen in Rome in 1866, the year he had his Scandinavian breakthrough with *Brand*.

9. Christiania Theatre on Bank Square in the old Renaissance quarter of Christiania. The theatre was built in 1837, and was Norway's main stage until it closed down in the summer of 1899. That autumn, the newly erected National Theatre opened its doors on Karl Johans gate.

10. Via Capo le Case, Rome, around 1865. The Ibsen family lived down the street around the bend, not far from the Spanish Steps.

11. Bjørnstjerne Bjørnson (1832–1910) returned to Christiania in the autumn of 1859 after having succeeded Ibsen as director at the Norwegian Theatre in Bergen for two years.

12. Georg Brandes (1842–1927) as a young man. Brandes is often presented as Ibsen's ally in the Scandinavian cultural debate of the 1870s and 1880s, but their relationship was more complex than that. Nevertheless, the Danish critic was to become an important ambassador for Ibsen's plays.

13. Danish-born Magdalene Thoresen (1819–1903) was a productive writer as well as Suzannah's stepmother and Ibsen's mother-in-law.

14. In Rome in 1868, Ibsen alternated between modelling for the sculptors Walter Runeberg and Herman Wilhelm Bissen. 'The challenge is to see who will achieve the greatest resemblance,' said Bissen. This bust is his.

15. The jury for painting and sculpture at the Vienna World's Exhibition in 1873. Ibsen (far right) represented both Norway and Denmark.

16. The Ibsens on a summer visit to Consul Thomas J. Heftye's summer house Sarabråten in the woods outside Kristiania, 1874. Fifteen-year-old Sigurd is to his father's left, while Suzannah is sitting on the veranda.

17. Ibsen's first address in Dresden, An der Frauenkirche 6, is in the background on the right-hand side. On the right we can also see a part of the Frauenkirche, one of the largest baroque churches in Europe.

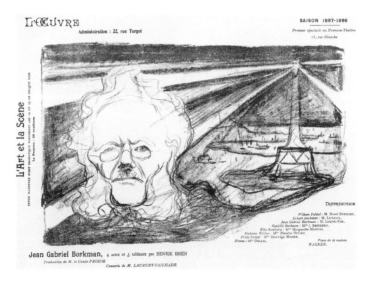

18. Edvard Munch drew hundreds of sketches of Ibsen as well as motifs from his plays. He also made posters for productions, such as this one of *John Gabriel Borkman* at the Théâtre de l'Oeuvre in Paris in 1897.

19. Herman Bang (1857–1912) was a Danish writer and journalist who followed Ibsen for decades with his elegant pen. His ambitions as an actor, however, never recovered from a disastrous performance of *Ghosts* in Bergen in 1885, where, playing Osvald, he was overwhelmed with nerves and failed to deliver his lines.

20. Ibsen photographed in 1878, the 'resting year' between *The Pillars of Society* (1877) and *A Doll's House* (1879). For the rest of his career, he would write a new play every second year.

21. In this detail of Per Krohg's painting of the Grand Café, Ibsen can be seen entering the famous Kristiania establishment, a haunt for bohemians, artists and writers. After he returned to Norway in 1891, Ibsen was in fact granted his own table here with an engraved copper plate mounted on the chair reading 'Reserved for Dr Ibsen'.

22. At the inauguration of Ibsenplatz in Gossensass, 21 July 1889, Ibsen was carried aloft by the locals and brought to a celebration on the hillside above the town. That very same summer he met Emilie Bardach, the 27-year-old daughter of an affluent Jewish merchant in Vienna. To the 61-year-old author she was just a summer fling, while he became an obsession to her.

23. A cartoon of Scottish writer and theatre critic William Archer (1856–1924) kissing Ibsen's feet. Archer was an early and eager advocate of Ibsen's plays in Great Britain.

Kristiania. Dr. Henrik Ibsens bolig.

24. In 1895 Henrik and Suzannah Ibsen moved into a newly erected apartment building in Arbins gate, where they spent their remaining years. Seen here, it is the first-floor corner apartment facing the intersection.

25. In 1892 Sigurd Ibsen married Bergliot, the daughter of Ibsen's main competitor Bjørnstjerne Bjørnson. Thus the families of the two dominating figures of Norwegian literature were united, not altogether to their parents' liking. They are photographed here around 1900.

26. August Strindberg (1849–1912), painted here by Christian Krohg, loathed and admired Ibsen, and struggled – as many a young dramatist did – to escape the shadow of 'the sphinx'.

27. Henrik Ibsen at his desk in Arbins gate. The room was exactly as he wanted it: spacious, with a high ceiling and large windows to ensure the flow of fresh air.

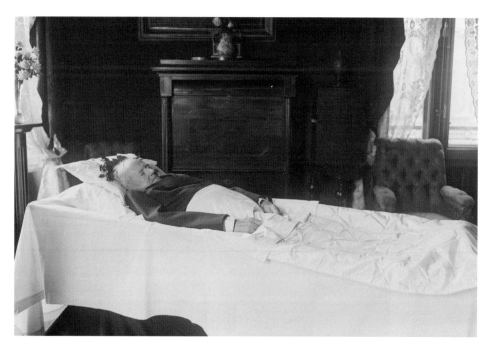

28. Henrik Ibsen lying in repose in his home, Arbins gate 1. He died at 2.30 p.m. on 23 May 1906, and was buried at Vår Frelser's cemetery in Kristiania.

29. The sculptor Stephan Sinding beside the sculpture that formed the basis for the bronze statue of Ibsen outside the National Theatre in Kristiania, unveiled on 1 September 1899.

Solveig's song came easily to him. Less easy was the Hall of the Mountain King – 'this is the sound of cowpats, Norwegian Norwegianness and smug self-satisfaction!'

Grieg had his work cut out. In January 1875 he complains again, this time to Bjørnson: '*Peer Gynt* is coming along the way you said it would. It's a nightmare and I can't see myself finishing it before the spring.' He confesses that it was probably the prospect of a healthy fee that had motivated him, a reason that may well now have struck him as a pretty thin basis on which to build inspiration. Another winter and spring would pass before Grieg was finally able to deliver his music for the play.

By that time, Ibsen had long given up hope of making a quick and triumphant journey home in the autumn of 1874.

Because that was what it was about, at least in large measure. When Ibsen dusted off *Peer Gynt* early in 1874 it was partly another recycling of his early work, with a new edition of the play scheduled for the coming winter. It may, however, also have been because he wanted to test the waters back home in Norway. His countrymen had accepted his ridicule of Norwegian public life in *Love's Comedy.* Would they be as indulgent towards the nationalist satire on display in *Peer Gynt*? That this should be a matter of such moment to him now was because he had finally decided to pay his home country a visit. For this reason he stressed to Ludvig Josephson that the play had to be performed in Christiania *before* Copenhagen and Stockholm, and at the most advantageous time in the company's programme, in the autumn.

But it was not to be. It mattered not that he had finished his part of the job so long as Grieg had still not delivered. He would have to go to Norway without *Peer Gynt.* In the spring of 1874 there was a new edition of *Brand*, followed in the autumn by *Peer Gynt, The League of Youth, The Vikings at Helgeland* and *Lady Inger of Østråt.* In May he received news that *Vikings* was to be performed at the Kongelige Teater in Copenhagen, the initiative this time coming from the theatre itself. Business was moving along nicely. New editions followed hot on each other's heels, performance succeeded performance, and his market was expanding almost under its own steam. Hegel also intimated in the spring that America was beginning to show an interest in his work. Ibsen himself was convinced that his plays would attract Scandinavian-American audiences; the only problem was that postal and customs charges were prohibitively high.

Otherwise he spent his time working on the new edition of *Lady Inger*, which he also hoped to offer for production to the main theatres in Scandinavia. But before things got to that stage, Georg Brandes reappeared one day in June. The last time these two met, two years previously, their friendship had been at its most intense, fostered by the moral support Ibsen had offered during the controversies over *Main Currents.*

Now the magic was gone. All the old problems Brandes had with the Norwegian dramatist had returned, along with a few new ones.

'The man sits there with his restricted inner resources and is in no condition to imbibe spiritual nourishment from the world around him,' he reports to a friend a few days after his visit. By this time Brandes has travelled on to Munich, where he is daily in the company of the German writer Paul Heyse, with whom he was completely besotted.

Ibsen he regarded quite differently:

He only really knows and cares about one thing, and that is what is going on back home, all that old-fashioned stuff back in Norway and Denmark. But he lacks culture, and this makes him very limited.

What on earth had happened to Ibsen?

Not necessarily all that much. Maybe he was simply in a bad mood during Brandes' short visit. As ever it was almost unendurable for the intellectual and widely read Brandes to have to sit and listen to the Norwegian's amateurish observations on society – unless, that is, Ibsen had once more succumbed to the temptation to provoke the humourless Dane.

'Can you imagine,' wrote Brandes, 'that he genuinely believes in a time when "the intelligent minority" in the world's countries will be compelled to use chemistry and medicine to poison the proletariat in order not to be politically swamped by the majority.'

Poison the proletariat to keep the masses down – tell that to Marcus Thrane. Ibsen finds Brandes easy to tease, but what is more interesting is that Brandes feels that Ibsen has become increasingly isolated in Dresden; he had no German friends and read no German literature, according to Brandes. On his previous visit Ibsen had struck him as a European; now the Norwegian seems provincial to him. He seems to have been incapable of understanding that Henrik Ibsen was both, a clumsy European from Norway, and that his very special qualities as a writer derived from just that mixture of Norwegian provincialism and a European perspective. Ibsen himself was in no doubt about what he *wanted* to be. Prior to Brandes' visit he had written a letter in which he identified himself with the other's struggle against provincialism in Denmark. And in the letter that followed the visit, brandishing his European credentials to the utmost, he asks why people such as himself and Brandes – 'who occupy a European standpoint' – should be so misunderstood at home.

Ibsen was certainly a European, but behind that glamorous facade the Norwegian in him was still fully present. His thoughts revolved constantly around his home country, and probably the more intensely so as the date of his departure for Norway approached.

NORWAY 1874

Early in July 1874, Henrik, Suzannah and Sigurd left Dresden and travelled northwards. They made a stopover in Copenhagen to see Frederik Hegel, who had invited them to visit him at Skovgaard, his country home, north of the city. On Saturday morning, 18 July, the steamer *Aarhus* left Copenhagen with the Ibsen family on board and the following day, at six in the evening, the ship berthed in Christiania harbour.

Ten years after he had left the country, Henrik Ibsen stood on Norwegian soil once again.

He was forty-six years old, more than halfway through his life. Behind him he had a career no Norwegian writer, living or dead, could match. Now he was back in that city where, as a student, a writer and a theatre manager he had wandered and drifted, not leaving it before it had left its mark on him. Many years later he would recall the visit in an unequivocally negative light. Even as the ship began its approach to Christiania he claims to have felt 'an unpleasant and oppressive tightening in the chest'. And this feeling remained with him throughout the remainder of the visit – 'beneath all these cold and uncompre-hending Norwegian stares from the windows and along the pavements I was no longer myself'.

Well, maybe. Ibsen wrote that in 1884, ten years after the visit – and one year before his next visit. In the intervening years he had provoked the Norwegian public with works such as *A Doll's House* and *Ghosts*, and in addition had his application for a rise in his annual writer's wage rejected. Resentment towards his home country remained an important motive for his continued exile. Only Ibsen knows whether his chest really did constrict in the way described. Seen from the outside, however, his visit to Norway was a success and a personal triumph. He was received as a hero, or – even better – as a poet. While still standing on deck with Sigurd and looking towards land he could hear the acclaim from the crowd assembled on the quayside, old friends and enemies, journalists and the curious. Ibsen was the summer's big news. Everybody wanted to catch a glimpse of him, everyone wanted a piece of him.

'This last week most of the talk has, of course, been about Henrik Ibsen,' according to the report in the *Ny Illustreret Tidende*. 'Have you seen him, have you spoken to him, what does he look like? Well, that at least is pretty easy to answer. You can easily spot him walking down the street wearing a black velvet coat and looking, as it happens, extremely like the latest portraits of him.'

Ibsen was well known back home in Norway, not just for his works. The *image* of him was also familiar to Norwegians, not from their memories of the scruffy and bushy-bearded theatre manager, but from the portraits and busts of the successful writer. Had Henrik Ibsen, on his way to Henriette Hofgaards Private

Hotel at Pilestredet 7, where the family were lodging, walked down Kongens gate and looked into the window of Adolf Vollmanns Gift Shop, he would have seen small busts of himself in unglazed porcelain, exhibited alongside busts of Bjørnson, Vinje, Sverdrup and other well-known Norwegians. With his elegantly trimmed beard, his bushy sideburns and broad forehead he was already an established icon in the popular imagination. Now the full-scale Ibsen walked among them, which was good news for the smaller versions: 'Sales of Henrik Ibsen's bust will probably once again pick up now,' the newspapers predicted.

The demand for the original was proving popular too.

'Ibsen is in town and doing the rounds,' Jonas Lie reported to Bjørnson, who was in Rome at the time. He noted that his friend looked older, which was reasonable enough, but also that he exuded a greater self-confidence than before. Lie had known Ibsen since the 1860s; in the intervening years Ibsen had become both a Scandinavianist and a European. He was more confident in his judgements, noted Lie, but more conservative as well. It was harder to say whether he had changed as a person.

'The extent to which his life as a writer has been of benefit to him as a person,' Lie continues, 'whether it has led him to love or ignore his fellow man, these are matters on which I would not risk an opinion.'

He received so many invitations that he had to turn some of them down. But in general it seems that he was well disposed towards his fellow country-men; he paraded the streets of Christiania, his decorations immodestly dangling from his breast, attended celebratory dinners and allowed himself to be feted by editors, consuls and the prime minister himself, Fredrik Stang.

The wealthy and socially distinguished were always sure of a positive response to their approaches, as were his old friends from the Learned Holland, Jacob Løkke, Ludvig Daae and Michael Birkeland. Daae recalls that during the course of a nine-week period he attended seven dinners, eleven afternoon gatherings and four breakfasts in the company of Ibsen. According to him there was general rejoicing at having their 'old and loyal friend Ibsen back' and Ibsen himself was 'as happy as someone of his nature can be'.

There were three portraits absent from this gallery of old friends. Aasmund Olavsson Vinje, Paul Botten-Hansen and Ole Schulerud were all dead, and with them Ibsen's closest friends and helpers from the first period in Christiania.

He was surrounded by the past, by memories. Perhaps he found it oppres-sive. But it wasn't the past coming back to haunt him. He was the one who had gone back, who had returned home to Norway in triumph. One day while visiting the university's museum he noticed the presence of a distant acquaint-ance from the Grimstad days. Ibsen approached him and began a conversation, at which the other, anxious not to say the wrong thing in the great writer's presence, hastened to assure him of his great respect and admiration. But Ibsen was sociable and friendly, and concluded by expressing a wish to see Grimstad again. In similarly relaxed fashion he talked about Skien with an old acquaintance from his schooldays there, J. F. Ording, whom he met at Daae's house. Ording was probably surprised, for his host had advised him not to mention Skien in Ibsen's presence.

Perhaps the past was not, after all, as oppressive as Ibsen later claimed? But some of the encounters must surely have had their difficulties. Previous biographers have assumed that Ibsen did not visit his family during his stay in Norway in 1874. And perhaps he did not, but they certainly visited him. Ibsen had been invited to a get-together at the house of a relative on the Paus side of the family who had invited as many of his old friends as possible. At some point his youngest brother Ole Paus turned up at the door. The brothers had probably not seen each other for twenty-five years. What did he expect, Ole? A warm handshake? An embrace?

'What do you want?' was all Henrik said. 'I'm in no position to support you.'

'I came to see you, Henrik,' replied the other. 'And now I've done it. Adieu.' After which he turned his back on his famous brother and set off back home. And Henrik? Yes, perhaps it was *now* that he felt his chest tighten.

* * *

The original plan had been to return home to Dresden before the start of Sigurd's school year. But the season at the Christiana Theatre did not open until 1 September, and because Ibsen wanted to see how things were progressing there under Ludvig Josephson the return journey was postponed. This was of particular interest to him in view of the planned production of *Peer Gynt*. There were also plans for a formal celebration of Ibsen from the stage of the main Norwegian theatre.

That was something he absolutely could not miss.

On 10 September the Christiania Theatre's production of *The League of Youth* opened. Already it was becoming something of an old war horse there. Ibsen's feelings as he anticipated visiting his old place of work again, with himself as the main attraction, must have been mixed. The climax for him came earlier in the evening, before the curtain went up. The students had arranged a torchlight procession in his honour. At about six o'clock a large procession marched up Pilestredet to Fru Hofgaard's private hotel, where Henrik Ibsen with his family and a couple of old Learned Holland friends were waiting for them. When the procession arrived, a delegation went up into his apartment and delivered a formal greeting, while those outside in the street raised their voices in a song of praise. Shortly after the writer appeared on the doorstep to meet the people.

He had clearly decided not to beat about the bush. He wanted to speak of his feelings for his homeland, and of his fellow countrymen's feelings for him.

With the cream of Norwegian youth around him and in the presence of
reporters, he was for the first time going to speak openly to Norwegians about
Norway – and without a Peer Gynt or a Steensgaard to hide behind.

> Gentlemen!
> On those occasions, during my stay abroad, when it became clear to me,
> with an ever-increasing clarity, that it was time for me to see my homeland
> again, then I will not hide from you the fact that it was not without consid-
> erable doubt and unease that I began taking steps to arrange for my journey.

Weakness is a strength, and nothing wins hearts like the modesty of a great
man. In addition he was being honest: he *had* been dreading it; how would his
countrymen greet him? Not his works, for their success was obvious, but *him*?
There was no denying that, for a long time, there had been a distrust and a
suspicion of him, he acknowledged that. In his view the complaints were of two
types:

> People have believed that I have regarded my personal and private affairs
> and experiences here at home in the light of an unforgiving bitterness, and
> I have also been accused of attacking certain events in our national life
> which, in the opinion of many, deserved a very different response than one
> of mockery.

He knows exactly how he is going to put forward his defence. In the first place,
it had never been his intention to rebuke only his fellow countrymen but to
rebuke himself too for the way in which they had all betrayed their ideals and
their Danish brothers. He was *complicit* in everything with which he had
rebuked the Norwegians. Secondly, it was not the case that he had made his
'private affairs' the subject of his writing; writing was not about 'what was experienced' but about what was 'lived through' – and lived through not just by
himself but by the Norwegian people.

This, he explains to his listeners, is his literary project: he writes from both
the best and the worst in himself, from what is 'great and noble in me', as well
as what emerges from the 'dregs of one's own being'. His art involved a dissection of himself and of his people, of all the greatness and the degradations
that Norwegians had experienced together, the exalted and the humiliating
simultaneously:

> And where amongst us is the man who has not now and then felt and recog-
> nised within himself the contradiction between the word and the deed,
> between will and duty, between life and learning?

In this way he formulates his poetics as an extension of the national-romantic ideal of the poet as interpreter of the people, only now the gaze is directed not at the nation's future but instead inwards, towards the individual mind. How to judge a person who ceaselessly judges himself, a writer who offers no answers but only questions? As he had done most recently in his play about the tragic hero Julian? This was what he wanted to say to his fellow countrymen, and thus make his peace with them without at the same time betraying himself. He was the poet-prophet returned to his own with the assurance that he had never forsaken them. He was, in other words, inviolable.

And what was the reply of the people?

'The speech was followed by bravos and resounding cheers,' *Morgenbladet* reported the following day. The students' choir performed a second song before the procession disbanded, while the leaders of the Students' Union and the choir accompanied Ibsen back up to his apartment, where refreshments were served and Fru Suzannah's health was drunk. Later the group made their way to the theatre for *The League of Youth*. The curtain fell to resounding applause and there were calls for the author to take a bow. Ibsen must have loved every minute of it. What a triumph! The chorus of whistlers had fallen silent, and indeed the newspapers took great delight in pointing out that the trouble-makers from the premiere in 1869 were the same ones now heaping praise on the dramatist. At the close of events he returned to the private hotel and rounded off the evening with a pipe.

It was obvious now; he *was* a poet-prophet in his own land. Did that trouble him? In play after play he had cracked the whip over his countrymen. And now here they were, sighing with pleasure under his lashes!

Given Ibsen's make-up, the dilemma was something he could live with: where Ibsen the poet enjoyed the provocation, Ibsen the man savoured the warmth of the applause. That was what he was like, and it was what he would remain. A week after the torchlight procession he writes contentedly to Hegel: 'I have been greeted with extraordinary goodwill by everyone. The suspicion and distrust are things of the past.' Indeed, so buoyant was his mood that he considered buying a house in Norway. But on this occasion there is nothing to suggest he ever seriously considered ending his life in exile, and any thoughts of a house in Norway were soon forgotten. But if the decision satisfied *him*, Suzannah probably felt differently about it. During the visit to Christiania she is said to have made a serious attempt to persuade her husband to return home for good. True, she had once written in a letter to her brother that her happiness was to be where her husband was – but what if that happiness could be had in Norway?

Henrik, Sigurd and Suzannah said farewell to Christiania on 29 September. As soon as they had vacated the rooms at Fru Hofgaard's private hotel, the

young boys living there sneaked in and helped themselves to the pens the great
writer had used. The family took the train to Sweden and on from there to
Germany. Behind them were over two months of almost continuous feasting,
and for the writer of the house a massive reparation for every humiliation, real
and imagined, his country had dealt him in his younger years.

That he would later recall the visit as an anxiety-ridden trial is another
matter altogether. Norway had, after all, given him the gift of sorrow, and *that*
was a gift he did not propose to relinquish so easily.

THE BREAK

Safely back in Dresden, Ibsen devoted himself completely to the revision of
Lady Inger of Østråt. By the end of November he had finished, and early in
December he sent it to the Gothenburg Theatre, the Kungliga Dramatiska
Teatern in Stockholm, the Kongelige Teater in Copenhagen, and, of course, the
Christiania Theatre. The only slight disappointment was that a delay in the
post to Norway meant that he missed out on the Christmas sales that year.

While Ibsen was still hard at work on the final revisions he received a sad
letter from Magdalene Thoresen in Copenhagen in which she related that
Suzannah's sister Marie was seriously ill and had not long left:

> Each passing hour brings her ever closer to the grave, and there is no longer
> any doubt about the nature of her illness.

Henrik and Suzannah already knew of Marie's condition, and Suzannah was on
her way to Copenhagen to nurse her sister. Henrik remained in Dresden, with
Sigurd and Thomas Thoresen, who was still living in the city. While still en
route to Copenhagen, Suzannah writes home:

> Dear Ibsen, thank you, thank you for letting me make this journey, both
> yesterday and today my mood was bleak, but now a peace has descended on
> me, and I can only pray I do not arrive too late.

She arrived in Copenhagen on the morning of 31 October and was met by
Magdalene. They went at once to the hospital where Marie lay. She was not too
late – 'God give me the strength to ease her pain in the final struggle.' Suzannah
remained at her sister's side through the first weeks of November, sending
greetings from herself and Marie home to Henrik. 'She sends a thousand greetings to you and thanks you for the love you showed her.' The thought of losing
her sister made her feel as if her heart would break. But Suzannah is not only a
sister, she is also a wife and mother:

Write to me and tell me how you are getting on, tell Sigurd he must be really grown-up and a good boy and do everything right. The washerwoman who comes on Thursday is due 1Th. 15 Groschen.

Henrik assures his wife she has no need to worry about the boy, who was now fourteen years old. The older Sigurd grows, the more strikingly protective does his parents' love for him become: 'You need not worry, I am keeping a close eye on him,' Henrik replies. 'I daren't let him be on his own too much, he gets up to far too much mischief if he is.' Henrik took no chances, meeting the boy from school every day. On 12 November, Suzannah writes home again. After a long and painful last struggle, Marie had finally died. Henrik was much affected, and offered to pay for the burial and the rental on the grave for twenty years. He complained bitterly that Marie had been sent to the hospital in the first place, and that Thomas had not visited his sister when he was in Copenhagen.

While Henrik was away in Egypt, Marie had told Sigurd that she could hardly sleep for worrying about him. During the short period they were in each other's company they had become very close, and whatever else they might have felt for each other beyond friendship was something they took to the grave with them. The death of Marie meant saying goodbye to a person of whom Ibsen had become truly fond. Was it the severing of this tie that led him to seek to re-establish ties with his own family, the family he had neglected for so many years? No one knows what motivated Ibsen to sit down a couple of months after Marie's death in February 1875 and write to his old father, but there is no reason to suppose that it was evidence of any deep-seated desire to renew contact. More likely it was related to the recent visit to Norway – perhaps at the urging of members of the family he had met in Christiania. Or perhaps he felt the tugs of obligation and conscience more strongly during the first visit to his homeland in ten years, though not strongly enough to visit either his father or his birthplace.

Henrik's letter is lost. But Knud Ibsen's reply survives, the letter of an old man, melancholy in his inadequacy, pathetic in his respect for his learned son, the great writer.

This is how a wounded father writes:

My dear son,

I have had the pleasure of receiving your welcome letter of 25 February, it was indeed a rarity, for as you say in your letter I haven't seen you or heard from you in twenty-five years, all the same I have heard from you in your writing: *Brand, P. Gynt, Love's Comedy*, the *League of Youth* have all been given to me. Brøndlund let me have *Emperor and Galilean*, but I don't know if I can keep it.

It's a trial to write a letter now, I wrote quite well when I was young, but now age takes its toll, just think, I'll be eighty in two years' time, so writing tires me out, and my best years are behind me and now I just wait for the end. You're coming to Norway in the summer and so I expect we'll hear from you in Skien. I would like that very much. Hedvig has probably given you the family news in her last letter, so I won't repeat it, everything is just the same as usual. But I have got some news, Peder Lendsmand who went up to Confirmation at the same time as you got married a few weeks ago. First he was engaged to the sheriff's daughter, but she changed her mind, so he had to make do with something awful – one of his own servants. Now I must cease this chatter and stop bothering a learned son with all my nonsense.

I tried to read your letter, but I couldn't understand it, I felt ashamed and so end here simply with a friendly greeting to you, your wife and son from your affectionate old father.

Knud Ibsen

We do not know whether Henrik replied. There are no further traces of contact between father and son after this. Knud Ibsen died two years later, eight years after the death of his wife Marichen. Henrik Ibsen was without parents, as indeed he had been for most of his life. Marie was gone, but he had his Suzannah and his Sigurd. When all was said and done, that was what mattered. It was these two who enjoyed the love and the concern that Knud Ibsen was denied.

The visit to Norway and the letter to his father were not the only steps Ibsen took down memory lane in the winter of 1874–5. He had decided that he wanted to celebrate his twenty-fifth anniversary as a writer by publishing a new edition of *Catiline*, timed to coincide with his forty-seventh birthday on 20 March 1875. The months preceding the anniversary had seen the success of *Emperor and Galilean* and the triumphal return to Norway. Third print runs of both *The League of Youth* and *Peer Gynt* appeared in the autumn of 1874. Delays in the production of the latter at the Christiania Theatre were a slight disappointment, but *Lady Inger of Østråt* had also been accepted. He was not so lucky at the Kongelige Teater in Copenhagen, where Christian Molbech took the same line as his predecessor Carsten Hauch had done the previous time Ibsen submitted this play, by declining the offer. *The Vikings at Helgeland*, however, was revived for a performance on 19 February. In that same month it was proposed, with the backing of others including Birkeland, that Ibsen be given a rise in his annual writer's wage by the Norwegian Storting.

All in all, it was an auspicious time to take a look back along the winding path that led to his success.

Early in December he starts revising *Catiline*. He worked on the style and the construction but avoided any major changes, and at the end of January

1875 sent the manuscript to Hegel. The book was ready for publication by the beginning of March. Ibsen sent copies to friends and connections both near and far, new and old – sometimes very old and very far back indeed. Back home in Norway, Ibsen's birthday was celebrated by the Students' Union and the Artists' Union, *Lady Inger* had its premiere at the Christiania Theatre – and of course what remained of the Learned Holland gathered to dine and drink his health. He was indeed a poet-prophet in his own land, that land to which, by his own account, he rode home every single night, and yet which he could see clearly only from a distance. So it was only natural that he should follow up success at home by moving ever further away from it, this time further south, to Munich. According to Ibsen the decisive factor behind the move was concern for Sigurd's schooling. Dr Hölbe's school in Dresden had run into financial difficulties and the quality of the teaching had declined. The school had to sell off equipment and possessions to make ends meet. The crisis passed, but the two final years in the curriculum were withdrawn, and that decided the matter. Dresden could offer the boy no viable alternative – in Ibsen's words, 'in their structure and methods the state schools here are not suitable for foreign pupils'.

Concern for Sigurd's future was hardly the only motive behind the choice of Munich. Ibsen writes to Daae that wanderlust had overcome him again. Most likely the trip to Norway, closely followed by his twenty-fifth anniversary as a writer, had seemed to him epochal moments in his life and career, so that now was the right time to move on from Dresden. In Munich they were also closer to Italy and the Alps. The climate was warmer, the cost of living hopefully lower than in Dresden and, moreover, it would be pleasant to live among Catholics again. As had been the case with Dresden, the matter of how long they would remain in Munich was left open – before the move Ibsen hinted that they might stay there two or three years. That the move took them ever further from Norway was clearly not a problem for the family. Or, at least, not for the head of the family.

VIII

MUNICH

LIFE BELOW THE ALPS

On 22 May 1876, Bjørnstjerne Bjørnson writes a letter to a friend in which, with ill-concealed relish, he passes on a recent rumour he has heard:

> Henr. Ibsen has dropped the respectable exterior and started drinking again. It *had* to end that way. There is no peace in him, no pleasures beyond the pleasure of ambition; and that is a thing that is easily provoked.

Bjørnson might well hope that Ibsen had reached the end of the road after the success of *Emperor and Galilean*; a month earlier he had again complained that the other had usurped his position as the poet of the Danes, and he can hardly have failed to notice that Ibsen, much like himself, was now paying literary court to the Germans.

In the spring of 1875, Ibsen left Dresden and settled in Munich, capital of the most southerly of the German states, the kingdom of Bavaria, and by the end of the following year still no new play had appeared. Was there, perhaps, something in those rumours of his dissolution? A year or two later the politician Ludvig Daae, a keen diarist, noted that Ibsen was 'apparently partying a lot and was generally regarded as living a disreputable life'. And indeed it was true enough that Ibsen was enjoying access to the excellent Tyrolean wines he drank daily with his evening meal. He absolutely loved the large glasses of dark, malty Bock beer that was served in the cafes.

But rumours of his decline were a considerable exaggeration.

Bavaria and Munich held a much more independent and prominent political position in Germany than Saxony and Dresden, a prominence that was reflected in the sciences, theatre life, literature and the arts. Both states had allied with Austria against Prussia during the unification campaign, but Bavaria was never invaded by Bismarck's troops, and maintained a much greater independence within the German empire. Under the Bavarian monarchs, Munich developed into a dominant cultural centre, on a par with Berlin, a reputation that was cemented by the presence of a number of foreign writers and artists among its residents. It seemed a place where Ibsen might thrive.

There are a lot of Norwegians living here, and the air here is fresher and more bracing than the Dresden air, a natural consequence of the proximity of the Alps.

Before arriving he had written to a German professor of law, Konrad Maurer, who was friendly with many Norwegians in the city. On Maurer's recommendation Sigurd was enrolled at Maximilian's College. After searching around for a week or two they found a comfortable apartment to rent in Schönfeldstrasse 17, in the centre of Maxvorstadt, close to Sigurd's new school and within walking distance of the city's great cultural institutions. Where the pattern of moves in Dresden had been characterised by social climbing, Ibsen's finances were now sound enough for the family to move into a fashionable district straightaway. It meant that he could accept with unusual composure the news that the Storting had rejected the request for a rise in his annual writer's wage.

'So I did not get the rise. Well, I can manage alright without it,' he writes to Johan Hermann Thoresen in May, though he is careful to point out that Sweden and Denmark appear to appreciate him more. He had received a bonus royalty of 1,000 kroner from Dramaten in Stockholm for the production of *The League of Youth*, while the Kongelige Teater in Copenhagen had awarded him a double royalty for *The Vikings at Helgeland*. He had, moreover, read in *Morgenbladet* that King Oscar II intended to award him a medal, something the king had strangely neglected to mention in the letter Ibsen received from him just before leaving Dresden. Early in December he received not just one but two medals, both the 'Achievement Medal' (King Oscar's Medal), introduced at Oscar's coronation two years earlier, and a medal cast to celebrate the unveiling of the statue on Slottsbakken in Christiania of King Carl Johan on horseback – or *Kristiania*, the spelling of the name adopted from the middle of the 1870s.

Much of the spring was spent on literary business. In addition to the new edition of *Catiline*, in the course of the year Gyldendal published new editions of *The Vikings at Helgeland*, *The Pretenders* and *Poems*. Ibsen also did his best to keep his promise to Brandes to contribute something to *The Nineteenth Century*, the magazine Georg ran with his brother Edvard which was now the foundation for the literary campaign Brandes was hoping *Main Currents* would inaugurate. Ibsen found the work difficult. Correspondence between the two men in the spring of 1875 reflects the cooler tone in their relationship following the meeting between them the previous summer. At the beginning of June, Ibsen sends the first poem, accompanied by a solemn promise to send something every month from now on. All that Brandes ever received was 'A Letter in Rhyme' and the nonce poem 'Far Away', written for a students' rally in Uppsala. Along with 'Greeting in Song to Sweden' and 'At the Millennial Celebrations July 18 1872', these two were the only verses he added to the new edition of *Poems*.

Brandes must have been deeply disappointed, though perhaps not surprised, at the modest nature of Ibsen's contributions to his magazine. Only the 'Letter in Rhyme' had the qualities appropriate for a literary battleground such as *The Nineteenth Century*. More interesting than both the new editions and the contributions to Brandes' periodical was the news that Karl Perfall, manager of the Kongelige Teater in Munich, had accepted *The Pretenders* for a production. It was all the more important for Ibsen because Bjørnson was now beginning to make a solid name for himself on the German stage, and with Munich as his base of operations.

The competition between them continued.

THE MOUNTAIN KING REVISITED

Bjørnson had written two dramas with contemporary settings, *A Bankrupt* and *The Editor*, in the summer of 1874. Publication was delayed until after the staging of the plays and the first was not premiered until January the following year, at Nya Teatern in Stockholm, with *The Editor* opening in February. Following these premieres both appeared in book form.

There had long been rumours concerning Bjørnson's new plays, expectations were high, and there was no lack of attention when the dramas reached the public. *The Editor* was controversial in Norway because Bjørnson had used *Morgenbladet*'s editor Christian Friele as his model, and the play was rejected by the Christiania Theatre. *A Bankrupt*, on the other hand, did well in Scandinavia, and following its German premiere in Munich on 12 June it marked Bjørnson's breakthrough in Germany.

'Bjørnson's "The Newly Weds" and "A Bankrupt" have been staged here,' Ibsen writes drily to Hegel a few days later. 'The former didn't do well at all; the latter, however, was more successful.'

He could have afforded to be a little more generous; *Die Neuvermählten* (*The Newlyweds*) was performed four times, and *Ein Falissement* (*A Bankrupt*) was staged twenty-three times during 1875 and 1876. That was sensational in a city in which few plays ever managed more than five performances in the course of a season, and where the great German dramatist Paul Heyse didn't manage more than seven performances in one season of even his most popular play.[1] Bjørnson's success must have affected Ibsen more than he lets on in his letter to Hegel, and it is hardly coincidental that he now starts work on the play that will mark *his* decisive change of direction towards realistic dramas with contemporary settings, and also give him his great breakthrough as a dramatist in Germany. In February he had revealed to Hegel that he was planning a new 'contemporary play' in five acts. The following month he asked his publisher to send him Bjørnson's two plays, and in August he was able to tell him that he had a timetable for his own play. Once again they followed closely on each other heels, Ibsen and Bjørnson. Both had written plays with a contemporary setting in the 1860s (*The Newlyweds* and *The League of Youth*), and Bjørnson had started work on *A Bankrupt* as early as the summer of 1868, while Ibsen had been nurturing plans for a 'serious drama of contemporary life' since at least the autumn of 1869. The first notes for what would become *The Pillars of Society* are dated 1870 and refer to the play as a comedy. Both struggled with their new ideas over the following years, and it was Bjørnson who first broke the literary mould with a play set in the present that featured a hitherto unprecedented degree of realism.

'*Finally!*' exclaimed an enthusiastic Georg Brandes. 'Finally it looks as though we too, up here in the north, are about to enjoy dramas in which those two great powers, the Present and Reality, get the respect and attention they deserve.'

Throughout the following autumn Ibsen worked steadily on his play. By the end of October the first act was ready, as was the title: *The Pillars of Society*. But the work did not proceed as quickly as he had hoped and it would take him another two years to finish it. Henrik, Suzannah and Sigurd planned to spend the summer of 1875 in the little country village of Kitzbühel, in the Austrian Alps. Just before their departure he receives a letter from Edvard Grieg, who has finally finished the music to *Peer Gynt* and now wonders where he should send the score. Ibsen asks Grieg to send it direct to Ludvig Josephson at the Christiania Theatre. On his arrival in Kitzbühel he receives a letter from the theatre's censor, Hartvig Lassen, confirming its arrival.

Rehearsals began, and on Friday 24 February 1876 the public could enjoy, for the first time, Peer Gynt as a character in a stage play. The role was created by Henrik Clausen, whose performance was hailed as a work of genius.[2] The scenery and props, the work of Frits Thaulow and other artists, also played an important part in the play's success. Indeed, the entire production was a tour de force that overshadowed anything that had previously been seen on a Norwegian stage. In consultation with Ibsen, Josephson had cut the play by eliminating scenes from the fourth and fifth acts. Even so, the play was long, and it speaks volumes for the enthusiasm of the audience that people sat from seven o'clock until close to midnight, and still had the energy to demand curtain calls of the cast, and finally, of the play's director himself, Ludvig Josephson. Thus it was that 'the foreigner' who had been greeted with abuse and booing on his arrival four years earlier could now crown his achievements in Kristiania with a performance that was as Norwegian as anyone could wish.

Peer Gynt, that swingeing satire of everything Norwegian, was rapturously received by those who were its principal target, the Norwegian public. At least that was the way it looked. Was there even a single member of the audience who reflected on the paradox of it all – that the premiere of *Peer Gynt* was given in, of all places, Kristiania, the very heart of the Hall of the Mountain King?

Apparently not, but then Ibsen and Josephson had muted much of the satire in the play and given it a more 'Norwegian' and melodramatic tone.[3] In addition, Grieg's music gave the play an element of precisely the sort of national romanticism that much of the irony of the original text was directed at.[4] So Ibsen himself was responsible for the fact that Norwegians experienced a more benign Peer Gynt than the creation they had first encountered in book form. Without a hint of irony, *Aftenbladet*'s reviewer could hail it as 'an important national epic'.

Thus began the Norwegian tradition of *Peer Gynt* as a national-romantic epic. The play was performed thirty-seven times before the end of 1877, and there might well have been more performances had not a fire on 15 January almost completely destroyed the theatre. That year alone Ibsen earned over 500 spesidaler from performances in Kristiania, a reward in part for his persistence in urging Lassen to do everything he could to attract audiences:

> Were I to hear that a large sum of money was coming my way it would be most welcome news; life out here in the big world is not cheap.

But was it true, as he had heard, that Bjørnson was being paid a higher fee than he was? If that were the case then Lassen must know that he would never again be offered a play by Henrik Ibsen!

AMONG ARTISTS AND CROCODILES

Socially, probably the greatest difference between life in Munich and Dresden was that relations with Suzannah's family practically came to an end. When Magdalene Thoresen visited the city in the summer of 1876, Henrik and Suzannah were away. The following year Dorothea and Conrad Falsen moved from Berlin. From this time onwards, what kept the family together was the correspondence among the living and memories of the dead. Marie had passed away, and in the spring of 1876 Henrik and Suzannah were saddened to learn that Thomas too had died of tuberculosis.

Locally, the writer rapidly entered the literary and intellectual life of society; it seems likely he worked assiduously to establish contacts: 'I would very much like to meet Paul Heyse,' he writes to Brandes, who had become friendly with the famous German writer the previous year. Ibsen did get to know Heyse, as well as a number of other authors, artists and intellectuals in the Bavarian capital, and by the spring of 1876 he looked to be riding the crest of a social wave that might at first sight have been reminiscent of the happy days in Rome. In addition he had the company of one of his old friends from those days – Lorentz Dietrichson, who had arrived in Munich at the end of the previous year. He remained in the city until February 1877, apart from an interlude of a few months when he was back in Norway in connection with his appointment as Professor of Art History. Dietrichson recalls from that time a sociable Ibsen, happy to open his door to his fellow countrymen and equally sociable when out visiting.

As there had been in Rome, there was a large contingent of Scandinavians here, including a number of Norwegian painters. Norwegian artists still had to go abroad to acquire a respectable training and make a name for themselves, and Germany remained the favoured destination; not until the 1880s did Paris become an artistic centre for Norwegians in Europe. In the 1870s, Munich was the place to be for Nordic artists who wanted to study historical painting, portraiture and life drawing. Naturally, Ibsen sought the company of his fellow countrymen.

About a month after his arrival he turned up one day in Eilif Peterssen's studio.

'He is a very quiet man, who doesn't say much,' wrote Peterssen to his parents. 'But unless I misinterpreted his nod, he was pleased with the visit and said he would be back.'

Ibsen did return, not least because Peterssen had asked whether he might paint his portrait. Thereafter he arrived at the studio every afternoon at five o'clock. Words were still at a premium, but 'he becomes more interesting with each visit'. This was how the first portrait painting of Ibsen emerged. It shows the writer from the front, standing and turned slightly to the right, his right hand underneath his waistcoat and those grey and imposing sideburns hanging down either side of his face. The expression is severe, the eyes searching, the mouth a gruff line. At forty-seven years of age Ibsen was well on the way to mastering his pose, his sphinx-like aura, but the features were still younger and the expression milder than in the portraits done in his later years. As for the painter, it is tempting to think that he painted Ibsen more as he *saw* him, uninfluenced by the heroic, almost geometric iconography that would be characteristic of later studies. Eilif Peterssen's portrait of Ibsen is *good* and probably captures the man rather than the sphinx that Ibsen later became.

Peterssen was not the only Norwegian to enjoy an acquaintanceship with Ibsen. Harriet Backer relates that the Norwegian painters were frequent guests in the writer's home, and for a period he seems to have held open house for his fellow countrymen once a week. But in the end Munich wasn't really like Rome after all. There is nothing to suggest that Ibsen really was an integrated part of the Norwegian circle of artists, and he was probably not often seen at the studio parties or the bohemian bars the young painters frequented in the evenings. His name is not associated with the Scandinavian community in Munich, and definitely not with wild parties, fancy-dress balls and such like.

Probably this reserve seemed only natural to him. Ibsen was approaching fifty and had long ago exchanged his bohemian ways for the routines and disciplines of family life and domesticity. It is not easy to say whether his encounters with painters in Munich had any influence on Ibsen's view of art. There is little evidence that he tried to follow the latest trends and developments in the artistic world. Much later he revealed something of his views on art to the painter Hans Heyerdahl. Art, he maintained, should not be tied up in various schools and programmes, like Impressionism. Art had to be *individual*, and the artist a *whole* person, creating out of what was inside him. The interest in formulating theoretical views of art and literature was a thing of the past. A friend was struck by the writer's lack of interest in Munich's art exhibitions and museums, and even noted that he rarely attended the theatre.

There is not much here that recalls the Ibsen who allowed himself to be enthused and seduced by Michelangelo's paintings and the tragic muse in Italy; increasingly he gives the impression of being an island unto himself, the works emerging from an encounter between the world and the writer's eye, whipped on by that creative imperative that had its source deep within him.

* * *

That the spring of 1876 was a time of socialising for Ibsen was only partly because of these Norwegians. In the main he preferred the company of Germans, and in particular an exclusive circle of writers and intellectuals with which he and Dietrichson soon became closely associated.[5]

'I've become part of a large literary crowd here,' he writes to Johan Hermann Thoresen in February, 'who treat me with great friendliness and courtesy. It makes life down here very pleasurable.'

This circle came together in a literary society called Gesellschaft der Krokodile, founded in 1857 and disbanded in 1883. Its members included Paul Heyse, Hermann Lingg, Wilhelm Hertz and Heinrich Leuthold, a Professor of Art History and Aesthetics named Moritz Carrière, a young doctor called Oswald Schmidt, the 'dialect poet' Karl Stieler, the historian and writer Felix Dahn, and not least Franz Grandaur, the director of the Königliches Hoftheater in Munich. The society was a much more exclusive club than the Literarischer Verein in Dresden. A small group of like-minded writers would meet in each other's homes or in the city's cafes to discuss aesthetic questions and give readings from works in progress. Ibsen had been a more or less passive member of the Literarischer Verein in Dresden, whereas here in Munich he was much more active as both debater and raconteur.[6]

Once again he had found himself a select circle of intimates able to function as an audience for his witticisms and paradoxes, as formerly he had found such groups in Grimstad, Kristiania and Rome, but not in Bergen, and hardly in Dresden. Again he knew the pleasures of life 'on the heights', visiting places such as the Achatz restaurant where he and his friends would gather to enjoy a 'Frühschoppen' – a glass of foaming bock beer – between noon and one o'clock. He was also present at the annual gatherings to celebrate the emperor's birthday and the little group's evening get-togethers. Indeed, he occasionally hosted such gatherings himself, not at home, but at one of the city's finer restaurants. It was probably evenings such as these that gave rise to those rumours back in Norway that he had started drinking again.

The origins and character of the Krokodile tell us much about the special cultural and political life in Munich and Bavaria, and so give us an insight into the world Ibsen inhabited and wrote from at this time. In Bavaria the regents had struggled for a long time to limit Catholic influence on the liberal and secular state. Part of the campaign involved turning Munich into a scientific and cultural centre in Germany, built on an apolitical classicism, and supported by a growing mass market among cultural consumers in the expanding bourgeoisie and bureaucracy. The Bavarian regents Ludvig I (1825–48), Maximilian II (1848–64) and Ludvig II (1864–86) consciously worked to attract North German Protestant writers, painters, composers and architects to the city. Stately new buildings, a national theatre, art collections and broad boulevards all bore witness to these ambitions to make Munich the capital of a new secular state in which the overriding aim was to unite the bourgeoisie and the nobility within a culture of refinement that was both classicist and loyal to the state.[7] In this way Munich developed within the course of a few short years into an intellectual centre in Germany that could compete with Berlin, at the same time as the North German intelligentsia helped to tie Bavaria more closely to the rest of Germany. It was from this dual starting point that the so-called 'Munich naturalism' of the 1880s arose, in opposition to the classical aesthetic, but less radical than the naturalism in Berlin. Writers such as Michael Georg Konrad and Karl Bleibtreu adopted a more ambivalent attitude towards modernity; here the concern was rather with the darker aspects of life in the big city, and an admiration for tradition (*Volkstum*) and what was local (*Heimstadt*).

How did Ibsen fit into this landscape?

Traditionally, Ibsen at this period of his life has been associated with the work of youngish naturalistic German writers with partly socialist and radical profiles such as Gerhart Hauptmann and Hermann Bahr.[8] And from a literary-historical perspective this seems fair enough, since this was the period in which

Ibsen started to write realistic dramas of contemporary life with *The Pillars of Society* as the first of them. But if we look at the writers whose company he actually kept in Munich, the picture is very different. Ibsen's friends in the Krokodile were in no way part of the school of naturalism but were solid supporters of the cultural politics of the time of Maximilian II. The group's aesthetic programme was a classicist post-Hegelian idealism that was clearly opposed to naturalism, anarchism, the radical *littérature engagée*, and indeed everything that threatened the status quo. Instead, elegance was cultivated, and the formally well-structured work, with motifs from bygone eras, exotic locations, or explorations of a 'timeless' idealism far removed from the problems of the day.

Paul Heyse, founder and leading light of the group, was an outstanding example of this. In the field of the aesthetics of idealism he was among Germany's leading writers. He was a charming and extremely cultured court-poet, a passionate advocate of the beautiful, in life as in writing, adored by women and admired by his colleagues and his numerous readers.

It seems he can hardly have come across Ibsen's like before, for he was greatly taken aback after their first meeting, which was at the behest of Georg Brandes. Brandes, to be on the safe side, had warned him what to expect – 'a closed, rather shy and taciturn but highly original and bizarre Norwegian'.

Not surprisingly, Heyse looked forward keenly to their meeting.

'I spent a half hour with Ibsen,' he relates to Brandes afterwards. 'But I cannot say much more than that I was, in a human sense, deeply attracted to him, in spite of his many peculiarities, the decorations on his velvet jacket, his uncommonly stiff, formal and yet not especially self-assured bearing, so that despite his self-consciousness one feels that he is begging for help to be released from himself.'[9]

Clearly Ibsen had got dressed up for his meeting with the great writer, but no velvet coat could adequately disguise the fumbling attempts of a Norwegian merchant's son to conform to European codes of sophistication. Yet Heyse was courteous enough not to let this cloud his judgement. He saw something in the other's eyes that convinced him they had quite a lot in common. To Brandes he had already expressed his great admiration for *The Pretenders*, and though he was disappointed by *Brand* he admired Ibsen's genius and hoped that they would meet again.

So while Ibsen, in his writing, would come to stand for a revolutionary break with a backward-looking aesthetic that cultivated the beautiful, he enjoyed the company of the defenders of that very aesthetic. The situation was the same with the Norwegian painters in Munich; Ibsen seems to have been closer to the Romantic painter Marcus Grønvold than to the nascent realist Eilif Peterssen. The paradox is striking, the more so if we also take into account

Ibsen's social, political and literary development. A man who despised politics, who had long ago turned his back on the social battles of everyday life like a 'poet-prophet in the desert', a man who looked down on the crowd and hailed monarchy and aristocracy, indeed, who found his friends among aristocrats, romantics and idealistic artists – this was the man who would blaze the trail for the realistic, problem-focused drama of contemporary life. *His* were the works that would be embraced by socialists, feminists and others who marched to the beat of modernisation in the century to come.

LIKE A SKALD AT THE FOOT OF HIS PRINCE

Ibsen's social entry into Munich's literary circles coincided with his break-through on the city's main stage. In the autumn of 1875 it became evident that the Hoftheater in Munich was not, after all, going to be offering a production of *The Pretenders*; instead he was promised a performance of *The Vikings at Helgeland* the following spring.[10] German translations of *Brand* and *The League of Youth* already existed. Now Ibsen was about to make his debut on the German stage – almost a year after Bjørnson. The premiere on 10 April 1876 was a resounding success. Ibsen, who watched the performance from the wings, took five curtain calls and was royally celebrated by friends from the Krokodile into the early hours of the morning. And as though applause and good reviews were not enough he was also offered the personal congratulations of Ludvig II, the theatre-loving king himself. The reviews were marvellous; this 'curious' Nordic play appealed to the Bavarians' fondness for historical drama; the thematic material was, moreover, derived from the same saga sources as Richard Wagner's great operatic cycle *Der Ring des Nibelungen*, which would shortly have its world premiere at Wagner's newly opened opera house in Bayreuth.[11]

Ibsen moved quickly to follow up his triumph. He provided a strikingly long list of people and institutions who were to receive complimentary copies of the German edition of *The Vikings at Helgeland* that included heads of thea-tres, actors, newspaper editors, professors, writers and aristocrats, new friends in Germany and old friends in Norway. A copy was also sent to the Burgtheater in Vienna, where the visionary director Heinrich Laube had now been replaced by another leading director, Franz Dingelstedt.

And Dingelstedt didn't take long to accept the play.

Yet the next great stage event in Ibsen's life took place not in Vienna but in Berlin. One day early in June, Ibsen did not arrive as usual for lunch at the Hotel Achatz at twelve o'clock. He was not there the following day either, and his friends had no idea where he was until he reappeared a week later. It turned out that the Duke of Saxe-Meiningen had invited him to Berlin, where his private theatre group intended to perform *The Pretenders*. Meiningen was a little duchy in Thüringen, in the heart of Germany. In the 1860s it was home to a modest population of 13,000 people. In 1866, Georg II had acceded the dukedom. Artistically talented and with a lively interest in drama, he also took over the running of the theatre. Heavily influenced by developments in France, his group laid great stress on ensemble playing, a natural acting style, authoritative and well-planned direction, and a thoroughgoing realism in its props and scenery that made it one of the leading theatres of the day. Its fame spread through numerous guest appearances in major cities across Europe.

Among directors, rising stars such as André Antoine and Konstantin Stanislavski learned much from their encounters with the Meiningen group. And Ibsen was well aware of what an opportunity this would be for him when the invitation from the duke arrived. He immediately wrote to Hegel with a request for money so that he could travel to Berlin, where the premiere was to take place. The play was not particularly well received.[12] Ibsen took several curtain calls on the first night, but the reviews were mixed. According to one of the theatre company Skule and Håkon were presented as equal pretenders to the throne, which made it hard for the audience to take sides. The production ran for seven performances in Berlin; by way of comparison, the theatre's production of Bjørnson's *Between the Battles* was played twenty-one times, and *Maria Stuart* an impressive eighty-nine times at various European houses. Poorly attended plays were of little use to a commercial theatre such as Meiningen's, and after *The Pretenders* was taken off it did not produce an Ibsen play again until 1885 with *A Doll's House*.[13]

Ibsen was nevertheless content. Following the premiere he was invited to the duke's country castle at Bad Liebenstein, and on Ibsen's departure the theatre-loving duke made him a Knight First Class of the Saxony Ernestine Order. Back home in Munich he wrote a letter of thanks to the duke; his stay there had been like a 'lovely fairy tale', a dream come true. He was reminded, he writes, of the old Icelandic skalds, who travelled south through Europe, visiting the courts of princes along the way to chant their verses, and returning to their remote island in the north laden with splendid gifts.

That was how he saw his place at the court of Georg II of Meiningen – as that of a skaldic poet at the foot of his prince. And there were certainly worse places to be. Culture-loving amateurs among royalty and nobility in nineteenth-century Europe often turned out to be talented cultural entrepreneurs.[14] Ludvig II was another, although on a quite different scale. Confronted with the unification of Germany under Prussian leadership, the ruler of the tiny state of Meiningen used culture to compensate for the loss of political power, while the kings of Bavaria used cultural politics to consolidate their position within the empire.

The influence of the Meiningen theatre on Ibsen's drama is hard to assess. The theatre was one of the most creatively advanced in Europe. Classic historical dramas – Shakespeare, Schiller and Kleist – were approached in radically new ways. There was no place for prima donnas in this theatre, for here even the minor parts were treated with great seriousness. Even the extras were carefully rehearsed. Georg II's right-hand man, Ludwig Chronegk, was responsible for the authoritative and well thought-out direction, the props were historically accurate – for preference genuine antiques were used – and the scenery carefully considered with an eye to the overall effect. In other words, the externals of traditional directing were further developed at the same time as a psychological element was introduced into the acting that signposted the way towards the modern theatre. Ibsen may have seen some of this in Paris, but hardly as consistently and comprehensively practised as here.

It is probably best to assume that his experience in Meiningen served to confirm and consolidate his own development. This coming together of ideas is perhaps seen to best advantage in *Emperor and Galilean*, published three years before his meeting with Duke Georg. Here Ibsen writes a historical drama featuring a high degree of detailed realism; he consciously introduces a range of 'everyday and insignificant characters' and does not force them to speak in the 'tongues of the gods'. All this is done without sacrificing the spectacular and tableau-like elements of the historical drama. It is not unthinkable that this detailed realism, the lengthy and explicit stage directions and the rounded portraiture of both central and peripheral characters in *The Pillars of Society* owe something to the Meiningen theatre. But the influence can only have been marginal, for Ibsen had already written the first act and parts of the second by the time of his visit to Meiningen, and there are no signs in the remaining acts of any change of direction in the wake of his visit.[15]

It was rather the case that the Meiningen theatre learned from him. As the theatre's bold production of *Ghosts* in 1886 showed, their new ideas and approaches could also be applied to the new drama of contemporary life. By that time, however, responsibility for the rejuvenation of European theatre along naturalist, modern lines had passed into the hands of men such as Otto Brahm in Germany and André Antoine in France.[16]

LATE SUMMER IN TYROL

Early in August 1876, Henrik, Suzannah and Sigurd fled from the noise and chaos of the big city and sought the quieter surroundings of the mountains. This time their travels took them to Gossensass, a small mountain village just south of the Brenner Pass. It was a very average sort of place – a nest of houses, a station and a church, ringed around by tall mountains. Ibsen was accompanied by Lorenz Dietrichson and other friends from Munich. Throughout the month a number of other travelling Norwegians visited the family.

One of these was Edvard Grieg, who had arrived in Germany to attend the premiere of *Der Ring des Nibelungen* in Bayreuth. On the train journey down he had got to know a young Norwegian writer named John Paulsen, who was travelling to broaden his education. Ibsen had invited Grieg to pay him a visit, and when he did so he took Paulsen along with him. This was how the young writer got to meet the great man who would play such a significant role in his own life.

He never forgot that first encounter. It took place when they arrived in Gossensass on a grey, cloudy August evening, just after the rain had cleared. He saw the writer walking along the dirt track leading up to the station in his black velvet coat 'with decorations and ribbons, the blindingly white linen, the elaborately knotted necktie, the very correct black top hat, those discreet gestures, that reserved manner'. More than anything else he reminded Paulsen of a bridegroom off to meet his beloved.

The Ibsens spent the next two months in these idyllic surroundings, along with Dietrichson, Grieg and Paulsen. Bracing walks in the mountains, long meals taken at the village's solitary restaurant, convivial evenings drinking and telling stories. Ibsen frequently invited Paulsen to accompany him on his walks, and a friendship arose between the two. Ibsen quickly took the young native of Bergen under his wing, offering him fatherly advice and supporting his applications for stipends. Gestures such as this were as rare for him as they were everyday matters for Bjørnson. The meeting between Ibsen and Grieg must have been accompanied by slight tension on both sides. It was the first time they had met since the performance of *Peer Gynt* at the Christiania Theatre in February. It seems, however, that they had managed to put the difficulties associated with that enterprise behind them, and Grieg remained a great admirer of Ibsen's work. At the personal level, however, his expectations were always guarded:

> A person who has abandoned himself so completely to a suspicion of others can never seem warm and friendly in company, no matter how truthful he may be.

Paulsen also noticed the way Ibsen kept his distance, and something of that same suspicion. That Ibsen had good reason to be suspicious of Paulsen is another matter. He would know why soon enough.

THE LONG WINTER

Winter arrived early in Gossensass that year, with the first snow falling in September. The Norwegians decided it was time to leave. Grieg returned home to Norway, while John Paulsen accompanied the Ibsen family to the little country village of Kaltern, a few hours' train journey away, where the summer lingered on. Ham and beer gave way to grapes and wine. In company with Paulsen, Ibsen took up fishing again, one of the few outdoor activities he had become interested in during his walking trips in the Norwegian mountains. It seems he still had the knack – he got bite after bite while Paulsen's line drooped limply over the side of the boat. By the end of September the family were back in Munich, in time for Sigurd to begin school. John Paulsen accompanied them and spent the autumn in the city.

Even before leaving Kaltern, Ibsen had written to Hegel that his future on the German stage was looking bright: in October *The Vikings at Helgeland* was being staged at the Burgtheater in Vienna and the Hoftheater in Dresden, it was in rehearsal in Leipzig, and was being revived in Munich. The following month *The Pretenders* was due to be performed in Schwerin. Emma Klingenfeld's translation of *Lady Inger of Østråt* was now complete, and theatres in Meiningen and Munich had expressed a wish to perform it.

'I'm well on the way to becoming a German writer,' he writes to Emil Stang in Kristiania. 'There's no denying it pays much better than being a writer at home, and I really can't afford to ignore that side of things.'

He was probably counting on a good income from these German productions, but in his enthusiasm he overlooked one thing: in the absence of a copyright agreement between Norway and Germany there was no guarantee he would enjoy the same advantages as German writers. Back in Munich he imposed limits on his social life. Out with drinking, in with work. He followed a daily routine of almost military precision: after a breakfast of black coffee and a slice of wholewheat bread he worked until lunch at one o'clock. In the early afternoon he strolled the streets alone among the shop windows and the people. After supper it was back to work, this time with his pipe for company. He was still in touch with the Krokodile, but by the winter the daily Frühschoppen at the Hotel Achatz had become a weekly affair. Occasionally he would meet Dietrichson after work for a glass of wine in one of the city's cafes.[17]

* * *

Three years had passed since his last completed play, and a year since he had started work on the new one. This was not necessarily a case of writer's block, for his sustained efforts to break through into the German market had taken a great deal of his time. He probably felt under pressure. One evening, when Didrik Grønvold visited, he found Ibsen pacing back and forth in the living room in a rage. It turned out that he had told John Paulsen about his new play. Naturally, the budding young writer had been unable to keep quiet about it and spoken of it to a Norwegian journalist. He had, however, misunderstood the title, so that Ibsen suffered the shock not only of reading about his own unfinished play in a Norwegian newspaper, but of reading that the play was to be called *The Pills of Society* (*Samfundets Piller*)![18]

The Grønvold brothers understood that friendship with Henrik Ibsen had to be based on discretion and respect for the great writer's private affairs. There is nothing to suggest that John Paulsen was blessed with the same insight.

The fact that Ibsen spent much of his time alone in the autumn of 1876 need not necessarily have been because he needed peace in which to write. His increasing attraction towards the idea of dramas of contemporary life involved a break with the aesthetic ideals of his friends in the Krokodile: perhaps he felt he was moving away from them? Paul Heyse complained to John Paulsen of how difficult it was to get Ibsen to visit or meet somewhere for a drink. He was welcome, but would not respond. Yet this was hardly a question of a formal break with his circle of German friends, and as late as the summer of 1878 Ibsen and Heyse were in each other's company almost daily.

Ibsen had become increasingly dismissive of his Norwegian acquaintances too, apparently because he had learned that people spoke disparagingly of Suzannah's talents as a hostess and of the family's living quarters. The justice or otherwise of these complaints about Suzannah's cooking has never been finally established, but a number of visitors were moved to comment on the furnishings in the Ibsen home.

'I can still see that very large living room,' wrote Herman Bang many years later, 'a strangely empty-seeming room, with pieces of rented furniture that stared at each other like strangers. A random selection of paintings hung on the walls, along with family portraits of people looking either very shy or highly astonished, as though these Norwegian ladies and gentlemen were asking themselves, in confusion, why and how they had arrived at such a place.'

Within this impersonal room sat Henrik Ibsen like a man 'who by chance found himself here and at any moment might be here no longer'.

The description of the Ibsens' apartment as a hotel room masquerading as a home for itinerants is striking, and yet it is hard to gauge really how much the domestic interior and the quality of their hospitality meant to the social life of the tenants. Whenever Ibsen was fully preoccupied with writing his life was organised to facilitate the process as much as possible, which meant daily routines divided into sessions of writing followed by visits to cafes. On a daily basis, and always at the same hour, he was to be found at the Café Maximilian, always in the same seat and directly opposite a mirror that gave him a view of the entrance, so that he could see all the comings and goings without turning round. Here he would read newspapers and observe the life around him. Once, when a German writer was tactless enough to approach him at his table not once but several times, he complained to Paulsen: Can you imagine, the man thought he was simply sitting there drinking beer and completely failed to understand that he was actually hard at work?

There were other and more welcome interruptions to work than tiresome Germans. During the spring a new edition of *Love's Comedy* appeared in Danish, and Ibsen sent the German edition of *Lady Inger of Østråt* to a long list of German theatres. In April the play was accepted by the Nationaltheater in Berlin, and *The League of Youth* was announced for Munich in the autumn. All the while he continued to work on the new play. He had promised Hegel it would be completed in the summer. Work was interrupted in late April and early May when the family left Schönfeldstrasse and moved into an apartment on Schellingstrasse 53, on the third floor, in the same central part of the city. Ibsen complained that the old apartment was too noisy for him to work properly. By the middle of June he had finished, and at once set about making the fair copy. Over July and August he sent the play to Hegel one act at a time, as was his habit.

Ibsen could lay down his pen, relax his daily routines and meet his friends again. The long winter was over.

LAUREL WREATHS AND NEW LEATHER GLOVES

There was no repeat of the trip to Tyrol that summer of 1877, but the autumn involved a lot of travelling. Ibsen had been invited to Sweden to attend celebrations of the 400th anniversary of the University of Uppsala in September, and offered the award of an honorary doctorate. Ibsen was not a man to say no. In fact, he had been using the title of Doctor from at least 1869, though lacking the necessary qualifications. Perhaps he thought that, as a recipient of an annual writer's wage, the title was his by right; after all, Andreas Munch received his literary wage in the form of a chair as associate professor, and it was common among German writers to assume the title – why should he be left out?

Now the title would become official in Sweden, while Suzannah and Sigurd enjoyed an extended stay in the west of Norway. On 9 August mother and son boarded the train to Hamburg, from where their journey would continue by steamer to Bergen. This left Henrik a grass widow at home in Munich, a rare event. Usually he was alone only when he was away travelling. At home there would almost always be the three of them.

The sudden change was noticeable.

'Dear Ibsen,' Suzannah writes on the day of her arrival in Bergen, 'how are you, I think of you every day, you will drop us a couple of lines, it feels like such a long time since I left but it's only 5 days.'

Now there was only him, but Henrik knew how to make good use of the stolen happiness that comes with life as a grass widower. Work continued, the final act of the new play was despatched to Hegel on 20 August. He ate his main meal alone, or with friends at Schleich, one of his favourite restaurants. He spent the evenings in peace at home or in company with Marcus Grønvold, and in the course of the summer a couple of friends who were passing through called in. Ole Bull, who was giving a concert in the city, dropped by, so did – wonder of wonders – Georg Brandes. Recently married, he arrived with his wife Gerda, who had previously been married to Adolf Strodtmann, both his and Ibsen's translator.

This meeting was hardly more successful than the last. Brandes soon realised that Ibsen had not read anything he had written since their previous encounter three years earlier.

'I can't tell you,' he wrote later to Holger Drachmann, 'how disappointing it was to discover that he was completely unfamiliar with my development over the last few years.'

Otherwise Ibsen made ready for the trip to Sweden and wrote anxious letters to Suzannah and Sigurd, who had arrived in Bergen in mid-August. It was the first time Sigurd had visited his mother's home town, and the second time he had been in Norway after leaving for Italy with his parents at the age of four. People were impressed by his worldly ways and how well he spoke Norwegian. The hotel swarmed with old friends from Suzannah's Bergen past. All of them asked Suzannah to say hello to Henrik for them, and in return each received a portrait photograph of the great writer.

Suzannah was back home again, and yet still a stranger who observed the city and its people with a calculating distance that was as continental as it was Ibsenian. On the steamer from Hamburg she forgot that she was surrounded by Norwegians and in a loud voice confided to Sigurd that she thought she was dressed much more elegantly and fashionably than the other women. To Henrik she wrote that the inhabitants of Bergen seemed to her like people 'straight out of *The Pillars of Society*, even including Rörlund, so much so that Sigurd said he couldn't fathom how you could have known all this, including how the townspeople all flock down to the harbour, yes, it was all there'.

Like any German tourists they went walking in the mountains, where for the most part they found themselves surrounded by English ramblers. Henrik was slightly alarmed at her news.

'I hope you are enjoying yourselves up there; but be extremely cautious at all times,' he urges his wife. 'And look after Sigurd, and your money, and don't let the locals fleece you.'

He writes the same day to his son:

Now you promise me you will be careful on land and at sea; the slightest carelessness can have the most dreadful consequences.

The dangers are plenty for an eighteen-year-old boy travelling in Norway; the fact that he was being looked after by a mother hen was no reassurance to the cockerel back home in Munich:

> Of course, you must try to meet some of the schoolboys in Bergen; but be careful you do not spend too much time on the water, and no sailboat trips!

Suzannah's reply was hardly going to reassure him. In this letter she described how she and Sigurd had set out on a walk from Odda and been surprised by a storm. With the help of a local guide they were lucky enough to find shelter in time. So all ended well, and Henrik should just see how well Sigurd looked after all the exercise and the home-cooking. But he probably felt more at home in Bergen.

Nothing had changed in the Ibsen family physiognomy, the natural state of which remained on display in the form of everyday life as lived in urbane Munich. One who witnessed this everyday life was Ludvig Josephson, who visited the family as often as he could during his summer holidays in Europe. Like other visitors, he was struck in particular by the rituals surrounding the evening meal, in which Sigurd arrived last at the table, bowed deeply to his parents – 'like a stranger' – and silently took his seat. This silence lasted almost throughout the meal. If something were said, whether by Suzannah or Henrik, Sigurd's reply was brief, and delivered in a slow and formal manner. At the end of the meal he again bowed deeply before leaving the room in silence. Josephson had observed the same rituals in Dresden, and wondered greatly at them, as did all who have described their observations of Sigurd at home with his parents.

However, Bergliot, Sigurd's wife in later life, noted that things were not necessarily quite so subdued when guests were not present. But the stories show how important it was for the family of three to protect their inner lives from the outside world.

* * *

While Suzannah and Sigurd were still wandering in the mountains Ibsen made his way to Stockholm, travelling via Stettin. On 4 September he made his way to Uppsala, where celebrations of the oldest university in Norden were due to get under way the following day. He knew what was in store for him – 'after the programme tomorrow the DEMON drink runs riot, that's to say, the Uppsala train leaves'.

There would be no shortage of the demon drink, or of anything else for that matter. Never before had the ancient university celebrated itself with so much pomp and circumstance. The award of the honorary doctorate took place on 6 September at a ceremony held in Latin, and conducted by the archbishop and three professors. Ibsen and the other honorary doctors were crowned with laurel wreaths, which they wore for the remainder of the day. Following the ceremony there was a banquet in the presence of the king in the Botanical Gardens, in a large pavilion specially constructed for the occasion. Mock turtle soup was among the delicacies served to the 1,500 guests. After the meal a party was held in the gardens attended by some 8,000 people. The climax of the evening was a firework display and a spectacular 'electric sun' which, alas, malfunctioned.

Perhaps it was all a bit too much. Dietrichson and Ibsen retired to a small cellar bar where several other guests of honour had sought refuge, Carl Snoilsky and Viktor Rydberg among them. Ibsen at once began to direct the conversation, as he was capable of doing if the atmosphere was good and the gathering small. In the evening he was among the guests at an exclusive gathering in Uppsala Castle, still with the laurel wreath on his head – by this time of day probably slightly askew.

'I have spoken daily to the king in Uppsala,' he proudly reports to Suzannah, 'and he at once made me feel warmly welcome.'

Between monarchs and meals he used the time to promote his new play. Before leaving, he had asked Hegel to send the play to theatres in Copenhagen and Gothenburg. He planned to deliver a copy personally to Erik af Edholm, Lord Chamberlain and director at the Kongelige Teater. In Stockholm the dinners and the receptions continued. Ibsen was invited to a banquet hosted by Oscar II at Drottningholm with 700 guests. He used the occasion to deliver *The Pillars of Society* to Edholm. In response Edholm invited him to dine at the Rydberg, the hotel he was staying at, and arranged an evening in Ibsen's honour that included a performance of *The Vikings at Helgeland*, which had had a run at the theatre the previous autumn.[19]

All in all, the stay in Uppsala and Stockholm confirmed to the full the status Ibsen had acquired following the publication of *Brand* eleven years earlier. Female members of the cultural elite were particular admirers. It was said that Fredrika Limnell, who had been his hostess during his visit in 1869, immersed herself in the most profound passages of his works: 'The more impenetrable it all was, the more impressed did she become.' Fru Limnell's fascination with Ibsen was powerful, and typical of the audience she represented. Of *Emperor and Galilean* she wrote that 'I could not stop myself from wondering and thinking about it, because to me it seemed possessed of something magnificent and mystical – to be an enormous riddle to which a solution *must* exist. It addressed me ceaselessly with its unanswered question.'

In Sweden as elsewhere in Europe, women were important consumers and communicators of literature. Women such as Fredrika Limnell, Anne Charlotte

Leffler, Alfhild Agrell and Ellen Key were not only readers with an unusual dedication to Ibsen; they were also hostesses and participants in an extensive circle of literary salons that thrived in Stockholm, just as Magdalene Thoresen had been in Bergen, though there in a more modest form. For over a century the literary salons had been important intermediaries of art and culture in Europe, arenas in which the traditional monarchical and aristocratic production and consumption of culture were open to new cultural impulses from bourgeois society. The continuity was exemplified by the Limnell family, in which the husband held a prominent position in the railways, while the wife cultivated her literary salon. In this way they were very much typical of their times and social class, introducing the cultural institutions of the aristocracy into the bourgeois world.

In a practical sense it was Lorentz Dietrichson who introduced Ibsen into these circles, both on his visit in 1869 and now in 1877. The art historian was a much respected man in the Stockholm salons; years after he had introduced him to the treasures of Rome, he was still acting as Ibsen's cicerone.[20]

* * *

On 12 September, Ibsen writes the only letter of the trip to his wife. He simply did not have the time. He admits that the ceremonies, the dinners and the receptions were almost too much. Anyway, Suzannah and Sigurd were able to follow proceedings in the Bergen newspaper that carried daily reports from the celebrations.

But the newly created honorary doctor longed to be back home in Munich. En route he stopped over in Copenhagen, spending the night at the Hotel d'Angleterre at Hegel's expense. It was the second meeting between the two, and the publisher honoured the celebrated writer with a large dinner party at his country home. The award of the honorary doctorate was news in Denmark too; Ibsen noticed that the newspapers thought him the most celebrated of the guests at Uppsala, a view that he shared. Quite simply, he was the centre of attention wherever he went.

Georg Brandes felt rather differently. If he had expected Ibsen to get in touch with him while in the capital he was mistaken. Brandes was absolutely not a welcome figure in the sorts of circles in which Ibsen was now moving.

The following summer Brandes shares his distrust of Ibsen with Bjørnson.

'He seems to me shy and deeply inhibited,' writes Brandes. 'Not especially articulate, not very forthcoming, suspicious and cautious even towards those who have never done him anything but good.'

He goes on to criticise Ibsen's shameless social climbing and his eagerness to please the upper class, his pathetic chasing after decorations, and especially his never risking his popularity by 'supporting causes that are not popular among the "right sort" ' – in other words that he did not put his pen at Brandes' service in his recent struggles. Maybe the Danes' recent enthusiasm for Bjørnson after *The Editor* and *A Bankrupt* had increased the distance between him and Ibsen but, regardless of that, the gap between them had been getting wider all the time. So the traditional view of Brandes and Ibsen as allies over-looks that Brandes at this juncture must have entertained grave doubts about whether he and Ibsen were fighting the same battle at all.[21]

A month after Ibsen's departure from Copenhagen, Brandes faced the consequences of his exposed position at home and moved to Berlin, where he remained for the next six years. With that he had acted upon Ibsen's passionate advice to make himself the enemy of all and had chosen the life in exile that Ibsen had been urging upon him all along.

Back in Munich, where he arrived on 20 September, Ibsen spent a few days wandering, alone and listless through the empty rooms in Schellingstrasse – 'I can't taste my food, the evenings are long, cold and sad, I spend the entire time alone at home.' Marcus Grønvold was out of town, and he didn't care for any other company. But surely it couldn't be long now before Suzannah and Sigurd returned, if the boy was to be in time to register at Maximilian's College for the last term before his final exam? Henrik writes a letter to his wife; will she do him a favour on the way home?

> I would be so pleased if you could find the time to buy 6 pairs of gloves for me in Copenhagen. Top-quality thin leather, preferably dark brown, size 8?

He had bought such a pair himself in Copenhagen for only one krone and seventy øre in a shop on Kongens Nytorv. If Suzannah did as he asked then Henrik could look back on a decent profit from the autumn: an honorary doctorate from the Swedes, a flood of receptions, banquets and dinners, and seven brand new pairs of leather gloves. Minimum requirements, with winter around the corner, for a man who was about to give society a real shaking up with his latest play.

PILLAR OR PILLORY?

The action in *The Pillars of Society* takes place in a small Norwegian coastal town. Consul Bernick, owner of a shipyard and a respected local citizen, lives here. He is married to Betty, and they have a son named Olaf who is thirteen years of age. On the surface everything seems idyllic, until Bernick's murky past gradually emerges. In his youth he betrayed Betty's half-sister, Lona Hessel, in order to get his hands on Betty's inheritance. He was also unfaithful to Betty during the period of their engagement, being caught in his lover's bedroom.

The consequences of the revelation are dramatic, but Bernick manages to wriggle out of them. He persuades his brother-in-law Johan to take the blame, since he is about to emigrate to America anyway. In his long absence Bernick spreads rumours to the effect that Johan is also a thief. In fact it is Bernick himself who is responsible for the empty bank box.

As the action begins, no one in the little town is aware of the consul's misdeeds. In the opening act he is seen among a group of respectable citizens who are planning to bring the railway to the town. That these same respectable citizens have bought up the land through which the railway is planned to run is another secret that will presently be revealed. The first crack in the idyll occurs with the return of Johan from America, with Lona Hessel. Johan threatens to reveal what he knows of Bernick's past. Bernick is afraid; his whole life rests on his reputation as an upright and responsible pillar of society. Initially, Johan plans to return to America. He takes Lona with him, and Dina Dorf, the daughter of the woman Bernick had the affair with. Dina and Johan plan to marry over there, but Johan promises his brother-in-law that he will return, and that the truth will emerge.

Bernick has one last hope, and it is one that he hardly dare admit even to himself: he thinks Johan and Dina will be sailing on *Indian Girl*, a ship that he, as a shipyard owner, knows to be unseaworthy. Hopefully the truth about all his misdeeds will soon be lying at the bottom of the sea. But the travellers choose another ship, and at the last minute *Indian Girl* is prevented from sailing. Bernick realises just how far he was prepared to go, and finally, under pressure from Lona, he confesses his sins – or at least most of them – in front of the crowd that has come to hail him as a pillar of society. With that the consul can start a new life, free from hypocrisy and lies, a life lived 'in the spirit of freedom and truth'.

* * *

Oddly enough, among Norwegian newspapers both *Morgenbladet* and *Dagbladet* neglected to review Ibsen's new play when it was published on 11 October 1877; and of the reviews that did appear the verdict was mixed. Arne Garborg was surprised at the edifying thought that underpinned the play, instead of the 'bitter and venomous bile' that had become Ibsen's signature. But if this was indeed the case, Garborg asks, then what lies behind this remarkable turnabout?

> It was 'doubt' that made a writer of him; if he should relinquish doubt, then just maybe that means the end for him.

Wasn't Ibsen too old to be changing direction?

> I have a hunch that, with *The Pillars of Society*, we see a talent in decline.

So much for Garborg's hunches.

Writing in *Aftenbladet*, Ditmar Meidell shook his head over the fact that contemporary writers appeared to have swapped their lyres for a microscope. It no longer seemed as though they wanted to 'build stairways to heaven for us mere mortals', now they were grabbing society by the collar and subjecting it to an inquisitorial cross-examination. Unlike both Garborg and Meidell, Kristian Elster in *Dagsposten* by and large rejects the idea that *The Pillars of Society* is social criticism but reads the play as a moral and psychological drama. In Denmark, too, opinions were divided over whether it was social criticism or a psychological study of morality. Edvard Brandes was in no doubt: *The Pillars of Society* was so artfully constructed that 'both press and public are able to pretend it expresses no particular message'. Georg Brandes was more positive, but by no means wildly enthusiastic, and saw no grounds to review the play.[22] At the other end of the scale was Johanne Luise Heiberg, who sent a letter to Ibsen deeply regretting the turn his writing had taken. She visited the 'Temple of Art' to get away from 'the pressures of reality' and could not understand why a spiritual talent like Ibsen wanted to drag the corruptions of society onto the stage when the proper place for them was in a court of law!

And yet Fru Heiberg had no doubts that Ibsen had written a hit play. And a hit it was. *The Pillars of Society* conquered stages not only throughout Scandinavia but also in Germany. Ibsen had handed performance rights outside Copenhagen to August Rasmussen, and Rasmussen was responsible for the world premiere at Odense Theatre on 14 November 1877. According to the newspapers it was well received, as it was when it opened in Copenhagen four days later. Edvard Fallesen, the director, had tried to persuade Ibsen to postpone publication until after the premiere, but Ibsen had refused. He earned more in royalties from the book, in his opinion, because theatres paid him at a lower rate than they did Danish dramatists. It was, moreover, artistically undesirable that the public should get to know the play through a performance, which was, after all, an interpretation, rather than through the printed text. This was a principle to which Ibsen adhered for the remainder of his career.

The disagreement with Fallesen and the theatre reflects an interesting if rather obscure development in the history of literature. By giving the book precedence over the stage performance, Ibsen was claiming an increased artistic and economic control of his work.[23] The same may be said of the detailed instructions he increasingly pressed upon theatres so that performances should follow his own intentions as closely as possible. Together these developments bear witness not only to Ibsen's growing status as a writer, but to an increased autonomy for the writer and the work in general – not least in relation to the theatre as institution. In this Ibsen became a model for others, and *The Pillars of Society* marked the turning point. Which is to say: Fallesen got his way in one sense, because newspapers waited until four weeks after the premiere to review the book, and by all accounts did so at his request.

But it would be his final victory; henceforth it would be Ibsen who decided the terms under which his plays would be introduced to the public.

The Christiania Theatre was among those to feel this new power. Ludvig Josephson had resigned as director the previous spring because the committee had vetoed his prestige project, the production of opera. Ibsen was outraged that the theatre would dare to replace a talented man such as Josephson with a litterateur like Johan Vibe, in his eyes 'an absolutely incompetent man'. He simply boycotted the theatre, and sent *The Pillars of Society* instead to Den Nationale Scene in Bergen, where the play had its premiere on 30 November.[24] By that time a Swedish company had already given the play its Norwegian premiere at the old theatre in Møllergaten. In Sweden *The Pillars of Society* opened at Dramaten on 13 December 1877, where it had a highly successful run, according to the director Edholm, possibly stimulated by the revival of *Lady Inger of Østråt* and the author's personal visit to the capital a few weeks previously.

Ibsen's greatest hopes, however, were vested in Germany. And with good reason. Following the completion of a German translation of *The Pillars of Society* in November 1877, a number of German theatres put on productions of the play. In one single week it was being performed simultaneously at five different Berlin theatres. *Nationale Zeitung* wrote that its success was unique in the history of Berlin theatre. By the end of 1878 the play had been performed on twenty-seven stages, and over subsequent decades Ibsen's dramas of contemporary life would achieve at least a thousand performances on fifty Germany stages. After the performance at the Residenz-Theater in Munich, the *Allgemeine Zeitung* and the *Müncher Neueste Nachrichsten*, the two biggest newspapers, were full of praise for the play's conscientious realism and its sheer exoticism.

Its reception in Germany, however, was just as Edvard Brandes had predicted. Reviewers tended to overlook the play's social criticism and instead concentrate on its morality and its study of individual psychology. No doubt this had much to do with Ibsen's drama, but it is probably also true, as some have maintained, that literary life in Germany was disposed to this sort of interpretation. German literature and philosophy had very different concerns to the social realism that had for some time been dominant in France, and in due course in Scandinavia too. It remained dominated by a poetic realism and a deep idealism that could have a neutralising effect on provocative tendencies in literature. So Germans embraced the works of Ibsen, as they did the works of Bjørnson, Garborg and other Norwegian writers, without reading them in quite the way intended by the writers, or in the same way as these were read in Scandinavia.[25]

While *The Pillars of Society* gave Ibsen his definitive breakthrough in Germany, it is important to remember that it was as an author of historical plays that he first came to the attention of German audiences. It was actually a perfect progression: Ibsen broke through in Germany by appealing to the fascination for history in German literature at about the time this was starting to wane, and then with even greater force became a model for a younger generation of naturalists who in the 1880s had started to reject the fashion for spectacular historical dramas that had dominated the German stage for so long.

One of that younger generation was Otto Brahm, whose theatre company Die Freie Bühne in 1889 created an arena for the performance of naturalistic drama in Germany. Looking back on his career, Brahm recalled that it was during the production of *The Pillars of Society* that he and others like him had their 'first inklings of a new sort of creative art, and felt for the first time that we stood face to face with people from our own times – people we could believe in – depicted with a critical insight that was valid for the whole of existing society'.

* * *

The position of *The Pillars of Society* as the first of Ibsen's dramas of contemporary life and, with that, the beginning of that run of plays that would bring him international fame and historical status, remains unchallenged; yet it is nevertheless difficult to place the work within the context of his oeuvre.

The formal development is the easiest to trace, the dramatic techniques that so impressed the critics. Ibsen gives us a tightly plotted play in which the main and the sub-plots are bound together in a natural and unforced way, something which could not be said of his only previous drama of contemporary life, *The League of Youth*. The everyday dialogue flowed with the same natural ease, crafted in such a way that each character had his or her own characteristic way of speaking, adding to the impression of the characters as rounded and living human beings. Most of the action takes place in Consul Bernick's conservatory, in which the rear wall largely consists of plate glass, giving the audience a view of the garden and the road outside. The furnishing is careful and economical. Ibsen introduced here the main features of the dramatic setting he would develop further in later plays: the bounded space (the bourgeois living room); the elegantly achieved connection between indoors and outdoors (here: through the plate-glass wall), which enabled a combination of inside and outside without recourse to a change of scenery; and not least that in *The Pillars of Society* the scenography becomes a meaningful element that can be played off against the dialogue, as when, for example, Lona Hessel says that she is used to the air on the prairie, and Bernick replies: 'Yes, there really is something quite suffocating in here.' Many will also find a metascenic level in Rummel's remark that 'a person's house ought to be like a glass cabinet', in other words, a stage at which the surrounding world can peer, rather as the audience peers at the events taking place on the stage. The glass cabinet thus becomes a metaphor for the theatre itself.[26]

Seen from this perspective, it is obvious that *The Pillars of Society* was not just Ibsen's first realistic drama of contemporary life, but also his textbook example of the advanced, multi-dimensional and self-reflecting drama that points beyond realism, in the simple sense of reproducing reality. From this some might go on to assume that Ibsen was an early modernist, whereas others interpret the metatheatrical dimension as an expression of the complexity of realism that does not necessarily make Ibsen a modernist.[27] Either way, the play seems like a transitional work, and in the light of what was to follow a number of the techniques seem undeniably immature. The question is, how much of the play does one understand by interpreting it in the light of posterity rather than using a contemporary perspective? One problem, pointed out by both Edvard Brandes and Kristian Elster, concerns the final scene, which appears to weaken the play's social criticism in favour of a vision of reconciliation and idealism concerning 'the spirit of truth and freedom – *they* are the pillars of society'.

Should *The Pillars of Society* be read as a social drama or a didactic exercise in morality and psychology? Is it fundamentally critical, or idealistic?

Posterity remains undecided whether the play's closing scene should be read literally or ironically. The former reading implies that the play conveys a 'naïve' and idealistic belief that the truth can liberate, that a man like Bernick can learn from his mistakes and grow. An ironic reading implies the opposite, that Bernick's confession is tactically determined and that, through his senti-mental and selective confession he actually avoids taking responsibility for his sins. A third possibility is to read the play in a heroic-existential light, in which Bernick's motives are accepted at face value, his striving for power and desire to harmonise his own motives with the general well-being of all.[28]

What was Ibsen's own view?

In a letter to Frederik Hegel he points out that the play can be considered an 'antidote' to *The League of Youth* and stresses that it will 'probably stir up quite a few debates about some of the most important questions of our times'. One of these important questions he had got straight from the newspapers. For several years, the English parliamentarian Samuel Plimsoll had been campaigning for the state to take action against cynical ship-owners who let unseaworthy ships set out on voyages in the knowledge that they would collect the insurance when the ships sank. The cause attracted international attention not least in a maritime nation such as Norway, and the Plimsoll 'coffin-ships' were written of in *Dagbladet*, and debated in *Norsk Veritas* during the time Ibsen was in Norway in 1874.[29] The critical bite was all the sharper because the play reflected a recognisable social reality in a broader context. The conflict between industrialist and worker, for example, illustrated by Bernick and Aune, the ship-builder. Both the environment and some of the themes were obviously based on Ibsen's own memories of Grimstad.[30] So there were good reasons to read the play the way Garborg did, as a social drama containing a critique of the business ethics of the upper class, though for many the concluding scene subverted the criticism. Additionally the play highlighted the position of women, principally through Lona Hessel. She is critical of the patriarchal society and demands the right to become herself, though some will protest that even this issue is dealt with cautiously.[31]

But if Ibsen was indeed preoccupied with toning down the potential for social criticism present in the play, what might the reasons be? A possible answer may lie hidden in a letter he writes to King Oscar II in September 1827. He opens the letter by pointing out the tendency in literature to attack institutions on which, in his view, society is dependent:

> I therefore think that it might be advantageous to guide the views and thoughts of the public in a different direction, and demonstrate that the dishonesty lies not in the institutions but within the social individual; that it is the spiritual life of the individual that needs to be cleansed and liberated.

It would be easier to dismiss this as an opportunistic toning down of the controversial elements for the benefit of 'Your Gracious Majesty' were it not for the fact that the words are remarkably similar to those used several years earlier to Brandes, in Ibsen's tirades on the subject of the revolution of the human spirit. In the earliest notes for the play, from 1870, he expresses similar ideas:

> There is a hidden meaning; something symbolic, liberation from all the restrictive decrees; a new life, free and beautiful. This is what the play is about.

No matter how much the play changed in the course of the writing, he may well have held on to this fundamental idea, and indeed it can only have been reinforced by the impressions made on him by the Franco-German war, his reckoning with the heritage of revolution, his contempt for politics and the institutions of the state, the feeling of living through a time in which everything was breaking up, and in which the individual formed the only fixed point. In the 'Letter in Rhyme' in 1875 he had written of how 'we are sailing with a corpse in the hold!', how the burdens of history and the complexities of society's demands were stifling the individual urge to self-realisation and the revolt of the human spirit. But how to depict this revolution in dramatic form? How could the inner demand for freedom be expressed without its being drowned out by the general din of society? This was something he had tried to write about in *Emperor and Galilean*, but there he had the advantage of dealing with the past. Did he perhaps find it difficult to apply his literary programme to a drama of contemporary life? At the very least he had no intention of allowing the social criticism in the play to overshadow his principal theme, which was the need for inner freedom.

Whether the concluding scene is read literally or ironically, Ibsen's literary project remained at heart the same; if the world was to become a better place, then the change must begin at the level of the individual.

LAURA KIELER'S MARRIAGE

The Pillars of Society appeared in a first edition of over 6,000 copies and was swiftly followed by a second printing of 4,000.[32] The figures must have impressed Ibsen's literary colleagues in Germany, where the average first edition of a novel was under 1,000 copies, while a dramatist could hardly count on any book sales at all. In this respect the Scandinavian book market was well in advance of the German. The play was largely responsible for a record income of 17,554 kroner in 1877. Most of this came from Scandinavian book sales, while income from stage performances was relatively modest. He had obviously overestimated the potential of income from German theatres, largely owing to the lack of a rights agreement between Norway and Germany.

The greater the success he enjoyed abroad, the greater the relative economic loss he suffered, even if his income increased in real terms. Some years he earned most from book sales, other years it was from the theatres. Ignoring the unusually high income from the sale of his collected works in 1898, he earned about the same from stage performances as he did from book sales in the years between 1870 and 1900. To this must be added the dividends from his shareholding, which became significant from about 1877 and which evened out the disparities in income from the other two sources.

Still, the lack of a rights agreement was costing him money; this was particularly noticeable following the publication of *The Pillars of Society*. From the twenty-seven productions of the play in German theatres he earned not a single krone in 1877, and in the following year just a few hundred.[33] Ibsen must have felt a massive irritation, not just at the financial loss, but also at his failure to prevent the publication of pirate translations of dubious quality. Emma Klingenfeld's authorised version of *The Pillars of Society* was rapidly challenged by pirate translations made by Emil Jonas and Wilhelm Lange. Only the Nationaltheater in Berlin and the Hoftheater in Munich used the authorised translation.[34] In the spring of 1876 Ibsen had enrolled in the German Dramatists Union and allowed it to collect royalties owing from most of the German theatres, but the amounts involved were insignificant.[35]

For Ibsen the demand for a rise in his annual writer's wage was closely related to the financial loss he suffered owing to the lack of an international rights agreement. Norway, he pointed out in a letter of 1877 to Sverdrup, president of the Storting, profited from the lack because it meant European literature and drama could be published and performed free of charge back home. He used this argument to advance his claim for a rise in the annual wage as compensation for the loss that he (and a handful of others) endured as writers in foreign markets so that Norwegians might enjoy free access to the literature of other countries:

> Give each of us a 200 spd. increase in the Writer's Wage as compensation for what we must sacrifice out of consideration for the needs of others.

This was his reasoning, and it was sound: the writer's wage was not a bounty but a legal right to financial compensation for the lucrative and lawless state of affairs that no one with any real understanding of the situation could deny. Sverdrup was duly convinced, and in February he put forward a motion for a general increase in the Writer's Wage along the lines suggested by Ibsen. Once again, the motion was defeated.

Ibsen was left hoping for an improvement in the copyright protection laws. An important step had been taken the preceding year with the 'Law of June 8 1876 concerning the protection of the so-called literary copyright', which guaranteed that a play could not be performed in Norway without the consent of the author, with the exception of performances of extracts without scenery and props. This latter was largely a matter of interpretation, and on several occasions Ibsen protested against readings and performances of extracts that in his opinion contravened the spirit of the law. Then on 1 January 1878 a decree came into force that guaranteed the same legal protection in both territories to Norwegian and Swedish writers. There was thus a degree of control over the Swedish market. The following year a similar agreement came into force in Denmark. The Bern Convention of 1886 finally brought order to the chaos of copyright control. Ten years later Norway became the first of the Scandinavian countries to sign the agreement. Until then the bilateral agreements prevailed and these, to Ibsen's great frustration, did not apply to the new market that had opened up for him in Germany.[36]

So despite his success in Germany, the main sources of his income remained Norway, Sweden and Denmark, and in that respect Henrik Ibsen was and remained for many years primarily a Scandinavian writer.

* * *

One of his most fervent admirers back home was a young girl who had devoured *Brand* with such intensity that, still only seventeen or eighteen years old, she went ahead and wrote a sequel to the drama. She was far from being the only person whose life was changed by Ibsen's work, but she was one of the few who had the experience, in return, of changing *his* life.

Laura Kieler was born and raised in Norway and at the age of twenty-three had settled in Denmark. There she made her literary debut with *Brand's Daughters* (1869), by her own account as help for 'those anxious souls in whom Ibsen's "Brand" had caused such distress'. Following some good reviews she sent a copy to Ibsen, who wrote a long and admiring letter in return. When the two met each other in Copenhagen in the autumn of 1870 he invited her to Dresden. She accepted the invitation, and the following year they were together almost daily during the period of her visit. She thus became the first in that succession of young girls with literary interests with whom Ibsen formed attachments for shorter or longer periods. 'Songbird' (Lerkefugl) was the sonorous nickname he gave her, but Laura could do rather more than sing. In due course she became a recognised writer in Norway and Denmark.[37]

Something else that distinguishes her from Ibsen's other songbirds was the tragedy that struck her in the spring and summer of 1878, which would have such serious consequences for her, for Henrik Ibsen, and for world drama. A couple of years earlier, her husband Victor Kieler had contracted tuberculosis. His doctor advised him to travel south, but there could be no question of that. Victor, it emerged, was an extremely unpredictable man capable of flying into a rage in matters concerning money. Laura took out a loan in secret and was able to persuade her husband to take the advice anyway. He probably believed that she had made the money from her writing. Her plan was indeed to pay off the loan through writing, but it turned out to be more difficult than she had anticipated. Victor recovered, and on their way back home through Europe the couple visited the Ibsens in Munich. Here she confided in Suzannah the truth of what she had done. It seems that Suzannah then told Henrik.

From this point on things rapidly went downhill for Laura Kieler. Difficulties in meeting her repayments led her to take out a new loan, with the help of two guarantors. When the date for repayment of this loan arrived she was still in bed following childbirth, one of the guarantors was insolvent and being threatened with debt collectors by the other guarantor. Everything was falling apart, but she clung to one last hope. In March 1878, Suzannah received a manuscript with an accompanying letter in which Kieler begged Henrik to recommend her to Hegel.

She saw acceptance of her manuscript at the respected house of Gyldendal as her only way out.

'I can assure you that I am deeply concerned on your account and sympathise with you, who must carry such a heavy burden on your slight shoulders,' Suzannah replies. 'Believe me, I shall plead your case as forcefully as I can to Ibsen.'

On 26 March, Henrik writes to her:

> I neither can nor will recommend the enclosed manuscript Última Thule to
> Hegel.

From a purely professional point of view he gives the only answer he
reasonably can. The manuscript bears all the signs of having been hastily
written, and a recommendation from Ibsen would have left Hegel unmoved.
But even so, isn't he a little hard? He knows what lies behind her request – or
does he?

'You write in your letter of circumstances that have made this pressured
work necessary,' he continues. 'I do not understand. In a family in which the
husband is still alive it can never be necessary that a wife, such as yourself,
should have to tap her own spiritual resources in this way.'

There had to be something she was keeping quiet about, thought Ibsen. If
this was indeed the case then she should tell her husband everything as soon as
possible.

> It is inconceivable that your husband knows the full story. You must
> enlighten him; he must assume the pains and the troubles that are now
> distressing and worrying you so greatly. You have already sacrificed more
> than is acceptable.

Was he unaware of Victor Kieler's unpredictable nature, his 'demonic temper'?
Maybe he was, but was it conceivable that Victor would not, in spite of all, be
there for the wife who had sacrificed so much for him, indeed, who had perhaps
saved his life, and who now lay with their newborn child in her arms as her
world came tumbling down around her? She could not bear this alone, in
Ibsen's view. But that is precisely what Laura Kieler chooses to do. She does not
confide in her husband, and this is the very moment at which she receives a
letter from one of her two guarantors who is now on the point of losing
everything he owns for her sake. In desperation she tries to forge a promissory
note, but it doesn't work. Fears of her husband's response consume her and she
begins to behave irrationally. One day a new and beautiful item of furniture
appears in the apartment, bought by Laura to please her aesthetically inclined
husband. Finally the bubble bursts, and her husband reacts in precisely the
manner she had feared. He rages, demands a separation, and refuses her access
to the children. By this time Laura has already started to crack up; she is
admitted to a mental hospital, paralysed in her distress, wholly unable to look
after herself.

Early in August, Ibsen writes to Hegel:

As regards Fru Laura Kieler it ended, as you probably know, in a dreadful tragedy. Her husband informed us briefly that she had been admitted to a mental hospital. Do you know any more details of the matter, and whether she is in fact still there?

Hegel's reply has not survived, but a draft has, in which he relates that he has learned from several sources that Laura has been involved in a fraud, that the fraud was probably committed while she was of unsound mind and that she had probably been exploited by some usurer. That, at least, was what rumour was saying. But there was still hope for Fru Kieler. After only a month she was able to leave the asylum, and a year or two later her husband asked her if she would please come back to him. She replied that she would, reportedly so that she could be with her children again.

And it all might have ended there. Perhaps Laura Kieler would have come through this painful episode and even the most damaging and hurtful rumours would have faded over the years. But it was not to be. It would be art and not life that inflicted the greater pain on Laura. And that is worse, because while life, at its best, mutes and soothes pain, art has a tendency to nurture it and keep it alive for decades.

At least if it is art created by a writer of Henrik Ibsen's stature.

* * *

In July, Sigurd took his final exams at Das Königliche Maximilians Gymnasium. The results were, of course, outstanding. Sigurd was now ready for adult life. But not without his parents. There is nothing to suggest that any of them were considering breaking away at this juncture. The plan was for the whole family to spend the coming winter in Rome. There Sigurd would begin his studies, before all of them returned to Munich. Henrik must have looked forward to visiting Italy again. It was there he had enjoyed his most fertile period. Now he brought with him an idea for a 'new play from contemporary life', as he told Hegel in May. He does not discuss the contents, but he hoped to finish it in Rome in the course of the winter.

Did their long-term plans include Norway? According to Bergliot, Sigurd's future wife, the idea was that Sigurd would conclude his studies in his home country. But this idea seems to have appeared later, for in the summer of 1878 Munich was the home to which the family were planning to return. In the autumn Ibsen writes to his right-hand man in Norway, the bookseller Nils Lund, and cancels his order for a consignment of sour-milk cheese – 'since I no longer need it'. It is Italian wine he is longing for now. And yet he had been thinking much of his homeland in recent days, not about what awaited him there, but about all that he had left behind. A few months earlier he had sat down and written a letter to his uncle, Christian Paus:

Though one of your closest relatives, I have good reason to fear that I might almost be thought of as a stranger when you now receive these lines from one who is so far away.

So cautious, so humble.

In the eyes of outsiders it does indeed look as though I have deliberately made myself a stranger to my own family and once and for all turned my back on it. But I believe I may claim that harsh circumstances and difficulties concerning this are what are largely responsible.

What harsh circumstances? His father's tyrannical ways, the curse of the Lammer's movement? The secret pain that tore the family apart, the literary calling that compelled him to break with everything and everyone that stood in its way? But then why these confessions to an uncle who was a stranger, and why that frightened tone? It was something he had stumbled upon by chance. In a German newspaper he had read of the death of a pathetic old former merchant in a provincial Norwegian town, well known, despite his poverty, to the inhabitants of the town as the father of the writer, Henrik Ibsen. Subsequently he received a letter from Hedvig, and now, compelled by decency, he acknowledges the debt he owes to all of those who carried the filial burden for him, not just for his father's sake, but for the sake of his long-dead mother too:

And as I now offer a thank-you to all of those who have offered the departed a helping hand, that thank-you goes also for all the help and support I have known on my way through life. Dear Uncle, let me tell you, and please pass this on to my other relatives, that the burdens and responsibilities they have relieved me of in life have played an important part in making my ambitions and my aspirations here in this world come true.

He freely admits his betrayal. But the betrayal had been necessary, and the sacrifices made by the family had eased his road to literary success. And the road led on, perhaps it even ended back in his homeland? Uncle Christian learns that Henrik and Suzannah have considered moving home in a year's time, once Sigurd was fully immersed in his studies and they were free to act for themselves. Yet Ibsen remained unconvinced that he would be able to write in Norway:

The circumstances of my daily life here are much more favourable; there is spiritual freedom out here in the big world, a breadth of vision about things.

No, Norway would have to wait a while yet. Henrik, Suzannah and Sigurd spent a little over a month in the late summer warmth of the Tyrol before heading south. The original plan had been to stay in Florence for a couple of months, but Henrik longed to settle to work in familiar surroundings. At the end of September the family left Gossensass and travelled to Rome, the city that had once before been his catalyst.

IX

ROME – MUNICH – ROME

SCANDAL AMONG THE SCANDINAVIANS

Following the incorporation of the Vatican into the kingdom of Italy in 1870, Rome had finally become a part of the modern age. In 1871 the city became the capital of the country. Two years later the first area development plans were presented, followed by the building of large residential complexes, streets and public buildings. The picturesque banks of the Tiber, where Ibsen had spent his first evening in Rome with Dietrichson in 1864, were developed and walls built to counter the flooding that had plagued the city for centuries.

Yet Rome was still the Eternal City, even if Pope Pius IX felt himself a prisoner, and travellers from the north still arrived to enjoy the wine, the life, the history and the art. Jonas Lie came here in 1872 and stayed for a couple of years, and in January 1874 Bjørnson returned after completing his historical drama *King Eystein* in Florence. He spent a productive winter and spring in Rome, where he completed those two plays with contemporary settings – *The Editor* and *A Bankrupt* – and made a start on several other works. Ole Bull visited Rome at about this time too, broke and newly divorced, but a breath of fresh air as always. Other visitors included Johanne Luise Heiberg, the sculptor Christen Daae Magelssen, the painters Eilif Peterssen, Ernst Josephson (the nephew of Ludvig Josephson) and P. S. Krøyer, and the writers Victor Rydberg and Sophus Schandorph. These and others maintained and refreshed the Scandinavian colony and the Scandinavian Society and kept up traditions such as the eating of a goose on St Martin's Eve, the Christmas party and the drinking in the city's taverns.

Rome was certainly changing, and yet there was much that remained the same. Ibsen noted that the rents had risen slightly, but it was still quite cheap to live here, and the wine was as good as it had ever been. The family moved into an apartment at Via Gregoriana 46, not far from the Spanish Steps. In the early days they lived a quiet life. Dinner was brought to the house, and the rest of their meals were provided by the landlord. A few of Ibsen's old friends were still living in Rome. One was the composer Niels Ravnkilde, another the painter Julius Kronberg, whom he knew from Munich, and Magelssen, a relative of Suzannah's. Most of the remaining Scandinavians were young and unknown, though he struck up friendships with a couple of them, such as Gunnar

Heiberg, and J. P. Jacobsen, an ailing Brandesian. Edvard Brandes paid a fleeting visit and met Ibsen for the first time.

Sigurd at once enrolled at the University of Rome where he studied philosophy, history, international law, constitutional law and economics. After just a short while in the city where he had grown up he spoke fluent Italian. As for Ibsen, he dedicated his time to finishing his latest play. A new sense of purpose seemed to have possessed him, a real commitment to the new play. But Rome was no place for solitude, and soon he was to be seen out and about at the dim bars and at the Scandinavian Society, where the season's first big event was the goose party in November. Rome was wine, it was gatherings, conversations, and in due course Ibsen was helping himself to all it had to offer. After one late evening at the society, Jacobsen and Heiberg had to take an arm each and guide the drunken and irritable poet home, listening as he cursed the world for making such slow progress, mankind for its general wretchedness, and his own writing, not least his own writing.

'Poetry! – Poetry – Just poetry!' he raged as Heiberg tried to cheer him up by quoting a few lines from his verse.

Once again he moved among the Scandinavians like an enigmatic lion, giving way to outbursts, indulging his idiosyncrasies. One of these – his vanity – had become even more striking since his previous stay in Rome. At this particular time Prince Gustav, crown prince of Sweden-Norway, was visiting the city. According to Gunnar Heiberg, Ibsen and the crown prince engaged in a shadow dance with each other, each waiting for the other to proffer an invitation. As time passed and no invitation was forthcoming, Ibsen began to rage against the crown prince, casting aspersions on his intelligence, his suitability for office, even criticising his appearance. When Crown Prince Gustav finally got in touch, it was apparently on the orders of his father, King Oscar, who instructed him to bring an end to the war of attrition. Ibsen welcomed the prince's approach and responded with an invitation to visit the family at their apartment.

When he was later invited to attend a royal banquet he is said to have enjoyed himself thoroughly, and entertained the guests with amusing stories from Egypt. And as though by magic the crown prince's intelligence and appearance both underwent a dramatic improvement.

Others besides Crown Prince Gustav enjoyed Ibsen's hospitality. Young and old, the famous and the unknown were invited to the family home. Just like the crown prince they too would be treated to stories from his travels in Egypt – clearly Ibsen had found a winner to offer his guests at table. But of course this wasn't getting any plays written. All he managed that autumn were a few sporadic notes. But social life in Rome wasn't entirely a waste of time; in particular the conversations he probably had with J. P. Jacobsen on the theory of evolution were important to him. Jacobsen had translated Darwin's *On the*

Origin of Species and *The Descent of Man* into Danish, and written several articles about him for the *New Danish Monthly Magazine*.[1] Over the next few years ideas on the origin of species and the theory of evolution were the subject of passionate debate throughout Scandinavia, and elements of those same ideas would later show up in Ibsen's thought and his writing.

One thing interested him particularly at this time, though there are no reports that he ever brought the subject up in conversation. Not until the new year did he open up and reveal what it was that preoccupied him, doing so in a highly untypical way. At a meeting of the board of the Scandinavian Society on 28 January 1879 Ibsen expressed his disappointment at the fact that the society's rules made it impossible to appoint a woman to the post of society librarian. On top of this he suggested the possibility of modifying the conditions that excluded women from board meetings. When the Danish consul asked whether a female librarian should also sit on the board Ibsen replied, possibly as a tactical compromise, that she should be given an advisory vote only. At the next board meeting, on 13 February, he proposed full voting rights for women in the society, and that it should be open to women to apply for the post of librarian. As if this were not radical enough, he went on to suggest that women ought in fact to be 'favoured' when considering the appointment of a new librarian, an example of what would now be described as positive discrimination. The other board members were, to put it mildly, taken aback, perhaps most of all by the source of these revolutionary proposals.

'Ibsen descending from his seat of judgement and involving himself in an issue of the day! Ibsen as agitator!' Gunnar Heiberg marvelled that, of all places in which to make his debut as a practical politician, Ibsen should have chosen a lazy social club in peaceful Rome. The atmosphere was almost embarrassing, it seemed to him. But Ibsen's choice of venue was not accidental; he was not comfortable in open terrain, on the larger stage. The size of the community in Rome better suited his campaigning talents, just as it did earlier when he urged Norwegians and Swedes to support Denmark in the war against Prussia in the 1860s.

Ibsen's suggestion was discussed on 27 February. Sigurd was present, and witnessed something he had probably never seen before: his father passionately trying to persuade an audience to join him in his way of thinking. Ibsen offered a list of reasons why women should be considered for the post of librarian. Was the board unaware that more and more women were entering working life? And doing so often at a wage below that of their less talented male colleagues? Was the board unfamiliar with the advances in women's education? Could any of them deny the organisational talents of women, and their attention to detail in business matters? Likewise there were many reasons why women should be given full voting rights.

The prospect of women joining the society was certainly not one that alarmed him:

> I'll tell you what I am afraid of. I'm afraid of the common sense of old
> codgers, men of small vision and small anxieties, men whose entire thought-
> processes and whose every action is dedicated to the end of gaining small
> advantages for their own servile little personalities.

No one could be in any doubt after this that Ibsen was talking about something
more than just librarians and voting qualifications. But of course it was the men
of 'small anxieties' who were to decide on the matter. During his presentation
Ibsen had stuck to his script, but it was every man for himself in the debate that
followed. The chairman, a Danish lawyer named Liebe, announced that, in spite
of his great respect for Ibsen, he could not possibly support such a revolutionary
proposal. On the other hand some of the more radical members were disappointed that Ibsen had not suggested that official posts in the society be open to
women, in addition to their being allowed to vote. When the vote was taken the
proposal that women be permitted to apply for the post of librarian was
accepted, but the suggestion that they be given voting rights failed by one vote
to achieve the necessary two-thirds majority (nineteen for and eleven against).

To Ibsen the victory was pyrrhic. He was furious, demanded the vote be
taken again, and when this was rejected went from one to the other in a threatening manner demanding to know: 'Did you vote?' The atmosphere must have
been highly uncomfortable. All were aware of the fact that Ibsen's proposal was
something of an event, and everyone knew how touchy he could be. Now, as he
came towards them with finger raised, ready to question their contribution,
they sidled away.

Later that evening Heiberg called in at their local bar. Here he found Ibsen
sitting alone at a table, with several of his friends at a nearby table. It was clear that
the atmosphere of the meeting had been transferred to the bar. Heiberg, as one of
the believers, joined Ibsen. As other guests arrived they took their places in silence
at one or the other of the two tables. When the Scandinavians gathered for the big
annual banquet later that winter, no one expected him to attend. But there he
stood, as elegantly attired as ever, medals glinting on the lapels of his jacket, his
greying hair neatly combed back. He offered a friendly general greeting to the
gathering that was not addressed to anyone in particular, and took a seat off on his
own. Had he forgiven them? Did he regret his behaviour? Yes, that must be the
explanation. Spirits rose. Glasses were raised in toasts, and people settled to enjoy
themselves, secure in the knowledge that harmony reigned again among the
Scandinavians. At this point Ibsen rises to his feet. He walks over to stand behind
a large table that gives him a view of the whole assembly: 'Ladies and gentlemen . . .'

He passes a hand across his hair. And then he begins, his voice subdued and
deadly serious. He had tried to perform a service of great benefit to the society,
he said, in attempting to introduce some of the most important currents of

modern thinking to the society's members. There was no getting away from big ideas, not even in a little duck pond such as this. He did not *say* duck pond, Heiberg relates, but one could clearly sense the word in the contemptuous twisting at the corners of his mouth. But how had his gift been received? As an attempted assassination! A robbery! Voted down by the tiniest of majorities. And how had the women responded? By intriguing and campaigning against his reform! What sort of women are these?

By now his voice is no longer subdued. It shakes with anger, his lower lip juts out, his arms are folded:

> What sort of women are these, what sort of ladies, what manner of females, ignorant, in the most profound sense uneducated, immoral, on a level with the lowest, the most wretched – the . . .

A loud thud as a duchess falls to the floor in a faint. She is carried out. Ibsen continues to abuse the human race and its opposition to new ideas. And now his words are flowing and articulate, they fly from his mouth, pouring forth in a contemptuous stream. And once he is finished he marches out the door, takes his coat and walks out, leaving behind the astonished guests, some angry, some inspired. He was, after all, not without supporters. Heiberg, Jacobsen and Josephson and a number of others stood firmly on his side in the question of the women's right to vote.

'How wonderfully direct he was!' Jacobsen exclaimed later. On the other hand a naval officer, a certain Captain Buchwaldt, was apparently so incensed he was on the point of challenging Ibsen to a duel.

* * *

For some time after this, Ibsen kept away from his fellow Scandinavians. It gave him the peace he needed to get on with his new play. By Rome's standards the winter had been a harsh one, but early in March the cherry trees were in bloom, and the violets glinted blue in the sun-warmed grass. The preceding autumn he had scribbled down a few notes on the theme of the new play:

> There are two kinds of spiritual law, two kinds of conscience, one for a man, and one quite different for a woman. They do not understand each other; but in practice the woman is judged by the man's version of the law, as though she were not a woman but a man.[2]

These are the rudiments of what would become *A Doll's House*. Even at this early stage Ibsen reveals his fundamental understanding of a woman as *essentially* different from a man, just as he had maintained in his speech at the

Scandinavian Society. Like the young and like the artist, woman was possessed of a sensibility that separated her from the male-dominated society of adults, innocent by the terms of that dominant society, and therefore the potential agent of society's regeneration, as well as its hope.

> A woman cannot be herself in contemporary society, which is an exclusively male society, with laws written by men and with prosecutors and judges who judge female behaviour from a male perspective. She has committed forgery, and is proud of it, because she has done it for the sake of her husband, to save his life. But this husband sees the matter only through the filter of conventional honesty, as a matter of law. He sees it with male eyes.

It was Laura he wanted to write about, Laura Kieler's life-tragedy that was to be kneaded and transformed into literature. He headed the note 'Notes for a tragedy of contemporary life'.

> Mental battle. Repressed and confused by her belief in authority she loses faith in her own moral right to raise her children. Bitterness. A mother in contemporary society, like certain insects that crawl away and die once they have done their part for the regeneration of the species. Love for life, her husband, her children, her family. Tries in female fashion to shake free of the thoughts. Recurring angst and fear. Has to carry all this alone. The catastrophe approaches inexorably, unavoidable. Despair, struggle, annihilation.

He did not start the actual writing until the beginning of May 1879, and by the end of the next month he had finished the first act and almost completed the second. Summer was approaching, and the Scandinavians made their preparations to leave the city. Originally the Ibsens had planned to go to one of the small mountain villages outside Rome, but in the end decided on southern Italy. On 5 July they set off for Amalfi, not far south of Naples. They moved into two small rooms with three iron beds at the Albergo della Luna, a converted monastery built on a point overlooking the sea. Here Henrik would surely find the peace he sorely needed in which to work – in that sleepy little fishing town there really wasn't much else to do.

Between sessions of writing he went for long walks in the hills around the town. There was a good beach at Amalfi and all three of them took up swimming again until the middle of September when the water began to be too cold. Otherwise Henrik spent most of his time indoors writing. One day he approached Suzannah:

'I've just seen Nora. She came right up to me and put her hand on my shoulder.'

'What was she wearing?' his wife asked.

'A plain blue woollen dress,' he replied.

By 3 August he had completed a first draft of the play. He wanted to give himself plenty of time to revise the text to make the 'language and the dialogue as formally perfect as possible', so it was not until early in September that Hegel received the fair copy, in good time for the Christmas market. Ibsen at once started making plans for the launch of the book. He had a good feeling about it.

> Of this much I am sure, that I can't recall any of my previous books bringing me greater pleasure in working on the details as this one.

INTERMEZZO IN MUNICH

At the end of September 1879 the family left Amalfi and spent a few days in Sorrento and Rome. On 14 October they were back in Munich, where they moved into a new apartment at Amalienstrasse 50a, in the same district as they had lived earlier. From sunshine and sea it was, so to speak, straight into thick winter coats in an autumnal Bavaria.

What had the sojourn in Rome and Italy done for Ibsen this time? He had found peace in which to work, drunk good wine, caused a scandal at the Scandinavian Society and finished his new play. Sigurd had been able to refresh his second native language, and completed a term at the university. Italy was a good place to be, but otherwise much had changed since his first visit. The train journey over the Alps in 1864 had been like a dream, a deliverance from darkness into light. Rome had been a place outside space and time, exactly what was necessary to give him the artistic liberation he needed. Rome had changed, but then so had Ibsen. He still appreciated the city, but he was no longer there in flight from the world. On the contrary, he wanted to be where things were happening, in the thick of life, a place where he could enlarge his literary market. He was also growing tired of the peripatetic life. He wanted to settle down.

It did not take him long to resume old habits such as visits to the cafes and long walks. He was once again to be seen in the Achatz drinking dark beer and eating salted pretzels with Paul Heyse, Professor Carrière, Dr Schmidt and other well-known and less well-known German writers and men of science. It seems, however, that he never frequented the Café Probst, a favourite haunt of Norwegians and a place where Norwegian newspapers could be read. He also avoided social gatherings. Not that it was always easy. As Ibsen became ever more well known the invitations began arriving in a steady stream, as did journalists, critics and Norwegian tourists, who rang on his doorbell to catch a glimpse of the great writer or exchange a word with him.

When, in later years, Ibsen would acquire a reputation for being withdrawn and testy, this is the prosaic explanation for his response. He had quite simply to keep his door shut in order to get any peace.

Henrik, Suzannah and Sigurd were still tenants at Amalienstrasse, the furnishings still rented. The walls, however, began to reflect the family's personal taste. In Rome, Ibsen had bought paintings, twenty of them – 'some of them very large and very valuable'. At least, so he believed. The collection consisted largely of old Italian paintings that were hardly as valuable as he supposed. He spoke of the collection entirely as an investment; it is also evident that, for the first time in a long time, he was feeling a need to furnish his home with possessions of his own.

That autumn Bjørnstjerne and Karoline Bjørnson passed through Munich on their way to Meiningen and Vienna. Neither Ibsen nor Bjørnson gave any sign of wanting to meet, but Sigurd sneaked down to the Café Probst to catch a glimpse of his godfather. There had been minimal contact between godfather and father in recent years. Two years earlier Ibsen had written to thank Bjørnson for his support for Brandes when Brandes had to flee Denmark. He had enclosed a copy of *The Pillars of Society*, for some reason or other insisting that it was meant for Karoline. It was a friendly gesture, but hardly an overture to anything further. The previous summer, while Ibsen was still in Amalfi, something else had come up between them. Along with a handful of other liberals, Bjørnson had provoked both Norwegians and Swedes with his demand for a 'pure' Norwegian flag to replace the union flag of Sweden-Norway. There was little support for Bjørnson's proposal, even in liberal circles, and Ibsen wasn't enthusiastic either.

'Let the sign of the union stay; but remove the monkish markings from people's minds,' was his reply when Bjørnson asked him to sign the petition. It was typical of Ibsen not to be concerned with the politics of symbol, with the little freedoms, as long as Norwegians remained bound in their thinking.

> It really doesn't matter if the politicians hand out more freedoms to society
> if they remain unable to provide freedom for the individual.

And then one in the eye for Bjørnson:

> In the whole of Norway there are not 25 free and independent personalities.

Later Bjørnson explained that the reason he avoided Ibsen in Munich was over the issue of the flag, but a contributing factor must have been that he was going through a difficult period in his own life at the time. Facing opposition as a politician, he found himself ignored by the theatres and was struggling financially. On top of it all he suffered a religious crisis that led to his breaking with Christianity. As if all that wasn't enough, once *A Doll's House* was published it completely overshadowed both plays from Bjørnson that same year, *The New System* and *Leonarda*. Before travelling to Munich, Bjørnson had met Georg Brandes at a dinner at Hegel's at which Brandes had suggested to Karoline that she and Suzannah arrange a reconciliation in Munich.

But Karoline dared not – 'Bjørnson would never forgive me'. And sure enough, the next day her husband turned up at Brandes' door to express his indignation at this interference.

If there was no reunion with Bjørnson there was at least a visit from Magdalene Thoresen, who was passing through Munich on her way to Rome. She was accompanied by her youngest son Aksel. Aksel soon returned to Copenhagen, however, leaving his mother to spend another two weeks in the city. It meant long evenings in conversation about art and literature, conducted in a light-hearted and frivolous tone that was nothing like the usual atmosphere in the household. 'You're so demonic, Ibsen!' Magdalene exclaimed one evening as she enfolded the diminutive writer in a big, warm embrace. Ibsen, who did not favour spontaneous embraces, pulled himself free. Over the years she had come to respect him more and more, but she always remained too much of a woman for him.

WHERE DID NORA SPRING FROM?

A Doll's House was in the shops by 4 December, in time to hit the Christmas market. From October onwards Ibsen had been sending the play to a long list of theatres in Scandinavia and on the continent; in Germany, Wilhelm Lange immediately started work on a German translation. Once again the head of the Kongelige Teater in Copenhagen tried and failed to persuade Ibsen to postpone publication of the book until after the premiere. Was he supposed to sacrifice the proceeds of the lucrative Christmas market just to please Fallesen, who had even tried to insist on having the world premiere of the play?

Fallesen had clearly not understood that Ibsen's fame was now such that it was he, and not the theatre, that set the conditions.

A Doll's House is the story of Nora Helmer who is living an apparently happy life with her husband Torvald and their three small children in a comfortable and secure bourgeois home. There is only one cloud on her horizon. Shortly after they were married, her husband fell ill, but declined to take the doctor's advice and travel south for the sake of his health. Nora then acted on her own initiative; she forged the signature of her recently deceased father in order to take out a secret bank loan and used the money to persuade her husband to go south with her. In so doing she believes she has saved his life, though he does not know it. What she initially fails to realise is that she has committed a crime, and that her actions have shattered the foundations of her marriage and her life. She finds out soon enough, however. Over the course of two or three days around Christmas the deceit is uncovered, and Nora is forced to take responsibility for her actions and for herself. She breaks out of her doll's life and insists on her right to discover herself as a human being, which in her case means leaving her husband and children.

Nora goes. She does what is almost unthinkable for a bourgeois woman in the nineteenth century: she puts herself before her marriage and her family, the institutions at the very heart of society. She defies the ideals of Christianity and the tradition that a woman's duty is to sacrifice herself, not to make demands.[3]

Ibsen must have known that the play he had written was scandalous, so the uproar when it was published can hardly have surprised him. He observed to Hegel that he hoped the book would be given a 'lively' reception. As for Hegel, it was not his habit to involve himself in Ibsen's choice of theme, but on this occasion he was unable to resist: 'I only wish that the play could end differently,' he wrote in November. Pretty soon he would realise that a publisher could hardly have hoped for a better ending.

But what was it that had excited Ibsen's interest in the position of women in the first place? No one knows where Nora went, but where did she spring from?

In *A Doll's House* Ibsen displayed one of the more subtle sides of his talent – an ability to pick up on something in the air and give it a radical and deeply original expression in dramatic form. The liberation of women and the rights of women outside marriage had long been a subject of discussion in Scandinavia. Nora had her predecessors, and over the years Henrik Ibsen had had the opportunity to learn from their experiences. It has often been claimed that one of Nora's midwives was his own wife. There is a family tradition to the effect that it was *she* who insisted that Nora must leave, an idea that Ibsen originally opposed. Stories such as these are difficult to assess properly. It may well be the case that a sort of 'compensation myth' concerning Suzannah has arisen, not least within the family, in which she is given a compensatory role as the woman who is said to stand behind every great man. It is often claimed that it was she who forced Henrik to go on writing when he wanted to give up; in their early years she is said to have driven his drinking friends from the door in order to save him for literature, and in other stories is given credit for Nora's famous exit. The difficulty is how little certain knowledge we have of her influence on Ibsen. He willingly granted his wife's role as model, as inspiration and support, and there is no doubt either that in her he found a stimulating and intelligent conversational partner. On the other hand, tales of wives influencing other writers made him indignant – that was no way for a serious writer to work!

In the matter of the position of women in society, however, there is clear evidence of how Suzannah felt. Some years later, in a letter to Camilla Collett, she offers fulsome thanks for her books and all they contain: 'Your every word and every opinion is priceless. May they fall on fertile ground, and may society be shaken into wakefulness.' When we know, too, how enthusiastic Suzannah was about the writings of John Stuart Mill, there can be no real grounds for doubting her influence on her husband when it came to the status of women. And yet she cannot be counted among those often referred to towards the close of the century as 'the new women', those who broke radically with the conventions either in their writing or their lifestyles. Like thousands of upper-class women before her, Suzannah was intellectually inclined and well read. But her life was in the home, and she was no rebel.

Magdalene Thoresen, her stepmother, on the other hand, most certainly was. So too, in the highest degree, was Camilla Collett. In 1854, three years after the death of her husband, Collett had written her breakthrough novel *The District Governor's Daughters*, the first realistic tendentious novel to appear in Scandinavia. In her insistence on being taken seriously as a human being and a professional writer she was one of Norway's first feminists. As a person she was rather chaotic and eccentric, as the Norwegian artists in Munich quickly realised, seeing her get into one argument after another with the city's cab-drivers, whom she was convinced were overcharging her because she was a woman. She forgot umbrellas and galoshes wherever she went, and had a regrettable tendency to forget the name of the hotel she was staying at.

Ibsen encountered her one day wandering back and forth through the Munich streets. He sensed that something was up and asked her which hotel she was living at.

'What, you mean you don't know, Ibsen?' she cried rather shamefacedly.

Collett is said to have let slip to one Norwegian painter that she was not particularly enamoured of Ibsen as a person, while Ibsen apparently once said of her that she was not fighting for the 'women's cause' but the 'ladies' cause' – 'and for her right and the right of a few other ladies' cause campaigners to be as mad as they want'. The sarcasm probably was only skin-deep. Ibsen greatly respected Camilla Collett, even before he met her in Dresden in 1871. Naturally he was familiar with her work. In *Love's Comedy* he had made use of elements from *The District Governor's Daughters*, and Collett was absolutely convinced that she was the model for Svanhild. She did not emerge as a polemic feminist until the 1870s. In 1868 she wrote an essay entitled 'On Woman and her Position', which was published in *Sidste Blade* (*Last Leaves*) in 1872. The following year she wrote under her own name for the first time – a demand that she be taken seriously as a writer, and not just as an 'interesting woman'. For Collett the liberation of women was primarily an inner process, of which the goal was that the woman herself and the society around her should recognise her value as a human being and liberate her spiritual talents.[4] The social, external freedoms were secondary considerations, and in this she and Ibsen were in agreement. But Collett was not alone at her barricade. In 1878, Aasta Hansteen's *Woman Created in the Image of God* discussed the question of the Church's attitude towards women. Hansteen travelled and lectured in Scandinavia in support of the women's liberation movement, and both book and lectures created a scandal. Hansteen was mocked and ridiculed, and in 1880 took the decision to emigrate to the United States.

Although women had achieved a degree of social prominence earlier, it was not until the 1870s that the women's liberation movement became a prominent part of public discourse. Over the next decade the subject of votes for women was energetically debated. In 1871 the Danish Women's Society was founded, two years later the Swedish Society for Married Women's Property Rights, and in 1884 the Norwegian Women's Liberation Society. The new movement was highly controversial, not only among the defenders of the civil-service state, but also among Liberals who feared that the question of women's rights might split the movement.

In other words, Ibsen was not especially ahead of the times when he raised the question of the role of women in *A Doll's House*. Nor had he shown any special interest in the subject earlier. When Georg Brandes' translation of John Stuart Mill's *On the Subjection of Women* caused such an uproar in Scandinavia, his reaction was one of scepticism. We do not know of any directly positive statement of support for women's rights from Ibsen during this time. On the contrary, Collett was apparently dismayed by the conservatism of his views on women when the two got to know each other early in the 1870s. They were, she claimed during one particularly heated exchange, more suited to an Old Testament prophet. She expressed her frustration in a letter to her son Alf in February 1872:

> From top to toe he is an egotist, and most definitely as a man in relation to women. His own domestic situation appears to have had no influence on him at all in this matter. Note his heroes: every one of them is a *despot* in his dealings with women.

In *From the World of the Dumb* (1877) she analysed the women in his writings and came to the conclusion that neither Agnes in *Brand* nor Solveig in *Peer Gynt* was a good role model for the modern woman. But the women in his historical dramas were quite different. In these, 'Devotion was paired with Will and Character; she did not merely obey, she initiated, she played an active role; she did not merely *give*, she also *took*; and she forgave, as a queen forgives, not as some cowed slave.'

Ibsen's view of women's rights changed in the 1870s, in part at least owing to Collett's influence. Reviewers had long been aware of the fact that his female characters tended to be more complex than his male ones. Lady Inger and Hjørdis were both notably complicated and interesting characters. In Selma Brattsberg and Lona Hessel he introduced a new and unprecedented dimension to his depiction of female characters, a dimension with clear social implications. This particular development reached its apotheosis in Nora Helmer. What was controversial about her was not her complex psychology but her rebellious and socially challenging actions.

THE DEATH OF THE LARK

A Doll's House was discussed throughout Scandinavia wherever literary people met. 'I know of nothing more perfect,' enthused Alexander Kielland, who had published his first book in the same year, *Short Stories*. 'You know,' wrote a less enthusiastic Bjørnson to a colleague, 'this is technically outstanding, but all the same, it's written in an embarrassingly mean spirit.' No one was indifferent. Was Nora right to leave? What about the children? Yes, but then what about her rights as a woman? The literature-loving women of society's upper echelons had plenty to talk about in their salons, and Scandinavian activists and radicals of both sexes hailed the book as a partisan contribution to the cause. Amalie Skram had admired Bjørnson more than Ibsen, but confronted by a creation such as Nora Helmer she openly proclaimed her conversion.

The play was a masterpiece, its message revolutionary:

Once the woman has taken her stand, she will no longer give way for anything. Like Nora, she will let those duties accruing to her through her life as a doll fall away into nothingness, because the task of working on her own neglected self consumes her completely, to the exclusion of all else.

To appreciate the explosive power in *A Doll's House* one has to remember that the traditional idealist aesthetic equated the ethical and the aesthetic. 'Beauty is the ideality of art,' wrote a reviewer in *Aftenbladet*, 'because what is beautiful is a natural external expression of the good in the universe.'[5] On these terms, Ibsen's play was an offence to both the beautiful and the good, an assault on the norms of art as well as the foundations of society. It was not made any the less provocative on account of the elegance and formal mastery with which it was written. Contemporary critics were almost unanimous in praising its technical brilliance; it was, in a word, unprecedented. By comparison with the preceding play Ibsen had advanced his minimalistic staging, concentrated as it was around the bourgeois living room, by cutting down the number of parts from nineteen to five. With its tight plotting, its natural and economic dialogue and its distinctive individual psychologies, contemporaries recognised that *A Doll's House* was a ground-breaking piece of theatre, regardless of what one made of Nora's departure.

'There was not a single declamatory phrase, not a melodramatic step taken, not a drop of blood spilled, indeed, not so much as a tear shed. Not for an instant was the dagger of tragedy raised.' Erik Bøgh was mightily impressed by Ibsen's ability to create great art out of simple everyday life when he attended a performance at the Kongelige Teater: 'There is no superficial dialogue, every exchange moves the plot one step forward, and there is not one extraneous effect introduced throughout the entire play.'

From a literary-historical perspective it is tempting to divide the reviewers into two camps, with one claiming that the aesthetic of idealism was the standard of the age, and the other claiming with equal certainty that idealism was long dead.

'Our literature is now well past the stage at which one sought only beauty in a work of art, in which the value of the literary work lay in how well it had fulfilled the aesthetic demands and challenges of its art,' Erik Vullum writes in *Dagbladet*. P. Hansen, writing in *Nær og Fjærne*, maintained that the play had to be weighed against 'the old, enduring considerations that demand that a work of art be neither depressing nor upsetting but uplifting and liberating'. In similar fashion Fredrik Petersen in *Aftenbladet* rebukes Ibsen for a play from which one departs without that 'elevated mood that, as long ago as the time of the Greeks, was considered a necessary precondition for any work of art'. *Morgenbladet*'s reviewer, on the other hand, insisted that a conciliatory conclusion to the play would have marked a fundamental breach in the play's own aesthetic logic.

On closer consideration, however, it is too easy to speak of two camps; on the one hand there were those critics who dismissed the play's ideas but realised that a simple moral condemnation of Nora's decision was naïve, and instead attacked the play on its own terms (in particular the inherent unlikeliness of Nora's abrupt change of mind, and her monologue in the final scene). Others asserted that Nora's revolt, which in real life would be despicable, was artistically necessary in terms of the play. A number of reviewers bemoaned the fact that Helmer is destroyed for his sins, whereas Nora gets away with hers, in particular the egotistical demand for self-realisation that comes at the cost of her innocent children and remorseful husband. In this way these critics hoped to undermine the heroine of the play – and its author too – little realising that in doing so they revealed their failure to understand Ibsen's poetics. For Nora is no traditional heroine, and she was never intended to be spotless. In Ibsen's view of his own plays, there are no authorial mouthpieces, or even roles, but only human beings.

Herman Bang was someone who realised this:

The writers of our own times are themselves searchers, doubters, children of the age. So Ibsen simply says 'This is not the truth' – and moves on.

On the other hand there were many who cared not a jot for aesthetic considerations and judged the play either as propaganda for women's rights or as a crude attack on society's values and institutions.

This last perspective was particularly in evidence in Växjö.

As Hegel had noted before Christmas in 1879, Ibsen's new play reached audiences well beyond the usual market for serious literature and theatre. On 11 May 1880, *Smålandsposten* carried a report of curious happenings in Växjö, a provincial town in southern Sweden, four days after C. W. Åbjörnsson's theatre company had performed *A Doll's House* at the local theatre:

Eighteen married men of the town have handed in a petition to the board of the theatre demanding that no theatre company with *A Doll's House* in its repertoire be allowed to perform in Växjö.

The eighteen husbands involved related that eleven women had ended their relationships with their fiancés on the grounds that they had noticed 'Helmeric tendencies' in their intendeds. Furthermore, three married men living in the area would no longer leave the house without first locking their wives in, and one married woman had already moved out and was living somewhere in the surrounding countryside and waiting for 'the most wonderful thing' to happen. There were a number of contemporary claims that Nora's revolt was having a direct effect on the institution of marriage. Marcus Grønvold in Munich related that the play created disquiet in several marriages, referring probably to the marriage of his painter friend Johan Nielssen and Clemence Lederer, a painter and the daughter of the mayor of Vienna. Ibsen spent Christmas Eve 1879 with them, and presented the Vienna society lady with a signed copy of his play. Johan and Clemence's marriage started coming apart, and when, a few years later, they were divorced, it was generally accepted that Clemence was following the example of Nora.

Ibsen is said to have taken the news philosophically, remarking that the liberated woman would soon enough discover the difference between being 'the divorced fr N., and the respectable wife of hr. N.' But Clemence never returned to her husband, and when the time came she even renounced her inheritance from him. Whether or not *A Doll's House* really had this kind of effect on marriages is hard to say. But the numerous stories of deserted husbands and women running loose are, in themselves, a part of the play's reception history.

It is much easier to gauge the play's effect on the stage, the book market and in public literary life. Although the first print run was 8,000 copies a second printing of 3,000 was needed by early the following year, quickly followed by a third of 2,500 in March.

'This looks like being a memorable year for me financially,' the satisfied author wrote to his publisher in February 1880.

That was putting it mildly. Ibsen's income in 1879 had been 17,609 kroner. In 1880 it rose to 26,953 kroner. The main source was royalties from the various theatres for his most recent play, while royalties from the sales of the book were dented by the availability of Wilhelm Lange's German translation in Denmark, for which Ibsen received not a penny.[6] In 1879, Gyldendal published a fifth edition of *The Pretenders* and a third of *Poems*, and the following year third and fourth editions of, respectively, *Emperor and Galilean* and *The League of Youth*. That same year saw the first German edition of *Peer Gynt*, though Ibsen was initially sceptical about its chances.

'Of all my books, it strikes me that "Peer Gynt" is the least likely to be understood outside the Scandinavian countries,' he wrote to the publisher Ludwig Passarge in May 1880.

How wrong is it possible to be? Over the years *Peer Gynt* would become one of Ibsen's most performed plays on the world's stages. On the other hand he quickly saw the potential of *A Doll's House*, and the play was soon translated into German, Swedish, Finnish and Polish.

* * *

In the theatres too *A Doll's House* was an immediate success – in part at least a *succès de scandale* – initially on the Scandinavian and German stages, by the end of the 1880s across all of Europe, and in time, in every corner of the world. The world premiere took place at the Kongelige Teater, just as Fallesen had requested. When the curtain rose on 21 December 1879 a nervous Ibsen paced the floor in Amalienstrasse and awaited the telegram. The play was a break-through for modern drama in Copenhagen, even though the performance at the Kongelige Teater still had traits of the acting styles of the recent past.[7] No doubt inspired by his experiences in Paris, the director H. P. Holst attempted to give it a realistic staging. But Betty Hennings' and Emil Poulsen's outstanding portrayals of Nora and Helmer were nevertheless Romantic in style, and they seemed more like stars of the stage than part of an ensemble. The public were delighted, however, and despite its controversial content the play was a box-office success.

It was Stockholm's turn on 8 January 1880. Once again, Dramaten and Nya Teatern competed for the right to perform the play, and on this occasion it was Edholm and Dramaten that won, and not Ludvig Josephson, who had taken over at Nya Teatern.[8] Not until 20 January did the play reach the Christiania Theatre. 'All very moved – huge success,' the theatre informed the author in a telegram. Elsewhere August Rasmussen's company obtained the rights in Denmark outside Copenhagen, while the Danish theatre managers Christian W. Foght and Oscar Salicath at the Folketeatret in Christiania competed so bitterly for the Norwegian provincial rights that in the end Ibsen took Salicath to court. During the spring the play was also performed in Bergen, Gothenburg, Helsinki and Åbo, while the German premiere was at Flensburg, moving on then to Munich, Berlin and a long list of other towns.[9] Over the next few years Nora conquered Vienna (1881), St Petersburg (1881), Warsaw (1882), London (1884), Brussels (1889) and Belgrade (1889). Wherever it was performed, the play occasioned debates and articles in newspapers and magazines.

If Ibsen had been nervous about the reception of the play in Scandinavia, he had particular reason to be anxious about its staging in Germany. The German actress Hedwig Niemann-Raabe had announced that she would be touring with the play. She had also stated that she had no intention of allowing Nora to leave for, as she said, 'I would never leave my children.'

Shortly afterwards Ibsen received a letter from his German translator, Wilhelm Lange, warning him that an edited version of the play might become the preferred version in the north German theatres. Under the circumstances Ibsen chose to change the ending himself – conceding that it was 'an act of barbarism' – and to allow this version to be performed. In the barbaric version, Helmer stops his wife as she is about to leave and persuades her to peek into the children's room. At the sight of the sleeping children she breaks down and realises that she *cannot* leave them, even if her change of mind amounts to a self-betrayal.

To this day Ibsen's alternative ending remains an embarrassing postscript to the story of *A Doll's House*, the play with perhaps the most uncompromising final scene in all of stage history.

'It's not possible that Ibsen could have done this,' writes Magdalene Thoresen in distress to Fru Heiberg in March 1880, having heard rumours of how Ibsen has mutilated his own drama.

She was probably not the only one to find the rumours incredible. But they were true alright, and in February, Ibsen felt under so much pressure that he finally did something he only ever did as a last resort: he wrote a letter of explanation, to the editor of the Danish *Nationaltidende*. He was, he explained, helpless to protect his play from the mistreatment of others as long as there was no effective copyright protection for writers. That he, by providing an alternative ending of his own, might make it easier for producers to choose this version, seems not to have occurred to him. But what was really at issue here? Was it his artistic integrity? Or was it about money? By rewriting the end of *A Doll's House* did he save the play, or was what he was offering actually a different and less interesting play? Would it not have been better for him, who believed he was writing for all eternity, to have left his signature on the original and allowed others to append their names to the travesty?

Is there, indeed, any other credible motive for allowing Nora to remain other than that her creator was willing to bow to the demands of the market?

Not that he did it with an easy conscience.

'It is expressly against my wishes,' he wrote in *Nationaltidende*, 'when this version is used, and I hope that it will not be used in many German theatres.'

He was not so lucky. In February 1880, when the German premiere took place in Flensburg, it was with his alternative ending. Even Heinrich Laube at the Burgtheater in Vienna dithered over which version to use and, of course, it was the alternative version Fru Niemann-Raabe took with her on her tour of Hamburg, Dresden, Hanover and Berlin. It soon became apparent, however, that audiences and critics alike, including those in Berlin, disapproved of the mutilation, and in the spring Fru Niemann-Raabe began performing the play in its original version. 'This is unquestionably the only right thing to do,' Ibsen wrote in relief to his German translator. 'My experiences here in Munich encourage me in this belief. I can't think of another play that has aroused so much interest and passionate discussion as this has here – and the main reason for that is the way the play ends.'

In Munich he had seen with his own eyes the effect the play had on audiences. The premiere took place on 3 March, the first performance in Germany of the original version. Ibsen watched from the wings, out of reach of the theatre-glasses that would otherwise inevitably have been focused on him. Out front sat Sigurd and John Paulsen. In the interval Sigurd ran home to give his mother a report – she had simply been too nervous to attend. And with good reason: as early as the end of the second act Ibsen was called up to acknowledge the acclaim of the audience. He bowed several times, hand pressed against his chest, before departing. He probably knew what was coming, and sure enough, at the end of the third act, 'a raucous disharmony arose among members of the audience', a disturbance that was carried out into the cloakroom afterwards. The performance over, Sigurd hurried home to his mother again, followed by John Paulsen and his father, arm in arm.

Paulsen noticed, as they walked, that Ibsen's whole body was trembling.

The audience's reaction was echoed by the critics; here too the disagreement was over the third act and the final scene.[10] 'Down here *A Doll's House* has caused the same uproar as back home,' Georg Brandes reported from Berlin. 'People take sides passionately. I doubt whether any other play has ever been the subject of such lively discussion as this.'

Any reaction, any protest seems only to have increased interest in the play: over time 60,000 copies of Reclam's German edition of *A Doll's House* were sold.[11] Nora's scandalous exit had harmed neither the play nor the *oeuvre*. Ibsen was not, however, the only one to offer an alternative version of the play; before long a plethora of curious variations and meditations on Nora and Helmer's marriage began appearing.[12] In both Germany and Denmark the legal aspects of Nora's forgery were subjected to close examination and fictional court cases conducted in the pages of newspapers, with legal documents and sentencings. A number of parodies appeared, but above all it was that final scene that inspired others to provide a conciliatory fourth act or postscript with titles such as 'How Nora came back home again', 'The impossible possibility' and 'Thoughts on Fru Nora Helmer's departure'. In a German version Helmer appears again two years after his wife's dramatic exit. A shadow crosses Nora's face when she sees her husband. 'Have you now truly forgiven me?' she asks. Helmer observes her calmly. He doesn't answer at once. And then at last he produces a bag of macaroons from his pocket. As she pops a macaroon into her mouth she gives a shriek of joy and cries out (probably in a spray of crumbs): 'The most wonderful thing!'

No, all in all, it was probably best to mutilate the play oneself.

* * *

And yet there was likely one person who missed a conciliatory fourth act more than most. How did things work out for the real Nora? Of course, Laura Kieler's unhappy marriage was not simply the raw material for Ibsen's play; in its own right it put the issue of women's rights high on the political agenda. Rumours had it that Laura's story was what inspired the poet-priest Jens Christian Hostrup's attack on married women's lack of legal rights in Denmark, and the politician Fredrik Bajer's work in the Danish parliament to secure the rights of married women to income generated by their own efforts. But it was *A Doll's House* that made Laura's tale immortal. It was also a burden for most of the rest of her life, for – in case anyone was wondering – there was no pleasure in being the model for Nora Helmer.

Whether one viewed the play as a masterpiece or a scandal, *A Doll's House* did not reflect well on Laura Kieler. Those who condemned Nora naturally condemned her too. And at the same time, she did not live up to the ideal of Nora as a role model. Laura had not left her husband and children with head held high. She had been thrown out, lost her children, and committed to a lunatic asylum. Literature's Nora left, reality's Nora clung on for as long as she could, and when the opportunity arose she returned to her family because she could not endure the thought of being apart from her children, like the Nora of the alternative German version. Just before Christmas in 1879, *Aftenposten* carried a feature about 'the real Nora', an anonymous Danish woman who had spent a fortune in doing up her home and ended up writing false promissory notes to cover her expenses. The story spread in various guises until the anonymous woman was anonymous no longer. Things weren't made any easier when Laura Kieler later became a controversial author in Denmark, and her personal history could be used against her by her enemies.

Although she always held Ibsen's writing in the highest regard, she felt that Nora had 'killed her soul'. She wasn't the only one; Camilla Collett also thought Ibsen had 'taken the real Nora hostage in his triumphal and ambitious pursuit of world fame'.

What did he have to say about all this?

Laura Kieler put off writing to Ibsen for a long time, and he had not sent her a copy of the play. Perhaps he really believed that it would exonerate her, even though the flood of rumours should have suggested otherwise. In 1885 they met again when Kieler interviewed him for *Morgenbladet* in Copenhagen. They were like strangers to each other now, master and lark. He seemed visibly nervous and uncomfortable to her. There are no indications that they cleared the air between them. In the pen-portrait Kieler wrote she praised him unstintingly, and wrote that the woman who more than any other was responsible for his involvement in the struggle for women's rights was – Suzannah. She does not even fleetingly refer to her own story.

This doesn't mean that Nora had disappeared completely from Laura Kieler's life, or that she was gone from Ibsen's life either. A few years later the rumours surrounding her flared up again, this time so fiercely that she chose to confront Ibsen, first in the form of a gripping correspondence, and then face to face. So in the end, the model caught up with the author. It was not a situation of Ibsen's choosing, for face to face, he had never been a courageous man.

PORTRAIT OF IBSEN

The spring of 1880 was spent chasing up translations, sales figures, and performances of *A Doll's House* and other plays; the writer's work was done, now it was the turn of the businessman. At Easter, Suzannah and Sigurd travelled to Oberammergau to see the passion play, leaving Henrik at home. In April he writes to Stockholm and requests that Julius Kronberg's large portrait from the celebrations in Uppsala in 1877 be sent to him.

The painting is one of the best known of Ibsen. He stands, draped in his doctoral robes with the Order of the Turkish Commander glinting on his chest, a pen in his right hand and his doctoral diploma in the other. The setting is a dimly lit room with a desk and a window through which a classical and timeless Mediterranean landscape can be seen. There are the outlines of a column and an olive branch. Ibsen's gaze is raised towards the light in a pose that accentuates the forehead and the hands. The whole painting is suffused with an aristocratic, academic dignity, with triumph and status. Two sculptures of him had already been made, by Herman Wilhelm Bissen and Walter Runeberg, both in Rome in 1868. Eilif Peterssen's study was from 1876, but most of the portraits would appear in the years to come. Yet Kronberg's portrait marks a watershed, for it is the first to show Ibsen in the sort of heroic posture that corresponds to his growing status as a writer. It positively oozes authority and success; the features of the sphinx are already largely in place, and all the details that would later characterise Ibsen's personal iconography are present.

But Ibsen could do more than ponder his image during the spring of 1880; he could read about himself too. At the end of March he writes to the Finnish literary scholar Valfrid Vasenius to thank him for his study *Henrik Ibsen's Drama: The First Phase*, which Vasenius had presented at the University of Helsinki the previous autumn. Interest in Ibsen came late to Finland, but when it did come it was highly positive, in the first instance through Swedish translations and a handful of articles, before the Swedish Theatre in Helsinki introduced him onstage in 1878 with productions of *The Vikings at Helgeland* and *The Pillars of Society*. In February 1880 *A Doll's House* was published in Finnish and performed at the Finska Teatern with a young Ida Aalberg playing the part of Nora. The result was, unsurprisingly, a furious debate in the newspapers and magazines. Later both older and more recent plays were translated into Finnish and performed on Finnish stages.[13] Vasenius' doctoral thesis discussed the work up to and including *The Pretenders* and is the first objective critical analysis made of Ibsen's writing. Yet its reputation remains slight among literary historians, despite Ibsen's wholehearted approval of its conclusions:

'It is of course difficult, not to say impossible, for me to sit in judgement over my own work,' he writes to the Finn after reading his book. 'But this much I can say, that I could not wish for a better advocate for my work and myself than you show yourself to be here.'

Vasenius had simply hit the nail on the head:

> Everything that you write on the subject of my intentions, the basic idea that lies behind each of the plays, the characters and the inner dynamic of their relationships, all this and much, much more is exactly what I should most of all wish to be asserted and demonstrated publicly.

These words make Vasenius' thesis a central document in our understanding of Ibsen, not necessarily on account of its qualities, but because it so clearly reflects the way the writer himself wished his work to be viewed. So what does the thesis tell us about Ibsen? The year before Vasenius had spoken out against the Finnish literary establishment's admiration for Friedrich Vischer's aesthetic of idealism.[14] Writers should instead take up the 'burning issues' of the moment, as Georg Brandes urged. He found this same concern for contemporary affairs in Ibsen, who 'has written for those able to see that the biggest and most important questions of the age, more crucial than any social and political question, is this: how may the *individual* become whole, harmonious, truthful and free in his inner self?'

How may a person become whole, harmonious, truthful and free in his inner self, that was the question for Vasenius – and for Ibsen too.

As a whole the thesis reads like a defence of Ibsen's work against those critics who over the years had either accused him of plagiarism (*The Feast at Solhaug*), or misunderstood or misrepresented him. In that sense Vasenius most certainly was Ibsen's 'advocate', not only in his thesis, but also as a participant in the Finnish debate on *A Doll's House* that took place in the spring of 1880.

For Vasenius, Ibsen's early plays are original masterpieces, and what is more important: the themes of those first works recur in his subsequent oeuvre. In other words, he stressed the continuity in the complete works, as Ibsen himself did. For Vasenius, Ibsen is a *realist*, not just in his external descriptions, but because he 'penetrates to the very heart of the phenomenon'. It was a matter of an inner, psychological realism. He claimed that, in addition to this, Ibsen was in complete command of the historical, external reality he was describing, even though the historical is, in the final analysis, subordinate to the 'inner core' of the main characters' psychology. The argument differed radically from that of Georg Brandes, for even though Vasenius, in his rejection of Vischer, revealed a degree of admiration for Brandes, in his doctoral thesis of the following year he distanced himself sharply from what he regarded as Brandes' one-sided insistence on the social and socio-political dimensions of Ibsen's work.[15] In Vasenius' view, Brandes read Ibsen according to the tenets of his own demand that the duty of literature was to debate problems. This was not to say that Ibsen's contemporary dramas were not also dramas of this type, but that Ibsen had qualities of a more universal and existential nature that took his plays beyond the confines of a politically engaged literature, or, as Vasenius later expressed it in a private letter: 'Ibsen's programme was *at one and the same time* concerned with social matters and the inner life of the individual.'

Of course, this appealed hugely to Ibsen, not least because the central ideas of the thesis were the same as those he had expressed himself in his own Foreword to *Catiline*.

* * *

So after *A Doll's House* Ibsen spent time studying portraits of himself done by others, both painted and written, and at some point it occurs to him to create a self-portrait. In May he sends a remarkable letter to Frederik Hegel in which he refers to the great interest his Foreword to the new edition of *Catiline* in 1875 has aroused, in particular its description of the genesis of the play. Ibsen has a suggestion to make:

> What if I now write a complete short book of some ten to twelve sheets containing similar accounts of the outer and inner conditions under which each of my plays came into being?

Ten to twelve sheets would make a book of somewhere between 160 and 192 pages. It would be a literary autobiography that would also include his own memories from the places and the settings in which the works were created. The initiative might seem surprising, given that Ibsen generally preferred to let his plays speak for themselves. On closer consideration, however, it seems like a natural step. From the early 1870s onwards he had shown an interest in watching over the contexts and interpretations of his own work, and the way in which he appeared as a writer. As his own enigma and fame increased it must have seemed very tempting indeed to incorporate his own life into his literary universe. It was about control, about a remarkably self-conscious writer's desire to weave together his written and unwritten works, and from there to attach the works to the author, not in order to reduce the works to life, but to bring the life and the work together in a 'Gesamtkunstwerk'.

Hegel was not convinced. A personal foreword like the one Ibsen had written for *Catiline* was fine, but a whole book containing material of a 'semi-private nature' would not, in his view, arouse much interest. His argument continues:

> Your works stand on their own as clear and distinct entities, and their importance ought not to be connected to distracting asides of this kind. Albeit unconsciously, they will work their way into the reader's awareness, and in due course introduce a new and distracting element into the reception of the work, since the whole and the pieces no longer harmonise.

Literary historians have often regretted Hegel's advice, and the quotation above suggests that he did not realise that it was not Ibsen's intention to disrupt the perception of his writing with a lot of irrelevant anecdotes but, on the contrary, to bring it into harmony with his life. In a draft of the letter, however, Hegel had edited out these lines:

> The nature of your whole personality as a writer is such that, for the time being at least, you would do well not to involve the public in revelations concerning the secrets and motives that lie behind your work, but to

continue as before to raise these issues and give the readers something to think about and something to mull over.

Frederik Hegel probably understood a thing or two alright. The aura of enigma surrounding Ibsen, and the anticipation that preceded each new play, were, from a publisher's point of view, invaluable, and something to be preserved at all costs. Hegel was, however, open to the possibility that Ibsen might, when the time was right, write a conventional memoir of the 'aus meinem Leben' type. With hindsight it is easy to see that his advice was sound. Writer and publisher both could safely leave it to the readers and the literary historians to combine Ibsen's life and work on the basis of memoirs, anecdotes, letters and Ibsen's own stray remarks about his life, not to mention the more obscure areas of his biography, leaving these open to be coloured in by all manner of speculation and literary motifs derived from his own works.

The following January he sat down to start work on the autobiography. As his working title he chose 'From Skien to Rome', but he got no further than a description of the town in which he had grown up and his memories of the time before his father's bankruptcy in 1835. Yet the few pages he did write are of great interest, not primarily for their content but for the literary self-construction that is the deeper subject of the text. This is especially evident in the two specific tales from his earliest childhood. The first concerns his earliest memory, from the steeple of Skien church, where his nanny had taken him. He would always feel a connection with this steeple, he writes, not only because of how striking the view of the world was from up there, but also because he connected the experience to the story of a mysterious black poodle that had once caused the death of a watchman. And that poodle was the devil himself, as it was in Goethe's *Faust*. In other words, what we have here is a variant on the Faustian pact, in which the ageing Ibsen, in describing his childhood, gives a mysterious account of how he entered into a pact with the devil that gave him the power to see the world from a vantage point outside, and on high, divorced from the society of humans, represented by the congregation in the nave beneath the steeple. In this way Ibsen uses autobiography to create a mysterious prelude to his own career as a writer.

In its entirety, the second tale reads like this:

Among my christening presents was a large coin with a man's head on it. The man had a high forehead, a large, bent nose, and a protruding lower lip; he was bare-necked, which seemed strange to me. The nanny told me that the man on the coin was 'King Fredrik rex'. Once when I was playing with it, rolling it across the floor, unfortunately it disappeared down a crack. I think my parents saw this as an inauspicious omen, since it was a christening present. The floor was taken up, and a thorough search made, but King Fredrik rex never saw the light of day again.

The little tale can be read as an account of how Ibsen was cheated of his inheritance; the crown and the throne, power and honour, symbolised by the coin's trivial face value, and its associations with dignity through the royal portrait. This is about declassing, the fall, and the difficult years preceding the departure from Norway in 1864, implied in the way his parents saw an ominous warning in the disappearance of the coin. But as we all know, Ibsen finally won back the crown and the throne.

These childhood fragments were all that Ibsen's dream of writing his own life produced. He could, however, a few years later, read the first full-length biography of him, written by the literary historian Henrik Jæger. Not quite the same as an autobiography, perhaps, but then Jæger did write his book under the watchful eye of his subject.

SATURDAY EVENING AT THE LIES'

As usual, the first part of the summer of 1880 was spent at home in Munich; in central European fashion the Ibsens preferred to take their holiday in the late summer. And as usual, Scandinavians arrived, on their way through the city, Ludvig Josephson and the actor August Lindberg among them. Valfrid Vasenius arrived with the Finnish Nora, the actress Ida Aalberg. The moment she passed through the door, Ibsen said later, he had thought: 'This is Nora.' We do not know what Ibsen and Vasenius talked about, but the Finn had certainly hoped that they might discuss his coming monograph on Ibsen, and received a collection of 'Nora polemics' which Ibsen himself had assembled.

At the beginning of August, Suzannah and Sigurd travelled home to Norway. The purpose was not merely to see the old country again, but to investigate the possibility of Sigurd continuing his studies in Christiania. Before their departure, Henrik had requested of King Oscar a royal resolution that would allow Sigurd to continue his legal studies at home without submitting to the 'second exam' (equivalent to the university preliminary entrance examination). Sigurd had been studying law at the university in Munich since the previous October, and the time had come to plan ahead:

> If my son is to consider becoming a Norwegian citizen, it will now be necessary for him to continue his law studies in Christiania.

Norwegian citizenship then, that was the plan. Sigurd, who had grown up a citizen of the state of Ibsen, was finally considering emigration. Why? Because common sense dictated it, and because Henrik and Suzannah thought the way any responsible parents would. For all his learning, his gift for languages and education, Sigurd had never established any contacts in his chosen professional field, never set foot on any career ladder. If he was to have a future, then he must quite simply have a home country – no matter how late in the day. It seems likely the parents planned to accompany their son, though there is no direct evidence in the sources for this. At any rate, Ibsen's opinion of Norway came increasingly to depend on the degree to which the country would accept his son.

And that acceptance, as it turned out, was hard to come by – or at least so it seemed from the perspective of the Ibsen family.

With wife and son out of the way, Henrik began to make preparations for his own travels. He had planned to spend the latter part of the summer in Berchtesgaden with John Paulsen. As was his habit he began his packing a week in advance, and when the day of departure arrived, he stood waiting on the platform, impeccably clad in a travelling outfit, at least an hour before the train was due to leave. On Ibsen's recommendation, Jonas Lie had also made his regular summer home in the town, and this little group spent time together in that green oasis between the snow-clad Alpine peaks.

Ibsen was booked in at the Hotel Salzburg and was soon to be seen tripping about the little town in a newly purchased Tyrolean hat with a long, bobbing feather. Daily rituals were established. In the morning he would stroll down to the marketplace and carefully study the list of the day's walking tours arranged for visitors by the local guides. After that it was down to the teashop where he would read the day's newspapers, and then off to the kiosk in the local park where he would study the thermometer, the barometer, and the latest telegrams from the meteorological stations in Munich. After that the day's work could begin.

Ibsen spent a lot of time on his own, but on Saturdays the gang assembled at Jonas Lie's place – the same house as the one Ibsen had stayed in when he first came to Berchtesgaden. It was a home from home, with an evening meal of roast beef, vegetables and potatoes, followed by toddies and cigars and a quickening of the atmosphere. Ibsen and Lie behaved like the two old friends and intimates they indeed were. The longer the evenings went on, the more stories were told. As usual Ibsen regaled the gathering with anecdotes from his visit to Egypt; for example, the one about how, on taking his leave of the khedive, he was presented with a 'pretty young negress', a gift he desperately tried to reject. He did, however, write home to Suzannah, warning her to be ready to meet her new, black co-wife.

Ibsen was usually in good form on these evenings, tossing off his paradoxes and his sarcasms, his cynical attacks on the state, on the Church and marriage, alarming his hostess Thomasine Lie so much that she found it necessary to equip herself with a copy of the Bible. He talked about Goethe ('that divine egotist'), and about the excellence of the aristocracy.

'The age needs great men,' he announced, 'and not just a pack of so-called democrats who think themselves "radical" because they support the last word in so-called progress. A modern human being is an anarchist.'

Pause. More toddy.

And they spoke of death. Ibsen wasn't afraid to die, he just didn't want to die in the middle of writing a play. The mood rose and fell with the topic of conversation, but friendship and laughter were the keynotes of those Saturday evenings at the Lies' house.

'When we were together in Berchtesgaden,' Lie recalled later, 'it always seemed to me that I saw two front teeth that became more and more visible with each passing hour; two front teeth with a gap between them. And the higher the mood rose, the more radiant did he become, laughing and laughing like any kindly, good-natured, chatty old midwife!'

Blessed is the man who has known the gap between Henrik Ibsen's front teeth. Jonas Lie must be, in addition, the only person ever to refer to Ibsen as a 'chatty old midwife', though several other stories confirm that he was fond of children. He spent a lot of time with the Lies' boys, fishing together, or listening to what they had to say. Only the daughter of the house was disappointed; she thought a famous toy-maker was coming to visit, and entertained secret hopes that he would be bringing her a doll's house.

Unfortunately for Ibsen and Lie, they were not the only ones to have discovered the beautiful Berchtesgaden landscape. Tourism was on the rise, not least because the presence of Ibsen and other celebrity guests had increased the renown of the place. Fame was beginning to become a burden. Back in Munich he had almost had to turn his home into a fortress to avoid being invaded by journalists and aggressive tourists. Now he couldn't find peace even in the mountains, what with journalists, writers and young ladies wanting and him to sign their poetry books, or local dignitaries who sent him invitations that were hard to decline. The summer of 1880 was the last he ever spent in Berchtesgaden.

* * *

While in the Alps, Ibsen heard of the death of Ole Bull. The whole Norwegian colony was preoccupied by the news. Ibsen had always had a taste for the old adventurer and loved to tell stories about him. 'Ah, so he thought he'd get away with it!' he observed, on hearing that Bull had lain on his deathbed with a flower in his hand and thanked the Lord for everything.

Late in August he received a letter from the Department of Church Affairs informing him that Sigurd would, after all, have to sit his university entrance exam. Judging by the letter he then wrote to Sigurd, Henrik does not seem to have been unduly bothered. He presumed it was just a matter of a few formalities, and that the boy would only have to take exams in a few disciplines. However, when Sigurd presented himself at the university at the beginning of September he was informed that he would have to go through exactly the same procedures as all the other students. His father's initiative had been unsuccessful, obliging Sigurd to spend another year on extra studies in order to qualify for the Faculty of Law, regardless of the fact that the last exam he sat had already qualified him for the title *canditatis juris.*

In Berchtesgaden the atmosphere around the table at the evening meal was oppressive on the day Sigurd's letter arrived. John Paulsen noted how Ibsen's face darkened. His mouth became a thin line, his fingers trembled as they clasped the knife. He said nothing, ate nothing except a little bread and salt – the sound of salt crystals being crushed by the knife was all that disturbed the oppressive silence round the table. Once again, Norway had given the Ibsen family the cold shoulder.

In fact things weren't quite that simple. A closer reading of Sigurd's letter reveals that it was not merely Norwegian bureaucratic petty-mindedness that stood between him and his choice of study. In the letter he concedes that his grasp of the studies involved in the preparatory exams was inadequate. So the university bureaucracy probably had a point after all; Sigurd's education from continental Europe was not entirely compatible with the Norwegian course of study. But neither father nor son was wholly willing to admit it. So great was the son's self-confidence, and so unshakeable the father's belief in his son's outstanding intelligence, that the fault in the matter *had* to lie with Norway.

'Don't imagine I would feel any regret at leaving Norway, even if it be for ever,' Sigurd continued. 'I have to say that I never – and certainly not after this visit – have felt any particular sympathy with or understanding of Norwegian ways and practices.' He had, after all, grown up in 'bigger societies':

I felt depressed and disheartened from the moment I set foot on Norwegian soil this summer, from the first word I exchanged with a Norwegian.

Like son, like father.

'What would you have gained by sitting your legal exams in Norway?' Ibsen wrote back. After all, he wasn't going to be a government official, he was going to be a professor, or a diplomat, and he didn't need legal exams for that. He could simply continue his education in Italy. And yet it is worth noting that his father's suggestions all operate on the assumption that Sigurd will finally settle to a career in his own country. Sigurd's immediate response was to apply to study law at the university in Rome. The family were together again in Munich by the beginning of October. A few weeks later, suitcases packed again, they gave up the apartment in Amalienstrasse and boarded a train going south. They were back in Rome on 4 November. Some two weeks before their departure Ibsen had written to Hegel expressing a revived hatred for his home country:

> As for that gang of black theologians who currently rule the Norwegian Department of Church Affairs, when the time comes I will give them a literary monument all their very own.

And when the time came he would indeed create just such a monument, in the best way he knew how – with his pen.

'I NEVER DRINK TEA'

In Rome the family settled into a pleasant and spacious apartment at Via Capo le Case 75, in the same area they had lived in earlier. There were a number of old acquaintances in Rome in the winter and spring of 1881. The writers Camilla Collett and Marie Colban were staying there, as was Kristofer Janson, a supporter of *nynorsk*, the New Norwegian language, with whom Ibsen had argued so much during his first sojourn in the city. From Munich he knew John Paulsen, Eilif Peterssen, Christopher Meyer Ross and Julius Kronberg. He also met Verner von Heidenstam, at that time still a young and unknown Swedish writer. Lorentz Dietrichson and his wife had come to the farewell party in Munich, on their way to Egypt. On their way back they were staying for a while in Rome. J. P. Jacobsen, however, had gone home. All in all they formed a large Scandinavian colony that crossed each other's paths endlessly, at gatherings, in cafes, on street corners, in the squares.

As ever, Rome was a place in which solitude had to be combated. In the years to come, Henrik and Suzannah would practise a social openness, holding regular soirées for other Scandinavians, Italians and Germans, an openness that suited the elegant living quarters they had chosen. At the Ibsens' soirées at Via Capo le Case 75 one might meet celebrities, famous people, artists, scientists, distinguished travellers. The soirées usually started at about nine or ten in the evening. An Italian waiter served tea, while wine and fruit were available from the buffet. Ibsen wore his black frock coat and gave a dignified greeting to new arrivals. There is no doubt that the family stood out from the other Scandinavians in Rome. Henrik, of course, as the celebrity that he was, Sigurd with his cosmopolitan, pleasant and reserved manner, always immaculately attired whatever the occasion, exactly like his father. And finally Suzannah, described in several sources as a dignified and commanding hostess. Suzannah also had her own circle of Scandinavian women, duchesses, artists' wives and artists who regularly visited each other in their homes. To the Swedish artist Georg Pauli the family was 'distinguished bourgeoisie', unlike other and more unruly members of the Scandinavian colony.

Ibsen's fame is one obvious reason why he now kept the company of prominent people, including non-Scandinavians. Another is that the Scandinavians in general were now living less isolated lives than they had done previously. For example, the painter Christian Ross's studio, in the same street as the Ibsens, had become a regular meeting place for artists, writers, scientists and diplomats from a number of different countries. Rome was no longer just a miniature version of Scandinavia but had become a genuinely international meeting place.

Swedish royalty visited that winter, in the form of two princes, Carl and Oscar. The previous year, when Crown Prince Gustav had visited, he and Ibsen had each waited for the other to extend an invitation. This time King Oscar II had even sent a letter asking Lindstrand, the Swedish minister, to arrange for 'the boys' to meet Ibsen. Alas, it went wrong again: Lindstrand had arranged a banquet in honour of the two princes, but without inviting Ibsen, who was, after all, neither a baron nor a consul. Instead he was invited to take tea later that evening.

Ibsen took umbrage and returned the invitation with the following comment: 'I never drink tea.'

With the coming of spring he and Dietrichson went on an outing together. They travelled by train to Frascati and Tusculum, and by donkey to Castel Gandolfo, the same route they had taken seventeen years earlier. In Genzano they visited the boarding house Ibsen had stayed in, and then travelled on to Lake Nemi. Neither the landscape nor the towns were much changed; but both travellers had. They spoke of various things, with Ibsen complaining as usual about the wretched state of society, about the appalling lack of idealism.

Suddenly he interrupted himself:

> I haven't changed. People think I have changed my views over the years; that is a great mistake; actually, my development is completely consistent; I can trace the clear threads of my own development, the unity behind my ideas, and the gradual way they have unfolded, and I'm writing down a few notes that will show the world that I am exactly the same person now as I was when I first discovered my real self.

Unity and consistency in everything – that had become essential to him, especially now that he was once again passing through the same landscape as when he achieved his great breakthrough, and moreover had had the idea for what would be his major work, *Emperor and Galilean*. Although, in his own opinion, he had found his real self long before; he had been himself ever since his debut play *Catiline*, and he intended to carry on being himself. The intensity of his words to Dietrichson shows that he was now looking both forwards and backwards, as does the reference to the planned autobiography, which he had still not completely given up on.

* * *

National Day, 17 May 1881, was celebrated at the Ibsens' home. The guest of honour was sixty-eight-year-old Camilla Collett, Henrik Wergeland's sister, both of them children of Nicolai Wergeland, one of the fathers of the Norwegian constitution. On that very same day a statue of Collett's brother was unveiled in the Student Gardens in central Christiania. Ibsen was apparently asked to write a poem for the occasion, but declined. Everything pointed to the fact that this would not be any ordinary national day in the Norwegian capital. Tension between the governing officials and the Liberal opposition was nearing breaking point. For the past ten years Liberal politicians in the Storting had regularly put forward proposals that government ministers should have access to the Storting, but on every occasion the king had exercised the royal veto to block the motion. Such a move would involve a diminution in the authority of the ruling powers, since it would give the Storting a much greater degree of control over the government.

On 9 June 1880, however, the proposal had been adopted by the Storting regardless of the royal veto, a move that clearly announced that the elected body no longer recognised the king's right to a veto in constitutional matters. To the conservatives this was a revolutionary provocation, and from this point onwards the struggle for power in Norway entered a last, intense phase that would end in electoral victory for the Liberal Party in 1882, an impeachment case against the Selmer government, and finally pave the way for the introduction of parliamentary rule in 1884.

This atmosphere of mounting tension was the background against which the celebrations of National Day took place in 1881, as the long procession of students, artists, artisans, shooting-club members and farmers – lots of farmers – marched from Tullinløkken, past Henrik Wergeland's old home in Grotten, and down to Eidsvoll Square, where the unveiling was to take place at four o'clock. The air must have been dense with patriotic fervour and politics as the main speaker of the day stepped forward. Bjørnstjerne Bjørnson had just returned from a visit to the United States, where he had been travelling and lecturing since September the previous year. Now he stood in front of the sea of umbrellas surrounding the drenched and glistening statue. He was not any kind of compromise speaker; the conservative papers had started rattling their sabres the moment the name of the day's main speaker was announced, and as he stood there now, in the houses facing Eidsvoll Square decent citizens drew their curtains.

And yet Bjørnson's speech that day is said to have been, by his standards, both dignified and temperate. The mood was tense enough as it was, and Bjørnson was moved to make a peace offering.

The same could hardly be said of Ibsen and the speech he gave for the little group of Norwegians gathered at his apartment in Rome. 'Norway has ninety-nine freedoms, but it doesn't have freedom,' he had announced. That spring he had once again campaigned for an increase in his writer's wage to compensate him for the losses he suffered in the absence of copyright laws. In a letter to the politician Hagbard Berner in March he had requested compensation in the form of an increased stipend for both himself and Bjørnson. Sweden and Denmark had entered into a bilateral agreement on literary copyright, so the problem was not here. In countries outside Scandinavia the situation was very different. Moreover, as he specified to Berner, this matter had assumed particular importance for him now that Sigurd had been refused immediate entry to the university in Christiania, since this had the effect of obliging the whole family to continue living abroad.

Berner probably got the message: if the Norwegians wanted to carry on calling Ibsen 'their' writer, then they had better show some appreciation. Without beating about the bush Ibsen explains to Johan Hermann Thoresen the consequences for him personally of the Norwegian educational system's rejection of his son:

> An Italian or German citizenship would have many advantages for me, and now that the Department of Church Affairs has turned away my son, I really don't know that I have any more business up there.

Ought he to sever his ties to Norway for good? That was up to the Norwegian state.

A 'FARRAGO OF SYPHILIS AND FILTH'

Quite when Ibsen had the idea for the play that would come to bear the title *Ghosts* is not known. But when John Paulsen asked him, in the summer of 1880 in Berchtesgaden, what he was working on, he is said to have replied:

> It's the tale of a family, as grey and sad as today's weather.[16]

Not surprisingly, rumours had long circulated that he intended to write a follow-up to *A Doll's House*. Georg Brandes feared the worst – 'it can only be an attempt to win back the bourgeoisie, who are appalled by Nora, by arranging a reconciliation between the couple. But Ibsen is too good for that.' Would the dramatist finally reveal what everyone was wondering about – just exactly where did Nora go? Of course he did no such thing. In November 1880 he reveals to Hegel that he has an idea for a new play, and the following March his publisher receives a peculiar letter:

> In strictest confidence I can reveal to you that I am writing a new book and that it will be finished in the course of the summer.

Hegel must have been left scratching his head. Not even Ibsen was usually so obscure. There was no word about the content, no one was to know what he was working on. And then, in the middle of June, came a partial revelation:

> The work I mentioned in a previous letter has been temporarily set aside, and at the beginning of this month I started shaping material for a stage play, an idea that has long preoccupied me and that has lately pressed so insistently on me that I was no longer able to ignore it.

It seems likely that it was ideas for *An Enemy of the People* he now set aside. There are no extant drafts of the play, but it can hardly be coincidental that at about this time Ibsen began expressing more forcefully than ever before his notion of aristocratic individualism. 'The majority?' he expostulated to Kristofer Janson in the winter of 1880–1. 'What is the majority? The ignorant mob. Intelligence is always to be found in the minority. How many, do you suppose, of those who are in the majority are qualified to have opinions? Most of them are ignorant clowns.'

These outbursts must have seemed particularly striking in Rome, where radical artists, conservative aristocrats, language reformers, Swedes, Danes and Norwegians all lived together within a closed environment. Doctor Stockmann was on his way, until this insistent idea for a new play obliged him to wait his turn. Ibsen promised to get the manuscript ready over the summer and send it to Copenhagen in the middle of October. At the end of June the family left Rome and travelled to Sorrento. They moved into the same hotel as they had stayed at two years previously, the salubrious Tramontano, beautifully situated atop precipitous cliffs that descended to the Bay of Naples, with views of Vesuvius on one side and Ischia on the other. Goethe, Byron and Keats had lived there before them, and it was here that most of Ibsen's new play was written.

By 30 September, Ibsen was able to inform Hegel that the play was finished, only the fair copy remained. And now at last the publisher was given a title. It was to be called *Ghosts*. The content was revealed to him only gradually, since Ibsen followed his custom of sending each act separately as he finished it. But that wasn't the end of the secretive shenanigans; he insisted to Hegel that at all costs the manuscript be kept from the prying eyes of strangers. He knew that, once they left the printers, these bundles of pages he was putting into envelopes would cause a scandal that would exceed even that caused by Nora's departure. No reason to risk the bomb detonating too early. On 4 November he despatches the second act. The following day the family leave Sorrento. Ibsen plans to send the third and final act from Rome. That's cutting it very fine for the Christmas sales. In November the play is despatched to various Scandinavian theatres.

While still waiting for the book to be printed he writes to Hegel about yet another play, the one he had laid aside earlier to concentrate on *Ghosts*. Rome had revived the ideas and he was working well. It looked to him like a comedy in four acts, but for the time being that was all the publisher was allowed to know. The priority now was this year's play.

> *Ghosts* will, I expect, cause alarm in certain quarters. Let it. If it did not, then it would not have been necessary to write it.

On 13 December 1881, Ibsen's new play – rushed through the printers – was published in Copenhagen. The first print run was a huge 10,000, which suggests that Hegel was expecting the sales at least to match those of Ibsen's previous play. That is not what happened; 13,500 copies of *A Doll's House* were printed in its first year, but no second Danish printing of *Ghosts* was needed until 1894. Nor had a simultaneous German translation been commissioned as had been done with the former play. An obvious reason was that the content of the new play was so daring that it would give a new meaning to the word 'scandalous'. Hegel is said to have received whole consignments of the book as returns from Norwegian booksellers.

Ibsen's top-secret drama had appeared. According to him it was a play that had to be written. How many would agree with him?

Ghosts is a play about chamberlain Alving's widow, Helene, who lives in isolation at Rosenvold with her maid, Regine. She has survived marriage to an alcoholic and debauched husband, sacrificed her love for Pastor Manders, and sent her son Osvald abroad to shield him from his father's profligate ways. As the play opens her son is home again, and the following day she is due to open a children's home funded by the chamberlain's money. This is how she hopes to exorcise the ghosts of the past. But the past will not so easily be driven away; in the course of a single day in Helene's living room the ghosts return with a vengeance. She is compelled to reconsider her own personal history, the part she has played in perverting her husband's joy in life, and the way she has hidden the truth from her son. And when her son tells her of the terrible illness that afflicts him, and asks his mother to give him death, as she once gave him life, Helene realises that she has lost. Even Regine abandons her when Helene reveals that the chamberlain is her true father, making Regine's love for him impossible. As night closes in all hope is suffocated, the children's home burns down, leaving only the son, vainly crying for light as syphilis reduces him to a babbling infant.

The play caused alarm. No question about it.

'Ibsen's book is brilliant, but suicidal,' said Holger Drachmann not long after publication. And that was really about all there was to say. *Ghosts* has long been regarded as the paradigm of Ibsen's dramas of contemporary life. The action takes place in the course of a single twenty-four-hour span, the setting is confined to Fru Alving's living room and the adjacent conservatory with its glass wall in the background. In other words the unities of time, action and place are all observed, with the crucial proviso that Ibsen makes use of *the retrospective technique* which remains inextricably bound up with his name. The story told in the play includes a long prehistory that gradually unfolds through the characters' dialogue. That a drama should open with a presentation of events preceding it was not in and of itself unusual; what is novel about Ibsen's use of the technique is that the unfolding of the past continues throughout the whole of the play, so that much of the plot strictly speaking precedes what is happening onstage; the past is, so to speak, conjured in dialogue, with the moment of realisation occurring at the point at which the unfolded past finally lies fully revealed. Ibsen had used retrospective techniques like these in his two previous plays of contemporary life, but not as consistently as here.

The result was a concentrated and charged drama, reinforced by equally charged dialogue. Ibsen makes greater use than before of the *doubly motivated remark*, a technique of ambiguity in which the characters say one thing, but something else lies beneath. The scenography is equally deliberate, such as the glass wall's symbolic representation of the divide between life inside the Alving household and the threatening reality of the outside world, or the way the flowers underscore the protective greenhouse environment that Fru Alving tried to create for her son Osvald.

Five living and one dead. The drama at Rosenvold is a tragedy of family life that takes place inside a narrow, airless room from which not even sunrise can drive the shadows.

A number of reviewers made the connection to the tragedies of antiquity. One was Peter Olrog Schjøtt, a professor in classical philology. And the relationship was not merely formal, in his view – classical tragedy at its best also dealt with social problems and the challenges of the age. He does not specifically mention the closest parallel, but others have done so. In the Osvald–mother–dead father triangle it is difficult not to see echoes of Sophocles'

Oedipus Rex. The central thematic complex of the inexorable heritage from the father and the suffocation of the maternal attachment gave rise, in due course, to a number of psychoanalytic readings of the play. Others complained that the play was not, strictly speaking, a drama but an epic, in that so much of the plot is retrospective, conveyed through long conversations rather than acted out onstage.

August Strindberg in Sweden was pleasantly surprised by Ibsen's new play. He had previously thought Ibsen 'cowardly' in his development; but was he now really prepared to defend the ideas in his latest play? Georg Brandes responded in similar fashion – 'who would have thought that the tight-lipped and hirsute old man, so cautious for so long, would have been capable of something so young?' Arne Garborg was less enthusiastic. In his review for *Dagbladet* of 14 December he acknowledged the play's power and its formal expertise, but ended on a note of resignation and regret:

> The overall impression of this book is distinctly unpleasant. Having read it, one finds oneself inevitably recalling all that good old poetry which one could read without distressing one's nerves.

He writes to Bjørnson:

> This has put our work back ten years. I cannot comprehend why our hopes and plans for the future need to be served up in the form of this farrago of syphilis and filth.

It is important to remember, when words such as 'unpleasant' recur in the reviews, that this was a perfectly natural reaction among Ibsen's contemporaries, and that he was well aware of just how offensive it was to write about syphilis and incest in a play – not to mention performing that play onstage. Many readers who had followed Ibsen with a fascinated interest now felt that he had overstepped the bounds of good taste. Even those who had admired *A Doll's House* now washed their hands of him – this was going too far. *Aftenposten*'s reviewer found no trace here of the 'healthy bitterness' of preceding plays. Ibsen was no longer a writer who held up a mirror to society. Instead he had turned his back on society, and joined the corrupted ranks of those who preached the 'lesson of the morality of pleasure in all its varieties, heredity, naively understood as freedom from responsibility, free love, the dissolution of family ties, a "painless death" for the sick and the unhappy etc'. What was Helene Alving other than an egocentric and frustrated woman who regretted the only decent thing she had ever done, namely going back to her husband on the instructions of the man she lusted after, Pastor Manders?

All in all Nora Helmer and Helene Alving's revolt against society earned their creator a reputation for unbridled egotism and hedonism – to such a degree that many contemporary readers convinced themselves that these two characters were the author's mouthpiece. This was one of the points Bjørnson raised in a public defence of Ibsen that appeared in *Dagbladet* on 22 December:

> When a newspaper goes as far as to suggest that the author presents Oswald Alving 'as a model', then in the first place one should remember that modern writing no longer concerns itself with 'models', and in the second place that Ibsen is not an idiot.

The following day a second article appeared in *Dagbladet*, entitled 'My Attitude towards *The League of Youth*'. In this Bjørnson explained why he and Ibsen had parted company and, more importantly, that the two of them – Norway's leading writers – had now settled their differences. Now *that* was a contribution guaranteed to attract attention! And yet it was not Bjørnson's version of the nature of Ibsen's literary project that characterised the continuing debate but rather the inevitable ethical question of whether or not *Ghosts* was an attack on marriage, and whether it was acceptable for two people to live together without being married. And what about the children, what about society? Was Ibsen attacking marriage as an institution, or was it rather the case, as Bjørnson claimed, that his attack on 'immoral marriage' actually represented a defence of real marriage? All things considered, literature wasn't much talked about in Norway during that Christmas of 1881, but morality most certainly was.

'This book has no place in a Christian home this Christmas,' wrote *Morgenbladet*, which just about summed up the situation for most people.

* * *

So *Ghosts* caused a literary sensation. But Ibsen had caused literary sensations before; what was it about this play in particular that aroused such furious reactions? An obvious reason is that here, more mercilessly than ever before, Ibsen confirmed his revolt against the aesthetics of idealism, and against an institutionalised social morality. In the home of the Helmer family there was at least a glimmer of hope; but Rosenvold is sunk in pitch blackness, and Osvald's invocation of the sun is merely the helpless sigh of a dying man.

But the reactions went deeper than this. The real shock must have been the actual experience of being confronted by a world suffused with the ugly, the degenerate and the hopeless, and one conjured by the exercise of a complete mastery of dramatic means. In particular the portrayal of the dying Osvald must have seemed like a mockery of all human dignity – this 'repulsive mollusc in human form'. Unease at the character of Osvald was heightened by a scientific determinism that mercilessly propels the characters in the play towards their ruin. At a time when the theory of evolution was emerging as a threat to the prevailing view of the world and of human beings, it was difficult to see the syphilis theme as just a simple parallel to the mental determinism involved in the power of 'dead thoughts' over people. The heredity theme was a provocation in itself because it seemed to eliminate all notion of human freedom and responsibility, and to wipe out the distinction between humans and animals. For a tragic character in a drama it was quite simply meaningless to suffer defeat at the hands of a hereditary illness (as syphilis was believed to be at the time).

Marcus Jacob Monrad concentrated on this aspect of the play. His review in *Morgenbladet* is a subtle text in which, disguised as a resigned idealist, he constructs a sharply polemical and elegantly ironic response. Monrad had been an important philosopher and critic in Norway for a great many years by the time *Ghosts* appeared. Posterity has cast him in the role of the very incarnation of the old society, a man deeply associated with the age of the civil-servant state, someone firmly entrenched in Hegelianism and the aesthetic of idealism. He had followed Ibsen with a benevolent interest throughout his career, but now the society he knew had all but vanished, and with it Monrad's benevolence towards the younger writer.

It is an old, but by no means beaten man who now enquires in *Morgenbladet* what one may learn from *Ghosts* – 'because the time is long gone now when one looked in a work of literature for what was once called poetry and beauty'. The trinity of idealism was broken, the beautiful, the good and the true were no longer one.[17] But what in fact did the naked truth in Ibsen demonstrate? In the first place, said Monrad, that the fight against religion, which was by no means a new phenomenon, now also implied a fight against morality. And that was new. Secondly, an extensive individualism and egotism that defied Christian teachings on community and togetherness as represented by, among other things, the dogma of original sin. Ibsen had exchanged Christianity's original sin for the original sin of the laws of nature – but was anything really gained thereby? Was not the view of human life in *Ghosts* in complete accord with the Christian view, the only difference being that Ibsen's characters were doomed to destruction according to the laws of nature? And did that not in turn mean that the only conceivable salvation from the determinism of nature was to be found in a principle that lay outside the order of nature – in other words, in Christ?

Monrad undeniably has a point here; whereas Ibsen's previous plays had offered freedom and necessity as *possibilities*, here freedom and salvation are announced as effective *impossibilities*. That is certainly one way of reading the play; *Ghosts* is the closest Ibsen ever came to naturalism, and in no other play is he quite so far from idealism.

But how was the play read by those who took an opposite point of view to Monrad's? Amalie Skram, whose *Constance Ring* (1885) established her as one of the most explicitly naturalistic writers in Norway, also found herself shaken by the play's 'naked reality', but unlike Monrad she didn't object. In her eyes, Ibsen was a scientific researcher who had dissected the social organism and was here displaying his findings. Thus both detractors and admirers of the play compared Ibsen to a researcher or a doctor, but in different ways. Skram's ideal was an objective exposure of real life, but in Ibsen she also detected a genuine power of *compassion*; he had been 'blessed with the gift of universal sufferings. He must have carried within his soul all the sorrows of earthly life.'

Ghosts was a slice of raw life, and if the play had a message, it was as a 'warning to society, a frightening call for repentance directed at every thinking person, no matter what their particular beliefs'.

No matter how anti-idealistic the play was, it was also an object lesson in how literature could create a better human being, a better world, not by holding up ideals, but by laying bare the truth. Literature should be neither exemplary nor affirmatory but instead a call to action.

* * *

Not surprisingly, and yet still disappointingly for Ibsen, *Ghosts* was rejected by the main theatres in Copenhagen, Christiania and Stockholm; even Ludvig Josephson refused to consider a performance at the Nya Teatern. At the Kongelige Teater, Erik Bøgh had succeeded Christian Molbech as censor, but even this change couldn't save the play. Bøgh saw it as his 'sworn duty' to reject a play that had a 'repulsive pathological phenomenon' as its main theme. Significantly, his views were more positive in a review of the book in *Dagens Nyheder* of 17 December. Bøgh's two responses illustrate the difference between the written and the spoken word, between book and stage. As a public arena the theatre was more potent, and therefore more dangerous, than the printed book, and censorship of plays all the more strict.

Even before the end of 1881 it was resoundingly clear to Ibsen that it might be a long time before the play was performed on the Scandinavian stage; and that a German theatre might put on a production was, in his view, a 'complete impossibility'. In view of this it is perhaps not so surprising that *Ghosts* was first staged in the United States, the land of opportunity. On 20 May 1882 the play was premiered at Aurora Turner Hall in Chicago by an unknown cast, though Mrs Alving was played by the Danish actress Helga von Bluhme, so the performance was not wholly amateur. This is believed to have been the first time Ibsen was performed in America, and the location was not accidental. Chicago was a city with a large contingent of Scandinavian immigrants. It had a Norwegian-language press and an interest in the theatre that in 1913 led to the establishment of a local 'Norwegian Peoples Theatre', with Holberg, Bjørnson and Ibsen among those in its repertoire. The city's attitude towards gambling, alcohol and prostitution was also liberal. It meant that the threshold of shock was high enough for *Ghosts* to be given a good reception, without protest or interference from the Church. Afterwards the company set out on a tour of Minneapolis and other Scandinavian settlements in the Midwest. The European premiere did not take place until the following year in, of all places, a provincial theatre in the Swedish town of Helsingborg. Several more years would elapse before it found its way onto the great stages of Europe.

Nevertheless this does not mean that the play was not performed in the Old World; according to Herman Bang it was performed 'semi-privately' by amateur actors in Copenhagen not long after publication. And in Germany, where it was published in 1884 but where performance was banned, drama students rehearsed the parts and acted out their own interpretations of the play in obscure salons far from the glamour of the large theatres. It was the young who read the play – 'out on the bridges, away out in the suburbs'.

Had Ibsen known of the secret activities of these youngsters, it would have strengthened the conclusion he had come to regarding the controversy over *Ghosts*, one he articulated in a letter to Georg Brandes in January 1882, his first for five and a half years: 'In my view, the one on the side of what is *right* is the one who is most in tune with the future.'

SOCIETY'S SILVER VEINS

If *Ghosts* shocked contemporaries, it did so in a very different way than *Brand*. Whereas in 1866 Ibsen had managed to confuse and seduce Scandinavian audiences with a drama that defied all expectations of what a drama should be, *Ghosts* to a much greater degree confirmed well-established literary and moral norms. For several years there had been talk of a watershed dividing the 'old' from the 'new' literature, between the traditional idealistic aesthetics and the sort of tendentious modern literature of which the Brandes brothers were Scandinavia's foremost advocates.

This literary schism reflected the deep divisions in the way people looked at Darwinism, positivism, Christianity, freethinking, sexual morality and the left and right in politics, which together formed the essence of the struggle surrounding the breakthrough of the modern in the Scandinavian countries. When the exchanges over *Ghosts* became as heated as they did this was not only a reaction to the content but also because the play was seen as a radical contribution in a profound culture war in which both sides came to adopt extreme positions.

The polarisation and focus of the two sides led also to a gathering of forces in each camp. For Ibsen this involved a strengthening of his links to Georg

Brandes and Bjørnstjerne Bjørnson. While in the United States in the winter of 1980–1, Bjørnson had written warmly about Ibsen, and later put all his considerable authority to work in defence of *Ghosts*.

He got his thanks in March 1882:

> I have been meaning to write to you for some time now to thank you for the open and honest way in which you came to my defence at a time when I felt myself under attack from so many quarters.

For the first time since their correspondence of the 1860s, Ibsen opens his heart. He had been so worried during Bjørnson's trip to America, he had read that Bjørnson had been ill, that there had been a storm at sea:

> I recalled so vividly then how infinitely much you have meant to me, to all of us. I felt that if anything should happen to you, if such a disaster should befall our country, then all my joy in writing would desert me.

Fine words, and an unalloyed declaration of love that is at once conditioned by the subsequent generalisation. As though suddenly made shy by his praise he hastens to hide himself in the crowd – 'all of us'. Bjørnson's response is equally fulsome:

> The truth is, dear Ibsen, that not until I received your letter did I realise how fond I was of you, then as now.

In his next letter Ibsen goes even further and expresses open admiration for Bjørnson's talent for politics – this from a man who had always believed that political engagement marks a betrayal of the writer's call. If he could choose the epigraph on Bjørnson's gravestone, he declares, he would be in no doubt about what to write: 'His life was his finest work.' A magnificent compliment – or is there just a hint of ambiguity there? As much as it appears to praise his human qualities, might the formulation not equally imply a slight on Bjørnson's activities as a writer? Bjørnson appears oblivious to any potential ambiguity:

> Damned if I know what's happened, but all this is very nicely done. I take my hat off to you.

Not that any of this meant that Bjørnson was a particular admirer of *Ghosts*. 'Actually I am repelled by Ibsen's book,' he confides to Georg Brandes. 'He uses people merely to deliver lines, he has no loving understanding of them.'

Bjørnson's strategy of a dual response to Ibsen's play – reservations in private but defence in public – was one shared by Georg Brandes. At one point he feared that in his new play Ibsen would give the audience the closure they had been cheated of in *A Doll's House*. But when the time came Ibsen did the opposite; instead of sending Nora back home again he described the terrible fate of the woman who never walked out. Helene Alving is a woman defeated by those very demons that Nora rebelled against. This dark consistency of vision appealed to Brandes, and in the review he wrote for the Danish *Morgenbladet* of 28 December 1881 he stresses the point that the play is a literary expression of the scientific theory of genetic heritage. And, opponent of Christianity that he was, Brandes was gratified that the villain of the piece was a man of the Church. Brandes had certain reservations, however; he found it technically unsatisfactory that the entire play involved an exposure of the characters' past; in other words he, too, experienced the retrospective technique as a breach of the conventions of drama. In the analysis, though, all was subordinate to this one thing, that Ibsen had more or less risked his bourgeois respectability for the sake of his artistic vision:

> Despite its great importance, this book is not the most perfect drama he has written. It is, however, the most noble act of his literary life.

Georg Brandes' review in *Morgenbladet* is the single most influential document that links Ibsen and Brandes as allies in the modern breakthrough in Scandinavia. There is also no doubt that Brandes saw *Ghosts* as supportive of both himself and the movement of which he regarded himself as the leader.

Nor was he in any doubt about the 'disreputable literature' that lay on Mrs Alving's table – 'the lady is reading "Main Currents", isn't she?'

It is evident, however, that the Danish critic's enthusiasm was highly conditional, and primarily related to the play's strategic importance in the culture wars. *Ghosts* was grist to the mill of the breakthrough movement, tactically exploited by Brandes to unite literary Scandinavia under his leadership. In private his objections to the play were far greater than anything he expressed in his review, not only on the formal level but also as regards its content. As Brandes read it, the play's main thrust involved its challenge to the prohibition against marriage between half-brother and sister:

> But what use is *that* opposition? Speaking personally, none at all.

No, what the breakthrough movement needed was a literature that could convince and attract supporters, and not frighten people away. That said, there was naturally an obligation to defend Ibsen from the 'rabble' – out of respect for him, and for the continued solidarity of the movement. It was on this point that Garborg had made his mistake; he should have kept his antipathies to himself, and defended the play in public, as Bjørnson and Brandes had done. But there were those who feared that Ibsen's drama was too much even for the movement's own people. What if, instead of uniting the movement, it did the opposite and occasioned a split into a radical and a moderate wing? This was what the liberal Johannes Victorinus Pingels feared. Brandes didn't share the fear. In his view *Ghosts* was almost a miscalculation; Ibsen had abandoned his usual caution and mounted 'a furious attack' in the belief that the Scandinavian public were ready for it. The miscalculation arose, according to Brandes, from the fact that Ibsen, in remote exile, obtained his ideas of the mood back home in Norway from the novels of Alexander Kielland and others. Now he knew better. After this he would 'improve his plan of attack' and resume his former caution.

There were several indications that this was indeed just what was happening. On 6 January 1882, Ibsen wrote a letter to Schandorph that was printed in the Danish *Morgenbladet* shortly afterwards, and presently spread throughout Scandinavia. In it Ibsen stressed that not a single view expressed in *Ghosts* could be ascribed to the author personally. Never had he written a play from which his own voice was quite so absent. His only goal had been to describe reality, and the book was certainly not intended to promote nihilism: 'It doesn't in fact promote anything at all.' What else could this be but a wretched retreat? For the supporters of the breakthrough Ibsen's exercise in fire-fighting was embarrassing. Behind the scepticism lay profound doubts about Ibsen's social courage: 'Hand on heart,' wrote Bjørnson to Georg Brandes early in 1882, 'do you really think he would have published that last book had he known the kind of reception it would get?'

Was Ibsen really trying to put out a fire he himself had started? There was no simple answer to the question, not even in his own responses to the criticism. His initial reaction to Brandes was at once tolerant and patronising:

> In Norway I think the nonsense has been for the most part involuntary, and there is a very obvious reason for this. Up there criticism is the province of those who are more or less theologians in disguise.

His aim had been to announce their death by erecting a tombstone over 'that band of theologians back home', so it was only to be expected they would do their feeble best to respond. Moreover, his plays had whipped up storms before. 'The outrage will fade away this time too, just as it has done before,' Ibsen wrote to Hegel. Nevertheless, in the letter to Brandes the temperature rises line by line:

And what is one to say of the so-called liberal press? These leaders who talk and write about freedom and freethinking, and at the same time make themselves the slaves of the presumed opinions of their subscribers?

Then comes this:

> Bjørnson says: the majority is always right. And as a practical politician he is more or less compelled to say so. I, on the other hand, am equally compelled: the minority is always right.

Thus the maxim of aristocratic individualism. Ibsen's view of society begins and ends with a sense of his own superiority: 'The future belongs to my book. Those chaps who have made such a fuss about it don't even really know much about their own times.'

Yet his defence of *Ghosts* is not completely unconditional. In the summer of 1882 he writes to Sophie Adlersparre, who had lectured on the play in Stockholm: '. . . I am in complete agreement with you when you say that I dare not go any further than *Ghosts*. I have a feeling that the general mood in our countries will not sanction it, and nor do I feel any urge to go further. A writer cannot distance himself so greatly from his people that there is no longer any understanding between them.'

It is quite possible that Ibsen feared for his social reputation after the publication of *Ghosts*. Maybe he had misjudged his public. He had, of course, anticipated the storm, but maybe not its strength, or that his artistic motive would be called into question. But literature was a serious matter for Ibsen, and in the final analysis he *had* to stand by what he had written. He admitted that the play had been 'rather daring', but he had acted under a compulsion to move 'a few boundary markers'. Beyond this he had only a limited interest in being drawn further into the political debate. When the dust stirred up by social discourse threatened to overshadow art, well, his response was to retreat into his shell. This was what Brandes and Bjørnson found difficult to accept. Ibsen stood behind *Ghosts*. He never again wrote a play that so directly challenged the social norms of his time, but he continued to provoke, albeit in ways that Brandes could hardly have foreseen.

Does this then mean that it is wrong to count Ibsen among the supporters of the men of the modern breakthrough in Scandinavia? The title of Brandes' 1883 book gave its name to a period in literary history. But of course the modern breakthrough in Scandinavia is not a historical fact; it is an ideologically loaded description, formulated in a specific set of circumstances which has, over the course of the years, become the standard designation for the entire period.[18] In reality 'the modern breakthrough' covers personalities and currents of the time with a handful of defining qualities in common but which might otherwise be very different from each other. There was, for example, a considerable distance between Brandes' socially constructive idealism and Ibsen's *tabula rasa*, and between Bjørnson's populist and collectivist attitudes and the radical individualism of Ibsen and Brandes (significantly, in the later years of the 1880s, there was another break between Brandes and Bjørnson in their views on the 'chastity question'). Nor was everything centred on Brandes; in Norway, people such as Aasmund Olavsson Vinje, Ernst Sars and Olaus Fjørtoft had adopted positivism, Darwinism and Spencerism independently of Brandes, even though his lectures had been landmark occasions in Norway too.

In the same way it is important to be careful with a typically Scandinavian concept such as 'cultural radicalism'. It has been used not only to group writers of the movement together, but also to reinforce the idea of the existence of a liberal, democratic and humanist line running from the Age of Enlightenment via the modern breakthrough to the left-wing intellectual groups of the twentieth century. One effect of this has been that the authoritarian, anti-democratic and aristocratic tendencies in Ibsen have been partly overlooked, and partly toned down to avoid association with the fascist eras of the twentieth century. To put it crudely, Ibsen is usually portrayed as a 'frustrated cultural radical', sometimes losing his way a little but fundamentally good.[19] In reality the division between liberal and illiberal positions in the nineteenth century was much more fraught and complex than twentieth-century left-wing intellectuals like to admit.

Georg Brandes appears to have had his doubts about whether Ibsen should be counted among those writers associated with the breakthrough. In articles and speeches about the literature of the movement he hardly mentions Ibsen. This changed in the autumn of 1881, in a series of lectures that formed the basis for his article 'Bjørnson and Ibsen', included in *The Men of the Modern Breakthrough* in 1883. That was how long it took Brandes to place Ibsen unequivocally among the writers of the modern breakthrough. Perhaps he found it difficult to judge him in a way commensurate with his own ideas – as late as the autumn of 1879 he had referred to Ibsen as a 'dyed-in-the-wool conservative'. The dilemma is reflected in *The Men of the Modern Breakthrough*. The entire chapter on Ibsen veers between belittlement and aggrandisement, a contradiction reflecting Brandes' efforts to censure Ibsen's anti-social, conservative, enigmatic and pessimistic sides while at the same time hailing him as a leading figure in the breakthrough movement.[20]

Might it perhaps have been wisest for Brandes to accept the consequences of his many reservations and simply exclude Ibsen from the programme of the modern breakthrough? If we take this line it opens up a whole new way of looking at Ibsen's oeuvre, one in which the realistic plays involving social criticism comprise only a limited, if important, part of his work, from *The Pillars of Society* (1877) to *An Enemy of the People* (1882). Starting with *The Wild Duck* (1884), he moves away again from tendentious realistic drama and towards the symbolic drama of ideas. Indeed, if we stress the relationship between the early plays of ideas (*Brand, Peer Gynt* and *Emperor and Galilean*) and the symbolic phase (from *The Wild Duck* to *When We Dead Awaken*), the intervening dramas might almost seem a socially critical raptus in which Ibsen deviates from a line to which he returns for the final phase of his career.[21] A theory such as this has value if it confines itself to the way in which the dramas with contemporary settings examine the externals of social life, social institutions and politics. But in general the most useful way to look at Ibsen is as a writer who, through a unique mix of symbolism and realism, broaches existential and universal questions in most of his mature work. Nor is it difficult to find in the dramas of contemporary life threads that are further developed in the later works, for example in the portrayal of female protagonists, in the critique of idealism, and the examination of day-to-day life.

Regardless of which approach one uses, there is a certain logic to placing Ibsen in the same landscape as Brandes, Bjørnson, Kielland and the other writers of the modern breakthrough, and thus also as an ally of Brandes, whether he liked it or not. For there was no getting round Brandes. He became the unifying figure as the cultural battle in Scandinavia intensified in the 1880s. Indeed, ever since the controversial lectures on Kierkegaard in Christiania in 1876, his power as a force for unity and division had probably been greater in Norway than in Denmark. The movement's most fundamental common denominators are also to be found in Ibsen's dramas of social criticism: middle-class marriage, the place of women, the morality of capitalism, sexual morality, Christianity's hold over people. He also made use of scientific ideas such as genetic heritage and evolutionary theory.

On the question of whether Brandes had any direct influence on Ibsen's writing, it is commonly asserted that the influence went, for the most part, the other way. When they first got to know each other, Brandes was the apprentice, Ibsen the master. And yet there are clear signs that in particular the first volume of *Main Currents*, entitled *Emigrant Literature*, may have influenced Ibsen; there are, for example, obvious similarities between *Ghosts* and Mme de Staël's *Corrine*, which Brandes discusses in his book.[22] On the other hand there is a danger of confusing a similarity of ideas with an influence. And if Ibsen *was* in fact influenced by Brandes then that would be all the more reason for him to deny it.

He had the same attitude towards the literary giant whom contemporary observers identified as a role model for both Brandes and Ibsen. From the 1870s onwards Émile Zola was French naturalism personified, the name above all others associated with the desecration of the temple of art as the man who had dirtied his own hands in the sewers of Paris. Brandes himself, who introduced Zola's work to Scandinavia, had certain reservations about the Frenchman, possibly tactical in origin. Ibsen, of course, acted similarly, often claiming that he merely knew the great French naturalist by repute (only towards the end of his life did he admit to having read many of his books). When a Swedish painter once suggested that he was getting close to French naturalists such as Guy de Maupassant and Émile Zola, Ibsen responded with barely controlled anger:

> Yes, with this little difference, that Zola goes down into the sewers to take a bath, while I do so to clean them.

Ibsen's description of the difference between himself and Zola is contentious. Zola's expressed aim was to 'clean' the sewers. As a writer his approach was that of the investigative journalist, and as a naturalist he had clear ideas for a programme of practical social reform. There are no grounds for suspecting Ibsen of anything similar. He also had a 'purifying' agenda, in his case to 'clean', not society's institutions, but the mind of the individual, to open up the possibility of a freer and more authentic life.

Perhaps we can go no further in comparing Ibsen's dramas and the literary programme of leading naturalists such as Zola and Brandes. In his revolt against the aesthetic of idealism Ibsen was in full accord with the earthbound focus of realism and naturalism, in which art concerned itself with the inadequacy of human beings in the sensate world, and not with their possible perfectibility in the sphere of ideas and metaphysics. At the same time freedom, not truth, was Ibsen's goal, and it must be this visionary dimension in his plays that explains their popularity both historically and globally, far beyond the contexts in which they originally appeared. It is not difficult to understand the ambivalence Ibsen must have felt at the reception accorded *Ghosts*. Certainly he wanted to shake society to its foundations, but he wanted to do so from the outside – as an artist. He wrote literature, but was read as a polemicist. Everybody wanted a part of him, friend and foe alike, to the degree to which friend and foe could be separated.

'What disheartens me most,' he writes to Otto Borchsenius, 'are not the attacks, but the fear that so clearly reveals itself in the ranks of the so-called liberals up in Norway. Poor material to man barricades with.'

For Ibsen the whole circus round *Ghosts* must have seemed rather like the Chinese proverb that says when a finger points at the moon the idiot looks at the finger. Yes, he wanted to write about society; but what preoccupied him above all was society *within* the individual, not the institutions surrounding the individual. Seen in this light, it is hardly surprising that after *Ghosts* he chose to take a different direction in his writing – but not until he had first given the critics his resounding literary response.

FOR THE BUSINESSMEN AND THEIR WIVES

While the storm around *Ghosts* was still raging, Ibsen sent a letter to Hagbard Berner, a prominent figure on the left. In March 1881 he had asked the member of parliament for help in getting a raise in the writer's wage of which both he and Bjørnson were recipients, and early in 1882 he read in *Dagbladet* that Berner really had put his request to the Storting. Ibsen's hopes were raised, but in reality it was by no means a foregone conclusion that the Storting would give the author of something as 'smutty' as *Ghosts* this sort of public recognition. And sure enough, even though a number of members expressed their understanding for Ibsen's request for financial compensation in view of the lack of copyright protection abroad, the moral concern was overriding: when it came to it the Storting unanimously voted against the motion.

There was little Ibsen could do but pick up his pen again. Indeed, even as he awaited the result of the vote in the Storting, he had decided to start on something new. His plans for a literary autobiography were dropped; the demand that he should be open about his own position after *Ghosts* seems almost to have had the contrary effect of encouraging him to mark an even clearer distinction between himself and his work. A new drama began to press upon him, probably the one he had laid aside the previous year. Just as *Peer Gynt* had followed *Brand* almost of itself, so too did *An Enemy of the People* seem like the natural follow-up to *Ghosts*. In both cases the second play can be seen as a dramatic expression of the reception of the preceding play. And yet it was not simply artistic necessity at work when Ibsen followed up the black pessimism of the tragedy with a comedy.

'It's going to be a peaceable play this time,' he wrote to Hegel in March 1882, 'something that can be read by cabinet ministers and businessmen and by their wives, and that won't see the theatres shying away. It won't take long to finish it, and I am certain I will have it ready by early autumn.'

He had every reason to want to regain the support of the cabinet ministers, the businessmen and their wives, not to mention the theatre managers. Ibsen's income for 1881 had fallen by almost 40 per cent from the preceding year. In particular his income from the theatres had been affected. The result was an increase in the number of requests to Hegel for an advance – and a comedy. The ability to combine the artistically uncompromising with a sound business sense is one of Ibsen's most remarkable characteristics, and it was never more evident than on this occasion. The autumn before he had worked hard to finish *Ghosts* in time for the Christmas market; he really was hoping that this uncompromising, bleak drama about syphilis, incest and ruin would find itself under every Christmas tree throughout the land! Aware as he was of the play's potential to offend, still he drove himself on to finish it in time for Christmas. Later he wrote to Hegel anxiously enquiring whether he thought the play's contro-versial contents had damaged its sales potential. Artist and salesman, hot and cold at one and the same time.

The same thing now happened with *An Enemy of the People*. It might seem cynical, and it probably was too. At the same time we should bear in mind that he acted in keeping with his own self-image as a state-appointed satirist; his job was to crack the whip, and it was the public's job to jump, in the same way as it was the state's job to raise his writer's grant so that he could continue his assaults on the establishment in his work. That had been the nature of his contract with the public for years, and it had brought him both artistic and financial gain. In this light *Ghosts* was an exception. The public had failed to uphold their side of the contract with their writer, and it would be a long time before he would forget it.

The play was finished as early as 20 June. He had his title, but debated whether to describe it formally as a comedy or a drama. In the end he decided on the latter, but made no secret of the fact that his play had 'much of the comedy in it, though its heart is serious'. He would be sending the fair copy to Hegel in due course; on this occasion they still had plenty of time before the autumn sales market. But could Hegel keep the title a secret? And simply leak the news that a new comedy in five acts was to be expected from Ibsen?

The tactics were ready. Bring on the autumn.

* * *

In the meantime Ibsen's attention was focused on the other writer in the family. Still only twenty-two, Sigurd had, in the course of June 1882, finished his exams and finalised his thesis on *La camera alta nel governo reppresentativo* – 'The Place of the Second Chamber in a Representative Form of Government'. He defended his thesis at the University of Rome on 4 July in the presence of eighteen professors, and once he had finished he received a standing ovation.

'He is the youngest doctor of law in Rome,' writes the proud father to Bjørnson. And how was Bjørnson's son Bjørn, who was already making his name in the world of Norwegian theatre? 'He's a future head of the theatre, there's little doubt about that.' Familiar and friendly, as though there had never been any harsh words between them. But Sigurd's future was by no means assured. The next stage was to get him a career, and even here it was impossible to reckon without the Norwegian authorities. The struggle went on. Not long after the ceremony the newly created doctor of law and his parents travelled to Gossensass, where they lodged at the Hotel Gröbner. The weather was atro-cious that late summer, the rain poured down, and an autumnal chill kept them indoors for most of the time.

But work continued apace. At the end of August, Ibsen sent the first four acts to Hegel, and the rest on 9 September:

Working on this has given me much pleasure, and now that I'm finished I miss it, and feel empty. Dr Stockmann and I got on so well together. There were so many things we were in agreement on; but the doctor is more confused in his thinking than I, and has a lot of other oddities as well, so that people will accept things from him a lot more readily than if it had been I who said them.

Hegel must have been rubbing his hands in anticipation. A protagonist who resembled Ibsen but was even more outspoken – it sounded like strong stuff after all the furious outbursts in the wake of his previous play. Unfortunately, both play and dramatist were subject to delays. Just as the Ibsens were due to return news came that heavy rains had washed away the country roads and railway lines in Italy. Early in October the family at least managed the trip down from the mountain, lodging at the Hotel Elefant in Brixen, where they were able to enjoy the last of the summer heat between the vineyards as they waited for the roads to open again. Time passed, there were further delays, more flooding, and in Rome the Scandinavians started to wonder. The day before the traditional goose festival of 10 November the Swedish artist Ellen Kylberg noted in her journal:

No sign of Ibsen yet – he hasn't written – no one knows if he'll be coming this year.

Hegel had managed to keep the play a secret, but now the time had come to break the news. In Brixen, Ibsen had heard from Hegel that the play had been delayed. His anxiety increased; he simply could not afford to miss out on the Christmas sales this year. A few days after the goose festival the roads were opened at last, and the Ibsens were able to return to Rome. On 28 November 1882 *An Enemy of the People* was published in a first edition of 10,000 copies. The poor sales of the previous year were forgotten, now it was all about winning back the businessmen and their wives.

AN ENEMY OF THE PEOPLE

Although *An Enemy of the People* is full of comic elements, its theme is serious enough. At the centre of events is the truth-loving doctor Thomas Stockmann and his struggle against the 'compact majority' in the home town he has returned to after an absence of many years. In the beginning all is sweetness and light. Over a long period Thomas has been carrying out scientific measure-ments at the spa, the town's most important source of income. When he discovers that the water is a danger to health he at once suggests that the spa be closed – serenely confident that the townspeople will thank him for his discovery. And indeed they do, until it emerges that the necessary improvements will cost the town a great deal of money. Under the leadership of his own brother Peter Stockmann, the local judge, opinion now turns against Thomas. Peter manages to get the backing of the local liberal newspaper, which had first taken up the case as a way of attacking the town's conservative leadership. Presently the conflict moves on from the specific question of the spa to the more general question of whether the majority or the minority is in the right.

At the large public meeting in the fifth act, Thomas confronts the people of the town with his *new* discovery – that 'the most dangerous enemy of truth and freedom among us is the compact, liberal majority. Yes, that damned compact liberal majority – *that's* who it is. So now you know.'

The meeting ends as the doctor is declared an enemy of the people. The family is evicted from their home, the daughter Petra loses her teaching job, and Thomas's own patients desert him. Finally his only supporters are his family and his friend, Captain Horster. Thomas considers leaving town, but decides that it's better to remain and teach the people to understand the true nature of freedom. He proposes to start a school, with his own two sons and the urchins of the town as his first pupils: 'This time I'm going to experiment with the mongrels; now and then some of them turn out to be quite remarkably bright.'

So he ends as the purely aristocratic individual, dedicated to making something better out of a people whom he despises for their lack of nobility. Almost everyone is against him, and yet still he claims to be the strongest man in the world – precisely because he stands alone.

* * *

This was yet another formally perfect play from Ibsen, with a dramatic and ironic turning point perfectly placed in the middle of the third of the play's five acts.[23] The local judge turns up at the print shop and wins over Hovstad and Aslaksen, the journalists who initially supported his brother on the issue of closing the spa. From this point Thomas Stockmann moves rapidly from being an optimistic leader of public opinion with the wind in his sails to being an outcast enemy of the people with a deep contempt for the general public.

Technically the play is a masterpiece, something the critics remarked upon almost *en passant*, being no less than what was expected of a new play by Ibsen. Beyond this it divided the critics deeply. Erik Vullum in *Dagbladet* interpreted it as an ideological treatise on the conditions for individual freedom in a modern democracy. Here Thomas Stockmann appears in a heroic and decidedly non-ironic light as a hero with a prescriptive programme for the liberation of the individual from the assaults of society.

Indeed, Stockmann is, according to Vullum, so completely rounded that his character requires no interpretation. It was an understanding he shared with Henrik Jæger, who describes the portrait of the main character as 'an outstanding piece of modern psychology'.

By contrast, other critics found the spa doctor a highly problematic figure. Marcus Jacob Monrad finds him ridiculous, but not comical. Stockmann is motivated not by a thirst for truth but by vanity: there was nothing edifying about the play, its lessons were entirely negative. The play was neither tragedy nor comedy; there was no liberating humour, no inspiring conclusion, nor a genuinely tragic dimension. Monrad was not the only contemporary reader who, in his genre-led approach, found the format of the play disturbing. Was the idealist spa doctor depicted comically or heroically? He was at least no Steensgaard – his cause was much too good for that – and the play had too much bitterness in it. At the same time it was difficult to take Stockmann's obstinate individualism seriously, if indeed it was meant to be taken seriously at all. If only one could identify in Stockmann the dramatist's own voice. But Ibsen had expressly rejected the idea that his plays contained authorial mouthpieces, so what was one to believe?

The minority is always right. Those were Ibsen's own words, weren't they?

It was as though Ibsen wanted to test the public's ability to accept his poetics by presenting a literary alter ego for whom he could nevertheless disclaim all personal responsibility. Somewhere between the extreme responses of Vullum and Monrad was Arne Garborg, offering his familiar mixture of admiration and doubt in reviewing his old role model. After the slaughtering of *Ghosts* one might have expected Garborg to adopt a milder tone, but he did not. With something close to relish he points out the many contradictions and inconsistencies in the play, not least in the huge gap between Stockmann the social revolutionary, and the prosaic conclusion he draws from his revolt. Stockmann uses a lot of big words to decry the uselessness of the conservatives, the cowardice of the liberals, and the stupidity of the crowd, but ends up doing what anyone else who wants to improve the world does, the only thing that actually *can* be done: he begins modestly, hoping that society can be reformed one step at a time. The social revolutionary's call is that of the schoolteacher, that's about as spectacular as it gets, says Garborg.

A problematic aspect of the Stockmann philosophy is, of course, the *legitimacy* the minority bases its right on. Garborg has no problem with the play's assertion that the minority is always right. For critics of a more Christian and idealistic cast of mind, such as Monrad, and Carl David af Wirsén, the leading Swedish critic of the time, the minority's claim to be in the right was harder to swallow. And which minority was Ibsen thinking of? Surely not Georg Brandes and his circle? It is symptomatic that the most severe criticism of aristocratic individualism came from the conservative–Christian–idealistic quarter. Here the Christian ideal of brotherhood and community is raised against elitism and the cultivation of genius, the dichotomy between minority and majority replaced by the divine principle as this is manifest in a superior principle (God) and the individual (which makes everyone equally valuable).

In other words, the way in which the play exposed contradictions in liberal secular society invited a critique of the premises on which society itself was based – on the rights of the majority as well as the minority. Bearing in mind the anti-clerical thrust of the 1880s cultural struggle, Monrad's and af Wirsén's thoughtful reviews are worthy of note: as conservative and idealistic as their views might have been, there was little of the inflexible Pastor Manders about them. And though several contemporary critics noted the dramatic irony in *An Enemy of the People*, there was striking uncertainty on the question of what conclusions one might draw from an ironic reading of the work.

'The main character obviously enjoys the dramatist's sympathy,' writes Garborg, 'but at every stage the light of irony plays over him, even when he is most keenly urging "the voice of truth".'

Fair enough, but why build up a hero and then pull the rug from under his feet? Of all the critics it is Garborg who is most inclined to accept Ibsen's approach: he sees *An Enemy of the People* as a typical Ibsen play about the individual's struggle to be himself, despite the pressures of society. Monrad notes the dramatic irony too, but sees no purpose in it if the play has no constructive message. Valfrid Vasenius, the self-appointed defender of Ibsen's writings, notes the flaws in the spa doctor's character but does not seem to have spotted the dramatic irony. Instead he finds it necessary to campaign as Stockmann's defender. The spa doctor does his best, says Vasenius, failing completely to see the knife Ibsen has plunged into the character's back.

There was one thing at least the critics were all agreed on: Ibsen's play was excellent material for the stage, even though some thought there was altogether too much swearing. So no opposition from the theatres this time. On the contrary, they queued up for the play. The premiere at the Christiania Theatre on 13 January 1883 was greeted with real enthusiasm. 'This was a premiere – not something we get every day up here,' wrote the reviewer for *Aftenposten*. Judging by the bursts of laughter from the audience, the play was performed and greeted as a comedy, though 'irony could be glimpsed everywhere behind the apparent seriousness'. This balance between seriousness, farce and irony seems to have been crucial to the play's success as a piece of theatre.

And Ibsen must have enjoyed a quiet chuckle too when the Christiania Theatre accepted his demand for the unusually large fee of 4,000 kroner for the play; clearly he wanted compensation for the rejection of his previous play. The next performances came at theatres in Bergen and Gothenburg, both in

February, before it opened at the Kongelige Teater in Copenhagen, in March. Four years later it was staged in Berlin, the first performance outside the Scandinavian countries.[24]

* * *

Over a century later, *An Enemy of the People* still seems like an apparently simple play that is somehow also strangely diffuse and disturbing. Thomas Stockmann is too pathetic and abstract to work as a tragic hero, but at the same time too serious to be a straightforward comic character. Yet the play is simultaneously comic and tragic. This is especially apparent in the final act, where Stockmann's furious reckoning with the compact liberal majority is shown to be every bit as ironic as it is heroic. It is hardly surprising that it has been read and performed in such radically different ways. While Erik Vullum read it as an attack on the pillars of society, in his production at the Kongelige Teater in Copenhagen, William Bloch stressed the way it could be seen as a rebuke to the political left – to the enthusiastic applause of a conservative audience.[25] This presented a particular problem for one of the possible models for Dr Stockmann, Georg Brandes. He was at that time on his way home to Denmark hoping to gain influence within the Danish left in its struggle against the country's conservative minority government. He certainly did not need to be associated with Stockmann's struggle against the 'compact, liberal majority' and in a speech given at the Students' Union he explicitly dissociated himself from the play.[26]

So the reactions were many and varied, as might be expected of an Ibsen play. An analysis of the structure shows patterns from several different genres are woven together; the play is partly a realistic social comedy that borrows traits from the comedies of character and of traditional intrigue associated with Molière and Holberg, and yet borrows as much from the characteristics of tragedy.[27] Historically, attention has been focused on Stockmann and his beliefs. Indeed, the heroic reading has been historically so dominant that when the idea of presenting Stockmann not solely as a hero but also as a clown was voiced in the 1960s it aroused controversy.[28]

The earliest responses included such a notion, so it was nothing new. But to see Stockmann as *merely* a clown is to go too far; for does he not have, like Osvald, a sanguine, happy nature? Yes he is naïve, but he is also visionary. And objectively speaking at least, the truth is on his side in the question of the health risks associated with the spa waters. On the other hand, Stockmann shows a complete lack of understanding of the bourgeois society to which he belongs when he blithely ignores every aspect of the economic realities, and every need for organised co-operation and beneficial engineering projects. It is no accident that Stockmann's closest ally is Horster. As a sea captain he stands in many ways outside bourgeois society, he is 'the skipper of his own ship', an image of benevolent aristocratic authority.[29]

Ashore, however, the skipper has as little authority as his spiritual companion the spa doctor does at the public meeting. In other words Stockmann's rage is the rage of resignation, he is the aristocrat who wants to 'torpedo the ark' but merely ends up a schoolmaster. And yes, this is the rage of a Henrik Ibsen, dissected and offered up to the judgement of the public by Ibsen himself. Like Horster, Ibsen stood in many ways on the edge of society, and in his exile he was as far from land as any ship's captain.

If we replace the spa doctor with the poet, we recognise at once Ibsen's own image of himself as the outsider, the man who stands alone because he is one of the advance guard of his culture. Called to be a leader, he cannot live in the world but must go out into the desert, to the fringes of society. The writer is the one who stands most alone. Yet there is one crucial difference between them: Stockmann is most reminiscent of Ibsen the man in his thunderous oration, categorical and free from doubt. But as a writer Ibsen had a dual image of himself: he was of the anointed at the same time as he was one of the guilty, a doubter with a limited talent for citizenship.

Perhaps the most fruitful biographical aspect of the play is that Ibsen the writer, through his portrait of the doctor, Stockmann, exposes and dethrones Ibsen the man, and in so doing demonstrates the simultaneous 'tragedy and comedy' of mankind that is also Ibsen's own.

With his ambiguities and complexities Ibsen had once again demonstrated his ability to confound and seduce his audience. But the play shows several natural points of connection with a number of his earlier works. As a drama of social life it relates to both *The League of Youth* and *The Pillars of Society*, the former in particular. In *An Enemy of the People* we meet Aslaksen the typesetter once again, we learn that Steensgaard is Hovstad's predecessor at the newspaper, and that the teacher of Stockmann's sons is none other than Rørlund. Digging deeper into the thematic content of the work, we can also see that Thomas Stockmann is driven by an intense and uncompromising idealism reminiscent of another of Ibsen's heroes: according to Garborg, Stockmann is a Brand who has been 'taken down from the heights and turned into a taxpayer'.

This typical Ibsen trademark explains much of the success of the play. But success had another side. Increasingly, Ibsen was emerging as a polemicist, a writer with a surprising ability to promote debate. The result was that audiences were focused ever more on the plays' ethical and political aspects, and paid less attention to their literary and artistic qualities. In other words, the plays were read and experienced as political pamphlets to a degree that must have dismayed Ibsen. Along with this, his eccentric personal obscurity and ambivalence created a considerable degree of interest in him as an individual.

Whether one viewed him as a poet-prophet or a public enemy, people were becoming as interested in the writer as in the work. He had no objection to being cast in this sphinx-like role, and actually played up to it. But it meant he had to struggle to remind people it was literature that was his business, not politics. Be that as it may, these three elements – the politics, the poetry and the poet himself – acting together, combined to make him an explosive force in Scandinavian public life.

FIRST MEETINGS

He was a writer, head of a small business concern, and an enigma inextricably bound up with obscure dramas. And still the cult surrounding his person was in its infancy. But celebrity was a mixed blessing. Between 1879 and 1885, during his time in Italy, Ibsen found that everyone wanted a piece of him, both residents and visitors to the country. Increasingly, he felt the need to guard his privacy and his working life. Women in particular were strangely attracted to him. One was particularly memorable, and not just on account of her fondness for cigars. She was from Bergen and her name was Fanny Riis. As a sixteen-year-old she had known the doubtful honour of being asked to dance by Ibsen at a Bergen ball. Now she was a grown woman, on a *Bildungsreise* through Germany and Italy. In the autumn of 1881 she arrived in Rome, where she met her old dancing partner again.

Would he remember her?

'That is not possible,' replies Ibsen firmly as Fanny introduces herself, 'because I have never danced there.' Suzannah replies in more or less the same fashion. 'That cannot be the case, my husband has never danced in his life.'

Not long afterwards he approached her again. 'Yes, you're right. Now I remember.' And with that he starts to recall the evening they spent together almost thirty years earlier, the pink woollen dress she was wearing, what jewellery she was wearing – everything, down to the smallest detail. In so doing he made full reparation for that poor first impression she had gained of him all those years ago in Bergen, for he was, indeed, a dreadful dancer. One evening he spent two hours in Fanny's company at the Scandinavian Society – 'so much of what he said seemed like very striking ideas,' she writes in her travel diary. He talks about strange things, about the future, and how he would like to live to be a hundred or two hundred years old, to see how everything changes. Because everything is connected, everything develops and changes into something other than it originally was – 'Astronomy and alchemy, religion and mythology'. Yes, even religion would disappear, the writer asserted, and the same went for poetry. At this Fanny protested vigorously, but Ibsen persisted:

Poetry will vanish completely; its time is past, and we as individuals are headed for annihilation; but our task is to create transitional routes for the benefit of future generations.

Tabula rasa. The old world must founder in order for a new one to arise. The writer's job was to destroy, to break society down to its smallest unit, the individual, and to leave it to those who came later to create a new and better world. Fanny began to feel dizzy. The room they were sitting in was hot, voices buzzed around them, and the man sitting beside her, the writer Henrik Ibsen, a man who had once led her clumsily across the dance floor but who was now a great man, the enigma, here he was, sitting next to *her* and speaking earnestly of strange and shocking things.

After he left she was both relieved and sorry, and more than a little confused:

Thank the Lord that I know my own immortal soul and its relationship and responsibilities to my Saviour and Redeemer.

Fanny Riis is just one of many who, in later years, wrote of their encounters with Ibsen in Rome. Taken together, these memoirs have created that corpus of quotations and turns of phrase that have done so much to fashion posterity's image of Ibsen as the poet-sphinx. Typically, these start with 'the first meeting'. An example is the account given by the art historian Frederik G. Knudtzon, from the Scandinavian Society in Rome in the 1860s:

The room was almost deserted, apart from one man who was pacing rapidly back and forth between the window and the piano, the piano and the window. He looked very distinguished. Stockily built, and impeccably well dressed, wearing a long coat that was buttoned up. Bushy-haired, mutton-chop sideburns and a very energetic chin were the most striking aspects of his face.

The most striking thing about the description is Ibsen's demarcation from his surroundings. He is his own universe, enclosed within himself. A sufficient and demarcated planet in empty space. 'There was something enclosed about his person, about the way he dressed,' Knudtzon concludes.

John Paulsen describes his first encounter with Ibsen thus:

Discreetly I studied that strange face, the small, blue-grey eyes behind the gold spectacles, the high, unusually broad forehead that seemed almost wrinkled with thought, the long, greying whiskers, the sensitive, closed mouth, its lines as thin as a knife-blade – but what it was that gave the face character, or to summarise my impressions in a single word, that was beyond me at that moment. I was standing before an impenetrable cliff-face – an impenetrable riddle.

Paulsen is Ibsen seen through male eyes. Fanny Riis gives us the female version:

His manner, attractively quiet and discreet, yet allowed one to see the half-hidden fire in his gaze that seemed to flare up and form a sort of halo around his powerful head.

In the winter of 1881–2, Rome was virtually invaded by elderly women from the Scandinavian countries, most of whom were rumoured to be spinsters. There were mutterings from many of the writers and artists at the Scandinavian Society and an insistence that the visitors should be excluded from at least some of their gatherings. But no protests from Ibsen. Again he defended the rights of women, in this case the rights of old maids, and happily invited them into his own home. Here he sat among them and told stories from his trip to Egypt until the eyes of the old women 'glowed with an intense gratitude'. According to one of the male visitors that winter, it was not uncommon to find that these ladies believed they possessed a deeper understanding of Ibsen's writing than the author himself, indeed, they seemed to regard him as one of the apostles, preaching in his writings the same truths as Jesus Christ.

If this were the case then very soon their Judas would make his appearance. In November 1882, after Ibsen had returned home from Brixen, he received a new book from Gyldendal. It was entitled *The Pehrsen Family*. It was about a tyrannical, mean, *noveau riche* businessman Pehrsen, his cowed wife who has read far too many novels, and his son Sverre, who hates his father and dreams of a career in the diplomatic service. Pehrsen himself has a drunken old father whom he refuses to recognise, and has his own history as a drunkard following a bankruptcy from which he has, over the years, recovered with the help of friends who got up a collection for him, enough for him to travel abroad. Despite his success he remains haunted by a feeling of inferiority and strives ceaselessly for the acceptance of the upper class and, more explicitly, for shining medals and orders to pin upon his chest . . .

The author of the novel was John Paulsen, and if anybody knew what he was writing about it should have been him – for there can be no doubt that the characters in the book are based on the Ibsens, and no doubt, either, that readers were to infer this. As in any *roman à clef* it is as hard to know the extent to which the characters should be regarded as portraits as it is to know how reliable the portraiture is. There is much that is familiar: that strange and formal tone between father and son, the mother's fondness for novels, the father's for alcohol, his upstart manner and denial of his own past. To the degree to which this is a portrait of Ibsen, it is a caricature.

The aim must have been to wound, but why? Paulsen had left Rome in the summer of 1881. Had he had enough of being Ibsen's lap dog, or had he quite simply fallen for the temptation to give his own career a boost at the expense of his mentor? Certainly that has been the view of many. But *The Pehrsen Family* is more than simply a brazen act of literary exposure. It is also a critique of the Ibsen family's betrayal of the left, of their conservative inclinations, of servility towards officialdom and the Swedish elite, and of indifference towards the practical, political struggle going on at home.

Ibsen must have been as furious as the Pehrsen depicted in the novel. And what had possessed Hegel to publish such a thing? From previous experience Ibsen knew that Paulsen was an unreliable character, but that was in small matters. Now the young literary apprentice had stabbed him in the back.

Ibsen responded immediately: 'Scoundrel!'

Short and sweet, that was the missive in its entirety. And with that one of Ibsen's disciples leaves the table. But new ones arrive. One of these was William Archer. Later Archer would become one of the writer's foremost advocates in Great Britain, but at this point in time his involvement was confined to an unauthorised translation of *The Pillars of Society*, performed once in London in 1880. The Englishman was naturally a little nervous when he introduced himself to Ibsen in stumbling Norwegian. It was an easy matter for Archer, as it was for anyone, to follow Ibsen in his daily routines in Rome – his addiction to routine was already legendary. Each morning he strolled up the steep incline of the Via di Porta Pinciana, through the Borghese Park, and on towards Monte Pincio. At about twelve o'clock he was to be found at the Café Nazionale, one of the most fashionable in Rome, glinting with gold, marble and mirrors. Here Ibsen had chosen a regular seat, as was his habit. Not one that was reserved exclusively for him, however – that would come later. He ate his main meal of the day between two thirty and three o'clock, the Italian preference for an evening meal not suiting his Norwegian stomach.

Suzannah and Sigurd were also regulars at the Café Nazionale. As the proprietor noted, the odd thing was that they came at different times and sat in different parts of the cafe, even when other members of the family were present. The host rushed anxiously from room to room, endeavouring to seat the family around the same table, until Ibsen explained to him in a friendly fashion that this was the way they preferred it. He added that he often worked in the cafe, and so needed to be left in peace – to the extent this was possible, what with all the tourists and others who turned up at the cafe in hopes of catching a glimpse of him.

The old Garibaldi redshirt who ran the cafe must have been surprised at this display of Scandinavian family life, so little like the Italian way, with extended families gathering in large groups to enjoy a meal together.

* * *

Ibsen had always been withdrawn and unpredictable; now he found himself forced to adopt a public mask in self-defence. The result was a considerable divide between the private and the public man. Those who gained his confidence through conversation in the Scandinavian Society, in cafes or best of all within the confines of his own 'castle' on the Via Capo le Case, were left with an impression very different from that of those who were excluded from this confidence. Particularly surprising was the discovery that in private Ibsen could be warm and friendly in a way that did not correspond at all with the image of the unapproachable sphinx of rumour.

What, then, was he like in private?

As a conversational partner Ibsen must have created a curious impression. Only very rarely do we find someone describing him as listening and interested. That is, he might well be listening, but as an *observer* rather than a direct participant. One of his acquaintances from Rome, the writer Kristian Gløersen, reports that Ibsen never spent a long time on a particular theme, and that he tended to withdraw from learned discussions on specific subjects. His preference was for desultory conversation, shifting from subject to subject and contributing in general terms in which paradox and pithy summation were notable characteristics. Judging by the memoirs, no one seemed to expect anything else of him. Voluble or silent, everyone knew that the master ceaselessly carried out his studies of human nature in his intercourse with ordinary mortals. That was why he tossed out his pithy summaries and paradoxes, as a way of testing the listener's reactions – 'observing them, entrenched behind his spectacles'. Ibsen could be entertaining, amusing and considerate; but what seems to have struck people most was when he was scrutinising another person, the way he 'studied the subject, analysed him in his mind'.

Once, after a gathering at the Ibsens, Gløersen walked home with another of the guests, a young lady, and explained to her what they had just been part of: 'Did you know, frøken, that you and I have just been modelling for Henrik Ibsen?'

Perhaps the socialising seemed different when he was among those whom he considered his intellectual equals, and yet the comments of men such as Georg Brandes or J. P. Jacobsen on Ibsen as a conversational partner are not notably different from those of someone like Gløersen, even though they did not share Gløersen's subservient admiration. Gløersen was one of 'the little people', observers and admirers of Ibsen who described their encounters with the writer in terms of awestruck admiration. When these 'little people' were invited into the Ibsen home they would often describe the visit as a sort of audience, an impression reinforced by their host's liking for medals and formal dress. If Ibsen received them wearing his finest regalia then his guests could do no less. The result was that a casual evening gathering at Via Capo le Case 75 could easily seem more like a high-class formal dinner. 'One was aware of the honour that came with the invitation, and the atmosphere reflected this awareness,' Fanny Riis recalled.

Georg Pauli, another guest, found the respectful and formal atmosphere unpleasant: 'I worried about revealing myself as I actually was, "very superficial", but managed to hide this by behaving suitably.'

In due course, however, the tray of cognacs would appear. The gentlemen and Fanny lit their cigars, and the mood relaxed. By the late evening little remained of the formal atmosphere. Pauli had in fact experienced the informal Ibsen on a previous occasion. One night, while he and Christian Ross walked home from a bar with the writer, Ibsen laid into them, labelling Pauli 'a wretched young pup' and accusing Ross of being 'a very nasty person'. He was better company for Fanny, whom he walked home each time she visited. Fanny became the Scandinavian Society's librarian the following summer, an appointment made possible following Ibsen's stance in the winter of 1879. He continued to support her through all the years she held the post, despite the fact that there was still considerable opposition to women in the society. Apart from that he kept a low profile. He protested vigorously when the committee decided not to bill *Svenska Aftonbladet* for a few stamps, but he wasn't interested in any deeper involvement. When Pauli suggested that Ibsen stand for chairman of the society he replied: 'I must tell you that I have to be part of the Opposition.' There were probably quite a few who preferred to see him there than in the chair.

LINDBERG'S STROKE OF GENIUS

In any other writer, life as a celebrity, a Christ and a social lion might have had an adverse effect on productivity. Not so Ibsen. As early as January 1883 he is writing to Hegel to inform him that he is planning a new drama of contemporary life in four acts; he hoped to begin the actual writing in a couple of months' time. Hardly had *An Enemy of the People* appeared, just a year after the play preceding it, and already he was noting down ideas for what would become *The Wild Duck*.

Spring came early that year. The grass was green by the beginning of February and the almond trees had already shed their flowers. In March, Sigurd had journeyed to Paris to study French society and culture. The trip was the parents' present to the newly created doctor of law. At the age of twenty-three Sigurd Ibsen was taking his first steps into independent life, and his mother was suffering.

'Dear Suzannah,' Magdalene consoled her, 'I can well understand your struggle at the loss of Sigurd; but thank the Lord, separation doesn't mean a bond broken for life, though the sorrow and fear never quite pass. It will be good for him to be off on his own.'

Sigurd was to spend two months in Paris. While his mother wept, his father took care of the practical side of things; he gets Hegel to send money, and asks Georg Sibbern, the Norwegian minister in Paris, to introduce his son to political life. Sigurd takes these expressions of trust seriously. In his first long letter home he gives a full account of what he's up to and what the money has been spent on. Perhaps he hoped that his father, who kept such a close eye on his own expenses and bills when he was away from home, would accept his accounting without further question.

He knew what his mother expected of him too:

Please tell mother, that my clothes are hanging in a row on a railing attached
to the wall, and that my socks, linen etcetera are kept in the chest of drawers
in the same order as in Rome.

Perhaps Sigurd really was as interested in correctly folded socks as she was in knowing that he was, but once outside the hotel room he knew how to enjoy everything Paris had to offer in the way of theatres, music and art. He spent time in the company of Norwegian and Swedish diplomats, but hardly became involved in any profound study of French political life. But in the main he seems to have tried to avoid other Scandinavians; twice he catches sight of Bjørnson but does not approach him – at least that's what he tells his parents. He reads a lot, and works on his new thesis on the evolution of the concept of the state.

As April advances he begins to feel homesick. In fact, he's felt that way most of the time. Moreover, he writes to his mother, two months in Paris is long enough for someone who already knew as much about France as he did. At the end of May he travels home.

Once again they were together, the three of them.

* * *

By the beginning of June 1883 the heat was starting to become oppressive. Ibsen was already looking forward to leaving the city at the end of the month to travel to Gossensass, which had now become the family's regular summer residence: 'Gossensass is what Berchtesgaden used to be – an ideal place in which to work free from the presence of inquisitive journalists or bespectacled students of literature.'

Here he intended to start work in earnest on the new play. Before leaving, he tells Georg Brandes in a letter that this new play 'won't be about the court of impeachment or the absolute veto, and not even about the pure Norwegian flag'. After four plays that in one way or another engaged with contemporary social issues he wanted to do something new: 'There's a compact grouping now occupying the ground where I once stood when I wrote my books. I am no longer there. I am somewhere else, further forward, I hope.' The obligations of the *avant garde*, always to be ahead of the game.

The family remained in Tyrol until the start of October. From Gossensass they moved down to low-lying Bozen, on the Italian border, arriving in the middle of the grape harvest. Temperatures were mild, and the weather so pleasant that the family postponed the journey home for as long as they could. Finally, at the end of October, they began the long twenty-hour train journey back to Rome.

While Ibsen was in Gossensass, work was patiently going on to mount a production of *Ghosts* in Scandinavia. The man responsible was the Swedish actor and theatre manager August Lindberg, whom Ibsen had met three years earlier in Munich, and who had attracted attention in February 1883 for his production of *Hamlet* in Copenhagen. After some thought Ibsen gave him the right to take the play on tour in Sweden, and then to perform it in Stockholm, Copenhagen and finally Kristiania. Ibsen would probably have preferred the prestigious national theatres, but there was still no show of interest from them.

Not surprisingly, Lindberg had problems finding a venue in Stockholm. The result was that the European premiere of *Ghosts* took place in the small southern Swedish town of Helsingborg. Lindberg invited Herman Bang to attend, knowing of Bang's own attraction to the theme of degeneration, and to the character of Osvald. Bang took the short trip across the Sound from Denmark, and he was not alone: something like a quarter of the audience were Danes. Famous writers, actors and journalists, as well as the cream of the local aristocracy, turned up. No one wanted to miss this occasion.

Gyldendal's Peter Nansen summed up the evening for the magazine *Vor Tid*:

> The performance was a success. Not a riotous one, but almost silent, as was appropriate for the dreadful seriousness of the play.

The success owed much to Lindberg's brilliant direction, and his own performance in the part of Osvald. Nansen found the final scene, with mother and son alone on the stage, particularly powerful, as did Herman Bang:

It is a simple scene, performed with all the abandon that Ibsen demands, allowing the tormented fear to rise almost to the level of mortal terror. I doubt whether our own audiences would be able to tolerate such a scene.[30]

The production brought Lindberg overnight fame throughout Scandinavia. And now, one after the other, the theatres began to open their stages to him – all save the main theatres in Copenhagen and Kristiania. Naturally this was something Ibsen regretted, but in terms of theatrical history there was nothing to regret, because the result was that *Ghosts* stimulated the world of alternative theatre in Scandinavia, notably Lindberg's travelling theatre company, but also smaller theatres that put their stages at the play's disposal. At the Folketeatret in Copenhagen, however, it appeared initially that Bang might have been correct in his prophecy; unlike the audience in Helsingborg the response from the house was so noisy that Hedvig Charlotte Winter-Hjelm, who was playing Mrs Alving, whispered to Lindberg in the middle of the play:

'Do you think we dare to go on?'

Lindberg dared. After Copenhagen he took the play to Stockholm, first to the Nya Teatern, then to Dramaten. The tour finally arrived in Norway on 17 October, though not at the Christiania Theatre, where the theatre manager Hans Schrøder confirmed his rejection of the play. Instead Lindberg took the stage at the old theatre in Møllergaten, having first convinced Ibsen that the venue was appropriate.

'As the curtain went up it felt as though the audience was holding its breath,' Lindberg recalled later. 'The scenes were played out in a silence almost befitting a spiritualist séance.' The silence persisted even after the curtain fell following the final act. Then came the applause. The mood had changed; two years previously the outraged had had their moment. Now it was the enthusiasts who set the tone, expressing their contempt for the Christiania Theatre, which that same evening was offering a trivial French farce. The contrast was too obvious to be ignored. Over the next few evenings there were organised demonstrations of jeering and whistling inside the Christiania Theatre and outside Schrøder's house, and even Garborg, who had originally been sceptical about *Ghosts*, supported *Dagbladet* in its condemnation of the theatre for refusing to perform it. He acknowledged that Lindberg's performance had stirred up a justifiable anger among the young.

Despite Lindberg's success it was some time before the established theatres followed suit, save for Dramaten and Nya Teatern in Sweden. Only a few days after the premiere in Møllergaten, Iver Olaus Olsen's travelling company put the play on in Fredrikshald, where it again went down well. Both Olsen and Lindberg took the play to Bergen the following spring. In May 1885 the third act of the play, with Herman Bang as Osvald, was performed at Den Nationale

Scene in Bergen, and four years later Fahlstrøm's Theatre put on a production in Christiania. Not until 1900 was *Ghosts* again performed in the capital, this time at the recently opened Nationaltheater. In Denmark the play was performed at the Dagmar Theatre in 1891, but not until 1903 could Osvald be heard calling for the sun at the Kongelige Teater. There was a performance in Germany in 1886, and in England and France early in the 1890s, though in the first two countries the censor made sure that the performances were private.[31]

So Hans Schrøder at the Christiania Theatre was still more or less in tune with the prevailing opinion as he made his way home from Møllergaten on the evening of 17 October 1883, convinced that he had done the right thing in refusing to let Ibsen's scandalous play be performed at his theatre.

'IN THE EVENT OF AN ACCIDENT . . .'

Ibsen didn't manage to get much work done on the new play over the last few months of the year, though he had been mulling it over for a long time; all that survives from the play's earliest days are a few undated pages of notes. But he had written letters, important letters that would secure a future for Sigurd.

One of these letters was addressed to his old Learned Holland friend Ole Andreas Bachke, who was now Minister for Justice in Christian Selmer's government. Could Bachke use his influence to ensure that Sigurd was considered the next time an attaché stipend was being offered by the Foreign Office? Ibsen was convinced that the diplomatic service was the right career path for his son, and gave assurances that Sigurd was prepared to take the necessary entrance exam at any time.

'But before that can happen it will be necessary for him to be naturalized.' That was why Sigurd's father had raised the question of the stipend; it was a last attempt to prevent Sigurd from permanently severing all ties with Norway.

For Ibsen to put his faith in Bachke shows how remote he was from the political realities back home. In the autumn of 1883, Bachke and the rest of the Selmer cabinet were on trial in an impeachment case which, in the early spring of the following year, led to conviction and the dissolution of the government. Following this came the so-called 'April government' of Christian Schweigaard, and finally the appointment of Johan Sverdrup's left-wing government on 26 June 1884. Social strife reached unprecedented heights in these years; town and country opposed each other, the divide between the left and right ran through the entire population. The whole political system was breaking up, the power-elite faltering, and royal power and even the union itself came under attack. There was talk of coups d'état, the military was put on alert – before the hand-over of power was effected in peaceful fashion.

A few days after the judgement of the court of impeachment, Ibsen writes to Bjørnson reiterating his old credo – 'I don't believe in the liberating power of politics'. But not even he could remain unaffected at such a time:

> If I had my way back home I would want all those without privilege to join together in a strong and resolute and confrontational party, and its policies would aim exclusively at practical and productive reforms, at a very generous extension of the franchise, a normalization of the position of women and the liberation of education from all manner of medievalism etc.

In view of who wrote it, the letter is striking: was Henrik Ibsen about to begin campaigning for the formation of political parties and an extension of the franchise, and take an interest in practical and productive reforms in the field of Norwegian politics? In his letter to Bjørnson he also enclosed a signed copy of a petition for the right of married women to retain ownership of their own property, a matter on which he, Bjørnson, Lie and Kielland were united. Thus he was taking, on behalf of Laura Kieler and Nora Helmer, a practical political initiative. Everything pointed to the fact that his political attitudes were on the verge of change; just how radical a change, and in which direction, would become clearer in the course of the following year.

In the middle of April he writes another letter, this time addressed to the Foreign Minister of Sweden-Norway, Baron Hochschild, in his efforts to secure his son a future in the diplomatic corps. Could His Excellency give Sigurd any grounds for hoping that his name might be considered the next time the attaché stipends were awarded? If so, then his son was prepared to travel to Stockholm to present himself, whenever necessary. The approach was unsuccessful, and in June the family decides that the best thing would be for Sigurd to travel to Norway to argue his case in person and to begin working on establishing the network of contacts he was so desperately lacking in the country of his birth.

* * *

The family go their separate ways at the end of June 1884, with Sigurd and Suzannah heading for Norway and Henrik to Gossensass, where he intends to finish his play – 'I have no other thoughts or concerns than work,' he assures Hegel. For much of the spring he had been preoccupied with concerns about his son's future, and distracted by the political struggles going on in Norway. Not until the middle of April did he find enough peace and quiet to get down to serious work on the new play. And now things really start to move. By June he has a draft finished, has made a fair copy of the first act and started on the second.

In other words, he had plenty of time to finish the play in Tyrol, enjoy the food and the company of the other guests at the Hotel Gröbner and, of course, keep up a correspondence with his wife and son at home in Norway.

Sigurd and Suzannah took the usual route north, the train to Stettin and then the boat to Kristiania, via Copenhagen. In Denmark they visited Magdalene and Dorothea, and were invited to Skovgaard, Hegel's country home. While they were there another guest rang the front doorbell – and in walked none other than John Paulsen. History does not record quite how he reacted at the sight of his literary models, but it seems that Hegel was visibly nervous. The atmosphere was uneasy in the extreme. Suzannah chose to be gracious, but Sigurd declined to say a word to the scoundrel.[32]

From Copenhagen their route took them to Kristiania and on from there to Trondheim. The plan was then to embark on an extended journey to the North Cape to enjoy the scenery and the midnight sun. At that time it was an exotic goal and travelling there almost an expedition in itself, which was precisely what attracted foreign visitors. Then, as later, the attraction of Norway was to places where there was as little visible evidence of Norwegians themselves as possible. Suzannah's letters are full of detailed descriptions of beautiful scenery, whereas the people themselves seem less attractive the further north she gets: 'As for the people here,' she writes from Trøndelag, 'they seem rather crude to me and lacking in sensitivity.' She seems to have adopted the continental upper-class tourist's mixture of fascination and condescension towards provincial Norway. But the main goal of their journey was not the North Cape but Kristiania. Here Sigurd would try as hard as he could to open doors that no one else could open for him.

'Don't let a single day go by without doing your utmost to establish the political and journalistic contacts that will be so vital for you,' his father adjured him. And then the usual advice: make sure you eat plenty of nutritious Norwegian food. Salmon in particular was a recurring theme for the fish-loving Ibsen. Horses were another matter; Sigurd must be very careful 'not to find yourself behind a Trøndelag horse, they are notorious for kicking'. Should he manage to avoid being kicked to death he should be equally wary of the dangers of being shot, his father warned him: 'In almost every Norwegian newspaper I read there are stories of accidents caused by the careless handling of loaded weapons. I should be extremely disappointed to hear that you have failed to keep your distance from people carrying this kind of weapon.'

Provided, then, that Sigurd steered clear of horses and armed Norwegians and made sure to eat fish, everything should be alright. In the event of bad weather, however, he and his mother must on no account take the boat home but travel overland, through Sweden. Come what may, it was of vital importance that he be kept informed of their progress:

In the event of an accident, I must be informed immediately by telegram.

Before heading north Sigurd had paid a call on the prime minister, Johan Sverdrup, in Kristiania, bringing a greeting from his father. Sverdrup received him warmly, and listened sympathetically as Sigurd expressed his interest in receiving an attaché stipend the next time these were due to be allocated. Sigurd was initially sceptical about the Left's 'great man', but warmed to him, and travelled north optimistically though well aware that Sverdrup could make no promises. The initiative paid off. By the time Sigurd and Suzannah returned to the capital, the decision had been taken: from November, Sigurd would be employed in the Department of the Interior, after which he would be posted as an unpaid attaché to the Swedish Foreign Ministry in Stockholm in January of the following year.

And so it was that Sigurd took his first firm steps out of the state of Ibsen and into the Swedish-Norwegian union, though he preserved links to what had been, not least because it was his father who was funding it all, that is, until such time as he, hopefully, received his stipend.

Norway had embraced the writer's son. At long last.

REUNION WITH BJØRNSON

While Suzannah and Sigurd were busy travelling up and down the coast of Norway, Henrik spent the summer in peace and quiet. He enjoyed his days in Gossensass, even though, as usual, he counted every penny and passed on detailed accounts of his outgoings to the family. The Hotel Gröbner was unusually full that summer, with guests from all over Europe. Gröbner himself extended the hotel to cater for the increased popularity of the resort.

Ibsen was one of the town's tourist attractions; he could see it for himself in the broad smiles of the other guests in the hotel's dining room. The attention did not entirely displease him, but he was careful to keep up his work discipline. The final stages of the play proceeded at a steady pace, made easier by bad weather that minimised the appeal of outdoor activities. He was finished by the end of August, and on 2 September despatched his fair copy to Hegel. When not working he spent a lot of time in the company of Niels Ravnkilde, Otto Sinding and one of the Grønvold brothers who were staying there that summer. He also kept Suzannah fully informed of how he and the other guests passed the time. One occasion was particularly notable. In September he became part of a small crowd gathered around a certain Frøken Schirmer, from Munich. She was interested in Spiritism, and Ibsen was clearly fascinated: 'She has the power, merely by touching another individual, to get that person to do as she says.' From among the hotel's other guests Frøken Schirmer picked out a nervous young woman named Pleuffer and carried out 'the most incredible experiments' on her, which probably did little to alleviate Frøken Pleuffer's nervous condition even while exciting Ibsen's admiration.

This was probably his first encounter with Spiritism, a belief in the possibility of contact with the Beyond. By the end of the century and well into the next the séance had become a craze among the fashionable set. For some it was only ever an innocent parlour game, for others a door opening onto another world. Both Henrik and Suzannah would become interested in Spiritism, an interest their son and daughter-in-law would inherit from them.

It's doubtful that Ibsen ever experienced the awakening of the dead at Hotel Gröbner. Very shortly, however, he did have the pleasure of renewing an old friendship. Back in January he had heard in a letter from Bjørnstjerne Bjørnson that he planned to spend the summer in the idyllic little Alpine resort of Schwaz, on the other side of the Brenner Pass, a short train ride from Gossensass. Was Ibsen interested in being part of a 'tri-poetical' meeting with him and Jonas Lie in Schwaz? Lie was at the time living in Berchtesgaden, but had to decline the invitation because he was hard at work. Ibsen, on the other hand, had just finished work, and Bjørnson too was just concluding a new book.

Twenty years had passed since the last time these two met. Years of warm correspondence, chilly correspondence, and no correspondence. And then the reconciliation after *Ghosts*. They were Norway's two greatest writers, but what were they to each other? Ibsen replied in the affirmative and did not regret it. In the middle of September he arrived at the station in Schwaz and was met by Bjørnson and his son Erling. Bjørnson looked well, but had gone grey, as was only to be expected. He led Ibsen to the guest house where the family was staying. Karoline's hair had turned grey too, and she was now quite deaf. Bjørn, the oldest son, wasn't with them, but their daughters Dagny and Bergliot were.

'Both daughters are unusually pretty, well-behaved, natural and spontaneous,' Henrik reported back to Suzannah.

He spent three days in Bjørnson's company. There was no room for him at the same guest house, so Ibsen had to stay somewhere else. It was probably best to observe a distance like this, but they spent a great deal of time in each other's company anyway, talking of politics, literature and many other things. One of the things they spoke of was the theatre, and it wasn't by chance. From December of the previous year Bjørnson had been conducting what was almost a campaign to persuade Ibsen to return home and take over as head of the Christiania Theatre. Again. How many more times was he going to have to turn down people who wanted him to return to a job that had almost killed him the first time around, and that no one had ever praised him for doing well? Certainly, Norwegian theatre had outgrown the swaddling clothes of those early days, but then so had he. He had told Bjørnson of his lack of interest back in January. Was he expected to put himself at the mercy of a group of actors who scarcely knew the meaning of words such as 'discipline' and 'unconditional obedience', not to speak of a national press that was at any moment liable to fly at one's throat? It was a job for Bjørnson, and for him alone. And if Bjørnson wouldn't take it, then at the very least his son Bjørn should be involved in some capacity at the theatre.

And yet throughout 1884 there were persistent rumours of Ibsen's return as head of the theatre, nurtured to some degree by the fading popularity of the current incumbent, Hans Schrøder. At the end of October, Ibsen had to issue a public denial of the rumours in *Dagbladet*, by which time Bjørn had already joined the Christiania Theatre as a director and actor. Bjørn Bjørnson had been educated in Germany, where he had spent time with the Meiningen group. He was a man with an obvious gift for the theatre who, at the start of the next century, would acquire legendary status as the first head of the new Nationalteater once it opened.

The days passed in fellowship and conversation. When Ibsen later describes the visit to Suzannah he stresses the degree to which it was a case of Bjørnson listening to *him*, how the other was regularly struck by what he said, and how Bjørnson would return to his words again later in the course of their conversation. They were the two most important writers in Norway, both now mature men, but beneath the surface that competitive element remained, the need on each side to weigh the other's importance against his own. This was every bit as true of Bjørnson as it was of Ibsen, and yet the former seemed genuinely impressed by Ibsen. Afterwards he described the visit to Jonas Lie as intimate – Ibsen was now 'a good and well-meaning old gentleman'. Naturally, they didn't see eye to eye on everything. But Bjørnson valued their exchanges, and he was able to see something in Ibsen that perhaps only a personal encounter could reveal, certain qualities in his friend that he knew he was lacking in himself, above all a cool calculating intelligence.

'He's more tenacious than you or I, more careful, more calculating,' he writes to Lie. 'Indeed, I am almost tempted to say that calculation is his most outstanding talent; you and I see more, and more clearly; our intellectual capacity is undoubtedly superior. But he is so good at managing what he has that he's able to get more out of it than we do.'

And shortly after, to Frederik Hegel: 'Calculation, foresight, and cunning are quite unusually prominent aspects of his intelligence; but his intelligence is not versatile, or his knowledge extensive.'

In other words, a tribute to Ibsen's cynicism, but not without a few digs from Bjørnson. All in all, however, the two old friends were well pleased with their reunion. And if family tradition can be relied upon then the meeting was fruitful in other ways, for according to that Ibsen said to Suzannah on his return: 'Now I've seen Sigurd's future wife.'

And sure enough, it turned out to be Sigurd and Bergliot. Not exactly delighting Ibsen – but *that* is another story.

By the middle of October they were together again. Suzannah and Sigurd had returned from their long journey and were safely ensconced in Gossensass. Now was the time they should have made their way back to Rome for the winter, but an outbreak of cholera delayed their departure. A few days later Sigurd returned to Norway to take up his post at the Department of the Interior. On 1 November, Henrik and Suzannah left Gossensass and stayed for a couple of weeks in Bozen. They were back in Rome on 13 November 1884, two days after the publication in Copenhagen of Ibsen's new play.

Sigurd had left the nest, and so had *The Wild Duck*.

THE DARK LOFT

In *The Wild Duck* we meet the little Ekdal family, consisting of the photographer Hjalmar Ekdal, his wife Gina and their only child, the fourteen-year-old Hedvig. With the exception of the first act, the action of the play takes place in the attic apartment where the family lives with Hjalmar's old father, Lieutenant Ekdal. The family faces many trials, and these multiply as a number of old secrets come to light in the course of the play. Hjalmar is an impractical dreamer with an exalted opinion of himself; his daughter Hedvig is gradually losing her sight; old Ekdal has never recovered from being sent to prison for crimes for which his former business partner, Werle, was actually responsible. As the play unfolds it emerges that Gina once had a relationship with Werle, in the days when she was a maid in his house, and that in all likelihood it is he who is Hedwig's real father.

As the action begins Hjalmar knows nothing of this, nor that his family is being provided for financially by the same Werle. He strolls around, polishing his exaggerated self-image and dreaming of the great invention he will one day create. Like his father, he cultivates an illusion that his life is free and authentic, an illusion that finds its symbolic expression in the wild duck the family keeps as a pet in the dark loft at the rear of the apartment. With the exception of the sensible Gina, they all regularly visit the loft to live out their dreams and prevent the cold realities of the world from invading their lives. It's a contented life, until the sudden return home of Gregers Werle, son of the squire and Hjalmar's old friend, determined to expose all the lies and lead the family to a life in truth and freedom. Gregers carries through his plan, only to discover that the truth does not liberate; instead it brings despair to the whole family, and in the end leads Hedvig to point a gun at her own chest.

All Gregers brings with his 'claim of the ideal' is misery, while his antagonist, Dr Relling, with his cynical maxim – 'If you take the life-lie from the average person you take his happiness in the same breath' – appears to be right.

* * *

In the letter accompanying the final pages of the manuscript sent to Hegel, Ibsen wrote that the new play 'occupies, in many ways, a unique place in my dramatic production'. Hopefully the critics would discover just what was new about the play – 'they will, at any rate, find a great deal to argue about and discuss. For this reason I think "The Wild Duck" might tempt some of our younger dramatists to try out this new path, a development I would find thoroughly welcome'.

Two who were not tempted were Bjørnson – 'How disgusted I am by Ibsen's new book!' – and Georg Brandes. Brandes had not reviewed Ibsen's previous play, and did not review this one either, leaving that to his brother Edvard. It was probably just as well. Georg was disappointed. After *Ghosts* he had hoped that Ibsen would serve the cause of the breakthrough movement – but this? In a mood of resignation he wrote to Kielland: 'The Ibsen was a sad experience for me, the thing seemed to be slightly empty. And why concern oneself exclusively with such completely insignificant people!'

No, the Ekdals were a poor set of allies to have in the great Nordic cultural battle.

Among critics and readers the sense of excited anticipation was at its usual high level for any new book by Ibsen. Rumours abounded, suggesting that one might expect the most cutting social drama yet from him. The shipment of books from Gyldendal arrived at Kristiania harbour at 1 p.m. on 11 November and were in the shops and on sale within ninety minutes. That same day the evening editions carried the first reviews.

One thing was certain; whatever it was people had been expecting, this wasn't it. One might suppose that the critics would by this time have ceased to be surprised by Ibsen, but they were not. It's striking to reflect that a play which is today considered a particularly suitable entry point to Ibsen's work for the young, left contemporary critics baffled as to what it was even about. Much of the confusion arose from the fact that the play neither promoted a traditionally idealistic aesthetic nor debated a recognisable and specific social problem of the type readers had come to expect from his most recent work. Instead here was a play almost devoid of plot or conflict, and in which Hedvig's death was not followed by any redemption or any tragic insight.

One thing at least was clear: Ibsen had added an element of the 'fantastic-allegorical' to his realism. To some this was something new, not so to others: for Alexander Kielland 'these endless symbols and allusions' gave the play a 'fussy and old-fashioned air'. In a similar fashion the reviewer in *Morgenbladet* was reminded of Ibsen's folk-tale drama *Peer Gynt*; what was unexpected here was finding the allegorical and the symbolic present in what was otherwise a realistic drama of modern life. In Edvard Brandes' view it was obvious what the play's most important symbol, the wild duck, was supposed to represent. Or was it? It seemed clear to the reviewer in *Morgenbladet* that the duck symbolised one of the characters, but he quickly abandoned the attempt to discover which one. He even managed to claim that the portrait of Hedvig was finely executed, spoiled only by 'the silly business with the wild duck'.

Like Ditmar Meidell and *Morgenbladet*'s reviewer, *Aftenposten*'s critic gave the play a traditional idealistic reading and found Gregers Werle to be the play's greatest disappointment. Gregers, who should have been its 'pure spirit, its element of nobility', turns out to be as confused and degenerate as the rest of those in and around the Ekdal household: 'And this anaemic, pathetic and delirious figure, in whom it is impossible to feel any interest, represents in this play the highest reach, the ideal.' It was fair enough to depict Hjalmar as an immature and naïve idealist – most of the reviewers were agreed Hjalmar was well described – but it was intolerable that his mentor and teacher Gregers should turn out to be just as bad. For the conservative reviewers it was clear that Ibsen was once again preaching negativity and doubt, and that the only lesson to be had from *The Wild Duck* was that one should simply 'take one's hat and leave, be thirteenth man at the table, pick up a gun and pull the trigger'.

Ditmar Meidell's conclusion could have come straight from Hjalmar Ekdal's own lips:

Ah, the good old days are gone, the time when a reviewer could conclude his review with words along these lines, that no-one will lay this book down without having first received a fulsome and harmonious impression from the exalted and beautiful poetry that suffuses this whole work of art.

Johan Irgens Hansen, writing in the radical *Dagbladet*, reached a quite different conclusion. For him it was precisely Ibsen's exposure of the frailties of idealism that made his positive message possible: 'Driven to their knees by these demands, in utter despair, we see his characters turning again and again to the only help they see – compassion, and love.' Irgens Hansen found the greatness of the play to reside at precisely the point the idealistic aesthete found its comfortless everyday normality repellent, and not least in the play's female characters. It was they who stood for 'forgiveness, understanding, reconciliation, leniency. They make life liveable, because they have the power of devotion, as well as that most wonderful of gifts: the ability to take the world as it is.'

The contrasting view of the women is the clearest divide between the idealist and the anti-idealist readings: Gina, who was, for *Aftenposten*'s reviewer, 'this simple woman with her shameful past', was for Irgens Hansen the possessor of the very qualities that make life bearable.

Significantly, Irgens Hansen insisted that Ibsen had by no means abandoned realism. In his view neither Ibsen nor Bjørnson had, in their earlier
plays, quite managed to free themselves completely from the Romantic heritage.
Both had been inclined to 'stretch reality a little too tightly across the last of the
idea'. Only now, with *The Wild Duck*, had Ibsen become a genuine realist. It was
not solely on account of the external realism, but because the way he had
chosen to tell the story led him to approach reality more closely than ever
before: 'In this book Ibsen has done something he has never done before; he
stands on humanitarian ground and speaks on behalf of humanity, even a
humanity as shabby as this.'

And yet it would be wrong to suppose that *The Wild Duck* was 'misunderstood' or 'understood' according to whether one was an idealist or an anti-
idealist, a conservative or a radical. Once again it is the Christian-conservative
Swedish critic Carl David af Wirsén who most clearly demonstrates this. With
his sceptical but intelligent reading he often displays a sharper eye for the
nuances of the play than his radical colleagues. Both Erik Vullum (writing of
An Enemy of the People) and Johan Irgens Hansen (on *The Wild Duck*) manage
to make Ibsen's characters simpler than they are, and the play's message less
ambivalent, than does af Wirsén. He is moved by the play: 'Perhaps Ibsen's
irony has never been at once as universal and as biting as in *The Wild Duck*.
Every last one of them is a sinner, that is the theme, and one would have to be
blind not to agree with the poet when he, in his sombre and sometimes dry
variations, repeats his "vanitas vanitatum vanitas".'

Every last one of them is a sinner. That was Ibsen's judgement on mankind,
and as a believer the critic had no choice but to concede that he was right. But
af Wirsén sees too that the judgement is directed at something quite specific:
'Increasingly his writing appears to be as the tolling of a funeral bell for the
nineteenth century. The chiming is dreadful, lacking in all sense of reconciliation, with all the destructive power of pitilessness, and speaks of corpses and
putrefaction and funeral drapes.'

Carl David af Wirsén hears the bells tolling for his own times. He acknowledges Ibsen's vision of mankind, praises his unique ability to express his critique
of civilisation in dramatic form. He is moved by the symbolism in the play,
shaken by the darkness of its vision. He insists only that hope does exist, a pale
beam that makes it worth while to struggle on. He also recommends that *The
Wild Duck* be staged.

He was not the only one. The critics were almost unanimous in agreeing
that on this occasion Ibsen had delivered a play that was, even by his standards,
unusually well constructed. By this time theatres were competing to be the first
to perform a new Ibsen play. At the Christiania Theatre, Bjørn Bjørnson, just
starting out as a director, began work on a production of *The Wild Duck*, but it

was the equally inexperienced Gunnar Heiberg at Den Nationale Scene who was first off of the blocks. Thus it was that Ibsen's new play received its world premiere in Bergen on 9 January 1885, two days before it opened in the capital. Despite suggestions that the play was beyond the capabilities of his theatre, Heiberg's production was given glowing reviews.

A delighted Erik Bøgh received the play at the Kongelige Teater in Copenhagen. William Bloch was responsible for the direction, and the premiere took place on 22 February. Bloch was the theatre's leading director and deserves much of the credit for bringing an end to the declamatory style of acting at Denmark's main theatre. His breakthrough came with *An Enemy of the People*, which he directed with great fidelity to Ibsen's stage instructions, paying particular attention to the psychological aspects of the characters. In Bloch's *The Wild Duck*, live hens and pigeons wandered about the stage, adding to the naturalistic realism of Bloch's production. It seems, however, that neither Bloch, the actors nor the audience really understood the play's symbolic language. As Ekdal, Emil Poulsen played the part for laughs, ignoring the balance between comic and tragic in the role. Ibsen intended the play to be *both* tragic and comic, but contemporary audiences, directors, actors, readers and reviewers all seemed to find the mixture of farce, comedy, melodrama and tragedy highly confusing.

Heiberg in Bergen almost certainly had a better grasp of the play, but regrettably Ibsen never saw that production. He did, however, see the Danish production when he passed through Copenhagen on his way to Norway from Germany in the autumn of 1885.

He was not pleased.

In Stockholm it was increasingly Dramaten that performed his plays, although it was Ludvig Josephson at Nya Teatern who gave *Catiline* its world premiere in 1881, and in the spirit of his *Peer Gynt* of 1876 directed a major production of *Brand* that had its premiere on 24 March 1885, the first time the play had been performed in its entirety, an evening that lasted a full six and a half hours.[33] Ibsen was delighted by reports he heard of the production, but in reality the fruitful co-operation between dramatist and director was over by this time. Josephson had little taste for the 'enigmatic playing with themes and paradoxes' that characterises *The Wild Duck* and the later plays. August Lindberg's response was different. He was responsible for the production of *The Wild Duck* at Dramaten, and in the years to come he took over from Josephson as Ibsen's interpreter on the Swedish stage.

* * *

What was it that was new about *The Wild Duck*, and why did contemporary critics find it so hard to categorise the play? In the first place, and most obviously, the symbolical and allegorical form. Certainly Ibsen had used these techniques before, but never so strikingly or so consciously. In *The Wild Duck* he limits himself to a small number of symbols that run throughout the whole play, most notably the duck itself and the dark loft. This relates *The Wild Duck* to plays of ideas such as *Brand* and *Peer Gynt*, and distinguishes it from them, pointing ahead to a similar use of specific and central symbols in the dramas of his old age, particularly *The Master Builder* and *When We Dead Awaken*. Nevertheless, in its external realities this play is also a realistic family drama of contemporary life, and the staging displays the familiar bourgeois home, if one more humble than any previously shown.[34]

The play lacks an obvious main character, which contributed to the confusions of contemporary readers and audiences.[35] The 'main character' is in many ways the Ekdal family. From here an interesting line can be traced back to Ibsen's previous play, *An Enemy of the People*. That play ends with Stockmann's famous observation that the strongest person is the one who stands most alone. But Stockmann is not completely alone, he has his family around him. The idea of the family was so integrated into the notion of individuality in the nineteenth century that 'alone', without any further qualification, could also mean the nuclear family.[36] The family was the link between the individual and society, at the same time as it represented an extension of the personal sphere, and society's smallest unit. In the light of this, Ibsen's fascination for the dynamics within the family is understandable. In *The Pillars of Society* and *An Enemy of the People* he had examined the individual's relationship to external society; *A Doll's House* and *Ghosts* concentrated on the development of the individual within the family. Here too he was keeping one eye on society, but on society as it operated *within* people and *between* people in the same family – supplemented by a small circle of family friends. And this is what he does too in *The Wild Duck*.

The central dichotomy in the drama is that between the idealistic demand for a life lived in wholeness and truth, and a realistic acceptance of the inadequacy of human beings as they live their lives, including their need to keep themselves going with a life-lie. It is tempting to identify Hedvig, her father and grandfather most closely with the fate of the wild duck, for they are the wounded creatures that have taken firm hold at the bottom of their illusions. But in doing this we run the risk of assuming the perspective of the warped idealist Gregers Werle. Is he not just as much a 'wild duck' as the others, believing he sees everything so clearly and yet hardly even aware of the extent to which his actions on behalf of the Ekdals are actually driven by a desire to avenge himself on his father? Recent scholarship stresses the critique of the idealistic project, particularly through Gregers' consistent use of a symbolic and metaphorical language.[37] He is, after all, the one who insists on interpreting everything around him in symbolic terms, and in so doing does great harm to those who try to keep language real and concrete – it is Gregers who persuades Hedvig that the wild duck is so important it must be sacrificed.

The strongest characters in the play are those with no illusions behind which to hide themselves, most notably the earthy Gina, but also her cynical supporter, the more disreputable Dr Relling. Where Gina is fully occupied in dealing with the realities of her own everyday life, Relling builds castles in the air for those whom he believes would otherwise be unable to survive.

In spite of the use of symbol this play too has clear ties to naturalism, not least in the doom-laden atmosphere that is in part connected to social situations (for example, Old Ekdal's fall from grace). Darwinist references point in the same direction; it is hardly coincidental that the animals living in the dark loft – pigeons, chickens, rabbits and a duck – are the same ones that Darwin writes about in the chapter on livestock breeding in *Origin of Species*, a book Ibsen could have read in J. P. Jacobsen's 1872 translation. Darwin's purpose is to show the effects of domestication on the evolution of these species. If Ibsen did indeed make use of this material, it is tempting to suppose that his purpose was to oppose the free, natural and authentic life in support of the civilised, unfree and tamed life. The Ekdals' wild duck thus becomes a deeply ironic metaphor for freedom, splashing around in its bowl in the dark loft. The duck is no more free than the people who look after it, and is an expression more than anything else of the human illusion of an authentic life with which the humans themselves have long ago lost touch.[38]

From this perspective, the conflict in the play is not primarily between realism and idealism, but between authenticity and inauthenticity. Of course, many commentators have preferred to see Hedvig's relationship to the loft and the wild duck as the expression of a more authentic experience, for unlike her father and grandfather she abandons herself to the ideal world of the loft with all the spontaneous honesty of a child; the loft is not, for her, a reduced version of reality but rather an extension and enrichment of it.[39] Others are less willing to idealise Hedvig in this fashion and claim that she, too, is a prisoner of illusions.

It is little wonder that interpretations of the play have been so many and so diverse. The striking thing about the variations in interpretation is that the symbols in the play are, in and of themselves, not especially difficult; even the most obtuse, like the reviewer in *Morgenbladet*, understood that the wild duck symbolised one or several characters in the play. The difficulty must have been to relate the metaphors and symbolic elements to each other and to the characters in such a way that the play 'worked out'. The task is not made any easier by the fact that the symbols mean different things for different characters (for example, the way in which Hedvig's loft differs from Gregers' loft), and that some are aware of the symbols whereas others are not. Some scholars have taken the consequences of this and maintained that the play must be understood as an 'open' work, a view not far removed from that of Mathilde Schjøtt's review in 1884. In her view, in this play Ibsen had reflected 'the many aspects of everyday life, of the life of the human spirit and of poetry – the Romantic, the realistic, the idealistic and the despicable – he uses it all and shines the fierce light of irony and satire upon his characters, the while remaining in the half-light himself, as a way of encouraging discussion and debate about exactly where he stood in all this'.

And yet, no matter how he tries to hide, the author can still be glimpsed between the lines of this play. Ibsen has clearly returned to memories of his own childhood in the creation of setting and character. Hedvig and the loft are probably based on Ibsen's sister and his memories of Venstøp. The book she refers to in the play – Harrison's *History of London* from 1775 – really was kept in the loft at Venstøp (while the wild duck symbol is also to be found in Welhaven's poem 'Seabird', about an injured wild duck that dives down to the bottom to die). The notes for the play reveal that one of the models for Hjalmar was the photographer Edvard Larssen, the man who took the oldest known photograph of Ibsen in Christiania early in the 1860s, along with various other vacillating and unstable persons known to Ibsen, much as was the case with Peer Gynt.

Others have been tempted to find links to Ibsen's own life beneath this superficial level. Edvard Brandes wrote that *The Wild Duck* was 'characterised at one and the same time by bitterness and self-irony', in the sense that Ibsen's reckoning with idealism had himself as one of its targets: 'He himself, Henrik Ibsen, is Gregers Werle, the man with the "claim of the ideal".' But when did Ibsen last portray an idealist whose stance he did not also sabotage? Brandes ends by suggesting that Ibsen has more likely split himself between Gregers and Relling, the idealist and the cynic, and in the dialogue between them expresses a bitter contempt both for the age and for himself. In this odd coupling cynical doubt meets the dream of wholeness and completion, the Romantic heritage that Ibsen undermined in so many of his plays but from which he was never able completely to free himself.

He understood this. Out drinking in Munich once he protested vigorously when his drinking companions began praising the idealism in his plays. His only aim was to depict life as he saw it, he claimed; but after a pause confessed that 'in the end it is possible to look at things in that way; because there is something Romantic hidden within all my themes, my points of view, and my characters.'

* * *

Recalling his miscalculation regarding *Ghosts*, Ibsen advised Hegel to be more cautious with the first edition of *The Wild Duck*. The print run for the follow-up play had been 10,000, but then that was a comedy – or at least fairly light-hearted. In his view 8,000 copies of *The Wild Duck* ought to be enough. By the following month, however, another 2,000 copies had to be printed.

Once again business was good for the firm of Ibsen and Hegel in Scandinavia. In Germany it was another story. *The Wild Duck* was not translated until 1887, and then in two versions for rival publishing houses, and not until the year after that did the play receive its first performance on the German stage. Indeed, for most of the first half of the 1880s it looked as though Ibsen had lost his appeal for German audiences, as a stage-dramatist at least.[40] *Ghosts* was still banned, and no one appeared interested in putting on a performance of *An Enemy of the People*. In fact, Ibsen had not been performed in Germany since 1880. The second half of the decade would see a revival of interest in the country, however, followed shortly afterwards by his breakthrough in Great Britain.

The pattern typifies Ibsen; acceptance first in Scandinavia, and then else-where in Europe with plays that had already been read and thoroughly discussed in Scandinavia. From this perspective the Scandinavian and the European Ibsen are two different phenomena. In the mid-1880s Ibsen was still predominantly a Scandinavian writer. It was here he had his market and here he waged his battles. It was not the conquest of Europe that preoccupied him in the spring of 1885, however, but the reconquest of the provincial nation which was, after all, his own.

NORWAY 1885

The decision must have been made quickly. As late as the end of April the plan had been to spend the summer in Tyrol or by Lake Constance. Six weeks later it was decided that they would be going to Norway, possibly inspired by a desire to see Sigurd again. He had by this time been transferred from Kristiania to Stockholm, but the plan was for the three of them to meet in Norway. In other words it might have been 'son-sickness' rather than 'homesickness' that drew Henrik north now.

On Friday 5 June their ship put into harbour in Kristiania. The dramatist's return was awaited with great anticipation, coming at a time when the level of public excitement was high anyway at the prospect of the first elections to the Storting under the parliamentary system that were about to take place. And that same summer the Storting was preparing to discuss the proposal to give a writer's wage to Alexander Kielland. In every way, public life in Norway was affected by the growing divisions of recent decades. By the first half of the 1880s these had turned into open conflict for political power and what form of government to choose. But the conflict was by no means confined to politics; city dwellers and country people squared up to each other, Christians were ranged against freethinkers, evolutionists were challenging established truths and the advocates of naturalism the traditional idealistic view of the purpose of art. The fronts extended far beyond the simple opposition of right and left. The split among the Left was perhaps most clearly evident in the gulf between radical authors and the lay Christian movement in the south and west of the country. Following the controversy over Kielland's stipend a new one arose over Hans Jæger's scandalous novel *From the Kristiania Bohemians*, published in November of that year. Jæger and his fellow bohemians addressed two of the most sensitive issues of the age, sexual morality and modesty. The cultural struggle definitively overshadowed the political struggle, and it was this that showed more clearly than anything how fragile the unity of those on the Left really was.

Ibsen did not take avoiding action. Originally the plan had been to travel direct to Trondheim to meet Sigurd, but out of loyalty to Kielland, Ibsen postponed his journey. On 10 June he and Suzannah sat together in the gallery of the Storting as the gathering debated a case exactly like the one he himself had been personally involved in twenty years earlier. Since then Jonas Lie, Camilla Collett and Kristofer Janson had all been granted a writer's wage. But the awards were considered on an individual basis, and this time around the discussion was not simply about the award of a stipend to one writer but about the Storting's attitude towards the new school of realistic, tendentious literature and the radical intelligentsia of the Left.

The government was absent during the debate, but a long list of representatives of the Left rose to be heard. Not a single voice from the right; they preferred to sit back and watch as the Left tore itself apart. As a movement, the Left had been an agglomeration of farmers, low-churchmen and radical urban intellectuals ranged in common cause against the civil-servant state. With the movement transformed into a political party in power, the challenge was to maintain their former unity. Sverdrup had turned out to be a lot more moderate than people had anticipated, determined to prevent a split within the party. On this occasion he did not succeed; when the vote was taken, Kielland's application was rejected when a minority within the Christian Left voted with the right. Ibsen watched from the gallery – disappointed, but also thrilled. In conversation with a friend the following day he regretted the result – 'but the good thing about it was the way the damned compact majority people back here have been cultivating split. I rubbed my hands in sheer delight.' The majority's betrayal did not surprise him. He was more disappointed by the failure of the leaders:

> The day Johan Sverdup came to 'power' and then found himself gagged and handcuffed was a sad day for progress in Norway.

The battle for freedom ennobled, freedom possessed was a corruption.

* * *

On 11 June, Henrik and Suzannah left the capital. A crowd gathered outside the Østbane railway station, many of them carrying bouquets. There were journalists, members of parliament and other local dignitaries. Inside the station Ibsen and his wife waited in the company of friends and acquaintances before climbing into their carriage, with the crowd surging forward for a closer look. Bjørnson was among those there to see them off. At their parting Ibsen shook his hand and urged him, in a voice loud enough for all to hear:

> Greet all that is young in Norway. Tell them to keep faith, and that I shall be with them as their pivot-man on the Left flank. That which might look like madness on the part of the young turns out, in the end, to be what triumphs.

The greeting was subtly ambiguous. Was he expressing his faith in the Left as a party, or in the madness of the young? Following his visit to the Storting it is tempting to suggest that it was the latter. As the train puffed out of the station Henrik and Suzannah could hear the rhythmic clunking of the steam engine and the sparks from the wheels that were taking them to Sigurd. It had been eight months since he had left them, they had never been apart for such a long time before. The plan was to spend some time together in Trondheim before travelling on to Molde, where they hoped to be able to enjoy a quiet summer.

But peace and quiet in Norway would prove to be elusive. Henrik Ibsen's return was simply too important an occasion to allow of it. People stood waiting in Trondheim, including one young man who could scarcely believe that the great writer had really come to town. Peter Egge, then sixteen years of age, had run all the way to the station, his heart pounding. After a delay of several minutes, which only increased the youth's sense of anticipation, the train eventually pulled into the station. A few minutes later Ibsen himself appeared in the doorway of the carriage. His old friend Karl Bomhoff from Dresden was there to greet him, as was Asbjørn Lindboe, the judge.

'For a few moments he looked at the two gentlemen, without smiling,' Egge noticed. 'There was nothing to indicate that he knew them, or was surprised or gratified to see them there.'

Ibsen was in character. Bomhoff might have been an old friend, but it was Ibsen, not Henrik, who carefully doffed his elegant top hat and held out his hand. On Sunday 12 June, two days after his arrival, a large procession from the Trondheim Workers' Union with flags flying, a band playing and a choir singing, made its way through the streets to the Britannia Hotel. Ibsen, bareheaded, stepped out onto the balcony to accept their homage. As the liberal newspaper *Dagsposten* wrote the next day: 'The absence of the city's aristocracy was entirely predictable.'

These were strange days in Norway. Wherever Ibsen travelled the waters parted into right and left. It was Moses crossing the Red Sea. Ibsen did nothing to encourage it; he was the author of *A Doll's House* and *Ghosts*, and that was enough to keep those on the left singing his praises, and those on the right away.

Once the choir had finished singing Beethoven's 'Sehnsuchte' and the leader of the Workers' Union his speech, Ibsen replied. He said what a pleasure it was to be home again, but spoke also about the disappointments he had experienced. Democracy, in its present form, he told them, would not be able to solve the problems facing them. No, something new was called for, an aristocratic element was needed in the government of the country. A nobility, and not just any old nobility; he was thinking of a nobility of character, of spirit, of the will. This was the nobility that would deliver liberation, and it must arise among the workers and the women, those who had not yet been irreparably damaged by the pressures of the party system.

He stood there as a spokesman for the women and the workers, but certainly not a supporter of the Left as a party. He wanted something new, but exactly what was it? He had spoken previously about the need for a nobility, and in years to come would do so many more times.

In Trondheim, Henrik and Suzannah and Sigurd were reunited. In the second week of July they travelled south along the coast to Molde. Here, surely, they would find the peace they longed for. The little town on the northern shore of Romsdalsfjord was, as Ibsen wrote to Hegel shortly after their arrival, 'one of the most beautiful places on earth'. The family took rooms in the newly refurbished Hotel Alexandra, which had just been awarded a star in Baedeker's travel guide. Over the next few days Ibsen was often seen on the quay, not far from the hotel, his gaze fixed on the sea: 'He stands there for most of the day – deep in thought.' Surprisingly, in view of his lifelong fear of the water, it seems that he occasionally allowed himself to drift across the fjord in a rowing boat. But something was, quite literally, driving him on, this remarkable, grizzled man, towards the sea, and towards silence.

In town peace and quiet were more difficult to come by; everyone wanted to meet him, and boast of it afterwards to others. 'There was Ibsen, and there was I,' as one of his female admirers is reported to have said.

A couple of Ibsen's old friends were living at the Hotel Alexandra that summer. Ludvig Daae was in Molde in this election year to take part in political meetings, and Lorentz Dietrichson was there to work on his book about Norwegian stave churches. Both men were now professors, the former of history, the latter art history. Both were conservative and chose their company from among the town's like-minded. Daae was also a contributor to the conservative *Morgenbladet* and throughout the 1870s and 1880s had become noted as a frequent and trenchant voice from the right. One of his opponents on the Left, Erik Vullum, was also living at the Alexandra. Vullum had been prominent in the booing and whistling during performances of *The League of Youth* in 1869. Now he was Ibsen's man.

As happened in Trondheim, the town's more conservative-minded citizens seem to have avoided Ibsen. He received no invitation in late August to attend gatherings to celebrate the presence in town – independently of each other – of the Prince of Wales (later Edward VII) and William Gladstone, until recently the British prime minister. Ibsen must have been annoyed. He was, however, well received by Hans Thiis Møller, the occupant of a stately old house called Moldegård. Møller was leader of the local chapter of the Left, and it was they who held a reception for Ibsen on 24 July at the Grand Hotel, in the east end of town.

The Grand Hotel was the gathering place for the town's liberals; the Hotel Alexandra, in the west end, was where the conservatives met. Between the two ran the River Molde, dividing east from west, left from right, in an almost perfect illustration of the political situation in Norway at that time.

Dietrichson was not quite sure where to place his old friend. Ibsen, it seemed to him, was unusually nervous, feeling as he walked around that Norwegians hated him. 'I kept thinking,' Ibsen told him later, 'whenever someone was walking behind me, that he was about to stick a knife into my back.' Ibsen's suspicions were directed not least towards Dietrichson himself. Under the political skies of his home country something seemed to have happened to him that Ibsen had not previously noticed under the fairer skies of Rome or during social evenings together in Stockholm. Not long afterwards, when both men returned to Christiania, the friendship would be replaced by a bitter hostility that culminated in a furious public confrontation.

There was no way round it, the river of political division flowed even between Ibsen and his old friends. Not so with a third old friend Ibsen met at the Hotel Alexandra. Carl Snoilsky had been through a lot since they last met. After several years in the Swedish diplomatic service which were also, in terms of literary productivity, barren years for him, the Swedish aristocrat had divorced his wife, abandoned his career, and travelled away to live in exile. Snoilsky was one of a small group of upper-class men who had renounced their privileges and entered the class war on the side of the underprivileged, driven on by a longing for solidarity with people from whom he was separated by reasons of birth and wealth, and yet whom he could never really count himself among, no matter how much he might wish to.

Snoilsky's impossible existential dilemma fascinated Ibsen. Later he would confess that during his stay in Norway he had been constantly on the lookout for possible new themes for a play. The most notable result of his searching, along with the political tensions in the country, would turn out to be this meeting with the renegade Swedish aristocrat.

* * *

At the end of July, Sigurd left them and returned to Stockholm, and on 5 September his parents departed too. The evening before they left, the Molde Singers accompanied by a brass band serenaded them outside their hotel windows. In response the dramatist gave a speech, the only one of his stay in Molde. If the summary given in the report in *Romsdals Budstikke* is accurate then it seems to have been a rather curious speech. He expressed his appreciation of the honour shown to him that evening. He could not, however, deny that what now seemed to him 'a necessity of life to bring to the attention of the world' was not something that was likely to please everybody. On the other hand, it was quite possible that the warm reception he had received in Molde 'would ameliorate, to some degree, what he felt himself compelled to say, and he asked that what he would in due course be sending back home from the south be viewed as a greeting, and a thank-you for his stay, which he would remember always'.

In other words, he was announcing that what he had experienced at home would emerge in his writing, and that he had no intention of pulling his punches – at least, not until the citizens of Molde had soothed his mind with their songs.

FACE TO FACE

Henrik and Suzannah continued their journey southwards along the coast to Bergen. Suzannah had visited her home town a few years earlier, but Henrik had not been back since the summer of 1863. In a number of ways the visit would be an encounter with the past. The overt reason for their presence was that Den Nationale Scene intended to stage productions of both *The Vikings at Helgeland* and *Lady Inger of Østråt*. With the passing of years the theatre in Bergen had become ever more important for Ibsen, in part because of the conflicts he had known at the Christiania Theatre, in part because the director, Gunnar Heiberg, had shown himself to be a courageous and visionary man of the theatre with a good grasp of what was going on in modern drama. It was he who had invited Olaus Olsen and August Lindberg's group to bring *Ghosts* to the city in 1884, and in February of the following year the world premiere of *The Wild Duck* had been given in Bergen.

Ibsen had met Heiberg in Rome and must have been curious to see what he had done with his old theatre. All the signs are that he liked what he saw. But being back in Bergen again cannot have been easy for him. As the ship berthed at Tyskerbryggen there was no crowd there to greet him, no official welcoming committee – just four of his drinking pals from the old days.

'Welcome, Henrik old chap!' one shouted as he caught sight of the drama-tist. Ibsen at once turned and went back below decks again, slipping ashore quietly later. When the board of the theatre suggested a gala performance in his honour he politely declined. And it was in vain that the audience cried out for the author at the premiere of *Lady Inger of Østråt*. Ibsen was not present. He had, however, arrived unannounced at a rehearsal and – wonder of wonders – even stepped out onto the stage to correct a point in Heiberg's direction. A sudden moment of madness, locking arms with the past, or perhaps an excited pleasure at once again standing face to face with actors on the stage.

He was reminded of the fact that he had not always been so courageous face to face when the love of his youth one day knocked on the door of his hotel room with a bunch of wild flowers in her hands. Rikke Holst was now a married woman with children, and yet she felt her heart pounding like a young girl as she waited for the door to be opened.

'I promise you, Ibsen, that I've looked at this old face of mine many times in the mirror today,' was the first thing she said to him when he appeared. 'Because I want to look just a little bit pretty now that I'm standing in front of you.'

He took her hands in his – this girl he had been so attracted to for one short summer back in 1853, from whom he had fled when her father disapproved of the relationship.

'I do so hope,' she went on, 'that you don't find me too greatly changed, so that you could still like me a bit the way you did in the old days.'

They spoke together about their lives, and about his writing.

'Have you spotted any traces of yourself and of our young love in my writing?' he asked her.

She laughed:

'Let me think . . . Well, then that would probably be "Mutter Stråmand" in *Love's Comedy* – with her eight children and always knitting something.'

She was memories for him, he was literature for her. But the reunion was warm, as warm as such reunions can be between old lovers when the passion has gone. After about a week in Bergen, Henrik and Suzannah continued their journey by sea back to Kristiania. The visit was not a happy one. The Christiania Theatre didn't have a single Ibsen play in their programme for the season and couldn't even offer a gala performance. August Lindberg, whom Ibsen met here, noted that he seemed in a dangerous mood. Others noticed the same. The whole thing began innocently enough. On 26 September a motion was proposed at the Students' Union to honour the writer with a torchlight proces-sion. The conservative students protested, but finally the chairman and a member of the committee were sent to inform Ibsen of the honour that was being proposed. The chairman was none other than Lorentz Dietrichson.

Ibsen declined. He was quite simply weary of torchlight processions. Dietrichson was offended, but what Ibsen had actually said, and the reason he had actually given, turned out to be a matter of dispute. According to Dietrichson, Ibsen replied with a simple no, and then expressed his appreciation of the thought and asked that his warm greetings be conveyed to the students. Dietrichson did as requested, and the following day, on 29 September, Henrik and Suzannah boarded the ship that would take them on to Copenhagen.

At this point the narrative heads off in two different directions, with one part continuing in Christiania and the other in Copenhagen.

* * *

In Copenhagen, Henrik and Suzannah moved into the Hotel d'Angleterre. A ceaseless parade of celebrations began. The Kongelige Teater gave a gala performance of *The Wild Duck*, and there was one dinner after another. One evening, as he and Suzannah were making their way back to their hotel, a man approached and presented his card. His name was Rasmus B. Anderson. He was a Norwegian-American professor and a diplomat, and currently the American ambassador to Denmark. Three years previously he had made a failed attempt to publish Ibsen in America, but since that time there had been no contact between them. To the man's considerable surprise, Ibsen embraced him, and told him how pleased he was to see him. Anderson soon realised he had been drinking. Now Ibsen took hold of his arm, sent Suzannah up to their room, and ordered champagne and cigars for himself and Anderson.

They sat up until the small hours, Anderson smoked, Ibsen drank – and talked. He talked ceaselessly about how from now on his writing was going to be more aggressive. He had only just started, he said, and before he was finished he was going to turn society inside out and upside down. He talked about how corrupt everything was, that a complete overhaul was called for, continuing until about three o'clock, at which point Suzannah came down in her dressing gown and guided him up to bed.

Anderson didn't like Ibsen, but it was the darker side of Ibsen he had encountered. Maybe his mood was unsettled after all his experiences at home in Norway. He had flown the political flag, entered the Norwegian social fray. Did he regret it? Did he know what his next step would be, what the consequences would be for his writing?

Throughout a dinner at Hegel's he sat in complete silence. Brandes rose to his feet and spoke in his praise. It was a good speech. Brandes praised him to the skies, thanked him for the way in which he had used his writing to expose the frailties in society, so that people could identify them and work to correct them. Only after a great deal of urging was Ibsen persuaded to respond. He wasn't going to give a speech, he said, he only wanted to tell Brandes that it was not his ambition to expose the world around him, he wrote only about himself, and to reveal himself to the scrutiny of readers in what he wrote.

He sat down, leaving the guests confused by what he had said – with the possible exception of Brandes. The atmosphere seems to have been better at a dinner Brandes gave for him. Here the host managed, with some difficulty, to persuade Ibsen to accompany him to a meeting of the radical Students' Union, formed three years earlier to oppose the conservative Students' Fellowship. On the evening of 3 October, Ibsen and Brandes attended the meeting together. Once again Brandes gave a speech, and this time, fortunately, Ibsen was in a good mood. 'I will be a student all my life,' he assured the gathering. 'The day I cease to be, I will no longer consider my life worth living.'

And in *this* company, surrounded by young people, he reaches out the hand Brandes had waited for in vain during that dinner at Hegel's; a writer's hand, offered to the world:

> If my life has been of any importance, as you say, then it is because between myself and the times there is a relationship.

So there *wasn't* a deep chasm between the writer and the world. But the writer's task in this fellowship was to be true to himself, and not to a party or a movement. That, in essence, seems to have been what Ibsen was saying in those two short speeches he gave in Copenhagen.

* * *

On the same evening that Ibsen was raising his glass to the Danish students, the Norwegian Students' Union in Kristiania was formulating its response to his refusal of the torchlight procession. After Dietrichson had given his version of what transpired, a Danish student named Ove Rode rose to his feet and said that he had talked to Ibsen too, and that what *he* had been told was that, in the first place, Ibsen didn't much like torchlight processions, and secondly, that he couldn't really believe the union was serious in their homage, because if they were then the first thing they would have done was to dismiss the current committee and choose a 'freethinking' chairman and leader. If that were done, he would be prepared to receive the students' homage.

What Rode said was tantamount to a declaration of war from Ibsen. It was a political attack on the academic community, which had so far managed to remain united through all the political turbulence. Two days later Dietrichson sent a telegraph to Ibsen, whose reply implied that Rode's version of events was closer to the truth:

'My deepest feeling was,' he wrote to Dietrichson, 'that I could feel no real sympathy with a Students' Union under your leadership. Convey this to the students.'

The rejection was personal, even though he must have realised its political implications. Or did he? Had he given Dietrichson a spontaneous answer, and thereby become involved in something that rapidly turned into a public political row? It was no less personal for Dietrichson, who was obliged to convey the humiliating response to the gathering of students. Dietrichson defended himself in front of the students, ridiculing Ibsen as cowardly and fickle, and when the punch was served it came with a drinking song about Ibsen that he had composed himself, an extended lampoon directed not just at Ibsen but at the minority of freethinking students who had supported him. To this must be added that the gathering now knew that Ibsen had been a guest of the radical Students' Union in Copenhagen. Word was that Brandes had revealed that Ibsen's real reason for declining to receive the torchlight procession was that in his opinion there were no real students in Norway. Ibsen, apparently, nodded his affirmation at these words.

Dietrichson's strategy now became apparent; Ibsen had left himself vulnerable here, and this presented an opportunity to challenge both him and the radical circles to which he belonged. Hence the lampoon which, naturally, created the uproar it was intended to.

The following day the scandalous meeting was the talk of the town. The debate continued in the pages of the newspapers, at which point politics became a major part of it. 'At last,' wrote Camilla Collett in *Nyt Tidsskrift*, 'a real rift in the verbal fig leaf that is used to cover everything in this town.' But nothing really changed. Those who agreed with each other before were now even firmer in their agreement, and those who disagreed with them disagreed even further. On Friday 16 October a protest meeting was arranged in Lieutenant Wettres's gymnasium on the corner of Pilestredet and Rosenkrantz gate. The liberal students assembled here, having first driven the conservative troublemakers away, then marched inside to send a greeting to Ibsen.

You have written yourself into our hearts, just as you wrote your thoughts into our minds.

Ibsen was touched, and sent a warmly appreciative telegraph. On 23 October he sent a lengthy confirmation of his dislike of the conservative majority in the Students' Union under Dietrichson's leadership, at the same time reaffirming his support for the radical minority. Encouraged by this, on 12 November the radical students resigned from the Norwegian Students' Union and formed their own Union of Freethinking Students.

With that the political strife had divided the students too, just as it had in Denmark. In the new organisation 'the great writers' were given honorary membership. Alexander Kielland declined, with thanks; he had no faith in the freethinking of the students, and held that the opposition was best served by remaining an opposition. Ibsen, however, was not a man to decline an offer of honorary membership of anything and enthusiastically accepted.

A month later he wrote to Hegel:

My battle with the Norwegian Students Union has ended in the way I thought it would. Dietrichson has been swept away, and a new organisation of freethinkers has been established. I must for the time being be content with this.

Quite possibly the whole business had assumed greater proportions than Ibsen had ever imagined or wanted. But when it did, he picked up the gauntlet Dietrichson had thrown down, and concluded his visit home with this very public demonstration of support for the liberal side in Norwegian politics.

* * *

At the beginning of October, Henrik and Suzannah left Copenhagen and boarded the steamer that was to take them to Stettin, travelling on from there by train through Germany. On board the ship was another Norwegian whom Ibsen had probably never met before, and whom he did not recognise on this occasion either. Arne Garborg was on his way to Loschwitz, outside Dresden, and it is little wonder that his heart began beating faster at the sight of the hero of his youth.

He longed to approach him, but how? Ibsen ate, and appeared not to notice the young man who sat at his table for thirty minutes without introducing himself. When Ibsen rose and left after the meal, Garborg fumbled for his calling card, and when Ibsen suddenly returned he grabbed his chance. He told Ibsen who he was, and Ibsen suggested they have a drink – 'and it turned into a helluva session'. They sat and talked about the production of *The Wild Duck*, which they had both seen in Copenhagen. They spoke of the language debate and of politics, and at one point Garborg took the chance to quickly apologise for his review of *Ghosts*. Ibsen 'didn't exactly go out of his way not to be unpleasant', but the mood was soon restored. When Garborg went to bed that night he felt elated, and summed up the evening's drinking in the following words:

Bjørnson is the Big Chief; Alexander Kielland is the merchant, Ibsen the intelligent proletarian.

From this perspective, his trip to Norway had been remarkable: he had arrived in the country as the great sphinx, and was now leaving it as the intelligent proletarian. Ibsen was the liberals' pivot man, defender of the madness of the young, spokesman for women and workers. Above all, he had entered the social fray and fought against reaction in the person of Lorentz Dietrichson. The struggle had not been fought face to face; it had to wait until he was out of the country. And perhaps it was distance that enabled him to declare himself content with the outcome.

But just how deep *was* that contentment?

About a year after his return he summed up his feelings about seeing his home country again after such a long time:

> I have never felt so alien when faced with my fellow countrymen's Thun og Treiben as I have this past year. Never more repelled. Never more distressed and uncomfortable. And yet I do not abandon my hope that all this crudity will presently resolve itself and become a genuinely substantial culture.

Alienated, repelled, and yet still holding out hope for the future. What was it he was actually hoping for?

THE RAGE OF RESIGNATION

Was Ibsen moving to a liberal position in politics in the first half of the 1880s, as is usually assumed? Or did he remain the apostle of aristocratic individualism? A likely place to look for an answer is in the speech he gave to the workers in Trondheim in June 1885.[41] In Christiania he had expressed his solidarity with the young and the liberals in Norwegian politics. In Trondheim he sang the praises of women and workers in a way that seemed to take sides clearly in the ongoing political, social and cultural struggles that had split Norway. Had Ibsen, finally, become a party-political animal? Was he waving the flag for the Left, or had he become an out-and-out socialist?

It isn't quite as simple as that. Indirectly he is expressing a degree of hope in the liberal movement, but he complained so often of the liberals' betrayals that his hope cannot have been all that great. And under the parliamentary system there was still no room for either 'Freedom of belief or freedom of expression beyond certain arbitrary limits'. He was, of course, thinking of the Kielland affair, and, significantly, he ends by denying that the new, parliamentary democracy has the ability to bring the fight for freedom to a successful conclusion.

The battle for freedom continued, and in this battle one quality in particular is stressed, a single, decisive element – nobility. Not the nobility of a traditional aristocracy, not the nobility of wealth, nor yet the nobility of learning, talent or ability. He was talking about nobility of character, of the spirit and the will. It was towards this that the revolution of the human spirit must aim. That this nobility was connected to women, workers and the young is important, but does not of itself mean that he identified himself with the women's movement, or the labour movement. No, what distinguished these groups was that they had 'not yet been irreparably damaged by the pressures of the party system'. They were the as yet unsullied, the 'noble savages', who could be bearers of the hopes for freedom, on the simple grounds that they had not yet been incorporated into masculine, bourgeois society, neither the old civil-servant state nor the new, liberal democracy. To some extent this can illuminate his view of the 'noble savage'; when, in other contexts, he makes fun of Norwegian missionaries among the heathen, it is not concern for the 'poor Negro' that moves him, but rather a desire to ridicule the smug self-satisfaction of the Christians.

Having admitted as much, it is clear that Ibsen had, in general, a far more tolerant attitude towards women, Zulus, Jews and workers than did many of his contemporaries. And it is equally clear that his plays have had a considerable influence on the women's movement and the labour movement, indeed, with the coming of the twentieth century, on European Jews under Hitler's regime, and in African and Asian lands both before and after colonialism. From a biographical perspective, however, Ibsen's remarks about 'the others' confirm more than anything else his fundamentally ambivalent attitude towards his own origins: his revolt was directed against the same society as that into which he was born, which he was writing about and for, and which, in the final analysis, was the one he sought recognition from.

As regards the concept of nobility, the speech sheds light on Ibsen's aristocratic individualism. That he would distance himself from a hereditary aristocracy is obvious; it was the stuff of everyday liberal rhetoric, and a reflection of the historical truism that the European aristocracy could not possibly have the future on its side. But nor did Ibsen believe in the permanence of bourgeois society, so he also rejects its conceptions of aristocracy. In rejecting the nobility of wealth, learning, talent and ability he is in reality rejecting the liberal bourgeois society's entire notion of an elite, which was based on the concepts of *Bildung und Besitz* – the power of education and money.[42] What he actually does in his speech in Trondheim is affirm his belief in a historical *tabula rasa*, the sense of living through a period of profound transition. The only thing that would remain standing after his thoroughgoing demolition of Europe's society-building was the individual. Therefore the only nobility worth fighting for was nobility of the spirit, the character and the will.

That is how radical Ibsen's revolution was, and of all the many things that can be said about his anger and his rage over the conditions of freedom, the most important is that this was the rage of resignation. His goal was movement, his writing an ongoing dissection of human freedom, not just by exposing those who *maintain* its illusions, but also by exposing those who *expose* them, an unending game in the human struggle for authenticity against dead thoughts.[43]

Behind this vision lay an idea of some kind of totality, a vague vision of wholeness and harmony. Or should one rather speak of the memory of a vanished harmony? Visions of the third kingdom are often presented as utopian, but it is easy to forget that utopias are often closely related to a dream of a lost golden age. Did Ibsen's third kingdom lie ahead – or was it a thing of the past? Henrik Ibsen was profoundly shaped by Romanticism and the early stages of capitalist society. He was a stranger to the parliamentary Norway he returned to in 1885, and was never quite able to see beyond the confines of his own century. This is what distinguishes his elitism from that of others: Brandes believed in science and progress, Bjørnson changed his political and social ideas with the times, and the author of the decadent novel *Tired Men*, Arne Garborg, was himself energetic enough to offer, on the cusp of the new century, visions of a direct democracy. The young aristocratic elitists, who would later unite as the Freethinking Left, adopted much of Ibsen's scepticism towards democracy and a society of the masses. But at least they had a programme: 'We are prepared to change, we are open to new ideas', as the editor Ola Thommessen wrote on the occasion of the establishment of the Freethinking Left (Frisinnede Venstre) in 1909.

This sense of a vanished harmony is an important explanation for Ibsen's resigned rage.

So was he then just a negative and vague utopian? Was he never, not even for a moment, tempted to get involved in the social debate with a single constructive and concrete suggestion as to how society ought to be organised? Not even he was as resolutely steadfast as that. In the years of debate surrounding Norway's constitutional status within the union, there are signs here and there that Ibsen really was trying to get to grips with the issues of the time. On several occasions he expresses concern for the social challenges facing society, at the same time as he believed that these challenges could only be met from outside the political system (unlike Bjørnson, who asserted that political freedom was a precondition for solving social problems). Ibsen hints, however, that a solution might lie in a large party of 'all the underprivileged', with a programme 'devoted exclusively to practical and productive reforms, to a very generous extension of the franchise, to a radical normalisation of the position of women in society, the removal of every remnant of medieval thinking from popular education etc etc'. On another occasion he specifies that the society of the future must be organised by 'something like a system of insurance companies instead of, as now, through societies and states'.

There is no reason to exaggerate Ibsen's talents as a socio-political engineer. But the ideas he does express are something more than the sort of bar-room talk he disparagingly dismisses them as. If we combine the idea of a 'party' devoted exclusively to the achievement of practical and productive reforms with the rather more obscure idea of organising society on the lines of an insurance company, it seems clear that Ibsen is touching on the idea of a non-political professional leadership based on popular foundations. These ideas are encountered again in right-wing activist groupings such as the Freethinking Left, Our Nation (Vort Land) and the Fatherland League (Fedrelandslaget), which during the first years of the twentieth century proposed alternatives to parliamentary government in Norway. The leaders of these right-wing activist organisations, men such as Christian Michelsen and Fridtjof Nansen, propounded an elitist and aristocratic view of life that is reminiscent of Ibsen's, as was their scepticism towards the parliamentary system and democracy. Another point of similarity is in a shared Social Darwinism, opposing the universal equality that was the ideal of democracy with a belief in the natural inequality of the different parts of the social organism. In the spring of 1883, Ibsen had similar thoughts:

> Different people have different roles in life – allocated to them by nature; nature gives to one the ability and the need to do such and such a thing – and to another something different; so each acts according to his own abilities, and in so doing carries out the functions given to him by nature.

Sigurd provides a link between Ibsen and right-wing activism. In the course of the 1890s he developed an extensive social theory of his own.[44] He too was convinced of the validity of Social Darwinism: 'Never mind, that a number of individuals go to the dogs, this is the way of the world, the majority of the human race are canon fodder in the struggle for life,' he wrote on one occasion. Sigurd shared with the right-wing activists an optimistic faith in progress, in elitism, and in professional leadership, and an ideology of modernisation based on scientific principles. He was sceptical of the parliamentary system, and wished to slow the development of democracy. Many, but not all of these were ideas to which his father would have assented. Where Sigurd most clearly deviates from the right-wing activism of his day was in his internationalism, which gradually turned into an out-and-out anti-nationalism. Men such as Nansen and Michelsen were also cosmopolitans, but they combined it with an equally thoroughgoing nationalism. This would be an important factor in the sidelining of Sigurd Ibsen in Norwegian politics following the dissolution of the union in 1905.

Sigurd was concerned not with the nation as such, but with the cultural advance of civilisation. And here he was unmistakably his father's son.

The Freethinking Left is the best illustration of the fact that the division into right and left, conservative and radical, in Norwegian political history is of limited application. Most of the leaders in this party had their roots in the Left. This was true of Sigurd, and yes, Henrik Ibsen himself, in the final analysis, was closer to the Liberals than to the Conservatives. The question is, how useful is it to say, as so many do, that Ibsen went through a conservative phase in the 1870s, before sliding over towards the liberals in the following decade? In reality he, with his aristocratic individualism, placed himself beyond the confines of this dichotomy, and with his impatient dismissal of the political system and his radical demands for freedom he moved freely between positions in both camps in the political landscape.

It is of course problematic to draw comparisons between the views of the nineteenth-century writer Henrik Ibsen and the right-wing activism of the twentieth century. For men of the right such as Michelsen and Nansen democracy remained, in spite of all, a fixed point in their thinking, and – for some of them at least – prevented them from slipping over into the totalitarian ideologies that would come to characterise their century. In the 1880s no such threat existed, which meant that Ibsen was able to attack the parliamentary system in the relatively forthright way he did. Where the conservative spokesmen urged a strong, national leadership, Ibsen was more preoccupied with the ennoblement of the individual: 'Democracy's vital duty is self-ennoblement.'[45] Since his interest in the pursuit of constructive political arrangements was at best slight we never hear him calling for 'the strong man', and in all his work there is not a single example of a strong man who is not ultimately toppled from his pedestal.

Nor did he share to the same extent the fear of socialism that characterised the Conservatives. As early as the revolution of 1848 the European bourgeoisie had viewed the lower class as a threat. Following the Paris Commune of 1871 the fear of socialism developed into outright panic. In Germany the bourgeoisie allied itself with the state, the nobility, and the aristocratically dominated officer-class against socialism and the working class. Two assassination attempts on the life of Kaiser Wilhelm in 1878 gave Bismarck the excuse he needed to abandon the hopeless cultural campaign against the Catholics and introduce the so-called 'socialist laws'. In so doing he managed not only to direct hostilities against the Social Democrats and the Socialists, but also to pacify the national-liberal bourgeoisie.

Ibsen was living in Germany while all this was going on, and though the issue itself was of no particular interest to him he no doubt shared the general fear of the advance of the proletariat – the masses. In inspired moments, however, he could express his admiration for the vigour of the socialists. 'To be honest,' he confided once, 'the only ones I feel sympathy for are the nihilists and the socialists. Their goals are absolutist, and they are consistent.'

But again, what appeals to him are the spirit of revolt and the willingness to act, not necessarily the aims.[46] His gestures towards a constructive social ideology remained vague and unfinished. Ibsen was always and ever a poet, and it was through his works that he remained best able to express himself. Perhaps his visions are most clearly articulated in the poem 'Stars in Nebula' of 1886, in which he finds a symbolic representation of the dissolutions and divisions of the times in the movements of the comets and stars through space:

> A different chaos hemmed me in, I found,
> of wills at variance and of paths contested,
> reluctance to accept the middle ground,
> to follow any change of route suggested.

But something was afoot, a gathering of chaos into a star in the north. This was the dream of Nordic unity, an expression of Ibsen's own dream of wholeness and totality. But dare he believe in the unity?

> The nebula, though formless, I believe in,
> chaotic though the weltering North may be;
> believe it is on course for unity –
> a brilliant star in process of conceiving.

He believes in the law of unity, even though it is still in its earliest stages. In the dramas he still had to write, however, it is not this law that preoccupies him, but another law, the same as that of all the work of his mature years, and which, in the final part of his life, emerges with ever greater clarity:

Not the law of unity, but the law of transformation.

X

MUNICH

'DIESER PLATZ IST DEM HERRN DOKTOR IBSEN VORBEHALTEN!'

Henrik Ibsen's life is like a long, gradually drying plaster cast; slowly but surely the living human being solidifies into the mask that posterity knew as *Diktersfinksen* – the Poet-Sphinx. Life comes to a halt, but that does not mean that the life's work does too. On the contrary, Ibsen carries on writing into his old age, and the plays from this late period have proved among his most durable.

The situation gives rise to a biographical paradox: the writer's literary powers continue undiminished long after the writer himself has gone into hiding behind the shell of his own monument. Life withers, art continues to flower. Not that the life had ever been especially spectacular. If Ibsen was right, and Bjørnson's life was his best creation, then most of his own life – his external life – was, on the surface, workaday prose of the most trivial sort. But only on the surface. Because Ibsen was the poet of the riddle. His veins of silver lay hidden inside the mountain; so too did the poetry he made out of his own life.

* * *

After their summer and autumn of 1885 in Norway, Henrik and Suzannah decided to settle back in Munich – if, that is, they had ever really left the city. While they lived in Rome all their furniture and paintings were kept in storage in a Munich loft; in that sense the Bavarian capital was their home in all the years that had elapsed since Dresden. The furniture had all been bought with the idea of establishing a home of their own. In reality only one place was home, though the visit to Norway had not been a particularly encouraging one. As on his previous visit, Henrik toyed with the idea of buying himself a summer residence. He got a little further with his plan this time, before eventually abandoning it. There would be another six years in Munich before he would finally give up his exile.

The couple moved into an apartment on Maximilianstrasse 32, not far from Maxvorstad, the artists' quarter where they had lived previously.

'We've got comfortable and spacious accommodation here in Munich's most exclusive and fashionable street,' he boasted to Hegel at the end of October, 'and the rent is just half of what we were paying in Rome.'

Cheap indeed, and Maximilianstrasse really was an elegant street. Historically, it was the monumental Ludwigstrasse that was the city's main street, but in modern Munich it was Maximilianstrasse that took pride of place. The Ibsens' old quarter, Maxvorstadt, remained the city's artistic centre, but as Munich grew and the population increased the artists migrated to the Schwabing area north of Maxvorstadt. It was here that the artist Olaf Gulbransson found his natural environment around the satirical magazine *Simplicissimus*, here that Albert Langen published Hamsun's *Mysteries*, where Thomas Mann wrote *Buddenbrooks*. Stefan George's circle thrived here, as did the Art Nouveau (*Jugendstil*) movement, the Blaue Reiter artists, Rainer Maria Rilke and others.[1]

Schwabing belonged to the new bohemians; Ibsen's bohemian days were over long ago. He felt thoroughly at home in fashionable Maximilianstrasse. The apartment satisfied his need for a home in which the ceilings were high and the rooms well ventilated, features that had become necessities of life for him. The spring of 1886 was a quiet one for the couple, and with Sigurd no longer living with them life was even quieter. The previous December the young man had been made attaché in Washington, a posting worth 7,500 kroner annually, and before setting out on the long journey he called in to celebrate the new year with his parents. He was now financially independent, and thus well beyond their reach.

Henrik had not kept in touch with many of his old Munich friends while living in Rome; he corresponded with Oswald Schmidt, as well as the Grønvold brothers and Otto Sinding, but that was about it. A lot of things had changed since the last time he lived here, or rather, he had changed a lot. His literary development following *The Pillars of Society* made it difficult for his old friends from the Krokodile – now disbanded – to follow him. Paul Heyse was now the defender of an idealist aesthetic that promoted beauty, and as such found himself a target for those young German naturalists who were such fierce defenders of Ibsen's plays on themes from contemporary life. Not that Heyse had responded with immediate hostility to his old friend's change of direction. He had expressed his appreciation of *The Pillars of Society*, even while regretting the use of prose in the play. *A Doll's House* had impressed him greatly, and he defended the last act as an artistic necessity, contrasting it favourably with what seemed to him the cheap compromise of a happy ending in the preceding play. But with *Ghosts* his admiration turned to disappointment, and for the rest of his life Heyse would lump Ibsen in with all the other naturalist writers who, in his view, destroyed everything that was beautiful and good in art.

It was not easy for either of them. Ibsen was almost embarrassed at the way his name was used to condemn his old friend, and where necessary he defended him. But Heyse was fighting a losing battle. He died in 1914, just before the outbreak of the First World War. With the war Europe's *belle époque* was finally over for good, and with Heyse's death the last of the great idealistic poets of the nineteenth century was gone. Once the 'Dichterfürst' of Munich, and one of Germany's leading writers of the last half of the century, his name was quickly forgotten.[2]

New names entered Ibsen's life, both in Munich and Berlin, literary supporters such as Julius Elias, Julius Hoffory (Danish, but living in Berlin), Paul Schlenter, Paul Lindau, Otto Brahm, Max Bernstein, Ludwig Fulda, Leo Berg, Felix Philippi and Michael Georg Conrad.[3] But it does not seem as though he had a circle of friends in his home town, or at least nothing comparable to the Krokodile.

Ibsen resumed his structured life, more structured now than ever before, if such a thing were possible. In the summer he rose at seven, a little later in the winter. He dressed slowly, and spent a whole hour in the bathroom, following this with a light breakfast before sitting down to work at nine. When the hands of the clock showed one o'clock he went out for a walk, returning for the main meal of the day at three o'clock. Afterwards he would read. Supper was at seven, followed by a toddy and bed at nine. Ibsen slept soundly, was rarely ill, and had a healthy appetite.

Such were the excitements of the life of an artist in Munich.

These descriptions of Ibsen's daily routine come from observations made by Henrik Jæger during a holiday in Denmark. In all likelihood he followed the same routine in Munich, with one exception: his visit to the cafe. A couple of blocks away from the apartment he found his new haunt, Café Maximilian. He went there daily, come rain or shine, between six thirty and seven thirty in the evening, to enjoy a tankard of beer or a small cognac, now and then lifting his gaze from the newspaper to observe the people entering and leaving through the door. Café Maximilian was the focal point of literary Munich, and in typical German fashion Ibsen was given the honour of his own regular seat and table. If someone were tactless enough to sit in his seat, a waiter would at once approach:

'Bitte, entschuldigen Sie: Dieser Platz ist dem Herrn Doktor Ibsen vorbe-halten!'

His presence in the city had not exactly been overlooked previously, but now his status was as one of 'the sights and celebrities of Munich', as one Danish newspaper put it.

Arne Garborg put it another way: 'You know, to be in Munich and not see Ibsen is like being in Rome and not seeing the pope.'

HOME AND AWAY

Even though Ibsen had spent almost five years in Rome, it was Germany that was his second home during the years of exile. And of the two German cities in which he lived, it was Munich that was closest to being his adopted home.

But was he really, in the strictest sense of the word, an exile?

His own version of his situation was ambivalent. On the one hand Ibsen described his exile as a 'banishment', accompanying the description with bitter recriminations against the Norwegians who had made his life at home impossible. Yet on numerous other occasions he stressed the necessity of putting 'distance' between himself and his homeland in order to be able to write. If the criterion for exile is that one has been *compelled* to leave one's country, then he was not an exile. From that perspective it was Georg Brandes – more or less driven out of Denmark – who was more genuinely an exile than he was.

Brandes had literally *fled* from Denmark. Ibsen had, to be pedantic about it, simply *moved* from Norway, a state of affairs that he nevertheless preferred to describe as 'living in exile'. But if we compare the two men's fates, the picture looks slightly different. Where Brandes quickly became part of social and intellectual circles in Germany, Ibsen lacked the cultural and social capital to do the same thing. Although in time he did cultivate acquaintanceships with non-Scandinavians, his social circle remained dominated by Scandinavians. And in *that* respect he was the genuine exile, whereas Brandes, intellectual cosmopolitan that he was, crossed borders with much greater ease.

And there is one sense in which it is not exactly wrong to say that Ibsen was driven into exile, for if he was not forced out by external factors, there may have been factors deep within that nevertheless necessitated his leaving. His contempt for his homeland remained as strong as ever, but it might well be the case that the Norwegian he had the most difficult relationship with of all was himself. If so, it makes it easier to understand the antipathy he felt towards those who connected him to his homeland through ties of blood. While visiting Norway he had received a letter from his youngest brother Ole. Like the letter from his father following his earlier visit home, this one too mingled familiarity with humility.

'Compared to you I am no poet or letter writer, my dear brother' – Ole begins – 'but since we have never corresponded at all with each other, which seems unnatural for brothers, I decided today to make a start, and so fraternally enquire: how are you keeping, dear Henrik?'

Ole had read in the newspapers of his brother's return and wanted to put an end to the strained relationship between them. But it soon emerges that he wants something else too. Ole knew what a burden Henrik had carried through his life, and that he was now a 'pioneer' for his people. He had suffered much, as pioneers do – but then gold must first pass through the fire before it glitters. And had not Jesus Christ, the greatest pioneer of them all, struggled his way through life in order to carry out *his* mission? The way Ole saw it, Henrik had punished people, in order to purify them:

This is the calling of the shepherd, and perhaps in time it will become your calling too?

According to Hedvig, Ole was a shy, introverted and brooding man, inclined to pessimism. He had been a storekeeper in Skien and now ran a small farm shop in Tjøme, but was not really cut out for business. He was still deeply religious and keen to share his faith with his celebrated brother. The language of his letter is suffused with the low-church rhetoric of the time, pompous and Romantic, with a fanaticism that the philosophical turns of phrase cannot disguise. With its convoluted phraseology and its hapless philosophical ambitions the letter is actually a folksy variation on Henrik's own self-projection as poet-prophet. If Henrik did see himself in Ole, it can hardly have quickened a desire to pay him a visit. He declined the invitation, and as far as is known never met his brother again. Yet two years later he did provide Ole with a letter of recommendation for a job as a lighthouse-keeper, and through Hedvig he was kept informed of how things were going with his pessimistically inclined brother – the man who became what he might have become had he never left Skien, his dark mirror-image.

No, perhaps, when you get down to it, the exile was not all that voluntary. Ibsen had that fundamental feeling of alienation and *tristesse*, that combination of hatred of and longing for his homeland which defines the distinction between the exile and the cosmopolitan. Yet he also benefited from the positive aspects of exile through the liberating power of distance from his native land.[4] James Joyce once observed that it is less wretched to live the life of a rootless man in exile than to suffer the tyranny of the mediocre at home. Ibsen probably also felt the same way. The advice he gave to the young Kristian Elster in 1880 was the same as he had given Grieg many years earlier – travel:

> For my part, I know what I owe to my knowledge of life and the world in general, and I sympathise with those many talented souls back home who are held back by the constrictions of smallness.

Home represented all that is narrow and close, whereas the continent represented breadth of vision and openness. In many ways he cultivated his status as an exile, possibly inspired by Georg Brandes' first book *Main Currents*, largely on the subject of French emigrant writers. But status as an exile harmonised also with his own self-image as the outsider, the lofty aristocratic individualist and 'poet-prophet', analysing society from his vantage point on its outer limits. Distance was necessary in order to see the home country more clearly, Ibsen maintained. But did he really see so much more clearly from a distance, or was it rather the case that exile gave him a *simplified* picture of his homeland? While

Ibsen sat in the cafes of Germany and Italy and handed down categorical judgements on the doings of his countrymen back home in Norway, it was muchderided party men, such as Bjørnson and Sverdrup, who actually entered the daily fray and its world of compromises and changes of policy in a complex political and social reality. Only in rare moments of self-awareness did Ibsen find himself able to praise the workhorses back home:

> When I think of you all at home up there, carrying on the struggle day in and day out, it makes me feel ashamed of myself; but I'm not really equipped to struggle in any other way than I do.

As a Norwegian at home Ibsen was inadequate, but distance did not necessarily make him any more efficient as an analyst of society either. It is not unreasonable to suppose that what distance did do was simplify and universalise the characters and settings in his plays (the provincial coastal town, the bourgeois types), and in so doing make the conflicts more accessible to a European public unfamiliar with the details of Norwegian society but who nevertheless inhabited the same bourgeois world as that depicted in the plays. He once told Magdalene Thoresen that living abroad gave him the advantage of imbibing a version of life at home in a purified and extracted form. Perhaps one might equally say that he abstracted the European from the Norwegian?

The relationship between home and abroad is manifest in various ways in Ibsen's dramas. Here is a world of people who flee from their homes, or return after long absences and find themselves at odds with the steady, stable local society. In *Brand* and *Peer Gynt* absence is connected with flight or eviction from the home, in *The Pillars of Society* and *Ghosts* it is respectively America and Paris that symbolise a life in freedom, and in *An Enemy of the People* and *The Wild Duck* Stockmann's life in the north of Norway and Gregers' year at Høydalsverket represent lives lived in isolation. Yet it would be unwise to go too far in identifying all of this as variations on a theme of exile; when Ibsen introduces an outsider into a small, clearly defined environment, what he is doing is making use of one of the techniques of classical drama to generate conflict and action. The encounter between the outside and home becomes an encounter between different ideas and interests. Past actions are revealed, fears and longings are aroused.[5] The theme of exile is more directly broached in the contrast between the narrow, cold north and the light, open Mediterranean, which Ibsen made use of as early as *The Burial Mound*, and later in *Ghosts*, alongside *Peer Gynt* and *When We Dead Awaken* (which of course is about an artist returning from exile).

* * *

Although Ibsen liked to convey an impression that his life abroad brought him into touch with a cosmopolitan world, he never made use of Dresden, Munich or Rome in his writing. With the exception of his first sojourn in Rome it is striking how superficially he describes the places in which he lives in his letters: the numerous references to good beer, the cost of living and the climate are more like entries for a Baedeker than a naturalist's programme. And yet the European experience may well have played its part, even though that part may be difficult to assess. It is hard to say whether Ibsen was a *European* writer who located his European themes in Norway, or a *Norwegian* writer who abstracted the European essence from Norway. What is certain is that he liked to regard himself as European (or Germanic), and what is equally certain is that whenever he talks about 'society' it is almost always Norwegian society to which he is referring.

By contrast with the rest of Europe, Norwegian society was lagging behind in a number of ways. This makes it tempting to suggest that the reason Ibsen's plays had such a strong appeal for European audiences was because they were set in an environment that was recognisably the same as their own, but simpler. It is equally interesting to turn the postulate on its head and ask whether Ibsen's status as a provincial and an 'immigrant' into the mainstream of European culture might not have given him certain advantages that were not available to those who had grown up within that culture ('the heirs'). As a provincial he may have had a greater sensitivity towards European culture and the large-scale social revolutions of his age, at the same time as his provincial background made him more disposed than the European cultural 'heirs' to cross the boundaries of the different aesthetic categories.[6]

Provincial and European, only a combination of these designations can explain *Brand* and *Peer Gynt* – those revolutionary dramas that made Ibsen Ibsen.

However, the axis was not simply 'home' in Norway and 'away' in Europe. The Scandinavian writers, artists, intellectuals, publishers, actors and directors who congregated in the large cities created what was in many ways a Scandinavian 'homeland' of their own, united as they were in a common cultural and economic sphere that linked their own domestic culture and the wider culture of the rest of Europe. Ultimately, it was probably this Scandinavian community that Ibsen felt most comfortable in, not least because it was the company that was chosen, and it was both free and incorporeal. In many ways he was made for just such an incorporeal homeland, located inside the borders of a shared Scandinavian culture. Typically his social life was characterised by the fellowship of correspondence and short visits. A noncommittal life, one that did not partake of the common fate. The same is true of his family life. Henrik, Suzannah and Sigurd lived a life much like that of any other bourgeois family, but for the most part in rented accommodation and with rented furniture.

Freedom above all; throughout his life, Ibsen made money not to build and settle, but to buy the freedom to keep moving.

THE WHITE HORSES

Just how much Norway still meant to him emerged clearly in the new play he worked on in the spring of 1886. Even before travelling to Norway he had told Hegel he had the framework for a new play, and the first notes are dated to the winter of 1884–5. But the trip to Norway and re-establishing himself in Munich both delayed the writing and gave it a new direction.

'The impressions, the experiences and the observations I made on my trip to Norway in the summer of last year continued to disturb me for a long time afterwards,' he later confided to Georg Brandes. 'Not until I had finally come to the full realisation of what I had lived through was I able to start to profit from it all in my writing.'

Only once experiences became transformed into something *lived through* could the writing process begin. But as time passed he was forced to admit that work on the new play was going slowly. By mid-June he had made a start on the third act of a play to which he had given the working title 'White Horses'. Then he stops, lays it aside and starts a complete rewrite, now with the title *Rosmersholm*. He remains in Munich throughout the summer, working to have the book ready by Christmas. July and August were spent at his writing desk, and not until 27 September was the fair copy ready to be sent to Hegel who, over the years, had got used to knowing next to nothing of what the plays were about until he had the finished manuscript in his hands.

Ibsen reveals a few of its secrets in his covering letter:

> As far as I can see the play is not open to attack from any quarter. But I hope that it will arouse a lively discussion, and I certainly expect there to be one in Sweden.

Hegel must have wondered what it was Ibsen had said about the Swedes in the new play, but apart from that it looked once again as though this was not going to be an acidic social satire. But lively discussions there were once the play was published on 23 November 1886, with a first print run of 8,000 copies.

* * *

In *Rosmersholm* we meet the apostate pastor Johannes Rosmer, last in a line of proud public officials who have lived in Rosmersholm for generations. The significant events in Rosmer's life have for the most part taken place before the action of the play opens. His mentally disturbed wife Beata drowned herself in the mill race; rumours suggested that she took her own life because she was unable to give her husband the child that would ensure the survival of the line. Now Rosmer lives alone, in company with a young woman who joined the household on the recommendation of Beata's brother Kroll, a headmaster. A close friendship has developed between Rebecca West and Rosmer, with Rebecca supporting Rosmer in his dream of transforming people into 'happy noble people'. In doing so she takes over the role formerly played by Ulrik Brendel, the tutor who had introduced the young Rosmer to radical ideas. Rosmer gives up his living, breaks with his conservative friends and, encouraged by Rebecca, becomes involved in politics on the left. He is all the while unaware that he is also in love with Rebecca.

Rosmer's political awakening leads to a break with the conservative Kroll, who in turn sets in train a web of intrigue in the course of which it becomes clear that Rebecca's motives while at Rosmersholm have sometimes been less than pure. At one point she admits that she deceived Beata into thinking that she herself was expecting her husband's child, and was going to take her place in the household. Rosmer now realises that his wife took her own life in order to clear the way for the two of them. But Rebecca too learns something new about her past when Kroll reveals that the stepfather (and lover!) she grew up with was, in reality, her biological father.

Dejection, doubt and not least guilt descend upon the sensitive and idealistic Rosmer, and he abandons his dream of ennobling the human race. It is this gloom that characterises the 'Rosmerian view of life', a view of life that perhaps is ennobling, but one which has killed the joy of life for the family, and for those who are drawn into the family's orbit. When Rosmer finally asks for Rebecca's hand she rejects his offer, crushed by guilt. For no apparent reason they conclude that life is not worth living, and happiness an impossibility as long as the ghosts of the past (symbolised by white horses) won't let go. They decide to abandon life by throwing themselves into the mill race at the same place as Beata drowned.

Alfred Sinding-Larsen voiced a common response when he borrowed Rosmer's own words from the closing lines of the second act for his review in *Morgenbladet*:

'What – is – this?'

And really, what was it? If *The Wild Duck* had provoked the reviewers, *Rosmersholm* did so even more. Never before had Ibsen written a play that seemed quite so obscure and confusing to readers. While the anonymous reviewer in *Aftenposten* wrote that it would have been no great loss to the world if all the 'deranged beings' in the play had jumped into the mill race, *Morgenbladet*

regretted the appearance of yet another glamorisation of suicide. Most conservative critics regarded the play as a political attack on the conservative view
of society, a reading that probably owed something to difficulties they had
in saying anything at all about its dramatic qualities. The response of the
radicals was not markedly different. Erik Skram conceded there was a certain
fascination in what he considered to be the main theme of the play – the burden
of one's ancestry – but regretted Ibsen's move away from realism, and found the
characters and the conflicts obscure and abstract.

Edvard Brandes did not understand everything about the play either, but
then he did not demand that a literary masterpiece be immediately accessible:

What is there to praise, if one will not praise this!

Edvard reads the play in the light of the political situation in Norway, but it is
the artistic qualities that compel: 'The writing in this play – powerful, cutting,
shining like gold script on a marble base – is something no other dramatist in
our time could manage.'

Georg Brandes, on the other hand, had as little use for Johannes Rosmer as
he had had for Hjalmar Ekdal:

But what on earth is all this irrational preaching about the *purifying*,
cleansing influence spouted by the sexless Rosmer!

For Georg, the association of idealism and purity showed that Ibsen was still
'up to his neck in the old theology', and the hostility towards sexuality was one
of the things he found most difficult to accept in the play. Bjørnson's reaction
was less predictable. Although fascinated by the content of the play, he objected
that Ibsen had picked the wrong literary form. *Rosmersholm* should have been
a novel, not a drama – quite something to demand of Henrik Ibsen, but understandable. Others besides Bjørnson found it odd that its decisive events
had occurred before the action of the play began, and that not much happened
on the stage, though these had by now become familiar aspects of Ibsen's
retrospective technique.

* * *

Rosmersholm is one of Ibsen's darkest and most complicated plays, subject to
numerous and widely divergent interpretations. It has even proved difficult to
identify the main character, with our understanding of the play changing quite
strikingly according to whether we identify this as Rosmer or Rebecca. The
differences emerge clearly if we pose two central questions: why does Rebecca
reject Rosmer's proposal of marriage if that is what she has been looking for

ever since her arrival at Rosmersholm? Why do they really end their lives in the mill race, and who leads whom?

An idealistic-tragic reading of the drama will tend to play down Rosmer's obvious weaknesses of character and underscore his genuine desire to transcend himself in the name of renewal. Within this tradition the ending is understood to show that the two gladly go to their deaths, that through this sacrifice they become *one*, as Rosmer says, and in this way realise their love for each other, in other words, a 'positive' tragic ending, in the classical sense. The religious reading, which stresses the idea of penance and sacrifice, is also part of this tradition. For many, Rebecca has *every reason* to take her own life in penance for what she has done at Rosmersholm. A critical-ironic reading turns this upside down, finding the play a criticism of Rosmer's idealism, with Rebecca presented as a victim of the Rosmerian view of life. Rosmer has crushed the spirit of life in her, and (unconsciously) manipulated her into making the fatal sacrifice.[7]

Between two such undeniably rather simplified extremes other possible interpretations exist; among these are the attempt to forge a third way that distinguishes between a positive tragic level in the 'supratext', and a number of negative signals in the subtext implying that the entity that Rosmer and Rebecca sacrifice themselves to in the mill race is in reality a delusion.[8]

What most agree on at least is that *guilt* and *freedom from guilt* are essential elements of the text. Both Rosmer and Rebecca are crushed by a guilt that in the end drives them to make their own retribution. In like fashion it is impossible to ignore the erotic element. Rebecca has been a woman of passion, driven by her desires, a classic *femme fatale*, save in the special case of the unintended incestuous relationship with her father. As the play gets under way, however, her passion has died down. Under the circumstances it can surprise no one that the most famous commentary on the play is that published by Sigmund Freud in a collection of essays in 1916. Here he explains Rebecca's rejection of Rosmer's offer of marriage as a projection of her own incestuous relationship with her father onto him. In this Oedipal light Beata becomes her mother, and under the shadow of this guilt-complex it becomes impossible for her to realise the relationship with Rosmer. This interpretation accords with an idealistic-tragic reading in that it provides a tragic motive for Rebecca's suicide.

In a critical-ironic reading one is inclined to take Rebecca at her word (ironically enough, in this instance). She does, after all, freely admit that her passion has left her under the influence of the Rosmerian view of life, and that she now cultivates the same ideas of purity and the ennobling of the spirit as Rosmer. She has, quite simply, changed, and no longer wants the same thing as he wants. As they end in the mill race both are equally unsuited for life in this world. From *their* perspective at least, suicide must appear in a genuinely

Romantic and tragic light. Both are in thrall to the Rosmerian vision, unable to see how the ennoblement of the spirit might be realised in daily life.

It all leaves one of the minor characters, the newspaper editor Mortensgård, as the victor. Mortensgård is a man who is neither weighed down by guilt nor spurred on by visions but instead plays the hand life has dealt him with an unusually pragmatic skill.

* * *

Few of these complex interpretations of the play can be seen in contemporary responses to it. The problem for most critics, and probably for the average reader as well, was that the play did not 'contribute to the debating of problems' in the way people had become accustomed to expect but was 'merely a psychological experiment' in which two people end up dead for God knows what reason. To some extent these criticisms echoed the reception of *The Wild Duck*. But there at least the oppositions involved in the 'claim of the ideal' were reasonably clear to the public; in *Rosmersholm* it was hard to get any idea at all of what the conflict was about.

All of this has led many to see this drama as a watershed in Ibsen's oeuvre, though the criteria have varied. For Georg Brandes, who always looked for a political and social message in the plays, *Rosmersholm* was the last in a line of dramas of contemporary life that began with *The Pillars of Society*. The play is also undoubtedly a reckoning with political life; the question is, how much weight should be given to the political and social dimensions of the preceding plays? *The Wild Duck*, for example, is hardly a political play. From the point of view of dramatic technique, what makes *Rosmersholm* remarkable is the element of symbolism. In this light, it is not the last in a line but the first of the symbolic plays with which Ibsen's writing life would conclude. While Ibsen had used *symbols* earlier, there are those who would say that he does not write as a *symbolist* until this play. In *Rosmersholm* the symbols and images can no longer be related to a concrete reality (such as the wild duck in the loft) but almost live lives of their own, independent of the characters and ideas in the play. The white horses simply *are* – pregnant with meaning, a mystical, mythological addition to the play's realistic, psychological and moral dimensions.

Ibsen does not abandon the realistic drama of contemporary life, nor does he cease to write about psychological and moral problems. But the prevailing mood of *Rosmersholm* is something different; the perspective is turned inwards towards the mind, so deeply and darkly that the words become meaningless. And it is here that Ibsen makes a dramatic connection between what is ineffable in the human mind and what is inexpressible in nature, introducing a symbolism that recurs in subsequent plays. In large measure this change takes place within the play itself. In the opening act Rosmer has a clear social and political agenda; he wants to break free of the cloistered life in his ancestral home and participate in the life of society. By the last act he has abandoned himself completely to feelings of guilt and the seductive power of the dead and, with Rebecca, sacrifices himself to the powers of the mill race.

'Out there. In the mill race. Help! Help!' From the window Madam Helseth sees everything.

'No. No help to be had here. – The good lady took them.'

One should probably be cautious in announcing dividing lines too sharply in Ibsen's oeuvre, for there is a real danger of losing sight of the continuities. He wrote sketches for the themes and characters of both *The Wild Duck* and *Rosmersholm* that functioned as deposit accounts for future plays. His notes for *Rosmersholm*, for example, contain this passage:

> *Her*: governess for his two daughters, liberated, passionate, rather reckless but hides it well. Regarded by those around her as the bad conscience of the house; the object of suspicion and gossip.
>
> *Oldest daughter*: on the point of being broken by idleness and loneliness; richly talented but with no outlet for it.

* * *

The two daughters have disappeared from the finished play, but crop up again two years later in *The Lady from the Sea*. In this note one can also see traces of Ellida Wangel and Hedda Gabler as well as several of Ibsen's other female characters.

But themes from *Rosmersholm* can also be traced far back into Ibsen's oeuvre. The parallels with the themes of genetic heritage and the ghost-symbolism of *Ghosts* are obvious, and in similar fashion Rosmer can be seen as a weaker and more disillusioned version of Dr Stockmann. Less obvious, but strong nevertheless, are the links to *Emperor and Galilean*. Like Julian, Rosmer is torn between tradition, family heritage and the Christian demands for punishment and order on the one hand, and the 'pagan' ideals of freedom and spontaneity, represented by Rebecca, on the other. And like Julian, Rosmer the Apostate cannot serve either kingdom. The dream of freedom, authenticity and somehow surpassing or exceeding oneself recurs in many of Ibsen's plays – in the kingly thought in *The Pretenders*, in Brand's tragic attempt to create the new human being in himself, in Peer Gynt's dream of empire, Maximos' vision of the third kingdom for Julian, Nora's dream of 'the most wonderful', Hedda Gabler's longing for 'vine leaves', Arnold Rubek's sculptural vision of 'Resurrection Day', and, of course, Rosmer's dream of the noble human being.[9]

In his outline for *The Wild Duck* Ibsen wrote for the first time about the nobility of the mind, the will and the character; he returned to the theme in his speech to the workers in Trondheim in 1885. In *Rosmersholm* he gives us a *poetic* treatment of the theme. But the way in which he does so is unique. Who else but Ibsen could have put his own political visions into the mouth of a dreamer such as Rosmer? Like Dr Stockmann, Rosmer borrows lines from his own creator; yet Ibsen exposes both to his merciless dramatic doubt. He builds them up only to tear them down.

There can be little doubt that the visit to Norway in 1885 had a marked effect on the development of the play. Ibsen himself said so. It was there that he found the most important model for Rosmer in the person of Carl Snoilsky, the Swedish aristocrat who wanted to put his pen at the service of the underprivileged but who found himself unable to shake off the curse of his background.[10] It was this that made Hegel realise what Ibsen meant when he said that the play might raise eyebrows in Sweden. On the larger scale, Rosmer's withdrawal from political and social involvement reflects Ibsen's own *critique* of the political struggle back home – though hardly his *withdrawal* from it, given the very limited nature of his previous involvement. Ibsen had given up on politics long before writing *Rosmersholm*, even though Georg Brandes had difficulty in swallowing the fact.

DIRECTING BY POST

Prior to the publication of *Rosmersholm*, Ibsen insisted on an unprecedented degree of secrecy. Wilhelm Lange was given the job of translating the play for Reclam Verlag, the same publisher who had earlier done so well out of *A Doll's House*, though it hadn't benefited Ibsen in any way. In order to foil potential pirate translators Lange received each act individually as it emerged from the printing press, and only learned the title at the end of the whole process.

Ibsen was similarly cautious in his dealings with theatres. As usual, he insisted that the play be published before it was released for performance, this time adding the proviso that the theatres should not even be given the manuscript until after publication day. Could he really trust the theatre's own employees not to pass a manuscript around among friends and associates? A new play from Ibsen should arrive with an explosive force, there must be no leaks to the press. Expectations were, in any event, so great that silence was the best form of advertisement. Additionally, he worried that public anticipation of the stage performance might damage sales of the book. Ibsen's hostility towards the theatre was increasing – economically, because performances threatened to harm sales of the book; and artistically, because theatrical interpretations had a way of getting between author and audience.

In a word, the theatres threatened Ibsen's control of his own plays, and he watched over them like a hawk.

Rosmersholm had its world premiere on 17 January 1887. Once again the honour fell to the Bergen Theatre, and if we accept the word of the anonymous reviewer in *Bergens Tidende* it was very well received. The play opened in Sweden at the Gothenburg Theatre in March, and at Dramaten in Stockholm the following month, while August Lindberg toured Sweden and Denmark with it and *A Doll's House*, playing, of course, the part of Rosmer himself. Things did not go quite as smoothly at the Kongelige Teater in Copenhagen, where Edvard Fallesen once again objected to the demand to delay a production until after publication. This time it led to a break between the two men. It meant that Copenhagen audiences did not get to see the play until August Lindberg's company gave a guest performance at the Dagmar Theatre in November, at the same time, as it happens, that a parody entitled *Dozemersholm. Idiotic, hippological hauntings during an attack of insanity* was playing at Nørrebros Theatre. Things didn't go all that smoothly at the Christiania Theatre either, where the director, Hans Schrøder, waited in vain for the play. In the end he contacted Ibsen, only to be told that in Ibsen's view, the play was unsuitable for his theatre.

Schrøder must have wondered what was going on. Granted, the writer had failed to send them *The Pillars of Society* some years previously, but since then the theatre had generally put on productions of each new play as it appeared. But it is clear from the letters he wrote that Ibsen had never had any particular faith in the theatre. His letters to Schrøder go over points of direction one by one; there isn't a detail he doesn't have a strong opinion on. The correspondence isn't just evidence of the theatre's incompetence; it says as much about a dramatist's efforts to break down the established theatrical conventions of the time where these created problems for his own artistic ambitions.

In this sense, Ibsen never stopped being a director. On the contrary, he cultivated the role – even if only by post.

The same demands are put forward each time the Christiania Theatre proposes to produce one of his plays. He is absolutely clear about which actors are best suited to which parts, he urges a generally quicker tempo to the acting, as well as a 'quick but well-rehearsed delivery of the lines'. The actors are not to overplay their characters as though they were stock characters but portray them as real people. In the event of a crowd scene, as in *An Enemy of the People*, they must not all flock to the front of the stage and behave as a homogeneous unit: 'The more these minor characters display individual characteristics in a crowd scene the better.' That sounds very much like something he might have learned from the Meiningen group.

Schrøder did not protest. Instead he made a practice of contacting the writer for instructions before starting rehearsals for a new play.

When the theatre announced its intention to stage *The Wild Duck*, yet another of these letters of advice arrived. Particular attention must be paid to the lighting, Ibsen explained, since this was 'designed to underscore the basic mood of each of the five acts'. Moreover, Hjalmar Ekdal must not be played for comedic or parodic effect: 'His sensitivity is honest, his melancholy attractive; there is no hint of affectation.' Only thus could Ekdal display an interesting psychology, as a *person,* not just a character.

And Schrøder did as he was bidden.

In retrospect these instructions might appear to reinforce the views of those who regard Ibsen as a naïve realist, typified by comments on *An Enemy of the People,* in which Ibsen opposed in the strongest possible fashion the suggestion that Stockmann's two boys be played by adult actors:

> The viewer must feel that he is invisibly present in Dr Stockmann's front room; everything here must be realistic, and that goes for the boys too.

The audience, in other words, should not be aware of the fact that what they are seeing is a performance, but feel instead that it is really happening. Naïve? Maybe, but then what of the many meta-theatrical elements in Ibsen's plays, for example, the glass wall in *The Pillars of Society* that turns Bernick's front room into a stage within a stage, as well as a symbol that turns the private life of the bourgeoisie into a play performed in public. Or Hjalmar Ekdal's 'scenic construction' of his own illusory forest in the dark loft? These meta-theatrical aspects of Ibsen's plays can hardly be described as naïve. On the contrary, his plays appear as advanced, multi-dimensional creations that consciously reflect the relationship between theatre and reality.

Why is this multiple dimensionality not expressed in Ibsen's own stage directions? Is it because the metatheatrical aspects have in the main been pointed out by scholars primarily concerned with the play as text rather than as performance? Not necessarily. Gunnar Heiberg was presumably a good interpreter of Ibsen's intentions when he directed *The Wild Duck* at Den Nationale Scene in 1885. Here, it seems, the players almost intuitively gave their parts the most enigmatic and mysterious interpretations possible, probably because the play's combination of enigmatic symbolism and everyday realism had left them feeling confused. Heiberg knew how to counteract that: the more natural and realistic the acting, he explained to them, the clearer would the symbolism become. This was directing in the spirit of the letters of instruction and advice that Ibsen himself was sending out to theatre directors.

The symbolism, the subtext and the metatheatrical elements should *not* be acted; instead they should be hidden behind the realistic exterior, in the ambivalence of the dialogue, the staging, the props and the lighting. In other words, the audience should dive for the pearls themselves, not have them served up on a plate by the director and the actors.

The uncertainty of actors and directors did not become any the less as Ibsen's writing developed ever further in the direction of symbols and symbolism, and here is the explanation for Ibsen's initial refusal to send *Rosmersholm* to the Christiania Theatre in December 1886. He simply did not believe the theatre was up to the challenge of producing it. He did, however, hint that he might change his mind if he was given a say in the casting. One result was that he preferred to see the twenty-three-year-old Constance Bruun cast in the part of Rebecca rather than the fifty-three-year-old diva Laura Gundersen. In the theatre, too, he spoke up for the young, those as yet untouched by the most persistent clichés of theatrical convention. Ibsen's importance for actors was twofold: on the one hand it was correct to say, as one reviewer did as early as January 1885, that it was 'in playing an Ibsen part that an actor was likely to achieve a breakthrough'. It also meant that older actors could find themselves sidelined. And everyone, actors and directors alike, could feel how their own artistic freedom was compromised by the strictness of Ibsen's stage directions, supplemented by the equally strict demands contained in his letters. August Lindberg was left in no doubt about this as he set about directing *The Wild Duck*:

> After Hedvig has shot herself, she must be positioned on the sofa in such a way that her feet are in the foreground, so that her right hand with the pistol dangles down. When she is carried out through the kitchen door I suggest that Hjalmar holds her beneath the arms and Gina takes her feet.

Lindberg was actually a director who was very likely to be in sympathy with Ibsen's ideas about the theatre. At Dramaten he had in many instances given leading female parts to younger and unknown actresses in preference to the company's prima donnas; the role of Hedvig was played by an eighteen-year-old drama student, while the part of Gina went to the wife of the theatre's stage manager. Inevitably there was trouble; even Ibsen was alarmed by Lindberg's experiments. In due course, however, Lindberg's production of *The Wild Duck* in 1885 became renowned as a breakthrough for naturalistic theatre in Scandinavia, not solely on account of the natural acting styles of the performers, but also for its scenography; on Lindberg's stages the door handles were real, not merely painted, and in one of the rooms he used a genuine commode, which later came to symbolize Lindberg's whole approach to directing.[11]

But older actors felt offended, and not all directors were like Lindberg. The Ibsenian theatre could seem undeniably controlled and constricted. In 1898, Emil Poulsen voiced his frustration at Ibsen's tendency to finalise his characters on paper – and in so doing limit the actors' interpretative options. On the other hand, Ibsen's drama contributed to a change in acting styles. Poulsen was just one of the company at the Kongelige Teater who managed, with his help, to develop a realistic and psychologically credible acting style.

Thus Ibsen could both liberate and confine his actors and directors, in much the same way as he has his readers and audiences.

A NEW SPRING IN GERMANY

Despite the Christiania Theatre's efforts to follow Ibsen's instructions, *Rosmersholm* was not a box-office success, nor was it in the rest of Norway. Things went slightly better in the rest of Scandinavia, but the play did not receive its Danish premiere until a year after publication. By that time it had already been performed in two German cities, and over the coming year Ibsen concentrated most of his efforts on Germany rather than Scandinavia.

By 1887 sales of his books in Germany had started to rise again for the first time since the stasis of the early years of the decade. Now he was on the point of a breakthrough on the German stage. It had already started the year before, with *Ghosts* at the Stadttheater in Augsburg, in April. The production had come at the initiative of Ibsen's supporters in Munich and seems to have been the first new production of an Ibsen play in Germany since *A Doll's House* in 1880. In November, Otto Brahm's study of him appeared in the *Deutsche Rundschau*, and a month later a certain duke decided to put the Alving family onstage at his famous theatre. *That* would be the real turning point.

Ibsen travelled by rail to Meiningen on 19 December 1886 and was back in Munich by 23 December. While the guest of the duke he lived like an aristocrat, with four enormous rooms and a manservant at his disposal. He had his own carriage too, but the snow lay deep, and he saw no good reason to miss out on any of Duke Georg's excellent hospitality. The performance itself was on 22 December, in the Meiningen theatre, and was a triumph for Ibsen, not only on account of the quality of the production, but because the venue itself was considered so prestigious. There was a reception after the performance, and before his departure the following day yet another glinting order was fastened to the dramatist's chest, this one making him a Commander, First Class, of the Saxon Ernestine Order.

The Meiningen performance left the Germans wanting more of Ibsen, and early in the new year the Residenz-Theater in Berlin announced a production of *Ghosts*. In the 1880s Berlin was gradually beginning to oust Munich as the cultural centre of Germany, a development related to the explosive growth in population following the unification of Germany, from 826,000 in 1871 to 1,600,000 by 1890. To a greater extent than Munich, Berlin was developing into a big modern city, with a growing industrial and working class. And with urbanisation came the writers and artists with new and radical ideas. A unique

'Berlin naturalism' arose in the latter years of the 1880s and early 1890s that rejected the old literary school in Germany led by figures such as Heyse, Geibel and Freytag, and in its stead hailed new heroes from outside the national borders – Ibsen, Bjørnson, Tolstoy, Dostoyevsky, Turgenev and Zola. Berlin was also a city of theatres, so it was natural for Ibsen to make it his new power base in the country.[12] Although he never actually lived there Ibsen rapidly acquired a status in the city that was unique among Scandinavians. The decisive moment came with the performance of *Ghosts* in January 1887. Even though censorship laws meant that the performance was private, there was no doubt that this was a public occasion. When it became known that the dramatist himself would be present, his supporters arranged a large reception. The guest of honour, however, remained unconvinced that things would turn out well as he boarded his train, just fourteen days after his return from Meiningen:

'I expect considerable opposition from the conservative press in Berlin,' he wrote to Hegel before his departure. 'But that is another good reason for me to be there.'

He had reasons to be worried; *Ghosts* was and remained a deeply controversial play in Germany. Things had gone well in Meiningen, but Berlin would be the acid test, not just for Ibsen, but for the nascent naturalism in the country.

All went well. It went more than well.

On the afternoon of Sunday 9 January the Residenz-Theater was filled by an invited audience in celebratory mood; that Ibsen was among friends was confirmed by the salvo of applause that greeted the end of the first act. But when Fru Alving sank down at her son's side at the end of the final act not a sound came from the audience, and when the house lights went up a sigh of relief passed through the gathering. Then came the applause, and Ibsen had to take a bow from the stage and deliver a few words of thanks. Two days later there was a dinner in his honour in the Hotel Kaiserhof's banquet room, attended by representatives from the academic world, the worlds of art and literature, civil servants, politicians, the theatre and the press.

News of Ibsen's triumph in Berlin soon spread far beyond Germany's borders. 'The Berlin production of *Ghosts* has really made waves,' writes Sigurd from New York at the beginning of February. 'Every newspaper is full of reviews and anecdotes.' The waves would take some time to subside. The theatre remained a particularly potent medium, but of course there were other reasons why Ibsen made his definitive and lasting breakthrough in Germany at the end of the 1880s. One was the cheap editions of his works published by Reclam Verlag. Once news of the Residenz-Theater's plans became known, copies of *Ghosts* flew off the shelves. Five thousand extra copies had to be ordered from Leipzig.

But at the most profound level the explanation must be in the satisfaction of a mutual need: Germany needed Ibsen as much as he needed Germany. For many years censorship laws had kept naturalistic drama off the stages, and when the curtain was at last raised for *Ghosts* it burst that particular bubble for good. Ibsen was the midwife for the modern breakthrough in Germany, he was the old man who opened the door for the young. Berlin was at the centre of all this, as it was the centre for the spread of a whole wave of enthusiasm for Ibsen that now swept across not only Germany but the whole of continental Europe. On 5 March the Ostendtheater followed up the Residenz-Theater's success and gave *An Enemy of the People* its German premier. Later in the spring the Residenz-Theater put on *Rosmersholm*, and the year after that *The Wild Duck*, *Lady Inger of Østråt* and *A Doll's House* were performed at the Lessingtheater. Henceforth all Ibsen's new plays were performed soon after publication, and though the premieres were often in different cities, it never took long for the plays to reach the Berlin theatres. At the same time a stream of critical studies, essays, books and parodies began to appear.[13]

This wave of enthusiasm reached a temporary climax when Otto Brahm chose *Ghosts* to open his naturalistic theatre Freie Bühne, on 29 September 1889. With this, the alliance between Ibsen and the young German naturalists was sealed.

This is not to say that opposition to Ibsen disappeared. The press quickly split into two camps: one, which hailed him as the 'standard bearer of a new age', and a second, which condemned him as 'a spirit of darkness'. Based on the reviews and the debate in Berlin in the spring of 1887, Julius Hoffory was able to assert that the division was not necessarily into a radical and a conservative press. In fact, Ibsen had opponents and supporters in both camps. Ibsen has never been loved by everyone at the same time. The crucial factor is that at the beginning of the 1890s he was, so to speak, *naturalised* as one of the great dramatists, and it was natural to read, perform and talk about him in German public life.

He no longer feared the conservative critics; bad performances were of much greater concern to him. A notable example was the premiere of *Rosmersholm* at the Stadttheater in Augsburg on 16 April 1887. Ibsen was present at the dress rehearsal, along with Suzannah, Julius Elias and several others. It was a shattering experience. Standing in front of the stage he cringed at every line: 'Oh my God, my God.' And when Rosmer came bounding on in bright yellow spats and shiny calfskin shoes he shuddered as though struck by lightning:

'Look. Will you just look . . .'

The others were afraid he might stop the whole performance, but then he suddenly stood up straight:

'I'll just have to forget all my ideas, then it might work out alright.'

He stood there, mumbling and repeating these words, and stayed until the end of the performance, no doubt compelled to recognise that success could be a mixed blessing, if only because it meant the custody of his own works passed completely from his control.

DER WASSERMANN

The summer of 1887 was one of the sea. Henrik and Suzannah had long planned to travel north, and at the beginning of July they set out for Fredrikshavn, on the northern tip of Jutland. Henrik needed quiet in which to work, yet he enjoyed strolling along the Fredrikshavn docks and chatting with the seamen. Suzannah, however, was not enthusiastic about the area. As a compromise they headed south ten days later for Sæby, an idyllic little Danish town with no rail or steamship connections. There were small, whitewashed houses surrounded by fields of swaying corn, with a magnificent beech wood behind it and open sea views. There was a windmill, a church spire and an old bridge. Henrik and Suzannah took rooms at the Hotel Harmonien and remained there until the end of August. Henrik enjoyed the fine summer weather and walked on the beach every day, accompanied only by his thoughts. The locals must have been puzzled by him, just as they had been in Molde when he stood on the quay staring down into the fjord. Even in the mountain village of Gossensass, to which he would return two years later, the same attraction to water was evident. The youngsters nicknamed him *Der Wassermann* because each day he was to be seen down by the River Eisach gazing down at the waters.

Just what *was* it about Henrik and water?

As isolated as the little town was, visitors still found their way to Ibsen's house. Late in July, William Archer turned up. He met a welcoming and relaxed Ibsen who had no objection at all to being disturbed; city-dweller that he was, he later confessed that life in Sæby had been almost too quiet. Being too polite to ask Ibsen in any detail about his writing, Archer found the conversation disappointing. They spoke instead of trivialities and politics. Ibsen held forth about the compact majority, but failed to impress the Englishman:

'It might seem harsh to say so,' he wrote afterwards to his brother Charles, 'but the truth is that I am more and more convinced that as an all-round thinker, or, more properly, as a systematic thinker, Ibsen really doesn't fit the bill.'

Had Ibsen not been a great writer he would have been a wretched philosopher, in Archer's view; yet the same was true of so many of the great names of the century, such as Thomas Carlyle and John Ruskin:

But of course, Ibsen is Ibsen, and I should be the last to complain that he is not Herbert Spencer.

One day two strangers approached the proprietor of the hotel. They had come to Sæby for the sole purpose of meeting the great writer. One of them, Peder R. Møller, was a dramatist himself and had this as a sort of excuse. As they entered Ibsen's apartment their awestruck nerves got the better of them; they forgot to introduce themselves, and an embarrassing silence ensued. Ibsen, however, was cordiality itself and invited the two travellers to dinner. During the meal he presently brought the conversation around to – what else but the sea?

'I have the sea,' he said, with such pathos that one of the guests thought: 'That was the poet speaking there.'

Suzannah, however, had heard Ibsen speaking of this before, and interrupted time and time again to contradict him as he delivered one of his pithy formulations. There was nothing unusual in him and Suzannah quarrelling, but for the unsuspecting guests it was a surprise to hear the great writer so openly challenged by his own wife. It may have been that the relationship between the couple was by this time in trouble. One reason for that might have been Ibsen's growing interest in young women.

No fewer than three women would play a part in Ibsen's life that summer, though there is no suggestion that anything untoward ever took place.

One was a thirty-year-old teacher named Julie Jørgensen, who enjoyed walking along the beach with the writer. When she disappeared without saying goodbye, he sent her a letter in which he thanked her 'for the ray of sunshine which you with your bright youthfulness have cast over an old man's journey along the road to his death'. Engelcke Wullf was considerably younger. She also liked to be down on the beach where she would sit daydreaming with her long brown plaits. One day she noticed a small, elderly man walking along the beach. As she watched he stopped, pulled some kind of plate from his pocket, screwed it into the end of his stick and then sat down on this peculiar seat and stared out at the sea, now and then making notes on a piece of paper in his hand. The following day he was there again, and by this time she knew who he was. They spoke, and Ibsen asked her what she was doing down by the water.

'I always see new life in the waves,' she answered. 'The woods are always the same, but every breaking wave is like the quivering sound of some instrument. The waves always have music in them.'

They met each other many times after this, and at the close of the summer he gave her a gift in the form of an assurance that one day she would appear as a character in one of his plays. It was a gift Engelcke kept for the rest of her life.

The third young woman was Adda Ravnkilde, and she had died several years earlier. At the age of just twenty-one Adda had taken her own life, drinking poison, cutting the artery in her left arm and finally putting a bullet through her right temple. She left behind a number of pieces of writing, and in 1884, the year after her death, the novel *Judith Fürste* was published. The publication attracted widespread attention, for the man responsible was none other than Georg Brandes. He saw great potential in the 'description of this young girl's vain struggle against an agonising and ecstatic love' – love for a man whom she knew did not deserve her. Brandes was fascinated, as was Ibsen. He visited both the home and the grave of the unhappy young writer in Sæby.

* * *

Towards the end of August, Henrik and Suzannah left Sæby and travelled to Fredrikshavn. Early in September the Norwegian critic and literary historian Henrik Jæger joined them. A year earlier he had proposed that he write Ibsen's biography, and Ibsen himself suggested that it be published to mark his sixtieth birthday in 1888. He also demanded a degree of control over the contents. Between Friday 2 September and Sunday 4 September, Jæger walked along beside Ibsen and listened as he spoke openly about almost every aspect of his writing. The biographer also got a taste of what life was like with Ibsen *the man* – his pedantries, a daily routine that slavishly followed the clock, the fact that each day as he rose to leave the dinner table he walked over to the window and looked at the thermometer. Why didn't he do that *before* he sat down, thought Jæger? Or why not just ask the waiter?

Jæger's description of his visit conveys a certain repressed irritation:

> Throughout the three days in which I have lived intimately with him, inhabiting the same four walls, eating at the same table, we have followed the clock from morning to evening to a degree that I would find intolerable in the long run.

The observation is telling; Ibsen's great need for control and predictability in everyday life meant that those closest to him were also subject to the same discipline. Jæger put up with it for three days, Suzannah for a lifetime. Ibsen also told Jæger of how he could walk for hours along the beach and look out over the sea, or just stare down into its depths:

'There is something remarkably compelling about the sea,' he tells him. 'If you stand and stare down into the water, it's as if you see the life that moves around up here on earth, only in another form. There are connections and similarities everywhere.'

And he adds: 'The sea will have an influence on my next play.'

One might almost suppose that Engelcke Wullf had read Jæger's account of Ibsen's words, as indeed she may well have done if she came across Jæger's article on his meeting in the summer with Ibsen that appeared in the Christmas edition of *Folkebladet* in 1887. Here new features are added to the mythology of the sphinx through all these references linking the writer and the sea: Ibsen with his literary gaze looking down into the water. He enters into a mystical relationship with the elements, nature itself tells him about the people and the life on earth. The sea heaves, and the writer – the seer – wrestles its secrets from it. Thus Ibsen, through the loyal medium of Henrik Jæger, advertises his new play in the pages of *Folkebladet*. At the same time it is important to note that this nature mysticism also reflects a genuine metaphysical fascination in Ibsen that is closely related to his critical view of the positivist understanding of nature.

'I have therefore formulated my own personal and independent view of nature,' he writes to the Norwegian epidemiologist Ernst Lochmann in the spring of 1888. 'I think that both the theologians and the natural scientists are much too restricted in their thinking. "Nature" isn't as material as many seem to believe. But *what* lies behind it – that is the great riddle, the as-yet undiscovered secret.'

Ibsen's words put him at the heart of contemporary thinking. During the last decades of the nineteenth century there were many who believed that the solution to 'the great riddle' was located beyond the material world. As orthodox psychology advanced, there appeared alongside it a number of movements concerned with Spiritism, telepathy and hypnosis. In the world of art symbolism, decadence and expression appeared. What they all had in common was an opposition to the mechanical determinism of the natural sciences, and an interest in the unconscious life of the mind. At the same time they were deeply influenced by the ideas of the natural scientists. The result was a golden age of pseudo-scientific theories mixed with religious, scientific and philosophical ideas. In his mixture of psychology and metaphysics, realism and symbolism, Ibsen reflects this trend in the series of plays that begins with *Rosmersholm*. Several plays show him openly indulging his interest in telepathy and hypnosis, and in the 1890s his orientation towards Spiritism was widely recognised.

Ibsen's interest in the enigmatic side of human beings was nothing new. Essentially, our modern fascination with 'the unconscious' derives from Romanticism, and in this sense Ibsen, the old Romantic, became fashionable once again towards the end of his life. But as with politics, there is nothing to suggest commitment to a specific set of beliefs. If his view of life was Christian he kept it to himself (though he never hid his fascination for the Bible). If he believed in anything, it was the art of writing. And as a writer, he must have found the positivist worldview inadequate. Certainly, he made use of theories of heredity and evolution in his works, but if science had pretensions to reveal 'the great riddle' then it soon became the enemy of literature.

Ibsen was and wanted to be the poet of the soul and the sea. Here is where he wanted to do his diving – but without reaching the bottom.

THE POET AND THE LADIES

A few days after Jæger's departure Henrik left for Sweden, and Suzannah paid a visit to Kristiania. Henrik spent six days in Gothenburg. It says a lot about his status that even though his trip was more or less spontaneous, and without planned dates of arrival and departure, Swedish high society exerted itself to offer him reception after reception. The banquet that was held at the Gnistan literary society on 12 September was just a foretaste of what was to come over the following weeks. Two days later, after attending the opera and a performance at a private theatre club, he travelled by boat up the Göta canal to Stockholm. His fellow passengers included the young Swedish writer and feminist Anne Charlotte Leffler and the young explorer Sven Hedin. Leffler was an admirer of Ibsen's work, but after meeting him her admiration seems to have changed into something closer to puzzlement:

> His is a remarkably solitary nature – he doesn't seem to read anything – has read far less than me – he socialises with almost no one, he just walks and dreams, or walks in silence, watching life without living it himself.

An undeniably curious observation concerning a man who, all the while Leffler was with him, was busily making his way from one gathering to the next. That he seemed to have read so little might be explained by the fact that in company with Leffler and other intellectuals he preferred to appear as the autodidact he actually was, secure in the knowledge that his work and his success created the desired mixture of puzzlement and admiration. To Victor Rydberg he once claimed that he had hardly done any historical research for *Emperor and Galilean*, a claim that understandably astonished Rydberg. As was usual when the Norwegian writer was visiting Stockholm, his social programme was packed. 'I suppose we must have a dinner in his honour,' sighed Leffler, who knew what was required of her as a Stockholm society lady. On Thursday 22 September she hosts an exclusive dinner for Ibsen and twenty-five other guests, including Leffler's Russian-born friend, the mathematician Sofia Kovalevskaja, and the writer Victoria Benedictsson, who wrote under the *nom de plume* of Ernst Ahlgren.

Benedictsson found Ibsen much more open and approachable than Leffler had done and later shared her impressions of him with Georg Brandes:

> He seems honest and human, he doesn't seem pretentious. He inspires confidence. He looks as though one could talk about anything with him, I mean all sorts of things that have happened – bah! I sound so silly! You're laughing? – I mean that he seems so harmonious, so complete, so whole.

Ibsen was in excellent spirits. He gave the ladies good advice and patted them affectionately on the shoulder, noted Benedictsson, adding, rather acidly: '... and they worship him like God the Father'. As for her, the naked admiration on display struck her as unpleasant, yet she was herself among those who flocked around Ibsen as he appeared in the doorway.

'Have any of you been following the debate between Georg Brandes and Bjørnson?' he asks unexpectedly, referring to a difference of opinion over moral questions between the two. Some reply yes, others no.

Ibsen's eyes start to flash:

'It could be that he feels bitter', he said, referring to Brandes. 'He might well have behaved recklessly. But one has to remember how he has been attacked, how he has been treated. – And the Danes should realise just what sort of a man they have in him.'

Faced with a choice between Brandes and Bjørnson, he went for Brandes. And Victoria Benedictsson would not have liked him any the less for that, unhappily in love with Georg Brandes as she was. For many this unrequited love was the reason she took her own life in a hotel room in Denmark the following year, at the age of thirty-eight. Another early death in the ranks of the women of the modern breakthrough. Yet there were other disappointments in Victoria's life, including the fact that she, though one of the foremost realist writers in Scandinavia, was unable to write under her own name and reveal her sex:

This horrible fate not to be allowed to be a human being but always a woman, a woman, a woman!

Two days later, on a Saturday, it was time for the official reception. Gustaf af Geijerstam thought he noticed that Ibsen didn't seem to be feeling well. As usual when in large gatherings he was withdrawn and formal. The whole of Stockholm's academic and cultural elite was assembled, speeches were given, eloquent but empty, in Geijerstam's opinion. But then Ibsen rose to speak, and what he said was both eloquent *and* meaningful, and Geijerstam was completely taken by surprise. The following morning Ibsen was invited to breakfast by August Lindberg. This was the sort of atmosphere Ibsen preferred, surrounded by young people, many of them actors who had recently performed in Lindberg's productions of *Rosmersholm* and *A Doll's House*. In an environment such as this Ibsen too became young, informal and light-hearted. And the following evening, after attending a gala performance of *An Enemy of the People*, he almost had to tear himself loose from the women who surrounded him as he pulled on his overcoat in the foyer.

After this Ibsen said his goodbyes and set off for Denmark. There he followed up his defence of Georg Brandes by attending a party organised by the

society of conservative students, to Brandes' great disapproval. Shortly afterwards he had dinner at Hegel's house, and once again spoke of the compelling
power of the sea, and of the influence this would have on his writing. He could
not have known it, but this would be the last time he would see his loyal
publisher. Frederik Hegel died during Christmas week 1887, and the business
was taken over by his son Jacob. Although the two men had never been close
they were never in any doubt about their importance for each other, from the
time back in 1866 when Hegel accepted *Brand* for publication before he had
even read the play.

Jacob Hegel was not the man his father was – but then what son is? Moreover,
Ibsen's writing career had a momentum all its own by now, so the changeover
at the publishing house had little effect. All that was required was a little oiling
of the wheels.

THE ANGRIEST MAN IN EUROPE

The day after the evening at Hegel's, Ibsen set off home for an autumnal and
chilly Munich; for the time being, the party was over. Suzannah's rheumatism
had grown worse in the cold northern climate and she was unable to get out or
climb the stairs without pain in her legs. Henrik had not managed to write
much that year; the winter and the spring had been spent in following up
productions in Germany, and in the summer he had only made notes and
plans. Now there was a pile of letters waiting to be dealt with, connections to be
nurtured after all the socialising.

One of the letters he answered was to Österling, a bookseller in the Swedish
town of Helsingborg. He had sent Ibsen a copy of August Strindberg's play *The
Father* while he was in Stockholm, but only now did Ibsen find time to read it.
Strindberg and Ibsen never met, though they did come close; in February 1884
the Swede asked Bjørnson and Lie to arrange for him to visit Ibsen in Rome:

I want to meet the angriest man in Europe before I die!

But the meeting never came off, and it probably wasn't just chance that decreed
it so. The relationship between Ibsen and the only Scandinavian dramatist with
whom he could compare himself is a curious chapter in the history of the
modern breakthrough. Strindberg, born in 1849, was part of the generation
that was deeply influenced by *Brand*. But if Brand, that 'fanatical doubter', made
him a disciple, Nora arranged for his apostasy – and comprehensively so. In a
long list of letters and writings, of which *Getting Married* (1884) is the most
well known, Strindberg attacks both Nora and Ibsen. For him, Ibsen was 'the
poet of women and therefore of the young. That is why men hate him! That is

why I hate him, particularly since he urges the young and their equals, the married women, to rebel against nature's aristocrats and masters – the men!' For Strindberg the relationship between men and women was one of war, and no Scandinavian writer has described the battle more intensely than he. Strindberg's anti-feminism can seem unbalanced and raving. And it is, but not thoughtlessly so. In his view, the liberation of women, from a Rousseauian standpoint, was simply contrary to nature.

What did Ibsen make of his furious opponent? As far as we know, the first time he mentions the name is in the letter to Österling the bookseller, in November 1887:

> Strindberg's observations and experiences in the area *The Father* deals with do not accord with my own, but that does not prevent me from recognising and being stirred by the author's great strength in this new work.

So despite the reservation, Ibsen appreciated Strindberg, and when Strindberg heard of the letter he was keen to have it published. In subsequent years, whenever Ibsen mentioned his Swedish colleague, it was almost invariably in positive terms. And Strindberg's treatment of marriage and the relationship between man and woman undeniably relates in a dynamic sense to his own work, both in similarities and differences. The kinship between their characters, such as Laura in *The Father* and Hedda Gabler, are evident – and were probably evident to the writers themselves. Not even Strindberg's furious attack on *A Doll's House* seems to have struck Ibsen as especially provocative. He never referred directly to the criticism, though it is easy to imagine the Norwegian satirist chuckling at the Swede's unbridled outbursts. If anyone could appreciate Strindberg's madness it would have to be him. And he did read Strindberg.

Added to this is the fact that, while Strindberg appeared on the literary scene too late to offer any real competition to Ibsen, for Strindberg the situation was the opposite. While Ibsen sat securely on his throne, Strindberg struggled to come out from under the shadow of that throne. He despaired of the way in which the debate around his own novel *The Red Room* drowned in the storm that followed the appearance of *A Doll's House*. Later he would find critics in Germany implying that the theme of *Gillet's Secret* was borrowed from *The Master Builder* – this despite the fact that his play appeared twelve years before Ibsen's! The competition for a place on foreign stages grew more intense as the 1880s drew to a close, and no matter how hard Strindberg tried to insist that Ibsen was yesterday's man, Ibsen continued to be the more popular in Germany until well into the next century.[14] At times there is something paranoid about Strindberg's outbursts; when *The Wild Duck* appeared he was certain that Hjalmar was intended as a parody of himself, and he read *Hedda*

Gabler (1890) as a direct admonition from Ibsen that he ought to shoot himself, like Ejlert Løvborg:

> And now that decrepit old mountain king seems to be handing me a revolver for the second time! But he'll regret it! Because I'll survive him – and all the others – and the day 'The Father' kills 'Hedda Gabler' I'll stick a revolver in the hands of that old troll.

Strindberg refers to seventeen of Ibsen's plays in his writing. *A Doll's House* alone is mentioned forty times. In 120 different textual contexts, spread across nineteen works, he discusses Ibsen. The statistics are eloquent of the importance Ibsen had for him. Yet Strindberg was sane enough to acknowledge Ibsen's importance for drama and Scandinavian literature in general, and even maintained that the public misunderstood him. Once, while complaining in his usual fashion about Ibsen, he suddenly stopped short:

> But it's true – he wrote *Ghosts*! I can't hate him! No! I shall follow his example and become Moses on the mount!

The trouble was, there was only room on the mount for one Moses at a time.

* * *

When not out travelling, Ibsen worked hard to protect his privacy. His sixtieth birthday, however, had to be celebrated. Michael Georg Conrad, who had known Ibsen for several years, now found himself invited to the writer's home for the first time, to be met by the celebrant himself in splendid spirits. The list of thank-you letters he received reflects both his hard-won status in Scandinavia, and the new wave of enthusiasm from Germany. The Christiania Theatre celebrated the day with a gala performance, other theatres sent their congratulations, as did Bjørnson, the Storting president Johannes Steen, and fifty-three other members of the Storting. The Christiania Workers' Union and a number of other institutions and private individuals were among others who offered their congratulations. Irgens Hansen wrote a series of articles on 'Ibsen in Germany' for *Dagbladet*, and he was even celebrated in the pages of *Aftenposten* by Bredo Morgenstierne. Only *Morgenbladet* remained silent. In Germany he was the subject of articles in every serious newspaper and periodical.

As part of the celebrations, Henrik Jæger's book *Henrik Ibsen 1828–1888: A Picture of a Literary Life* appeared, just as Ibsen had hoped. At first Ibsen turned down the invitation from Hegel to proofread the biography, maintaining that they ought to rely on Jæger's 'literary tact'. In other words, no inappropriate interference. And when, later, he was given J. B. Halvorsen's entry on him for the *Encyclopaedia of Norwegian Writers* to read through, he limited himself to correcting and expanding on the factual material and left the interpretative side of things as it stood.

So what did Jæger have to say about Ibsen's life and work? Did he function as the voice of the writer himself, as Valfrid Vasenius had done? The answer is both yes and no. Jæger had not always been a great admirer of Ibsen's work. In his capacity as artistic advisor to the Christiania Theatre he had advised against a performance of *Ghosts*. He later changed his opinion, but retained some of his former reservations, for though the biography is fundamentally sympathetic towards its subject it is not a simple uncritical defence of Ibsen. He gives a factual picture of Ibsen's life that accords with Ibsen's own self-mythologising, but the literary analyses – which dominate the book – bear witness to critical and independent readings that do not necessarily always correspond with Ibsen's own.

Jæger's book was independent, but largely in line with Ibsen's own presentation of himself. In the degree to which Ibsen influenced it, it was through the medium of his own aborted autobiography, which Jæger quotes from and to which he gives considerable importance. Moreover, the writer had the opportunity to form an opinion on and influence his biographer during those conversations in Fredrikshavn. Several biographical articles were already in circulation prior to Jæger's book, including the one by Paul Botten-Hansen, as well as the monographs by Valfrid Vasenius and Ludwig Passarge. But Jæger's must be counted as the first complete biography, with material derived from more important sources than his predecessors had access to. The biography sold well and was quickly translated into German and English. The year 1889 also saw the appearance of J. B. Halvorsen's article on Ibsen, the one that was later used in expanded form in the *Encyclopaedia of Norwegian Writers* that included a comprehensive overview of publications, translations, performances and reviews. Together these two works formed the basis for a burgeoning industry of Ibsen biographies over the next hundred years, with each new biography able to build on material from the previous one.

* * *

The sixtieth birthday was the event of the spring. Only with the approach of summer did Ibsen begin to find the time to start work on the new play he had been mulling over. The first notes are dated 5 June:

> The compelling power of the sea. The longing for the sea. People profoundly attached to the sea. Bound by the sea. Must return to it. A species of fish that forms one of the first links in the chain of evolution. Do elements of this remain in the human mind?

The theory of evolution is evidently present here, but it is not science that makes the sea attractive for Ibsen: 'The sea exerts an atmospheric power that operates like the will. The sea can hypnotise.'

LADY OF THE FJORD

It was to be about the sea, but the writer himself remained on dry land and wrote his way through its five acts in Munich in June and July 1888. Then came the revision. But the summer had other pleasures to offer besides those of writing. After an absence of almost three years, Sigurd visited his parents in July. For most of the time he had been attached to the legation in Washington, spending the summers in Newport and the winter of 1886–7 in New York. In letters home he had described the conflicts at the legation, and how bored he was by high society, with all its gossip and intrigues.

In letters to his parents he also reveals his literary ambitions, but confesses that he feels inadequate to the task of following in his father's footsteps. He mentions again and again his loneliness, his industry, and repeatedly stresses how few pleasures he allows himself, probably with the intention of reassuring his father, who was supplementing his stipend. Yet he gives the impression of having matured since the break with home and in his encounters with the world of international diplomacy. When in the autumn of 1887 he told his parents he might possibly be posted to St Petersburg they reacted with alarm. He must on no account throw away all his ambitions and prospects on a move like that. It was, however, something Sigurd himself wanted, and he explained how living in the United States had given him new ideas about life – indeed, a feeling of *having a life*:

> My wisdom was taken from books; my experience of life and my thinking
> in recent years have opened up vistas for me infinitely greater than those I
> knew before.

Sigurd's is the letter of a man who feels he owns the whole world and yet is unable to find his rightful place in it. Over the new year he suggested he might travel to Germany – or Venezuela 'or some other half-barbaric land'. No doubt his parents breathed a sigh of relief when he finally decided to spend the last of his stipend years in Vienna, being neither half-barbaric nor all that far away from them. When Sigurd stepped down from the train in Munich to spend some time with his parents before travelling on, Henrik had been waiting on the platform for an hour and half.

Ibsen needed the whole of August and most of September to make a thorough revision of the manuscript, and then another, before sending off the fair copy on 25 September. The play with the working title 'The Mermaid' had become the five-act drama *The Lady from the Sea*.

In the following letter to Jacob Hegel he writes:

> I am confident this play will attract widespread attention. Because in many ways it marks a change of direction for me.

Once again he was announcing something new, but he clearly knew his readership: this time he was about to shock them with a play that was *not* shocking.

* * *

The Lady from the Sea was published in 28 November 1888 in a first print run of 10,000 copies. This was a couple of thousand larger than his previous two publications and turned out to be more than adequate.[15] It is another play set in a small coastal town in Norway, located in the north of the country. Here live Dr Wangel, his wife Ellida and his two daughters from a previous marriage, Bolette and Hilde. A shadow descends over Ellida following the loss of a son in infancy. She and her husband do not share a marital bed and he worries about her mental state. Ellida is the daughter of a lighthouse-keeper and feels a strong attraction towards the sea. Ten years previously she was engaged to a sailor who had to flee after committing a murder, but not before assuring Ellida that he would return. The sailor has the same compelling power over her as the sea, and even though she had tried to break off the engagement she continues to walk about in a kind of sleepwalker's trance, partly dreading and partly yearning for his return – 'the Stranger'.

Bolette yearns too; she chooses to accept a proposal of marriage from Arnholm, the tutor, not because she loves him but because he looks like her only chance of a better life. Once again the theme is that of a woman's dilemma, caught between the demands of responsibility and self-sacrifice, and her longing for freedom. But here the conflicts end in what looks like a rather un-Ibsenian resolution.

When the Stranger finally turns up, Dr Wangel realises he must acknowledge Ellida's freedom to choose between him and this other, and with this acknowledgement Ellida makes her choice to stay with her husband. The magical power of the Stranger is broken, and the Wangels enter a new phase of married life, in freedom with responsibility.

No suicide, no slamming of doors. Not even a hint of incest.

* * *

'How tame Ibsen has become,' wrote Bjørnson to Kielland. 'Do *you* know of sea-ladies like this washing up on the beach up there in Molde? Helped along by English steamships, hauntings and mysterious Finns?'

Although memories from Sæby were closer in time, Bjørnson was right in assuming that Ibsen's stay in Molde had influenced the new play. A couple of local legends may also have inspired him, for there were indeed hauntings in Molde. During his stay there he had heard the story of a Finn who, with his hypnotic gaze, had caused the wife of a priest to leave her husband and children and run away with him. Another story concerns a sailor whom everyone had presumed drowned at sea but who one day returns, to find his wife married to another man. But experiences in Sæby influenced the play too. Several critics have pointed to the similarities between *The Lady from the Sea* and *Judith Fürste*, the novel by the Sæby writer Adda Ravnkilde. According to Suzannah, the model for Ellida Wangel was Magdalene Thoresen. Magdalene had grown up in a small Danish coastal town, and shared with Ellida a yearning for the sea, for love and life on a larger scale. In her youth she had been infatuated with the Icelandic writer Grímur Thomsen, a 'wild, strange character' who exerted a powerful hold over her. After the two parted, Magdalene moved to the Sunnmøre coast where she met Suzannah's father, a man with distinct similarities to Wangel. The parallels with the Thoresens' story are clear enough. At the same time, Ellida's boredom in her marriage, her longing for erotic fulfilment, freedom and self-realisation, reflected the everyday trials of nineteenth-century women, especially intellectual and creative women. Not surprisingly, Camilla Collett saw something of herself in Ellida. After seeing the play in Copenhagen, she wrote to Ibsen:

> I too am a sort of 'Lady from the Sea', or call me rather: 'The Lady from the river depths'. From Eidsvold's deep, shadowy valley. For many years during my youth I wandered about here alone with my dreams, until in the end I joined the valley nymphs myself and was compelled to play that part for the others.

Young Camilla even had a 'Stranger' in her life, she heard his voice in the rushing of the river and behind every bush. She had no difficulty in empathically entering the world of Ibsen's play, as must have been the case with many women. It's striking too, to notice the way Collett transfers Ibsen's symbolism into her own life, almost writing herself into the play using an image taken directly from it. There are many instances of this kind of subjective identification with the characters of Ibsen's plays, but *The Lady from the Sea* also tempted the reader to apply the symbolism of the play to its *author*.

A striking example of this occurs in Johan Irgens Hansen's review in *Dagbladet*:

> Up there in Molde he wandered alone along the path by the beach. Down in Fredrikshavn he was often to be seen on the dock, staring into the sea for

hours on end, or watching the play of the waves in the Kattegat. The sea sounded its changing chords through his thoughts and his moods. Its terrors and its fascination seemed to him life forces that we must contend with in all their impenetrable mystery, in all their laughing play through our thoughts and senses.

In speeches and interviews Ibsen had encouraged this association between the writer and the forces of nature, and Irgens Hansen rewarded him royally: here the poet's spirit is related to the depths of the ocean in a consistent series of images. The sea reflects the human mind, the forces of nature become 'life forces', and the writer is seen as the interpreter of life's secrets.

The most surprising aspect of the play was that Ibsen had provided it with a happy and harmonious ending. One might imagine, according to Irgens Hansen, that 'it amused him to cause people to be astonished at seeing him surface so far from the place where he had last been seen'.

Ibsen, the great 'asker' of questions, had finally provided an answer!

But precisely what was that answer? Was it as simple as saying that the demand for freedom must be balanced by a sense of responsibility? The golden *via media*? Irgens Hansen and the Swedish critic J. A. Runeström both seem to have been content with that. But here too Ibsen had dropped a hint that obscured as much as it revealed. In the speech he had given in Stockholm in 1887, which had been read all over Scandinavia, he had announced the impending third kingdom. Did this mean he was finished with the literature of anger, of social criticism and scandal? Had the new age arrived? Was his battle against the ghosts over, and was this what his writing had been pointing towards all along – 'the "third kingdom" of freedom, responsibility, the joy of life and love'?

Was the rallying cry of the third kingdom the need to 'acc-limat-ise' oneself?

The critics had plenty to go on, but strictly speaking there is no reason to believe that Ibsen had achieved any new insights into his theory of the dawning of a new age. In the next play he wrote it would be obvious that he had not yet finished experimenting in his dramatic laboratory. He could still make a sudden reappearance far from the point at which he had last been observed, still finish off his characters by shooting them, drowning them and burying them beneath an avalanche, to the wondering confusion and bewilderment of audiences.

Even though *The Lady from the Sea* generally got better reviews than *Rosmersholm*, there were still many who had little time for Ibsen's impenetrable symbolism. The humourists were busy again, witness the title of one German parody *Die Frau von Mehreren. Psychiatrischatavistisch-bigamisch-metaphysisch-maritimes Ur-Schauspiel in fünf Abteilungen für Unheilbare, nach Henrik Ibsen's «Frau vom Meere» für das Neulietzegehrsdorfer Burgtheater frei bearbeitet*. A number of people pointed to the psychiatric aspect of the play: if Ellida Wangel was suffering from a mental illness, what then was the value of the play as a psychological study? And who could guarantee that she would not renege on her promise to Wangel if her illness grew worse? There are echoes here of the criticism of Osvald's hereditary illness in *Ghosts*, and it illustrates the problems many of Ibsen's contemporaries had in relating to his realism by ignoring the fact that these were, after all, literary creations and not real people, and certainly not real patients. In the same sense, Lars Holst, writing in *Dagbladet*, complained that the psychological realism in the play was undermined by the symbolism and mysticism, echoing the criticism Erik Skram had made of *Rosmersholm*. It was clear that critics on the left were alarmed to note the weakening of elements of social criticism in Ibsen's later plays.

Ibsen's new play was premiered at two venues simultaneously. On 12 February 1889 *The Lady from the Sea* opened at both the Christiania Theatre and the Hoftheater in Weimar. In Kristiania the first night was sold out, the first time such a thing had happened in five years. The box-office takings were the third largest in the theatre's recent history and twice what was normal for plays by both Ibsen and Bjørnson. The explanation is that the theatre had put ticket prices up for the premiere, and for those who bought tickets on the black market the seats were even more expensive. If Lars Holst, *Dagbladet*'s theatre critic, is to be believed, expectations were even greater than usual on this occasion, as audiences were looking forward to the staged version of this play that was to inaugurate the drama of 'the third kingdom'.

If this assessment is correct then there can be no doubt about it: Ibsen was a genius, not only in his writing, but in his ability to mould and control his audiences' expectations. Never before, and not since, have people entered a Norwegian theatre in hopes of witnessing the birth of a new era in human history.

The reviews were not universally favourable. Lars Holst was of the opinion that here, as in the book, the abstract symbolism weakened the play's psychological realism, whereas Johan Vibe, in *Aftenposten*, thought that the psychology itself was a weakness; the play had no plot, it was simply about Ellida's inner world. Once again Ibsen found himself being advised to write novels rather than plays. Nor was the production at the Kongelige Teater in Copenhagen considered particularly successful. In customary fashion the director, William Bloch, ignored the symbolism in the play, and matters were not improved by his attempts to liven up the rather static plot by introducing a great deal of gratuitous movement around the stage. Fru Eckman's performance as Ellida was notably unsuccessful; as a former ballet dancer she interpreted the role using a series of poses and gestures that recalled the Romantic and mannered tradition of the dance in which she had been trained, and which had no place in an Ibsen play. In Germany too the play was greeted with some scepticism;

four theatres had requested permission to stage the premiere, but all ended up rejecting it.[16] On 5 March, however, a month after the premiere in Weimar, it was performed at the Schauspielhaus in Berlin during an Ibsen Week in which performances of *The Wild Duck* and *A Doll's House* were also staged.

All in all, the reception of *The Lady from the Sea* bore witness, on the one hand, to the profound respect in which Ibsen was held as a dramatist, and to the authority he enjoyed: regardless of one's position in the cultural debate, a new play from him was not to be lightly dismissed. On the other hand there was growing bewilderment and irritation at the ever more obscure and mystical elements in his recent plays. And on this occasion he was, quite simply, boring. The difference of opinion was not confined to the public reception of the play; Ibsen's own colleagues found themselves divided. Jonas Lie was ecstatic in his enthusiasm, but for Garborg, Ibsen had once more revealed that he had not left Romanticism behind completely. He was still there, 'half-hidden behind the bushes, with the light of the moon shining down on him'.

Romantic, mystic, psychologist, realist – the labels were adding up. But just how different is *The Lady from the Sea* from Ibsen's other dramas with contemporary settings?

THE LITTLE LOVE

The Lady from the Sea is another play with threads that extend back through Ibsen's writing. Here are the themes of love and marriage from *Love's Comedy*, here is the dream of the 'something wonderful' that Nora longs for, and that Ellida perhaps experiences. But the most obvious connections are to *Rosmersholm*. In both plays Ibsen uses elements from folk beliefs, nature mysticism and symbolism.[17] Rebecca and Ellida are closely related through their passion and their 'heathen' wildness, which in both cases are constricted and repressed by the life situations in which they find themselves. If we add the next in line, Hedda Gabler, we have a trio of unusual female figures struggling with their desires and their irrational impulses, in each case with very different results.

In *The Lady from the Sea* a contrast is created between the narrow and stifling and the open and free, represented respectively by the fish pond in the Wangels' garden and by the sea. This divide relates to the contrast between valley and mountain in *Brand*, and between stuffiness and fresh air in *The Wild Duck* and *Rosmersholm*. In the new play, however, something emerges between the two extremes – the waters of the fjord, in which Ellida bathes as often as she can. These waters are not as fresh as the sea, and yet not as closed as the waters of the fish pond. The compromise reveals the way in which an accommodation – an acclimatisation – is reached between freedom and responsibility that enables the sea lady Ellida and the landlubber Wangel to find themselves as people of the fjord.[18]

But is the play really as harmonious as many will have it? And why did Ibsen choose such an untypical – for him – ending? But Ibsen had never committed himself to writing scandalous tragedies; he wrote what he pleased, and now he wanted to show what might happen where two people do *not* go their separate ways, like Nora and Helmer, nor yet die, like Rosmer and Rebecca.

And yet the play is not so different that it can, without further ado, be described as harmonious and devoid of social criticism. On the contrary, here too there is incisive criticism of the institution of marriage and the idealistic notion of ideal love. Both Ellida and Wangel acknowledge that the relationship between them began as a trade, and Arnholm is guilty of straightforward exploitation when he tells Bolette that his offer of marriage is her only chance to escape a life of 'sitting here at home and watching life pass you by'. And there is a sharp sting in the tail: when Ellida chooses to stay with her husband, she does not at the same time withdraw her threat to leave him if he fails to acknowledge her right to freedom. This demand for freedom is *more* radical than Nora's, because Wangel is, after all, a decent man, who has not let his wife down in the same way as Helmer. Ellida dismisses any question of duty and sacrifice in marriage, making the premises for her return every bit as provocative as Nora's leaving. A conservative reviewer such as Bredo Morgenstierne understood this, as did Carl David af Wirsén.

But doesn't some of this criticism disappear in the reconciliation of the final scene? To some extent it does; the message seems to be that a 'truthful' relationship is possible within a marriage. And yet still there are those who will feel that something has been lost in this spirit of compromise. The Stranger acknowledges Ellida's freedom to choose, and not until Wangel does the same does she decide to stay with him. But her wildness and her uncontrollable need for freedom are sacrificed. This involves a loss for Wangel too, because the fact that she was different is one of the reasons he loves her.[19] In other words, this is yet another Ibsen play that one might lay down with a certain sense of disquiet.

How, then, are we to understand Ibsen's own words about *The Lady from the Sea* representing a change of direction in his writing? As his subsequent plays demonstrate, the change did not involve 'optimism'. He no longer wished, however, to write dramas that the world consistently interpreted as polemic. In *Rosmersholm* he had relegated politics to the background; now it disappeared over the horizon. Henceforth he would concern himself with something that was certainly not new for him, but which came to preoccupy him more and more – the complex, contrary and irrational human mind. And it is in pursuit of this new direction that he introduces elements of mysticism and symbolism into the world of realistic drama.

Psychology and metaphysics; the contrasting relationship between them is illustrated by Ellida's mystical view of the world and Wangel's scientific view. As several commentators have pointed out, Wangel's conversations with Ellida prefigure the emergence of psychoanalytical therapy, while the power the Stranger exerts over Ellida relates to popular contemporary phenomena such as hypnosis and telepathy.[20] Playing at the same time with the evolutionary theory that human life came from the sea, Ibsen makes it clear that, for him, there is no absolute distinction between science and metaphysics.

In this context it is interesting to note Lars Holst's observations on the place of *The Lady from the Sea* in Ibsen's works. In his view, Ibsen was the Romantic who became an evolutionist. But now a new note of Romantic idealism had entered his writing, an idealism that opened with a belief in the future that was at odds with the pessimistic determinism of *Ghosts*. This change first becomes evident in *Rosmersholm* which, despite its tragic ending, shows that people are not necessarily at the mercy of nature and circumstance. In *Rosmersholm*, people are ennobled to their deaths; in *The Lady from the Sea* Ibsen shows that it is also possible to be ennobled into life – a life of freedom with responsibility.

Holst's analysis can be understood in the context of a contemporary tendency to read idealistically. But how reasonable is it, in fact, to maintain that the ennobling thought in *Rosmersholm* and the reconciliation in *The Lady from the Sea* bear witness to a new idealism in Ibsen? The Rosmerian view of life is actually extinguished in the mill race, and the reconciliation between Ellida and Wangel is precisely *not* the expression of an idealistic love. What really happens here is that the notion of idealistic love is obliterated; it is the little love that turns out to be the survivor, not the great love. Wangel is no hero, he doesn't talk about love in the expansive and dramatic way of a Torvald Helmer, and he does not, like Rosmer, demand sacrifice. If anyone demands anything then it is Ellida, and what she demands is to be seen, heard and respected as an equal. Wangel is the only male hero in Ibsen who is capable of meeting such demands, and the two are able to find each other again using simple, everyday language.[21]

Something has been sacrificed, something lost – romantic passion, desire, perhaps. Or can passion still be found among people of the fjord, between the fish pond and the wide, wild sea?

EMILIE AND HELENE

Early in July 1889, Henrik and Suzannah travelled to Gossensass again for the first time in five years. This was a special occasion: the town intended to name a square after its most celebrated visitor. For Gossensass, as for other small towns around the Brenner Pass, tourism had become an important source of income. But the town wasn't the only idyllic spot, and to attract visitors it was necessary to exploit all available resources. Next to the majestic scenery, Henrik Ibsen was the prime tourist attraction Gossensass had to offer.[22]

Five years had elapsed since his previous visit; so the town did what such towns commonly do to create an association with a celebrity, the simple – and cheap – expedient of naming something after him. For Ibsen, tourism had become a good reason to keep away from places such as Berchtesgaden and Gossensass. On the other hand, he was not the man to reject an honour of any kind. It also meant that Sigurd would be able to visit them that summer. At the naming ceremony for the Ibsenplatz on 21 July the guest of honour was carried in triumph through the streets of the town. At the Ibsenplatz itself there was a reception and concert in his honour.

It wasn't, however, these celebrations that would make that summer in Gossensass so memorable, nor was it even the reunion with Sigurd. Another guest at the Hotel Gröbner was a certain young woman who was there on holiday with her mother. Her name was Emilie Bardach, she was twenty-seven years old and the daughter of an affluent Jewish merchant in Vienna.[23] She was a typical society lady of her time, educated in the art of conversation, attending balls and concerts, and living a life of cultured aimlessness. Between this young woman and the sixty-one-year-old writer there arose a sort of love affair that has been the subject of a remarkable amount of attention. Books have been written about Henrik and Emilie, and her presence in his plays has been much studied.

Was he really in love?

Of the fact that *she* was there can be little doubt. Most of what we know about this passion of hers can be gleaned from her diary. And therein lies the difficulty. The diary itself has long since vanished. It was first spoken of after the Great War, when inflation had rendered Emilie's fortune worthless, and she attempted to sell her diary and letters from Ibsen to raise money for her children. The American writer Basil King was the first person she offered them to. He did not buy the material, but published an article in *Century Magazine* in 1923. Five years later Emilie contacted a French writer named André Rouveyre. He too took the matter no further than an article in the periodical *Mercure de France*. So far so good. The problem was that quotations from the diary used in the two articles turned out to be different from each other in several particulars. In addition, in a letter from Emilie to Rouveyre she says that she is not sending him the actual diary but instead a dictation based on the diary and taken down by a secretary. The dictation, it becomes apparent, was made several decades after the summer in Gossensass, and Emilie does not hide the fact that she has made some changes.[24]

Did an original diary ever even exist? Probably it did; Basil King claims to have held it in his hands. But why has the original never seen the light of day, in spite of its owner's efforts to make a living from it? Is it possible that the original was a lot less sensational than the later, edited versions? No one knows. But even if we accept that the text reflects Emilie's thoughts from that summer of 1889, can we still rely on her account of events? In King's text there are several passages that give rise to doubt:

'His words arouse a chill and a fear in me,' writes Emilie. 'He speaks of the most serious things in life, and puts great trust in me. He expects so much of me, far, far more than I can ever hope to fulfil, I fear. He says that never, in his whole life, has he been happier to know someone. Never has he admired someone as he has admired me.'

Emilie Bardach as the person Ibsen admired most in his life? Did he say that, or did she simply hear it? Or have the memories expanded with the years, as her fortune diminished, and her love for the writer emerged as the greatest thing in her life? The impression given by the text is of an immature and dreamy person, strikingly so when one bears in mind that Emilie was, after all, a grown woman when she met Ibsen. And if he did indeed say all that she claims he says, then of course, this may have been because he was head over heels in love with her – or was trying to seduce her. She writes of all the promises he made to her, of how much she meant to him. 'This is real love, ideal love, he says,' she writes. But then there were all those barriers – 'his wife! – his son! – everything that stood between us'. If only he had been free!

She was probably nothing more than a summer flirtation for him; for Emilie he became an obsession.

The summer passed. Ibsen was taking a sabbatical from writing, but as usual he had plans and drafts going through his head – when he wasn't busy with Emilie. Did wife and son notice anything? Sigurd certainly had enough on his own mind. His stipendiary engagement ran out that year, now he was worried about whether the Foreign Office would extend it. And Suzannah? According to Emilie, who was in the company of both husband and wife, she knew nothing. On the other hand, her husband's taste for young women was nothing new to Suzannah. According to John Paulsen, he preferred to employ pretty servant girls in the house – 'he can't get on with the old and the ugly,' Suzannah apparently explained. She was convinced that her husband's fascination was strictly aesthetic. What could she do? In later years the relationship between them was so cold that she was certain he would leave her. But he denied it, denied ever even considering it.

There was only one indisputable fact: Suzannah was no longer the only one.

If the flirtation between Henrik and Emilie was not common knowledge, at least one other guest could see what was going on. 'Frøken B. absolutely crazy about Ibsen,' wrote the young Munich artist Helene Raff in her diary for 21 September. But Helene herself was not indifferent to the writer's presence either, nor he to hers. Emilie would soon have competition; she would not long remain his only one either.

The snow came early in Gossensass that year, and in September the guests began leaving the resort. On the night of 28 September, Emilie and her mother boarded the train to take them back to Vienna. A few days later, Henrik, Suzannah and Sigurd also left. Back in Vienna, Emilie waited impatiently for a letter. A couple of telegrams arrived, but no letter from Ibsen. Finally she wrote to him herself. Sometime in the middle of October his reply arrived:

> Esteemed young lady, I thank you from the bottom of my heart for your most gracious and welcome letter, which arrived on the final day of my stay in Gossensass and which I have read over and over again,

And yes of course – both this and subsequent letters show a considerable degree of devotion on Ibsen's part. But there are also small signs of unease between the lines of these letters. In her letter of reply, Emilie rebukes him for the distant and formal tone he adopts – 'I am no *frøken* to you.' In his next letter Ibsen accepts the rebuke and adapts the form of address: 'dear child, because you are certainly *that* to me'.[25] In this way he conveyed to her that she should lower her expectations and accept that this was all there was ever going to be between them. The summer was over for him, but autumn brought with it new joys. Three days after his last letter to Emilie he bumps into Helene Raff in the street. Helene was twenty-four years old and had been living in Munich for the past six years. She had made a name for herself as a portrait painter and writer. In this sense she was a different type from Emilie, more independent, and with both feet firmly planted on the ground. But she too found herself helplessly attracted to the small man with the big ideas and had been walking up and down Maximilianstrasse for days in the hope of meeting him. When the encounter did take place they arranged to meet the following day at an exhibition of paintings. A few days later she again sought him out on the street. He took her back to his home, and they kissed each other.

Four days later he writes to Emilie, now condemned to be addressed as his 'dear child'. No promises, but friendly and inviting. Will she write to him again when she has a free half hour? He is very busy himself. On 8 November, Helene calls at Maximilianstrasse 32, but this time Suzannah is also at home. Three days later, he is the one who visits her home. 'He walked me home,' she confides in her diary, 'A tender parting.'[26] A few days later he turns up at her studio with a gift, Henrik Jæger's biography. She asks him straight out exactly what it is he sees in her.

'You are you, child, youth personified,' he replies, 'and I need youth – for my work, my writing.'

These are the words of a man fully aware of his capital, but in Helene's case he overreached himself. For she reveals that Emilie has told her about what happened in the summer, and asks him politely not to use the same words to her as he has used to Emilie! But Ibsen maintains his composure:

'Oh, that was in the country. One is more serious in the city.'

He had a way with words, you'd have to give him that; and he wasn't bad when it came to writing them down either. The following day he sends another letter to Vienna, accompanied by a portrait:

'Warmest thanks for your most welcome letter! What must you think of me who haven't even answered it yet? But you know that you always are and always will be in my thoughts.' And then, a little more sharply: 'A lively correspondence is, from my side, an impossibility. I have already told you this. You must simply accept me as I am. –'

On the back of the photograph he had written: 'To the May sun in a September life'. Now it was November. The year was drawing to a close, and with it, love. That's to say; first of all, Helene begins to have second thoughts. After an evening at Maximilianstrasse at which Suzannah was also present, he writes a curious letter:

> As you sat there in the twilight and spoke so sensibly, so understandingly, do you know what I thought, what I wished? No, you don't know that. I wished: Oh, if only I had such a sweet and lovely daughter.

So now Helene too had been turned into a child, and a very confused child. He hadn't, after all, kissed her like a man kissing his daughter, had he? Later she again called at the apartment, only to find herself almost dumped on Suzannah. Helene felt affronted. Still she went on meeting him, and still he wanted to kiss her. As late as 1892 he wrote in a dedication to her: 'A voice inside me cries out for you.' But Helene had realised long ago that there would never be anything between them. Suzannah, as far as is known, never referred to the relationship, though she may have had her suspicions. In the late autumn of 1889 his fascination for Emilie flares up again: having previously warned her not to expect so many letters from him, in December he writes two letters in which he calls her his princess. He says he continues to dream about her, but ends on yet another cautionary note: 'But in all honesty, dear princess – in many important respects we differ greatly from each other.'

In this fashion he found a way out of the relationships; as his erotic passion died down, he turned his young female friends into children, and in this way removed their threat. In February 1890 he writes to Emilie requesting that their correspondence come to an end. His conscience will not permit him to continue, he claims. And she should get on with living her young life. He cannot remain in half a relationship with someone, he must give himself wholly and completely. But should they ever meet again . . .

Emilie gets the message alright – 'isn't it natural for me to suppose that you don't want to see me again?' In this letter from Emilie, one of the few to have survived, it as though she is begging for a straight answer, but one that she would rather not hear; he keeps giving her grounds for hope, even as he rejects her. Finally she announces that she will not write again. She can wait. Seven months later, in September, she receives a note of condolence on the death of her father. She writes back, and on the penultimate day of the year Ibsen sends yet another letter in which he asks her not to write to him again.

* * *

So ends the tale of Ibsen and his two princesses from Gossensass, Emilie Bardach and Helene Raff. He had told Emilie that it was fate that brought her into his life, and it was presumably fate that introduced him to Helene too. Fate was good to Henrik Ibsen. But the fate of the women was not to be compared with his, for where they were a breeze in his life, he grew to become a storm in theirs.

In the literary histories it is Emilie Bardach in particular who has acquired a status as Ibsen's muse, the model he needed in order to create Hedda and Hilde in his two next dramas. But by elevating her to the level of muse people have, in reality, obliterated her and all she represented in her own right. The mythology of inspiration might be seductive, but it is also misleading. For Ibsen, Emilie and the other princesses were objects of his fascination and very probably his sexual desire. In the matter of his writing their role is trivial. Ibsen created his characters from the world and the people around him. What might the dreaming Emilie have *added* to Ibsen's writing? Was it not more likely the case that he *took* what he needed? And the literary characters he created from these impressions, what do they say about her? Several years later, while working on *The Master Builder*, he told Julius Elias that he was basing one of the female characters on a young woman he had met in Gossensass.

'She at once made him her confidant,' relates Elias:

The essence of it was that she wasn't interested in marrying some handsome and decent young man or other, she would probably never marry. What tempted and trapped and thrilled her was the thought of luring other women's husbands away from them. She was a wicked little destroyer, often she seemed to him like a little bird of prey who would happily also have counted him among her victims.

Elias concludes by quoting Ibsen's own words:

She didn't catch me, but I caught her – in my writing. And I suppose she found comfort with someone else.

In Emilie he had found a woman who was educated in the social graces, an upper-class young woman born, quite simply, to get married. It is easy to imagine such a woman resorting to coquetry, intrigue and seduction, to the extent that she rejected her lot in life. But Ibsen had depicted 'dangerous' women both before and after encountering Emilie. Sometimes these are literary stereotypes, such as the demonic Furia (*Catiline*), sometimes modern 'raptor-women' such as Hedda Gabler, who reflected a profoundly existential dilemma that existed for bourgeois women in the nineteenth century who longed for significance in a society that only had aimlessness to offer. In the plays these women are among the most gripping of his creations, but their real-life models played no more important a role for Ibsen than they would have for any other man: he used them for his own ends, and in that respect Ibsen was every bit as much a raptor as Emilie Bardach.

SLIPPERS AND PISTOLS

By the end of 1889, Ibsen had other things to occupy his mind than his young princesses Emilie and Helene. Now it was the crown prince who demanded his full attention. In the course of the autumn it had become apparent that Sigurd was not, after all, going to have his stipend renewed. Once again the Swedish Foreign Office used his lack of a Norwegian examination against him; moreover, it was felt that the stipend had not earned him the necessary credits for a career in the full diplomatic service.

Sigurd was furious and complained to the Norwegian prime minister in Stockholm, Gregers Gram, who in January 1890 replied that he had raised the matter with the Swedish Foreign Minister, but without success. It meant that, as far as he could see, the Norwegian authorities' hands were tied.

But there were more than merely formal hindrances in his path, and Sigurd knew it. In Stockholm, Washington and Vienna he had experienced the patronising and disrespectful attitude towards Norway, and protested by submitting his reports in Norwegian rather than Swedish. As his scepticism towards the Union increased, so did that of his own superiors towards him. The Swedish Foreign Office was not interested in having a Trojan horse within its walls. Not long before Christmas 1889, Carl G. Fleetwood, the head of the department's security service, was quite specific about the danger Sigurd might pose for Sweden:

'Ibsen acts systematically and with great deliberation; I have for this reason always been afraid of him, and more than ever now that he is in a position to do real harm.' The subject of his fears was, of course, the growing opposition to the Union in Norway:

> The unfortunate aspect of this business is that Ibsen is a name that might very easily acquire a political significance.

Fleetwood was afraid of Sigurd in his own right, but he feared as much the potential political power in the Ibsen name. Now Henrik himself used it to once again try to further his son's career. On 11 December he wrote to Emil Stang, prime minister in the new Conservative government that had just taken over after Johan Sverdrup. Ibsen could not believe that the Norwegian government was powerless in the matter, but tactfully conceded that the blame was partly his in allowing his son to grow up abroad. But if Sigurd had acquired his education at home that would also have required *him* to live in Norway, and had he done so, Norway would have had one less world-famous writer. He goes on to remind Stang that in a year's time he will celebrate his fortieth anniversary as a writer; was it not the normal thing for a writer to receive some form of recognition or other on such occasions? Would it not be a remarkable irony were Norway now to bestow on him 'the most bitter and offensive sorrow' he could imagine?

But Henrik had to swallow the offence, and so did Sigurd. In anger he left the diplomatic service, bitterly rejecting offers of a job without pay as an attaché or trainee in London. Back at last in Kristiania he wrote a series of articles in *Dagbladet* in which he was open about his experiences at the Foreign Office. The articles were noticed, and meant that Sigurd was soon a member of the group of left-wing intellectuals critical of the Union, a group that had developed around Bjørnstjerne Bjørnson and Ernst Sars.

So once again, an Ibsen was an established name actively involved in Norwegian political matters, on the left and working closely with Bjørnstjerne Bjørnson. We can only guess what Ibsen senior made of it all. He would, in any event, soon have grounds for worrying about a much closer tie between his son and the Bjørnson family than this *political* alliance.[27]

* * *

By the start of the 1890s, Henrik Ibsen was in a position to claim that he was moving beyond the boundaries of the Scandinavian and German worlds and had established himself as a *European* writer. *Hedda Gabler* was the play with which he finally broke free of his Norwegian cultural roots. Ironically, the play appeared just a few months before he himself returned to Norway for good. So the paths of writer and work crossed for a second time: in 1864 he had left his home country to write plays that principally addressed matters of interest to

Norwegian and Scandinavian audiences. Returning home in 1891, his plays were well on the way to conquering all of Europe.

The new play had a difficult birth, even though rumour had it that Ibsen was able to produce plays with the same punctilious regularity as he took his walks. Audiences and readers could see for themselves that a new play now appeared every two years. And Henrik Jæger had been made privy to the writing process itself. Five distinct phases were involved. First came the period of *thinking through* the idea; in this so-called sabbatical year Ibsen hardly put pen to paper. During this phase he was at work all the time – whether dressing in the morning, or out walking. Following this came the *draft*. Even though he was by this time able to see the whole play in rough outline he wrote chronologically, to accommodate new ideas as they arrived. The third phase, which was usually a quick one, involved the *development*. Here he made a point of always stopping work while he still had lines unwritten in his head, making it easier to resume the next day. If he encountered difficulties and couldn't find the right words, he remained seated at his desk until the problems were solved. Ibsen kept office hours and did not clock himself out until the day's stint was done. Once he had a finished manuscript it was time for the fourth phase, the *revision*, and it was only at this stage that he felt he knew his characters well enough to give the play its finished form. Finally there was the *fair copy*, which was what he sent to Hegel. Ibsen wrote almost all of his plays in the summer (the exceptions being *The League of Youth* and *Emperor and Galilean*), and while writing he ate frugally. He insisted on absolute silence, plenty of fresh air, and three or four rooms through which he might pace back and forth.[28]

This was the timetable at the Ibsen School of Creative Writing. This was how masterpieces got written.

If we look more closely at the genesis of the individual works it becomes apparent that things weren't quite so systematic, not even in the case of *Hedda Gabler*. He had been planning the drama as early as September 1889, and in November he tells Emilie that the writing is well under way. He then gets distracted, and not until the end of June does he feel able to inform the publishing house that he is 'once again making good steady progress'. He drops the holiday in the Tyrol, declines an invitation to visit Vienna, and prepares to spend yet another summer at his writing desk. And yet by 13 August he has still got no further than the second act, and over the next three weeks he manages only three lines of dialogue and a few stage directions. By that time a year had passed since his first notes:

The pale and apparently cold beauty. Great demands on life and on happiness.

A long list of sentences, descriptions and dialogue. Some appear in the finished play, some don't. Still others appear in later plays. A lot of it is related to women's position in society:

Main points:
1. Not all of them are born to be mothers.
2. They are sensual, but are afraid of scandal.
3. They sense that life offers certain callings, but they cannot grasp them.

Gradually he reveals Hedda's formative background: 'Women have no influence on external matters of state. For this reason they wish to exercise influence on souls.' And the raptor image appears again: 'Speaking to Thea in the first act, Hedda says: I can't imagine how anyone can fall in love with an unmarried man – or someone who is not engaged – or not in love – with someone else –.' But deep down she is a victim, squeezed between her lust for life and the conventions she lacks the courage to defy: 'There is a deep poetry in Hedda. But her surroundings frighten her. Imagine – to make oneself appear ridiculous!'

He worked carefully onwards, writing and excising, and by 17 November he was ready to send off the fair copy. On 16 December, Gyldendal published *Hedda Gabler* in a first edition of 10,000 copies. With his previous play Ibsen had announced a change of direction in his writing, the reconciliation of the third kingdom – at least, that was the impression readers got. What was the 'acclimatisation' looking like in the new play?

Hedda Gabler is the first play since *Brand* to use the name of the main character as its title. And indeed it is mostly about what happens to the general's daughter who marries beneath herself, to Jørgen Tesman, a student of art history. Hedda demands a social life that corresponds to the life she experienced growing up, and she does not hide her disappointment at the life Tesman has given her. Nor does she share his interest in Flemish handicrafts of the Middle Ages. Jørgen Tesman is a well-intentioned but naïve man who is spoiled by his two old aunts and feels a touching devotion to his old slippers. But where he is content with life, Hedda is almost dying of boredom. She despises what is common and everyday, and cultivates dreams of beauty and greatness but does not herself have the ability to make her dreams come true. The knowledge that she is pregnant fills her with disgust.

As the play opens, the couple have just returned from a six-month honeymoon to the splendid house in Kristiania that Tesman has bought to satisfy his wife's demands for a certain standard of living. The house, its furnishings and even the honeymoon have all been well beyond the means of a student, but Tesman is banking on being awarded a chair in art history in the very near future. On his return he learns that he has a rival for the position. And now things start to happen in Hedda's life, for the competitor is none other than her old suitor Ejlert Løvborg, a man who has long been presumed lost to dissolution and drink. In recent years, however, he has managed to pull himself together and, with the help of Thea Elvsted, written two books. Thea loves Ejlert, and has left her husband in order to join him. Hedda's life suddenly becomes very much more interesting when first Ejlert and then Thea arrive in the city. She persuades Ejlert to abandon his hard-won sobriety and attend a bachelors' party being thrown by Judge Brack, a family friend. He gets drunk and loses the manuscript of his next book. Jørgen finds it and hands it to Hedda, but instead of giving it back to Ejlert she burns it. She then hands one of her father's pistols to the unhappy Ejlert, to enable him to commit suicide, so that *he* can live out her dream of greatness and beauty, in dying a beautiful, magnificent and tragic death. And Ejlert does die, but not in beauty; instead, he dies accidentally shooting himself in the balls in one of the city's brothels.

Hedda's plan fails, but now it is Brack's turn to set his traps. He knows where the pistol comes from and tries to blackmail Hedda into being his lover. Meanwhile, Tesman and Thea decide to work together on a reconstruction of Ejlert's manuscript. This leaves Hedda completely isolated. She has no task in life, no purpose, no one needs her, and with Brack's threat hanging over her she takes her father's other pistol and shoots herself – through the temple.

One thing the reviewers were agreed on: there was no trace here of 'acclimatising', the dramatist's announcement of a new writing had not manifested itself:

> The pendulum has now swung to the other extreme. The intellectual threads of earlier productions, specifically *Ghosts* and *Rosmersholm*, are picked up again here, and the obscurity, the bizarre and abnormal psychology illustrated, and the empty and comfortless impression left by this whole vision of life depicted more starkly than ever.

Bredo Morgenstierne in *Aftenposten* was disappointed; this time Ibsen had gone too far. He was a magician, that was true, but 'we neither understand nor believe in Hedda Gabler'. Alfred Sinding-Larsen agreed wholeheartedly:

> All things considered, Hedda Gabler can hardly be described as anything other than an unpleasant product of the imagination, a monster in female form conjured up by the playwright himself and without a corresponding model in the real world.

The old fronts appeared to have established themselves once more. The conservative critics despair of this bizarre monster of a woman, and accuse her creator of 'the pursuit of sensationalism and voyeurism'. Representing the opposite camp, Gunnar Heiberg attacks the critics – those who 'sit there and know what writers and artists should have done differently in order to get the thing *completely right* by the end of the book'. Heiberg's personal opinion was that there was 'something magnificently immoral about Hedda Gabler', and he is caustically ironic about the protests of those little critics against the great artist who 'allows himself to find, in an immoral woman, a suitable theme for artistic treatment'. The protest is aimed at the idealistic demand that art be edifying, but is as much about the fact that Ibsen had by now acquired a European reputation; it is *he* who now sets the benchmark for Europe's drama-tists, not a group of provincial Norwegian critics.

Heiberg's review is a paean in praise of the free and untrammelled writer whose only goal is the creation of art, the one who does not build walls but tears them down. 'Everywhere there are females you will find women with Hedda Gabler-like qualities – among the Eskimos, and in Paris.' Where many regarded Hedda as alien, un-Norwegian and unlikely, Heiberg sees her as expressing Ibsen's breakthrough as a European, even a universal writer.

But the fact that Ibsen had once again sowed dissension between the young and the old, the traditionalists and the avant-garde, should not lead us to suppose that *everything* was as it had been during the furore over *Ghosts* nine years previously. For by this time, both supporters and opponents had devel-oped an understanding of what characterised an Ibsen play. Whether they liked it or not, people had undergone a learning curve. This didn't stop Ibsen from still being a nose ahead of his readers. Never before had he written such a compact and economical drama. *Hedda Gabler* consists throughout of dialogue that is short, and charged, and only occasionally retrospective. Theatregoers hardly had time to digest one line before the next came along. Things were simpler with Nora's monologues and Werle and Stockmann's short, program-matic declarations. The information offered by Ibsen in this play was so sparse that the consumer, according to Morgenstierne, had to 'resort to his own imag-ination in order to form even a rough approximation of the train of events, the result of which is characters who, in large degree, lie beyond anything we have encountered in our lives'.

Never previously had Ibsen so consistently stuck to his technique of hiding the message of the work, like a vein of silver in a mountain. The problem was that contemporary audiences were simply not used to relying on their own imaginations in this way, almost as Ibsen's co-writers. The consequence was that the more he perfected his own dramatic techniques, the more inaccessible did he become to his audiences.

The most perceptive reviews came, in the end, from Ibsen's own supporters, people such as Henrik Jæger, who reviewed the play in *Dagbladet*. But even the conservative critics showed a greater insight than one might have expected.[29] Carl David af Wirsén acknowledged the masterly way in which the drama was constructed and Hedda's 'aesthetic egotism' was depicted, even though he ends by dismissing the play on principled grounds. The Swedish critic held onto the idealistic definition of a 'beautiful art', whereas Ibsen wanted to revolutionise the purpose and meaning of art, and tear apart the beautiful and the good. In the century that followed, literary historians and biographers have caricatured his contemporary opponents, and in a mistaken show of sympathy with the aims of the modern breakthrough depicted them as prejudiced and unable to understand what he was doing. In reality, the struggle was between different worldviews, not necessarily between insight and bewilderment.

THE DEATH OF BEAUTY

Who is Hedda Gabler? Ibsen was, as ever, reluctant to say too much about her:

> I haven't really wanted to deal with so-called problems in this play. My main purpose has been to describe people, their moods and fates, against the background of the social views and attitudes obtaining at the moment.

But we need not let him get away with it that easily.

Henrik Jæger once described Hedda as 'Hjørdis in a corset', and he is not the only one to have noticed the similarities between Hedda and Ibsen's demonic female character in *The Vikings at Helgeland*. By 'corset', he explains, he is thinking of a 'sort of spiritual straitjacket she wraps around her real self. She has voluntarily agreed to wear it; she does so as an unavoidable necessity; but it pinches and constricts her, it bites into her very flesh – until, at the moment of her death, it finally bursts open.'

The voluntary nature of this is debatable; from a sociological perspective, the play can be read as the study of an encounter between two levels of bourgeois society, an aspiring bourgeoisie, and an upper class consisting of the grand bourgeoisie and the aristocracy. And if that aristocratic element might have seemed alien in a Norwegian context, the fusion of the aristocracy with the higher echelons of the grand bourgeoisie was a phenomenon Ibsen was familiar with from the Germany he lived in, as was the upper class's general need to distance itself from the threatening expansion of the lower classes. As the tight compartmentalisation of society gradually dissolved into a more fluid world of workers, technocrats, bureaucrats, politicians and parvenus, the requirements of education, social conventions and cultural capital became ever more important as a way of sustaining the exclusivity of the upper class.

These demands are the fabric of Hedda's corset, and she has hardly put it on voluntarily.

Hedda chose Tesman because she thought he was a safe choice. In obedience to the demands of convention she repressed the passion and the need for freedom which, in the privilege of her youth, she had enjoyed with Ejlert Løvborg. When Tesman cannot, after all, offer her the life she has been raised to live, she becomes homeless in the world. All she has left is this unresolved lust for life for which she is unable to find any kind of constructive expression. Hedda lacks the courage to break away that Nora had. She is cowardly, afraid of scandal; she is, to borrow an expression from *Ghosts*, among those 'afraid of the light', illustrated by her preference for keeping the curtains shut (that at the same time she longs for fresh air underlines how deep the split is between her longing for freedom and her need for security). Hedda's cowardice makes her a relative of Helene Alving, but she differs from the widow at Rosenvold in not having a *cause* to live for. This was what contemporary society found so provocative: Hedda doesn't want anything, she has nothing to fight for, and so lets herself be driven by egotism and destructive impulses. As she says herself: what she wants is power over another person. And the victim of this lust for power is Ejlert Løvborg, whom Hedda tries to win in competition with the play's 'bright' female character, Thea Elvsted.

Ultimately, however, at the deepest level it is Hedda herself who is the real victim. If we add a feminist perspective to the sociological analysis, it becomes easy to see that this is a play about a certain type of woman in a specific society, and at a specific time. For contemporary audiences it was obvious that this was a *fin de siècle* play, and its main character regarded as a demonic variant of the new woman. In this sense the play is also a study of the *Zeitgeist*, and in a wider sense a critique of bourgeois civilisation at the close of the nineteenth century. Hedda belongs to an upper-class environment characterised by stagnation, ennui, meaninglessness, compensated for by a culture of social etiquette and the overripe Victorian interior that Ibsen describes in such detail in the stage directions for the first act. At such a time and in such an environment, nothing was more superfluous than the upper-class woman.

Hedda's cowardice and her boredom can also be explained by the fact that she is caught between two epochs. Her aestheticism and longing for greatness and beauty suggest, at the deepest level, a longing for an aristocratic world that has vanished, one personified by her late father.[30] Ibsen himself explained that she is given her maiden name in the title 'because, in terms of personality, she would rather be seen as the daughter of her father than the wife of her husband'. The father, General Gabler, is the one who has shaped her character, and who still watches over her from the portrait at the back of the stage, just as Rosmer was bound to the past by the gallery of ancestors on the walls at Rosmersholm.

Trapped in a dead past, Hedda is helpless in the face of an unknown and uncertain future – the future seems to belong to men such as Judge Brack, the smart and cynical pragmatists who don't care a damn about laurel wreaths around the forehead but instead know the world from the perspective of financial and judicial power. And this is the advantage Brack uses in his scheming in the Tesmans' home. With the possible exception of Løvborg, he is the only one who does not live in the past, though Løvborg's visions of the future are of a very different order. While his formal description makes him appear to be a historian, he seems more the artist-genius type, albeit a resigned and bohemian *fin de siècle* version. Jørgen Tesman, on the other hand, is most definitely a historian of the conventional sort. Ibsen could not have expressed more clearly his dissatisfaction with the kind of historicism with which he had grown up, and which still exerted a considerable influence on everything from art to architecture.

Here, as the century is drawing to a close, he announces that history is dead; all that remained now was an open and uncertain future.

If we look at the play from the perspective of class, sex and the times then there is every reason to dismiss the myth of the demonic Hedda. She is certainly bad, but in a structural sense also a victim, trapped as she is in a dead, idealistic world, corrupted by her own uselessness, and incapable of constructing a meaningful life from the world of trivialities she inhabits, devoid of greatness and beauty. In desperation she tries to recreate a moment's magnificence by arranging a beautiful death for Løvborg, and when that plan fails, she turns her father's pistol on herself. But Hedda Gabler does not die a beautiful death; the idea of beauty is what dies with her. Once again, Ibsen depicts the failure of the dream of the aristocratic human being – and as an aristocratic *woman* Hedda's is a double defeat.

Is it any wonder Norwegian readers found her somewhat exotic?

'She does not belong in our city, occupying the same space and time as ourselves,' wrote Camilla Collett. 'Imagine a Hedda Gabler wandering down Karl Johan, large as life, with a gun held to her bosom!'

But was Hedda really as alien as Collett suggested? Norway too had its share of world-weary young people who romanticised beauty and death, a *fin de siècle* generation turning in revolt against a mechanical and soulless naturalism and towards the mystical and inexplicable. In a literary and artistic sense they turned to movements such as symbolism and decadence, living out their lives as wasted wrecks or scrupulous dandies. Both the new young decadents and the older generation of bohemians were romantically attracted to suicide, and Ibsen had the fates of Adda Ravnkilde and Victoria Benedictsson in recent memory. Although the statistics show that the suicide rate in Norway was unchanged between 1876 and 1900, the *idea* of suicide was a part of the *Zeit-*

geist in Norway as in the rest of Europe, as is evident from Émile Durkheim's classic 1897 study, *Suicide*.

Ibsen's suicides were, in other words, recognisable to contemporaries, and the same is true of Hedda's existential boredom and her longing for the beautiful – attracting some and provoking others. 'He enjoys firing his revolver, that Ibsen,' commented Arne Garborg, while in Edvard Grieg's view there had been enough suicides, what with Hedvig's death, Rosmer and Rebecca drowning themselves, and now Hedda:

> But what's the point? Idiots can go on living, but everybody else should shoot themselves. A fine lesson for the future! And all that cold mastery expended on this.

August Strindberg, on the other hand, was most interested in Ejlert Løvborg, in whom he saw a malicious portrait of himself:

> How could a talented bloke be 'ruined' just by getting drunk, visiting a whorehouse and getting in a fight with the police? He's supposed to shoot himself for that?

No, Strindberg had no plans to shoot himself, and gave assurances that he never felt so 'restored and inspired' as he did after a really good night out. As a literary motive, of course, suicide was nothing new. But previously there had always been some purpose to it, a profound and tragic dimension, and it was this element that so many found lacking in both *Rosmersholm* and *Hedda Gabler*.

'TOO FAR FROM PICCADILLY'

In *Hedda Gabler* Ibsen had offered his growing European market a play that captured the spirit of the times. In Germany the rise of his reputation had taken place in two stages. First came the moderate breakthrough with the historical dramas of the 1870s that culminated in the success of *The Pillars of Society* and the scandal of *A Doll's House*. This wave was over by the early 1880s, but it rose again at the end of 1886. What characterised it this time was how important Ibsen had become for the nascent naturalism in the country; indeed, scholars have with good reason pondered the question of why German youth had to turn to an ageing *Norwegian* writer to help them carry out their literary revolution.[31] One explanation is the lack of native role models. Until the close of the 1880s the epigonic historical play dominated German stages, and emergent naturalism was kept out of theatres by the censor. Generally speaking, literary development in Germany was marked by a more abrupt transition from the long drawn-out phase of poetic realism to modern naturalism, whereas what typified Scandinavia was an earlier and more gradual move towards realism that broke with idealistic and Romantic ideals. Otto Brahm had good reasons for opening his naturalistic Freie Bühne theatre with *Ghosts* on 29 September 1889, even though some have suggested that Brahm's naturalism can best be described as an 'idealised' or a 'poetic' naturalism.[32]

So the German Ibsen was something different from the Scandinavian Ibsen. As his reputation spread from country to country, it became ever more obvious how both opponents and supporters managed to adapt his plays to the contemporary cultural and literary currents of the local society. His name aroused enthusiasm and contempt everywhere, but in different ways, and for different reasons.

In England his name had been known almost as long as in Germany, but only among those with a special interest.[33] Edmund Gosse had written articles and reviews and translated *Poems*; among the plays, *Emperor and Galilean* was available in Catherine Ray's translation from 1876, and six years later Frances Lord's *Nora* appeared. But for most people in Britain, Ibsen remained an unknown name. In January 1886 a group of enthusiasts gathered at a house in Bloomsbury for an amateur reading of *A Doll's House*. The part of Nora was read by Karl Marx's daughter Eleanor, Helmer by her husband Edward Aveling, Fru Linde by William Morris's daughter May, and Krogstad by George Bernard Shaw. Whereas Ibsen's feminism was generally regarded as both non-political and humanist, the enthusiasm of this particular group meant that it was associated in England with socialism, something which would, in due course, arouse the antipathy of conservative critics. Eleanor Marx translated several of the plays, but it was above all Shaw who managed to requisition Ibsen for his own agenda in British political life and public debate with his book *The Quintessence of Ibsenism* from 1891.

But Ibsen did not become an Englishman overnight. A performance of William Archer's unfortunate adaptation of *The Pillars of Society* as *Quicksand* in 1880 was followed by another heavily edited adaptation in 1884, this time of *A Doll's House*, under the title *Breaking a Butterfly*. On both occasions the performers were amateurs, and Archer was led to the exasperated conclusion that Ibsen was impossible to perform on British stages. But in due course it was he, with his large output of translations and articles, who became Ibsen's most important advocate in the country, competing to a degree with Gosse and Shaw.

Things began to happen in 1888, the year in which Archer published an inexpensive volume of translations of *The Pillars of Society*, *Ghosts* and *An Enemy of the People* that sold surprisingly well. The decisive breakthrough came the following year. On 7 June 1889, *A Doll's House* had its premiere at the Novelty Theatre in London, in a production by a married couple, Janet Achurch and Charles Charrington. The performance excited enthusiasm and outrage in equal measure, setting the tone for the strongly polarised reaction that would characterise Ibsen's reception in England. For supporters the occasion was shattering: 'This was either the end of the world or the beginning of a new world for women.' Ibsen himself, who was initially a little sceptical as regards the English, was delighted:

'What is happening in London marks a high point in my life and is far beyond anything I might have dreamed of,' he writes to Archer, who kept him informed of events.

The leading conservative critic of the time, Clement Scott, who wrote in the *Daily Telegraph*, the biggest newspaper at the time, was considerably less enthusiastic. He would become the foremost opponent of Ibsen and everything associated with him in British public life, though here his irony is mild enough as he amuses himself at the sight of this 'socialist Nora, the apostle of humanity's newest creed'. Another critic wondered whether Ibsen was a missionary or an artist, and concluded with a patronising assertion that there was no reason to be too hard on the man:

Ibsen isn't suburban. He isn't even provincial – he is from Scandinavia.

And so it went on. A month after the premiere of *A Doll's House*, Ibsen's supporters, already being spoken of as a congregation of 'Ibsenites', staged a production of *The Pillars of Society* at the Opéra Comique in Paris. It played for only one night, but the debate continued. Writing in December 1889, Robert Buchanan, along with Scott the most influential of Ibsen's critics, likened him to the French naturalists:

Filth from the gutters and sewers of the continent has, as I have said, polluted the sources of English literature, and a kind of literary typhoid has struck down our most able writers. A degraded sexual pathology, expressed in a language that cannot claim to be literature, now threatens our drama.

Buchanan was not the only conservative critic with a taste for the metaphors of disease and degeneration, but his complaint is interesting because he sees Ibsen as both provincial (Scandinavian) and continental, two sides that he unites in his characterisation of the Norwegian writer as perfidious, as 'Zola with a wooden leg'. In 1890 the first four volumes of Archer's five-volume *Ibsen's Prose Dramas* appeared, and the following year saw the publication of Shaw's *The Quintessence of Ibsenism* and the opening in London of *Rosmersholm* in February, *Ghosts* in March, *Hedda Gabler* in April and *The Lady from the Sea* in May.

Not surprisingly it was *Ghosts* that opened the gates of hell. The play had actually been banned by the strict British censor, but, as happened in Germany, the enthusiasts of the Independent Theatre found a loophole in the law by organising a private performance. No one, however, was in any doubt that the evening of 13 March 1891 was a public event, and indeed posterity judges it to have been the most controversial theatrical performance of the entire nineteenth century. Journalists, editors and critics launched a furious attack on the play. The editorial in the *Daily Telegraph* for 14 March 1891 has acquired a legendary fame:

> An open drain; a loathsome sore unbandaged; a dirty act done publicly; a lazar-house with all its doors and windows open.

This represents the zenith, or nadir, of the storm that broke around Ibsen in England in the years around 1891. Ibsen was the man of the moment, at times the most talked-about writer in the country. So hostile was the opposition to *Ghosts* that William Archer decided the best response was to publish an article that consisted in its entirety of quotations from the most vituperous pens:

> This disgusting performance . . . bestial and cynical . . . offensive cynicism . . . Ibsen's melancholic and noxious world . . . Completely repellent and stinking . . . Hideous, almost crude indecency . . . Literary carrion . . . dreadful matters . . . new and dangerous unpleasantness . . . This chaos of vulgarity, egoism, crudity and absurdity . . . unspeakably repulsive . . . Disgusting play . . . Scandalous . . . Naked repulsion . . . A completely worthless and repelling production . . .

And so on and so forth. One thing is certain: if the minds of Ibsen and the Ibsenites were dirty, they had nothing to teach the conservative critics, neither in their imagination nor their literary creativity. In the opinion of some, Archer's little collection of quotations and the argument presented in the *Pall Mall Gazette* of 8 April 1891 marked a turning point for Ibsen in England. But just exactly *what* was it about Ibsen that so provoked and enthused the British, and that led to coinages such as 'Ibsenites', 'Ibsenism', and 'Ibscenity'?

Fundamentally, it was the same here as elsewhere, that he challenged the traditional demands of idealistic aestheticism for beauty and edification. For a man such as Clement Scott the matter was simple: 'the play you see on the stage *after* dinner should never exceed the bounds of decency observed *during* dinner'. A play such as *Ghosts* was most definitely not considered an appropriate side-dish to lamb chops and Yorkshire pudding. But other factors involved contributed in a unique way to Ibsen's reception in England, both for his supporters and his opponents.[34]

In the first place Ibsen came late to the British, and he came very suddenly. Audiences in Scandinavia and to some extent in Germany had followed his development from the historical dramas via *Brand* and *Peer Gynt* to the dramas with contemporary settings; but until he broke through as a scandalous writer of modern drama he was practically unknown in England. Those who missed humour and poetry were left to seek out *Love's Comedy*, *Peer Gynt* or *Emperor and Galilean* for themselves. Secondly, English theatre censorship was an efficient watchdog for the highly developed moral standards of Victorian England. Defiance or avoidance of censorship was therefore also a provocation against the power of the authorities. Additionally, drama in the Victorian era had developed in a non-literary direction. A combination of censorship and problems related to copyright laws meant that printed drama had gradually disappeared from the book market. So if the censor banned a play from the stage, then it quite simply vanished. Given this background, it is easier to understand the shock occasioned by *A Doll's House* and *Ghosts* in England.

In the fourth place, Ibsen was not only a foreigner, he was a Norwegian – which is to say *provincial*. And this is significant. For a large country with a rich cultural tradition provincialism can be seen either as a positive or a negative quality. In Germany, Ibsen's nationality is generally regarded as having worked in his favour; in German eyes, Scandinavia appeared as a 'präkapitalistische Idylle', a culture related to German culture, but simpler and more authentic.[35] This Romantic notion was probably what made the Germans receptive to the historical plays as well as to *The Pillars of Society*. In England, by contrast, Ibsen's Norwegian origins were largely used against him. The essence of a long list of reviews and commentaries is that 'Norwegianness', as represented by Ibsen, was associated with radicalism, pessimism, immorality, self-centredness, mental illness and a deadly lack of humour. A. B. Walkley, who was among Ibsen's admirers, wondered why his characters were always so melancholy, introverted and obsessed with their own 'dirty little souls'. Everyone wonders why they were born and what their mission in life is.

Are Norwegians really made that way, I wonder? And if so, why?

On the other hand, there were others besides Walkley who were aware of the invigorating potential of the provincial on Europe's old-established cultures. To those astonished that 'the new gospel of dramatic revelation should have come from such a remote Nazareth', Walkley explained that when a new drama did emerge, it would have to be precisely from a source 'far removed from the main currents of European life'. Others pointed to the similarities linking Ibsen and Walt Whitman, Dostoyevsky and Tolstoy, and history shows that they were right. There *are* good reasons to view the spread of Ibsen's writing in Europe in the light of the cultural awakening that took place in sites away from the centre in the latter years of the nineteenth century. This awakening became apparent during the 1848 revolution, and was related to the process of modernisation itself that transformed, and to some degree united, the whole of the West technologically, politically, socially, economically and culturally, though at different times, and with many local variations. As citizens of the world's greatest colonial power the British probably also projected some of their feelings of superiority towards their colonies onto provincial Norway, though Ibsen himself could easily have passed as a bureaucrat from the civil service in almost any European country.[36]

In the final analysis he probably lacked, in the eyes of many Britons, the style necessary, in both form and content, to make the grade – as the American Henry James put it, he was quite simply 'too far from Piccadilly and our glorious standards. Therefore his cause may be said to be lost; we shall never take him to our hearts.'

The provincialism was not least related to the complete absence of humour in Ibsen's plays. 'There is nothing very droll in the world, I think, to Dr. Ibsen,' observed Henry James (who nevertheless became a convert to Ibsenism). The English, on the other hand, have never lacked for either humour or wit. A number of people found the characters in Ibsen's plays unintentionally comic, and according to some malevolent reviewers audiences sometimes burst out laughing during performances. A sub-genre of satires and parodies presently arose in the satirical magazines and on the stage. Of theatrical parodies J. M. Barrie's *Ibsen's Ghosts, or Toole up to Date* (1891) is reckoned the best, while the most famous print parody would have to be *Mr Punch's Pocket Ibsen* from 1891 in *Punch*, which appeared in Norwegian two years later. It includes the following alternative stage direction for *Hedda Gabler*:

> A sitting room cheerfully decorated in dark colours. Broad doorway hung with black crepe in the wall at back leading to a back drawing room in which, above a sofa in black horsehair hangs a posthumous portrait of the late General Gabler. Over the piano a pretty winding sheet. Through the back window a thick wall and a cemetery can be seen . . .

The fifth factor in explaining what was unique about Ibsen's reception in England must be sought in his supporters. In that highly industrialised class society, socialist and feminist activists were both noticeable and controversial, and it was among these that Ibsen found his most dedicated supporters – most notably George Bernard Shaw. We do not know what Ibsen himself made of *The Quintessence of Ibsenism* – he could not, after all, read English – but in the view of many the book says more about its author than it does about Ibsen. It was based on a lecture Shaw gave at the premises of the Fabian Society in 1890 as part of a series of lectures on 'Socialism in Contemporary Literature', and it sets the new, realistic drama against the aesthetics of the traditional, idealistic play. According to Shaw, Ibsen's contribution to the drama is the way in which he integrates the discussion of social problems into the dramatic structuring of the play, so that the plays acquire a didactic function by making 'the spectators themselves the persons of the drama, and the incidents of their own lives its incidents'.

The Quintessence of Ibsenism had an undeniable influence in England; but it is also partly responsible for the persistence of a rather rigid perception of Ibsen as a dramatist of social realism, something that created difficulties with his turn to symbolic writing in the 1890s.

Although Ibsen could not read Shaw, he reacted angrily when the *Daily Chronicle* followed Shaw's lectures with an interview in which it was claimed that Ibsen dissociated himself from social democracy. In a letter to one of his contacts in London he writes that he has studied the question of social democracy closely, and that the journalist had misrepresented what he said:

> In reality I simply expressed my surprise that I, whose principal task was always to describe human characters and human fates, realised that at certain points – and without any conscious intention on my part – had reached the same conclusions as the moral philosophers of social democracy through scientific research.

This was the only occasion on which Ibsen became personally involved in his reception in England, and the reasons may be complex. In the first place he had no interest in denying a political interpretation of his writing that was so central to his English supporters; in other words, his motive might have been tactical. Secondly, he remained fascinated by socialism's opposition to the status quo, though he had no wish to see his own name used to further the cause of a political ideology.

Yet again, he establishes an elegant balance between the practical concerns of business and his artistic integrity, at the same time as he confirms his part in the social concerns of the day without the sacrifice of his independence.

THÉÂTRE LIBRE

After the excitements of the breakthrough in Great Britain in 1891, Ibsen had a quieter year, before the spring of 1893 arrived with a host of productions in which Elizabeth Robins, one of the most important actors in the English-speaking world, played a leading part. It was she, in company with Marion Lea, who had hired the Vaudeville Theatre at her own expense and given *Hedda Gabler* its English premiere two years earlier. This introduced audiences to a more fashionable notion of Ibsen, and among the play's well-known admirers were Oscar Wilde, Henry James, Thomas Hardy and George Meredith. Herbert Beerbohm's production of *An Enemy of the People* at the Haymarket Theatre in June 1893 was the first time an Ibsen play had been performed at a commercial theatre having no connection with the Ibsenites. It was beginning to look as though Piccadilly was about to be conquered. Although he continued to be controversial, there were fewer and fewer willing to question Ibsen's place in the repertoire and, if Archer is to be believed, his editions of the dramas of contemporary life had sold over 31,000 copies by the end of 1892.

Some of the credit for this ought perhaps to be shared with Clement Scott, whose passionate campaign of opposition acted as a highly effective if involuntary advertisement for the Norwegian's scandalous and titillating dramas.

Ibsen's arrival in France took place almost simultaneously with that in England, and there too he divided critics and audiences. But in most other respects, his reception was very different. However, in the early phase of his acceptance, Ibsen was hailed by the young naturalists here as well. As in England, his writing was initially of interest to a small and esoteric group, beginning in the 1870s. There were a few articles, and in 1887 a major assessment of his talent appeared in the pages of *La Revue d'Art Dramatique* by the critic Jacques Saint-Cère. Of even greater significance was the presence of André Antoine in Belgium in the summer of 1888, where he had been an enthusiastic member of the audience at the Meiningen Theatre's performance of *Ghosts*.

And with that the story of Ibsen and France really begins. The year before, Antoine had started the Théâtre Libre as an experimental amateur theatre with a strong orientation towards naturalism. That same autumn he decided to mount a production of *Ghosts* on his own stage.[37] The play was given a reading at the Théâtre Libre in September, and Émile Zola urged them to follow it up with a production – he clearly saw in Ibsen proof of his own international influence. Antoine's problem was that he lacked a satisfactory translation, with the result that his plans had to be postponed indefinitely. Then, in January and February 1889, new translations of *Ghosts* and *A Doll's House* appeared in *La Revue Indépendante*. The man responsible was Moritz Prozor, a Lithuanian count of all things, who had been deeply impressed by *Ghosts*, which he saw while a secretary at the Russian Embassy in Stockholm. The translations were published in book form in 1889, occasioning a debate to which the influential critic Jules Lemaître contributed several articles.

On 30 May 1890, an Ibsen play appeared on the French stage with Antoine's production of *Ghosts* at the Théâtre Libre on the Boulevard de Strasbourg in Paris – the theatrical capital of the world. Antoine himself played the part of

Osvald with such intensity that he could hardly remember any of the performance after the second act. Osvald was a dream part for Antoine – 'the most
beautiful part any actor could play'. August Lindberg and Herman Bang were of
the same opinion, and their fascination is an important corrective to the notion
of Ibsen as the creator of great parts for women. Opinions have differed greatly
as regards the success or otherwise of the production. In fact, there were two
performances, since the dress rehearsal of 29 May was open to members of the
theatre, while the premiere itself was open to all. When Antoine describes in
his memoirs how the audience moved from surprise, to irritation, to anxiety
during the final act, he is referring to the first performance, when the hall was
filled with supporters of the theatre. Following the premiere proper the reaction was as divided as one might expect. Foremost among the hostile critics
was Francisque Sarcey who, like Clement Scott in England, almost single-
handedly created an anti-Ibsen campaign in the French media.

The chief objection, among both opponents and supporters, was the lack of
that clarity – 'la clarté' – that was so central to the French theatrical tradition.
Ibsen was obscure, and associated with 'la brume scandinave' – the Scandinavian
fog. Questions were raised about his retrospective technique; one of those
working in the theatre had even suggested adding a prologue in which Alving's
story could be played in the place in which, chronologically speaking, it
belonged. But the lack of clarity wasn't only Ibsen's fault; in the first place,
Antoine had made cuts to the script that left certain crucial connections obscure.
Secondly, those in the audience who had read the play beforehand (including
Sarcey) made use of what was then the only published text available, which was
Prozor's inadequate translation.

Additionally, it is important to remember that reviewers of plays do not, in
the first instance, concern themselves with the play itself but with the production, in this case Antoine's experimental naturalistic style. Here the focus was
on ensemble playing rather than bravura individualism, darkness in the house
as a way of focusing attention on the stage, and a naturalistic acting style in
which declamation was replaced by conversational exchanges, often with backs
to the audience. All of this provoked conservative critics every bit as much as
the play itself.

Antoine, on the other hand, was delighted with the provocation he had
given, and at once decided to follow it up with a new production, this time of
The Wild Duck, which had its premiere in April 1891. By that time opinion was
divided along clear lines, for and against Ibsen. This play was seen as more
accessible than the previous one and was generally given a better reception.
Antoine had obtained genuine Norwegian pine for his scenery, but it was the
mysterious bird that attracted most attention, providing as it did yet another
instance of 'Scandinavian fog'.

French critics asked many of the questions Scandinavian reviewers had done when the play first appeared: What is all this about the duck?

'Ah, I won't flatter myself by pretending I understand the duck,' Sarcey confessed to his readers. 'Don't expect me to explain it to you. I have already read a number of theories concerning this enigmatic duck; they do not satisfy me; some have prepared it with olives, some à la rouennaise, others with oranges; for my part I can recommend no particular sauce.'

In France they eat ducks, not give them leading roles on the stage – and Sarcey was by no means the only one who felt an urge to be sarcastic; according to some reports, members of the public quacked away like ducks during the performance itself.

Was that highly intelligent critic trailing his intellectual coat when he claimed that 'no one will ever know what the duck is, what it's doing in the play, or what it means'? Must we assume that he was actually well able to say something about the wild duck's symbolic function, but chose instead to make fun of an obscure and absurd element in the play? Writing in Ibsen's defence, Lemaître said that 'it seems to me that most critics have made the duck a lot more enigmatic than it really is'. He then goes on to explain that the duck, which had once been free but now grew fat in the family's loft, quite simply symbolised the Ekdals, father and son, who were now likewise living on the charity of the man who had dishonoured them.

It is hard to believe that Sarcey was incapable of understanding that. His criticism must be at deeper level; he could not understand the more profound significance such a symbol might have in a drama, and declined to make the effort to do so, since his point of departure was that the whole thing seemed to him meaningless.[38]

With these two performances Ibsen had arrived in France. He was now a famous name, with supporters among the young and opponents among the establishment, along very similar lines to what had happened in England. In reality the French Ibsen was very different from the English Ibsen, and both were different from the German and Scandinavian Ibsens. As the 1890s progressed what was unique about his reception in France would become ever more apparent as he became increasingly the province of the experimental symbolists rather than the experimental naturalists. And here there were no difficulties with either wild ducks or white horses.

EUROPE – AND BEYOND

Having made it in Germany, England and France, Ibsen was now well on his way to conquering the world, and for the remainder of his life he would see his plays crossing borders and claiming new territories. In the long run it was the anglicisation of his work that proved most important for his status as a world dramatist. But just as the Norwegian Ibsen differs from the English Ibsen, so did his reception differ in different parts of the English-speaking world. In the United States the performance of *Ghosts* in Chicago in 1882 suggested that the Americans were receptive to his radical dramas of contemporary social life, but in fact the occasion was anything but typical. Ten years later, when Ibsen was introduced to the New York stage, it became obvious how incompatible his plays were with the puritanism and conservative values of the American middle class. Newspapers on the East Coast described his plays as incomprehensible, pedagogic, obscene, and on top of all that, Ibsen was a foreigner – in the sense of not being an American. As in England, he was idolised by a small group of leftist Ibsenites, and it was not until the general radicalisation of American society that took place after the turn of the century that he acquired a larger audience in the New World.[39]

In Ireland he played a very different and interesting role.[40] Like Norway, Ireland was a small, provincial nation living in the shadow of a larger and more powerful culture. Towards the close of the nineteenth century there was great interest in Ibsen among Irish nationalists, not least on account of his activities as a writer and a man of the theatre. Ibsen's participation in the Norwegian theatre movement of the 1850s and 1860s was something the Irish nationalists found easy to relate to as they struggled to establish their own national theatre, the later Abbey Theatre. They saw Ole Bull's theatre, the language struggle, Ibsen and Bjørnson's nationalist contributions, and the whole Norwegian nation-building project as an example for their own fight against English influence. There is a certain irony in the fact that Ibsen thus became associated with a background which he had himself rejected many years earlier.

But there was a second group of Irishmen who admired Ibsen precisely *because* he had freed himself from the national context and the pressures and external demands exerted on the artist by society. It was Ibsen *the exile* who so fascinated the young James Joyce that he went on to spend most of his life living abroad. Informed by William Archer in 1900 that Ibsen had appreciated his review of *When We Dead Awaken*, his response was:

> I am a young Irishman, eighteen years old, and the words of Ibsen I shall keep in my heart all my life.

Joyce regarded Ibsen as a genuine cosmopolitan intellectual who had, through his career, demonstrated the autonomy of the artist. Thus there was both a nation-building and a cosmopolitan Irish Ibsen tradition. There were elements of conflict in the relationship between the two; Joyce, for example, in an article in 'The Day of the Rabblement' (1901), attacked the Irish theatre movement for its reluctance to free the artist from the pressures of social involvement. The nationalists, for their part, identified with Ibsen's national role, but not necessarily with his literary programme, leading to criticism from Joyce when no one dared to mount a production of *Ghosts* in Ireland. For the first group it was a question of uniting the nation, for Joyce of liberating the artist. So while the national and the universal were, for Norwegians, chronologically successive sides of the same writer's production, these two facets operated simultaneously and with divisive effect in Ireland. Thus the Irish Ibsen was different again from the American and the English Ibsen.

In southern Europe too his reception and repute were coloured by local conditions. France was Ibsen's most important market, but in his own lifetime his name became well known in other Latin countries. For a long time Italians had to be content with the sight of the Norwegian writer strolling through the streets of Rome or barricaded behind a newspaper in the Café Nazionale, but by the end of the 1880s a number of enthusiasts were campaigning to make his work better known in the country.[41] Here as elsewhere much of the interest was concentrated on *A Doll's House*, with *Ghosts* close behind. Early in 1885, Ibsen was contacted by an Italian lawyer name Alfredo Mazza requesting permission to publish his translation of *A Doll's House* with the title *La Casa della Bambola*. Mazza had taught himself Norwegian in order to read Ibsen, and published the opening of his translation in a newspaper. But for some reason or other a full translation was never published.[42] In 1891, Luigi Capuana published the play as a supplement in the Rome newspaper *Carro di Tespi*; three years later it appeared in book form.

On 15 February 1889, Ibsen was performed for the first time on an Italian stage.[43] *A Doll's House* had its premiere at the Teatro Gerbino in Turin, with Emilia Aliprandi Pierei playing the lead. The production was not particularly successful. As in England, naturalist drama was making a breakthrough here too, though there were no equivalent theatres dedicated to the promotion of the style as there were in Germany and France. That left matters in the hands of a few enthusiasts. The most significant of these was Eleonora Duse, who became one of the most important interpreters of Ibsen onstage, attaining a celebrity that reached well beyond the borders of her native land. It was her interpretation of the part of Nora at the Teatro Filodrammatici in Milan on 9 February 1891 that marked Ibsen's real breakthrough on the Italian stage.

A characteristic of Ibsen's reception in Italy was the way his plays were regarded as *exotic*. Here too his work found supporters and detractors, but it seems that criticism did not lead to anger so much as bewilderment at this strange art from the north. Even hostile critics conceded that they lacked the background to understand the Scandinavian tradition. Supporters admitted much the same thing. Nervous of the audience's response, before his production of *A Doll's House* in Milan in 1891, Capuana had asked Ibsen's permission to change the ending, as had been done in Germany some years previously. This time Ibsen declined. He was convinced that Italian audiences would understand the play just as he had written it. But, he added in a letter to Moritz Prozor, whom Capuana had contacted while working on the translation:

> If it turns out that it really doesn't work, then Herr Capuana may himself use your version of the ending, though I cannot formally recognise or authorise such a move.

Ibsen's response to Capuana's request has traditionally been seen as a sign of his artistic integrity. Yet what it actually shows is that he did not expressly forbid a change of ending but saw this as an acceptable solution if it transpired that the market there was not yet ready for Nora's departure. The difference here is that, unlike in Germany, he would not give his formal blessing to the alternative ending. Another difficulty was that in Italy his works were usually translated from German or French versions, as Capuana had based his on Prozor's French edition. The result was that Italian readers were presented with texts that varied greatly in quality and accuracy. Other Ibsen plays were translated and performed in Italy throughout the 1890s, these too giving rise to enthusiasm and debate. When *The Wild Duck* was performed in 1891 the audience is said to have called out for 'that bloody duck' to be shot; but in the following year a successful production of *Ghosts* was mounted in Rome. Yet Ibsen's reception was nothing like as stormy as it had been in Germany and England. *Hedda Gabler* and *The Pillars of Society* were performed in 1892, *The Master Builder* in 1893, and in the following year *Rosmersholm* and *The Lady from the Sea*. Many of the plays were performed in Milan, with two names recurring in particular: Ermete Zacconi and Eleonora Duse. It was Duse whose name would become so closely connected with Ibsen and Italian theatre. She also took her interpretations of the roles on tour in Europe and the United States.

North, south, west – how were things looking in the east? Ibsen was able to tell Hagbert Berner in 1882 that *The League of Youth* had been performed in Russia, *A Doll's House* in Warsaw, and that *The Vikings at Helgeland* had been translated and was due to be performed in Hungarian. As elsewhere he gained a foothold in eastern Europe through the efforts of enthusiasts who translated him, wrote articles, and arranged performances of varying degrees of success and quality. The actress Helena Modjeska had played Nora in both St Petersburg and Warsaw in November 1881 and February 1882, on both occasions in Polish. Not until 8 February 1892 was Ibsen performed in Russia in Russian. The play was – of course – *A Doll's House*, which had its premiere in St Petersburg, though it does not appear to have been a success. Not until

1892 did the Russians try again, and three years later August Lindberg took productions of *Peer Gynt* and *Little Eyolf* to St Petersburg.[44] The translations followed the same pattern; following the publication of *A Doll's House* in 1883 translations appeared on a regular basis through the 1890s, and in due course a six-volume Russian edition of Ibsen's collected works appeared in 1896 and 1897.

Ibsen must have been curious to see how he would fare in Russia. Notoriously unwilling to admit his admiration for any other writer, late in life he conceded his fondness for Russian literature, and especially Dostoyevsky's *Crime and Punishment* and Tolstoy's *Anna Karenina* and *Promoting a Devil*.[45] He was, however, well aware that his admiration was not reciprocated by Tolstoy; in the Russian's opinion, Ibsen's drama was 'artificial, false and very clumsily written, in the sense that none of his characters are credible and real. His reputation in Europe demonstrates only the poverty of creativity in Europe.'

Tolstoy largely dismissed Ibsen's drama as non-religious and amoral; not surprisingly, he had more taste for Bjørnson. Nonetheless, his letters and diaries reveal that he was familiar with the Norwegian's work and, if it was any comfort, he disliked him for the same reasons that he disliked Shakespeare and Dante.[46] Ibsen also enjoyed reading Ivan Turgenev, though we know nothing of his opinion of the person who, along with himself and Strindberg, is regarded as the greatest of modern dramatists – Anton Chekhov. According to the great theatrical revolutionary Konstantin Stanislavski, Chekhov regarded Ibsen as dry, cold and over-expository, though he admired his talent. Chekhov's own letters provide few clues beyond the fact that he was curious about and familiar with the Norwegian writer's work, until a year before his death when he described Ibsen as his favourite writer. Opinions differ on the question of any influence Ibsen might have had on the younger Russian dramatist, but there are those who hold that *The Seagull* shows the influence of the bird symbolism of *The Wild Duck* as well as the open ending of *A Doll's House*.[47]

When it finally happened, Ibsen's major breakthrough in Russia came when Stanislavski made him part of the repertoire at the Moscow Arts Theatre in 1899 – though the real Ibsen expert at the theatre was Stanislavski's partner, Vladimir Nemirovitsj-Dantsjenko. The play chosen was *Hedda Gabler*, with Stanislavski himself playing the part of Løvborg. Stanislavski regarded Ibsen as an interesting but exotic writer. He was Scandinavian, and Stanislavski admitted that he did not understand Scandinavians. *An Enemy of the People* was the only real success the theatre had with Ibsen, probably on account of the fact that the play could easily be adapted to reflect Russian conditions. When the theatre gave a guest performance in St Petersburg on the same day as demonstrating students had clashed with the police in Kazanski Place, audiences had no difficulty in identifying with the play's public-meeting scene, creating such a disturbance that the actors had to abandon the performance. In other words, the audience took over the roles and brought the action down from the stage and into the stalls.

As it happens something similar took place when Aurélien Lugné-Poe put the play on in Paris in 1893, with 'students and anarchists and starving artists' rioting inside the theatre. Similar responses are reported elsewhere.[48] Along with *A Doll's House*, *An Enemy of the People* has shown a unique ability to be revitalised within different historical, social and political contexts.

Before the outbreak of the First World War, nine of Ibsen's plays had been performed by the Moscow Arts Theatre, and by that time other theatres had introduced him into their repertoires as well. Thus Ibsen influenced the breakthrough of modern theatre in different countries at different times, first in Germany in the 1880s, then in England and France, and finally in Russia from the turn of the century onwards.

A DIVA AT THE END OF THE TOUR

In country after country, Ibsen was translated, read and performed. In 1882 *A Doll's House* was translated into Polish, and the following year *An Enemy of the People* was published in Holland. In 1887 *Rosmersholm* appeared in Czech, while *A Doll's House* was published in both Hungary and the United States in 1889. Three years later *The Vikings at Helgeland* was published in Icelandic. The following year, on 14 April 1893, Ibsen was performed for the first time in Spain, when *An Enemy of the People* was staged in Barcelona.[49] Five more plays appeared in Spanish the next year, and so it continued. It is in the light of this that we must view Ibsen's decision to make a European drama out of *Hedda Gabler*. In the autumn of 1890, and before he had finished writing the play, he was arranging for its publication in Scandinavia, Germany, France and England. He also anticipated translations into Russian, Hungarian and Italian. The level of ambition was high, but not unwarranted.

In Germany the house of S. Fischer had established itself as the country's leading publisher of Ibsen after 1887.[50] The company had close links to the nascent naturalist movement, and on the initiative of Julius Hoffory decided to publish all Ibsen's works in its Nordische Bibliothek series. Hoffory was a Danish-born Hungarian, professor of Nordic philology in Berlin since 1887, and to him goes much of the credit for a more reliable and consistent publication of Ibsen in Germany. He was said to be a brilliant man, but unstable, with a taste for alcohol and brothels – Ibsen used him as a model for Ejlert Løvborg. At the time *Hedda Gabler* appeared, Hoffory was ill; he developed a mental illness and died three years later. Instead it was Julius Elias who became Ibsen's contact with S. Fischer. Elias was a literary scholar based in Berlin, German-born, and known for the pleasure he took in sorting through other people's papers – a man who gave Ibsen some of the characteristics he used for Jørgen Tesman.

A disagreement arose, however, over the company's plans to publish *Hedda Gabler* as a supplement to a weekly journal before it appeared in book form. For Ibsen such a thing was, of course, completely unacceptable. In the ensuing delay he feared that his book would miss the Christmas market – and German theatre managers were already waiting in line for performance copies of the script. Last, but not least, there was the risk of pirate editions appearing now that the book was available in Scandinavia. And Ibsen was *definitely* not interested in losing any more money from his German market:

'The play must be published in its entirety, as a book,' he wrote angrily to Elias on 17 December. 'And it must be published immediately. With no further delays.'

He got his way; a few days later Fischer's edition of *Hedda Gabler* reached him in the post. Unauthorised editions were not always, however, a bad thing. A case in point was Reclam Verlag's editions of his work. As long as these did not compete with Ibsen's authorised translations for the theatre, he had nothing against the company's cheap editions because they generated sales of his books 'among those who would not otherwise read them'. Reclam also paid him a voluntary royalty on sales, showing that Ibsen knew how to turn the chaotic and lawless state of the publishing business to his own advantage.

In most respects, Ibsen's plans for the publication of *Hedda Gabler* had succeeded. In 1891 the play appeared in England, the United States, France, the Netherlands and Germany, in the latter both in Fischer's authorised version and in Reclam's best-selling 'authorised pirated edition', as well as a third version that appeared over which Ibsen had no control.[51] The following year an Italian translation appeared. All things considered, it was as much a triumph for Ibsen the playwright as for Ibsen the businessman. His departure from Norway in 1864 had marked the start of his search for a position of artistic freedom untrammelled by the constraints of external obligations. The publication of *Hedda Gabler* marked the culmination of this process. With it, he gave proof of his status as an independent and free writer who governed the conditions of his activity himself, both in regard to *what* he wrote, and in *how* he ran his literary business. In all of this he became a model for other writers, a pioneer in the creation of the modern literary world. The fruit of success was – freedom.

It must have been particularly satisfying to observe that the more provocative and difficult his plays became, the more successful they were. The process is demonstrated by the reception accorded *Hedda Gabler*, both as book and as play. In its allusive and economical form, the play was as much of a challenge to directors as it was to critics. Hedda herself provided actresses with an even more daunting challenge than Ellida Wangel; over the years, Hedda has been portrayed as everything from existentially weary to an out-and-out psychopath, and, as was the case with Ellida, there are many who believe that Eleanora Duse was the first to bring the role to life. At the premiere at the Residenz Theater in Munich on 31 January 1891, at which Ibsen himself was present, the play was received with both boos and cheers. As much as a reaction to the play, the ferocity of these responses reflected the loyalties of the different parties in the ongoing German cultural wars.[52] Ibsen was the spark that ignited the audience's passions. The play was no less controversial at the Lessingtheater in Berlin, and in Copenhagen the curtain had to be brought down and the whistles of the audience silenced by the gong.

In April he was invited to Vienna, where he had not been since attending the World's Exhibition in 1873. As ever he loved being the centre of attention, though there was always a price to pay: 'Constantly besieged by journalists and other visitors,' he complains in a letter home to Suzannah.

In Vienna he attended a successful production of *The Pretenders*, followed by a banquet at the Hotel Kaiserhof at which his youthful supporters hailed him with poems and speeches. While Ibsen was still in the city a local version of a Freie Bühne, a free theatre, opened. The same thing had happened in Munich. Ibsen was an automatic choice for honorary membership, as he was for membership of a society devoted to the furtherance of the cause of higher education for women. And still the trip had not reached its climax. Before leaving for Vienna he had met the Hungarian translator Bela Lázár and told him of his poem 'To Hungary', written in his youth to honour the Magyars' struggle for freedom. Learning that Ibsen was to visit Vienna, Lázár hurriedly invited him to extend his trip to Budapest. Ibsen accepted – and did not regret it. On 19 April he left Austria to attend the Hungarian National Theatre's production of *A Doll's House* the following day.[53] His presence was greeted with the proverbial storm of applause. He was repeatedly called to take a bow, until finally he was carried through the theatre by a group of young men, the tears pouring down his cheeks. 'His old, hard face seemed transfigured,' *Morgenbladet*'s reporter wrote in his account of the evening. He gave a moving speech of thanks at the banquet that followed, and reminded the guests once again of his old poem in support of Hungary.

Thus did a political gesture from his early days provide an unexpected bonus for the ageing writer who had left politics behind long ago. He was greeted as a king, this man who was supposedly 'the lonely man with no homeland'.

For August Strindberg the irony was intolerable:

'And Ibsen! The "Great Solitary" has descended to the level of a touring diva!' he growled contemptuously on reading of how Ibsen was feted in Austria and Hungary. 'The prophet as coquette! Flaunting his so-called loneliness in the middle of the banquet hall! A so-called artistocrat who welcomes the new aristocracy of journeymen and women. For Christ's sake!'

* * *

Indeed, the diva himself was beginning to tire of life on the road. At some point in the spring he decided to make a trip back home to Norway, intending to spend the summer there. He had received a letter from his sister Hedvig, inviting him to Skien for the opening of a new community centre in the town; it is not hard to imagine that several of the town's leading men prevailed upon her to try to get Skien's greatest son to pay a visit to his home town.

Hedvig tells him that the town has celebrated his birthday, something which Henrik might also have read about in the newspapers. His reply is warm and friendly. He writes that nothing would give him more pleasure than to visit Skien once again, though he did not expect to see many of his childhood friends: 'I would have been among complete strangers.' And he was aware that the great fire of 1886 had burnt down his childhood home in Stockmannsgården, as well as the church and the whole of the old town around the square in the centre of Skien: 'All the things that were part of my earliest memories – burned, all of them.'

His parents were dead, as were two of his brothers in America, Johan and Nicolai. When Sigurd was posted to the United States, his father asked him to find out what had happened to Nicolai. Was it Hedvig who nudged him? Or did he have a soft spot for this brother, crippled after a fall in childhood, a man beloved of all with his attractive and sunny disposition? Of his brothers only Ole was still alive, but Henrik can hardly have wanted to meet him again. No, the past could rest in peace as far as he was concerned. Hedvig could probably have guessed that he would not come to Skien, despite all the fine words. But he would be with them in spirit at the opening of the centre: 'And if indeed I do, as I hope, come to Norway – then yes, I would like to see home again – the old one that is now a new one.'

The letter is dated 13 March, and there is nothing to suggest that he has plans for an imminent trip to Norway, unless, that is, he is keeping it secret from his sister to avoid being obliged to visit Skien. A mere two months later, however, at the beginning of May, he reveals to his business agent in Kristiania, Nils Lund, that he and Suzannah have been thinking they might take a trip north. The question is, just *how far* north. On 6 June he tells Didrik Grønvold that he is still not sure whether he wants to travel all the way to Norway, that he might prefer instead a few weeks near the Øresund 'where I can see hundreds of ships sailing in and out'. But the choice finally fell on Norway. Early in July, Henrik and Suzannah left Munich and travelled north. The furniture and paintings were left behind. The plan was to spend the summer at home, and one can only speculate whether Henrik would have made the trip at all at this juncture had he known that he would, in fact, be living in his native land for the rest of his life.

XI

KRISTIANIA

IMAGINE BEING FROZEN

On a visit to Ibsen in Victoria terrasse at some point in the early 1890s, Herman Bang was struck by how unhomely the apartment was. The large, cold rooms seemed almost designed to hold receptions in; Bang felt as though he had entered the offices of a man from the ministry. But then the apposite nature of the association struck him – 'in reality Ibsen did, during these years, run a Ministry – the ministry of his own fame'.

He had made a long journey from the counter of an apothecary in Grimstad to a life in which he shared tables with the crowned heads of Europe. *Hedda Gabler* had extended his fame to the whole of Europe and beyond. These are the circumstances under which Ibsen decided to return home to Norway, among the smallest and most insignificant of European nations. He would spend the remainder of his days in Christiania. Here he would conclude his career as a writer, and husband his growing fame around the world. As usual, Bang's observations were accurate:

> He wanted the best of everything; of his writing as well as of its fruits. Therefore he took as much care in managing his name as he did his fortune. That's it. But he did not sacrifice his humanity . . .

No, he did not sacrifice his humanity, though there were times when it might look as though he had done. During the last years of his life Ibsen would undergo the final metamorphosis, from man into mask. He became his own statue, an icon, a tourist attraction. And yet over the last decade of the century he continued, with striking energy, to produce ground-breaking new work, plays in which he would explore human nature in a way that no celebrity can, only an artist.

* * *

On 16 July 1891, Henrik and Suzannah set foot on Norwegian soil. Sigurd stood waiting for them on the quayside at Kristiania harbour, along with a pack of journalists. The couple checked into the Grand Hotel, and later that same day invited the journalist Peter Rosenkrantz Johansen to join them for coffee on the hotel's glass veranda. They informed him that they would shortly be travelling on to the North Cape – or even the North Pole, why not, joked Henrik:

'Imagine,' he said, 'if one could reach the North Pole, freeze solid and remain there for the rest of one's life.'

A few days later they set off, but not, as they had planned, together. While Henrik took the train to Trondheim, there to board a ship to the North Cape, Suzannah and Sigurd headed for Valdres and the mountains. Mother and son then returned to Kristiania before travelling on to Italy for the winter. Not until early in the new year did they return to Kristiania.

Things were not as they ought to have been between Henrik and Suzannah, but for the time being no one outside the family had any idea of what the problem might be.

Ibsen arrived in Trondheim on 24 July and booked in at the Hotel Britannia. The next day, after dining with his old friend Karl Bomhoff, he continued his journey on board the steamer *Nordland* to Hammerfest and the North Cape. On the night of 31 July he reached the most northerly point of Norway, and there cast a bouquet of roses into the sea. On the outward and homeward-bound journeys he kept himself to himself, perhaps depressed by his marital problems. The mere fact of being home again seemed to depress him too. He told one of the few fellow passengers he spoke to that all the time he was walking in the streets of Kristiania he felt as though someone was following behind him and getting ready to jab a lighted cigar into his back.

By 7 August he was back in the capital, where he once again booked into the Grand Hotel. Georg Brandes was living in Lysaker at the time and decided to host a dinner in honour of Ibsen at the hotel. The plan would turn out to be more hazardous than he could have imagined, although he should probably have known better by this time. There had still been no reception for Ibsen in Kristiania, which would have been almost unthinkable in either Copenhagen or Stockholm. When he arrived for the dinner, he wore an expression of such overwhelming dourness that few dared to engage him in conversation. He had been promised that the gathering would be intimate, but rumours of the occasion spread, and the guest list expanded accordingly. As if that were not enough, the guest of honour had been seated next to the forty-eight-year-old painter Kitty Kielland. Everyone knew that Ibsen preferred the company of young ladies on such occasions, and now he sabotaged all Kielland's brave attempts to engage him in conversation. When she began to tell him how little she liked self-sacrificing women such as Thea Elvstad in *Hedda Gabler* he brusquely interrupted her:

> I write to describe human beings, and it is a matter of complete indifference to me what the fanatics of the women's movement do and do not like!

To lighten the atmosphere the decision was taken to serve champagne with the fish and get onto the speeches straightaway. But Brandes had on several previous occasions displeased Ibsen with his speeches, and this time was no exception:

> Dear Ibsen, you have, over the years, become so astonishingly celebrated that it is only with great difficulty one can praise you.

At least he made an effort:

> The foreigners have spoilt you. But, am I not correct, it is we in the north who understand you better than the foreigners.

Ibsen sat shaking his great white head throughout Brandes' speech. Brandes noticed, and it made him uncertain, and the more he insisted that Ibsen's writings were better understood in the north, the more demonstratively did Ibsen shake his head. With the speech over and a toast drunk to the guest of honour, he half-rose from his seat and remarked that there were a number of things one could say about *that* particular speech, but that this was neither the time nor the place. Later that evening someone told him that Brandes was applying for the chair left vacant by the death of the university's professor of literature, Olaf Skavlan.

'Well,' said Ibsen, 'in that case he better stay away from Norwegian literature, because he has no understanding of it at all.' But later on, it seems, his mood improved, and lightened even more so once he had Erik Wereneskiold's wife and her sister on his arms.

His humour had not improved much by the autumn when he was invited to a buffet dinner by the country's newly appointed prime minister, Johannes Steen. 'So, the animals are to be paraded!' was his comment. Bjørnson was another guest, and it was impossible not to notice how Bjørnson stood at the centre of a large and attentive group of people, while Ibsen stood holding his plate by the stove in a corner, his back turned. He took rather more pleasure in the gala performance given in his honour at the Christiania Theatre on 14 September. Suzannah was by this time back from Valdres and spending a few days in the capital before travelling south with Sigurd. The play chosen was *The League of Youth*, which received its hundredth performance that night; that this particular play, which had in its time created a rift between the playwright and his native land, was chosen to celebrate Ibsen was, in itself, a gesture of reconciliation. Following the performance they were cheered by a large crowd and then driven on to the Tivoli, where they enjoyed a splendid dinner in the company of the actors and actresses, the directors and the management. Hans Schrøder, the manager, gave a speech in which he praised the writer in conventionally extravagant terms. In his reply, Ibsen used the occasion to say that it was about time the country acquired a new theatre. This was a subject much debated at the time, and his suggestion that the foundation stone should be laid on 18 October that same year – the date of the first performance of *The League of Youth* at the Christiania Theatre back in 1869 – was greeted with wild enthusiasm.

Thus did he garner support for the idea that the future of the theatre in Norway should be built on his own writing, just as the foundation stone of the country's new theatre would be the foundation stone of his own monument.

HILDUR AND HAMSUN

Ibsen was a prophet in his own land, but there were dissenters. The country remained split in its attitudes to the old and the new literature, with the right and left still in opposition. On the personal level, Ibsen and Lorentz Dietrichson managed a reconciliation, no easy matter after the disagreements that had come between them six years earlier. With Ludvig Daae, however, his old conservative friend from the days of the Learned Holland, Ibsen was not even on speaking terms. Rumour had it that Daae was deeply offended at the suggestion that Ibsen had used him as a model for Rector Kroll. In any event, Ibsen had no plans to get involved in Norwegian politics:

> Since my return I find myself in the happy position of knowing that I enjoy the support of both the right and the left.

He was in Norway to write. Others could get on with whatever they wanted to.

Yet there was one group that entertained a natural ambivalence towards his status as a writer, and that was his younger colleagues. Ibsen was old, celebrated, and wore medals on his chest, for which he deserved to be knocked down from his pedestal. But at the same time he was still producing potent dramas that undeniably captured the *Zeitgeist* and were still regarded as avant-garde. So what did they do? Nothing, until Knut Hamsun began a lecture tour of Norwegian cities and towns in which he dismissed the whole generation of older writers, and in particular Ibsen.[1] Hamsun had had his breakthrough in 1890 with *Hunger*, regarded as one of the earliest modernist novels. The express purpose of his lecture tour, which started in Bergen the following January, was to clear a space for himself and his generation. What is striking, however, is the way in which Hamsun's disrespectful assaults on the great poet-sphinx were received:

'It is quite simply a joy,' wrote *Bergens Tidende*, 'to get the feeling that a stormy opposition is brewing, a storm that can shake things up in our rather rusty old literary world.'

Similar sentiments could be encountered in all the Norwegian towns that Hamsun visited. Ibsen was rusty, he needed shaking up. Some journalists felt that he was perhaps being a little hard on the great writers, but in the main the journalistic response was one of sensational curiosity and a vindictive pleasure at Hamsun's insolence. He was an excellent speaker and aroused the same sort of wicked delight as a Confirmand who swears in church. The question was, would he dare to swear as loudly in the presence of the priest himself? It was the turn of Kristiania in the autumn. Hamsun was to appear at the premises of the Hals brothers' piano factory in Stortingsgaten on 7, 9 and 12 October. According to one source he had been cocky enough to send a personal invitation to Ibsen who, having read the newspaper reports, was well aware of what to expect should he accept.

The venue was packed. No one wanted to miss this; Johannes Steen was present, as were Fridtjof Nansen, Edvard Grieg and other well-known names. On the evening of the first lecture Ibsen arrived too, but not alone. During the autumn he had made the acquaintance of a twenty-seven-year-old pianist named Hildur Andersen, the granddaughter of Helene Sontum, his landlady during the years in Bergen. In fact, his association with the family had lasted many years. Helene's son-in-law and Hildur's father, Oluf Martin Andersen, was Sigurd's godfather, and another of Helene's grandchildren, Christian Sontum, was Ibsen's doctor from the time of his return to Norway until Sontum's death in 1902. Hildur had been educated in Dresden and Leipzig, and was living in Vienna at the same time as Sigurd was there. According to Bergliot there was a budding romance between the two that was broken off by Sigurd. Instead Hildur became his father's regular companion in Kristiania, and of all his young princesses was the only one who left a lasting trace after her, to Henrik's delight and the despair of Sigurd and Suzannah.

Perhaps it was as well that it was Hildur sitting beside Ibsen in the front row that October evening in 1891; there's no knowing how Suzannah might have reacted to the tirades that came flooding from the podium. Hamsun's criticism of Ibsen was related both to his choice of genre – the drama – and to his failings as a writer. In Hamsun's view, drama was poorly suited to convey deep psychological insights because the form required simplification and visible realisation in order to be understood. Indeed, according to Hamsun, 'the dramatist has not been born who is also a good psychologist'. Ibsen contented himself with an 'arid and over-simplified character psychology' and was not a talented thinker. In his efforts to be profound he succeeded only in being diffuse and woolly.

Ibsen's perfectionism in general was a source of irritation to him, as were his carefully composed dialogue and his character psychology – 'characters' were exactly what he himself was trying to get away from. A look at Hamsun's novels makes his position easier to understand. It is not easy to imagine the irrational, impulsive and split narrator of *Hunger* (who, significantly enough, does not even have a name) as a character in one of Ibsen's plays. Ibsen is about finding one's self, Hamsun about whether a 'self' even exists. Hamsun's need to commit this act of literary patricide is understandable, as is the fact that he reserved his most severe criticism for Ibsen precisely because Ibsen had taken out a 'patent' on psychological drama that made it difficult for Hamsun to get an audience for his own kind of writing.

Throughout the lecture Ibsen stared expressionlessly up at the lecturer. He is said to have observed to Ola Thommessen afterwards that 'if this were a civilised land then the students would have beaten that chap's brains out tonight', but apart from that he seems to have tolerated Hamsun's act of lèse-majesté well enough. After the second lecture a member of the audience observed that Ibsen even appeared to be enjoying himself. Earlier in the day he had said to Hildur:

'You haven't forgotten that we are attending Herr Hamsun's second lecture this evening?'

'Do you mean to say you want to hear that shameless man again?' was Hildur's surprised response.

'Surely you understand that we have to go and learn how to write!'

What passed through Ibsen's head during those evenings, and what was Hamsun thinking? The latter seems to have been delighted with the results. In his next novel *Mysteries* (1892) he puts a number of attacks on Ibsen into the mouth of his main character, Johan Nagel. And the following year he gave a revised version of the lecture at the Students' Union in Copenhagen in which he removed the discussion of Bjørnson, Kielland and Lie and instead developed his attack on Ibsen:

> For the last twenty years Ibsen has managed to persuade people of the depth and profundity of his thought. What an achievement! Now people study him more seriously than they study the bible. They find hidden significance in his least word, they study his punctuation, his underlinings, they ponder the meaning of the starched collar Solness wears. And every last word of it is most enchantingly impenetrable.

For Ibsen, Hamsun must have been a reminder of life's merciless inexorability. He was, after all, the man who wrote for the future, the guiding star in the firmament for Germany's young intellectuals. And along comes Hamsun and wants to put him in a museum! On the other hand, Ibsen was well aware that his position as a writer was unassailable, and he appreciated a worthy and articulate opponent, as he showed in his response to Strindberg. He must have known, moreover, that the success of Hamsun's lectures had no real effect on the profound respect he enjoyed among young Norwegian writers, many of whom were in the habit of sending him a copy of their most recent book.

He was well able to survive Hamsun, but it must have been disturbing to note that very few newspapers voiced any particular criticism of the content of Hamsun's lectures. He had reached the top alright, but that did not make him inviolable.

* * *

The young were the threat, as the young were also the hope. In Suzannah's absence, Henrik and Hildur openly enjoyed each other's company throughout the autumn, whether out promenading or attending concerts, exhibitions or the theatre together. Just how close they became at this time is shown by a cabinet photo of himself which he signed: 'Viele Grüsse von Hildur und Henrik Ibsen 20.10.91.' Greetings from Henrik and Hildur! It was in the midst of these flirtatious and irresponsible autumn days that he resolved to rent an apartment in Kristiania – without consulting Suzannah. She had by this time already left the country in a state of some distress. For the time being the plan is to spend the winter in Kristiania, he writes to Jacob Hegel in September, but there are signs that he had already decided to make the capital his home base:

> Naturally we don't intend to live here all year round but to travel, as we have done previously.

Victoria terrasse, completed the year before in upper Vika, was one of the city's most fashionable apartment complexes. Intended to give the city a European and cosmopolitan air, it occupied an entire block. The apartments were large and luxurious, and boasted such modern amenities as baths. From here Ibsen could look down on the poor quarter of the town where he had lived when he first arrived in the capital in 1850. On 21 October he moved into his new quarters at Victoria terrasse 7b. Princess Hildur helped him to furnish the apartment.

He had not been living there long before another of his princesses – the first – came knocking at his door. She had sent him a letter in advance, so he was not entirely taken by surprise. The woman had long held a grudge against him, but had been an admirer for even longer. Now she sought a reconciliation with her old teacher, the man who had once called her his 'little lark'. Laura Kieler had never quite managed to escape the rumours surrounding her name after *A Doll's House*. The previous year she had published *Men of Honour*, a play that was regarded as a personal attack on Georg Brandes. The play was rejected by the Kongelige Teater, but accepted at Casino in a production that was slaughtered by reviewers. The newspapers used the occasion to remind readers of Kieler's earlier marital trials, and indeed, even before that, Brandes had spoken publicly and disparagingly of her troubles.

It was following this that Kieler wrote to her friend Fredrika Limnell and asked her to persuade Ibsen to deny that she had forged documents, to publically announce that *she was not Nora*. Fru Limnell wrote a letter on 10 June 1890, enclosing a number of documents that illuminated Laura's case. On the first day of the following month Ibsen replied:

> Any statement from me to the effect that she is *not* Nora would be both meaningless and ridiculous since I have never made any claim to the opposite effect.

Why did she and her husband not simply deny the rumours themselves, he asked. In any case, there was little he could do. Laura's personal tragedy had become public knowledge, so what good would it do to be acquitted as Nora as long as she remained Laura Kieler? But now here she stood on the pavement outside Victoria terrasse and wanted to come in. Their conversation lasted four long hours. She took him back in time, to their first meetings in Copenhagen and Dresden. She described her life to him, her marriage to Victor, the pain Nora had caused her – and the rumours, those indelible rumours. By her own account, much of what she told Ibsen was new to him, until finally he was so moved that he burst into tears:

> Ah Laura, Laura, I feel as though I can't let you go, but you must not return tomorrow. No no, that's impossible. I can't. It's not possible!

He understood her pain. But to act personally and on his own initiative liberate her from the curse of the doll's house, or at the very least do what he could to restore her honour, that was something he would not, could not, do.

It was impossible.

THE LOSS OF A SON

In January 1892 Suzannah and Sigurd finally returned from Italy. The marital reunion can hardly have been a warm one. What was it that had come between Suzannah and Henrik? When had the marriage begun to fail?

The atmosphere in the Ibsen family had always been characterised by a polite silence punctuated by furious quarrelling, though this did not necessarily indicate that the relationship between them was bad. On the contrary, Suzannah's lack of subservience may well have indicated an equality in the marriage with which both were comfortable and yet which might well have confused outsiders.

Undoubtedly she had to put up with a great deal from him, not least when he was drunk, and as a result of his popularity with the opposite sex. On a number of occasions, 'hysterical and deluded' women forced themselves upon him, threatening the stability of family life, obsessed by a desire to call themselves Ibsen's intimate and hoping to become his next model.

These female admirers were probably as unwelcome to him as they were to her, but the moment he returned their admiration Suzannah's patience ran out.

Suzannah had a very clear idea of the role she played in her husband's career: he created the writing, and she created the writer. Her obligations ranged from being an intellectually stimulating companion to putting him to bed when he was too befuddled by drink to do it himself. Whatever ambitions she may have had in life she realised through him. Suzannah undoubtedly put up with a lot, and in return she demanded respect. Quite why *he* stopped showing her this respect and became involved with his young princesses probably requires less explanation. He was a man, he was famous, and he was getting old. They were young, pretty and obliging. The more pathetic her husband's pursuit of princesses became, the more indignantly did she respond, on behalf of them both. His life's work was her life's work, and his dignity was her dignity.

That was how Magdalene Thoresen saw the situation too:

You have been more important to your husband than he probably realises himself, and the world that places its tributes at his feet probably owes you as much as it owes him. Without you he may well have gone to the dogs – one can never know for sure – but with you it was impossible.

In the summer of 1891 there was also a second and very concrete source of conflict between the couple. Suzannah simply could not tolerate the climate in Norway. Whereas before she was always the one who wanted to return home to Norway, now it was the other way round. She must have shuddered as she recalled her previous stay in the country six years previously; on their return to Munich her rheumatism was so painful she could hardly walk. On their return to Norway this time, Henrik must have hinted that he was interested in staying for some considerable length of time, at least over the winter, so that he could finish his new play. Suzannah must have responded angrily, for their parting was not on good terms. The fact that he had rented an apartment without even consulting her can hardly have improved matters. The rooms in Victoria terrasse were cold and damp and only made Suzannah's rheumatism worse. She may have met Hildur Andersen during her stay in Kristiania in September, and it cannot have improved her mood when she returned in the new year to find herself not merely a prisoner in a home she never wanted, but that the home had been furnished by one of her husband's princesses! It must have been a great relief to her when Hildur returned to Vienna in February to resume her music studies, even if Henrik and Hildur continued to stay in touch by letter.

Her stepmother tried to comfort Suzannah, saying she could not believe that Henrik really wanted to return to Norway for good:

> Trust me, he will soon enough feel the need for a different spiritual atmosphere.

But, like Brand, Ibsen was immovable. Just as the uncompromising priest had sacrificed the health of his son to follow his calling in a village with a hostile climate, so now Henrik sacrificed Suzannah's health and contentment in order to spend his final years in Christiania. Each spasm of pain that wracked her rheumatic body must have made her think of him. He, for his part, could add the final verse to that poem in which he had most clearly expressed his dream of returning home one day. When the players at the Christiania Theatre asked him to autograph a collection of his own books for an auction to raise money for a new theatre, he added a verse to the poem 'Burnt Boats':

> For huts of the Norsemen
> from scrub bathed in light
> there rides forth a horseman
> unfailing, each night –
>
> Recently he dismounted,
> found open every door –
> could not that wandering guest
> have returned before?

The poem was quickly picked up by the newspapers, and it is easy to suppose that many Norwegians were charmed by the writer's conciliatory tone. One who was not was Suzannah Ibsen. Quite *why* it was so important for him to remain in Norway, especially bearing in mind the price his wife paid, is difficult to understand. But he entertained always, of course, the thought of a return. That it happened now might, in the first instance, have been because of his age; if he was ever going to move back home, now was the time. Secondly, the fact of his international breakthrough may have proved decisive. It had become difficult to find peace and quiet in Germany. There were endless invitations and premieres, and as the hero of the young naturalists he found himself at the very centre of the German culture wars. It was hardly a position in which he was comfortable. He had left Norway in search of independence, but now found himself requisitioned for the social struggle in Germany too. In Norway, on the other hand, he had finally won for himself that freedom and independence he had so desperately missed when he left the country in 1864. His position now was somewhere 'above and beyond parties'; he was financially independent, enjoyed complete artistic freedom and the general respect of all. Wherever he went he paid the price of fame, but now it was Norway that offered him the optimum freedom as a writer he had always looked for.

That this also involved Suzannah remaining away in southern Europe for months on end, as she henceforth did, was something he could live with. It left him in peace to live the life of a disciplined bachelor, alone, or with Hildur Andersen.

* * *

As Henrik and Suzannah's love life slowly withered, Sigurd's started to bloom. After settling in Kristiania, he had spent much time in Bjørnson's company. A month before his parents arrived he paid his first visit to Aulestad, where he promptly fell in love with Bjørnson's daughter Bergliot, who had just returned from her singing studies in Paris. The love was reciprocated, and soon the two were a couple. On a visit to the Bjørnson family in Schwaz, Henrik had apparently once predicted that something like this would happen, but now that it came to pass he was anything but pleased.

Marriage to one of Bjørnson's offspring was not part of his plan for Sigurd's future – and certainly not for his own!

Nor was Suzannah especially thrilled. Meeting Karoline one day she did not say a single word about the engagement, and when Karoline mentioned the rumours that Ibsen was about to settle in Norway she responded sharply:

'No, he belongs to the world, he will not be staying here in this little country.'

Back came the equally sharp reply:

'God, how self-important you are, Suzannah. Just the way you always were.'

Suzannah received step-motherly advice from Copenhagen to the effect that she must put her son's happiness before her own displeasure. Moreover, Magdalene added conspiratorially, she should not forget that Bergliot's Bjørnsonian nature could be tamed: 'I think there is something about her – something untouched, that Sigurd will be able to mould to his own will.' The anxieties were not unfounded; the Ibsen and Bjørnson families were as unalike as could be. Bjørnson realises that the two families will have to work this out, and in the beginning of September he invites himself to Victoria terrasse – without Karoline, but with the newspaper editor Ola Thommessen as support. Thommessen later related that Bjørnson was visibly nervous, Ibsen cordiality itself. Presently the tensions dissolved in nervous humour and good-natured irony. It did not mean, however, that anything had changed between the two of them.

As the day of the wedding approached, Suzannah realised that she must do the right thing and support her son in his choice. Henrik, on the other hand, absented himself from the ceremony on the dubious grounds that he was feeling unwell. In Ibsen's defence, things weren't easy for him at the time. Suzannah was angry with him, and his son had fallen in love with the daughter of his greatest rival. The close relations between Sigurd and Bjørnson also distressed him – '*you* of course will immediately gain Sigurd's confidence', he complains to Bjørnson in January 1892, 'something I have never had and never will have.'

This was hardly how he had imagined his homecoming. But things weren't all that easy for the young ones either. Bergliot didn't just have to struggle to win over her prospective father- and mother-in-law; she was also fully aware of how close Sigurd was to them. Scarcely a month after they met each other at Aulestad in the summer of 1891 he disappeared again with his mother, and stayed away for most of the remainder of the year. With mother and son in Italy, Bergliot feared that Suzannah would do everything in her power to persuade Sigurd to stay with her. In November both fiancée and father wrote urging Sigurd to return, but were told that Suzannah wished to stay on a while longer. Sigurd, poor man, had to choose between a jealous sweetheart and a sick and demanding mother. If Sigurd is to be believed, it was only for his and Bergliot's sake that Suzannah agreed to return to Norway in the dead of the winter; she would greatly have preferred to wait until the bitter Norwegian cold had passed. But Bergliot was not pacified, especially when Sigurd, after his return in January 1892, wrote that he was still not able to visit her at Aulestad; this time it was his father who couldn't do without his company.

If she hadn't done so before, Bergliot would have realised it by now: one didn't get engaged to Sigurd Ibsen, one got engaged to the Ibsen family.

The wedding took place at Aulestad, with Bjørnson, Karoline, Suzannah and Johan Hermann present. Bergliot's parents had refused to attend if the ceremony were to be held in a church, a crisis solved when the couple agreed to get married in Bjørnson's own study. Exactly nine months after the wedding Tancred Ibsen was born, the first citizen of the world in a direct line of descent from Norway's two greatest writers. The little family settled at Øvre Toft, close to Aulestad, remaining there for a year before moving to Kristiania. Henrik was friendly if formal towards Bergliot. With time the relationship grew warmer. As early as May he had written, in conciliatory terms, a note in which he advised her: 'Just go on being yourself, just the way you are now. I can't think of a better wish for you.' Wise words, for with all the travelling Suzannah and Sigurd would do over the coming years, Henrik and Bergliot would end up spending more time together than they could ever have imagined.

Were they happy, Sigurd and Bergliot? She had, at least, the capacity for happiness. Typical of her was her rejection of Sigurd's suggestion that he buy her an engagement ring – she told him she would rather he gave her an accordion. They sat out in the fields at Aulestad, Bergliot playing for him, and Sigurd lying on his back in the grass, laughing until the tears ran down his cheeks. The warmth and vitality she brought into Sigurd's life were something he sorely needed, for his taciturn and cold ways could drive her to distraction. By Bergliot's own account, against all odds, they did indeed find happiness. The price she paid was the suppression of her own spontaneity, and an acceptance of the fact that she would never really be allowed entry into the circle that enclosed the three of them.

THE TOWER

For the whole of the summer of 1892 Ibsen had paced the Victoria terrasse apartment in a grim silence. Family matters soured his humour, Hildur was abroad, and work on his new play was not going smoothly. He wrote drafts and rejected them; not until 9 August did he finally manage to get going on what would turn out to be the play's final form. A couple of weeks later he promises to send Hegel the manuscript by the end of September, at the same time reassuring him that the new play does not have 'the slightest thing to do with social and political questions'.

Now he really got going. In a mere six weeks he had all three acts, and by 29 September he was ready to begin the fair copy. The whole manuscript was sent to Copenhagen at the end of October, and six days later Gyldendal published it in a first edition of 10,000 copies. As usual the title was kept secret for as long as possible, but now the time had come to reveal *The Master Builder* to the world. In addition to England, Germany and France the play was soon available in the United States, Russia, Italy, Poland and the Netherlands.

* * *

Halvard Solness is the master builder, a self-made man who is plagued by his conscience; his professional breakthrough came about as a result of building projects that came his way after the fire that burnt his wife Aline's childhood home to the ground. A further burden on his conscience is the loss of their twins, who died shortly after the fire.

Although Solness is well into middle age, he has no thoughts of retirement. Fearing the competition of younger men he does all he can to keep his young assistant Ragnar Brovik down. Another of Solness's employees is his own former master, who is also Ragnar's father, a man now sick, and bitter because of the obstacles Solness puts in his son's way. So great is the master builder's cynicism that he even tries to marry Ragnar off to his third employee, Kaja Fosli, to prevent him from starting up in business on his own. Solness has a peculiar power over Kaja which does not solely derive from the fact that she is in love with him. He reveals to Dr Herdal, his physician, that he possesses a suggestive power that enables him to make others do his will; he even admits that he once wished his wife's childhood home would burn down, and that was exactly what happened. It leaves Solness a haunted man, and he reveals to the doctor that there are times when he fears for his own sanity.

A turning point in the play comes with the appearance of the young and vivacious Hilde Wangel, who has been out hiking in the mountains. She too represents youth, though in a different way from Ragnar. Solness has forgotten her, but Hilde reminds him that they met when she was a child and he dedicated a church steeple in her home town. He kissed her back then, she claims, and promised to come back for her in ten years time and give her a kingdom.

Now ten years have passed, and Hilde has come to claim her kingdom.

Hilde Wangel is a strong, free woman with whom Solness at once feels a kinship. And just as he has power over her, she has power over him. Now she encourages him to climb the steeple of the house he has just built for himself and Aline. Solness suffers from a fear of heights, but in the days when Hilde was a child he had managed 'the impossible'. Now she challenges him to do it again. He climbs up, and as he reaches the top she waves at him triumphantly with her white shawl. The next moment he falls to his death.

Many were interested to see whether Ibsen's return home would be reflected in his writing. The reviewer in *Dannebrog* could see no sign of it and asserted that Ibsen had, once again, written a European drama. And that is true enough, though it is equally valid to point out that the play reflects a continental development in Norway and Kristiania. Between 1875 and the turn of the century the population of the capital rose from 100,000 to 250,000. Ships arrived here from all over Europe, here were hotels and restaurants with international reputations such as the Grand Café with international reputations. Around 1880 telephone wires and electric cables were strung between poles and houses, and soon the streets were lit by the first electric arc lamps. At the end of the 1880s a period of economic stagnation gave way to a wave of prosperity that saw a building boom in Kristiania. Housing for workers shot up in the east, fashionable apartment blocks in the west of the city. Victoria terrasse was the prime example of a luxurious and distinctly continental residential area, while the businesses and shops with their plate-glass windows and the wide range of goods for sale demonstrated the presence of a modern, capitalist and industrialised economy. With these changes came social mobility and the chance to get rich quick, as well as the risk of social ignominy, crises and bankruptcies. Few businesses illustrate this better than the profitable but high-risk world of the builder. When Ibsen, after returning home, chose to write a play on the subject of a master builder's rise and fall, he was in the highest degree reflecting contemporary Norwegian – and European – reality.

* * *

The Master Builder can be read as a psychological account of the fall of an ageing man of power, or perhaps as a critical study of a cynical capitalist contractor with one foot in the old order and one in the new. But the most common interpretation sees the story of the master builder's ambitions and his fall as an allegory of the writer's relationship to art and life. Not surprisingly, a great many people have read the play as a *biographical* allegory, as Ibsen's reckoning with himself:

'He is himself the master builder,' wrote Kristofer Randers in *Aftenposten*, 'The buildings are his plays.'

The axis of this biographical-allegorical interpretation lies in the parallel linking the master builder's three phases as a builder of churches, homes for the people and castles in the air to Ibsen's national-romantic, realistic and symbolic dramas. It has also been suggested that the threat from the young, in the person of Ragnar Brovik, might be a reference to Knut Hamsun, with the alluring young Hilde Wangel as a version of Emilie Bardach, Helene Raff and Hildur Andersen. The one who suffers most in this jigsaw puzzle is, of course, Suzannah, since the marriage of Halvard and Aline was, naturally enough, related to the dramatist's own marriage.

Clearly this kind of one-to-one relation of the work to the life can easily tip over into banality. And yet the biographical thread in the play is both present and relevant, not least because of the influence it has had on how the play has been received. Contemporary critics did indeed mention the biographical parallels, but it seems almost as though the critics, uncertain as they were when confronted by an Ibsen play, were afraid of being lured into an authorial trap. They see the parallels between Solness and Ibsen, but are wary of making too much out of them. Only later did the biographical reading come into prominence, largely due to the influence of a handful of Norwegian literary historians who, in the first half of the twentieth century, created what might be termed a received understanding of Norwegian literature of the nineteenth century.

Typically, Edvard Brandes outlined the theme of the play without drawing attention at all to the biographical parallels:

This is not a play about old age, or about genius, as has been claimed. No, *The Master Builder* is about those men who, though no longer young, have not yet given in to the resignation of old age – who dare not hope, and yet will not renounce hope.

Edvard's conclusion was clear enough: 'This is a masterpiece.' And his brother was of a similar opinion:

There has never been a more impressive demonstration of technical prowess, never before has there been dialogue like this.

Georg Brandes too thought that the main theme of the play was the unease of an old man facing dethronement by someone from the coming generation, but noted specifically that this was an allegory of 'the tragedy of the ageing artist'. He also noted something that others would remark upon: Ibsen had largely raised himself above the struggle between the young symbolists and the older generation of naturalist writers: 'For over a dozen years now his work has demonstrated an easy harmonisation of naturalism and symbolism.' The observation may well have been occasioned by Brandes' wish to make his peace with Ibsen (as perhaps also with the symbolists). And yet his point is a valid one: Ibsen certainly challenged the conventions of the realistic bourgeois drama, but he never abandoned them completely, as Strindberg would do after his *Inferno* crisis. Just like Solness, Ibsen had one foot in the present and one in the past.

Although it had many admirers, there were others who were bewildered by this plotless play with its 'spiritual pathology', and found it either meaningless, immoral, or both. Reactions to Hilde Wangel provided a straightforward test of where the individual critics stood: for the negatively inclined she was as despicable as she was refreshing for the play's admirers.

With hindsight it is as easy to understand the admiration for the play as it is the confusion it engendered. *The Master Builder* really is a peculiar play. It begins in a way familiar enough from Ibsen's previous work, but things take an unexpected turn with the arrival of Hilde Wangel a little over halfway through the first act. All the other characters apart from her and Solness are relegated to the background as the external action dissolves, to be replaced by long, densely symbolic dialogue. Even though things remain realistic on the outer plane, the drama acquires an ever stronger allegorical, even unrealistic character. But if the play breaks new ground, it still finds its place neatly in the overall scheme of Ibsen's writing. In this as in the following plays, Ibsen returns to the theme, familiar from his earlier works, most notably *Brand*, of a man with a call. It marks a resurrection for the male protagonist, following the female heroines Ibsen had placed in the foreground in so many earlier plays. Now it was the man's turn to dominate as an interesting, conflicted and complex personality.

With regard to the Brandes' brothers observations on the subject of the conflict between the old and the young it is worth noting that Ibsen was not the only one to be preoccupied by the cult of youth. A fascination with the strength and beauty of the young was typical of the time. When Hilde Wangel makes her entry wearing hiking clothes with the skirt tucked up, the knapsack, the staff and her sunburnt face, she represents the same ideal of youthful athleticism as the explorer Fridtjof Nansen. Her self-assurance and easy eroticism were very different from the buttoned-up and inhibited correctness that characterised the preceding generation, Ibsen's own. Not surprisingly she has been credited with a certain Nietzschean vitalism. But Hilde does not just represent youth, she also stands for sensuality and the pleasure of the moment. The obsession with the conquest of the steeple, which she shares with Solness, is drenched in eroticism, power and death – it would be hard to find a more apt phallic symbol than a steeple. So her meeting with the master builder in her youth can be seen as a sexual awakening followed by an erotic obsession, while his vertigo involves the fascination for and fear of sex (impotence), and power (destruction).

If we relate this erotic fear to uncertainty about the new, capitalist society, the play becomes a mirror reflecting Norwegian and European society as the nineteenth century draws to a close. Indeed, the approach of the end of the century was in itself a source of anxiety.[2]

Halvard Solness is fundamentally split; though he belongs to a bygone age, all his life has been devoted to creating something new. Aline, on the other hand, is irrevocably a part of the old, moribund society. In losing her childhood home and all the things she grew up with, not least her beloved collection of dolls, she also lost the foundation upon which her life was based. She is an old-fashioned, average and conventional person. Her life is, one might say, horizontal, in contrast to that of Solness and Hilde, who see life as a struggle along a vertical axis in which there are two options – up onto the heights, or down into the depths. Solness describes his wife as someone who died a long time ago, while Hilde says that visiting her was like going down into a burial chamber. But Solness is wrong when he supposes that his wife is grieving for the dead children whom it would have been her life's work to raise. Aline is no educator, she has no mission to renew; it is the dolls she misses, and through them a life in which she once felt at home.[3] Again the links to earlier plays are clear: Aline is like Beata in *Rosmersholm*, or like a Nora who never left the doll's house. Hilde, on the other hand, is like Rebecca West, Ellida Wangel, Nora – those who reject their obligations and impatiently seek renewal. Unlike them, however, she has a male partner who is not bemused by her longings, and indeed, who shares them.

From start to finish this play is, in one sense, a 'social drama', but done in such an allegorical and symbolic way that it could not be taken as a contribution to the social debate. It is also quite possible to regard it as a purely psychological and existential drama that moves far beyond its contemporary context, and this is probably the form in which the play has survived. Seen in this light it can be read as a drama of revelation, in which Solness is unmasked as a self-deceiver of epic dimensions. In line with this, some have taken the main character's allegorical and self-mystifying language as an attempt to create meaning in a meaningless existence.[4] There is much that might be said about the master builder's grasp of reality; he is clearly wrong to fear competition from Ragnar Brovik, who seems to be a mediocrity; in the final analysis, it is the seductive Hilde Wangel who brings him down. Nor are his intense feelings of guilt easy to understand, for in what way has he really committed crimes against Aline and old Brovik?

Is it not rather all about his own exaggerated self-image, his uncontrollable urge to climb, to conquer, to win, in a world that has no more prizes left for him?

Some will see the master builder's fall from the steeple as the execution of poetic justice, a punishment for his hubris. But it is also possible to see a genuine heroism in the master builder's life struggle.[5] For is he not, indeed, a strong person with a string of major achievements behind him, and is the climbing of the steeple not an expression of his power to transcend himself in an attempt to achieve the impossible? He does, after all, reach the top of the tower, he realises his own and Hilde's vision. What is there left to do after that but fall?

If we disregard the amateur reading in London in December 1892, the play had its premiere at the Lessingtheater in Berlin on 19 January the following year. The head of the theatre was the writer Otto Blumenthal, and it had become an important venue for Ibsen in Germany, despite being overshadowed by Otto Brahm and Freie Bühne. The play opened to a packed house of expectant members of the public and critics, but *The Master Builder* was not particularly successful in Berlin. *Aftenposten*'s correspondent reported that anticipation soon gave way to boredom; in particular the long sequence of dialogue in the second act persuaded many that the play was poorly suited to the stage. The cheers of Ibsen's supporters quickly faded, and when the master builder at last tumbled to his death the audience began to laugh.

The day after the premiere in Berlin, William Petersen's travelling company performed it in Trondheim, and in the course of February it opened in London, Helsinki, Kristiania and Copenhagen. It didn't do particularly well anywhere. In England it caused a split in the Ibsenite camp on account of the symbolism, though both Henry James and William Archer defended it. It meant that Archer was once again able to compile a collection of disparaging remarks from the English press following the performance at the Trafalgar Square Theatre.[6]

* * *

Despite a mixed reception for *The Master Builder*, 1892 turned out to be a good year for Ibsen financially. These were no longer the rarities they once had been. Yet his international breakthrough did not bring immediate financial rewards. Not until 1887 did he start to earn significant sums from countries outside Scandinavia, principally through royalties for performances. In the 1890s his income from these sources made up about 34 per cent of his total royalties and performance fees from Norway, Sweden and Denmark. The proportion varied greatly from year to year, but throughout the 1890s there were only four years in which he earned more from non-Scandinavian sources than from Scandinavian countries. The international breakthrough that came at the end of the 1880s did not mean that Ibsen the businessman could forget about his Scandinavian market, even if he did eventually earn good money from Germany and England.

The Norwegian tax authorities were among those who were glad to see Ibsen's return to settle in Norway. In Munich he had only paid tax on the small amount he earned in Bavaria. In Norway the authorities proposed to tax him on an annual income estimated at 25,000 kroner, and on a fortune of 400,000 kroner. Ibsen protested, and the authorities agreed to reduce their demands by half. In point of fact it was impossible to get any clear view of his financial affairs. His money was often held in the publisher's account in Copenhagen, or it was quickly converted into shares and obligations. Although his income increased considerably over the following years, his tax assessment remained the same.[7]

A FRENCHMAN IN KRISTIANIA

During the summer of 1893 Ibsen had once again met Edvard Grieg, at Grefsen sanatorium, and Georg Brandes had visited Kristiania with his family. Otherwise it seems that Henrik and Suzannah largely stayed at home. They had a grandchild to enjoy now that Sigurd, Bergliot and Tancred had finally moved to the city. Sigurd had no full-time job and was keeping his family on what he earned from writing. In the spring his father had made yet another failed attempt to persuade the Norwegian authorities to secure his son's career, repeating his old threat to abandon his Norwegian citizenship – in spite of the fact that his daughter-in-law had recently given him a very good reason to remain in the country.

The grandparents had their first encounter with the little wonder at the Grand Hotel, Henrik tripping in a circle around little Tancred in Suzannah's lap, bending down each time in sheer delight.

The fact that Hildur Andersen was away travelling for most of the year also contributed to an improved atmosphere at home – as long as Suzannah didn't sneak a look at her husband's correspondence. In one of the few surviving letters to Hildur he writes: 'Oh how I long for my princess! Longing down from the height of my dreams. Longing to walk on the ground again and do what I said – so many times!' He could find no better way to seduce her than to make her a part of his writing, inviting her up his master builder's steeple. To put the matter beyond all doubt, the letter was signed 'Your very own master builder'. He spent the autumn of 1893 yearning for her, now and then walking past the empty windows of her home. He was completely consumed by her. On one occasion he even dedicated his entire life's work to her. She was youth itself and she must never change.

> I want you to be just the way you always were. Do you hear me, Hildur? Do you promise me?

A year later Ibsen found out what the young thought of him, for good and ill. It became obvious how difficult his fame and unique status could make life for younger writers when, on 7 May 1894, he paid a visit to the offices of the Society of Authors that had been formed by Erik Lie and a few other young writers the previous November. Not a born joiner of organisations, Ibsen had nevertheless enrolled. Prior to the meeting, the young decadent writer Gabriel Finne had published an article in *Dagbladet* in which he asked how one could expect support from a society in which 'most of the members will be old, or talentless'. He was particularly critical of Ibsen – 'a man whose entire output is a defence of the aristocracy of the individual'. But Finne too turned up at the meeting, and proceeded to get exceedingly drunk.

Yet it was not he but Nils Kjær who was responsible for the scandal. With the formalities out of the way, and after a great many glasses of punch and hot toddy, Kjær decided he would give a speech in praise of woman. Older writers, he claimed, had never managed to describe the woman, but the new literature was all about her – 'and there', he said in conclusion, gesturing towards Finne slumped drunkenly in his seat, 'there sits the man who is, today, our finest writer about women!' Embarrassing silence. The author of *A Doll's House* sat, remote and majestic, an enigmatic smile playing about his lips, maintaining a silence even when Vilhelm Krag tried to make amends in a speech in praise of him. Jacob Breda Bull leapt to his feet, outraged:

'Shame on you, you curs,' he howled. 'You come here boasting, you who have achieved nothing, who can't do anything and don't want anything. And Henrik Ibsen has to sit there and listen to all this.' He ended by hurling his glass to the floor, where it shattered into pieces. And that was the end of Ibsen and the Norwegian Society of Authors. As he was leaving, he said to Lorentz Dietrichson:

> That is the most unpleasant gathering I have ever attended; I shall never set foot inside these premises again.

He encountered a very different attitude from the group of young French actors who visited Kristiania in October.[8] The French were experiencing a fresh wave of enthusiasm for his plays. André Antoine's productions of *Ghosts* and *The Wild Duck* in 1890 were followed the year after by a less successful production of *Hedda Gabler* at the Théâtre du Vaudeville. Following this the initiative passed to the young director Aurélien Lugné-Poe. In him Ibsen found not only a new champion in France, but also one of the most original – when he was not downright bizarre.

Lugné-Poe had been a student of the naturalist Antoine, but was soon converted to symbolism under the influence of the Belgian symbolist Maurice Maeterlinck. In 1892, at the age of twenty-three, he started the Théâtre des Escholiers, and that same year produced *The Lady from the Sea*. The following year, with his team of young amateurs, he established the Théâtre de l'Oeuvre. The result was one of the strangest experiments in the history of modern theatre. Lugné-Poe opposed the acting styles of naturalism and instead culti-vated an obscure and mannered performance in which the players moved in a dream-like way around a dimly lit stage. They were not to *act* the parts or *declaim* the lines but intone them in a monotonous and hypnotic style as 'mouthpieces' for the text. Scenery and props were reduced to a minimum, the back cloth painted by symbolist painters in an 'allusive' way. From a contempo-rary perspective one could hardly imagine a less Ibsen-like performance, not least when weighed against the dramatist's own, clearly expressed stage direc-tions. But Ibsen became a central part of the theatre's repertoire, and during its lifetime (1893–7) there were productions of *Rosmersholm* and *An Enemy of the People* in 1893, *The Master Builder* in 1894, *Little Eyolf* and *Brand* in 1895, *The Pillars of Society* and *Peer Gynt* in 1896, and *Love's Comedy* and *John Gabriel Borkman* the year after. Lugné-Poe abandoned the symbolist style after *Borkman*, and later came to see it as a wrong turning.

It was a rather bedraggled little group of French players that wandered up Karl Johans gate from the railway station on the morning of 3 October 1894. They were young, they were broke, and they had come to seek the master's blessing for their experimental reworkings of his plays. They were due to play *Rosmersholm* at the Karl Johan Theatre in the Tivoli, the following day Maeterlinck's *Pelléas and Mélisande*, and the day after that *The Master Builder*. Ibsen arrived for the first evening at the Karl Johan Theatre and sat stony-faced throughout the entire performance. Things had not gone particularly well. The players were nervous, the language French, and the acting style, to put it mildly, unfamiliar to the Norwegian audience. At eleven o'clock the following morning Lugné-Poe arrived at Victoria terrasse, accompanied by Herman Bang as his interpreter. The Frenchman's first impression was that Ibsen was not particu-larly happy. And yet he also turned up for the performance of *The Master Builder*, and now, it seems, he was moved. Although later he complained that the French had made a little too much of the symbolism in his plays, immediately after the performance he approached Herman Bang and said:

This was the resurrection of my play.[9]

If Lugné-Poe's experimental symbolism was not really to Ibsen's taste, he was not the man to turn on his supporters, and in the case of Lugné-Poe his instincts proved sound. By the middle of the decade Ibsen was making ever greater inroads into French theatrical life. Besides Lugné-Poe's repertoire there was a successful production of *A Doll's House* at the Théâtre du Vaudeville in April 1894, with Gabrielle Réjane playing Nora. Lugné-Poe's central role in all this, despite his experimental style, demonstrates how open French theatre of the time was, notable especially by contrast with English theatre.[10] France had a tradition of experimental theatre that was absent from the British Isles, where Ibsen had been viewed with considerable distaste by a small but dominant group of critics. In Paris there were numerous small, independent theatres, a wide range of audiences, and an equally varied range of radical periodicals. Nor was there state censorship of the theatre in France, and in general the country had an openness to foreign writing, particularly from Scandinavia and Russia. Where Ibsen in England was regarded as 'provincial' in a negative sense, the opposite was the case in France, as it had been in Germany. Bjørnson and Strindberg both profited from this, each gaining access to French theatres in the wake of Ibsen's success.

If we look at the reception as a whole, we can detect in the French an openness that extended to things that were not understood, something that the English lacked. This is not to say that Ibsen did not encounter resistance in France, but the great difference here was that there was a healthy and vibrant alternative culture, and in this tradition André Antoine and Aurélien Lugné-Poe were the leading exponents of, respectively, the naturalistic and the symbolic theatre. Whereas in England, Ibsen had almost to be 'smuggled' in and adapted to the needs of conventional theatre, in France he was adopted by the alternative theatre movement and exploited for all he was worth.

From all this we can deduce that Ibsen made a stronger and more radical impression in England. The reason for this is not merely that the French were more tolerant, but also that the attention Ibsen attracted in France had as much to do with interpretations and directing styles as with the plays themselves. In England, it was Ibsen's actual *texts and ideas* that created the shock. This is true even in the longer perspective. While his position in England went from strength to strength, his explosive entry on the French scene in the 1890s was followed by a period of diminishing interest. Ibsen never gained quite the same foothold in France as he did in Germany and England, a state of affairs highlighted by the fact that he was not performed at the country's leading venue, the Comédie Française, until the 1921 production of *An Enemy of the People*.[11]

* * *

With the visit of Lugné-Poe and his company to Christiania in the autumn of 1894, Ibsen had proof that he still had the attention of the young, and not only the young naturalists but also the even younger symbolists. That the younger generation of Norwegian writers were more divided in their attitude towards him is perhaps not all that surprising. For them he was no exotic breath of fresh air but instead a dominating and omnipresent father figure whose hirsute authority and provocative youthfulness seemed oppressive. As long as the sphinx still exuded a literary vitality it was hard to knock him off his pedestal; thus far only Hamsun had managed it with a certain class.

What of the unhappy Nils Kjær? Well, he reviewed Ibsen's new play when it appeared at the end of the year – a review fawning with admiration, naturally.

THE LAW OF CHANGE

The summer months that lay between the visit to the Society of Authors and the guest performances by the Théâtre de l'Oeuvre were mostly spent by Ibsen at his writing desk in Victoria terrasse. By the middle of June he was hard at work on the new play he had been thinking about since at least the previous September. Suzannah stayed at home too; even at the warmest time of the year her rheumatism continued to trouble her, and she was planning another trip to Italy in the winter.

In the early stages the writing went well and by 7 August he had a draft of all three acts. The revision proved a little more difficult, however, and the fair copy was not despatched to Copenhagen until 13 October. Sigurd was again entrusted with the German translation, Archer the English, and Prozor the French. Again the publishing machine ran smoothly – or almost smoothly. Before publication there was an episode that demonstrates what an event any new book by Ibsen had become. Almost every stage of the process was followed by the press and the public; even something as prosaic as Gyldendal's sending the manuscript abroad to each of the translators was noted. The secrecy of both title and content, until the day of publication, ideally the same in every country, was in itself a calculated part of the launch. For this reason, Hegel despatched the proofs in batches, as they arrived from the printer, to enable the translators to get on with their work.

A triviality? Not in the least. The American actress Elisabeth Robins described these manuscript batches as 'in small, in very small, violently agitating spurts – or as one might say, in volts, projected across the North Sea in a series of electric shocks'.

In a word, these postal despatches were described as, quite simply, an orgasm. However, while *Little Eyolf* was still at the printer, something happened that was not supposed to happen – information about the content was leaked.

The writer Thomas Krag, brother of Vilhelm, was sent the proofs of two acts of Ibsen's play instead of his own – whether deliberately or in genuine error was never clear. Unaware – or perhaps only too well aware – of what a scoop this was, he gossiped about the contents of the play in such a way that the press got hold of the story. It meant that Ibsen, outraged, naturally, could read about his own new play in the pages of *Politiken* on 14 November. From here the rumours spread like wildfire across Europe. There was speculation about the possible meaning of some of the more enigmatic lines ('The crutch is floating'). In due course Thomas Krag regretted his indiscretion, but the episode did nothing to harm sales of the new play; in fact, the effect was quite to the contrary.

On 11 December *Little Eyolf* was published in Copenhagen, London and Berlin. American and French editions appeared shortly after, and by the close of 1895 the book had also been published in Finland, the Netherlands, Russia and Romania.

The title character, nine-year-old Eyolf Allmers, is, like Hedvig Ekdal, a neglected child. While still an infant he fell from a nursery table while his parents were making love in another room. The accident left the boy partially lame, and now as he limps about with his crutch he nurtures his parents' feelings of guilt by his very presence. The relationship between the couple has always been tense. Rita Allmers has a jealous and possessive nature, and an open sexuality that has caused Alfred to withdraw from her. Following the tragedy he immersed himself in his work on a philosophical treatise on the subject of 'human responsibility', leaving Rita plagued by thoughts of the things that prevent her from having him wholly and completely to herself, whether that be his work, their son, or his half-sister Asta, to whom he is close.

As the play opens, Allmers has returned from a walk in the mountains with the resolution to give up all work on his treatise and devote himself completely to his son. Rita's response is a jealous one; she will not share her husband with anyone, not with his work and certainly not with their son. The turning point in the play comes with the arrival of the Rat Wife. She earns a living by enticing rats to follow her and leading them to drown in the sea, but Allmers and Rita assure her there is nothing 'gnawing away' in their household. Eyolf, on the other hand, is fascinated by the strange lady and follows her down to the sea, where he drowns. His death precipitates a crisis in his parents, already burdened by guilt, and a number of other secrets emerge from the past: Allmers admits his love for the half-sister Asta, while Asta reveals that the two of them are not actually related. She chooses to accept the proposal of a suitor named Borgheim, leaving the Allmers alone with their grief – and yet not entirely without hope.

As bleak as things look, they decide to stay together and to dedicate their lives to helping the town's poor children, hoping in this way to atone for the guilt they feel over Eyolf's death.

* * *

There are signs that Ibsen struggled with this play. A number of important features occurred to him late in the compositional process – Eyolf's disability during the final revision, and, not until the fair copy, the scene of his parents making love as he lay on the nursery table. So the guilt motive related to the child, which is such a crucial part of the finished play, did not emerge until late in the day, and hints at how uncertain the writer felt about the material.

A number of people have viewed this as a weak play. The objections are partly to the apparently obvious nature of the symbolism; to what seems inadequate motivation on the part of the characters; and in particular Allmers and Rita's 'conversion' at the end of the play, where they decide to solve their marital problems by dedicating themselves to philanthropic work. The dramaturgy itself has been criticised. Just as *The Master Builder* takes an unexpected turn with the arrival of Hilde in the first act, so too does the turning point in this play come early, with Eyolf's death at the end of the first act. But by contrast with the earlier play, the turning point does not lead to a heightening of the dramatic tension. Instead the plot slows down and dissolves into a series of long exchanges on the subject of the couple's grief.[12]

Nonetheless the quality of this play is very dependent on the reading one gives it. Here, too, commentators have historically split into ironic and non-ironic traditions. In this case, however, the objections to *both* readings are so strong that it might seem difficult to reach a clear conclusion. The ending has caused the biggest problems. 'Contrary to Ibsen's usual style,' writes Bjørnson, 'the scene comes without any warning – a sure sign that it is a last-minute insertion.' When Rita and Allmers decide to atone for their guilt over their dead son, it is, quite simply, hard to believe them. Has the self-centred and passionate Rita suddenly become an altruist? And can we really believe the irresolute Allmers when he asserts that he will dedicate the rest of his life to philanthropic work? The same doubts that arose concerning Ellida's choice in *The Lady from the Sea* appear again here.

Ibsen himself hinted that we ought not to take the Allmers couple at their word. On one occasion an acquaintance expressed sympathy for Rita and the work she had undertaken in helping the children of the poor. 'Do you really believe her?' replied Ibsen. 'Don't you think it was more a sort of Sunday morning whim?' In other words the doubt was intentional, but the question does not, in itself, invite an ironic reading of the play. For such a reading presents difficulties as well. If the irony is directed at anyone, it must be Allmers, who comes closest to playing the part of the idealist in the play. At the close of the third act he plans the way forward for himself and Rita in a series of idealistic flourishes:

RITA: Which way must we look, Alfred – ?

ALLMERS: (*Fixing her with his gaze*) Upwards.

RITA: (*With an approving nod*) Yes, yes – upwards.

ALLMERS: Upwards, to the heights. To the stars. To the great silence.

RITA: (*Holds out her hand*) Thank you!

This would not have been the first time Ibsen had sabotaged an idealistic project. The problem lies in seeing what purpose irony would serve in this context. What constructive reading does it open up, when the subject of the irony is an indecisive and weak character such as Alfred Allmers? Unlike a Rosmer or a Gregers Werle, Allmers does not seem to represent an attitude towards life or a value system that is worth the trouble of being re-evaluated.

Perhaps, instead, the play should be read as an exploration of the relationship between art and life, the way Christen Collin does by introducing a biographical perspective. Ibsen too had pondered 'human responsibility', writes Collin, reminding readers of how the writer, while 'up on the heights of art and thought', had thought of death as a friend in need, and written about it in *Rosmersholm* and *Hedda Gabler*.

> But now here he comes, announcing that death – death is and always will be monstrously frightening.

So for Collin, the death motive in the play is related to the artist's turning away from life, and he suggests that Ibsen now acknowledges the primacy of life. But does Allmers really deserve to be compared to an artist or a writer? Is he in the same class as Solness, Borkman and Rubek in the other Ibsenian dramas of old age, those who pay the price for a relentless struggle to reach beyond themselves in the pursuit of power? Initially, Ibsen had made Allmers a successful writer, but in the final version he is not much of anything. There is nothing about him to suggest that he deserves a place alongside Ibsen's master builder, his banker and his artist.

Not surprisingly, contemporary critics of the play were also split. What is more surprising is that, generally speaking, the play was well received by critics and audiences alike. The first edition of 10,000 copies sold out within a few days, and a second printing of 2,000 appeared just in time for Christmas. There was a third printing of 1,250 copies in January 1895. Although the play is not usually regarded as particularly well suited to the stage, the first productions were a success. The premiere took place on 12 January at the Deutsches Theater in Berlin, with Otto Brahm directing. The response here was mixed, but *Aftenposten*'s correspondent deemed it a success; the few attempts to set up a chorus of whistling and jeering were soon silenced. And the play was well received at the Kongelige Teater in Copenhagen and in Kristiania. Ibsen attended rehearsals at the Christiania Theatre and was at the premiere, nervous and uncomfortable, even when the applause broke out as the curtain fell.

Kristofer Randers probably spoke for many when he wrote in *Aftenposten*:

Has our elderly writer become young again?

Like others, he had thought of *The Master Builder* as the writer's 'last will and testament', and was expecting him thereafter to retire and leave the stage to the young. Nils Kjær's enthusiastic review was proof that the young still could not get enough of Ibsen, though Kjær suggested that other young writers were disappointed that Ibsen seemed to have abandoned symbolism in favour of a return to the realistic-psychological drama. Not even the openly symbolic presence of the Rat Wife could persuade them otherwise.[13] Still others, such as Carl David af Wirsén, considered the play *far too symbolic*. In the main, contemporary critics were much more preoccupied by the relationship between realism and positivism in the play than by whether it should be read ironically or positively. Few of them questioned the volte-face in the third act, though both Wirsén and Just Bing suspect Rita of using the social project to silence her own bad conscience. But readers of the time were much more disposed to accept such a 'great reconciliation' than subsequent generations of readers, even in a play by Ibsen.

Many critics showed a particular interest in the play's construction. Reviewers of the time were keenly aware of the conventions relating to drama, and were engrossed by the ways in which Ibsen challenged these conventions – as in the early occurrence of the peripateia, the use of symbols, and the use of dialogue with a double layer of meaning. Whether one rejected or rejoiced over the dramatist's technique, it remained a subject of intense interest. The criticism of *Little Eyolf* also displays the fascination for reading Ibsen's work in context, with critics constantly picking up threads and themes from earlier plays. In this instance, *The Lady from the Sea* was frequently invoked, though others found connections linking back to the dramas of Ibsen's early days (for example, the similarities between Rita and Hjørdis). Ibsen's writing was becoming a branch of literary studies all of its own, a development that undoubtedly stimulated the critics. Indeed, it is tempting to suggest that Ibsen's writing was also an important inspiration for the development of modern textual and literary studies in Norwegian academic life.

For the writer himself this development signalled a unique success; for decades he had urged critics to regard his writing as an organic whole. Now he could reap the rewards, and among the rewards were these: his overall grasp, not just of the individual work but of the whole corpus of his writing, created a respect among critics that made it very much harder to dismiss the play. To read an Ibsen play was to engage in the search for a hidden pattern. The critic who dismissed the play risked being accused of having given up on his task. This was particularly relevant in the case of *Little Eyolf*, where it was tempting to concentrate on the play's imperfections and conclude that this was a talent in decline.

But what if the master was plumbing new and uncharted depths? What if the pattern was there and it was the *critic*, and not the master, who was inadequate to his task?

Generally speaking, *Little Eyolf* was read as a realistic-psychological drama. And in this light it has much to offer. With the exception of Borgheim, the engineer, who is positively bursting with a robust love of life, the other adults – Alfred, Rita and Asta – are trapped and bound together in a complex net of repressed erotic ties, guilt and denial. But precisely because they cannot deal with their relationships with each other, not to speak of the little boy, in reality they live lives that are lonely and isolated. Rita emerges as the best of the three of them, for, unlike her husband, she does not deny her demons. It may seem surprising that, in spite of her overt sexuality, her egoism, and her weak maternal instincts, contemporary critics sympathised with her. Perhaps, by this time, Ibsen's 'dangerous women' had become recognised and accepted, and even admired, character types. Others must have found Rita acceptable because they read the play idealistically and saw her as abandoning the life of the appetites in assuming her new and philanthropic direction.

It is, moreover, easier to sympathise with her fear of death and emptiness than with her husband's longing for death. It is the Rat Wife who articulates this longing when she described how her 'poor little ones' – the rats – find rest in the sea. Like the rats, little Eyolf is a reject, superfluous – or rendered superfluous – in life. For Allmers, on the other hand, death is a flight from the emptiness he has created within his own life. So death becomes a resting place for the rejected and the resigned, but for a vivid person such as Rita, hungry for life, something to be feared.

And yet it is possible to read this play in *both* an ironic and a non-ironic light, and in the final analysis this is probably the most fruitful approach. For it is quite possible to concede that the text exposes the characters to irony, and at the same time accept the couple's motives for wishing to change their lives; they *want* to atone for the death of their son, they are honest in their desperate resolve to break out of their isolation.

This does not mean that they will succeed. When Allmers, in his final lines, indicates that their route lies towards 'the heights' and 'the stars', we realise that he is still in thrall to his idealism. Ibsen's irony pursues him to the very end.[14] And yet the point is not necessarily 'what happens' to Allmers and Rita, or whether, as the curtain goes down, they have finally rid themselves of all self-deceit. This couple don't seem made for great insights; instead, they seem driven on through life by circumstance. And yet they do have something, perhaps the most important thing of all: they have the will, and they have the potential to be 'transformed' through the way in which they use language. As the dialogue between the two demonstrates, they possess the power of self-insight – or more accurately: the *will* to self-insight. Catastrophe strikes, and burdened down by guilt and by fear of the great emptiness they hurl the most grotesque accusations at other. But they also take these accusations back, and *admit* their guilt. The dialogue goes back and forth in this fashion. A number of people have pointed out that the dialogue here, as in *The Lady from the Sea*, has a therapeutic function. But if such is the case then what we have here are two patients giving each other therapy.

Both Rita and Allmers are very largely the slaves of their own natures, their urges and ideals, but as the dialogue between them reveals, they also possess the ability to see themselves from the outside, and to reflect upon their own moral responsibilities. They have the tools, but they must learn to use them.

If we accept that these two are complex characters, weak but searching, then it ought to be possible to accept the final scene. Even if the transformation is incompletely motivated by the action (it comes with undeniable suddenness), it is not unreasonable to claim that it finds its motivation in Rita and Allmers' characters. And if this is correct, then the dialogue between them is ample demonstration of this. Few characters in Ibsen's universe are as genuinely *human* as these two. In furnishing two such weak people with ambitions to 'want the impossible', he takes one of his most central concerns to an extreme pitch: can a human being change him- or herself *fundamentally*? Is transformation, the power to go beyond oneself, possible? Ibsen has posed this question many times, but here the question is whether transformation is possible even for people such as Rita and Allmers. Read in this way, the fact that the play doesn't seem to add up is perhaps a strength rather than a weakness. After all, life itself rarely adds up.

IBSEN'S BODY

At about the same time as *Little Eyolf* was published, Suzannah travelled to Tyrol and Italy, once again accompanied by Sigurd. She would be away for almost a year; it was the longest parting between the two since Ibsen had travelled to Rome before her thirty years earlier. Once again Henrik could live the life of a grass widower in Kristiania. The year 1895 was a fallow one for Ibsen, nothing of a creative nature emerged from his study. He was, however, a favourite subject for the creativity of others. For some reason or other, a number of Norway's leading painters decided, in the spring of that year, that they wanted to paint, draw or sculpt him.

The queue formed even before the new year, with both Hans Heyerdal and Erik Werenskiold asking for permission to paint his portrait.

'You're very welcome to,' was Ibsen's reply to Werenskiold, 'but I'm working on something at the moment, and that means I'm thinking about it from dawn to dusk. It makes me very ill-tempered, and that won't bring you much joy. Once I've finished things will be much better.'

Werenskiold wisely took the hint. In January 1895, with *Little Eyolf* well on its way out of the nest, he made his first sketches of Ibsen, but work was interrupted when Bernt Grønvold invited Werenskiold to Rome. In the meantime, Heyerdal had completed his portrait, and his place in the queue had been taken by Eilif Peterssen. Heyerdal had to put up with a model in very poor humour, but the Ibsen whom Werenskiold encountered was in excellent spirits. As he sat or stood for hours on end he joked about previous experiences of having his portrait painted.

'There was one Danish painter who tried to paint me as a saint,' he related, 'but I don't think it was suitable at all.'

As he told the story, he laughed until his body shook and the tears ran down his cheeks, and later that same day Werenskiold made a charcoal sketch of 'the laughing Ibsen'. This is the only portrait that shows the genial and warm writer thus far familiar only to a select handful of friends. Three paintings and a number of sketches and drawings were the result of these spring sessions. One painting shows Ibsen standing with his hands behind his back, two show him seated with hands folded. With the exception of that 'unofficial' charcoal sketch of the laughing Ibsen, all the portraits show him looking as if he has never smiled in his life, and doesn't have any plans to do so either.

No sooner was Werenskiold finished than it was Stephan Sinding's turn. Sinding had been commissioned to make the statue of Ibsen that was to stand outside the new National Theatre once it was built. Sinding too found his model in high spirits, but struggled to find the right approach to his task. As he was about to begin work on his sixth study he suddenly had an idea and asked Ibsen to remove his glasses:

I felt a shock pass through me. Never before have I seen eyes such as these. The one large, I might almost say *fearsome* – that was how it struck me – conveying an overall impression of mystery; the other much smaller, like something screwed up, cold and clear, and calmly penetrating.

Rarely had Ibsen's face and body been subject to such close study as it was in the spring and summer of 1895. What did the artists see, and what did they depict? What can actually be said about Ibsen's body? In the first instance this: he has no body, at least not one of flesh and blood. For the men of Ibsen's generation, nothing exists but the head and the hands. His body is a geometric form, an attitude, a broad brushstroke. The clothing and hairstyles of the nineteenth century were characterised by elegant lines and shapes that could be rendered on paper by a single brushstroke or a pencil line. In the caricatures he appears as a stooping, lightly tripping figure connected to a cane; a refined and highly urbane vision.

Ibsen was short, around 5ft 3in in his stockinged feet. That so much power and energy could be concentrated in such a small frame was given a curious explanation by the Danish writer Johannes V. Jensen, who wrote that 'the same amount of vital energy is more tensely concentrated in small people, whereas in bigger people with slower reactions it is spread across a larger cubic content'. So Ibsen's character is measurable on the basis of energy per cubic centimetre, an approach rarely encountered in the history of literary criticism. Given the interest at the time in physical anthropology, however, the formula is not so surprising; indeed, Ibsen himself had once had his cranium measured by a German professor.

'It turned out to be the largest by volume of any he had ever measured,' he proudly told Werenskiold.

In 1885, Peter Egge, then a young man, saw Ibsen step down onto the platform in Trondheim, and was surprised to realise that the great writer turned out to be 'a small man, but broad and stocky'. And yet he was not disappointed, as is clear from his memoirs, in which Egge turns from Ibsen's small stature to focus on his expressionless – in other words, his highly expressive – face. That Ibsen's face showed no expression whatsoever was the most meaningful aspect of his appearance: he was not physically a big man, but his real size, his greatness, lay hidden behind that sphinx-like exterior. Others have almost denied that he was small. In Henrik Jæger's description from 1887 he seems almost to grow, sentence by sentence:

> As is well known, he is not a tall man; but his upper body is remarkably powerful, and atop those broad shoulders is the large and lively head, surrounded by a strutting halo of grey hair . . . it strikes me that he has never looked more powerful than he does now, as he approaches his sixtieth year. He is a giant, not only spiritually, but also in a physical sense.

Jensen also remarks on the *hair* in his description of the Ibsenian iconography: 'Ibsen's mane puts one in mind of those fearsome masculine attributes familiar from the animal kingdom, the manes of the lion and the hamadryas baboon, and the resemblance is not coincidental.' Jensen himself (born in 1873) was one of that first generation of well-trimmed heads who viewed their forefathers' manes with mild astonishment. The photograph of the young Karl Marx, for example, in tailcoat and with a wild brush of hair sprouting from his head, is strikingly similar to portraits of the young Ibsen. The thicket was tamed after *Brand*, and styled in the European manner. Men of Johannes Jensen's generation admired the shaved, athletic look, personified in Norway by Fridtjof Nansen, and found something unmanly, fussy and domesticated about the styles adopted by Ibsen's generation of men.

When Nansen returned from the Fram expedition in September 1896 he was given a hero's welcome in Kristiania. The scientist and explorer had earlier crossed Greenland on skis, and now he had come closer to the North Pole than any man before him. The city went wild, but not Ibsen. Edvard Brandes met him in the deserted streets and asked why he was not down at the docks to greet Nansen like everyone else.

'No,' replied Ibsen, his face stiff, 'that's Red Indian stuff, celebrated with a Red Indian dance. It's not for the likes of me!'

He was right about that. Nansen was the clean-shaven and virile Redskin, Ibsen the Paleface with his beard and his sideburns. To fully appreciate the significance of this hair business a brief excursus on the history of hairstyling may be helpful. After almost two beardless centuries the fashion for beards and moustaches returned in the nineteenth century. The beard had long been associated with something rough, unrefined and rebellious (Marx again), but by the middle of the century it had become respectable, and between 1860 and 1880 there was a constant plague of them. Whiskers in particular were cultivated in an infinite variety of styles. Hair is both part of a person and a foreign body to be ejected – along with excreta, nails and sweat. In this light it is a fascinating comment on the nineteenth century's preoccupation with individuality and personality that men of Ibsen's generation so intensely cultivated their own personalities by sculpting their faces with something that the body was actively trying to get rid of. By the 1890s beards were on the way out and only the moustache held out, until the requirements of the gas mask during the First World War meant the disappearance of the last of the stubble. Since then the trimmed and clean-shaven look has been the manly ideal, with brief exceptions in the 1960s and 1970s.

In a historical perspective these developments relate Ibsen even more firmly to his time, and reinforce the mythical dimensions of his beard.

When Ibsen responded to the success of *Brand* by drawing a wide swathe with his safety razor between the nose and the throat he was abandoning his rebellious exterior in favour of the expression of a European type of individuality. At the same time he reinforced the iconic nature of his own presence, turning his natural human face into a geometric icon. Sculptors had difficulty in rendering whiskers in a natural way, as the famous busts made by Herman Bissen and Walter Runeberg in the 1860s both demonstrate. Reproduced in stone, the massive side-whiskers simply look like stone, and the face something rather more solid and permanent than flesh and blood.

For painters it was easier to depict hair in a realistic way, but even here the artists usually chose to accentuate the geometry of Ibsen's face. This requires yet another short excursus on the subject of representations of Ibsen in paint. They can be divided into two main tendencies that succeed each other in the history of art. The first category is the *naturalistic-heroic*, noticeable in most of the portraits and sculptures done from life, and including those by Erik Werenskiold, Nils Gude, Hans Heyerdal, Bissen and Runeberg. Here the starting point is a human being, rendered as something greater than itself by techniques involving format, colouring and lighting. The second category is the *geometric-iconographic*, observable in contemporary caricatures of Ibsen as well as in Edvard Munch's portraits. This style became common in the modernist era, most notably among sculptors. It is hardly necessary to add that this art-historical development reinforces the impression of Ibsen as a mask, a stylised icon, a phenomenon rather than a human being.

As well as expressing virility, the mane of hair functioned as a frame for the broad, white *forehead* – the crucible of the writing. John Paulsen describes Ibsen's forehead as 'knotted in thought', as though the veins and wrinkles in the forehead were the physiological traces of the master's thought and spiritual struggle. The most common description of the forehead is that it was 'broad' and 'high', meaning its owner was intelligent. The immediate association is to Zeus, who gave birth to Athena from his forehead. Ibsen's forehead too hid a cranium big enough to give birth to a whole nation of literary characters. Unlike the forehead, the *hands* are rarely described in the literature, oddly, since it is the hands that hold the pen that produces the work. But this is not by chance, for Ibsen's most important attribute is his *spirit*, the transcendent part of the human being, lodged behind the forehead. The myth relates that it was in his head that Ibsen so to speak 'wrote' the finished works, and in that context the hands are plebeians, the fingers simple slaves that obey orders from the spirit. In other words, Ibsen's hands are uninteresting.

However, we catch a glimpse of the spirit in the *eyes*, those eyes that so overwhelmed Stephan Sinding. And Ibsen's eyes really are something special. From birth the left eye was somewhat larger than the right. In the mythology of the sphinx it is the small eye that is the important one, the penetrating one, the large eye being the one that is fascinated and far-seeing – two 'gazes' that represent respectively Ibsen the critical-ironical revealer of secrets, and Ibsen the heroic and existential seeker. The fascination of the eyes increases with age as the focus of a face that acquires a varied and dramatic physiognomy of its own; the heavy lids, the bags beneath them, the severe groove dividing them. Two flashes, clear and sharp, surrounded by heavy folds of skin that bear witness to a life lived. The small eye in particular attracts our attention, the one that looks straight through us. And painters have of course realised the importance of using dramatic lighting to underscore the surrounding topography, now and then allowing it to fall in a tiny starburst onto the golden rim of his spectacles. A physical deformity elevated to the level of mythical reality, transformed into the all-seeing eye of the poet-prophet.

There are alternative analyses of these eyes. One is that the small eye stares inwards towards his own centre, leaving the large one to observe the world – an analysis that is strikingly similar to Ibsen's own description of the eyes of the Muse of Tragedy, the sculpture from the Emperor Hadrian's villa, which made such a strong impression on him during his first stay in Rome. He noticed in particular the eyes, 'that seem at once to look both inward and yet to penetrate the far distances upon which they are actually focused'.

Like the hands, the *nose* has largely been ignored in the literature. It was reasonably large and rather snub – and snub noses never go down in history. Nor are the *ears* especially spiritual parts of the body, and as such have largely been left in peace by the memoirists (Ibsen was completely unmusical). The *mouth*, however, is an important part of Ibsen's facial landscape. It is often described as a line, occasionally a severe line, or as being 'sharp as a blade'. It is, above all, a closed, tight-lipped mouth. With so much going on in the head, the mouth must inevitably remain closed while the big ideas brew behind the forehead and come seeping out through the fingers. It is also, secondarily, a serious mouth, as the whole face is serious.

Although this is not quite the whole story. Henrik Jæger was among those who experienced Ibsen the mild and genial – 'and then a bright, soft smile spreads across his face, a smile that is one of the most charming I have ever seen'. The smiling Ibsen is quite simply sweet. But it is one thing to note down memories from personal encounters, and another to do as Erik Werenskiold did and paint his picture of the laughing Ibsen that revealed him to all the world as a good-natured old boy. From the perspective of the iconography of Ibsen as sphinx, Werenskiold's portrait is not far off blasphemous, surpassed in that respect only by the study for a statue made by Gustav Vigeland following Ibsen's death. This showed the writer reclining in full-figure, the upper half of his body naked, the rest of him partly covered by a toga-like garment. The study was displayed at Blomquist's in the summer of 1906 and became the subject of an intense debate. Appraised of such a monstrous memorial Ibsen – who was buried fully clothed – would have turned in his grave.

Naturally, most people realised this, and Vigeland's monument was never used. Ibsen wasn't always a sphinx, he was also once a human being. Several memoirists reflect on the metamorphosis that turned the man into the mask. The best of these is perhaps the account given by Magdalene Thoresen, Ibsen's own mother-in-law:

> When he came to us – about 27 or 28 years of age – he did not have the imposing appearance he now has. He was often timid and withdrawn, and yet one could see the great man in him. He was by nature a very quiet man and often remained silent while others without a tenth of his spiritual talents started holding forth. But following the changing expressions that passed through his eyes one realised that his silence was due not to ignorance but because he was thinking. He knew that one day it would be his turn to hold the stage – and until that day came he could hold his peace.

Ibsen entered Magdalene's home in 1856 as a silent, withdrawn, taciturn man. By 1901, when she wrote her memoirs, the silence had been turned into wisdom; he kept silent because he knew his day would come! She was only one of many who, with the wisdom of hindsight, reinterpreted the young Ibsen's silence and shyness to give it a sort of dignified authority; Jonas Lie, for example, described him as the 'silent centre' of the Learned Holland. The more his writing became controversial, the more striking did his silence become. In Germany they were especially impressed by the sovereign silence with which the writer responded to the endless attacks.

'Even the loneliness through which his life glides,' writes Herman Bang, 'makes him an attractive subject for the mass imagination. He becomes remote and full of remarkable secrets, Germany's great "foreign man".'

A similar metamorphosis can be observed in the description of his temperament. In his youth Ibsen was notorious for his irritability and quick temper, not least when he had been drinking. In the literature of memoirs this characteristic too has been refined and elevated; one of his friends from Rome, Frederik G. Knudtzon, wrote in his memoirs of Ibsen's 'inner turmoil' at that time, so disturbing that 'it was impossible for him to appear a harmonious personality'. In this fashion his ordinary human characteristics were transformed into meaningful elements, his weaknesses rendered as strengths.

* * *

So the question of who Henrik Ibsen *was* is in many respects a matter of the ways in which he has been *constructed* via texts and in visual images. Seen in this light, 'the sphinx' is a linguistic construction, a 'literary sculpture' based partly on Ibsen's own sayings, and partly on the numerous observers of Ibsen who, in letters, journals and memoirs, have provided literary history with memories and opinions on the subject of the great man – his spirit, his conduct, his body, his work, all of it coalescing into the literary sculpture 'Henrik Ibsen'. Work on this literary sculpture started in earnest in 1866, when he achieved his Scandinavian breakthrough with *Brand* – the year zero in the time of the sphinx, the year of rebirth that set in train this metamorphosis that would transform him from body into spirit, from flesh into marble, from man into myth.

Among the most significant contributors to this literary sculpture are those female devotees of culture who, from the end of the nineteenth century, have given us some of the most magnificent descriptions of the writer. Once again, Magdalene Thoresen is a prime example. On one occasion she describes her son-in-law as a 'scourge with a scythe in his hand, and every weed that hinders the growth of what is truly human must be cut down'.

He was writer and prophet, heaven and earth in one:

An eternal star shines above the name of Henrik Ibsen, *for what is made of spirit* can never perish.

But none can match the description given by Laura Kieler following her meeting with him in 1887:

A lonely man! This is how he describes himself, and how others describe him. A man who moves the boundary markers further and further out and keeps watch, looking for the rising sun. As soon as others catch up with him, he shyly withdraws and fights his way further up into the heights, across 'rocks and screes'. He does not wait to see whether others are following him. A pioneer, ahead of his time, and so always standing alone! He raises his banner, advances across the mountains, points into the distance and cries: 'Excelsior!'

Regardless of how exalted such descriptions may seem, there is no doubt that they represent an important branch of the many ways in which Ibsen was received, one in which the literary prophet seems almost to become a religious prophet and his works enigmatic messages of metaphysical dimensions, even though at times it is difficult to distinguish the religious from the erotic phraseology.

Of one thing there is no doubt, however: the little man with his large head was an image of masculine potency; pure spirit he might have been, but beneath the crinolines of those adoring women there might also have been a little condensation. Dyre Vaa's statue that was raised in the middle of Skien after the writer's death gives him a V-shaped, athletic body – as though the artist was trying to combine Ibsen's spiritual power with Nansen's athletic physique, and so fuse the masculine ideals of the nineteenth and twentieth centuries.

INCIPIENT MADNESS

The last artist to portray Ibsen in 1895 was Christian Krohg, who painted him standing on Karl Johans gate with his hat in his outstretched hand – very reluctantly, judging by the facial expression. But then he had every reason to look dour at that particular time.

In 1895 the Ibsen's marital crisis reached its climax. Suzannah had travelled with Sigurd to a spa centre in Meran in Tyrol, and Monsummano, near Lucca in Italy, in December, and she did not return until late in the autumn. They were apart for ten months. In the meantime, Henrik continued to take his daily walk through the streets, or stayed at home, reading and writing when he wasn't sitting for his portrait. Suzannah displayed a wifely concern for his well-being, especially around Christmas 1894.

Fortunately she had Bergliot:

'My dear Bergliot,' she writes in mid-December 1894, 'would you be so kind as to help Ibsen by buying what he needs for Christmas – maybe order 2 Christmas cakes at one krone each from Kirkeby's – I want each of the maids to have a bottle of sweet wine from Bøe's at one krone a bottle, you can also pick up there a couple of pounds of apples, a pound of walnuts for Lina and some gingersnaps . . .'

And so on. It seems as though Henrik got his cakes, and that he found his solitude tolerable, after all:

'Everything is going very well here,' he writes to Suzannah at about the same time as she was writing her anxious letter to Bergliot. He sometimes had his dinner delivered from Marie Blehr's School of Good Housekeeping in Victoria terrasse, but usually his food was cooked by the maid, Lina Jacobsen. Bergliot joined him for dinner on Sundays – and he also had Hildur to keep him company, though he does not mention *that* to his wife. Lina had joined them in the autumn of 1892, and though she wasn't a new princess she was a welcome addition to the household. Dr Sontum had put Ibsen on a special diet, but Lina cooked Ibsen whatever he wanted; when she served him meat broth with peeled raw potatoes in soup the tears welled up and he told her the food reminded him of his mother.

Although sentimental moments such as these probably owed something to alcohol, there is no doubt that he was attached to Lina, as his letters to Suzannah confirm. Through the winter and the spring of 1895 the couple continued to write to each other. There are no indications that anything is wrong; Henrik describes how he passes his time and adds small, chatty details. The winter that year was cold, and he spent most of it indoors. In February, Sigurd paid a brief visit to Kristiania before returning to join his mother. While in the city he persuaded his father to buy Christian Krohg's portrait of August

Strindberg. Sigurd dubbed it 'The Revolution', while his father preferred 'Incipient Madness'. Ibsen hung it in his study and later claimed that he was unable to write without 'that madman standing there staring down at me with his insane eyes'.

Early in May the cracks appear. On 7 May, Henrik writes a letter to his wife after receiving an upsetting one from her:

> It pained me to read your most recent letter, dated May 1. And I hope that now, having thought it over, you regret ever sending it to me.

Suzannah's letter has not survived, but from her husband's reply it is clear that she has persuaded herself that he intends to leave her. Henrik denies it, and assures her that he has never thought of such a thing, never wished for it. But Suzannah has obviously revealed the source of her suspicions, and Ibsen knows where to lay the blame:

> So it's your stepmother, that old reprobate, who has been up to her old tricks and tried to turn us against each other.

It was Magdalene who had persuaded her stepdaughter that Henrik wanted 'to be free at any cost'. Nor is he in any doubt about where Magdalene has *her* information from. For some time he had been at odds with Suzannah's sister, Dorothea. Indeed, he had taken to crossing the street when he spotted her walking towards him. Now she wanted her revenge. It was a conspiratorial theory, but in truth Magdalene had formed her own impression of the state of the marriage during a visit to Kristiania the previous year. In a letter written shortly afterwards she gives a depressing picture of the couple:

> They are two lonely people – each on their own – absolutely on their own.

Was Suzannah persuaded by her husband's reassurances? Did she manage to avoid thinking about Aline Solness, hanging like a living corpse on the back of her successful, ambitious husband – who in turn preferred the company of a young woman? Suzannah didn't need the gossipy insinuations of Magdalene or Dorothea to suspect that Henrik wanted out. From his letter we understand that she has taken this opportunity to air all her frustrations over their life together. She demands that they move from the cold apartment on Victoria terrasse and find somewhere that is better for her health. That was her simplest demand, and he accedes to it without a struggle. But the demand for a move is not *solely* motivated by her health worries, as is evident from his description of the new apartment he shortly afterwards acquires:

I'll have a large study with direct access from the hall, so that people who come to see me don't need to enter any of the other rooms in the apartment. It means you have a large corner salon with a balcony, exclusively for your own use, as well as a living room almost the same size with a door in from the dining room to do whatever you like with.

For two people contemplating divorce, physical separation is the quickest route. The layout of the flat was ideal for a couple more concerned with avoiding each other than being together:

From the dining room you walk straight into the spacious library, and from there straight into your bedroom, which is considerably larger than the one I have now here. My bedroom is next to it, and has a balcony. You won't need to use the corridor except when you want to use the bathroom.

On 15 October, Henrik moves into Arbins gate 1. It was a new block in an affluent part of town with a view of the royal castle and the trams rumbling by on Drammensveien. To help with the furnishing he had Bergliot, Lina and Hildur – again! Via Sigurd he sent a message insisting that Suzannah wait until everything was ready before she returned. She in her turn used her son as a go-between to demand that Lina be sacked. The housekeeper's fantastic skills as a cook and her concern for his well-being were things he greatly appreciated, but naturally enough Suzannah did not feel quite the same way. Once again Henrik accedes, though not without a ruffling of his feathers: 'as long as I am alone in the house and left to manage my own affairs then I will not tolerate this kind of supervision'. The implication seems to be that he would tolerate it once his wife returned. There was no doubt about it, Suzannah planned to take charge once she was back; it was her job to run the household, her role to be the writer's other. She was to serve him his porridge in the morning, and it was she who knew how to arrange the plants in the living room.

She returned in the autumn and seems to have found the apartment at Arbins gate acceptable. The crisis was over on this occasion, and the couple could resume their life together – when, that is, they chose to let their paths cross somewhere within the apartment's 320 square metres.

HENRIK IBSEN SUPERSTAR

Although Henrik could give the impression of wanting to live an isolated life in his apartment, that was only a partial truth. In general he carried out the social duties his position demanded, though sometimes he did try to wriggle out of them, as on the occasion when he declined an invitation on the grounds that he was an active member of the 'Anti-Visit Society'. But he accepted invitations to dinners, receptions and the theatre, and now and then attended meetings of societies such as Andvake and the Academy of Sciences. And if he was expected to wave from a window, well, he waved from the window.

The truth is, he could attend as many gatherings as he wished without making any impact at all on his reputation as 'the great and lonely master'.

He didn't just have Lina, Hildur and Bergliot around, there were others too – some invited guests whose visits were welcome, others uninvited and unwelcome. During the summer he had received visits from a Hungarian writer, the French Count de Contades, and the Russian Duke Galitzin. His French translator, Count Prozor, called in with his wife en route to St Petersburg. In August the Serbian Prince Bojidar Karageorgevitch arrived, and almost as soon as he had left Aurélien Lugné-Poe turned up in Kristiania again on a flying visit.

It was evident that a visit to Ibsen was a must for any celebrity tourist passing through Kristiania. And there were tourists enough, the less celebrated as well as the celebrated. Most of them were heading for the Norwegian mountains and fjords, but in the capital there was one attraction at least they absolutely had to see – Henrik Ibsen. The attraction himself was not entirely pleased by the development:

'There is a horde of tourists here this year, and they are a real annoyance to me,' he complains to Suzannah in August. 'But it is enjoyable sometimes –'

Fame was a two-edged sword. How else to interpret the strange incident that took place when he was stopped in the street outside the Grand Hotel to receive the tributes of a group of forty or fifty tourists led by an Austrian field marshal? Ibsen and the Grand had long been a familiar association in Christiania, and his daily walks from Arbins gate to the cafe have become an intrinsic part of Ibsen mythology. His punctuality was legendary, and of course, exaggerated. For though Ibsen was punctual, he was not a machine. Sometimes he took a detour in order to buy something, on some occasions he used the tram. But in general he was to be found at the cafe twice daily, first at around eleven or twelve o'clock, and then in the evening at around six to seven. On his first trip he often stopped by the old university building to set his watch. And he might also visit the cafe later in the evening if there was a special occasion, for example, a visit to the theatre.

In due course the seat in the corner became his own, and the manager, Herr Fritzner, arranged for the import of the German beer he drank in Munich (Spatenbräu). He also had a copper plaque mounted on the chair on which was written 'Reserved for Dr Ibsen', and after 1899 there are said to have been four glasses waiting for him, each for a different spirit, each engraved with his name.

All are agreed that he drank spirits at the Grand Hotel, even on his morning visits – though there is disagreement about how much. Bergliot, in an effort to counteract the rumours that he downed dram after dram, insists that he sipped from the same glass (cognac, in her version) the whole time. Certainly August Lindberg never forgot his lunch with the writer in the 1890s. At twelve they took their seats at Ibsen's regular table, where a carafe of spirits and a bottle of pale ale awaited him. Ibsen signalled to a waiter and ordered – another carafe of spirits and a bottle of pale ale for Lindberg!

'Yes, but what about the food?' asked Lindberg in surprise after they had drunk the first toast.

'Are you going to eat?' asked Ibsen.

'Yes, excuse me,' replied the Swede, 'but did the doctor not invite me to breakfast?'

'Are you hungry at this time of day?'

'Well I need some sandwiches at least.'

As a rule Ibsen seems to have preferred to sit on his own in the mornings, and not always in 'his' corner. Sometimes he preferred the peace of the Reading Room, separated both from the hotel and the restaurant. In the evenings he might enjoy a dram in the Palm Hall, often in company. Ibsen's routines were well known to the tourists, who stood waiting outside the Grand Hotel to watch the writer make his entrance. Once an American tourist even dared to sit in his seat in order to see what he would do. Another American managed to trick his way into Arbins gate and steal a pencil before hotfooting it out of there.

Young women were the admirers he most welcomed. When Anna Warberg Tharaldsen, then eighteen years of age, saw Ibsen on Drammensveien one day she gave in to an impulse to approach him:

I stood in front of him and bowed low and curtsied to the master.

Neither then nor later did she understand why she had done so, she just knew she had to. People who actually turned up at his door, or wrote letters to him, were worse. Autograph hunters were tricked by him disguising his handwriting when he replied, still others wanted advice – a priest who had lost his faith, a couple whose marriage was in trouble. And then there were journalists who prowled the Kristiania streets or set up camp outside Arbins gate to get a glimpse of the writer, and photographers taking paparazzi pictures.

In sum it seems as though Ibsen both loved and hated his fame. He cannot possibly have visited the Grand Hotel in hopes of finding solitude there. A waiter later recalled that he always wanted his evening dram served in the Palm Hall – 'right in the middle, so all the tourists could see him'. He wanted to be seen, but reserved the right to complain about it:

'Dammit,' he said to the waiter. 'There isn't a moment's peace to be had here. They want my picture, every one of them.'

On the other hand, it was hard to find somewhere outside where he *could* stroll around without being approached. He did have one bolt hole. In Queens Park, behind the castle, directly across the street from Ibsen's apartment, he would be left in peace; King Oscar II had personally presented him with a key to the gate. So the monarchy was still able to provide him with the freedom to live in the world of his own thoughts. Beneath the king's trees he found the solitude necessary for creation, and by 1896 another play was ready for publication.

FOOTSTEPS FROM THE FIRST FLOOR

Ibsen had worked without interruption throughout most of the summer, unhampered by the heatwave that affected the city. By August he had written the whole thing, leaving only the rewriting and the fair copy. On 20 October he sent the manuscript to Hegel, accompanying it with a few words of warning to the effect that Hegel must ensure no light-fingered literary thief got his hands on the proofs.

All went well; this time the launch went according to plan. *John Gabriel Borkman* was published on 15 December 1896 in a first edition of 12,000, the largest first edition of an Ibsen play thus far. The many advance orders meant that a second edition of 3,000 copies had to be printed and despatched at the same time as the first. As with Ibsen's previous three plays, Heinemann published an edition of twelve copies in order to secure copyright protection in England, accompanied by an amateur reading to secure the same protection for the stage rights. Shortly afterwards the play was also published in France, Russia, Holland and Germany. A disagreement arose with the German publisher, Fischer, who Ibsen felt made unreasonable demands in respect of the fee for translation; instead he gave the rights to the young German publisher Albert Langen, who already owned the rights to *Catiline*. The contact may have been established through Bergliot, for Langen had close ties with the Bjørnsons, and not only as a publisher. In March 1896 a double wedding took place in Munich, with Bergliot's youngest sister Dagny marrying Albert, and Albert's sister Elsbeth marrying Dagny and Bergliot's brother Einar.

* * *

John Gabriel Borkman is a bank manager found guilty of embezzlement. Released after serving a prison sentence of eight years, he has spent the next eight years living in isolation on the first floor of his home. His wife Gunhild lives on the floor below him, a woman embittered by life and despising the husband who has brought such shame on the household. Borkman himself has no regrets. He is the son of a miner and spent much of his youth down the mines before making a career for himself in banking. He regards himself as an 'exceptional man', a visionary human being with the natural right to place himself above the ordinary rules of society in order to pursue his destiny. And that is to bring the 'singing ore' up from the depths of the earth's interior, to liberate it, so that it may serve both him and society – that is why he embezzled the money, to invest and to create.

Now he lives up on the first floor, where he paces restlessly back and forth. He has only two visitors: young Frida, who plays the piano for him, and Frida's father, Vilhelm Foldal. Foldal is one of the victims of Borkman's dishonesty, but over the years they have developed a curious relationship in which each reinforces the other in his life lie. Borkman encourages Foldal's literary dreams, and Foldal supports Borkman in his belief that the day of his restitution will come, and the outside world will ask for his forgiveness and give him his old job back.

As the play opens Gunhild's twin sister Ella is visiting. When they were young, she and Borkman were in love, but he sacrificed her to his rival, Hinckel the lawyer, in return for the job as bank manager. Instead he married Gunhild, whom he never loved. They have a son, Erhart, now in his twenties and a student. Ella would not have Hinckel and remained a spinster. That, in Borkman's opinion, is why Hinckel reported the embezzlement – as a way of taking revenge.

The main reason for Ella's visit is not John Gabriel but Erhart. Following the scandal she took responsibility for the boy's upbringing, and now she and her sister compete for his affection. Gunhild's dream is that Erhart will restore the family honour, but Ella, who is mortally ill, needs all his love during the few months of life that remain to her. Borkman too expresses his need for the boy's support now that he has decided to emerge from his self-imposed isolation and rebuild his career. But Erhart wants nothing to do with all this; he just wants to live and enjoy being young. The turning point in the play arrives when he announces that he wants to marry Fanny Wilton, a divorced woman, and travel in southern Europe with her and Frida. The flight of the young ruins the plans of the old. Borkman, who at this juncture has emerged from his room, refuses to go back in. Instead he heads out into the winter night with Ella. They hear the sleigh bells ringing as the coach carrying the young people hurtles by. Shortly afterwards Borkman has a heart attack and dies, Gunhild arrives, and the sisters find reconciliation over his dead body.

* * *

A week or two before publication, *Aftenposten* carried a report indicating that expectations 'throughout the civilised world' were still high before the appearance of a new play by Ibsen. In Scandinavia, however, in the writer's opinion, the interest had fallen off; in Norway in particular, it seemed, he was beginning to be regarded as slightly old-fashioned.

It is hard to assess how accurate this claim was. His plays continued to cause surprise, and arouse enthusiasm as well as distaste, but it may well be that they no longer attracted quite the same degree of attention. Ibsen had simply been accepted, his dramas institutionalised, and his critics won over – at least the younger among them, those not brought up on the aesthetic traditions of the past. It was now possible to point to the epic element in the plays without this being regarded as a 'technical sin', and *John Gabriel Borkman* was praised as a tragedy without subjecting it to the strict historical criteria of classical tragedy. Most importantly, critics recognised Ibsen's supreme technical mastery, and allowed him the right to define his own work. And if there *were* criticisms, these were seldom of the sort that meant dismissing the work as a whole.

'But one must simply take Ibsen's writing for what it is,' wrote Valdemar Vedel as a commentary on his own few objections to *John Gabriel Borkman*. Elsewhere Just Bing conceded that Ibsen's characters might well be unnatural creations, possibly even insane the lot of them:

> Ibsenite characters really only belong in one place – and that is in the Ibsenite drama. And there they are completely at home.

He could not have made it plainer: Ibsen had become an institution, something fixed and permanent whom one could choose either to relate to or not relate to. In contrast, Carl David af Wirsén protested that *John Gabriel Borkman* could not be a tragedy as long as the demand for tragic guilt was not met. But af Wirsén was no longer a defining critical voice, and the aesthetic of idealism no longer the only one. An anonymous Swedish reviewer in the *Nordisk Tidskrift för Vetenskap, Konst och Industri* provides clear proof of the defensive position in which idealism now found itself: 'It is we poor, bullied idealists, we, who go around with the "claims of the ideal in our back pockets", who represent the opposition to Ibsen's later writing.'

It is hard to fight a war without an enemy; from this perspective the turn to symbolic drama, the theme of the call and the relationship between life and art, youth and age, had all been well-calculated moves. Indeed, it is remarkable how rapidly Ibsen was able to move from being shocking and rebellious to the position of contemplative old master. In two years, from *Hedda Gabler* to *The Master Builder*, he had become 'old' in the eyes of the world.

All in all the play received a rapturous welcome. The fact that the plot unfolded over just a few hours excited particular admiration. This was 'real-time' theatre, which did not neglect to unfold the past in the dialogue. All is compacted and tight in this drama, with Ibsen again demonstrating his mastery of scenography – as in the contrast between indoors and outdoors.[15] Life within the Borkman household is enclosed and claustrophobic; but the world seen through the windows in the conservatory is not the summery world it was in *The Lady from the Sea*, or the autumnal one of *Hedda Gabler*. Instead, the contrast is between heat and cold, between the heated room and the ice-cold snowy landscape outside. The contrast is echoed within the older characters who have all, in one way or another, been cheated of the warmth of love in their lives. Gunhild has probably never known that warmth, while Ella accuses Borkman of having killed her love as well as his own. Borkman sacrificed Ella's warm heart to win the cold metal, the ore in the mountain that he saw as his mission in life to bring up into the light.

Even when confronted by Ella with his betrayal of her, he remains true to his real love:

> I love you, there where you lie, seemingly dead, in the depth and the darkness! I love you, your values that demand the sacrifice of a whole life, with all your bright train of power and honour. I love, love, love you!

One of the play's main problems lies here, in Borkman's shameless love of money and power. Not that this was a problem for contemporary critics, who were more or less unanimous in their condemnation of the former bank manager, thoroughly convinced that this was the play's message. Precisely *what* was being condemned was rather more difficult to say: was the play about 'the punishment of cold egotism', or was it 'the life's lie, and the empty imitation of a life' that the writer was attacking? Or was this play too a 'disguised reckoning' in which the writer sat in judgement on himself? For there is no doubt that this is one of Ibsen's darkest plays, as well as his coldest. Contemporary critics turned the play inside out in search of a gleam of light, and found it in Ella Rentheim. Many simply ignored her darker sides; she openly admits that she does not feel mercy, and that her interest in Erhart is selfish. Yet as the plot unfolds she reveals an ability to love and a willingness for self-sacrifice.

It meant that most people regarded the play's main theme as being *the murder of love*, with Ella as the positive polar opposite to the negative extreme of Borkman's self-love. Borkman's fate in the final scene is to be overtaken by an 'ice-cold stony hand of rock' that takes a deadly grip upon his heart.

But is this the only possible interpretation? Is John Gabriel Borkman just a lost soul, a treacherous egotist, or is there, somewhere within him, a trace of the heroic? Does this play too allow interpretations that are both ironic and positive? It might be sufficient to read the play in the light of Ibsen's previous dramas to answer this aright. Or we might take a detour that involves the German philosopher Friedrich Nietzsche.

THE POETRY OF IMPOTENCE

We don't know whether Ibsen ever read Nietzsche, but we do know that Nietzsche had little time for Ibsen:

'I now see your Henrik Ibsen in a very clear light,' he writes. 'For all his robust idealism and his "will to truth" he has never dared to free himself from the moral illusion that speaks of "freedom" without acknowledging what freedom is.'

Nietzsche saw Ibsen as an 'old maid,' a closet idealist and moralist who did not have the courage to take his rebellion beyond liberalism's individualistic call for freedom. Not that Nietzsche had read much of him, and the works that *might* have interested him were mostly written after his mental breakdown in January 1889.

And yet the two men are historically connected; the question is, in what sense?

There is a widespread assumption that Ibsen first came across Nietzsche's ideas through Georg Brandes' series of lectures given in the spring of 1888 and published, in revised form, as the essay 'Aristocratic Radicalism' in the magazine *Tilskueren* in August of the following year. This essay introduced the German philosopher to Scandinavian intellectuals; shortly afterwards Nietzsche achieved a wider European breakthrough. Brandes tried to persuade Nietzsche and Ibsen to read each other's books, but with little success. Ibsen knew of the lectures, and in all likelihood read Brandes' essay, so that any Nietzschean influence on his writing can only have appeared from *Hedda Gabler* onwards.[16] But not until *The Master Builder*, and *John Gabriel Borkman* especially, does he appear to show a conscious awareness of the German philosopher. It is apparent in Solness' contempt for compassion, his revolt against God, the struggle between his urge to power and the voice of his conscience, and in Hilde's heedless vitalism, and her 'Viking morality', which corresponds closely to the superman morality, and the unyielding will with which she compels the master builder to attempt the impossible.

In 'Aristocratic Radicalism', Brandes writes about Nietzsche's view of the will:

> Nietzsche replaces the Schopenhaurian 'Will to life' and the Darwinian 'struggle for existence' with a 'Will to power'. The will is not to life and life alone, in his view, but to power.

It is hard to imagine that ideas like this did *not* influence Ibsen, and in *John Gabriel Borkman* the parallels are even more clear.[17] The play deals explicitly with the idea of the exceptional man and the will to power. Borkman does not actually use the term 'superman', but speaks of himself as 'exceptional', and relates the lawyer Hinckel to the idea of a 'supervillain'. Borkman's contempt for the feminine and his love of music also seem to suggest Nietzsche. But if Nietzschean ideas are indeed present in the play, we still need to understand *how* such ideas are used. Does Ibsen identify with Nietzsche, or distance himself from him?

A number of people have chosen to see *John Gabriel Borkman* as nothing less than Ibsen's reckoning with Nietzsche – and thus with Brandes. This tradition requires, of course, an ironic reading, one in which Borkman, the 'exceptional man', is unmasked and stripped bare. And one might as well admit it: of all Ibsen's male heroes, none is more pathetically described than he. He is a common criminal, a swindler, a loser who pads about in his loft swathed in Napoleonic delusions about himself. And as if this were not enough, Ibsen has given him his very own Sancho Panza, in the shape of Vilhelm Foldal, who acts as a distorting mirror for Borkman's own pompous self-image. Ibsen also appears to be having fun at Nietzsche's expense with coinages such as the 'supervillain' morality.

Any attempt to give this play a positive reading presents real difficulties. One option is to focus on the younger characters, and especially Erhart's desire to be young and free. He travels with Fanny and Frida to southern Europe, a goal synonymous in Ibsen's universe with light and the joy of life. But there are a number of difficulties in seeing *John Gabriel Borkman* as a play about youth. In the first place their project is not described in terms that are exclusively positive, and it is not easy to see Erhart as representing the future. What he longs for is the sensuality and spontaneous joy of the present moment – in quite specific terms, the temptations of Fanny's body. Secondly, the drama does not actually end with the departure of the young at the end of Act Three. In the concluding fourth act, in which we follow Borkman on his last journey through the winter night, the drama is reclaimed by the old – those who are left behind to contemplate their failed lives now that the young have gone.[18]

If Ibsen had wished to hold an aristocratic character such as Borkman to account it would have been very untypical of him. As a writer he saw the heedless pursuit of his calling as a necessity of life and, like the miner, it was also the writer's duty to bring hidden things into the light of day and ennoble them. He had once urged Brandes to pursue 'a really thoroughgoing egotism', and claimed that the best way he could serve society was by 'refining the raw metal inside you'.

In describing Borkman as a 'miner's son' Ibsen deliberately creates an identification of the main character with himself ('Bjergmanden' – The Miner). If the bank manager's vision of bringing ore up into the light corresponds to the writer's task, then it becomes hard to accept an outright condemnation of him. But doesn't the *text* itself reveal an understanding of the greatness in Borkman's work? Has he not indeed once *been* a great man, if not on the scale of a Napoleon? And is it obvious that Ella's need for love takes precedence over his love of the 'ore', of the possibility of creating something unusual, both for himself and for others? For both Ibsen and Borkman, self-realisation is an end in itself. Borkman is driven primarily by the urge to meet his calling, to open the dictates of his own nature, even if at the cost of the happiness of others, and even if he must commit a crime to achieve his goal:

> People don't understand that I *had* to, because I was myself – because I was John Gabriel Borkman – and nobody else.

Borkman is not the first of Ibsen's heroes to ignore the well-being of others as he pursues self-realisation. But there is no avoiding the fact that the *cost* of self-realisation is an important theme in this drama. After all, the conflict here is not between self-realisation and duty, dead thoughts or society's conventions. In Borkman's case, self-realisation comes at the cost of the ability to love, to love another. This is what makes it tempting to leave the play open to different interpretations, and dwell on that image of Ella and Borkman, lost in the bitter cold of a winter's night as they hold a reckoning with their lives. Two questions are asked, both directed at him:

Was it worth it? And could things have been otherwise?

If one recognises that there is at least an element of heroism in Borkman's life's work, the play can hardly be read as an unambiguous rejection of Nietzsche. But this is not to suggest that Borkman therefore appears as a figure straight out of Nietzsche. Although he clearly expresses his will to power, in the final analysis it is more natural to see him as a variant of Ibsen's heroic protagonists. The difficulty is that we are dealing with qualities that as categories simply cannot be compared if we set Nietzsche's *philosophy* up against Ibsen's *dramatic method*.[19] There are many examples in Ibsen's extra-literary sayings of a belief in the elite and a contempt for the masses, but as a *writer* he did not see it as his task to promote ideas but to test them out. Many have pointed out that the Nietzschean characters in Ibsen are 'weak Nietzscheans'. Hedda, Solness, Hilde, Borkman, all of those who bristle with the will to power and heedlessly follow their calling, all are depicted with flaws that prevent them from fully realising themselves. They are split people, and the depiction of them is split too. Usually there is a core of greatness in their urge to transgress, yet they are also always subjected to a bitter irony, in Borkman's case to outright ridicule. When Ibsen refuses to raise his heroes above the mass, but instead destroys them in impotence and disillusionment, this is not a result of his view of life or philosophy, it is a consequence of his dramatic method.

It is, moreover, easy to find elements in Ibsen's life and his work that do not accord with Nietzsche. Those dramas that stress the non-heroic, with *The Lady from the Sea* as the best example, have little to do with Nietzsche. The same goes for Nora's non-heroic revolt in *A Doll's House*, and in general for Ibsen's faith in women and workers. In Ibsen the Dionysian is not resolved, but crushed and disfigured (Hedda), even though in the later dramas the joy of life is more prominently expressed (Hilde).[20] Nor does Ibsen divide people into masters and slaves, but instead sees the ennoblement of *humanity itself* as his goal. Like Rosmer, he would like to turn everyone into aristocrats. This ambition underpins all his writing, expressed in the frequently quoted phrase, that 'democracy's consuming task is to become aristocratic'.

Such statements make Ibsen's elitism very conditional, and make it tempting to suggest that *if* he promoted a vision, then that vision did not involve the will to power, but the will to *freedom* – for everyone.

If, however, we are tempted to assess the ideological consequences of Ibsen's project for the pursuit of liberation and ennoblement, two objections may arise: in the first instance, it is natural for an elitist to wish to create a rhetorical harmony between the elitist and the democratic positions; Thomas Carlyle too insisted that the aristocracy represented 'the real' democracy. Secondly, there is an obscurity about Ibsen's view of the aristocracy that emerges in an exchange in *Rosmersholm*. In answer to a question from Kroll, Rosmer explains the nature of his project of ennoblement in these terms:

> ROSMER: To make aristocrats of everyone in the land.
> KROLL: Everyone – !
> ROSMER: As many as possible, at least.
> KROLL: By what means?
> ROSMER: By liberating minds and enfeebling the wills, I imagine.

When Kroll reacts to Rosmer's claim to want to ennoble *everyone* he hurriedly revises this to 'as many as possible'. Both Ibsen and Rosmer operate from a position that typifies aristocratic individualism; the presumption is that everyone can be ennobled, and there is no option for those who, in the real world, would never be able to live up to the ideals.

As many as possible are to be ennobled. But what of the remainder, what about the rest of us? There is, at the core of Rosmer's revision, the seed of elitism, and in this unresolved situation lies a possibility common to both Rosmer and his creator – in consequence if not in intention – of a distinction arising between masters and slaves.[21] In other words, the path that links Rosmer and Borkman need not be as long as one might at first sight think, and the same goes for the path leading from Ibsen to Nietzsche.

A UNIVERSITY CHAIR FOR SIGURD

On 10 January 1897, *John Gabriel Borkman* had its world premiere in Helsinki, opening at both the Svenska Teatern and the Finska Teatern. In Norway,

Lindberg acquired performance rights outside Kristiania, but following protests from Bergen the rights there went to Den Nationale Scene. Lindberg was quicker off the mark than either Bergen or Kristiania, however, and the Norwegian premiere on 19 January was in – of all places – Drammen, just south of Kristiania.

The Christiania Theatre pulled out all the stops in an effort to avoid the humiliation, but had to concede defeat. Lindberg even arranged for extra trains to be put on to tempt the capital's theatre-lovers to take the trip to provincial Drammen. Lindberg himself played Borkman in a performance that was greatly admired. In the course of the spring the play opened in Stockholm, Frankfurt, Berlin, Copenhagen, Amsterdam, London and Prague, and in the autumn in Paris, New York and Budapest.

As it happens, Ibsen had other things to occupy his mind that spring than the fate of his ambitious bank manager on the European stage. Once again the question of Sigurd's future had to be dealt with. On 29 April a government committee resolved to establish a chair in sociology for Sigurd, something he had been hoping would happen for a couple of years now. Sociology was a new discipline in Norway, but Sigurd was familiar with it from Europe and had been campaigning for its introduction into Norway. The previous autumn he had tested the waters by delivering a series of lectures at the university that were well attended and attracted considerable attention in the press. Henrik and Bergliot sat in the front row and studied the faces of the committee members, expressionless even when the audience, in a breach of academic etiquette, burst into a round of applause.

The committee's conclusion was that 'Dr Sigurd Ibsen has failed to demonstrate, in the series of lectures delivered, that he possesses the scientific qualities necessary for the university to be able to offer him with confidence a chair in the study of Sociology . . .'

In other words, he was incompetent. And this was broadcast to the entire world in all the Norwegian and foreign-language newspapers that had been following the story. Not surprisingly the Storting, acting on the committee's advice, declined to establish the chair in sociology. For a man with a pronounced superiority complex such as Sigurd Ibsen the rejection came as a total humiliation. All his old bitterness against Norway flared up, he felt himself betrayed on all sides and shortly afterwards left for Monsummano in Italy in the company of his mother. It is easy to understand that the Ibsen family felt deeply offended. But they should have realised much earlier which way the wind was blowing. In the Norwegian political world the university was not a neutral arena. Political appointments were nothing new, and when the Left promoted the social sciences, one of its reasons for doing so was to challenge the power of the jurists who made up the conservative bastion among the state's civil servants. Sigurd was one of those on the left with radical views on the question of the Union, and as if that were not enough, he was unlucky in that two of the most influential members of the committee were the deeply conservative professors T. H. Aschehoug and Bredo Morgenstierne.

In the summer the decision was taken to appoint a new committee and invite Sigurd to give a second series of trial lectures. But he was too proud to accept the invitation, and to accept a more humble post such as senior lecturer was equally unthinkable. The only thing that would satisfy his honour would be an unconditional offer of the professorship itself. Many, including quite a few on the left, thought him both touchy and arrogant; even his father advised him against an exaggerated stubbornness. It was one thing not to have many friends in the political world; what made it worse was that he didn't seem to want any either.[22]

In the end both father and son decided to remain in Norway – a disappointment, perhaps, for Suzannah, who might have seen a second exile as the chance for a new and better life in a warmer climate. Sigurd returned to his literary activities, from 1898 onwards in the pages of his own magazine, *Ringeren*. Not until the turn of the century did a career option present itself that seemed acceptable to him.

The problems over Sigurd's professorship affected Henrik. He was still worrying about it in December. In a letter to Prozor he tells him that he is no longer enjoying life in Norway. It wasn't just his son's difficulties that bothered him, the cold dark winters were getting him down too. He noticed his health was declining, he had less energy, and his legs were causing him pain. With Suzannah and Sigurd heading south he dreaded the prospect of being alone. Above all he wanted to get back to writing; ever since the summer he had been thinking about a new play:

'I feel the essence of it already,' he told Suzannah in June, 'but so far I only see one of the characters. Still, the others will appear soon enough, no doubt.'

And perhaps they would have done, had the author stayed put at his desk. Early in the year Julius Elias had suggested that Fischer Verlag publish his collected works, and over the summer Ibsen sent off all the plays that had been published by Gyldendal. It proved more difficult to get hold of copies of the two early works *The Burial Mound* and *Olaf Liljekrans*, but he finally tracked them down in the archives of the Norwegian Theatre in Bergen and the university library in Kristiania. He adamantly refused to allow *St John's Night* to be included, however, and despite Elias' protests the play was excluded. In 1898, Jacob Hegel at Gyldendal likewise suggested a collected works in the form of a cheap 'popular edition', an idea that Ibsen wholeheartedly approved of, though still refusing to allow the inclusion of *St John's Night*.

The timing of these two initiatives was not accidental. On 20 March 1898, Ibsen would be celebrating his seventieth birthday, an occasion that neither publishers nor theatres intended to pass over in silence.

PRIDE AND PAPIER-MÂCHÉ

Long before the great day arrived congratulations and gifts began streaming in: a painting from Ibsen's French friends, and a silver 'loving cup' from England with a greeting signed by, among others, the prime minister Lord Robert Cecil and the writers Thomas Hardy, Henry James and George Bernard Shaw. Gerhard Gran edited a *Festschrift* with a greeting from King Oscar and contributions from twenty-five writers, actors and critics from Norway, Denmark, Sweden and Finland. It seems no one had thought to invite Shaw or Hauptmann, and why not Zola? Five of the contributors, however, were women, though none of them Norwegian.

The centre of all this attention reacted in the only sensible way possible. 'If it was up to me,' he sighed to Jacob Hegel, 'I'd run off and hide somewhere in the mountains, somewhere nice and quiet.' On the day itself, 20 March, there were gala performances at both the Christiania Theatre (*The Feast at Solhaug*) and Centralteatret (*Ghosts*). There were gala performances in two Copenhagen theatres, three in Stockholm, four in Vienna, and six in Berlin. Two days earlier Ibsen had attended the Christiania Theatre's production of *The Master Builder*. Suzannah went with him, but insisted that her husband sat alone in the box.

'This is your evening,' she said, 'and I have no business being there.'

Suzannah's health did not allow her to participate in the celebrations that took place over the next few weeks in Denmark and Sweden. On Wednesday 30 March, Ibsen stepped onto the platform at Copenhagen station to be met by Jacob Hegel and Peter Hansen, who accompanied him to the Prince's Suite at the Hotel d'Angleterre. A small box lay waiting for him in the room. No doubt he was able to guess its contents. While the train was at Gothenburg station he had received a telegram from Hansen, who was now manager of the Kongelige Teater, informing him that he was to be honoured with the Dannebrog Great Cross, his most prestigious award so far. In great excitement he opened the box.

'But, what is this?' He held up the box's contents, his hands shaking.

'This isn't a decoration. It's made of papier-mâché.'

It was explained to him that the etiquette governing the award process required the recipient to visit the royal jeweller in person and buy the order with his own money. The following day, Hegel made it his business to buy the award for Ibsen, only to discover, on handing it to him, that Ibsen had already been presented with the proper version of the order by the king himself. In the evening he dined with Hegel, Nils Vogt, editor of *Morgenbladet*, and Alexander Kielland, who happened to be in town. The next day there was a gala performance of *The Wild Duck* at the Kongelige Teater. Ibsen sat alone in a box directly opposite the royal box, where the Danish royal couple were joined by the Russian tsarina and the Princess of Wales. The production was not to Ibsen's taste. Afterwards he was greeted by students who had gathered in Kongens

Nytorv to offer him a greeting that no one heard, for which he gave a speech of thanks that also no one heard. When he then expressed a wish to return to his hotel it seems that no one had ordered a cab for him. Peter Hansen had presumed he would be willing to walk the few metres back to the hotel.

In this he turned out to be catastrophically mistaken.

Peter Nansen, from Gyldendal, had walked ahead to the hotel with his wife Betty. There they joined Kielland, but before they had a chance to order something to eat and drink the hotel door was flung open and from the square outside came the sounds of shouting and cheering:

'We heard wild shouting,' Nansen related, 'cheers for Ibsen, mixed with the shrieks of women who were almost being knocked off their feet.'

And then, as though shot from a cannon, Ibsen suddenly appeared in the doorway – 'shaken, his coat torn, his broad-brimmed hat pushed back, his orders and medals dangling outside his coat, with Peter Hansen and his wife close behind him as a dense crowd of excited men and women, high-spirited youths and tipsy hooligans just looking for a good time jostling behind him.'

Henrik Ibsen superstar was in town. If he hadn't realised it before, Peter Hansen knew it now. But Kielland was furious: 'Christ above, isn't that typically Danish!' he exclaimed – 'Absolutely typically Danish!' Ibsen should have been conveyed across the square 'in a bridal chariot with white horses, with the theatre director as his gallant defender'. But Ibsen lived to tell the tale, and now he settled down to a meal of three open sandwiches, a beer and a dram, which he must have found very welcome, for Hansen had neglected to provide him with anything during the long evening at the theatre.

So he survived the first day, but more tribulations awaited. On the following day there was to be a gala banquet in his honour at the hotel. Here just about everything that could go wrong did go wrong. When the evening's main speaker, Professor Kristian Kroman, had to cancel at the last minute, Peter Hansen – again – had to step into the breach, and in all haste had to adapt his own informal words of welcome into something resembling a formal speech. It did nothing of the kind. Nor was Sophus Schandorph's speech particularly successful, not so much because the speech was poor as because the speaker was so drunk he had to be supported by two men while he delivered it. If the dinner had got under way in a rather tense atmosphere this was now dispelled by outbursts of laughter and ribald shouts. Schandorph would have none of it:

'You should bloody well keep quiet while I'm speaking!' he bellowed from his post, swaying behind the guest of honour, who presumably maintained his usual silence. That can't have been easy when he was accosted after the meal by the boisterous painter Thorvald Niss, who in a moment of pure enthusiasm put his arms around him and shook him heartily from side to side.

'God dammit, you really are something! Thank you for everything, my lad!'

Ibsen, rigid with fear, stretched out his hands in front of himself in self-defence.

'Get rid of this man.'

So much for Danish joviality, of which there would be more on his third day in Copenhagen, Saturday 2 April. At a reception at the Students' Union, Valdemar Vedel got things off to a bad start by addressing Ibsen with the familiar 'du' form instead of the formal 'de'. Ibsen's response was a simple 'Thank you and goodbye' as he stood up and left the gathering. On his way out he remarked: 'An able man, no doubt, although I cannot ever remember that he and I drank each other's health and agreed to address each other as "du".'

Yet again the boisterous and convivial Danes had managed to tread on his toes. A performance of *Brand* which he attended at the Dagmar Theatre the following evening proved a little more enjoyable. Here he was served a buffet dinner and as much champagne, beer, whisky, liqueurs and coffee as he wanted. That's all that was needed; he was, moreover, deeply moved by the performance and had to dry his tears several times. This may have been the first time he ever saw *Brand* staged, unless he was present at August Lindberg's production at the Eldorado in the autumn of 1895. After a much needed day of rest Ibsen's visit to Copenhagen concluded with a dinner at Jacob Hegel's country home Skovgaard. Here he had a final encounter with Danish joviality when Sophus Schandorph tried to make up for his disastrous speech by kissing him. But Ibsen was in no mood to be kissed by Schandorph and again left the gathering early. The following day he travelled on to Stockholm for a continuation of the celebrations. He would never see Copenhagen or indeed Denmark again.

* * *

On his way to the Swedish capital Ibsen came as close to meeting August Strindberg as he ever would. Strindberg arrived by the 15.31 train direct from Paris at Lund station on 6 April. There he was met by a student choir and a large flag-waving crowd that he quickly realised had not actually gathered to greet him. Strindberg did not like large gatherings and left as quickly as possible. At 16.10 Ibsen's train arrived. After a brief spell of speeches, songs and cheering he travelled on to Stockholm and more speeches, songs and cheering. Forty minutes separated them. Strindberg might have waited, but he didn't.

A week later Ibsen was interviewed in the newspaper *Dagen*. Here he praised Strindberg's talent and said that, while he had never met his Swedish colleague, he had read his work with the greatest interest; *Inferno* (1897) had impressed him particularly. It is not hard to guess Strindberg's response, and in the autumn he asked Gustaf af Geijerstam to send Ibsen a copy of *To Damascus* along with a greeting to the effect that he was ashamed not to have been part of the celebrations for 'the Master from whom I have learned much'.

'But,' he is careful to add, 'I greet the Master of the dramatic arts, not the philosopher!'

Ibsen sent a note of thanks, again using af Geijerstam. Strindberg was aware that Ibsen had bought Christian Krohg's portrait of him and was greatly amused by the fact. And Ibsen was no less amused at the fact of having his 'mortal enemy' hanging on the wall of his study.

Once in Stockholm, Ibsen checks in at the Hotel Rydberg on Gustav Adolf's Square. He spends the first couple of days quietly, but on 9 April he has an audience with King Oscar II, who awards him the Great Cross of the Order of the North Star. Six years previously he had received the St Olav Order, Commander, First Class, and the following year the Great Cross of the same order. With this he could adorn his broad chest with the most distinguished decorations it was possible to obtain in Scandinavia. During his audience Ibsen was careful to raise the matter of his son's career prospects. Bearing in mind that Sigurd had recently come out in favour of a dissolution of the Union and the establishment of a separate monarchy in Norway, the king was surprisingly open:

I know he doesn't want me as the nation's king; but no matter. Let us just hope that his wife does not influence him further in the direction of radical protest!

Ibsen assured him that Bergliot was not dangerous in her radicalism, but the king probably knew what he was doing. With Ibsen junior campaigning for his removal as king of the Norwegians, he attached Ibsen senior ever more closely to the royal house of Sweden with this expansive symbolic gesture. The following day the newspapers commented on how remarkable it was that a Norwegian should be awarded the Order of the North Star. It's hard to know whether Ibsen himself was aware of the political implications behind all this, but there are no reasons to suppose that he, the old prophet of Scandinavianism, shared his son's views on the Union. The episode shows how untenable was Ibsen's insistence that he was 'above politics'; whether he liked it or not, as long as he was Scandinavia's greatest writer and the father of Sigurd Ibsen, his embrace of the Swedish monarchy was a political act with a direct bearing on the question of the Union. And yet his freedom as a writer was paramount. At a dinner later that same evening, Oscar II ventured to criticise him for having written *Ghosts*. He sat in silence for some time, before finally exclaiming: 'Your Majesty, I *had* to write *Ghosts*.'

Two days later the Swedish Society of Authors invited him to a dinner at Hotel Hasselbacken in Djurgården, and on other evenings there were visits to the theatre (*The Pretenders* and *Lady Inger of Østråt*), and a banquet arranged for him by the city at the Grand Hotel. The recent decorations had had an immediate effect on Stockholm society, with everyone keen for the company of the writer and royalist. Verner von Heidenstam found it tasteless:

'All those people who despised Ibsen the week before and never read his work are now suddenly praising him.' Even Carl David af Wirsén, Ibsen's most severe critic in Sweden, turned up at the banquet to dine with 'the until-recently condemned enemy of the people and prophet of darkness'.

Owing to the great interest there were problems of space, and women were excluded from the banquet. There were protests. Ibsen had always valued his contact with the female social elite in Sweden, and enjoyed the respect of Sweden's female authors. So they managed to persuade him to postpone his return to Norway to enable him to attend the Ladies Ibsen Celebrations at the Hotel Hasselbacken on 16 April, spontaneously arranged by the Nya Idun and Fredrika-Bremer Society. The celebrations began at seven o'clock with the guest of honour occupying a gilded chair and surrounded by 250 guests. He was in his element here, and was no doubt delighted when the floor was taken by the young female members of the Friends of Folk Dancing.

One dancer in particular quickly attracted his attention. Rosa Fitinghoff was twenty-six years old and destined to be the last of Ibsen's princesses. Like Helene Raff she came from a good family that had been reduced to genteel poverty following the early death of her father. In spite of their poverty, the mother and daughter of the family remained in touch with prominent social circles in Stockholm, so their presence at Djurgården that evening was no surprise. Once the performance was at an end he made it his business to talk to her. She wrote in her journal that he 'touched my hair and said that you simply didn't find such lovely thick hair in Norway'. When he took hold of her dress to pull her towards him, she was putty in his hands:

> And he wanted me to pack my things and accompany him to Norway the next night – he said it lots and lots of times.

After the rain comes the sun, as day follows night. When Ibsen stood waiting on the platform the following day, Rosa and her mother really did turn up. He catches sight of her and asks whether she has packed her suitcase, which her mother does not find particularly amusing. A few days later he receives a letter from Rosa and writes back, regretting that they did not meet until just before he left. But she must write again. Rosa does, and with that another epistolary romance was under way. The following summer they met in Kristiania, first with Rosa's mother present, later alone in Arbins gate.

And as for what happened *there*, Rosa confided only in her beloved journal, equipped with the following warning on its cover: 'No honourable and decent person may read this book until long after I am dead.'

* * *

Ibsen had almost a month of continuous celebrating behind him in the three capitals as he took his seat on the train bound for Norway on 17 April. Was it all a triumph? A highlight in the ageing writer's career? Was this the crown of victory?

Not necessarily. Taken together, all the reports of the celebrations in articles, letters and memoirs display a certain ambivalence, a slightly sour sense of dutifulness beneath the superficial enthusiasm. Some, like the young journalist Albert Engström, were very far from impressed. He met Ibsen at the Society of Authors' dinner in Stockholm:

> Of certain personalities people say: as he spoke he seemed to grow. That was certainly not the case with Ibsen. The sphinx disappeared, transformed into a fat, spoiled, lion-coiffed black poodle. He was one of my great disillusionments.

That the phrase 'as he spoke he seemed to grow' is a quotation from *Brand* is something of which Engström seems to have been unaware, and in one sense that says all that needs to be said. Ibsen's writing had begun to percolate down into everyday speech. Already the whole 'sphinx' mythology was beginning to seem stale to many of the young, his legendary taciturnity merely peculiar, his heavy drinking obvious, and his taste for young women pathetic. They may indeed have been young, but Engström makes the point that the women who mobbed Ibsen in Stockholm were mostly elderly: 'Like a horde of termites they swarmed over him, crept inside him, into his ears and nostrils, and began to eat him alive. One or two in particular were almost insane in their desire to rub up against him, enter him completely and rub their souls up against his.'

The old women came of their own accord, the young he invited – and not only Rosa Fitinghoff. A number of young women are said to have visited him in his hotel room. He used the whole Hilde Wangel syndrome for all it was worth, handing out signed portraits with a kiss and the words:

> Just as I dreamed my Hilde.

The twenty-nine-year-old Engström was, by his own account, one of the 'young blasphemers'. But this was about more than a lack of respect among the young. In both Copenhagen and Stockholm it might seem as though all the fuss around Ibsen had got slightly out of control. One might call it all hysteria, whipped up by journalists in search of sensation, and by a public equally hungry for it. Ibsen was a superstar in an age that still lacked the structural mechanics for dealing with celebrity. Several speakers had addressed him as 'Master'. But how does a master behave, and how does one behave in his presence? Did a master make his own way across a public square after an evening at the theatre, or should he be driven? Ibsen himself behaved more or less as he had always done. He emptied the glasses of punch that were placed in front of him, flirted with the girls, kept quiet when he felt like it, and replied enigmatically when he did feel like replying. Many were impressed, many disappointed. At the Society of Authors' gathering in Stockholm he had turned to the woman sitting next to him:

'Can you tell me . . .'

At once the woman adopted an expression of profound interest, clearly anticipating a typical manifestation of the Ibsen enigma:

'Do you know, can I take the night train to Kristiania direct, or do I have to spend the night in Laxå?'

No matter what he did, he encountered his own reputation. Perhaps he tried to play down the expectations; for example, he made no mention of 'the third kingdom' in any of his speeches. After *The Lady from the Sea*, which many had expected to signal the start of a new period in his writing, it probably made sense to drop the whole 'kingdom' business from his repertoire. Of course he was ridiculed. But if the writer had started to turn into a parody of himself, it is worth pointing out that hardly any accounts of the celebrations of his seventieth birthday belittle the actual *writing*.

* * *

A month after Ibsen's return to Kristiania there was a small coda to the celebrations in Sweden. On 26 May the Norwegian Women's Union gave a banquet in his honour. Suzannah accompanied him on this occasion. In his speech of thanks, Ibsen said something that has acquired great significance for the understanding of his attitude towards the issue of women's liberation. Politely but firmly, he denied that his work had been to advance the cause of the freedom of women; he was, he said, not even really sure what the words meant:

> For me, it has been a question of the liberation of humanity. And careful readers of my books will understand this. It is of course desirable to settle the women question, but as a corollary, not as a primary aim. My task has been *the portrayal of humanity*.[23]

Ibsen's words have often been used in support of the view that his writing, and above all *A Doll's House*, cannot be considered polemical contributions to the feminist cause. But it is not that straightforward. In the first place, the validity of that conclusion depends on the degree of authority one ascribes to Ibsen's view of his own works. In the second place, the reasoning, as it stands, is not particularly clear. If we insist on the distinction between 'human liberation' and 'women's liberation', the implication is that the feminine does not represent the universal, with the further implication that the universal is represented only by the masculine. If, on the other hand, the feminine is regarded as being as universal as the masculine, then there is nothing to hinder *A Doll's House* being read as a feminist work that deals with specifically female problems and *at the same time* allows us to affirm that it is about 'human liberation'.[24]

It is highly unlikely that Ibsen himself was clear about these distinctions. The main point of his speech was probably to protest once again against the reduction of literature to the status of a socio-political pamphlet. There is no reason to exaggerate the radical nature of Ibsen's feminism. The preparatory notes for *A Doll's House* make it clear that he regarded women as being essentially different from men: 'There are two kinds of spiritual law, two kinds of conscience, one in the man, and a different one in the woman. They do not understand each other, but in daily life the woman is judged by the laws of men, as though she were not a woman but a man.' There is no generalised humanity here, no universality, only two sexes governed by different laws. In closing his speech to the Women's Union, however, he relates the contribution of women to humanity primarily to their role as mothers:

> It is the women who shall solve the question of humanity. They shall do so as mothers. And only *then* can they do so.

For Ibsen to demonstrate in this way that he was a child of his time and the world in which he actually lived need not have any repercussions for a reading of *A Doll's House*. What he demonstrated in his speech is that the work may be greater than the writer. Looking back from the perspective of over a century later, there are probably many who would grant him that.

THE MAN AND THE MASK

Over the summer Gustaf af Geijerstam, William Archer and his brother Charles visited Kristiania. Another arrival was Christian Morgenstern, from Fischer Verlag, who came to discuss plans for the publication of Ibsen's collected works. Morgenstern installed himself in Nordstrand on the outskirts of town and worked on the translations, under the close scrutiny of Ibsen himself.

Under the circumstances it was impossible to get started on a new play. By way of recompense he could reflect on the fact that turning seventy had been a very lucrative business. Gyldendal's popular edition alone, printed in an edition of 15,000 copies, netted him 75,000 kroner, and his total income for the whole of 1898 was 98,257 kroner. Between then and the turn of the century the popular edition appeared in nine volumes. The first two volumes of the German venture also appeared that year, edited by Julius Elias and Paul Schlenter, and by 1903 the complete edition in nine volumes had appeared.

Not until February 1899, against a background of speculation that had lasted throughout the anniversary year, could Ibsen inform Hegel that he was hard at work on the writing of a new play. On the day before his seventieth birthday, when a journalist asked what his next play would be about, Ibsen was his usual secretive self, though the journalist felt encouraged to report that 'Hr Ibsen's next book will probably be *a summing-up of his life's work*, a presentation of all that he has experienced and lived through over a lifetime. A book in which he will show how all his plays relate to each other, and that all of them were created in accordance with a definite plan.' In a speech at the birthday banquet four days later Ibsen revealed that 'I really am thinking about writing such a book now. A book that links my writing to my life in a way that will be revelatory.' Perhaps he really did intend to write an autobiography, or perhaps he was simply teasing his public. Because whatever else it was, what he actually wrote was not an autobiography. But never before had he come closer to himself and his own writing than he would do in his next play.

Through the whole of the spring and summer of 1899 he worked at his desk, but by the end of July he had still got no further than a draft of the first act. He felt his age now, everything took more time. Moreover, a couple of serious distractions occurred in the course of the summer. Not that it necessarily bothered him, and especially not when one of them had voluminous dark hair and was named Rosa Fitinghoff.

At last she had come, as she had promised she would – even if she did bring her mother. On 24 July the two Swedish ladies booked into the Teachers' Home, and met Ibsen at the Grand Hotel the same day. Rosa had been wild with excitement at the prospect of meeting her famous admirer again. The following day they were invited to Arbins gate, and later in the day Ibsen treated them to ice cream and cakes at the Grand. On the next day mother and daughter left town, but not before Rosa had taken the opportunity to meet Ibsen at the apartment in Arbins gate. This time they were alone. He was seventy-one, she was twenty-seven. He gave her his photograph, told her he wanted her to be with him the whole time because he found it so much easier to write then.

Then he pulled her close:

He kissed my hands over and over again, put his arms around me and kept touching me. – Didn't want to let me go.

When Rosa explains that her mother is waiting for her, he finally releases her – but carries on saying 'lots of strange, warm things' that Rosa dare not even commit to writing in her journal. And still he isn't quite prepared to let her go:

When I said goodbye, he kissed me, first on the cheek and then a long, full kiss on the lips, lots of times. – And his eyes were filled, filled with tears, he kept telling me. He was so upset he was actually shaking, followed me all the way out to the hallway and didn't bother in the least that a man was sitting there waiting to see him.

Rosa had gone to visit the sphinx and met the man. Trembling with excitement, Ibsen had reached out to grab the rose when it was finally within reach. She did not go back to see him again after that. In December she received a dedicated copy of his final play. In return she sends him a pillow for Christmas. Ibsen's response maintains the erotic undertones of their previous encounter:

Each day I lay my head on it and imagine it is my little fairy that has come to me.

The following Christmas she sends another gift. He thanks her, and calls her his 'princess from the fairy-story world'. After Ibsen's death Rosa made a single short entry in her journal: 'Ibsen died. Sent money for a wreath.' Later she was reluctant to talk about their relationship, claiming it would harm his reputation. Yet she did reveal that he had proposed to her. As it happens Rosa – like Emilie Bardach, Helene Raff and Hildur Andersen – never did marry. The thing about Ibsen's princesses is that they seem to have entered body and soul into their role as the master's muse, to the huge satisfaction of those who cultivate the mythology of inspiration, and who strenuously deny that the writer was in any way at the mercy of his private parts.

Only a brief journal entry about wet kisses and fumbling hands remains as evidence that the muses aroused desires in the master that were more than spiritual.

* * *

Not long after Rosa's visit it was time for the unveiling of Stephan Sinding's statues of Ibsen and Bjørnson outside the new National Theatre, which opened with three days of celebrations from 1 to 3 September 1899. Ibsen and Bjørnson were the guests of honour.

Those in charge of the arrangement must have been dreading it. Ibsen and Bjørnson guests of honour – at the same time and in the same place? And moreover: what play to choose for the opening performance? All of these matters were going through the head of the theatre's first director, Bjørn Bjørnson, when he bumped into Ibsen in the street one day. He enquired whether any decision had been reached. When Bjørn replied that he was considering his father's *Sigurd Jorsalfar*, with music by Grieg, Ibsen was quick to respond:

'Please let me remind you that I am the older of the two of us.'

'If Ibsen chooses to look at it in that light,' answered Bjørn, 'allow me to point out that Holberg is even older.'

The solution was to mount a Ludvig Holberg cavalcade the first evening, *An Enemy of the People* on the second night, and *Sigurd Jorsalfar* on the third. Bjørnson had been dreading the opening, at which King Oscar II was due to be present – 'for God's sake don't let me disturb things for him and Ibsen!' When the day arrived, he turned up anyway, as did Ibsen. Quite a sight, the two old 'poet-chieftains', taking their seats next to each other in the middle of the stalls, separated only by a garland of red and white roses. The audience went wild. Bjørnson had regained his composure, waved and bowed to acknowledge the applause, while Ibsen sat stiffly staring straight at the curtain and nervously drumming with his fingers. By the third evening he could tell that Bjørnson had won the draw anyway; though his own play had preceded it, Bjørn had mounted a much more lavish production of his father's work.

And then there were the statues. It would be stretching things to say that Sinding's enormous bronze statues were particularly well received when they were unveiled on the morning of 1 September. Didn't the two poets look more like a couple of cheese magnates? And didn't Ibsen look almost too hunched over and introspective? When he was asked later what it felt like to pass his own statue, Ibsen replied: 'One gets used to it.' And the rest of the population did too, and so he remained standing on that pedestal outside Norway's National Theatre – in bronze, and considerably larger than life-size.

RESURRECTION DAY

On 21 September the first draft of the new play was finished, and two months later Ibsen sent off the fair copy, with the working title 'Resurrection Day' changed to 'When the Dead Awaken'. By the time the play was published on 2 December 1899, a final change had been made and it appeared under the title *When We Dead Awaken. A Dramatic Epilogue.* Encouraged by the success of Ibsen's previous play Jacob Hegel printed a first edition of 12,000 copies, quickly followed by a second of 2,000. Over the following year translations appeared in Germany, England, France and Russia.

When We Dead Awaken opens with two people sitting in wicker chairs on a warm summer day in the grounds of a Norwegian spa hotel. The ageing sculptor Arnold Rubek has returned to his homeland with his young wife Maja. After completing 'Resurrection Day', the work that made his name, Rubek's talent has deserted him. Now he simply earns a living by making portrait busts.

Maja, young and vivacious, has little in common with her melancholic husband and no way of knowing what it is that plagues him. It is clear that the marriage has grown stale, if indeed it has ever been a good one.

Presently Rubek becomes aware of another guest, a woman dressed in white, who is constantly accompanied by a deaconess wearing black. They start a conversation, and Rubek realises that this is Irene, the woman who was his model for 'Resurrection Day'. His sculpture had originally depicted a vision of 'the earth's most noble, pure, and ideal woman', but later he changed it, placing the woman among a group of women with 'the hidden faces of animals'. This was the version that had made his name throughout the world. Only now does Irene learn of how he betrayed his original vision. Theirs is a strange and fateful encounter. Rubek is convinced that his creative powers deserted him when Irene left him, and that she, and she alone, can restore them to him.

Will she return to him? It is no easy matter for Irene. She sacrificed everything for him back then, she claims, gave him both her soul and her life. But Rubek had refused to see her as a living woman, in need of love; he saw her only with the eyes of an artist, not of a man. After she left him, things turned out badly for Irene. Following two failed marriages she ended up in a mental hospital, and she is still under the supervision of a nurse. Now she sees herself as one of the living dead, and accuses Rubek of having stolen her soul. But he too identifies more closely with death than with life.

In the course of the play's three short acts Rubek and Irene become a sort of couple, while Maja takes to the mountain in the company of a virile local squire, Ulfheim, a hunter who pursues everything from bears to women. Through a series of painful confrontations Rubek and Irene come to a decision to try to live one last time. They too head on up into the mountains, where they meet Maja and Ulfheim. Ulfheim, an experienced climber, advises them to seek shelter from a storm that is on the way. He takes Maja down the mountain, but Irene and Rubek continue on up into the heights where they are engulfed by an avalanche and die.

* * *

Although Ibsen denied it himself, it is obvious that the play represents yet another step in the direction of symbolism. In a letter of December 1900 he writes:

> The symbolism is something well-meaning and deep-minded that readers read into my generally quite realistic representations.

This is a piece of pure obscurantism from a writer who always denied his association with any literary trend, no matter how obvious it might be. If the strategy is a familiar one it is also understandable. Ibsen was in sympathy with the trend in the 1890s for symbolism, the irrational and the mystical in art. But he was no young rebel, he was an old man. What did he really have in common with the *fin de siècle* generation? Edvard Munch admired his symbolic dramas and was convinced that *When We Dead Awaken* was inspired by his own painting *Woman in Three Stages* of 1894. But where Ibsen greatly influenced Munch, Munch's influence on him was probably marginal, even though Ibsen may well have had the red, white and black woman from Munch's painting in mind when he created Maja, Irene and the deaconess.[25] Ibsen was an old man, his symbolism was not rebellious but eclectic and contemplative. It is not even certain that this was some kind of personal reckoning, for he had never been a programmatic positivist, naturalist or rationalist. On the contrary, he was able, in his final dramas, to make use of elements from the play of ideas and the heritage of Romanticism that he had never quite abandoned. In this sense he was right to distance himself from the symbolic camp in which others were so keen to place him.

In any event, to describe *When We Dead Awaken* as being essentially a realistic play is meaningless, and it is significant that those who have denigrated the play have done so based on a realistic reading. Most have either read it as allegorical or symbolical in some way or other. Contemporary responses were mixed, but respectful.[26] Some complained of its obscurity, its negativity, the amorality of its message, whereas others were ecstatic in their praise. In James Joyce's view the play was so masterfully realised that criticism was impossible:

> When the art of a dramatist is perfect the critic is superfluous. Life is not to be criticised, but to be faced and lived.

When Joyce read Ibsen, he did not read *about* life. The drama was in itself part of the formative experience of life. Joyce was under no illusion that his contemporaries would be able to understand this, however: 'Many years more, however, must pass before he will enter his kingdom of jubilation, although, as he stands to-day, all has been done on his part to ensure his own worthiness to enter therein.'

It is an extraordinary statement. The young Joyce declares that this ageing, world-renowned poet-sphinx belongs to the future; his final work is not the end but the beginning of something. He was undoubtedly right about his contemporaries having difficulty grasping *When We Dead Awaken* – in both book form and as a stage play.[27] The Brandes brothers' responses are especially worthy of note, not only because they have such divergent views on the play, but because their readings represent the two main traditions of interpretation that have developed. Edvard's admiration is exceeded perhaps only by Joyce's. Although he continued to find Ibsen inscrutable, the message of this particular play seemed clear to him: 'Without love, no life.' For him, the play was about the artist's betrayal of life, a reading that brings Irene into focus because she is the one who is sacrificed and who represents the judgement on the artist. Had he discussed the play with his brother? Georg too focused on the play's obvious theme, the relationship between art and life. But being an admirer of the concept of genius he had little patience with the accusations that Irene levels at Rubek. Was this not, finally, the old story of the woman's jealousy of the man's creative powers?

> Who has been around artists and their women and not, in some unguarded or overwrought moment, heard the outburst of female hatred for the chiseller, the dauber or the scribbler?

And how naïve of Ibsen to allow Rubek to be affected by Irene's recriminations, and to express regret at having placed art above love:

> Who in the world can believe that happiness in love would have resulted had the artist, in his past association with Irene, neglected all consideration for his work?

Georg Brandes' criticism might seem crude, and in a sense it is. But at the same time he raised an important objection to his brother's interpretation. Because is it, after all, so obvious that love for another is to be placed above a dedication to art, to the call? This leads us to one of two important questions one can ask regarding this play: ought it to be read as a condemnation of the artist's decision to choose his calling above life and love, or is it instead a play about the necessary cost of that calling? The second question is whether the play ends in negativity and hopelessness, or in redemption. And if the latter is the case, what sort of redemption?

* * *

Although Ibsen on this occasion had written a play set entirely in the outdoors, his scenographic signature remains unmistakable. Like *Brand*, this drama too moves along firmly vertical lines. As the three acts progress there is an ascent from the spa hotel to the scene at the mountain sanatorium higher up, and from there to the last act that is played out in the mountains themselves. In a symbolic sense the movement is a shift from the claustrophobic, sleepy non-life in the lowlands to the free and vital life in the mountains. But if there is freedom in the mountain heights there is also the danger of precipitous gorges and harsh weather conditions; death lurks wherever life is lived to the full.

The dialogue in the play is remarkable. It is rich in metaphor and, in the case of Irene in particular, characterised by a stylised rhetoric. The language is also full of so-called oxymorons, a putting together of disparate elements ('hearing silence', 'living dead').[28] In many ways the whole play is a montage of contrasts, between life and death, high and low, warm blood and cold marble. This is also reflected in the cast of characters. Maja and Ulfheim represent sensual and happy vitality. Ulfheim seems almost like an animal in human form (in the opinion of some reviewers he verged on caricature). As regards Rubek and Irene, it is tempting to ask whether Irene exists at all. Is she not actually a projection of Rubek's own imagination, the incarnation of a nostalgic longing for his old idealistic vision of the pure woman? Rubek and Irene are the living dead in the play, though she is the one who exhibits the symbolic manifestation of death: she walks in stiff, measured steps, her eyes closed, her arms crossed, like one dead. She wears a floor-length white gown that suggests a winding sheet and here, as in *Rosmersholm* and *The Master Builder* too, a white shawl that is the sign of death. Irene might also suggest a marble statue, something that is, for her, the same as being dead.

That she also seems to teeter on the verge of insanity was regarded by some reviewers as a weakness. But on this occasion Ibsen found a greater acceptance for his pathological creation than he had done with either Ellida Wangel or Hedda Gabler. A mentally disturbed female was recognised as being one of the master's gallery of characters, and one Danish reviewer reminded his readers that the ancient Greeks regarded the insane as holy. This acceptance is yet another example of the institutionalisation of Ibsen, and thereby of a weakening of his power to provoke.

Although contemporary critics were, as ever, largely reluctant to point to explicitly autobiographical elements in the play, it was impossible not to associate the sculptor Arnold Rubek with the writer Henrik Ibsen. Like Rubek he, too, was the aged artist returning home after a life in exile and failing to find peace. It meant, inevitably, that the play was read as Ibsen sitting in judgement over his own life. Like Rubek, he had sacrificed life for the sake of art, and now he acknowledged the cost of his decision. In Sven Lange's view, a rising sense of doubt and self-recrimination was traceable from *The Master Builder* through *John Gabriel Borkman* to *When We Dead Awaken*. Together they amount to a merciless conclusion: 'A wasted life! A failed poetry!' But then what, in that case, was the poetry that had failed? According to Valdemar Vedel, the play ought to be read as Ibsen's judgement on the realistic dramas of contemporary life and a longing for the 'Romantic idealism' that characterised his earlier dramas. Others have concurred in this, not least those of the Christian Ibsen tradition: 'The whole play is actually one long sustained confession,' writes the Danish priest Andreas Fibiger in 1928, 'a settling of accounts with the past, a bitter scourging of himself and of the writing that was so extravagantly praised by the world.'

The drama was a gift to all those who regretted the direction the writer had taken during the decades since *Brand*: 'In his last work he subjects himself to a profound humiliation,' Fibiger continues. 'The play is a personal confession and a return to the faith of his youth.'

'Resurrection Day' is commonly invoked in support of this theory: in the original version, the pure woman represents the poetry of idealism, and the figures with the hidden features of animals that appear in the changed version refer to Ibsen's own realistic phase. Right in the middle of them Rubek/Ibsen places the penitent artist.

But whether the play is read as a personal day of reckoning or not, the question of whether it ends in redemption or negativity remains. Vedel's view is that it ends in hopelessness, whereas Fibiger is in a tradition that holds that the personal reckoning leads to a new, idealistic and even religious insight. In recent years these edifying readings have been challenged by literary scholars who maintain that the play points forward to modernism rather than back in the direction of idealism and Romanticism. In various ways these critics interpret the play as an exposure of idealism and belief in the idea of the artistic calling; indeed, some claim that what Ibsen actually does here is abjure both art and his own writing.[29] Others point to the emptiness of the language and the allegories and suggest that the play questions belief in the possibility of redemption. One interpretation sees the drama as an inversion of the Pygmalion myth, with Rubek bringing death to the living instead of the dead being brought to life.

There are good reasons for seeing Rubek as a lost soul, as a betrayer. But the question then is, precisely *what* it is he has betrayed – is it life and love, or on the contrary, is it art?[30] As in *John Gabriel Borkman*, at issue here is whether following the call and submitting to one's own nature are worth less than the love of another, which is the question Georg Brandes raised. Just as Borkman has to be Borkman 'and no one else', Rubek too is clear that he must be the man he is – 'Because I was *born* to be an artist, you see. – And will never be anything but an artist, come what may.' Many have read *When We Dead Awaken* as a morality on the subject of the betrayal of love, but strictly speaking this drama, like its predecessors, is amoral. It is less about doing the right thing than about *being* the right thing. And Rubek is an artist. He does not regret his renunciation of life and love; for him, life is only possible through art. And the self-recrimination that is expressed in the final version of 'Resurrection Day' is motivated not by his betrayal of Irene but by his betrayal of his original vision of the resurrection of the pure woman.

No doubt it is correct to suggest that the play sheds ironic light on Rubek's choice of a *life in art*, not least in that Maja has the last word with her song about freedom just as the artist and his model are being swept down from the heights. But the irony is directed at Maja and Ulfheim too, those who choose *a life in life*. None of them live life to its limits – in the final act these two choose to come down the mountain in search of shelter from the storm. In the final analysis they, too, choose safety among the 'half-dead flies and people' down at the spa hotel.

Once again, Ibsen offers variations on the same themes, once again creating work that can be read in a variety of ways, some in direct contradiction of others. And once again it feels as though, in choosing one particular interpretation over another, something gets lost.

THE SPHINX'S SILVER VEINS

Along with *Love's Comedy*, *When We Dead Awaken* is the only one of Ibsen's plays that specifically deals with the theme of the artist, even though *The Master Builder* and *John Gabriel Borkman* can both be read as disguised versions of artist-dramas. Yet this does not mean that the play ought to be read in the light of Ibsen's own life as the contra-indications are just too numerous. Is it reasonable to suppose that Ibsen sacrificed life and love for art? Is it not rather the case that writing brought him victories in life as well as in art? That he might have sacrificed the *shared life* of marriage is a more interesting hypothesis, but not even this is a clear-cut solution. The idea that Suzannah might have directed the same accusations at Henrik as Irene does at Rubek is dubious. Was Suzannah one of the living dead, deprived of life and spirit by her husband? Granted, she sacrificed herself, but at the same time she lived and breathed for the things that her husband achieved in his work, and in which she also claimed a stake.

It is more rewarding to read the play as Ibsen's reflection on art's relationship to life in general, and to his life work – which is actually something other than life. There are, for example, good reasons for interpreting 'Resurrection Day' in the light of the oeuvre, but not necessarily in such a way as to suggest that Ibsen is here expressing regret for having written the dramas of contemporary life. And why indeed would he do such a thing, he who otherwise insisted that his entire production ought to be considered an organic whole? It is more reasonable to see the sculptured group as expressing the split in the artist between the conflicting demands of art and of the world as it is; throughout the 1880s he had frequent experience of the ways in which his plays were requisitioned for this or that political or social viewpoint, all the while insisting himself that they had to be read as literature.

Rubek's problems are Ibsen's problems, but Rubek's regret need not be shared by Ibsen – even though the play invites such a conclusion. And plenty have accepted the invitation over the years. The historical-biographical reading has endured into our own age, but scholars in the twentieth century introduced a counter-reaction that has been both proper and necessary. This does not mean that the historical-biographical method has nothing more to offer, but the problem with the traditional readings of the relationship between life and work is that they often fail to explain the significance of the biographical correspondences. That Ibsen's young female friends, from Emilie Bardach to Hildur Andersen, are of relevance in the context of *The Master Builder* is obvious – but what does it mean? What does Hilde actually say about Hildur, and Hildur about Hilde? And how important are the conclusions we may reach?

Not to mention Rosa Fitinghoff. Ibsen did not know her well, he met her twice before forcing a kiss on her. Some have related the episode to Rubek's unease on the subject of sex. But would Ibsen really need Rosa in order to write about sexual anxiety in his play? After all, the issue lay like a carpet across the entire Victorian era.

Things become more interesting when the historical-biographical reading is related to *the writer's strategies*: when Ibsen inserts references to his own life into the last plays, it relates to his self-constructing strategy of becoming one with the works, of creating a *Gesamtkunstwerk* of himself and his writing. As the reception history shows, Ibsen's readers were hopelessly oriented towards historical-biographical readings, an approach that contributed to the creation of the sphinx in such a way that Ibsen took note of it and recycled it for use in his work. Historically speaking, the fascination for the work is almost indistinguishable from the fascination for the man; it is one thing to admire a piece of work, another altogether to be seduced by a prophet. 'Ibsen' is and always has been more than 'text', he is a modern, European cultural-historical phenomenon. In order to understand the phenomenon it is both sensible and necessary to study the connections between the writer's life and his work – not by establishing simple correspondences between the works and the writer's spiritual life, but by pointing out the complex connections that link the text, the reception and the writer's strategies. If, for example, we read Ibsen's childhood memories from the steeple of Skien church in 1881 as a self-constructing text built from subtle literary effects, then it is difficult not to discover an association with *The Master Builder*. In these two pieces of writing – the one non-fiction, the other fiction – Ibsen combines his *origins* and his *final reckoning* as writer into allegorical myths on the subject of ascending towers.

Regardless of how false and untrue many of the myths about Ibsen might be, they remain a part of the truth of the sphinx.

* * *

What, then, are the veins of silver that run through Ibsen's life and work? What can explain the enormous success he achieved as a writer? The simplest explanation is, of course, the one offered by many of his critics – his choice of sensational and titillating themes. It is easy to forget that Ibsen, the icon of classical culture, was once regarded as tabloid. But one can also do as Otto Borchsenius did in his review of *Ghosts* and maintain that the controversy, 'the problems', were secondary. The simple fact was that what one had here was 'a drama that can take the reader's breath away'.

Might the explanation for Ibsen's success simply be that he is *good*? The question is as seductive as it is hard to answer. What can be gleaned from his contemporary reception is that respect for his talent made it difficult to ignore him, even for those who were against everything he stood for – such as Carl David af Wirsén. On the other hand, it is perfectly possible for a writer to be good or sensational, or both, and still not achieve anything like the level of success that Ibsen achieved.

What is extraordinary is probably best explained by what is extraordinary. The most important explanation for the success of Ibsen's dramas is, in the final analysis, that they were written by Henrik Ibsen – and nobody else. Ibsen's life and his writing consisted of a steady movement in the direction of ever greater freedom and independence. He attained a position of eminence that few, if any, Scandinavian writers before him had ever attained, and from this position he was able to dictate for himself the terms on which he wrote.

With freedom and eminence came power, the ability to set the agenda and exert his own influence upon it.

With this in mind, some have described him as a *miracle*, but where did this miracle come from? Ibsen took two quantum leaps in life.[31] The first was in Rome in the 1860s, when he wrote *Brand* and *Peer Gynt*. The second came with his revolutionising of European drama from the end of the 1870s. Of these two leaps the former is the more significant. When he left Norway and headed for Rome, he severed his ties to Norwegian society. Henceforth citizenship meant nothing to him other than a way of legitimising his claim for an annual writer's wage from the state. Certainly he remained Norwegian in his thinking, not to speak of his writing. But he had no institutional ties to Norway, and declared himself ideologically liberated from both the political debate at home and the whole national-romantic way of looking at life.

He was liberated from his origins in the sense of being independent of them. In timeless Rome he could explore art and his own creativity, and the result was a break with the aesthetic tradition in which he had grown up, in the form of the two verse dramas he wrote there. At the same time those dramas reveal his familiarity with European literature and culture. And it is here that we find the first condition of Ibsen's pre-eminence: he was both provincial and European. He was familiar with the cultural heritage of Europe, but felt neither oppressed by nor obligated to it. As an autodidact from a post-colonial European outpost he possessed the necessary lack of respect to break with the 'rules of beauty'. In Rome he created sufficient distance between himself and his origins to be able to reach beyond himself, as a Norwegian and a European, to create the basis for a new and original literature.

But pre-eminence and power cannot be achieved without a material basis. Ibsen's first book was self-published in 1850 in a land that lacked the most fundamental structural framework for a market-based literary careerist. When he published his last work forty-nine years later it was with the assistance of a well-oiled publishing machine, an affluent and interested public, a professionalised body of criticism, and newspapers and periodicals that amplified the work, spreading it from country to country. Ibsen contributed to this development, particularly in Norway and Scandinavia more generally. The story of Ibsen's journey into freedom is, then, also the story of the growth of a modern, market-based literary arena within a specialised cultural public sphere, with the role of the autonomous writer as its highest accomplishment.

It is also important that Ibsen broke through as a *dramatist*, not just as an author. To a far higher degree than other art forms, drama is bound to a heavily traditional institution, the theatre, which in turn is closely bound up with public political life and prevailing social structures. The theatre is conservative by nature, and renewal faces a stiffer challenge here than in other fields such as the novel and poetry. A vacuum appeared that Ibsen was able to exploit. He had few competitors and a large space within which to grow. As an avant-garde writer it might have been more natural to avoid a bastion of conservatism such as the theatre, but Ibsen was a theatre man through and through, he knew the conventions and the techniques and carried out his revolution from within. In the wave of modernisation that swept across European theatre in the latter part of the 1880s the ageing Norwegian writer was an absolutely central figure. His contribution was to liberate the drama from historicism, mimicry and superficial entertainment, turning it into part of the modern, contemporary world of art and communication.

* * *

But then what was it, more specifically, about *the plays* that had people reading them, going to see them, and discussing them? How did he conquer the market? Now that is a more difficult question to answer. Ibsen's dramas are fundamentally ambivalent. They do not preach, they investigate. Sympathies change, things are examined from different angles. His themes are both contemporary and existential, about the constitution of the individual in the world, about the relationship between the one and the many, about the human dream of exceeding oneself, about human inadequacy, about self-sacrifice and self-deceit. And the magic lies in the multiplicity of the ambiguities, in the absence of answers, and in the feeling that, ultimately, these plays are unfathomable.

And yet ambivalence and ambiguity are only one side of the magic of these plays. Another is the thematic *connections* that make an organic whole of the oeuvre. Ibsen's dramas, and to some extent his poetry too, are variations on a handful of themes spread over a writing career that lasted fifty years, deeply original and yet part of the currents of literary history. No wonder scholars have been busy. The texts can be compared to hidden codes in a book, in which one places a perforated sheet of paper over the page in such a way that the letters legible through the holes give access to a coherent meaning. For over a century literary scholars and others have been placing these perforated sheets across Ibsen's pages, and the code seems always to reveal itself, whether the goal has been to present the works as anarchistic, idealistic, political, feminist or even a critique of orientalism.

Ibsen himself liked to give the impression that there was a 'master plan' behind his entire oeuvre; what is more likely is that he continually looked back and organised the unity with hindsight – his famous letter to Peter Hansen and the Foreword to the 1875 edition of *Catiline* show that this 'unity project' can be traced at least as far back as the early 1870s. The later attempts to systematise his writing at the end of his life must be seen in the same light, not least in the addition of 'A Dramatic Epilogue' as the subtitle to his final play. Of course, audiences assumed that the master was announcing the conclusion of his work, but Ibsen vehemently denied it, saying he had no plans to lay down his pen as long as there was breath in his body.

But then what is the play an epilogue to? Even before publication, Ibsen had told *Verdens Gang* that he thought of *When We Dead Awaken* as an epilogue to the run of works that began with *A Doll's House* – 'it forms a unity, a whole, and with this I am now finished'. In March 1900, however, he conceded to Moritz Prozor that the play concluded the series that began with *The Master Builder*. If we look more closely at the play itself, however, it is also possible to regard it as an epilogue to the plays since *Brand*, in other words, the whole of the mature Ibsen's work. The point is that in one way or another, *all* such divisions can be justified, which brings us back to the idea that, in the final analysis, the whole oeuvre has to be viewed as a single creation. Ibsen said as much explicitly in the Foreword to the *Collected Works* published in 1898, and in April two years later he asked August Larsen to include the last play in his edition, 'where it belongs, organically, as the finale of this series'. In other words, he viewed his entire output as 'this series', as though he was contemplating, at the age of seventy-two, starting on a new one!

Instead of assuming a preordained vision or overall plan, one suggestion is that the writing develops in *dialogue*, with one play commenting on the preceding play and in which the same conflict is discussed using different situations, different settings and characters. Ibsen wasn't God, after all; he was a human being who changed over the years. But he was consistent in his development, of that there can be no doubt.

But there is something else behind the method, behind the strategic thinking – a deeply original personality, a man with unique powers of observation and a talent for transforming lived life into literature. Ibsen's dramatic method can only be understood in the context of who he was as a person. Like his final play, the writer himself is rich in oxymorons, the combining of disparate elements. He was doubter and believer, uncompromising and calculating, man and mask. He wanted to break things down, and yet longed for wholeness; as a man he was authoritarian, as a poet humble. He was a genius but almost dysfunctional in that he struggled to function within the social framework into which he was born. Before choosing exile he appears to have been the victim of this inept side of himself. That he managed to turn this weakness into a strength and create a position for himself independent of the social life he was unable to master might be deemed the human side of Ibsen the miracle. And the miracle is all the more impressive for the fact that, from his position as an outsider, he was able to exert such a powerful shaping influence on society.

One might wonder how it was that a man who lived so divorced from ordinary social life nevertheless managed to capture his time as well as he did. A number of answers have been suggested – his ability to see and describe, or the clarity that came with the perspective of distance. Another and more prosaic answer is that he read his newspapers. Ibsen was an almost fanatical reader of newspapers and regularly ploughed through them, Norwegian and foreign, on his visits to cafes. Several witnesses have recorded how he would begin at the top of page one and continue to the foot of the last page, reading everything, including the advertisements.

'What extraordinary happiness,' he exclaimed once, 'what desperate misfortune can be glimpsed behind an advertisement!'

Many have also pointed out the numerous references to newspapers in his plays, but on a larger scale the newspaper was a prism through which modern life was refracted – 'a place in which innumerable stories tangle with each other and talk over each other', as someone once said.[32]

Ibsen was an observer of contemporary life; what is even more important is that he was also, inevitably, part of it. He lived a life of spotless bourgeois respectability because he was a respectable member of the bourgeoisie. He belonged inside society, even if he lived on the periphery, as a writer with optimal autonomy – like a prophet in the desert. At one and the same time Ibsen is the great destroyer and jester-by-appointment to the bourgeoisie; he wrote of the problems of life faced by modern human beings, of the problem of personality, the fear of change, the ephemeral and the fleeting.[33] His subject was the psychological human being, not the commonsensical, the social or the ideal. When he was able to command such enormous attention, even with something as seemingly blasphemous and indecent as *Ghosts*, then one of the reasons must have been precisely that he was an insider – would the same thing have happened had he been a social rebel along the lines of a Marcus Thrane or a Hans Jæger? At the same time he distanced himself from the material sides of bourgeois life, from political activity, from organisations and from public controversies both great and small. Ignoring the base of society he was, so to speak, left free to float up into its higher regions. More than any other contemporary writer he occupied the role of literary poet-prophet, of truth-teller, of chastiser. He did not locate himself outside society but in his life and his work floated *above* the swamp of trivialities. This ascent was the result both of his artistic genius and of his social dysfunctionality, his strengths and his weaknesses. These tensions, these eternal doubts, were what he wrote about, giving life and form to them as literary alibis – not so very different from Kierkegaard's philosophical method. To understand Henrik Ibsen we have to understand this faith in ambivalence, in self-doubt, and the profound realisation that weakness is a strength.

Are we at the source of all things here? Is this as far as we can go? Ibsen was calculating to the point of being scheming, of that there can be no doubt. But above and beyond that he was an artist who must have believed in his calling with every fibre of his being. And the source of an artistic will cannot easily be uncovered. Some have it, and no one will ever be able to provide a complete explanation of what it is that drives them and why they succeed. Ibsen the miracle will remain unexplained, as is the fate of all miracles. Perhaps we must be content to affirm that, like Shakespeare, he belongs among the great human beings of history, those who have exerted such a powerful shaping influence on succeeding generations that we are no longer able to see the full extent of their originality, precisely because we ourselves are a product of it.[34] If so, this means that any attempt to understand Ibsen will also tell us something vital about ourselves, and for that very reason the study of his life and his works will always be worthwhile.

XII

ARBINS GATE

CAN IBSEN DIE?

In the spring of 1900, Ibsen suffered a mild stroke. He recovered in due course, but decided to be accompanied by Dr Sontum to the sanatorium in Sandefjord in June. Here he and Suzannah spent the summer with Sontum and his family. He enjoyed himself thoroughly, played with the children and took long daily walks along the quays, at least when he was able. At one point he contracted erysipelas in his foot and had to remain in bed for several weeks. Later he was able to hobble around with a stick, but in the autumn his health declined again and he had a second stroke, this one slightly more serious. Everyone was afraid he was going to die. A worried mother-in-law wrote from Copenhagen:

> How can it be that this giant is paralysed, this person who has occupied one of the most important watchtowers in our cultural life? Can he die?

Could Henrik Ibsen die?

His hour had still not yet come. But it came for Christian Sontum. In the summer of 1902 the loyal doctor and faithful family friend was struck down by cancer and died, just forty-four years old. A new doctor was summoned, but despite a glowing reputation, Peter F. Holst failed to win Ibsen's confidence and he was replaced the following year by Dr Edvard Bull. He was a relative of Ole Bull, the doctor attached to the National Theatre and a much loved physician to many of the country's cultural elite. When he turned up at Arbins gate on a May day in 1903 he was met by a suspicious, irritable and reluctant patient. In time, however, his quiet authority won Ibsen's confidence and he remained his doctor until the end.

Life was quiet in Arbins gate. But poor health did not necessarily mean the end of Ibsen's volcanic temperament. When Bull visited and asked Suzannah how the patient was, she might reply: 'Well, you know, not too bad – he's cursed a couple of times!' His taste for order and punctuality had turned into an obsession. When his barber, Carl A. Larsen, arrived on Tuesdays and Fridays at 10.30, Ibsen would be sitting waiting with his silver watch in his hand. If Larsen was two or three minutes late the message was clear: 'Come back tomorrow!'

Fanny Riis remembers that both she and others would often be told to leave the apartment if something they said upset the host. She also noticed that quite suddenly he would disappear into his study, apparently to drink a glass of wine. Was he an alcoholic? Henrik Ibsen's life was a dance with angels and demons. Maybe his ordered life and extreme punctuality were strategies for keeping the demons at bay – and not letting them get the upper hand, as they had done in his youth. Yet he was a man who acknowledged his own demons, those excesses in his own nature. In that sense he was like his plays, rebellious content inside a controlled and managed form.

Is one an alcoholic only if the alcohol has social consequences, if work is neglected, personal hygiene ignored and family life destroyed?

If so, Ibsen was no alcoholic.

Suzannah still had to put up with his outbursts of rage; but now it was *she* who was in charge. No more struggling to get her husband home from nights out binge-drinking with friends, no more princesses – Hildur Andersen was banned from the house. Perhaps it wasn't surprising that Ibsen swore and cursed from the chair that he was increasingly chained to, as Suzannah was chained by her progressively worsening rheumatism. After the turn of the century she was more or less housebound. Yet still she watched over her husband, day and night, and insisted on dusting the paintings twice a month, despite the great pain it caused her.

* * *

Such were their last years together, Henrik and Suzannah. Gradually the circle around them thinned out until it consisted only of close friends, nurses, Dr Bull, and Ibsen's regular masseur, Arnt Dehli. Apart from Johan Hermann they saw little of Suzannah's family. Henrik, however, had renewed contact with Hedvig and in particular her daughter Anna. As early as the autumn of 1891 he had written something in his twenty-three-year-old niece's commonplace book, and they had kept in touch afterwards. In May 1895 he accepted an invitation to attend the golden wedding anniversary of his uncle, Christopher Blom Paus. Following the great fire in Skien the Paus family had moved to the capital, and the occasion was celebrated at the home of Christopher's son, Ole. It seems that, at the gathering, Chamberlain Løvenskiold extended an invitation to Henrik to visit him at his mansion home in Skien, close to Venstøp.

But no, Henrik would not go back to Skien.

Figures from the past reappeared often during these years in Kristiania. One was Hans Jacob Hendrichsen, his illegitimate son. By his own account, he went to see his father at least once. Henrik almost certainly gave him the cold shoulder, and turned down his request for money.[1] It is highly unlikely he ever saw the boy's mother, Elsa Sophie, again either; she died, blind and in poverty, in the summer of 1892. Visits from his legitimate son were much more welcome, though after the turn of the century they became less frequent. In 1899, Sigurd's long and futile search for a career came to an end when he was appointed head of the Department of Internal Affairs. The aim was to build up Norway's own Foreign Office, which had been one of the most contentious issues in the Union debate. Two years later he became a member of the second consulate committee, and in the same year he was appointed to the Cabinet in Otto Blehr's left-wing government. Finally, it seemed, Sigurd was about to claim his rightful place in the world.

When Bjørnson turned seventy in 1902, Ibsen was too ill to attend the celebrations. Instead it was Bjørnson who came to see him. Bjørnson later described the emotional encounter to his youngest daughter Dagny, and the warm words that had passed between them:

'Of all the memories, and the people, it is you I most often think of,' Ibsen told him. And when Bjørnson was about to leave, Ibsen took his hand and added:

'You are dearer to me than all the others.'

There they stood, the two rivals, deeply moved. Bjørnson later told the same story to Kielland, adding: 'I couldn't say the same thing; but his words made me happy, and made both our families happy.'

In 1901 the Nobel Prize in Literature was awarded for the first time. Among the suggestions for candidates for the following year one proposed that the prize be awarded jointly to Ibsen and Bjørnson. Instead it went to the German historian Theodor Mommsen. Ibsen can hardly have been surprised; the committee's secretary and most influential member was none other than Carl David af Wirsén. The Swedish Academy's Nobel Committee was a bastion of the idealistic aesthetic; even parts of Bjørnson's oeuvre were too 'disgusting' for some members of the committee, not to mention his political radicalism. The presence of Carl Snoilsky on the committee cannot have helped his cause either. He resented Norwegian opposition to the Union, and was not an admirer of Ibsen's 'unhealthy' plays of the 1890s. The Nobel committee's expressed reasons for rejecting the joint candidature in 1902 are, however, interesting. The members asserted that individually neither Ibsen nor Bjørnson deserved the prize, and that jointly they were too important and imposing to share it.

On this latter score the two men might have agreed. Bjørnson was awarded the prize in 1903, while Ibsen's name was put forward in vain in both 1903 and 1904. His consolation must be that he shares his failure to win it with Tolstoy, Zola, Chekhov, Strindberg, Proust and Joyce. As long as he sat on the committee, af Wirsén had considerable influence on the awards, and he used it to promote his demands for idealism and moral dignity in literature, with the result that few of the prizewinners of the first ten years are read or even remembered a century later. The Nobel Prize was a great honour, but aesthetically it started out as a prize for yesterday's writers. Ibsen was never a writer for the past, not even at the end of his life.[2]

THE MASK

As he grew steadily weaker, Ibsen had begun to take his daily outings in town by horse and carriage, using a sleigh in winter. While out one day he caught sight of Hildur Andersen. He told the cabman to stop and held his hands over her:

'Bless you, bless you!'

It was the last time he would see his lost princess. In March 1903 he had a third stroke, more severe than the previous two. But he was tough. In the summer he resumed his daily drives, always in the company of his masseur Arnt Dehli, who was by now a trusted companion. That same year Sigurd had asked Halvdan Koht to oversee the publication of his father's letters. When the letters were published the following year, Suzannah had to sit and read aloud from them to Henrik – the fiery letters to Bjørnson and Brandes, the dry letters to Hegel, elevated thoughts about art, trivial demands for royalties and rights.

On his seventy-fifth birthday he was visited by Edvard Grieg and Jonas Lie. As they were about to leave, Grieg said: 'You must permit me to do this' – and then did what one never did unpunished to Ibsen. He put his arm around him.

This time there was no protest. 'Thank you, thank you,' was all Ibsen said.

Just over a year after Ibsen's death Grieg was gone too. And Lie the year after that. Alexander Kielland died the same year as Ibsen, fifty-six years of age. In 1910, Bjørnson died in great pain in a hotel room in Paris. Within the first ten years of the new century most of the writers associated with the golden age of Norwegian culture were dead and gone. Georg Brandes outlived them all, surviving until 1927. The literature of the Norwegian golden age had first seen the light of day through a Danish publishing house, and as the twentieth century got under way it looked as though that was where it would end. In 1905, Sigurd sold the Scandinavian rights to his father's works to Gyldendal for 150,000 kroner, and Bjørnson soon followed suit. In 1925 the head of Gyldendal Norsk Forlag, Harald Grieg, bought the rights back. Norway's great writers would continue to serve the nation.

* * *

Death was approaching, but it was in no hurry. In the autumn of 1904, Ibsen received a visit from Dr Sontum's daughter, Bolette. She met a small, wizened man, pale and thin. The proud lion's mane was a sorry sight now, and the glint in the eye all that remained of the great writer she remembered from her childhood. In November he had a serious heart attack. He recovered, but by now his decline was irreversible.

In his last years his suffering was constant, though Bull did not think he experienced great pain. The strokes had left him paralysed on the right side of his body, so he had problems speaking and finding the right words, and his memory and intelligence were both in decline. So was his sense of humour. At times he hallucinated. He was suspicious and irritable. During the day he spent a lot of time sitting at the window peering down at the tourists lined up on the pavement on Drammensveien to peer up at him. He slept quite well, and his appetite remained unchanged. His taste for alcohol, however, was gone.

The same was true of his writing. He had never *decided* to stop work. After the publication of his 'dramatic Epilogue' he was asked whether he had written his last work. 'No,' he replied, 'this is just one chapter that is over. I will presently start work on a new one.' And as late as March 1900, just before his first stroke, he writes to Prozor:

> I am not sure whether or not I will write any more plays; but if my health and strength permit it, then I do not see how I will be able to stay away from those old battlefields for long.

He didn't know anything else but writing, couldn't imagine a life in which he wasn't working. During Bull's time as his physician he was hardly able to write his own name. On the night of 30 January 1905 he cried out in his sleep:

'I'm writing! It's going really well!'

The last word he wrote was a greeting to Bull, dated 14 February 1904. It consisted of just the one word:

'Thanks'

* * *

The world was there outside his window, but moving ever further away. He was most interested in hearing news from the theatre. The news that Norway had broken from the Union with Sweden and become an independent monarchy does not appear to have made any particular impression on him, though he did say that he didn't much like the idea of dying under a president. According to Bull, not even Sigurd's fate had any profound effect on him, though he regretted what had happened.

And if anything was the result of his poor health it must have been that, for Sigurd's was indeed a tragic fate. After the Swedish prime minister in 1904 refused to allow the Norwegians to appoint a Norwegian consul, matters had moved rapidly towards a unilateral dissolution of the Union. Sigurd was in favour, but believed the right way was to call a new general election and change the constitution. Not everyone shared his patience. Sigurd found himself at odds with his own party, and when the Blehr government collapsed and Francis Hagerup formed his coalition government, Sigurd was appointed Norwegian prime minister in Stockholm. When the Union finally collapsed in 1905, however, and Christian Michelsen formed his government, Sigurd was left out in the cold.

He departed Stockholm that same year and returned to an uncertain future as a writer. At forty-five years of age his professional life was more or less over.

Again he felt himself unwelcome in Norway. Personally he had come to despise Norwegian nationalism and was moving towards a new Scandinavianism that would have delighted his father. He carried on writing and published his main work, a philosophical-historical study called *The Quintessence of Mankind*, in 1911. He also wrote a couple of plays, but even though one of them, *Robert Frank* (1914), was both translated and performed at the Norwegian National Theatre, there were no laurel wreaths for Ibsen junior as a dramatist. Like his father, he became more and more reclusive. After the death of his mother in 1914 he spent most of his time abroad, and in the 1920s he and Bergliot bought a house in southern Tyrol, not far from Gossensass. There, in the Villa Ibsen, they lived for the remainder of their lives.

The ring was closed. Sigurd had grown up in the state of Ibsen, and that was where he would end his days, in solitary majesty.

His father was spared all of this. He knew nothing of Sigurd's bitter fate, nor did he experience the new, independent Norway after 1905, nor the Great War that brought the ravages of war to the continent of Europe for the first time since the Franco-German war of 1870 – the war that had destroyed Ibsen's world, and which persuaded him that he was living through a transitional age in which all the familiar and the known would disappear. Afterwards he put all his faith in the individual, and in his diffuse vision of the third kingdom. And when in due course it did come, in the form of the German Third Reich, there was no reconciliation in it, and certainly no enlightened and contented nobility.

Ibsen did not belong in the twentieth century, and the few years he spent in it were borrowed time. There is an uneasy symbolism in the fact that he suffered his first stroke in 1900, almost as though he were being denied entry to the new age. He did not belong to the twentieth century, and yet his works carried on living and travelling throughout the world. He would also be of service to his country in the nation-building process that he had seen the beginnings of, and that seemed never to come to an end. In 1908 the Stavanger Preserving Company obtained the rights to use Ibsen's name as the brand name of their tinned sardines, and a hundred years after his death the nation celebrated him in lavish style, in speeches and on stages throughout the land.

* * *

By the spring of 1906 it was clear that the end was near. He could no longer walk, and had to be carried from the bed to his chair, where he sat for a couple of hours every day, always in the same position. After Sigurd's return from Stockholm, his son's visits became his greatest joy. If the wait seemed too long he became uneasy:

'Shouldn't Grimbart be here by now?'

In front of him on the table lay his silver watch and on each side of it a gold box. One held his snuff and the other his chewing tobacco. Each morning his daily ration was cut into strips of identical length. His red handkerchief lay there too, placed in an absolutely straight line. If it wasn't straight he would begin to pluck at it in distress.

Earlier that year Eleonora Duse visited Christiania. As one of the most important interpreters of Ibsen's female roles in Europe she was keen to finally meet the master himself.

She sent him a note:

I have come here to offer for a few moments my admiration to the genius who has bestowed upon us the power to believe in our own abilities, and who for that very reason gives me faith in my efforts and lights my way as I strive to achieve the right interpretation.

In reply she received flowers and a telephone message to the effect that Ibsen was unfortunately no longer able to receive visitors. She had arrived too late. Aurélien Lugné-Poe, who was also in town, met her shortly afterwards. She was devastated. The following day the two of them were waiting outside the Grand Hotel at twelve o'clock in hopes that the writer would appear, as he had done every day for so many years. Snow whipped through the Christiania streets, and Duse had invested in a pair of Norwegian boots to keep the cold out. But no writer.

Now the summer approached, and with it death. On the afternoon of 22 May he said his last words to Suzannah:

'On the contrary!'

Others claim that his last word was 'No!', while Bergliot remembers his turning to Suzannah and saying: 'My sweet, sweet wife, how good and kind you have been to me.' Different words for different ears. The following day he was unconscious, and at 2.30 in the afternoon of 23 May he breathed his last. Bull summoned Ibsen's regular barber to come and give him his last shave. For the first time in seven years Carl Larsen found that his hand was shaking. Afterwards he stroked the white cheeks, Ibsen's cold mask:

'Thank you, Doctor Ibsen, for the time we have spent together. It will be a long while before I have another customer like you.'

* * *

He was laid in his coffin fully dressed. Suzannah sat in Arbins gate as condolences streamed in from all over the world, from princes, governments, theatres and writers. The coffin was conveyed to Trefoldighets church, and on the evening of 30 May members of the public were allowed to view the body. Twenty-seven students, artists and writers were chosen to stand guard of honour over the coffin. Among them were Eilif Peterssen, Vilhelm Krag and Dr Bull's son, Francis. At the funeral service the next day the church was packed with ministers, ambassadors, and prominent members of the clergy, the military and the civil service. Shortly before 1.30, Norway's new king, Haakon VII, whom Ibsen did not live to meet, arrived to take his seat.

The funeral was paid for by the state and the proceedings were led by Christopher Bruun, the old Grundtvigian priest who had once been an inspiration for Ibsen's *Brand*. Pomp and circumstance. Speeches, and not a tactless word was heard.

The coffin was then conveyed to the new grove of honour in Vår Frelser's cemetery, with a vast procession following. Banners waved as the coffin was lowered into the ground, and students sang. So too did a choir of businessmen. A hammer had been carved into the black memorial stone – the miner's sign. No sculpture, no portrait. Suzannah did not attend the funeral, but a little later she arranged to be carried from the flat to visit the grave. In the remaining eight years of life left to her she never left Arbins gate. An old woman in a large and stuffy apartment always pleased to talk about her Henrik and all that they had meant to each other, and in particular what she had meant to him. Shortly after Henrik's death she received a letter from his sister Hedvig:

> Dear Fru Ibsen! My Henrik was probably so tired that to be able to rest was the best thing he could think of. I have laid him in God's sweet embrace, and there he shall rest for all eternity.

She had stood beside him once on Kapitalbjerget above Skien and listened as he told her his hopes and his dreams. He had wanted to reach the greatest possible heights in life, and then die. Up into the stars, deep into the dark earth of the churchyard grave and the great silence.

AFTERWORD AND ACKNOWLEDGEMENTS

As a genre biography moves somewhere between literature and science. I have tried to write a biography that meets academic standards and is also of interest to the intelligent general reader. My hope is that I have been so consistent in my writing that the methodological choices I have made will be readily apparent from a reading of the text.

Even so, I hope I may comment on the methodological question that usually attracts the most attention in a biography, and that is the relationship between the life and the work. As a historian it is natural for me to operate on the basis of a close connection between the life and the work. A literary text necessarily bears a causal connection to its human author, one that is both intentional and non-intentional. Ibsen's plays and poems are ink on paper, texts just like any other texts. But there are two factors that make the literary text a much more complicated source for the life than, for example, letters and diaries. In the first place, the *fictive character* of the literary text in itself creates a distance to the author that is difficult to navigate; this is particularly true of the drama, with its polyphonic character and its lack of an overarching narrative authority. There may also be, on the part of the author, a *deliberate* distancing and mystification in regard to the process that leads to the finished work. This distance is an expression of the notion of art as an autonomous product, a product of the mind detached from its origins in the writer's intimate life.

Of course, there are writers who reject this distance, who openly attempt to write directly from their own lives. Ibsen was, to put it mildly, not one of these. With a few exceptions, such as poems written in specific contexts and for specific occasions, he sought to maintain a clear distance between himself and his work, and as a rule he dismissed attempts to read his works biographically.

In principle I would therefore say that it is theoretically – and in some cases also practically – possible to argue for the presence of biographical elements in Ibsen's literary works, as I attempt to demonstrate at certain points. But in the main I am very careful to draw conclusions from the work on the subject of the life. I also see little reason to draw attention to the more superficial and banal biographical aspects of the work. It is, for example, quite possible that Knud Ibsen was a model for Jon Gynt, but what the literary character has to tell us about Knud Ibsen the individual, and his son's view of him, is far from clear. The same applies to what the Greenclad's troll changeling might have to tell us about Ibsen's relationship to his illegitimate son, and what the many variations on the theme of bankruptcy and ruin say about Ibsen's own experience of the family's misfortune.

In other words, I am quite open to the possibility of using an approach to the works that is academically reliable as history, and rigorous in its approach to the sources, but in practice I have found it to be of little use. I have, on the other hand, gained great benefit from reading non-literary sources using a literary-scientific approach. There is no reason to exaggerate the distinction between literary and non-literary texts; a letter or a journal can easily be of a fundamentally fictional nature. And some of Ibsen's prose texts are most revealing if we read them as works of fiction – such as, for example, his aborted autobiography, and a number of his letters.

All in all, my methodical approach has been pragmatic and manifold: I try to shed light on the more obscure areas of Ibsen's life using the tools that seem best to me. And where I do not find the necessary tools to hand, then my instinct has been to allow these dimly lit patches to remain dim, after a presentation of such speculation as seems warranted and defensible. On the other hand, I have tried to avoid the temptation to illuminate these dark areas with all sorts of material from the plays.

I cannot completely overlook the possibility that this is a terrible miscalculation, that the key to Ibsen's innermost life really does lie hidden between the lines of his plays, or in the totality of them. But to discover that life would require a biographer of considerably greater ability than I.

Instead I have concentrated on questions such as: what kind of writer did Ibsen *want* to be (what sort of literary programme did he follow); what kind of writer *could* he have been (what were the defining limitations on him); and what kind of writer *was he regarded as being* (what sort of reception did he get). I have been reluctant to give my own close readings of the works, preferring instead to trace the long lines that link them, and illuminate what seem to me the different traditions of interpretation based on my own observations, and the wealth of material available within the world of Ibsen scholarship. The goal has been to give a detailed description of Ibsen the man (the private individual) and Ibsen the writer (the social actor). In addition I wanted to offer an overarching presentation of the works, of their most prominent motives and the different possible lines of interpretation. The man and the work are two independent historical subjects, but I have not been shy of engaging with the points at which the two demonstrably interrelate.

A biography can never say everything, only something, and at best a lot. This is my contribution.

It has been a demanding process, and I would not have been able to write such a wide-ranging biography without the assistance of the many biographers who have gone before me. Halvdan Koht's biography from 1954 is an enduring classic and for anyone interested in Ibsen's life it remains essential. Likewise Michael Meyer's monumental biography from 1967. Meyer's great achievement is principally the breadth and range of sources he draws from in describing Ibsen's life. The third book that has been my companion throughout the writing of this one is Robert Ferguson's biography from 1996 – bold in its speculation, and often stimulating and challenging. In general the conclusions I reach often differ from those of my predecessors. But harmonious accord is not one of the characteristics of the fellowship of good scholarship; the ability to conduct a fruitful debate is. I am proud to have been allowed to take my place in the ranks of Ibsen's biographers.

I would also like to express my gratitude to the following individuals, who have read the manuscript either wholly or in part, or in some other way helped me in my work: Thoralf Berg, Hege Stølen Berstad, Joen Bille, Arnstein Bjørkly, Thor Arvid Dyrerud, Erik Henning Edvardsen, Harald Engelstad, Uwe Englert, Freddy O. Fjellheim, Narve Fulsås, Mai Britt Guleng, Bernt Hagtvet, Jonny Halberg, Jorunn Hareide, Ivar Havnevik, Kjetil Havnevik, Nils Kåre Jacobsen, Anne Lise Jomisko, Johnny Kondrup, Lars Roar Langslet, Kari Garder Losnedahl, Toril Moi, Klaus Neiiendam, Heidi Nordli, Aina Nøding, Tore Rem, Øystein Rian, Anne Lise Seip, Oda Skard, Olav Solberg, Odd Arvid Storsveen, Espen Stueland, Åsmund Svendsen, Eivind Tjønneland, Benedicte Treider and Vigdis Ystad; also Prosjektet Henrik Ibsens skrifter, Grimstad By Museum, Telemark Museum, Fredrikstad Bibliotek, Mária Fáskerti and Randi Meyer at the Centre for Ibsen Studies and the Scandinavian Society in Rome. Finally, my many thanks to Robert Baldock and the editorial staff at Yale University Press, to my copy-editor, Richard Mason, and last, but by no means least, to Robert Ferguson for the translation.

ARCHIVES AND ABBREVIATIONS

Letters

The most important group of sources in this book are Ibsen's own letters. The great majority of these have been published, some in the Centenary Edition (HU), some in Øyvind Anker's collection from 1979 to 1981, some in *Edda* 1/1998 and in *Ibsen Studies* 2/2002. In addition, a few letters, either copies or originals, are to be found in various archives. The overview below is of abbreviations for the different archival institutions I have made use of. More specific information on which parts of the archives I have consulted is contained in the notes.

BNP Bibliothèque Nationale, Paris
DKB Det kongelige Bibliotek, København (The Royal Library, Copenhagen)
  – Gyldendals Arkiv 1991–70. Gyldendalske Boghandel. Nordisk Forlag AS.
  (Herunder Ny kgl. Saml. 3742 – 4 II, Fr. Hegels brevkladder)
DSF Den skandinaviske forening i Roma (The Scandinavian Society in Rome, manuscript collection)
  – Protokoll övfer Skandinaviska Föreningens General församling
IKW Israelitische Kultusgemeinde Wien (Jewish Community of Vienna)
KBS Kungliga biblioteket, Stockholm (The Royal Library, Stockholm)
  – Rosa Fitinghoff's journals, L 53:11:1
NBO Nasjonalbiblioteket i Oslo (The National Library in Oslo)

No. 4:107 (letter from Suzanna Ibsen to Camilla Collett), no. 39 (letter from Henrik Ibsen), no. 88 (letter to Jens Brage Halvorsen), no. 143 (letter to Lorentz Dietrichson), no. 154 (letter from Magdalene Thoresen), no. 200 (letters to and from members of the Ibsen family), no. 209 (letter from Eilif Peterssen), no. 290 (corr. Sigurd Ibsen – Peter Nansen), no. 383 (letter to Johan Scharffenberg), no. 417 (letter from Ole Bull), no. 576 (letter from Sigurd to Bergliot Ibsen), no. 689 (letters to and from Christopher Bruun and his relatives), BB (letters from Bjørnstjerne Bjørnson).

Manuscripts

Ms. fol. 3704:7–8 (letters from Suzannah Ibsen to Johan Hermann Thoresen), Ms. fol. 4 2590 (letter from Johanne Luise Heiberg to Henrik Ibsen), Ms. 4 2415b (letter from Knud Ibsen to Henrik Ibsen), Ms. 4 3413:4 (letter from Laura Kieler to Henrik Ibsen), Ms. fol. 4110:3 (letter from Edvard Fallesen to Henrik Ibsen), Ms. 200 (Sigurd Ibsen to Henrik Ibsen), BB 922, Ms. fol. 3704, Ms. 8 1199, Ms. 8 1461, Ms. 4 2415, Ms. fol. 3998, Ms. fol. 942, Ms. 8 843, Ms. 4 2590, Ms. 8 785, Ms. 8 825, Ms. fol. 952, Ms. 740 8, Ms. 9 1199 (interview with Fanny Riis, Eitrem, Hans. Karakteristikk av Henrik Ibsen), Ms. 8 785 (Henrik Ibsen. Childhood Memories [From Skien to Rome], Ms. 8 785, NBO), Ms. 4 3681 (Fanny Riis' diary), Ms. fol. 907 (HI's corrections to J. B. Halvorsen's entry in the Norwegian Directory of Authors).

PA	Privat Archive
	– PA Joen Bille
RA	Riksarkivet (The National Archives, Oslo)
	– PA 164 (Axel Heiberg), PA 1111 (the Grønvold family), PA 258 (Halvdan Koht)
SiB	Statsarkivet i Bergen (The National Archives in Bergen)
SSD	Sächsisches Staatsarchiv Dresden
TA/UiB	Teaterarkivet, Universitetet i Bergen (Theatre Archives, University of Bergen)
TM	Telemark Museum
	– HD 179, 182 og 3377
	– Einar Østvedt's papers
TSark/NBO	Teatersamlingen, Nasjonalbiblioteket i Oslo (Theatre Collection, The National Library, Oslo)
	– TSarkA2: Christiania Theaters arkiv, TSarkA3: Kristiania Norske Theaters arkiv
UBB	Universitetsbiblioteket i Bergen (University Library, Bergen)
UBT	Universitetsbiblioteket i Trondheim (University Library, Trondheim)
UBiT	Universitetsbiblioteket i Tromsø (University Library, Tromsø)
WSL	Das Wiener Stadt- und Landesarchiv (Municipal and Provincial Archives of Vienna)
	– WStLA, Polizei, Bundespolizei Wien, Meldeunterlagen

Other abbreviations used in the Notes

HI	Henrik Ibsen
HIS	Henrik Ibsens skrifter (Henrik Ibsen's writings)
HU	Hundreårsutgaven (The Centenary Edition of Henrik Ibsen's collected writings)

NOTES

Chapter 1 Skien

1. See for example Meyer (1995: 10 and 13), where Knud Ibsen's ruin is firmly associated with a feeling of 'shame' and 'disgrace'. The same association is also found in Ferguson (1996: 18).

Chapter 2 Grimstad

1. In Robert Ferguson's biography of Henrik Ibsen the relationship to the illegitimate son is a recurring theme in Ibsen's life, a burden of guilt and shame that becomes an essential aspect of Ibsen's attitude towards Norway (the son who awaits back home) and his writing (e.g. the Greenclad's child in *Peer Gynt*); cf. Ferguson (1996: 26ff especially). In Björklund-Bexell (1962: 21ff) the main events of Hans Jacob's life are traced through church records and interviews, and the story that emerges is not a happy one: he worked as a smith and lived with his mother in Birkedalen, outside Lillesand. They lived on very limited means, and when Hans Jacob married at the age of thirty his mother had to rely on charity. He had a son, but his wife died not long afterwards. Less than a year later, in 1882, he married again and fathered a daughter, but within a year both mother and child died from illness. Shortly afterwards he married for a third time. He had five children by this wife, of whom four died young, while the fifth lived until the age of twenty-seven. Hans Jacob himself died in 1916. The fate of the only surviving son is unknown – and it is not possible to trace any further this branch of the Ibsen family tree. Those who knew Hans Jacob describe him as intelligent and well read. He was apparently very fond of history, geography and travel writing, and was also a good fiddle player and fiddle-maker. He had an unfortunate weakness for alcohol, and his consumption increased as a result of all the adversity he encountered in his life. According to several sources he visited his father in later life but was rejected. It has not been possible to verify any of these sources, and Henrik Ibsen himself makes no mention of it at all. A newly discovered source confirms the picture we have of Hans Jacob; in a letter from Wilhelm Scharffenberg, a schoolteacher at Lillesand school, to Johan Scharffenberg, 20 January 1895 (letter collection, No. 383, NBO), we read the following: 'Like his father in many respects, he might have made something of himself had Ibsen not cut him off completely. Now he is a smith, usually drunk or else attending a temperance meeting. The only time I ever had anything to do with him was once when he came staggering into the kitchen blind drunk. He has apparently several times tried to contact his famous father, but received no help. Ibsen did not write *Ghosts* without good reason. His father drank – and so did this son; you know the proclivities of the generation in between. Certainly Ibsen is very talented . . . but in many respects Ibsen is a little man.' Scharffenberg's theory of a hereditary weakness for alcohol in the Ibsen family may well have something in it but is difficult to prove. Knud, Henrik and Jacob all acquired a reputation for having an unhealthy attitude towards alcohol in the course of their lives. But as we have seen, Hans Jacob had good reason to drink as his loved ones disappeared one by one. Hans Jacob Hendrichssen's is a heart-rending story of a rejected child

and possibly also a wasted talent, but based on the information we have it does not deserve a prominent place in Henrik Ibsen's life.

In this context it is also worth mentioning that even in Ibsen's own lifetime there were rumours that *he* too was an illegitimate child. The rumour says that his mother had a relationship with a Telemark man named Tormod Knudsen when she visited bailiff Florentz in Kvitseid in the mid-1820s. Knudsen was employed as a clerk in the bailiff's office, and gossip soon suggested that there was something between the two of them – this despite the fact that Marichen was apparently engaged to Knud by this time. Even if there is any truth in this, a putative conception of little Henrik must have taken place later, after Knud and Marichen had married and settled in Skien. Usually the historian must abandon his quest at the bedroom door, but there seems little reason to give credence to the rumours of Tormod Knudsen's involvement, as Oskar Mosfjeld convincingly shows in what is the most thorough investigation of the rumour yet undertaken (Mosfjeld 1949: 31ff). Naturally such rumours may have influenced Ibsen's attitude towards his own illegitimate son, and perhaps even his relationship with his own parents. But there is very little to go on here, and the sources leave us with not much more than an open question.

2. Cf. Dahl (1958: 17).
3. Cf. Daniel Haakonsen's opposition to Kristian Elster and Erik Kihlman's characterisation of Ibsen's idealism as incompatible with life – giving rise to the expression 'paradoxical idealism'. Against this, Haakonsen claimed that Ibsen's idealism was characterised by a fullness of life, the implication being that, for Ibsen, ideals should be realised, with 'an earthly life, free from ideals' as the ideal result, cf. Haakonsen (1950).
4. Sørensen (1994).
5. Cf. the analysis of Ibsen's examination papers in Bø (2000: 31ff).
6. Cf. Thue (1842: 212–15). The following titles were apparently on the syllabus at Skien Latin School: 'Sallustius Crispus, Gaius. *Catiline et Jugurtha*' (publ. E. F. Bojesen), Copenhagen 1837, 'Cicero's 4 Speeches against Catiline, Tale pro lege Manilia, de senectute & de amicitia, een bog af Ciceros de officiis', and 'Sallusti bellum Jugurthinum & Catilinerium'. While Ibsen was not a pupil at the Latin School, it is likely that much of the school's syllabus was also in use at Hansen and Stockfleth's school. But, bearing in mind Ibsen's youth, it is doubtful that he ever got beyond a preliminary introduction to Latin grammar while living in Skien.
7. No fewer than eleven dramatisations featuring Catiline are known of before Ibsen's. Four of them show clear similarities to Ibsen's that go beyond the historical background given in the sources: Ben Jonson's *Catiline: His Conspiracy*, London 1611; Christophe Kuffner's *Catiline*, Vienna 1825; Alexandre Dumas and August Maquet's *Catiline*, Paris 1848; and finally C. E. Guichard's *Catiline Romantique*, Paris 1844. Ibsen is unlikely to have read Jonson's play, which was not available in either Danish or German translation at the time, and Dumas and Maquet's drama had its premiere on 18 October 1848 and was probably published shortly afterwards. If Ibsen knew of this play before writing his own, it would probably have been through references in the newspapers. We cannot know whether or not the remaining versions were ever available to him, although it is worth noting that in Grimstad he had access to a greater range of literature than has previously been thought. There are also good reasons to suggest parallels between Ibsen's *Catiline* and other plays, such as Shakespeare's *Julius Caesar*, cf. Larson (1999: 90ff), Smidt (2004: 17ff) and Downs (1946: 3).
8. It is worth noting that Ibsen himself, in his Foreword to the second edition (1875), stressed a more generalised theme in Catiline's revolt against 'the majority', and in doing so reflected Ibsen's own literary programme at that time. This does not hinder a reading of the play that stresses revolt against authority as part of the drama's social-revolutionary theme – a theme historically associated with the play, no matter which interpretation one chooses.
9. Thue's Reader: the full title is *Læsebog i Modersmaalet for Norske og Danske, tilligemed en Exempelsamling af den svenske Literatur og med æsthetiske og literaturhistoriske Oplysninger*, 1846. The author had close links with Grimstad, was a cousin of Emil Bie and friendly with the Monrad brothers, his fellow students. He was a headmaster in Arendal from 1844 to 1848. Thue's Reader contained an unusually varied selection of texts that included dramatists like Johannes Ewald, Adam Oehlenschläger, Ludvig Holberg, as well as an extract from Søren Kierkegaard's *Either-Or* and *Stages on Life's Way*. The texts were equipped with genre theory and information supplied by Thue himself and must have been a useful guide for a young writer.
10. Cf. Fraenkl (1955: 11ff). Here Fraenkl argues for the necessity of seeing the outlines of an 'inner genetic literary process' in the young Ibsen, in which the writer's deeply personal inner imagery is realised in its encounter with the outside world. In other words, the inner dynamic is the crucial element in Ibsen's literary development.
11. Foreword to the second edition of *Catiline*, HU 1: 123.
12. There has been speculation about which members of the family joined the Lammers' movement, and it has often been claimed that Ibsen's mother was among them. There is, however, no evidence

for this. On the other hand we have Hedvig's own word that she and her brother were the only ones who joined, cf. 'Opptegnelser etter samtale med Hedvig Stousland 28 July 1911', H. Kohts papers, ms. fol. 3704: 5, NBO, cf. Koht (1952) and Østvedt (1973: 136ff). An expressed disapproval of art might also have contributed to Henrik's antipathy – Lammers had been a talented amateur painter, but after his vision he turned against all earthly vanities, cf. Sem (2000: 107ff).

13.   HU 19: 163, cf. 'Opptegnelser etter samtale med Hedvig Stousland 28 July 1911', H. Koht's papers, ms. fol. 3704: 5, NBO, cf. Archer (1906). In addition Ibsen later used Lammers as a model for Brand, a model many find to be positive.

Chapter 3   Christiania

1.   On bourgeois life and culture in Europe see Kaschuba (1992: 39ff).
2.   The marketing fate of the earliest Norwegian writers is discussed in Linneberg (1992: 39ff).
3.   HU 1: 246, cf. the study of the development from *The Northmen* to *The Burial Mound* made in McLellan (1982).
4.   Cf. the analysis of 'The Man' in Koht (1928), cf. his introduction to HU 15. Botten-Hansen also writes about the magazine in the biography of Henrik Ibsen in *Illustreret Nyhedsblad*, 19 July 1863.
5.   *Norma* was written as a parody of proceedings at the Storting based on Bellini's opera *Norma*, which Ibsen had recently heard at the Christiania Theatre, cf. McLellan (1980–1).
6.   Ibsen's difficulties in paying his child support are described in Dahl (2001: 83ff).

Chapter 4   Bergen

1.   Rubow (1953: 56), Fenger (1992: 127ff) and Jørgensen (2005: 343ff).
2.   Rudler (1966: 240), cf. HI to Henrik Jæger 1887, Midbøe (1960: 163). Ibsen confessed his fascination for both Dawison and Høedt to Jæger, but with reservations about Høedt's interpretation of Hamlet.
3.   Hettner (1852), cf. Bjørn Hemmer's comparative reading of Hettner's and Ibsen's ideas about poetry in Hemmer (1978: 15ff), cf. the discussion of Hettner's importance for Ibsen in Koht (1954a: 84ff) and Francis Bull's introduction to *St John's Night*, HU 2: 12. In 1857 Ibsen wrote a programmatic declaration on the subject of historical drama that was in the spirit of Hettner: 'Of a genuine historical tragedy we have no real right to demand the facts of history, but of its potential, not the actual people and characters of history, but the spirit and thinking of its times', HU 15: 160. He differs from Hettner in the more extreme degree of freedom he demands for the 'poetic value' of a drama, if needs be at the expense of the historically correct, cf. Hemmer (1978: 17).
4.   In Danish literary history the late Romantic period (c. 1825 to 1850) is termed 'Romanticism'. What characterises the period is a new focus on the split and 'interesting' individual, as a reaction against what was seen as the naïve and harmonising idea of the individual typical of early Romanticism, cf. Jørgensen (2005: 252ff). The term Romanticism is, however, not commonly used in Norwegian literary history and I have chosen not to use it here.
5.   The most articulate advocate of Ibsen's abilities as a practical man of the theatre in Bergen and Christiania is Roderick Rudler, e.g. Rudler (1966), Rudler (1970b) and Rudler (1973).
6.   On the reception of *St John's Night* see *Bergens Stiftstidende*, 5 and 9 January 1853, cf. Blanc (1884: 150), *Bergenske Blade*, reported in *Drammens Blad*, 19 January 1853, cf. Rudler (1970b: 154) and Wiers-Jenssen (1923).
7.   Blanc (1884: 169ff) and Rudler (1970a).
8.   Blanc (1884: 169ff), Blytt (1907: 12), Koht (1954a: 108) and Rudler (1977: 63).
9.   Kaschuba (1993).
10.   In P. A. Munch's history, which Ibsen read at school, Lady Inger is briefly mentioned as someone who *might* have led an uprising against Danish rule. The two volumes of *Diplomatarium Norvegicum* already published, Gregers F. Lundh's collection of letters in the first volume of *Samlinger til det Norske Folks Sprog og Historie* from 1833 and Caspar Paludan-Müller's publication of *Documents* relating to the Counts' Dispute from 1852–3, were probably more relevant. Shortly afterwards Paludan-Müller published his own account of the Counts' Dispute, the second volume of which appeared in the spring of 1854. Of these Ibsen had probably read at the very least Lundh and Paludan-Müller. Here were the historical foundations of his own drama, cf. Halvdan Koht's introduction to *Fru Inger til Østraad*, HU 2: 115ff, and Ibsen in his 'Foreword to *Gildet på Solhaug*', HU 3: 27ff.
11.   Cf. Ibsen's foreword to the second edition of *The Feast at Solhaug*, HU 3: 32; cf. HU 15: 136.
12.   *Bergensposten*, 20 and 24 January 1856, *Aftenbladet*, 25 March 1856 (Hartvig Lassen), *Trondhjems Adressecontors Efterretninger*, 5 April 1856. In addition there is Bjørnson's warm defence printed in

Morgenbladet, 16 and 30 March, 11 and 27 April and 4 May 1856, and P. Botten-Hansen's review in *Illustreret Nyhedsblad*, 29 March 1856.

13. Ibsen discusses the reception of *The Feast at Solhaug* in 1856 in the Foreword to the second edition of 1883. Åse Hiort Lervik has examined the reception, and finds that Ibsen's description of it in the 1883 Foreword might be ascribed to his general touchiness in the face of negative criticism, as well as a psychological reaction to the accusations of plagiarism later levelled against the play by, among others, important critics like Georg Brandes and Erik Bøgh. In addition *Ghosts* had recently been the subject of severe criticism which, as we know, upset him greatly, so that he may have projected this reaction onto the reception of *The Feast at Solhaug* in his Foreword, cf. Lervik (1969a).

14. Rudler (1970a) and Berg (1998).

15. The most exhaustive treatment of this subject is in Mohr (1953) and Mohr (1956). None of the mature works are highly rated. Among them the most admired is, significantly enough, the water-colour of Store Follestad that Ibsen painted at the age of fourteen in Skien. Despite obvious flaws in its execution the painting is praised as promising for someone of that age. To J. B. Halvorsen, Ibsen claimed to have abandoned painting completely as *Love's Comedy* and *The Pretenders* came to take up all his time, cf. HI to Halvorsen, 18 June 1889, HU 18: 215. As of 2005 there are 137 drawings and paintings believed to be by Ibsen. Many are reproduced in Mohr (1953). Some are lost, however, and are known only by reference.

16. Blanc (1884: 213), cf. *Bergensposten*, 4 January 1857, and *Christiania-Posten*, 10 January 1857.

17. A point he probably came across in Johan Ludvig Heiberg's treatise on the Danish heroic ballads (Heiberg 1861: 167–288) from 1837, where Heiberg cites specifically the difficulties in adapting the epic to the dramatic, unlike the lyrical – not least the lyrical 'Heroic ballad'.

18. He is obviously basing this on Rudolph Keyser's theory of immigration, which proposed that the Nordic countries were settled by eastern tribes who entered the north of Norway and then spread southwards, driving out or subduing the native Gothic-Germanic tribes in Denmark and South Sweden. This theory, somewhat modified by P. A. Munch but not substantially challenged by contemporaries, formed an important historical basis for the national-romantic elevation of Norway to the status of a culture, and the Scandinavian land with the most 'authentic' historical lineage. However, Ibsen was the first to relate the origins of the folk ballad to this Ur-Germanic society. Unjustifiably so. Ibsen was probably simply guessing when he related the folk ballad to an accepted theory of immigration. It failed to convince. And with the abandonment over time of the immigration theory, little remains of Ibsen's attempts as a researcher into folk memory.

19. E.g. *The Vikings at Helgeland*, published as a supplement to *Illustreret Nyhedsblad*, 25 April 1858, in over 2,200 copies. The figure greatly exceeds a typical Norwegian book publication, and even in Denmark a printing of 1,000 copies was considered large.

Chapter 5 Christiania

1. Nordström (1963: 237).

2. See the discussion in Collin (1923: 38 and 98), Amdam (1993: 170ff) and Francis Bull's introduction to *The Vikings*, HU 4: 23. The similarity between Hjørdis and Halte-Hulda can otherwise be explained by the fact that both Ibsen and Bjørnson were inspired by Oehlenschläger's *Kiartan and Gudrun* (1848), in which Gudrun appears as the prototype of the difficult woman in the sagas – derived from the *Laxdøla Saga*, which Ibsen knew from N. M. Petersen's translation, cf. F. Bull, HU 4: 19.

3. C. Petersen's review of *Love's Comedy* in *Fædrelandet*, 18 July 1863.

4. *Illustreret Nyhedsblad*, 20 and 27 December 1857, HU 15: 163ff.

5. Ystad (1991).

6. Linneberg (1992: 23ff).

7. This and the following quotation are taken from Ibsen's application for government support for Kristiania Norske Theatre, 25 October 1859, HU 15: 224ff.

8. Contempt for politicians was in varying degrees characteristic of the whole generation of 1848 across Europe, the reaction following the 1848 revolution leading to a widespread and lasting disillusionment among artists and intellectuals. Jakobsen (2004: 167ff) places Ibsen in this tradition.

9. Amdam (1993: 232ff), Meyer (1995: 170ff), Arvesen (1912: 104) and Ole Hansen, 'Erindringer fra det norske Selskab', ms, BB 922, NBO.

10. Ibsen's reluctance to get involved in the language debate between 1857 and 1862 may have been because he was obliged to follow the line taken by the philologist Knud Knudsen at the Kristiania Norske Theater. After the theatre went bankrupt he was able to express his views more freely. The extent to which their views differed isn't easy to say, although both felt that the norm should

conform to some version or other of 'the normal, educated spoken language' (*Morgenbladet*, 5 October 1862, HU 15: 298). After his Scandinavian breakthrough Ibsen increasingly distanced himself from those urging the case for a more 'Norwegian' Norwegian. Yet we cannot ignore the possibility that Knudsen influenced the development of Ibsen's language during his most nationalist phase in the 1850s and 1860s; at any rate Ibsen was big enough to hail Knudsen's work for the language in the greeting he offered him on his eightieth birthday in January 1892 (HU 18: 306). Note also that there was probably little contact between Ibsen and Ivar Aasen. In the latter's correspondence and diaries there are only sporadic references to Ibsen, cf. Aasen (1957–60).

11. On Scandinavianism generally in the 1850s and 1860s see Seip (1971: 285ff, esp. 309ff) and Sørensen (2001: 234ff).

12. For Ibsen's annual writer's wage and his income tax debt see Dahl (2001: 36) and Edvardsen (2003: 73).

13. Ibsen's contributions to the theatre debate are quoted from HU 15: 236–73, other contributions in Lund (1925: 86–91).

14. Summary of the civil actions brought against Ibsen at Christiania Municipal Court, 1857–64, in Dahl (2001: 11ff).

15. Ibsen's suicidal thoughts are referred to in *Aftenposten* 4 October 1908, and the German translator Julius Eliasen is believed to have spread the rumours to Germany through his article 'Eine Christianiafahrt', *Neue deutsche Rundschau*, 1907.

16. The journey was reconstructed in *Aftenposten*, 31 January 1931, cf. Freihow (1936: 6ff), cf. Ibsen's travel diary HU 19: 82ff.

17. For references in *Love's Comedy* see Francis Bull's introduction to the play in HU 4: 127ff. The intertextual weave in the play is also analysed in Ystad (1996b).

18. Forfang (1990: 46ff), cf. Daae (1888: 323n).

19. The foremost proponent of Falk as an out-and-out aesthete is Halvdan Koht, cf. Koht (1954a: 160ff). Bjørn Hemmer, however, in a more recent reading of 'On the Heights' and *Love's Comedy* sees in Falk a forerunner of Brand, cf. Hemmer (2003: 62ff). Hemmer is right insofar as the hunter in the poem does not have to be seen as an aesthete and anti-hero, but as a person driven by a genuine sense of calling. In the play, however, this idea of a calling is treated with such irony and complexity that many will find that Hemmer goes too far in interpreting the character of Falk in a positive and serious light.

20. This reading accords with Hemmer (2003: 54ff, esp. 60ff).

21. Cf. the reading of *Love's Comedy* in Northam (1973: 10ff, esp. 30ff).

22. Francis Bull in the introduction to *Love's Comedy*, HU 4: 126.

23. Halvorsen (1892: 12ff).

24. Koht (1954a: 200), cf. Daae (1934: 242ff) and P. Botten-Hansen's Ibsen biography in *Illustreret Nyhedsblad*, 19 July 1863.

25. Andreas Munch is usually given the honour of this as early as 1869, and as far as it goes this is correct. But the award to Munch was made in the form of a salary as a lecturer at the university, where he was even given the title of professor with no teaching obligations involved. The writer's wage awarded to Bjørnson was something new, marking a final separation between literature and the academic institution, and a breach with an economic-liberal tradition unwilling to see the state take on obligations in the cultural life of the nation – witness the many rejections of applications for support for the theatre. Now, finally, writing was recognised *as* writing, and the writer *as* writer.

26. Critical reception of *Love's Comedy* given in Francis Bull's introduction to *Love's Comedy*, HU 4: 134, cf. Daae (1934).

27. *Fædrelandet*, 18 July 1863.

28. Se Halvdan Kohts' introduction to *The Pretenders*, HU 5: 9, and Hemmer (2003: 197).

29. In Hamre (1945: 122ff).

30. As fertile as the thought might be, it is worth noting that Ibsen himself on one occasion conceded his likeness to Jatgeir the Skald, HI to B. Bjørnson, 16 September 1864, HU 16: 101.

31. Quoted in Agerholm (1910–11: 276–80).

32. *Fædrelandet*, 2 April 1864.

33. See the discussion of this and subsequent collections for Ibsen's benefit in Modalsli (2001). Bjørnson has traditionally been ascribed a central role in this, largely based on his own account. New archival discoveries suggest that Dunker's role was at least as central.

Chapter 6 Rome

1. On Scandinavians in Rome in the 1860s see Nordhagen (1981), Eriksen (1997) and Villari (2002).

2. Bø (1996).

3. Wærp (2003).
4. Tysdahl (2003).
5. For *Brand*'s reception see, for example, *Morgenbladet*, 2, 9, 16 and 23 September 1866, cf. further articles in ibid., 1 and 4 December 1866 (Monrad), and *Aftenbladet*, 7 April 1866 (Meidell), *Dølen*, 8 April 1866 (Vinje) and (Danish) *Dagbladet*, 23 May 1866 (G. Brandes). In later essays on Ibsen's writing Brandes expressed a more positive view of the play, as in for instance his subsequent essay in *Dansk Maanedsskrift*, November 1867.
6. *Brand* as a symbolic drama of ideas, a tragedy and an existential drama of personality, see Hemmer (2003: 122ff), Eriksen (1997: 76), Kittang (2002: 36ff) and Ystad (1996a: 129ff).
7. The poem was included in the draft list of contents for *Poems* but did not appear in the published volume and was not found among Ibsen's papers after his death, cf. HU 14: 492ff.
8. Although other individual works achieved high sales figures comparable to *Brand*, these were rare – 3,000 copies of Oehlenschläger's *Axel og Valborg* (1810), for example, were published, but later sales figures hovered in the region of a thousand copies, cf. the analysis of Danish sales figures to 1870 by Kristensen (1965: 51–63).
9. Dietrichson (1896: 351), cf. the account of the change in Ibsen in Lie (1928: 24ff), cf. Sophie Møller, 'Henrik Ibsens håndskrift', ms. fol. 942, NBO. The conclusion of this handwriting analysis is that Ibsen changed his handwriting after *Brand*, but that it took some time before the final style developed.
10. Cf. the letter from HI to Peter Heise, 16 June 1870, *Edda* 1/1998, in which Ibsen describes himself as 'a musical monster, who has no right to express his opinion on musical works'; cf. the remark by Ibsen's friend Hildur Andersen that Ibsen was not musical, *Verdens Gang*, 4 March 1910; cf. Due (1909: 44) on Ibsen's lacking musicality.
11. The stories concerning Sigurd's childhood are taken from Ibsen (1948: 23ff) and Ibsen (1976: 11).
12. A rumour based on the tradition of Henrik as a non-erotic person, as well as a remark said to have been made by Suzannah to her lifelong friend Karoline Bjørnson to the effect that she was not going to have any more children after Sigurd. The story recurs in Ibsenian folklore, see e.g. Bull (1966: 44) and Koht (1954a: 163). Its origins are unclear. Koht claims to have heard it from Karoline herself, cf. Koht (1954b: 303). Regardless, this is a flimsy basis for depriving Henrik and Suzannah of the joys of sexual love for the remainder of their lives.
13. In Schindler (1942: 121ff).
14. The stories of Ibsen and Bergsøe on Ischia are from Bergsøe (1967).
15. Cf. Francis Bull's introduction to *Peer Gynt*, HU 6: 19ff. Ibsen's first encounter with the Peer Gynt figure may well have been in *St. Hansnats Eventyr* (*Midsummer Night's Tale*), written by P. Botten-Hansen in 1831, and printed in 1862, which contains the story of 'the terrible hunter Peder Jynt'.
16. Asbjørn Aarseth's commentary on *Peer Gynt*, cf. Ibsen (1993: 26ff), includes a useful list of the works quoted from or alluded to in the play. Cf. an extended study of the play's sources in Haakonsen (1967).
17. The use of such metres in a verse drama such as *Brand* was uncommon, but frequently encountered in lyrical poetry and in larger, descriptive and expository verse, cf. Lervik (1969b: 41ff).
18. For *Peer Gynt*'s reception see *Morgenbladet*, 29 November 1869, and *Aftenbladet*, 30 November and 4 December 1869, *Fædrelandet*, 30 November 1867 (C. Petersen) and (Danish) *Dagbladet*, 16 December 1868 (G. Brandes). The latter was reprinted in Brandes (1868) as part of a larger study of Ibsen. Brandes also reviewed the play in *Illustreret Tidende*, 29 December 1868.
19. The three readings (national satire, folk play, morality play) were established by Asbjørn Aarseth in Ibsen (1993: 187ff); cf. the presentation of the readings of *Brand* in Ystad (1996a). Halvdan Koht is a late representative of the satirical reading, cf. Koht (1954b: 300ff).
20. Bø (2000: 216).
21. *Aftenbladet*, 25–31 January 1876, reprinted in Hageberg (1967: 54ff).
22. Auring (1984: 532ff).
23. Dyrerud (1998: 85) highlights the theatrical and scenic aspects of Kierkegaard's style.
24. In Christopher Due's account of the period in Grimstad, 'we eagerly studied Søren Kierkegaard's *Either-Or, Deeds of Love* etc.', *Aftenposten*, 16 October 1904. Frøken Crawford, to whose library Ibsen had access, owned a copy of *Either-Or*, cf. Eitrem (1910: 47). The most thorough comparative examinations of Ibsen and Kierkegaard remain those of Beyer (1924: 114–91) and Eriksen (1923: 252–69), cf. also Kihlman (1921).
25. The image of 'the ring of forefinger and thumb' ('den hule hånd') in itself illustrates some of the dangers of reading Ibsen through Kierkegaard. Ibsen also used the image in 'On the Heights', which accounts for why so many have read the poem as his first reckoning with aestheticism. The problem is that the expression hardly had the Kierkegaardian connotations in the poem that it acquired in the later letter to Bjørnson; cf. the discussion in Hemmer (2003: 84ff).

26. He admitted to Henrik Jæger that he had read parts of *Either-Or* and *The Moment*, but no more than a few pages, HI to H. Jæger 1887, Midbøe (1960: 162). Fr. G. Knudtzon relates that he lent Ibsen the *Concluding Unscientific Postscript to the Philosophical Crumbs*. When Ibsen returned it, Knudtzon relates that Ibsen said 'I have read it, but read it like a half-wit': Knudtzon (1927: 161–6).
27. Helveg (1886); Brandes (1867), cf. Ibsen's dismissal of Helveg's book, HI to F. Hegel, 9 June 1866, HU 16: 158. Valborg Eriksen also stresses Ibsen's need to liberate *Brand* from associations with pietism, Eriksen (1923: 252); cf. the following lines from the diary of the Danish parliamentarian and later minister Andreas Frederik Krieger (1817–93): 'In a few days' time H. Ibsen's *Brand* will be published, a Kierkegaardian drama, apparently inspired by Norwegian religious movements', Krieger (1920: 352). See also Ibsen's remark to Laura Petersen about *Brand*, that it was 'an aesthetic work, in every respect, and absolutely nothing else'. Ibsen appears to be responding to the fact that Petersen read the drama as a sermon and not as poetry. It suggests a defence of the autonomy of the artist rather than a conceptual objection to Kierkegaard's theory of the stages along life's way, cf. HI to L. Petersen, 11 June 1870, HU 16: 302.
28. There has been little written about Clemens Petersen (C.P.) in Denmark. The most important discussions are in Hamre (1945: 13ff and 39–70), Westling (1985: 167–83), Norseng (1975), Schyberg (1937) and Jørgensen (1994: 189ff). It is striking that Georg and Edvard Brandes hardly mention the dominant critical voice from their own youth. The Brandes expert Henning Fenger denies any intellectual value to C.P's criticism, both as critic and as a possible source of inspiration for G. Brandes, cf. Fenger (1955: 96ff). The influence of C.P's idealism on Ibsen has been seriously neglected, for example the critic is dismissed by Meyer as 'a smart and superficial journalist' (1995: 219). It is, however, worth noting that not everything in C.P's critical writings coincided with Ibsen's literary views. C.P. was, for example, disapproving of the growing tendency towards scenic realism and the psychological interpretation of roles in the theatre. On the other hand Ibsen was in the 1860s principally concerned with the drama of ideas, not with realistic drama. Critic and playwright were thus closely associated in this particular decade, despite the fact that Ibsen's plays of ideas were never really to C.P's taste.

Chapter 7 Dresden

1. Siebold's translation was completed by 1869 but not published until 1872.
2. In Norwegian and Danish the preference was for Latin rather than Gothic script, the abolition of initial capitals in proper names, the introduction of å for aa, the removal of silent e and d in words such as *stoe*, *døe* and *vadske*, *dandse* and *ind*, likewise the long vowel in words such as *heel* and *muur*. There were fewer suggested changes in Swedish; they included the replacement of qv with kv in words such as *qvinna*, and f and fv with v in words such as *lif* and *lefva*, see Vinje (1978: 157–77).
3. In most respects Ibsen shared the general European notions of the people and culture of the Orient in both his literary and non-literary texts. He was in other words an Orientalist, as defined in Said (2003). Even when he writes of North African culture in the fourth act of *Peer Gynt* he is, in my view, saying something about his own culture. Conversely, a scholar such as Elisabeth Oxfeldt will maintain that the fourth act can be read as a critique of Orientalism, cf. Oxfeldt (2005: 133–60). I do of course agree that the play is critical of European complacency, but cannot see that the critique is advanced from a location outside the world of contemporary Orientalism of which Ibsen was a part.
4. Ibsen on his wanderings in Girga, HU 15: 340ff.
5. Montigny was employed at the Gymnase as early as 1844, but his real breakthrough as a director did not come until the production of Balzac's *Mercadet* in 1851. There is a thorough account of his work in Eriksen (1973), cf. Bergman (1952). Both draw a comparison with the German theatre tradition, see for example Bergman (1952: 8ff and 137ff).
6. Ibsen could have attended the theatre in Paris both on his way out to Egypt and on his way home, which is to say, at the beginning of October and the end of November/beginning of December. At the Comédie Française he could have seen the following: *Tartuffe* and *Les Fourberies de Scapin* by Molière, *Il ne faut jurer de rien* and *La nuit d'octobre* by A. de Musset, *Le Menteur* by Corneille, *Le Mariage de Figaro* by Beaumarchais, *Le cheveu blanc* and *Julie* by Octave Feuillet, *Mercadet*, a comedy by H. de Balzac, *Les enfants d'Edouard*, a tragedy by C. Delavigne, as well as a couple of comedies by Emile Augier, Feuillet and others. At l'Opéra Garnier *Faust* and *Don Juan* were among the plays performed. At the Théâtre de l'Odéon there was *Le Bâtard* by Alfred Touroude, with Sarah Bernhardt, and at the Théâtre du Gymnase *Frou-Frou* by Meilhac and Halévy. The references are from a list of performances in Paris theatres in the autumn of 1869 made by Marie-Christine Muchery, BNP.

7. In my view both Henning Fenger and Jørgen Knudsen are too extreme when they describe Brandes' review of *The League of Youth* as, respectively, an 'incontrovertible' and a 'complete' change in his view of Ibsen, cf. Fenger (1964: 184ff) and Knudsen (1985: 143). As Fenger points out, Brandes also moderated somewhat his initial enthusiasm for *Peer Gynt* in *Kritiker og Portraiter* (1870).

8. See the analysis of *The League of Youth* in Hemmer (2003: 177ff, esp. p. 188).

9. Nordström (1963: 237–62).

10. See the discussion of the draft in H. Koht's introduction to *The Pillars of Society*, HU 8.

11. Ibsen's financial situation is based on his own account books, which are thoroughly analysed in Jacobsen (2006).

12. Cf. the analysis of Hegel's strategies as a publisher in Rem (2002: esp. 121ff).

13. HI suggested a new edition to Hegel as early as August 1868, but the rights were not finally transferred from Johan Dahl to Gyldendal until November 1869.

14. See e.g. Koht (1912: 84) and Bull (1960a: 185ff). Later scholars have generally subscribed to the idea of a close literary and ideological association linking Ibsen and Brandes, see e.g. Gunnar Ahlström's authoritative work on the modern breakthrough (Ahlström 1974). In recent years the Danes Per Dahl and Jørgen Knudsen have subscribed to the same view, though with clearer reservations, cf. Dahl (1988), Dahl (2002) and Dahl (2006), and Knudsen (1985), Knudsen (1988) and Knudsen (2006). I am critical of this 'fence-sitting' and ask myself why it is so important to maintain this basic harmonisation of views between the two men when the points of difference between them are as obvious as they are. The most severe critic of the 'brothers in arms' theory is Erik M. Christensen (Christensen 1985), followed by Nicolas Reinecke-Wilkendorff, who in a 2004 article provides a good overview of the whole topic (Reinecke-Wilkendorff 2004).

15. In *Dagbladet*, 28 January and 11 February 1878, Brandes contributed anonymous reviews of the performances of *The Pillars of Society* in Berlin, likewise in *Dags-Avisen*, 24 November 1880, on *A Doll's House* in Berlin. After the review of *Emperor and Galilean* in 1874, Brandes did not review any new play by Ibsen until *Ghosts* (*Morgenbladet*, 28 December 1881). Over the succeeding decades he published several works that included Ibsen, cf. Dahl (2006: 339ff). Note also that Ibsen's name was conspicuous by its absence from a petition in support of Brandes when he left Denmark in the autumn of 1877. Hegel was among the forty-five prominent signatories, and Bjørnson wrote his own separate declaration of support, cf. Knudsen (1988: 16).

16. This is discussed in Christensen (1985: 39–75, cf. 217ff). The outstanding example is Brandes' essay in the German periodical *Nord und Süd* in November 1883. Here he writes, among other things, of Ibsen's hostility to the state, his anti-Prussian statements, and generally on the socially destructive consequences of his individualism. To put it mildly, a presentation such as this did nothing to promote Ibsen's popularity in Bismarck's Germany. The same is true of Brandes' contribution to Adolf Strodtmann's book *Das geistige Leben in Dänemark* (1873), which depicted Ibsen as hostile towards Germany (see pp. 94ff). In 1887 he also translated an article by Hermann Bahr in *Politiken*, in which Ibsen is criticised for his provincialism.

17. Ibsen writes to G. Brandes, 23 July 1872 (HU 17: 52): 'I have no fear of being taken as a party-political hack; and I cannot understand why people now consider that I am somehow "outside" the party political system.' Among all the numerous attacks on party politics this is especially remarkable. I can find no good explanation for this deviation. The letter was written following an untypical expression of his willingness to write for *Det nittende Aarhundrede* (*The Nineteenth Century*). Perhaps he was more interested in taking part in the social debate at that time; if so then he soon reverted to his position of principled indifference to practical politics.

18. See Helge Rønning's interesting comparative reading of Mazzini and Ibsen in Rønning (2002), in which he indicates clear points of similarity between Mazzini's and Ibsen's view of the heroic individual in history, the rightness of the minority, their ambivalent view of nationality and national identity, and scepticism towards the tendency to compromise in practical political life. The assertion that Ibsen, like Mazzini, supported 'democracy as an ideal' (p. 28) is more problematic.

19. See Russell (1947: 121ff). Bertrand Russell describes here a long tradition of ideas that includes Carlyle, Mazzini, Fichte and Nietzsche. This tradition is characterised by its anti-rationalist revolt against the commonsense beliefs of the Enlightenment, natural law and democracy, and is related to the Fascism of the nineteenth century. Russell's analysis is relatively imprecise and polemical, but it is hard to avoid the conclusion that certain of the traits he focuses on as being typical of the anti-rationalist revolt accord, in the main, with Ibsen's own political statements (although Russell does not mention him). Eric Bentley also stresses the emotional and unsystematic aspect of this tradition, which he calls 'Heroic Vitalism', cf. Bentley (1957: 239).

20. See the in-depth analysis of the concepts of 'aristocratic' and 'authoritarian elitism' in de Figueiredo (2002: 99ff).

21. The concept of 'the dilemma of freedom' is a central theme of Helge Rønning's interesting monograph on Ibsen and his writing, cf. Rønning (2006).

22. Ibsen supported capital punishment and late in life expressed the view that war is uplifting, cf. HU 19: 223ff and HU 15: 437ff and 441. In general his language in debating social matters is strikingly aggressive. His most brutal suggestions should probably not be taken literally, as when he tells Brandes that the proletariat ought to be kept in check by the use of poison. And yet it is hard to ignore an affinity with the exercise of power that is apparent in so many of his statements. It is of course quite possible not to take Ibsen's observations on society and politics seriously, and instead see his many unequivocal outbursts as deliberate provocation of the politically correct, or perhaps as emotional outbursts that cannot be taken literally as expressions of political and social views. And yet it would be a great mistake to dismiss the main thrust of these statements on account of their extremism, as, in my view, many Ibsen scholars have chosen to do – probably because the political Ibsen is difficult to reconcile with the literary Ibsen in a way that might make him, quite simply, ineligible for the nation's cultural canon.

23. This is in line with one of Atle Kittang's main points (Kittang (2002: 15). I agree with Anne Marie Rekdal when she claims that Ibsen's conception of freedom transcends the boundaries of social and political freedom and points in the direction of an overarching subjective and existential under-standing of freedom, cf. Rekdal (2000: Introduction and Afterword) and Rekdal (2001).

24. Here I am in agreement with Fredrik Engelstad when he relates Ibsen's aristocratic ideas to the idea and ethics of 'the call', cf. Engelstad (2003).

25. Cf. Erik M. Christensen who – despite his interesting objections to Georg Brandes' monopoly on the interpretation of Ibsen – goes much too far in ascribing an anarchistic programme to Ibsen, cf. Christensen (1985).

26. Letter from HI to Peter Hansen, 28 October 1870, in HU 16: 315ff.

27. Cf. the discussion of this quotation from the perspective of the conception of autonomy in Helland (2000: 26ff).

28. Toril Moi opposes Frode Helland's interpretation of the Ibsen quote in question and claims that it should be read as a 'passionate defence of his own freedom of expression', a passion that derives from a Romantic tradition rather than a modernist, autonomic aesthetic, cf. Moi (2006: 62ff). Here I am in agreement with Moi.

29. HI to M. Thoresen, 29 May 1870, and L. Kieler, 11 June 1870, HU 16: 297 and 302; cf. Ibsen's speech to the students' torchlit procession in Kristiania, 10 September 1874, HU 15: 393, cf. HI to L. Passarge, 16 June 1880, HU 17: 402. Per Dahl relates the idea of 'living through' ('gjennemleve') in a similar way to a subjective 'aesthetic of emapathy' in Ibsen, while Georg Brandes is aligned with a 'poetic of experience', which Dahl relates to a positivist objectivism, cf. Dahl (1988).

30. Kjetil Jacobsen expresses it thus: 'As a phenomenon, autonomy is inside society, not outside it.' Jacobsen (2004: 26). I prefer to use 'independence' rather than 'autonomy', but have otherwise drawn on Jacobsen here.

31. HI to F. Hegel, 8 January, 21 January and 8 February 1871, HU 16: 332ff, 339 and 344ff. Herleiv Dahl has undertaken a thorough reconstruction of the editing of Poems, Dahl (1958: 227ff). In letters Ibsen gives the impression that he wishes to describe the history of his own development in this publication, at the same time asserting that, in his view, the collected poems formed an organic whole, HI to Fr. G. Knudtzon, 19 February 1871, Edda 1/1998.

32. For expectations of and reactions to Brandes' lectures, see Brandes (1907: 63–5) and Knudsen (1985: 231ff).

33. Im neuen Reich, 40, 1871, and Constitutionelle Zeitung, 2 November 1871.

34. Strodtmann (1873: Foreword ix). This book led to ill-feeling between Ibsen and Georg Brandes, since Ibsen suspected Brandes of complicity in Strodtmann's discussion of him; Brandes had indeed contributed much to the book, cf. letter from G. Brandes to P. Heyse, 6 May 1875, Brandes (1966: 105).

35. At this point Dostoyevsky had already published Crime and Punishment (1866), The Gambler (1867) and The Idiot (1869), so Ibsen may well have been familiar with his name; indeed, it was in the 1870s that he became aware of Russian literature and art generally. But the chances of their having met are slender – not only did Dostoyevsky have a work rhythm that was the diametric opposite of Ibsen's (he wrote at night and slept during the day), but the two also lived in different parts of the city, cf. Magarshack (1962: 405ff), Meyer (1995: 321ff) and Kjetsaa (1977: 30).

36. Brenna (2002: 5, cf. 305–17).

37. Toril Moi here disagrees with Meyer and maintains that the English paintings in particular, with their mixture of realistic detail and moral and ethical idealism, were interesting as modern art at the exhibition. She also discusses the connection between Ibsen's writing and the visual world around him, cf. Moi (2006, esp. 160–70), and Meyer (1995: 379).

38. The whole business, both its legal documents and its correspondence, is the subject of a thorough account in Haugholt (1956).

39. Among the primary sources the most important was probably the account of Amianus Marcellinus, an officer in Julian's army, which Ibsen might have read in the German school edition *Römische Geschichte* edited by Trosz and Büchele. There are also a large number of secondary sources. Several scholars have discussed the literary sources for *Emperor and Galilean*, including H. Koht's introduction to *Emperor and Galilean*, HU 7, Svendsen (1932) and Chesnais (1937). Svendsen finds the most important secondary source to be August Neander's *Allgemeine Geschichte der christlichen Religion und Kirche* (1828 and 1846), whereas Chesnais inclines more to the writing of the French church historian Albert de Broglie. There is a succinct overview of all the relevant literature in Wærp (2000: 30ff). See also Aarseth (1999b). Aarseth shares the view that fidelity to the historical sources is detrimental to the play's literary quality.

40. In his classic study Ole Koppang draws attention to the obviously Hegelian aspects of the play. His conclusion is that Ibsen was not a Hegelian, but made use of elements of Hegel's philosophy for his own literary purposes, cf. Koppang (1948: 177–97, esp. 193). Brian Johnston is a more recent example of a scholar who stressed the Hegelian elements in *Emperor and Galilean*, and on Ibsen's drama generally, cf. Johnston (1980). The American Paul Sandvold Baxter is another who stresses Hegel's influence in his account of Ibsen's conception of freedom in Baxter (1998).

41. Collin (1906) is an example of this viewpoint.

42. See for example P. Reimann in *Nordisk maanedsskrift for folkelig og kristelig oplysning*, Odense 1874. Among scholars, Paulus Svendsen has interpreted the third kingdom as a worldly realisation of the Millennium, while Egil A. Wyller identified it more clearly with the biblical Millennium as described in the revelations of John, cf. Svendsen (1940: 485) and Wyller (1993: 140–8).

43. Halvdan Koht advances his Neoplatonic interpretation in a historical study of the idea of the third kingdom in Koht (1953: 132–5). In the introduction to *Emperor and Galilean*, HU 7: 20ff, he associates the conception with Schopenhauer's doctrine of the will.

44. In Bjørn Hemmer's extensive study of *Emperor and Galilean* it is precisely the interleaving structures of the conflict that give the play its unique character, the tension between human values of existence and the essential values of Christianity that are in different relationships to each other in the context of the two world visions presented in the play, the Christian vision and the vision of the third kingdom. In the Christian perspective the issue is 'Emperor or Galilean', whereas 'Emperor and Galilean' – in other words, the synthesis – is at the heart of the idea of the third kingdom, cf. Hemmer (1970).

45. This reading accords with Wærp (2000: 140ff).

46. Lisbeth P. Wærp criticises Brandes and the broad tradition of his successors who have criticised *Emperor and Galilean* for its failures as a historical-philosophical work. Wærp's point is that the obscurity of the work's ideas should rather be considered in the light of its literary and poetical complexity, cf. Wærp (2000). According to Wærp, the drama is characterised by an 'ironic mixture of critical-analytic disillusionment and visionary optimism' (p. 106), and it is in just this constant tension between optimism and disillusionment, idealism and scepticism, that she finds the essence of a 'typically Ibsenian dramatic complexity and ambivalence' (285).

47. A view that accords with Kittang's interpretation of the play in Kittang (2002: 124).

48. Moi (2006: 265ff), cf. on the concepts of theatricalisation and scepticism, pp. 292–304.

49. In a letter to Julius Hoffory, 26 February 1888, HU 18: 154, Ibsen writes of the problems of getting started on *Emperor and Galilean* in the 1860s: 'My viewpoint back then was still one of nationalist Scandinavianism and that made it hard for me to get a hold of this alien material. Then I experienced Germany's great time, the war and what happened afterwards. All of this brought about a change in me. Thus far my view of the history of the world and of mankind had been a nationalist view. Now it expanded to become a tribal view, and that freed me to write *Emperor and Galilean*.' As I have argued elsewhere, there is little reason to ascribe a deep-seated and profound pan-Germanism to Ibsen. It makes more sense to read the words as a reaction to his encounter with Dresden, which brought him into touch with a modern Europe that was very different from what he experienced in Rome – despite his resort to fashionable contemporary pan-Germanic jargon ('tribal view').

50. Jørgen Haugan discusses Julian as a portrait of Brandes in Haugan (1993: 157ff).

Chapter 8 Munich

1. For an account of the plays and the number of performances, see Perfall (1894: 78ff).

2. Blanc (1899: 293ff) and Josephson (1898: 58ff).

3. See the analysis of *Peer Gynt* and the Ibsen tradition in Norwegian theatre in Hyldig (2006: 7).

4. The contrast between *Peer Gynt*'s anti-national content and Grieg's Romantic music was noted as early as the first decades of the twentieth century. A progressive German director named Berthold

Viertel had Solveig's song sung from *behind* the stage. In Norway, Kristian Elster criticised the music as early as 1923, and in 1947 Hans Jacob Nilsen caused an uproar by mounting a production of the play at Det norske Teatret in New Norwegian with music by Harald Sæverud, cf. Nilsen (1967), Lyche (1991: 203) and Englert (2001: 140ff).

5. In Myhre (1908) Heyerdal, Ibsen, Leuthold, Carrière and the writer-director Emanuel Geibel are described as forming a single group. But Geibel, who had been a central figure in the Krokodile and literary life in Munich, had left the city by 1868, Dirrigl (1984: 1,495–9). Marcus Grønvold mentions Ibsen, Heyse, Lingg, Hertz, Stieler and Grandaur as the Krokodile gang that used to gather at the Achatz, cf. Grønvold (1925: 136ff). In a letter to L. Dietrichson, 29 April 1877 (HU 17: 260), Ibsen mentions that he is spending time with Schmidt, Heyse, Carrière and Grandaur. Dietrichson, who later joined them, describes these gatherings in his memoir. He also mentions that Heyse's friend Oswald Schmidt was a regular member of the group, Dietrichson (1913: 362). There are no indications of any close relationships between Ibsen and German artists, apart from the fact that he was a member of the Munich Society of Artists (HI to M. Grønvold, HU 17: 330). Ibsen had promised to visit Piloty to buy a painting for the Christiania Society of Arts, and Piloty had been one of Ibsen's fellow judges in Vienna, but beyond this there are no indications of any further contact, cf. HI to Thomas Rist Hesselberg, 27 February 1875, *Edda* 1/1998.

6. *Om Gesellschaft der Krokodile*: see Wülfing (1998: 155ff). A more extensive study is in Dirrigl (1984: 1381ff).

7. See Jelavich (1985: 1–26), Dirrigl (1984: 1,381), Breuer (1987) and Spindler (1978: 808–11).

8. For example, Brandes (1890) and Koht (1954b: 79).

9. The translation follows Moi (2006: 95). Moi has written the most thorough analysis of the relationship between Ibsen and Heyse, see pp. 92ff.

10. The Hoftheater in Munich may have dropped its plans to perform *The Pretenders* because the play had been read and given a trial production at the Meininger theatre in January 1876.

11. Fleischhacker (1995: 118ff).

12. Ibsen himself describes the production as popular with audiences, but adds that it displeased the Berlin critics. According to Ibsen the play was performed nine times in Berlin, but in a number of Meiningen sources the number is given as seven, cf. Grube (1926: 129, table), Osborne (1988: 176) and Koller (1984: 195). A Danish newspaper also wrote that the play had been performed in Meiningen in January but was not particularly successful. This was a misunderstanding; the performance at Meiningen had merely been a dress rehearsal. Theatre historians seem therefore to be in agreement that *The Vikings at Helgeland* in April 1876 must be reckoned Ibsen's first appearance on the German stage and not the dress rehearsal of *The Pretenders* in January, cf. Fleischhacker (1995: 118, n. 21).

13. It is clear from Reznicek (2000: 15) that there was a performance of *A Doll's House* at the theatre in 1885.

14. Osborne (1988: 2), Dirrigl (1984: 1,381) and Breuer (1987: 301ff).

15. My interpretation agrees with that of Michael Meyer, cf. Meyer (1995: 419).

16. On the naturalist criticism of the Meininger's historicism and of *Ghosts* 1886 as an exception in the Meininger's repertoire, see Osborne (1988: 76ff and 170ff).

17. The daily routines are described in Grønvold (1925: 137ff).

18. Grønvold (1945). 'Piller' here should be read in the sense of 'pilarer', so Paulsen's version was not completely wide of the mark – but wide enough for Ibsen.

19. Edholm (1948: 117). *The Vikings at Helgeland* was this time performed at the 'opera venue' Kgl. Stora Theatern and not at the Kgl. Dramatiska Theatern (Dramaten), where most of Ibsen's plays were performed. The previous autumn the play had been performed at Dramaten (premiere 11 November 1876), a year after the production at Nya Teatern (premiere 3 November 1875). Edvard Stjernström was the manager here, and there had been a bitter disagreement between the two theatre bosses Stjernström and Edholm over who had the rights to the play, cf. Lindberger (1964: 381ff).

20. See Dahlgren (1913: 264ff). Dahlgren also provides a general description of the salon world and the women who ran it in the last decades of the nineteenth century, cf. also Linder (1918).

21. Per Dahl and Jørgen Knudsen explain the breach between Ibsen and Brandes from the end of the 1870s as being intimately related to the closer relationship that developed simultaneously between Brandes and Bjørnson. Ibsen is said to have deferred to his Norwegian rival. But even though Brandes and Bjørnson got on well together and wrote disparagingly of Ibsen, it is hardly likely that Ibsen would break off a correspondence with an important critic such as Brandes because Brandes consorted with Bjørnson (as well as the rest of literary Scandinavia). It is more likely that the 'brotherhood of arms' linking HI and Brandes was not especially strong to begin with, or that it gradually grew weaker, cf. Dahl (2002: 15ff) and Knudsen (1988: 238ff). Meyer explains the break as being because Brandes was offended at not being invited to visit when Ibsen was in Copenhagen

in the winter of 1877 and is of the opinion that the long break in their correspondence owed much to the fact that Brandes believed Ibsen did not like him, cf. Meyer (1995: 434ff). There is support for Meyer's view in a letter from Brandes to John Paulsen, 13 October 1880 (*Edda* 1928), in which Brandes wonders why Ibsen has not written to him for three years, and does not hide the fact that, in his opinion, Ibsen 'owes' him a letter. My view is that Dahl, Knudsen and Meyer lay too much stress on observations and anecdotal evidence. Although all three were touchy in the highest degree, the shifting alliances in which they were involved need also to be seen against the background of the more fundamental tensions between their literary and intellectual projects, as I argue in this book. Another letter from 1880 illustrates this. Brandes writes to P. Heyse, 25 September 1880 (Brandes 1966: 221), that he hardly considers Ibsen a friend any longer, and he wonders about the veracity of a rumour he has recently heard to the effect that Ibsen had written a new and reconciliatory follow-up to *A Doll's House*. Such would be a great mistake, in Brandes' view, a giving-in to the respectable bourgeoisie. But he chooses to disbelieve the rumour; Ibsen was much too great a writer to do such a thing. The point here is that Brandes really doesn't know quite where he is with Ibsen, and is certainly not sure that they have the same literary and political programme.

22. In a letter to his brother Georg Brandes writes: 'In a literature as small as ours, it seems to me that it [*The Pillars of Society*] will always find a place', G. Brandes to E. Brandes, 27 November 1877, Brandes (1940a: 4). He is more severe when writing to J. P. Jacobsen: 'Ibsen's play is technically very proficient, but did not teach me anything new', G. Brandes to J. P. Jacobsen, 16 December 1877, in Brandes (1940b: 132). However, he did review a production in Berlin anonymously in *Dagbladet*, 11 February 1878.

23. See Tore Rem's analysis of the relationship between book and theatre in the Dano-Norwegian and British literary arenas in Rem (2006b: 89ff)

24. When the Christiania Theatre eventually produced *The Pillars of Society* in March 1879, Vibe was, at Ibsen's request, not its director. The following autumn he was replaced by Hans Schrøder. However, not even Schrøder remained in Ibsen's favour for long.

25. See Friese (1985: 134) and Fleischhacker (1995: 119ff), cf. the comprehensive study of the German reception history in Gentikow (1978: 33ff). See also Øystein Rottem's discussion of Gentikow's theories in Rottem (1981).

26. The analysis of the scenography in *The Pillars of Society* accords with Aarseth (1999a: 45ff).

27. Toril Moi uses Aarseth's focus on the metascenic elements in *The Pillars of Society* in support of the argument that Ibsen's dramas show modernist tendencies that go beyond the boundaries of the traditional view of him as a realistic and pre-modernist writer, Moi (2006: 308ff).

28. The traditional view of *The Pillars of Society* as an edifying play with a reconciliatory ending was first challenged by James McFarlane, cf. McFarlane (1966: 36–40). He suggests instead an ironic reading of the final scene that makes the play a more complex drama of revelation. The interpretative tradition is reviewed in Kittang (2002: 128ff). Kittang himself supports a reading in which Bernick's striving for greatness is seen in an existential and heroic light, while leaving open the possibility that the text also lends itself to the revelatory and the comic, cf. Kittang (2002: 153).

29. See H. Koht's introduction to *The Pillars of Society*, HU 8: 20ff. Plimsoll's campaign led to the first legislation on seaworthiness in 1873, but when this showed itself to be inadequate he took the matter up again in the House in the summer of 1875. This became a matter of international interest, and led to the passing of a new law. Ibsen may have read of the case in *Morgenbladet*, 30 July 1875, and the debate of the preceding year was described in *Dagbladet*, 18 July and 1 September 1874.

30. In a seafaring town such as Grimstad damaged foreign ships were frequently repaired and there were several parallels to actual personages here: a scandalous actress tried to make it in Grimstad but had to leave on account of gossip; Morten Smith-Petersen lived here, a high-flying businessman and local pillar of society; the schooner *Palmetræet* sailed from here, just as it does in the play; and Marcus Thrane had started a workers' union here six months before Ibsen left the town, cf. H. Koht's introduction to *The Pillars of Society*, HU 8: 24ff. But there were no grounds for relating Smith-Petersen to the 'plimsoll coffins' – he was one of the founders of the insurance company Norsk Veritas.

31. Toril Moi regards the play as a radical criticism of paternalism and an idealised view of women. Bjørn Hemmer is more moderate and believes that the play offers an 'ambivalent' view of women, which shows signs of a 'growing awareness' of the need for a new way of looking at women, as well as an image of woman as man's spiritual helper, cf. Moi (2006: 313ff) and Hemmer (2003: 53ff). Ibsen originally intended to devote much more space to the question of women, as the earliest drafts of the play show. These were, however, moderated in the final version, cf. early notes for *The Pillars of Society* 1870, HU 8: 154ff. The Swedish reviewer August Strömbäck, who discussed the play in the periodical *Tidskrift för hemmet* (2/1878) – a periodical that addressed itself to 'Norden's women' – found that Ibsen here managed something Bjørnson had not, a 'positive expression' of woman's position in the family and in society. However, what was positive about it was that Ibsen's female figures 'at the decisive moment support their men with all their resources, love and under-

standing'. In other words, *The Pillars of Society* was not necessarily read as taking radical issue with the contemporary idealised view of women, but as a play that gave women a heroic role within the traditional division of the sexes.

32. The figures are from Fulsås (2007).
33. Ibsen's own accounts show that he earned just 626 kroner from the German Dramatists' Union for the successful production of *The Pillars of Society* in 1878, cf. Jacobsen (2006a).
34. Halvorsen (1892: 57).
35. Ibsen was enrolled as a member of the German Dramatists' Union on 10 March 1876 and left it in May 1884, cf. HIS 13k: 109.
36. National and international copyright law, see Larssen (1976) and Francon (1986).
37. L. Kieler's life and tragedy are described in Kinck (1935).

Chapter 9 Rome – Munich – Rome

1. Tjønneland (1999).
2. 'Notes for a tragedy of contemporary life', HU 8: 368ff.
3. See Toril Moi's analysis of *A Doll's House* as taking issue with the idealised view of women, Moi (2006: 125).
4. Ørjasæther (2003: 143ff and 162ff).
5. My discussion of the reception largely accords with Moi (2006: 320ff), even though, as is apparent, I find the distinction between 'realists' and 'idealists' rather more complex than Moi does.
6. Discussed in a letter from HI to F. Hegel, 22 January 1880, HU 17: 380ff. At first Ibsen believed the sales were negligible, and was very worried when Hegel informed him late in 1879 that Copenhagen's largest bookshop had sold 600 copies of the German Nora. Early in the new year he receives another letter from his publishers, in which Hegel writes that Nora 'is doing no little harm to the original', cf. F. Hegel to HI, 27 December 1879 and 18 January 1880, F. Hegel's draft letters in Ny kgl. Saml. 3742–4, DKB. However, Ibsen himself had authorised Lange's edition, and there is no doubt that his edition was perfectly lawful. The primary indignation of both writer and publisher is, however, directed towards the lack of proper legal protection rather than at Lange personally.
7. See the discussion of the production of *A Doll's House* at the the Kongelige Teater in Wiingaard (2002: 18ff).
8. On the production of *A Doll's House* at Dramaten, see Österlund (1985). Josephson was also head of the Nya Teatern with Victor Holmquist.
9. Halvorsen (1892: 67).
10. For reviews in the Munich press of *A Doll's House* see Fleischhacker (1995: 120ff), cf. Paulsen (1900: 138ff). Paul Lindau in *Die Gegenwart* 18 (1880) also found the ending both immoral and illogical, while Karl Frenzel found Ibsen lacking as a dramatist and regretted his fascination for repellent themes, *Deutsche Rundschau* 26 (1881).
11. Friese (1985: 132), cf. Magon (1967: 222).
12. The variations are discussed in Halvorsen (1892: 62ff).
13. Ibsen in Finland: In 1871, M. G. Schybergson wrote the first Finnish essay on Ibsen in Åbo, 'Underrättelser' (on *Brand*); three years later Eliel Aspelin Haapkylä published a number of articles about *Brand, Emperor and Galilean* and *The Pretenders*. Following the productions of *The Vikings at Helgeland* and *The Pillars of Society* (the first Finnish translation, published in 1878), both new and older Ibsen plays were translated, produced and reviewed in Finnish newspapers and periodicals – not least by Vasenius, cf. Holmström (2005), Kjetsaa (1972), Silén (1977) and Seghedoni (2003).
14. Vasenius published his essay *Om skaldens ställning till tidens «brännande frågor»*, Helsingfors 1878, in which he attacked Friedrich Vischer's aesthetics, discussed in Holmström (2005: 350ff).
15. In a covering letter Vasenius stresses the differences between himself and Brandes. The letter has been lost, but Geir Kjetsaa found drafts for it at Helsingfors University, printed in Kjetsaa (1972: 80ff). In the first draft, dated 29 September 1879, Vasenius writes: 'It seems to me as though your work will, read in this perspective, offer a number of beautiful things to which Hr Brandes is quite blind, and I permit myself to conclude from this that my way of looking at it is the more correct.' So the indications are that Ibsen opened Vasenius' dissertation expecting to find something very different from Georg Brandes, and the contents show that this was indeed the case.
16. Paulsen (1906: 89). Note that Ibsen had already in the autumn of 1879 told Hegel that he was planning a new play, though it is not certain he was referring to *Ghosts*, cf. HI to F. Hegel, 13 September 1879, HU 17: 358.
17. The splitting of 'idealism's trinity' is fundamental to Toril Moi's analysis of the aesthetic of idealism, Moi (2006: ch.3).

18. See the discussion of the modern breakthrough as a periodisation in Aarseth (1988).
19. Cf. Jørgen Knudsen's presentation of Georg Brandes' 'aristocratic radicalism': 'Brandes' political ideal really had no place in the world but becomes firmly established in this period; an aristocraticism, an exclusive and demanding taste for quality, only the best, in everything – combined with a loving respect for the common people and an anger against those who oppressed them economically and in other ways' (Knudsen 1988: 82). The presentation gives what is practically a jovial impression of Brandes' elitism that permits an almost trouble-free enrolment of Brandes in the cultural self-understanding of left-wing cultural radicals.
20. There is a similar ambiguity in Brandes' article 'Henrik Ibsen and his School in Germany', *Tilskueren*, June 1890. Here Brandes tries to harmonise the negativity in Ibsen by insisting that his individualism contains a 'hidden socialism', in other words, that his pessimism might still be part of a project to build a new society.
21. Vigdis Ystad has considered the possibility that Ibsen's contemporary dramas mark a deviation from the line that runs from the dramas of ideas to the symbolic dramas, cf. Ystad (2001: 23ff).
22. The most thoroughgoing attempts to show the influence of *Emigrant Literature* on Ibsen's dramas with contemporary settings are those of Ahlström (1974: esp. 72ff, 108ff and 171ff) and Chamberlain (1977). Both offer interesting comparative readings, but in my view the arguments are stretched a little too far in order to make Ibsen's plays a part of Brandes' programme.
23. See the analysis of the dramatic structure of *An Enemy of the People* in Noreng (1969).
24. Halvorsen (1892: 74ff).
25. Wiingaard (2002: 20).
26. Reinecke-Wilkendorff (2004: 87ff).
27. See the discussion of genre and intertextuality in *An Enemy of the People* in Van Laan (1986), cf. Kittang (2002: 155ff).
28. Noreng (1969).
29. Rønning (2006: 201).
30. Local reviews in *Skånes Allehanda*, *Nyaste Öresunds-Posten* and *Helsingborgs Tidning* were all positive and praised Lindberg in particular for his interpretation. The almost total lack of criticism of the play's contents is striking. All the reviews are in Holmberg (1986), cf. Bang (1892: 229–45).
31. Performances of *Ghosts*, see Hyldig (1993: 180).
32. 'Scoundrel' is a play on Ibsen's letter to J. Paulsen above.
33. Ollén (1955: 50ff), cf. HI to L. Josephson, 9 April 1885, HU 1861ff. Earlier the fourth act was presented on certain occasions at the Christiania Theatre as part of its 1867–8 season, as was also the case in June 1876 and June 1877.
34. But note that Ibsen contrasts the affluent home of old Werle with the poorer bourgeois Ekdal home. In other words, the social dimension is more clearly present in this play, though distinctions of class, here as elsewhere in Ibsen, are not of decisive significance.
35. See John S. Chamberlain's discussion of various theories concerning the play's protagonist, cf. Chamberlain (1982: 109). His own conclusion is that there is no obvious protagonist in *The Wild Duck*.
36. Rønning (2006: 202).
37. See for example the analysis of the idealist language used in *The Wild Duck* in Moi (2006: 350ff) and Rønning (2006: 373ff).
38. Darwinian elements in *The Wild Duck* are discussed in Aarseth (1999a: 127ff).
39. Haakonsen (1957: 47) and Høst (1967: 188ff).
40. Narve Fulsås points out that the lull Ibsen experienced in the German book market was of shorter duration than that in the theatre. The period of Ibsen's absence from German stages was roughly from 1880 to 1887; but in the bookshops only from March 1884 to November 1886, Fulsås (2008).
41. HU 15: 407ff.
42. Jürgen Habermas traces the liberal conception of aristocracy back to the idea of education and economic power, discussed in Tjønneland (2006: 145ff). In the main I agree with Tjønneland's sharp analysis of Ibsen's (and Brandes') concept of aristocracy, not least when he points out that Ibsen deviated from the liberal conception of aristocracy in his speech in Trondhiem. However, I think it is a touch misleading to say, as Tjønneland does, that Ibsen reconsiders/undermines his own conception of nobility in *Rosmersholm* (p. 148). What characterises Ibsen's drama generally, unlike his extra-literary pronouncements, is precisely the constant shifting between the trying out of new positions and ideas and the undermining of them. Ibsen did not renounce his concept of the aristocratic after *Rosmersholm*, but as a dramatist it was his task to examine the consequences of all positions, his own included.
43. In Aage Henriksen's view, a chief characteristic of Ibsen's writing (as of Karen Blixen's) is that they test out society's tenets and beliefs using individuals in their everyday lives. The purpose of the

literary project is to analyse and demonstrate the cost of self-realisation and the free development of the personality. The writers side with their illusions, so to speak: their goal is not to unmask or explain the riddles but to identify with the very riddles they are investigating. So they are as inefficient as pillars of society as they are as revolutionaries. In regard to Ibsen, I follow Henriksen here, cf. Henriksen (1974).

44. Sigurd Ibsen's social views are thoroughly analysed in Steine (2005).
45. An isolated quote by Ibsen from November 1895, HU 19: 149, cf. letter to G. Brandes, 3 January 1882 (HU 17: 449), in which he maintains that a democracy that was not based on the 'refined mind' was the same as a 'plebeian' society.
46. Ibsen's only known response to the Commune is the following ironic remark made to Georg Brandes: 'How disgraceful of the "Commune" in Paris to spoil my beautiful state-theory – or rather, non-state theory! Now the idea has been ruined for a long time to come, and I can't even in all conscience offer it in the form of a poem. But the core of it is sound, I see that clearly, and the time will come when it will be put into practice without all the caricaturing.' HI to G. Brandes, 18 May 1871, HU 16: 368.

Chapter 10 Munich

1. Heitmann (1999: 358ff).
2. Heyse (1912: 95ff), discussed in Bernhard (1989: 366ff), cf. letter from P. Heyse to G. Brandes, 12 December 1879, 24 December 1881 and 15 January 1882, Brandes (1966: 206ff, 247 and 251ff). See also Toril Moi's portrayal of Heyse and the relationship between him and Ibsen in Moi (2006).
3. Note that all save J. Elias, L. Berg and F. Philippi are listed as members of Verein Freie Bühne as of 30 June 1889, reproduced in Pfäfflin (1983). According to Fleischhacker (1995), Philippi was the leading supporter in Munich.
4. Inga-Stina Ewbank stresses the liberating power of exile on Ibsen, cf. Ewbank (1997: 43).
5. Here I am in agreement with Atle Kittang who, partly in taking issue with Inga Stina-Ewbank, points out that the experience of exile is of little relevance for homeless characters such as 'the Stranger' in The Lady from the Sea and Ulrik Brendel in Rosmersholm, cf. Kittang (2006b: 215ff) and Ewbank (1997: 49).
6. The concept of the 'immigrant' heirs is established by Ketil Jacobsen, cf. Jacobson (2006b: 215ff), cf. Rønning (2006: 22 and 26ff).
7. As regards these positions Atle Kittang distinguishes between scholars who interpret the final scene as one of 'tragic reconciliation' and others who in various ways give it an ironic reading, cf. Toril Moi's related division of scholarly traditions into idealist and anti-idealist camps, Kittang (2002: 211ff) and Moi (2006: 408).
8. Kittang (2002: 191ff).
9. The theme of the individual transcending his or her own boundaries is the analytic thread in Atle Kittang's monograph Ibsens heroisme, Kittang (2002).
10. See the discussion of Snoilsky as a model for Rosmer in Tveterås (1933) and in F. Bull's introduction to Rosmersholm, HU 10: 323.
11. Lindberg (1943: 146ff).
12. For Berlin's growth and cultural leadership in Germany, see McFarlane (1991).
13. See the overview in Eller (1918: 136ff).
14. Sjönell (1987: 497ff).
15. The play was reprinted in Folkeutgaven, but a new general edition was not printed until 1902.
16. Eller (1989: 78ff).
17. See Nina Alnæs' examination of the elements of folklore and nature mysticism in Rosmersholm and The Lady from the Sea, Alnæs (2003: 219–322).
18. Aarseth (1999a: 194).
19. Garton (1994: 118).
20. Vogt (1930: 75ff) and Brandell (1961: 90ff).
21. I rely here on Toril Moi's acute analysis in Moi (2006: 412–40).
22. Gossensass, see Næss (1994)
23. The traditional view is that Emilie was eighteen when she and Ibsen met in 1889. According to the Vienna archives, however, the only Emilie Bardach registered in the Vienna area at that time was born on 5 August 1862. She was the daughter of a Sigmund and Minna Bardach. Sigmund, a merchant, died on 29 August 1890, which accords with the fact that Ibsen sent his condolences to Emilie on the death of her father on 18 September 1890, HU 18: 253, cf. the birth register of the Jewish population of Vienna no. 3170/1862: Emilie Bardach and register of deaths no. 2216/1890: Sigmund Bardach,

Israelitische Kultusgemeinde Wien (IKW). Emilie's date of birth is also confirmed in a document dated 16 May 1896, WStLA, Polizei, Bundespolizei Wien, Melde unterlagen, Das Wiener Stadt- und Landesarchiv (WSL). For E. Bardach's biography, see Templeton (1997a: 233ff).

24. Parts of E. Bardach's journal are in Basil King. Ibsen and Emilie Bardach, *Century Magazine*, New York October and November 1923, and partly in Meyer (1995: 618ff) and André Rouveyre, 'Le Mémorial inédit d'une amie d'Ibsen', *Mercure de France*, 15 July 1928. See Joan Templeton's discussion of the authenticity of the journal in Templeton (1997).

25. I agree here with Halvdan Koht in his objections to Else Høst, who finds a 'passionate love' in Ibsen's letters to Emilie of the autumn of 1889, Koht (1958: 355).

26. Extracts from Helene Raff's journal appear in HU 19: 173ff and in Koht (1958).

27. Sigurd's farewell to diplomacy is described in Steine (2005: 23) and Langslet (2004: 80ff).

28. Jæger (1887: 25ff).

29. Cf. Moi (2006: 323).

30. See Helge Rønning's analysis of *Hedda Gabler* in a social and historical perspective, Rønning (2006: 338ff).

31. Discussed in George (1968: 9ff).

32. Hansen (2001). For Ibsen's influence on the works of the German naturalists, see George (1967) and Brandes (1890).

33. For the reception of Ibsen in Great Britain I have largely relied on the account in Rem (2006a). Most of the quotations from English-language critics are also taken from Rem's book.

34. The following is based on Rem (2006a: Introduction) and Rem (2006b).

35. Gentikow (1978).

36. Rem (2006a: 26ff).

37. For the performance of *Ghosts* at the Théâtre Libre, see Swanson (1941) and Sanders (1964), partly in taking issue with Swanson, cf. the detailed discussion of the performance and reception in Templeton (1998).

38. Cf. Toril Moi's discussion of Sarcey's problems in interpreting the wild duck symbol. She believes, as I do, that he must have had a superficial understanding of the role of the duck in the play, as a simple parallel, but must have looked in vain for a deeper importance for it. Moi claims here, with support from Eroll Durbach, that Sarcey fell into the same trap as those many scholars who fail to realise that in searching for a deeper meaning one assumes the same attitude towards the duck as Gregers Werle – for he is the one who constantly insists that the duck involves such a meaning, cf. Moi (2006: 351ff) and Durbach (1982: 93). Yet I think it is worth remembering that understanding is closely related to motivation, and that a lack of motivation may well be the decisive explanation for Sarcey's failure to understand and his urge to ridicule.

39. Ibsen in the USA, see Øverland (2001) and Egan (1972: 25-37).

40. For Ibsen and Ireland, see Rem (2007). The relationship between Ibsen and Joyce is also discussed in Tysdahl (1968).

41. Ibsen in Italy, see Lokrantz (2002) and Pertici (2001).

42. Both Koht and Meyer mention Mazza's translation, but as letters from Ibsen discovered later make clear, the translation was never published. As a consequence of this, Ibsen broke off contact with Mazza. Ibsen would also break with Galletti, responsible for the translation of *A Doll's House* used for the performance in 1889. Galletti, however, published his translation in 1894, the same year as Capuana published his.

43. According to the tradition, the performance of *A Doll's House* with Eleanora Duse in February 1891 is accounted the first performance in Italy, cf. Meyer (1995: 659). As Margherita Giordano Lokrantz has shown, however, this play had been performed earlier, on 15 February 1889, Lokrantz (2002: 59ff).

44. Lagerroth (1990: 23).

45. Ibsen on Dostoyevsky and Tolstoy, see interview with Ibsen on 19 March 1898, HU 19: 214 and HI to Emanuel Hansen, 27 November 1888, HU 18: 191.

46. L. Tolstoy to P. G. Hansen, 14 September 1891, Tolstoy (1978: 483), cf. Nag (1967: 99ff). Tolstoy's diaries also show that he did not like *Love's Comedy* but found *Rosmersholm* 'not bad', Tolstoy (1985: 270, 291, 410ff, 475 and 484).

47. Chekhov on Ibsen, see Stanislavsky (1924: 345), Chekhov to A. L. Vishenskij, 7 November 1903, in Meyer (1995: 823). On Ibsen's importance for Chekhov's *The Seagull*, see Nag (1967: 113ff), Meyer (1995: 823n) and Deppermann (2005: 44).

48. Meyer (1995: 513n).

49. Meyer (1995: 513).

50. Ibsen on S. Fischer Verlag, see HI to J. Elias, 17 and 18 December 1890, and to S. Fischer, 25 December 1890, HU: 18, 266-8 and 269, cf. Mendelssohn (1970) and Pfäfflin (1985: see for example the overview of publications 65ff).

51. Ibsen in the Netherlands, see HI to Cornelis Honigh, 4 January, 11 March and 5 April 1891, *Edda* 1/1998. The play was also performed in the Netherlands that year.
52. Fleischhacker (1995: 127–30) and Hanssen (2006: 119ff).
53. Ibsen in Hungary, see Lázár (1918: 21–4).

Chapter 11 Kristiania

1. Hamsun's lecture tour and the newspaper reports are comprehensively described in Larsen (2002). See also the discussion of the relationship between Ibsen and Hamsun in Hemmer (1997).
2. This is the main point in the analysis of the work in Rønning (2006: 242–70).
3. The interpretation of Aline is based on Kittang (2002: 263).
4. Helland (2000).
5. Kittang (2002: ch. 5).
6. Meyer (1995: 709–12) and Rem (2006a: 216–20).
7. Ibsen's income tax, see Edvardsen (2001: 241ff).
8. The visit of the French Theatre to Christiania is described in Lugné-Poe (1938).
9. Bang (1906: 328). In conversation with Jules Claretie in the summer of 1897, Ibsen said that Lugné-Poe made too much of the symbolism in the plays, though he was grateful for all the French theatre manager had done for him, HU 19: 210.
10. The comparison of the reception in England and France is based on Shepherd-Barr (1999).
11. Swanson (1946). In 1925 the theatre followed this up with *Hedda Gabler*.
12. See the overview of criticism of the play in Helland (2000: 243ff).
13. As a number of critics have noted, what is fascinating about the Rat Wife is that although she obviously has a symbolic function she also gives the impression of having a lived life (unlike the Stranger in *The Lady from the Sea*). Perhaps she appears so lifelike because, according to Ibsen, she is based on an old 'aunt' he knew in Skien – probably 'Aunt' Ploug, who lived at Venstøp. Ibsen denied, however, any familiarity with Goethe's poem about the Pied Piper of Hamelin, though he admitted that he knew of the legend, cf. HU 19: 203ff.
14. Atle Kittang points out that the 'peaks' Allmers looks up towards in the final scene are the same 'heights' he has formerly wandered on, and identified with his longing for death – which represents his tendency to avoid the challenges presented in the real world, Kittang (2002: 354ff).
15. See the analysis in Aarseth (1999a: 309–33) and Kittang (2002: 278–317).
16. There is a more extensive discussion of the relationship between Ibsen and Nietzsche in the two-volume Norwegian edition of this biography, de Figueiredo (2007: 473ff).
17. Another Nietzschean influence on this play might have come via Brandes' Nietzsche-inspired book on Shakespeare, which Brandes sent to him. Ibsen thanks him in October 1896: 'I have not merely read your monumental work on Shakespeare, I have immersed myself in it more profoundly than probably any other book.' HI to G. Brandes, 3 October 1896, HU 18: 385.
18. Aarseth stresses the young in the drama, Kittang the old (Borkman himself), Aarseth (1999a) and Kittang (2002).
19. Although the methods of the philosopher and the dramatist make them, in the main, too disparate to compare, Fredrik Engelstad's article on Ibsen's and Nietzsche's view of power are very readable – especially the analysis of the different forms of power in Ibsen's plays. Engelstad acknowledges the problems involved in the comparison when he writes: 'The dramatist is observing and intuitive where the philosopher constructs syntheses based on concepts . . .': cf. Engelstad (2001: 283).
20. See the discussion of the relationship between pleasure and duty in Theoharis (1996).
21. Eivind Tjønneland has noted the elitism that lies hidden in this dialogue, Tjønneland (2006: 147).
22. For the controversy surrounding Sigurd Ibsen's professorship see Steine (2005: 92–8) and Langslet (2004: 143–69).
23. A speech at the celebratory dinner given by the Norwegian Women's Union, HU 15: 417.
24. See the discussion of the concepts of human liberation–female liberation in relation to *A Doll's House* in Moi (2006: 343ff).
25. Ibsen and Edvard Munch: the two met in the 1890s, in the street at the Grand, but there was no question of a friendship. Ibsen's appearance at his scandalous exhibition at Blomquists' in 1895 was crucially important for Munch. The exhibition consisted of the so-called *Frieze of Life*, which includes *Woman in Three Stages*. The exhibition had previously opened in Berlin, where it was subjected to vigorous attack. The same thing happened in Kristiania. Given Ibsen's orthodox tastes in art there is no reason to suppose that he should have been attracted to Munch's work. On the other hand, the writer was preoccupied with the young, and it is hard to ignore the similarities linking Munch's visually symbolic language in *The Frieze of Life* and the literary symbolism in the plays of Ibsen's old age. The only explicit source we have of Ibsen's alleged taste for Munch's art is

Munch's own account, written long after the event ('Livsfrisens tilblivelse', 1929). And Munch is not an especially reliable source. As a chronicler he is not merely imprecise, but he also had very good reasons for wanting to connect Ibsen to his own art. In the third place, the comparison linking *When We Dead Awaken* to his own paintings is dubious; especially where he believes he finds traces of 'Melancholy' and 'Jealousy' in the description of *Resurrection Day*. It is perfectly possible that Ibsen made use of Munch's paintings in *When We Dead Awaken*, but the most important influence has been from Ibsen to Munch. This is evident from Munch's numerous sketches, prints and paintings that refer to Ibsen himself and his plays. His first portrait of Ibsen was the lithographic theatre poster he made for Lugné-Poe's production of *John Gabriel Borkman* in 1896. Already he manages to capture the writer's geometric-iconic features, and these same features recur in his later portraits, the most famous of these being the painting of Ibsen at the Grand Hotel from 1898. In this picture Ibsen's head glows against a dark curtain, while the window to the right shows Karl Johan full of life and people: the writer who inhabits the darkness with his profound thoughts behind that jutting forehead, separated from the world of the small people outside. Whether this was a case of Munch nurturing the sphinx myth, or whether he has enrolled the writer in his own universe here, probably amounts to the same thing: for Munch the idea of the rejected and elevated figure of the artist was an important point of his identification with Ibsen. Over the years Munch did hundreds of illustrations for *The Pretenders*, *Peer Gynt*, *Ghosts*, *Hedda Gabler*, *John Gabriel Borkman* and *When We Dead Awaken* – often for use as posters or scenographic sketches for productions in theatres in France and Germany. In addition there are those pictures with obviously Ibsenian themes, regardless of their overt subject. Often he uses himself as a model. In 1909 he placed Ibsen in the company to which he felt he belonged, with Nietzsche and Socrates in the sketch entitled 'The Geniuses', cf. Langslet (2004) and the more critical Templeton (2000).

26. For reviews and the history of the reception of *When We Dead Awaken* see Wærp (1999: 16–38).
27. If we discount Heinemann's reading in London on 16 December, the play's real premiere was at the Hoftheater in Stuttgart in January 1900. In the course of the spring the play was performed on a number of stages in Scandinavia and Germany, and the general view seems to have been that the play was difficult to stage.
28. Cf. the study of the rhetorical figures in the play in Wærp (2000).
29. Haugan (1982: 101).
30. Kittang (2002: 318–58).
31. In what follows I use Kjetil Jacobsen's analysis of the preconditions for Ibsen's breakthrough as an autonomous writer in a European context, Jacobsen (2006b).
32. Jacobsen (2006b).
33. Rønning (2006: 27ff).
34. Here I follow Harold Bloom's sympathetic presentation of Ibsen's originality and greatness, Bloom (2007: 312).

Chapter 12 Arbins gate

1. In a letter to Johan Scharffenberg from his brother Wilhelm, who was headmaster at the Lillesand school, Wilhelm – who knew Hans Jacob – writes: 'He has, by his own account, several times applied to his famous father for help, but to no avail.' Cf. W. Scharffenberg to Johan Scharffenberg, 20 January 1895, brevs. 383, NBO, cf. Ferguson (1996: 394ff).
2. For nominations, awards and grounds see Svensén (2001), cf. the discussion of af Wirsén's idealistic influence on the Nobel Committee in Moi (2006: 147–52). In 1910, af Wirsén ended his period as a member of the committee by awarding Paul Heyse the Nobel Prize in Literature. Ibsen himself was invited to suggest candidates, but declined the offer. His reply to the committee is lost, but in a draft note giving his reasons for declining he writes: 'However, since I am afraid that my understanding of . . .' The rest is lost, but a single word, crossed out, is still legible: 'idealistic', cf. Anker (1979: 480).

BIBLIOGRAPHY

Aarseth, Asbjørn (1988). 'Det moderne gjennombrudd – et periodebegrep og dets ideologiske basis', in Bertil Norlin and Peter Forsgren (eds), *The Modern Breakthrough in Scandinavian Literature 1870–1905*, Göteborg.

Aarseth, Asbjørn (1999a). *Ibsens samtidsskuespill. En studie i glasskapets dramaturgi*, Oslo.

Aarseth, Asbjørn (1999b). 'Le dramaturge en tant qu'historien de la civilisation', *Europe*, no. 840 (April).

Aasen, Ivar (1957–60). *Brev og dagbøker*, Oslo.

Agerholm, Edvard (1910–11). 'Henrik Ibsen og Det kgl. Teater', *Gads danske Magasin*.

Ahlström, Gunnar (1974). *Det moderna genombrottet i Nordens litteratur*, Stockholm (1947).

Alnæs, Nina (2003). *Varulv om natten. Folketro og folkediktning hos Ibsen*, Oslo.

Amdam, Per (1993). *Bjørnstjerne Bjørnson. Kunstneren og samfunnsmennesket*, Oslo.

Anker, Øyvind (1979). *Henrik Ibsen. Brev 1845–1905. Ny samling*, Oslo.

Anker, Øyvind (1981). *Henrik Ibsen. Brev 1845–1905. Ny samling II*, Oslo.

Archer, William (1906). 'Ibsen as I Knew Him', *Monthly Review* (June).

Arvesen, Olaus (1912). *Oplevelser og erindringer fra 1830-årene og utover*, Kristiania.

Auring, Steffen (1984). *Borgerlig enhedskultur 1807–48, Dansk litteraturhistorie*, vol. 5, Copenhagen.

Bang, Herman (1892). *Teatret*, Copenhagen.

Bang, Herman (1906). 'Personlige erindringer om Henrik Ibsen', *Det ny aarhundrede. Maanedsskrift*, 3:2 (April–September).

Baxter, Paul Sandvold (1998). '*Caesar is my Captive': Hegel's Influence on Ibsen's Concept of Freedom*, Boston.

Bentley, Eric (1957). *A Century of Hero-Worship: A Study of the Idea of Heroism in Carlyle and Nietzsche, with Notes on Wagner, Spengler, Stefan George and D. H. Lawrence*, Boston.

Berg, Thoralf (1998). *Henrik Ibsen på teatret i Trondheim før 1865*, Trondheim.

Bergman, Gösta (1952). *Regihistoriska studier*, Stockholm.

Bergsøe, Vilhelm (1907). *Henrik Ibsen paa Ischia og 'Fra Piazza del Popolo'. Erindringer fra Aarene 1863–69*, Copenhagen.

Beyer, Harald (1924). *Søren Kierkegaard og Norge*, Kristiania.

Björklund-Bexell, Ingeborg (1962). *Ibsens 'Vildanden'. En studie*, Stockholm.

Blanc, T. (1884). *Norges første nationale scene*, Kristiania.

Blanc, T. (1899). *Christiania Theaters historie 1827–1877*, Kristiania.

Bloom, Harold (2007). *Vestens litterære kanon. Mesterverk i litteraturhistorien*, Oslo.

Blytt, Peter (1907). *Minder fra den første norske Scene i Bergen i 1850-Aarene. Et kulturhistorisk Forsøg*, 2nd edn, Bergen.

Bø, Gudleiv (1996). 'Fra Solhaug og Solbakken til Roma', in Kari Gundersen et al. *Veier til byen. En antologi*, Oslo.

Bø, Gudleiv (2000). *Nationale subjekter. Ideer om nasjonalitet i Henrik Ibsens romantiske forfatterskap*, Oslo.

Boeck, Albert (1940). 'Små randgloser til Ibsens biografer', *Nordisk tidsskrift för vetenskap, konst och industri*, Stockholm.

Brandell, Gunnar (1961). *Vid seklets källor*, Stockholm.

Brandes, Georg (1867). *Henrik Ibsen*, Copenhagen.

Brandes, Georg (1868). *Æsthetiske Studier*, Copenhagen.

Brandes, Georg (1890). 'Henrik Ibsen og hans Skole i Tyskland', *Tilskueren* (June).

Brandes, Georg (1907). *Levned. Et tiaar*, Copenhagen.

Brandes, Georg (1940a). *Brevveksling med nordiske forfattere og videnskabsmænd* (ed. Morten Borup et al.), vol. II, Copenhagen.

Brandes, Georg (1940b). *Brevveksling med nordiske forfattere og videnskabsmænd* (ed. Morten Borup et al.), vol. III, Copenhagen.

Brandes, Georg (1966). *Correspondance de Georg Brandes. Lettres choisies et annotées par Paul Krüger*, vol. III. *L'Allemagne*, Copenhagen.

Brenna, Brita (2002). *Verden som ting og forestilling. Verdensutstillinger og den norske deltakelsen 1851–1900*, Oslo.

Breuer, Dieter (1987). 'Der Münchner Dichterkreis und seine Anthologien', in Alfred Weber (ed.), *Handbuch der Literatur in Bayern*, Regensburg.

Bull, Francis (1960a). *Norsk litteraturhistorie*, vol. IV, Oslo.

Bull, Francis (1960b). *Nordisk kunstnerliv i Rom*, Oslo.

Bull, Francis (1966). 'Hildur Andersen og Henrik Ibsen', in *Vildanden og andre essays*, Oslo.

Chamberlain, John (1982). *Ibsen: The Open Vision*, London.

Chesnais, Pierre G. (1937). 'Les sources historiques de l'*Empereur et Galiléen*', *Edda*.

Christensen, Erik M. (1985). *Henrik Ibsens realisme. Illusjon, katastrofe, anarki*, vol. I, Copenhagen.

Collin, Christen (1906). 'Henrik Ibsens fremtidsdrøm', *Samtiden*.

Collin, Christen (1923). *Bjørnstjerne Bjørnson. Hans barndom og ungdom. Anden del*, 2 vols, vol. II, Kristiania.

Daae, Ludvig (1888). 'Paul Botten-Hansen', *Vidar*.

Daae, Ludvig (1934). *Politiske dagbøker og minner*, vol. I, Oslo.

Dahl, Herleiv (1958). *Bergmannen og byggmesteren. Henrik Ibsen som lyriker*, Oslo.

Dahl, Per (1988). *Det moderne gennembruds poetik: Brandes, Bjørnson og Ibsen*, in Bertil Norlin and Peter Forsgren (eds), *The Modern Breakthrough in Scandinavian Literature 1870–1905*, Göteborg.

Dahl, Per (2002). 'Den umulige treenighed: Bjørnson – Brandes – Ibsen', *P2-akademiet*, Oslo.

Dahl, Per (2006). 'Georg Brandes om Henrik Ibsen. En bibliografi', in Jørgen Dines Johansen et al. (eds), *Ibsen og Brandes. Studier i et forhold*, Oslo.

Dahl, Per Kristian Heggelund (2001). *Streiflys. Fem Ibsen-studier*, Oslo.

Dahlgren, Lotten (1913). *Lyran. Interiörer från 1870- och 80-talens konstnärliga och litterära Stockholm*, Stockholm.

Deppermann, Maria (2005). 'Modern Theatre in Russia around 1900: A Context for the Reception of Ibsen's Drama', in Knut Brynhildsvoll (ed.), *Ibsen and Russian Culture: Ibsen Conference in St. Petersburg 1–4 October 2003*, Oslo.

Dietrichson, Lorentz (1896). *Bergen og Christiania i 40 og 50-Aarene*, vol. I, *Svundne tider*, Kristiania.

Dietrichson, Lorentz (1913). *Svundne tider*, vol. I. 'Bergen og Christiania i 1840- og 50-årene', Kristiania.

Dirrigl, Michael (1984). *Maximilian II. König von Bayern 1848–1864*, Munich.

Downs, Brian W. (1946). *Ibsen: The Intellectual Background*, Cambridge.

Due, Christopher (1909). *Erindringer fra Henrik Ibsens ungdomsaar*, Copenhagen.

Durbach, Errol (1982). *Ibsen the Romantic: Analogues of Paradise in the Later Plays*, Athens, GA.

Dyrerud, Thor Arvid (1998). 'Den kierkegaardske "Reflex" i Ibsens dramatikk', in Finn Jor (ed.), *Filosofi og samfunn*, Kristiansand.

Edholm, Erik af (1948). *Mot seklets slut. Upplevelser under Oscar IIs tid intil författarens död 1897*, Stockholm.

Edvardsen, Erik Henning (2001). *Henrik Ibsen om seg selv*, Oslo.

Edvardsen, Erik Henning (2003). *Ibsens Christiania*, Oslo.

Egan, Michael (ed.) (1972). *The Critical Heritage*, London.

Eitrem, Hans (1910). 'Henrik Ibsen – Henrik Wergeland', *Maal og Minne*, Kristiania.

Eller, William H. (1918). *Ibsen in Germany 1870–1900*, Boston.

Engelstad, Fredrik (2001). 'Henrik Ibsen som maktutreder', *Nytt norsk tidsskrift*, no. 3.

Engelstad, Fredrik (2003). 'Frihet, adel og livskall. Henrik Ibsen som kritiker av demokratiet', *Sosiologi i dag*, no. 3.

Englert, Uwe (2001). *Magus und Rechenmeister. Henrik Ibsens Werk auf den Bühnen des Dritten Reiches*, Tübingen/Basel.

Eriksen, Trond Berg (1997). 'Ibsens *Brand* – en klassisk tragedie', *Egne veier. Essays og foredrag*, Oslo.

Eriksen, Valborg (1923). 'Søren Kierkegaards betydning for norsk aandsliv', *Edda*.

Ewbank, Inga-Stina (1997). ' "I Ijemland . . . fødeland!" Ibsen, Strindberg och landsflykt', *Ibsen-Strindberg seminar på Voksenåsen 15.–17. september 1995*, Oslo.

Fenger, Henning (1955). *Georg Brandes' læreår. Læsning ideer smag kritik 1857–1872*, Copenhagen.

Fenger, Henning (1964). 'Ibsen og Georg Brandes indtil 1872', *Edda*.

Fenger, Henning (1992). *Familjen Heiberg*, Copenhagen.

Ferguson, Robert (1996). *Henrik Ibsen. Mellom evne og higen*, Oslo.

Figueiredo, Ivo de (2002). *Fri mann. Johan Bernhard Hjort. En dannelseshistorie*, Oslo.

Fleischhacker, Sabine (1995). 'Ibsen im Lichte der Münchner Presse (1876–1891)', in *Contemporary Approaches to Ibsen*, Oslo.

Forfang, Halvard Grude (1990). *Paul Botten Hansen og Hollenderkretsen. Litterat og boksamler i en nasjonal grotid*, Lillehammer.

Fraenkl, Pavel (1955). *Ibsens vei til drama. En undersøkelse av dramatikerens genesis*, Oslo.

Francon, André (1986). *Bernkonventionen 100 år*, Stockholm.

Freihow, Halvdan Wexelsen (1936). *Henrik Ibsens 'Brand'. Litterær-psykologisk studie*, Oslo.

Friese, Wilhelm (1985). 'Das deutsche Theater und Henrik Ibsen. Ein historisches Panorama', in *Contemporary Approaches to Ibsen*, Oslo.

Fulsås, Narve (2007). 'Innledning til Henrik Ibsens skrifter', vol. 13, *Brev 1871–1879. Innledning og kommentarer*, Oslo.

Garton, Janet (1994). 'The Middle Plays', in James McFarlane (ed.), *The Cambridge Companion to Ibsen*, Cambridge.

Gentikow, Barbara (1978). *Skandinavien als präkapitalistische Idylle. Rezeption gesellschaftskritischer Literatur in deutschen Zeitschriften 1870 bis 1914*, Neumünster.

George, David E. R. (1968). *Henrik Ibsen in Deutschland. Rezeption und Revision*, Göttingen.

Grønvold, Didrik (1945). *Diktere og musikere. Personlige erindringer om noen av dem*, Oslo.

Grønvold, Marcus (1925). *Fra Ulrikken til Alperne. En malers erindringer*, Oslo.

Grube, Max (1926). *Geschichte der Meininger*, Berlin.

Haakonsen, Daniel (1950). 'Henrik Ibsens lyrikk', *Edda*.

Haakonsen, Daniel (1957). *Henrik Ibsens realisme*, Oslo.

Haakonsen, Daniel (1967). *Henrik Ibsens 'Peer Gynt'*, Oslo.

Hageberg, Otto (1967). *Omkring 'Peer Gynt'*, Oslo.

Halvorsen, J. B. (1892). *Norsk Forfatter-Lexicon 1814–1880*, vol. 3, Kristiania.

Hamre, Kari (1945). *Clemens Petersen og hans forhold til norsk litteratur i årene 1856–69*, Oslo.

Hansen, Thorbjørn Tønder (2001). 'Otto Brahm's Freie Bühne. *Ghosts* in 1889', in Pål Bjørby and Asbjørn Aarseth (eds), *Proceedings. IX International Ibsen Conference Bergen, 5–10 June 2000*, Larvik.

Hanssen, Jens-Morten (2006). 'Da Thea stjal showet', in Anne-Sofie Hjemdahl (ed.), *Ting om Ibsen. Tingene, livet og dramatikken*, Oslo.

Haugan, Jørgen (1982). *Diktersfinxen. En studie i Ibsen og Ibsen-forskningen*, Oslo.

Haugan, Jørgen (1993). 'Kejser og Galilæer – det antikke og det moderne', in Øyvind Andersen and Asbjørn Aarseth (eds), *Antikken i norsk litteratur*, Bergen.

Haugholt, Karl (1956). 'Henrik Ibsens sak mot boktrykker H. J. Jensen', *Edda*.

Heiberg, Johan Ludvig (1861). *Johan Ludvig Heibergs Prosaiske Skrifter. Fjerde Bind*, Copenhagen.

Heitmann, Annegret (1999). 'Letters from Munich: "En Masse Kunst og storartet Bier" ', in Michael Robinson and Janet Garton (eds), *Nordic Letters 1870–1910*, Norwich.

Helland, Frode (2000). *Melankoliens spill. En studie i Henrik Ibsens siste dramaer*, Oslo.

Helveg, Frederik (1866). *Bjørnstjerne Bjørnson og Henrik Ibsen i deres to seneste Værker*, Copenhagen.

Hemmer, Bjørn (1970). *Keiser eller Galiléer. Konfliktstrukturen i Henrik Ibsens diktning 1850–1873*, Oslo.

Hemmer, Bjørn (1978). *Ibsen og Bjørnson. Essays og analyser*, Oslo.

Hemmer, Bjørn (1997). 'Hamsun og Ibsen – Den gåtefulle og sfinksen', in Nils M. Knutsen (ed.), *De røde jærn. 7 foredrag fra Hamsun-dagene på Hamarøy 1996*, Hamarøy.

Hemmer, Bjørn (2003). *Ibsen. Kunstnerens vei*, Oslo.

Henriksen, Aage (1974). 'Det borgerlige oprør', *Kritik*, no. 32.

Hettner, Hermann (1852). *Das moderne Drama. Aesthetische Untersuchungen*, Braunschweig.

Heyse, Paul (1912). *Jugenderinnerungen und Bekenntnisse*, vol. 2, Stuttgart/Berlin.

Holmberg, Hans (1986). 'August Lindberg, Herman Bang och en historisk teaterpremiär i Helsingborg', *Kring Kärnan*, Helsingborg.

Holmström, Roger (2005). 'Att utforska en samtida. Ibsen reception i Finland med fokus på Valfrid Vasenius', in Vigdis Ystad et al. (eds.), *'Bunden af en takskyld uden lige'. Om svenskspråklig Ibsen-formidling 1857–1906*, Oslo.

Høst, Else (1967). *Vildanden av Henrik Ibsen*, Oslo.

Hyldig, Keld (2006). 'Ibsen-tradisjonen i norsk teater', *Norsk Shakespeare- og teatertidsskrift*, nos. 3–4.

Ibsen, Bergliot (1948). *De tre*, Oslo.

Ibsen, Henrik (1993). *Peer Gynt. Et dramatisk dikt*, Oslo.

Ibsen, Henrik (1999). *Samlede verker*, vols 1–21 (Hundreårsutgaven), vol. 2, Oslo.

Ibsen, Tancred (1976). *Tro det eller ei*, Oslo.

Jacobsen, Nils Kåre (2006). *Henrik Ibsens økonomi*, n.p.

Jæger, Henrik (1887). 'Fra et Besøg hos Henrik Ibsen', *Folkebladet* (Christmas issue).

Jakobsen, Kjetil (2004). *Kritikk av den reine autonomi. Ibsen, verden og de norske intellektuelle*, Oslo.

Jakobsen, Kjetil (2006). '"Gjennemlevet, ikke oplevet". Henrik Ibsens vei til virkeligheten' (from Ivo de Figueiredo, *Henrik Ibsen. Mennesket*), *Agora*, no. 4.

Jelavich, Peter (1985). *Munich and Theatrical Modernism: Politics, Playwriting, and Performance 1890–1914*, Cambridge.

Johnston, Brian (1980). *To the Third Empire: Ibsen's Early Drama*, Minneapolis, MN.

Jørgensen, Jens Anker et al. (2005). *Hovedsporet. Dansk litteraturs historie*, Copenhagen.

Jørgensen, John Christian (1994). *Det danske anmelderis historie. Den litterære anmeldelses opståen og udvikling 1720–1906*, Copenhagen.

Josephson, Ludvig (1898). *Ett och annat om Henrik Ibsen och Kristiania Teater*, Stockholm.

Kaschuba, Wolfgang (1993). 'German Bürgerlichkeit after 1800: Culture as Symbolic Practice', in Jürgen Kocka and Allan Mitchell (eds), *Bourgeois Society in Nineteenth-Century Europe*, Oxford.

Kihlman, Erik (1921). *Ur Ibsen-dramatikens idéhistoria. En studie i dansk-norsk litteratur*, Helsingfors.

Kinck, B. M. (1935). 'Henrik Ibsen og Laura Kieler', *Edda*.

Kittang, Atle (2002). *Ibsens heroisme. Frå Brand til Når vi døde vågner*, Oslo.

Kjetsaa, Geir (1972). 'Ibseniana i Helsingfors Universitetsbibliotek', *Edda*, no. 2.

Kjetsaa, Geir (1977). 'Henrik Ibsen og von Knorring', *Ibsen-årbok*.

Knudsen, Jørgen (1985). *Georg Brandes. Frigørelsens vej 1842–77*, Copenhagen.

Knudsen, Jørgen (1988). *Georg Brandes. I modsigelsernes tegn. Berlin 1877–83*, Copenhagen.

Knudsen, Jørgen (2006). '"Jeg har dannet mig et Billede af Dem". Brandes som Ibsens kongsemne', in Jørgen Dines Johansen et al. (eds), *Ibsen og Brandes. Studier i et forhold*, Oslo.

Knudtzon, Fr. G. (1927). *Ungdomsdage*, Copenhagen.

Koht, Halvdan (1912). 'Georg Brandes og Norge', *Samtiden*.

Koht, Halvdan (1928). *Henrik Ibsen i 'Manden'*, Oslo.

Koht, Halvdan (1952). *Hedvig, Ibsen-årbok*.

Koht, Halvdan (1954a). *Henrik Ibsen. Eit diktarliv*, vol. I, Oslo.

Koht, Halvdan (1954b). *Henrik Ibsen. Eit diktarliv*, vol. II, Oslo.

Koht, Halvdan (1958). 'Hedda Gabler. Förhistorie og symbol', *Nordisk Tidsskrift*.

Koller, Ann Marie (1984). *The Theater Duke: Georg II of Saxe-Meiningen and the German Stage*, Stanford.

Koppang, Ole (1948). *Hegelianismen i Norge*, Oslo.

Krieger, A. F. (1920). *Dagbøker 1848–80*, Copenhagen.

Kristensen, Sven Møller (1965). *Digteren og samfundet*, vol. I, Copenhagen.

Lagerroth, Ulla-Britta (1990). 'August Lindberg som visionär skapare av ett nordisk samarbete', in Claes Rosenquist, *Nordiska spelplatser. Studier i nordisk teaterverksamhet från sekelskifte mot sekelslut*, Gideå.

Langslet, Lars Roar (2004). *Sønnen. En biografi om Sigurd Ibsen*, Oslo.

Larsen, Lars Frode (2002). *Tilværelsens Udlænding. Hamsun ved gjennombruddet 1891–1893*, Oslo.

Larson, Philip. E. (1999). *Ibsen in Skien and Grimstad: His Education, Reading and Early Works*, Grimstad.

Larssen, Birger Stuevold (1976). *Til TONOs forhistorie. Komponistens fremføringsrett – forspill og intermezzo non troppo dignitoso 1868–1887*, Oslo.

Lázár, Béla (1918). *Írók és muvészek között. Száz vidám história. Képekkel*, Budapest.

Lervik, Åse Hiort (1969a). '"Gildet paa Solhaug" og samtidens kritikk', *Edda*, no. 1.

Lervik, Åse Hiort (1969b). *Ibsens versekunst i Brand*, Oslo.

Lie, Erik (1928). *Erindringer fra et dikterhjem*, Oslo.

Lindberg, Per (1943). *August Lindberg. Skådespelaren och människan. Interiører från 80- och 90-talens teaterliv*, Stockholm.

Lindberger, Örjan (1964). 'Ibsen och två svenska teaterchefer', *Nordisk Tidsskrift för Vetenskap, Konst och Industri*.

Linder, Gurli (1918). *Sällskapsliv i Stockholm under 1880- och 1890-talen. Några minnesbilden*, Stockholm.

Linneberg, Arild (1992). *Norsk litteraturkritikks historie 1770–1940*, vol. II, *1848–1870*, Oslo.

Lokrantz, Margherita Giordano (2002). 'Three Unpublished Letters by Henrik Ibsen about the First Performances of "Et dukkehjem" in Italy', *Ibsen Studies*, no. 1.

Lugné-Poe, Aurélien (1938). *Ibsen i Frankrike*, Oslo.

Lund, Audhild (1925). *Henrik Ibsen og det norske Theater 1857–67*, Oslo.

Lyche, Lise (1991). *Norges teaterhistorie*, Oslo.

McFarlane, James (1966). 'Meaning and Evidence in Ibsen's Drama', in *Contemporary Approaches to Ibsen*, Oslo.

McFarlane, James (1991). 'Berlin and the Rise of Modernism', in Malcolm Bradbury and James McFarlane, *Modernism: A Guide to European Literature 1890–1930*, London.

McLellan, Samuel (1980–1). 'Rhyme and Reason in Ibsen's Norma', *Contemporary Drama*, vol. 1.

McLellan, Samuel (1982). 'Ibsen's Expanded Idea in Kjæmpehøien', *Edda*, no. 5.

Magarshack, David (1962). *Dostoevsky*, London.

Magon, Leopold (1967). *Wegbereiter nordischer Dichtung in Deutschland. In 100 Jahre Reclams Universal-Bibliothek 1867–1967. Beitrage zur Verlagsgeschichte*, Leipzig.

Mendelssohn, Peter de (1970). *S. Fischer und sein Verlag*, Frankfurt am Main.

Meyer, Michael (1995; 1971). *Henrik Ibsen. En biografi*, Oslo.

Midbøe, Hans (1960). *Streiflys over Ibsen og andre studier*, Oslo.

Modalsli, Tone (2001). 'Ibsen, Bjørnson and Bernhard Dunker, 1864–66', *Ibsen Studies*, no. 2.

Mohr, Otto Lous (1953). *Henrik Ibsen som maler*, Oslo.

Mohr, Otto Lous (1956). 'Henrik Ibsen as a Painter', *Scandinavian Review*, no. 43.

Moi, Toril (2006). *Ibsens modernisme*, Oslo.

Mosfjeld, Oskar (1949). *Henrik Ibsen og Skien*, Oslo.

Myhre, Jan Eivind (1999). 'Århundreskiftet som sosialt vannskille. Borgerskap og middelstand', in Bjarne Rogan (ed.), *Norge anno 1900. Kulturhistoriske glimt fra et århundreskifte*, Oslo.

Myhre, Olov (1908). 'Ett och annat nytt om Henrik Ibsen. Hans Heyerdahl til minnen', *Svenska Dagbladet* (21 December).

Næss, Atle (1994). 'Ibsen, Gossensass – og Emilie Bardach', *Bokvennen*, no. 3.

Nag, Martin (1967). *Ibsen i russisk åndsliv*, Oslo.

Nilsen, Hans Jacob (1967). 'Peer Gynt – eit anti-romantisk verk', in Otto Hageberg (ed.), *Omkring 'Peer Gynt'*, Oslo.

Nordhagen, Per Jonas (1981). *Henrik Ibsen i Roma 1864–1868*, Oslo.

Nordström, Gertrud (1963). 'Den svenska urpremiären på Ibsens De unges forbund 1869', in Gösta M. Bergman (ed.), *Dramaten 175 år. Studier i svensk scenkonst*, Stockholm.

Noreng, Harald (ed.) (1969). *Ibsen på festspillscenen*, Bergen.

Norseng, Mary Kathryn (1975). 'The Ideal and the Real at the End of the Golden Age: A Study of the Aesthetics of Clemens Petersen', University of Wisconsin (PhD).

Northam, John (1973). *Ibsen: A Critical Study*, Cambridge.

Ollén, Gunnar (1955). *Ibsens dramatik*, Stockholm.

Ørjasæther, Kristin (2003). *Camilla. Norges første feminist*, Oslo.

Osborne, John (1988). *The Meiningen Court Theatre 1866–1890*, Cambridge.

Österlund, Bodil (1985). 'Ibsens dockhem då och nu, i Thavenius, Jan and Bengt Lewan', *Läsningar. Om litteraturen och läsaren*, Stockholm.

Østvedt, Einar (1973). *Henrik Ibsens barndom og ungdom*, Oslo.

Øverland, Orm (2001). 'The Reception of Ibsen in the United States 1889–1910', in *Proceedings. International Ibsen Conference, 5–10 June 2000*, Bergen.

Oxfeldt, Elisabeth (2005). *Nordic Orientalism: Paris and the Cosmopolitan Imagination 1800–1900*, Copenhagen.

Pasche, Wolfgang (1979). *Skandinavische Dramatik in Deutschland. Björnstjerne Björnson, Henrik Ibsen, August Strindberg auf der deutscher Bühne 1867–1932*, Basel/Stuttgart.

Paulsen, John (1900). *Mine erindringer*, Copenhagen.

Perfall, Karl von (1894). *Ein Beitrag zur Geschichte der königlichen Theater in München 25. November 1867–25. November 1892*, Munich.

Pertici, Alessandra (2001). 'Ibsen og Italia. Første mottagelse på slutten av 1800-tallet og begynnelsen av 1900-tallet', *Studi Nordici VII 2000. Henrik Ibsen*, Pisa–Rome.

Pfäfflin, Friedrich and Ingrid Kussmaul (1983). *S. Fischer Verlag. Von der Gründung bis zur Rückkehr aus dem Exil* (exhibition catalogue), Stuttgart.

Reinecke-Wilkendorff, Nicolas (2004). 'Våpenbrødre? Om Georg Brandes' forhold til og opfattelse af Henrik Ibsen og hans værker', *Danske studier*, no. 99.

Rekdal, Anne Marie (2000). *Frihetens dilemma*, Oslo.

Rekdal, Anne Marie (2001). 'Henrik Ibsen og friheten som dilemma', *Nytt Norsk Tidsskrift*, no. 3.

Rem, Tore (2002). *Forfatterens strategier. Alexander Kielland og hans krets*, Oslo.

Rem, Tore (2006a). *Henry Gibson/Henrik Ibsen*, Oslo.

Rem, Tore (2006b). 'Ibsen, ibskønitet og den victorianske blåblyanten', in Per Thomas Andersen, *Lesing og eksistens. Festskrift til Otto Hageberg på 70-årsdagen*, Oslo.

Rem, Tore (2007). 'Nationalism or Internationalism? Ibsen and the Irish Question', unpubl. ms.

Reznicek, Ladislav (ed.) (2000). *Dagbok for Norge 1849*. Hertug Georg II von Sachsen-Meiningen.

Rønning, Helge (2002). 'Ibsen and Italian 19th-Century Liberalism', in Astrid Sæther (ed.), *Ibsen and the Arts: Painting, Sculpture, Architecture. Ibsen Conference in Rome 2001*, Oslo.

Rønning, Helge (2006). *Den umulige friheten. Henrik Ibsen og moderniteten*, Oslo.

Rottem, Øystein (1981). 'Den kritiske funksjons nøytralisering', *Edda*.
Rubow, Paul (1953). *Heiberg og hans skole i kritiken*, Copenhagen.
Rudler, Roderick (1966). 'Ibsen som teaterstipendiat i Dresden', *Edda*.
Rudler, Roderick (1970a). 'Ibsen som turnéleder i Trondhjem', *Edda*, no. 3.
Rudler, Roderick (1970b). 'Den første norske teaterhistorien, og Sancthansnattens tilblivelse', *St Halvard*.
Rudler, Roderick (1973). 'Ibsens rolle som praktisk teatermann. En misforstått side ved hans virksomhet', *Forskningsnytt fra Norges allmenvitenskapelig forskningsråd*, 18:6.
Rudler, Roderick (1977). 'Uroppførelsen av *Gildet paa Solhoug* og *Fru Inger til Østeraad*', *Ibsenårbok*.
Russell, Bertrand (1947). 'Opprør mot fornuften', in *Frihet og fornuft. Essays*, Oslo.
Said, Edward (2003). *Orientalism*, London.
Sanders, J. B. (1964). 'Ibsen's Introduction into France: *Ghosts*', *French Studies*, no. 18, Belfast.
Schindler, Peter (1942). *En ungdom. Efterladte papirer af Martin Schneekloth*, Copenhagen.
Schyberg, Frederik (1937). *Dansk Teaterkritik indtil 1914*, Copenhagen.
Seghedoni, Stefania (2003). 'Kvinnen i dramaene til Henrik Ibsen og Minna Canth: Nora (Et dukke-hjem) og Johanna (Työmiehen vaimo), med et sammendrag av Ibsen-kritikken i Finland fra 1870 til 1890', in Eva Maagerø et al. (eds), *Italiablikk. Norsk og nordisk kultur og litteratur sett fra Bologna*, Høgskolen in Agder.
Seip, Jens Arup (1971). *Ole Jacob Broch og hans samtid*, Oslo.
Sem, Gunnar (2000). *Lammers*, Porsgrunn.
Shepherd-Barr, Kirsten (1999). ' "Too far from Piccadilly": Ibsen in England and France in the 1890s', in Inga-Stine Ewbank (ed.), *Anglo-Scandinavian Cross-Currents*, Norwich.
Silén, Beatrice (1977). *Ibsen på Nya teatern. Svenska teatern under åren 1878–1893*, Helsingfors.
Sjönell, Barbro Ståhle (1987). 'Strindberg om Ibsen', *Nordisk Tidsskrift*.
Smidt, Kristian (2004). *Silent Creditors: Henrik Ibsen's Debt to English Literature*, Oslo.
Sørensen, Øystein (1994). 'Nasjonalisme, skandinavisme og pangermanisme hos Bjørnstjerne Bjørnson', in Øystein Sørensen (ed.), *Nasjonal identitet - et kunstprodukt?*, KULTs skriftserie, no. 30, Oslo.
Sørensen, Øystein (2001). *Kampen om Norges sjel*, Norsk idehistorie, vol. III, Oslo.
Spindler, Max (ed.) (1978). *Bayerische Geschichte im 19. und 20. Jahrhundert*, vol. I. *Staat und Politik*, Munich.
Stanislavskij, Konstantin (1924). *My Life in Art*, London.
Steine, Bjørn Arne (2005). *Sigurd Ibsen. Nasjon, politikk og kultur*, Oslo.
Strodtmann, Adolf (1873). *Das geistige Leben in Dänemark*, Berlin.
Svendsen, Paulus (1932). 'Om Ibsens kilder til "Kejser og Galilæer" ', *Edda*.
Svendsen, Paulus (1940). *Gullalderdrøm og utviklingstro. En idéhistorisk undersøkelse*, Oslo.
Svensén, Bo (2001). *Nobelpriset i litteratur*, vol. I, *1901–1920*, Stockholm.
Swanson, Carl A. (1941). 'Ibsen's *Ghosts* at the Théâtre-Libre', *Scandinavian Studies*, no. 8.
Swanson, Carl A. (1946). 'Ibsen and the Comédie-Française', *Scandinavian Studies*, no. 2.
Templeton, Joan (1997a). *Ibsen's Women*, Cambridge.
Templeton, Joan (1997b). 'New Light on the Bardach Diary', *Scandinavian Studies*, no. 2.
Templeton, Joan (1998). 'Antoine versus Lugné-Poe: The Battle for Ibsen on the French Stage', in Maria Deppermann et al. (eds), *Ibsen im europäischen Spannungsfeld zwischen Naturalismus und Symbolismus. Kongressakten der 8. Internationalen Ibsen-Konferenz, Gossensass 23.-28.6.1997*, Frankfurt am Main.
Templeton, Joan (2000). 'The Munch-Ibsen Connection: Exposing a Critical Myth', *Scandinavian Studies*, no. 4.
Theoharis C. Theoharis (1996). *Ibsen's Drama: Right Action and Tragic Joy*, London.
Thue, Fredrik (2004). 'Norge som dannelsesprosjekt. Akademisk kultur, borgerlighet og samfunns-forståelse 1830–1890', in Anne Kristine Børresen and Mikael Hård (eds), *Kunnskap og kultur. Vitenskapens roller i det norske samfunn, 1760–2000*, Trondheim.
Thue, Henning Junghans (1842). *Norske Universitets- og Skole-Annaler*, Kristiania.
Tjønneland, Eivind (1998/1999). 'Darwin, J. P. Jacobsen og Ibsen', *ARR*, no. 4.
Tjønneland, Eivind (2006). 'Ibsen, Brandes og ideen om fremtidens aristokrati', in Jørgen Dines Johansen et al. (eds), *Ibsen og Brandes. Studier i et forhold*, Oslo.
Tolstoy, Leo (1978). *Tolstoy's Letters*, vol. II, *1880–1910*, ed. R. F. Christian, London.
Tolstoy, Leo (1985). *Tolstoy's Diaries*, vols I and II, ed. R. F. Christian, New York.
Tveterås, Harald (1933). 'Ibsen og Snoilsky', *Norvegica. Minneskrift til femti-årsdagen for opprettelsen av universitetets biblioteks norske avdeling 1883–1933*, Oslo.
Tysdahl, Bjørn (1968). *James Joyce and Ibsen: A Study in Literary Influence*, Oslo.
Tysdahl, Bjørn (2003). 'An Advocatus Diaboli Reading of Ibsen's Letters about Art from Rome', *Ibsen Studies*, no. 3.
Van Laan, Thomas F. (1986). 'Generic Complexities in Ibsen's *An Enemy of the People*', *Comparative Drama*, 20:2 (Summer).

Vasenius, Valfrid (1879). *Henrik Ibsens dramatiska diktning i dess första skede. Estetisk-kritisk undersökning*, Helsingfors.

Villari, Lucio (2002). 'The Roman Question', in Astrid Sæther (ed.), *Ibsen and the Arts: Painting – Sculpture – Architecture*, Oslo.

Vinje, Finn-Erik (1978). *Et språk i utvikling*, Oslo.

Vogt, Ragnar (1930). *Den Freudske psykoanalyse. Dens historiske bakgrunn*, Oslo.

Wærp, Lisbeth P. (ed.) (1999). *Livet på likstrå. Henrik Ibsens Når vi døde vågner*, Oslo.

Wærp, Lisbeth P. (2000). *Overgangens figurasjoner. En studie i Henrik Ibsens Kejser og Galilæer og Når vi døde vågner*, Oslo.

Wærp, Lisbeth P. (2003). 'Ibsen's Poetics: "The Tragic Muse", *Brand* (1866) and *When We Dead Awaken – A dramatic Epilogue* (1899)', *Ibsen Studies*, no. 3.

Westling, Christer (1985). *Idealismens estetikk. Nordisk litterturkritik vid 1800-talets mitt mot bakgrund av den tyska filosofin från Kant til Hegel*, Stockholm.

Wiers-Jenssen, Hans (1923). *Laurentius og andre krøniker fra den gamle by*, Kristiania.

Wiingaard, Jytte (2002). 'Henrik Ibsen and Denmark', *Ibsen Studies*, no. 1.

Wülfing, Wülf (1998). *Handbuch literarisch-kultureller Vereine. Gruppen und Bunde 1825–1933*, Stuttgart.

Wyller, Egil A. (1993) 'Ibsens "tredje rike" og Bibelens "tusenårsrike"', in Hans Kolstad, *Tanke og omtanke. Festskrift til Asbjørn Aarnes på syttiårsdagen*, Oslo.

Ystad, Vigdis (1991). 'The Young Ibsen – Critic and Theatre-Writer', *Contemporary Approaches to Ibsen*, vol. 7, Oslo.

Ystad, Vigdis (1996a). '– *livets endeløse gåde'. Ibsens dikt og drama*, Oslo.

Ystad, Vigdis (1996b). 'Dikteren som komediefigur. Litterær intertekst i "Kjærlighedens Komedie"', *Bøygen*, no. 1.

Ystad, Vigdis (2001). 'Fra Pygmalion til den dansende faun – Ibsen og "det uutsigelige"', *Acta Universitatis carolinae – philologica 2 germanistica pragensia*, XVII.

INDEX